Race, Class, and Gender in the United States

An Integrated Study

Third Edition

Race, Class, and Gender in the United States

An Integrated Study

Third Edition

Paula S. Rothenberg
William Paterson College of New Jersey

ST. MARTIN'S PRESS NEW YORK

Editor: Sabra Scribner
Manager, publishing services: Emily Berleth
Publishing services associate: Kalea Chapman
Project management: Omega Publishing Services, Inc.
Cover design: Heidi Haeuser

Library of Congress Catalog Card Number: 94-65241
Copyright © 1995 by St. Martin's Press, Inc.

Manufactured in the United States of America.
98765
fedc

For information, write:
St. Martin's Press, Inc.
175 Fifth Avenue
New York, NY 10010

ISBN: 0-312-09652-6

Acknowledgments

"Racial Formations," from *Racial Formations in the United States* by Michael Omi and Harold Winnat. Copyright © Routledge. Reprinted by permission of the publisher.

"The Ethics of Living Jim Crow," from *Uncle Tom's Children* by Richard Wright. Copyright 1937 by Richard Wright. Copyright renewed 1965 by Ellen Wright. Reprinted by permission of HarperCollins Publishers, Inc.

"Rethinking Women's Biology," from *The Politics of Women's Biology*, by Ruth Hubbard. Copyright © 1990 by Rutgers University Press. Reprinted by permission of the publisher.

"The Social Construction of Gender," from "Believing is Seeing: Biology as Ideology," *The 1992 Cheryl Miller Lecture*, by Judith Lorber. Reprinted by permission of Sage Publications.

"Ah, Ya Throw like a Girl!" by Mike Messner, from *New Men, New Minds*, copyright © 1987 by Franklin Abbott, Editor, published by The Crossing Press, Freedom, CA. Reprinted by permission of the publisher.

"The Social Construction of Sexuality," from *The Politics of Women's Biology*, by Ruth Hubbard. Copyright © 1990 by Rutgers University Press. Reprinted by permission of the publisher.

Acknowledgments and copyrights are continued at the back of the book on pages 501–504, which constitute an extension of the copyright page.

Preface

Like its predecessors, this third edition of *Race, Class, and Gender in the United States: An Integrated Study* undertakes a study of issues of race, gender, and sexuality within the context of class. A new first section introduces these issues simultaneously, examining how each has been socially constructed and the social construction of difference itself that underlies them. Issues of gender in this third edition now include more attention to the ways that males have been socialized to become boys and men and to the relationship between this socialization and misogyny and homophobia. Issues of class and heterosexism are fully integrated throughout.

The structure of this book is designed to focus on similarities and differences between and among forms of oppression and to emphasize the ways in which issues of race, class, gender, and sexuality intersect. These issues are addressed in every section of the book, drawing parallels, repeating themes, adding yet another layer to the analysis. My hope is that our understanding of each phenomena as well as the relationships among them will deepen as the student moves through the text.

Individual instructors will find many ways to modify the order of presentation of articles to conform to their own vision of how this complex and challenging material is best presented. For example, while I have chosen to place Suzanne Pharr's important discussion of the relationship between heterosexism, homophobia, sexism, and class privilege in Part VII, some may chose to use that selection early in the course, perhaps even integrating it into the material in Part I. Others may find it useful to assign Gregory Mantsios's analysis of class from Part III earlier. It might also work well in Part I. The newspaper article on gang rape that appears in Part II could be followed immediately by a reading of the article on pulling train in Part VI, which looks at the place of gang rape in college fraternity culture, and then by June Jordan's "Requiem for a Champ" from Part IV.

I have chosen to place the historical materials in Part V fairly late in the book because I continue to believe that students are more likely to read and digest this material when their interest has been captured by the more contemporary articles. This ordering helps students see that history holds answers to perplexing contemporary questions rather than simply provides background for them. Others will undoubtedly prefer to use the historical material earlier. Countless other possible reorderings will emerge from the contents depending upon each of our visions for the course we are teaching. I think this flexibility is one of the strong points of a collection that is genuinely interdisciplinary and firmly grounded in an inclusive perspective.

In this new edition, I have attempted to enlarge the vision and deepen the analysis that prompted this book in the first place. In this effort, I have been helped by conversations with faculty and students throughout the United States who have shared their experiences using this text with me. The fact that so many have found this book useful confirms my belief that these topics are an essential part of a liberal education. It is unthinkable that students graduating from college at the end of the twentieth century would fail to grapple with issues of diversity and inequality in the course of their studies. This book is designed to facilitate that inquiry and analysis.

Many people contributed to this book. First, I owe a profound debt to the old 12th Street study group, with whom I first studied Black history and first came to understand the centrality of the issue of race. I am also indebted to the group's members, who provided me with a lasting example of what it means to commit one's life to the struggle for justice for all people.

I owe an equally profound debt to my friends and colleagues in The New Jersey Project: Integrating the Scholarship on Gender and The New Jersey Multicultural Studies Project, and to friends, colleagues, and students at William Paterson College involved in the various race and gender projects we have carried out for some years now. I have learned a great deal from all of them. I am especially grateful to J. Samuel Jordan and Leslie Agard-Jones—colleagues, teachers, and friends.

Della Capers, Martina Nowak, and Judy Fronefield, as well as Gina R. Cassese and Lisa Schotts, have all helped with different phases of this book's preparation. I am indebted to them for their diligence and enthusiasm.

I am also grateful to the following questionnaire reviewers: Julie Andrzejewski, St. Cloud University; Jeanne Ballentine, Wright State University; Ellen Barry, Bowling Green State University; Jane Bradley, Virginia Polytechnic and State University; Noel Casenave, Temple University; Robert Claus, University of Northern Iowa; Donald R. Culverson, University of Wisconsin–Madison; Kathleen Daly,

Yale University; Norman Daniels, Tufts University; Christopher Dobb, Southern Connecticut State University; Carol Docan, California State University at Northridge; Laura Fishman, University of Vermont; Estevan Flores, University of Colorado; Thomas J. Gerschick, Illinois State University; Bobbie Groth, Shimer College; David Iacoho-Harris, University of Texas at El Paso; Leslie Hill, Bates College; M. Njeri Jackson, Southern University; Carolyn Jacobs, Smith College; Sue Ellen Jacobs, University of Washington; Alphine Jefferson, Southern Methodist University; Peter Kellogg, University of Wisconsin–Green Bay; Patricia Klein, Western Michigan University; Seena Kohl, Webster University; Dorothy Kurz, University of Pennsylvania; S. Kwame, Lincoln University; Jill Leeper, DePauw University; Margaret Nash, SUNY Cortland; Ann Parsons, University of Utah; Bronwyn Patulski, Syracuse University; D. Seider; Joan Strouse, Portland State University; Arlene Thorn, West Virginia State University; Karen Tolly, St. Lawrence University; Jacqueline Wilkotz, Towson University; A. J. Williams-Meyers, SUNY New Paltz; and Jacque Wunzelbacher, University of Kentucky. The reviewers' thoughtful comments and suggestions have greatly strengthened the book's final form.

Many other people contributed to the book in a variety of ways. Some helped me track down articles or information, others discussed issues, and others were simply part of a broad learning experience that provided the context for the book. My thanks to Bernadette Anand, Susan Cavin, Michelle Fine, Charley Flint, Laura Kramer, Chandra Talpede Mohanty, Clara Lomas, Greg Mantsios, Marcia Treffman, Sharyl Bender Peterson, Evelyn Shalom, Steve Shalom, Holly Sklar, Consuelo Lopez Springfield, Isa Tavares Maack, and Ros Winters. Thanks also to Vivian Scheinmann and Pamela Sheldrick of Pandora Book Peddlars, Haledon, New Jersey; Arlene Hirschfelder and Dennis White of the Association of American Indian Affairs; Kelly Jenkins of the National Committee on Pay Equity; Marilyn Saviola of the Center for Independence of the Disabled, New York City; and Paula Ettelbrick, director of public policy of the National Center for Lesbian Rights. Very special thanks to Marjorie Pryse, Beth Hess, Aubyn Lewis, Joan Griscom, and Judy Baker, and to Bob Greenwald for all those home deliveries.

Special thanks to the faculty and students, too numerous to name, at the many colleges and universities where I have lectured during the past several years. Their generous sharing of bibliographies, articles, insights, and questions has enriched this book immeasurably. I am particularly grateful to my friends at The University of South Carolina in Columbia; Frostburg State College in Maryland; Wooster College in Ohio; Central Missouri State University in Warrensburg; Middle Tennessee State University in Murfreesboro; Clemson University in South Carolina; Sangamon State College in Illinois; Bates College in Maine; Montgomery County College in Maryland; Rochester Institute of Technology in New York; Kenyon College in Ohio; and The State University of New York at Cortland, Binghamton, and Albany for their hospitality and lively conversation.

The book in both its versions has benefited greatly from the professional contributions of many people at St. Martin's Press. In particular, I would like to thank Andrea R. Guidoboni, Patricia Mansfield Phelan, Beverly Hinton, Michael Weber,

Louise Waller, Sabra Scribner, Randi Israelow, Huntley McNair Funston, and Kerry Abrams for their work on this book. I would also like to thank Rich Wright, who has twice helped make the mechanics of producing a bound volume as painless and professional as they can be.

Finally, continuing thanks to my family with whom I listen to the news each morning, clip the daily papers, and argue the state of the world at dinner every night. Each of their perspectives has helped to frame the issues in this book.

Contents

PART IV: MANY VOICES, MANY LIVES 173

PART VI: CREATING AND MAINTAINING HIERARCHY: STEREOTYPES, LANGUAGE, IDEOLOGY, VIOLENCE, AND SOCIAL CONTROL   367

PART VII: REVISIONING THE FUTURE   442

Race, Class, and Gender in the United States

An Integrated Study

Third Edition

Introduction

This book begins with the assumption that it is impossible to make sense out of either our past or our present without using race, class, and gender as central categories of description and analysis. Because issues of race, class, and gender are not merely topic areas like "pollution" or "health care," they cannot be treated in two-week course modules which adopt a smorgasbord approach to studying social problems. Rather, race, class, and gender are basic and central categories that must be studied in depth if we wish to understand our lives and our social, political, and economic institutions.

Developing an Inclusive Model

There was a time when theorists debated about the conceptual or structural primacy of these categories, arguing that one or the other was the most basic and important. Now the challenge is to find a model or a theory broad enough, flexible enough, and complex enough to capture and reflect the way these elements, functioning together; determine how we see ourselves and each other and circumscribe the opportunities and privileges to which each of us has access. Our task is made harder by the narrow intellectual training so many of us have received. In the U.S.

1

this training tends to be fairly narrow in orientation and perspective and often leaves out the rich intellectual traditions of the diverse cultures of the world and of many peoples in our own society, beginning with Native Americans. It has offered us a fairly narrow intellectual perspective and set of theoretical categories and treated them as if they were coextensive with human thought. This approach to conceptualizing reality overemphasizes oppositional thinking, individualism, and linear models. These are a few of the intellectual structures that limit our progress and make it difficult to deal with theoretical perspectives that emphasize complex interrelated elements.

Oppositional thinking and teaching encourage us to divide the world and its people into hard categories—"black and white," "rational and emotional," "strong and weak"—and then to divide these qualities among people or things instead of adopting a model for thought that posits continuums and complexities and embraces contradictions. Where models drawn from Native American cultures and many Eastern traditions posit opposites existing in harmony with each other and often see growth as the result of reconciliation among contradictory elements, education in a Western tradition leaves little room for these possibilities.

This way of thinking is an important part of the social construction of gender, race, and class as difference in the sense that defines what is different as utterly other and insists that we either destroy difference entirely (as in the melting pot approach to ethnicity) or be divided forever by differences that are unbridgeable. Such an approach tends to regard those who are not white, male, heterosexual, and middle class as the ones who are in fact different; so that the very notion of difference comes to include hierarchy and to carry with it a rationale for the unequal distribution of power, privilege, and opportunity that characterizes society.

The other part of the dominant intellectual tradition in America portrays reality as constructed out of simple and discrete (isolated) units or individuals and does not see relations and relationships as building blocks of reality (even though this contradicts the experience of so many ethnic and racial groups). This approach views relations among discrete individuals or units as linear and encourages simplistic thinking about social problems. Because of it, we are often inclined to look for the cause of events, feelings, and realities as if were possible to specify a single cause and then move on to the next effect in a simple linear progression. We must learn to spin theories that look more like cobwebs than railroad tracks and to construct models that look more like kaleidoscopes than pyramids. This is no easy task in a book that seeks to adequately reflect the incredible complexity of the ways in which race, gender, and class intersect and interact with each other and with other aspects of experience.

The most basic challenge presented by the subject matter is the need to explore each form or aspect of oppression in its own right while, at the same time, do justice to the enormously complex ways in which they overlap and intersect. While it may be necessary, for the purposes of analysis, to focus for a time on one or another in the abstract, we should never lose sight of the fact that any particular woman or man has a unique ethnic background, class identification, age, sexual orientation, and religion. It is always the particular combination of these identities that shapes who we are and locates us in society.

Language

At times, talking about racism, sexism, and heterosexism within the context of class may require that we generalize about the experience of different groups of people even as we affirm that each individual is unique. In order to highlight similarities in the experiences of some individuals, we often talk about "people of color" or "women of color," even though these terms are problematic in some respects. When we refer to "women" in this book instead of "white women" or "women of color," it is usually to focus on the particular experiences or the legal status of women as women. In this regard, language is used in much the same way that one might author a guide to "*the* anatomy of *the* cat." There is no such thing as "*the* cat" anymore than there is "a woman" or "people of color." Yet for the purposes of discussion and analysis, it is often necessary to make artificial distinctions that allow us to focus on particular aspects of experience that may not be separate in reality. One assumption that is reflected in the structure and contents of this book is that language both mirrors reality and helps to structure it. It is no wonder that it is so often difficult to use our language in ways that are adequate to our topics.

Beginning Our Study

Whereas students in an introductory literature or sociology class rarely begin the semester with deeply felt and firmly entrenched attitudes toward the subject, almost every student in a course that deals with issues of race, class, gender, and sexuality enters the room with strong feelings. These feelings can either provide the basis for a passionate and personal study of the topics, one which transforms its participants, or they can function as enormous obstacles that prevent our study from ever beginning in earnest. This means that it is important for us to acknowledge the existence of these strong feelings on the part of both students and faculty and commit ourselves to creating a classroom atmosphere that encourages candid and respectful dialogue.

The Structure of the Book

This book begins with an examination of the ways in which race, class, gender, and sexuality have been socially constructed in the United States as difference in the form of hierarchy. It treats the idea of "difference" itself as a social construct that underlies and grounds racism, sexism, class privilege, and homophobia. Parts I and II explain the claim that certain differences have been socially constructed in hierarchical ways and used to rationalize inequality, and then provides a definition of difference. What exactly does it mean to claim that someone or some group of people is "different"? What kind of evidence might be offered to support this claim? What does it mean to construct differences? And what does society do to people who are categorized in this way? The readings in Parts I and II are designed to initiate a dialogue about the ways in which this society constructs difference and the social, political, and personal consequences that flow from that construction. They do so in the context of encouraging us to think about the meaning of racism, sexism, and class difference.

Defining racism and sexism is always a volatile project. Most of us have fairly strong feelings about race and gender relations in our society and have a stake in the way those relations are portrayed and analyzed. Definitions, after all, are powerful. They have the ability to focus our attention on certain aspects of reality and to make others disappear. They may even end up assigning blame or responsibility for the phenomena under consideration. Here is another difference between this course and many traditional courses. In other courses, teachers write definitions of terms on the board and students copy them down. The definitions are memorized, the problems or issues that define the subject matter are agreed upon, and the remainder of the course is spent examining different ways of solving the problems. In courses about race, class, gender, and sexuality, definitions provoke intense reactions and inspire little agreement. Instead of copying definitions and memorizing them, students challenge, argue, and protest. Instead of spending the semester solving mutually recognized problems, we spend it trying to agree on what the problems are.

Parts I and II are designed to initiate this process of definition. They allow us to discuss the ways in which we have been taught to think about race, class, and gender difference and to look at some of the ways these differences manifest themselves. Carrying this enterprise further, deepening our understanding of these phenomena, their manifestations and intersections, is the project of this entire volume.

Part III provides statistics and analysis that allow us to examine the impact of race, class, and gender differences on people's lives. Where essays in the previous sections used words to define and describe discrimination and oppression, the material in Part III presents current data, much of it drawn from U.S. government sources, which document the ways in which socially constructed differences mean real differences in opportunity, expectations, and treatment. These differences are brought to life in the articles, poems, and stories in Part IV, which offer glimpses into the lives of women and men of different ethnic and class backgrounds, expressing their sexuality and cultures in a variety of ways. While many of the selections are highly personal, each points beyond the individual's experience to social policy or practice or culturally conditioned attitudes.

When people first begin to recognize the enormous toll that racism, sexism, heterosexism, and class privilege take on human lives, they are often overwhelmed. How can they reconcile their belief that the United States provides liberty and justice and equal opportunity for all, with the reality presented in these pages? How did it happen? It is at this point that we turn to history.

Part V highlights important aspects of the history of subordinated groups in the United States by focusing on historical documents that focus on race and gender issues in U. S. law since the beginning of the Republic. Read in the context of the earlier material describing race, gender, and class differences in contemporary society, history becomes a way of using the past to make sense of the present. Focusing on the *legal* status of women of all colors and men of color allows us to telescope hundreds of years of history into manageable size, while still providing us with the historical information we need to make sense of contemporary society.

Our survey of racism and sexism in North America, past and present, has shown us that these phenomena function in a variety of ways. For some, the experiences that Richard Wright describes in "The Ethics of Living Jim Crow" are still all too real, but for most of us they describe a crude, blatant racism that seems incompatible with contemporary practice. How then are racism, sexism, and class privilege perpetuated in contemporary society? Why do these divisions and the accompanying differences in opportunity and achievement continue? How are they reproduced? Why do we have so much difficulty recognizing the reality that lies behind a rhetoric of equality of opportunity and justice for all? Part VI offers some suggestions.

An early essay on sex-role conditioning draws an important distinction between discrimination, which frustrates choices already made, and the force of a largely unconscious gender-role ideology, which frustrates the ability to choose.* Our discussion of stereotypes, language, and social control is concerned with analyzing how the way we conceive of others and, equally important, the way we have come to conceive of ourselves help perpetuate racism, sexism, heterosexism, and class privilege. Our discussion then moves beyond the specificity of stereotypes to analyze how our modes of conceptualizing reality itself are conditioned by forces that are not always obvious. Racism, sexism, and classism are not merely narrow but identifiable attitudes, policies, and practices that affect individuals' lives. Rather, they operate on a basic level to structure what we come to think of as "reality." In this way, they cause us to limit our possibilities and personhood by internalizing beliefs that distort our perspective and make it more difficult to blame the socioeconomic system that benefits.

Finally, Part VII offers suggestions for moving beyond racism and sexism. These suggestions are not definitive answers. They are offered to stimulate discussion about the kinds of changes we might wish to explore in order to transform society. They offer the reader a variety of ideas about the causes and cures for the pervasive social and economic inequality and injustice this volume documents. They are meant to initiate a process of reflection and debate about these social ills and about the kinds of changes that can help address them. These solutions are neither

---

*Sandra L. Bem and Daryl Bem: "Homogenizing the American Woman," from *Beliefs, Attitudes, and Human Affairs* by D. J. Bem, Brooks/Cole Publishing Company, Monterey, California, 1970, pp. 89–99.

comprehensive nor definitive simply because we are light-years away from *global* change. Meaningful social change will occur first at the local level as individuals, working together, begin to identify ways in which the institutions of which they are part perpetuate domination and subordination so that they can then seek to alter those institutions. Part VII is meant to provide a framework in which this process of identification and alteration can occur.

The Social Construction of Race, Class, Gender, and Sexuality

Every society grapples with the question of how to distribute its wealth and power. In some cases the distribution is relatively egalitarian and in others it is dramatically unequal. Those societies that tend toward a less egalitarian distribution have adopted various ways to apportion privilege; some have used age, others have used ancestry. Our society, like many others, places a priority on sex and race. To this end, race and gender difference have been portrayed as unbridgeable and immutable. Men and women have been portrayed as polar opposites with innately different abilities and capacities. The very personality traits that were considered positive in a man, were seen as signs of dysfunction in a woman; and the qualities that were praised in women were often ridiculed in men. In fact, until very recently, introductory psychology textbooks provided a description of neurosis in a woman that was virtually identical with their description of a healthy male personality.

Race difference has been similarly portrayed. White-skinned people of European origins have viewed themselves as naturally superior in intelligence and ability to people with darker skin or different physical characteristics. As both the South Carolina Slave Code of 1712 and the Dred Scott Decision in Part V make clear, "Negroes" were believed to be members of a different and lesser race. Their enslavement, like the genocide carried out against Native Americans, was justified based upon this assumed difference. In the Southwest, anglo landowners claimed

7

that "Orientals" and Mexicans were naturally suited to perform certain kinds of brutal, sometimes crippling, farm labor to which whites were "physically unable to adapt."[1] Women from various Asian populations are said to be naturally suited to the tedious and precise labor required in the electronics industry (an appeal to supposedly innate race *and* gender difference).

Class status, too, has been correlated with supposed differences in innate ability and moral worth. Property qualifications for voting have been used, not only to prevent African Americans from exercising this right, but to exclude poor whites as well. From the beginnings of society, being a person of property was considered an indication of superior intelligence and character. The most dramatic expression of this belief is found in Calvinism, which taught that success in business was a sign of being in God's grace and similarly, that being poor was a punishment inflicted by the Almighty for transgressions in some previous life.

In Part I we begin with a different premise. All of the articles in this section argue that far from reflecting natural and innate differences among people, the categories of gender, race, and class are themselves socially constructed. Rather than being "given" in nature, they are culturally constructed differences that reflect and perpetuate the prevailing distribution of power and privilege in a society and they change as other aspects of social, political, and economic life themselves evolve.

On first reading this may seem to be a strange claim. On the face of it, whether a person is male or female or a member of a particular race seems to be a straightforward question of biology. But like most differences alleged to be "natural" and "immutable," or unchangeable, the categories of race and gender are far more complex than they might seem. While it is true that most (though, as Judith Lorber points out in Selection 4, not all) of us are born unambiguously "male" or "female" as defined by our chromosomes or genitalia, the *meaning* of being a man or a woman differs from culture to culture and within each society. It is this difference in connotation or meaning that theorists point to when they claim that gender is socially constructed.

Social scientists distinguish between "sex," which is, in fact, a biologically based category, and "gender," which refers to the particular set of socially constructed meanings that are associated with each sex. These are seen to vary over time and place so that what is understood as "naturally" masculine or feminine behavior in one society may be the exact opposite of what another culture considers "natural" for women or men. Furthermore, while it is true that most societies have sex-role stereotypes that identify certain jobs or activities as appropriate for women and others for men, and claim that these divisions simply reflect "natural" differences in ability and/or interest, there is little consistency in what kinds of tasks have been so defined. While in many cultures strenuous physical activity is considered to be more appropriate to men than women, in one society where women are responsible for such labor the heaviest loads are described as being "so heavy only a woman can lift it." In some societies women are responsible for agricultural labor and in others it is men. Even within cultures that claim that women are unsuited for heavy manual labor, some women, usually women of color and poor, white working women, have always been expected and required to perform back-breaking physical labor—on plantations, in factories, on farms, in commercial laundries, and in their homes. The actual lives of real women and real men throughout history stand in sharp contrast to the images of masculinity and femininity that have been constructed by society and then rationalized as reflecting innate differences between the sexes.

In addition to pointing out the enormous differences in how societies have defined what is "naturally" feminine or masculine, and using these disparities to challenge the notion of an innate masculine or feminine nature, some theorists, like Hubbard and Lorber, use the phrase "the social construction of gender" to make an even more profoundly challenging claim. They argue that the notion of difference itself is constructed and suggest that the claim that women and men are naturally and profoundly different reflects a political and social decision rather than a distinction given in nature. Anthropologist Gayle Rubin explains it this way:

> Gender is a socially imposed division of the sexes. . . . Men and women are, of course, different. But they are not as different as day and night, earth and sky, yin and yang, life and death. In fact from the standpoint of nature, men and women are closer to each other than either is to anything else—for instance mountains, kangaroos, or coconut palms. The idea that men and women are more different from one another than either is from anything else must come from somewhere other than nature.[2]

In fact we might go on to argue, along with Rubin, that "far from being an expression of natural differences, exclusive gender identity is the suppression of natural similarities."[3] Boys and girls, women and men are under enormous pressure from the earliest ages to conform to sex-role stereotypes that divide basic human qualities between the two sexes. Central to this construction of difference is the social construction of sexuality, a process Ruth Hubbard analyzes in Selection 6. In a society where parents thought of their job as raising "human beings" instead of boys and girls, we would likely find all people sharing a wide range of human qualities, and the belief that men and women naturally occupy two mutually exclusive categories would not structure social, political, and economic life.

The idea of race has been socially constructed in similar ways. The claim that race is a social construction takes issue with the once popular belief that people were born into different races with innate, biologically based differences in intellect, temperament, and character. Ethnicity, in contrast to race, focuses on the shared social/cultural experiences and heritages of various groups and divides or categorizes them according to these shared experiences and traits. The important difference here is that those who talk of race and racial identity believe that they are dividing people according to biological or genetic similarities and differences, while discussions of ethnicity simply point to commonalities that are understood as social, not biological, in origin.

Contemporary historian Ronald Takaki suggests that in the United States, "race . . . has been a social construction that has historically set apart racial minorities from European immigrant groups." Omni and Winant, authors of Selection 1, would agree. They maintain that race is really more of a political categorization than a biological or scientific category. They point to the relatively arbitrary way in which the category has been constructed and suggest that changes in the meaning and use of racial distinctions can be correlated with economic and political changes in U.S. society. Dark-skinned men and women from Spain were classified as "white" along with fair-skinned immigrants from England and Ireland, while early Greek immigrants were often classified as "Orientals" and subjected to the same discrimination that Chinese and Japanese immigrants experienced under the laws of California and other western states. In South Africa, Japanese immigrants were categorized as "white," not "black" or "colored" presumably because the South African economy depended on trade with Japan. In contemporary U.S. society, dark-skinned latin people are often categorized as "black" by people who continue to equate something called "race" with skin color. While U.S. society has long been organized around rigid distinctions of race, people in other countries, such as Brazil, show little interest in such a way of dividing people.

The claim that race is a social construction is not meant to deny the obvious differences in skin color and physical characteristics that people manifest. It simply sees these differences on a continuum of diversity rather than as reflecting innate genetic differences among peoples. Scientists have long argued that all human beings are descended from a common stock. Some years ago the United Nations published a pictorial essay called *The Family of Man*. It included numerous photographs of people from all over the world and challenged readers to survey the enormous diversity among the people depicted and point out where one race ended and the other began. And, of course, it was impossible to do so. The photographs did not reflect sharply distinguished races but simply diversity on the same continuum.

The opening line of the autobiographical account by Richard Wright (Selection 2) provides another opportunity to think about the ways in which race is socially constructed. Wright begins his account by announcing "My first lesson in how to live as a Negro came when I was quite small." While it is true that Wright was born with dark skin, an unambiguous physical characteristic, it was for others to define the meaning of being black. As the Wright selection makes clear, in the South during the early 1900's it was primarily whites who defined what it meant to be a Negro. They did so by making clear what behavior would be acceptable and what behavior would provoke violence, perhaps even death. In Part VI of this book William Chafe draws an analogy between the way (white) women and black men have been socialized in this country under the threat of violence to conform to rigid race and gender roles. The irony is that when this socialization is successful, its results are used to support the claim that sex and race stereotypes are natural and reflect innate differences.

Writing about racism, Algerian-born French philosopher Albert Memmi once explained that racism consists of stressing a difference between individuals or populations. The difference can be real or imagined and in itself doesn't entail racism (or, by analogy sexism). It is not difference itself that leads to subordination but the interpretation of difference. It is assigning a value to a particular difference in a way that discredits an individual or group to the advantage of another that transforms mere difference into deficiency.[4] In this country, both race and gender difference have been carefully constructed as hierarchy. This means that in the United States, women are not merely described as different than men, but also that difference is understood to leave them deficient. The same is true of race. People of color are not merely described as different from white people, but also that difference is understood as deviance from an acceptable norm—even as pathology—and in both cases difference is used to rationalize racism and sexism.

The social construction of class is analogous but not identical. Differences between rich and poor, which result from particular ways of structuring the economy, are socially constructed as innate differences among people. They are then used to rationalize or justify the unequal distribution of wealth and power that results from economic decisions made to perpetuate privilege. In addition, straightforward numerical differences in earnings are rarely the basis for conferring class status. For example, school teachers and college professors are usually considered to have a higher status than plumbers and electricians even though the latter's earnings are often significantly higher. Where people are presumed to fit into the class hierarchy has less to do with clear-cut numerical categories than its does with reflecting the socially constructed superiority of those who perform mental labor, or work with their heads, from those who perform manual labor, or work with their hands. In addition, the status of various occupations and the class position they carry with them often changes depending upon whether the occupation is predominately female or male and according to its racial composition as well.

Equally significant, differences in wealth and family income have been overladen with various value judgments and stereotypes so that identifying someone as a member of the middle class, working class, or underclass carries implicit implications about the moral character and ability of the individuals in question. As Herbert Gans suggests, various ways of classifying and portraying poor people in this country have been used to imply that their poverty reflected some failing in them rather than indicating a social problem for which society as a whole might be held responsible. In the nineteenth century, Calvinism and social Darwinism maintained that being poor in itself indicated that an individual was morally flawed and thus deserved his or her poverty—again relieving society of any responsibility for social ills.

Finally, class difference can be said to be socially constructed in a way that parallels the construction of race and gender as difference. In this respect, our society is organized in such a way as to make hierarchy or class itself appear natural and inevitable. We grade and rank children from their earliest ages and claim to be sorting them according to something called natural ability. The tracking that permeates our system of education both reflects and creates the expectation that there are A people, B people, C people, and so forth. Well before high school, children have come to define themselves and others in just this way and to accept this kind of classification as natural. All this means that quite apart from accepting the particular mythology or ideology of class difference that prevails at any given moment (i.e., "the poor are lazy and worthless" versus "the poor are meek and humble and will inherit the earth"), we come to think it natural and inevitable that there should *be* class differences in the first place.

NOTES

1. Takaki, Ronald. *A Different Mirror*, p 321.
2. Rubin, Gayle, "The Traffic in Women," in *Toward an Anthropology of Women*, Rayna R. Reiter (ed.), New York, Monthly Review Press, 1975, p 179.
3. *Ibid.*, p 180.
4. Memmi, Albert, *Dominated Man*, Boston, Beacon Press, 1968.

Racial Formations

Michael Omi and Harold Winant

In 1982–83, Susie Guillory Phipps unsuccessfully sued the Louisiana Bureau of Vital Records to change her racial classification from black to white. The descendant of an eighteenth-century white planter and a black slave, Phipps was designated "black" in her birth certificate in accordance with a 1970 state law which declared anyone with at least one-thirty-second "Negro blood" to be black. The legal battle raised intriguing questions about the concept of race, its meaning in contemporary society, and its use (and abuse) in public policy. Assistant Attorney General Ron Davis defended the law by pointing out that some type of racial classification was necessary to comply with federal record-keeping requirements and to facilitate programs for the prevention of genetic diseases. Phipps's attorney, Brian Begue, argued that the assignment of racial categories on birth certificates was unconstitutional and that the one-thirty-second designation was inaccurate. He called on a retired Tulane University professor who cited research indicating that most whites have one-twentieth "Negro" ancestry. In the end, Phipps lost. The court upheld a state law which quantified racial identity, and in so doing affirmed the legality of assigning individuals to specific racial groupings.[1]

The Phipps case illustrates the continuing dilemma of defining race and establishing its meaning in institutional life. Today, to assert that variations in human physiognomy are racially based is to enter a constant and intense debate. *Scientific* interpretations of race have not been alone in sparking heated controversy; *religious* perspectives have done so as well.[2] Most centrally, of course, race has been a matter of *political* contention. This has been particularly true in the United States, where the concept of race has varied enormously over time without ever leaving the center stage of US history.

What Is Race?

Race consciousness, and its articulation in theories of race, is largely a modern phenomenon. When European explorers in the New World "discovered" people who looked different than themselves, these "natives" challenged then existing conceptions of the origins of the human species, and raised disturbing questions as to whether *all* could be considered in the same "family of man."[3] Religious debates flared over the attempt to reconcile the Bible with the existence of "racially distinct" people. Arguments took place over creation itself, as theories of polygenesis questioned whether God had made only one species of humanity ("monogenesis"). Europeans wondered if the natives of the New World were indeed human beings with redeemable souls. At stake were not only the prospects for conversion, but the types of treatment to be accorded them. The expropriation of property, the denial of political rights, the introduction of slavery and other forms of coercive labor, as well as outright extermination, all presupposed a worldview which distinguished Europeans—children of God, human beings, etc.—from "others." Such a worldview was needed to explain why some should be "free" and others enslaved, why some had rights to land and property while others did not. Race, and the interpretation of racial differences, was a central factor in that worldview.

In the colonial epoch science was no less a field of controversy than religion in attempts to comprehend the concept of race and its meaning. Spurred on by the classificatory scheme of living organisms devised by Linnaeus in *Systema Naturae*, many scholars in the eighteenth and nineteenth centuries dedicated themselves to the identification and ranking of variations in humankind. Race was thought of as a *biological* concept, yet its precise definition was the subject of debates which, as we have noted, continue to rage today. Despite efforts ranging from Dr. Samuel Morton's studies of cranial capacity[4] to contemporary attempts to base racial classification on shared gene pools,[5] the concept of race has defied biological definition. . . .

Attempts to discern the *scientific meaning* of race continue to the present day. Although most physical anthropologists and biologists have abandoned the quest for a scientific basis to determine racial categories, controversies have recently flared in the area of genetics and educational psychology. For instance, an essay by Arthur Jensen which argued that hereditary factors shape intelligence not only revived the "nature or nurture" controversy, but raised highly volatile questions about racial equality itself.[6] Clearly the attempt to establish a *biological* basis of race has not been swept into the dustbin of history, but is being resurrected in various scientific arenas. All such attempts seek to remove the concept of race from fundamental social, political, or economic determination. They suggest instead that the truth of race lies in the terrain of innate characteristics, of which skin color and other physical attributes provide only the most obvious, and in some respects most superficial, indicators.

Race as a Social Concept

The social sciences have come to reject biologistic notions of race in favor of an approach which regards race as a *social* concept. Beginning in the eighteenth century, this trend has been slow and uneven, but its direction clear. In the nineteenth century Max Weber discounted biological explanations for racial conflict and instead highlighted the social and political factors which engendered such conflict.[7] The work of pioneering cultural anthropologist Franz Boas was crucial in refuting the scientific racism of the early twentieth century by rejecting the connection between race and culture, and the assumption of a continuum of "higher" and "lower" cultural groups. Within the contemporary social science literature, race is assumed to be a variable which is shaped by broader societal forces.

Race is indeed a pre-eminently *sociohistorical* concept. Racial categories and the meaning of race are given concrete expression by the specific social relations and historical context in which they are embedded. Racial meanings have varied tremendously over time and between different societies.

In the United States, the black/white color line has historically been rigidly defined and enforced. White is seen as a "pure" category. Any racial intermixture makes one "nonwhite." In the movie *Raintree County*, Elizabeth Taylor describes the worst of fates to befall whites as "havin' a little Negra blood in ya'—just one little teeny drop and a person's all Negra."[8] This thinking flows from what Marvin Harris has characterized as the principle of *hypo-descent:*

> By what ingenious computation is the genetic tracery of a million years of evolution unraveled and each man [sic] assigned his proper social box? In the United States, the mechanism employed is the rule of hypo-descent. This descent rule requires Americans to believe that anyone who is known to have had a Negro ancestor is a Negro. We admit nothing in between. . . . "Hypo-descent" means affiliation with the subordinate rather than the superordinate group in order to avoid the ambiguity of intermediate identity. . . . The rule of hypo-descent is, therefore, an invention, which we in the United States have made in order to keep biological facts from intruding into our collective racist fantasies.[9]

The Susie Guillory Phipps case merely represents the contemporary expression of this racial logic.

By contrast, a striking feature of race relations in the lowland areas of Latin America since the abolition of slavery has been the relative absence of sharply defined racial groupings. No such rigid descent rule characterizes racial identity in many Latin American societies. Brazil, for example, has historically had less rigid conceptions of race, and thus a variety of "intermediate" racial categories exist. Indeed, as Harris notes, "One of the most striking consequences of the Brazilian system of racial identification is that parents and children and even brothers and sisters are frequently accepted as representatives of quite opposite racial types."[10] Such a possibility is incomprehensible within the logic of racial categories in the US.

To suggest another example: the notion of "passing" takes on new meaning if we compare various American cultures' means of assigning racial identity. In the United States, individuals who are actually "black" by the logic of hypo-descent have attempted to skirt the discriminatory barriers imposed by law and custom by attempting to "pass" for white.[11] Ironically, these same individuals would not be able to pass for "black" in many Latin American societies.

Consideration of the term "black" illustrates the diversity of racial meanings which can be found among different societies and historically within a given society. In contemporary British politics the term "black" is used to refer to all nonwhites. Interestingly this designation has not arisen through the racist discourse of groups such as the National Front. Rather, in political and cultural movements, Asian as well as Afro-Caribbean youth are adopting the term as an expression of self-identity.[12] The wide-ranging meanings of "black" illustrate the manner in which racial categories are shaped politically.[13]

The meaning of race is defined and contested throughout society, in both collective action and personal practice. In the process, racial categories themselves are formed, transformed, destroyed and re-formed. We use the term *racial formation* to refer to the process by which social, economic and political forces determine the content and importance of racial categories, and by which they are in turn shaped by racial meanings. Crucial to this formulation is the treatment of race as a *central axis* of social relations which cannot be subsumed under or reduced to some broader category or conception.

Racial Ideology and Racial Identity

The seemingly obvious, "natural" and "common sense" qualities which the existing racial order exhibits themselves testify to the effectiveness of the racial formation process in constructing racial meanings and racial identities.

One of the first things we notice about people when we meet them (along with their sex) is their race. We utilize race to provide clues about *who* a person is. This fact is made painfully obvious when we encounter someone whom we cannot conveniently racially categorize — someone who is, for example, racially "mixed" or of an ethnic/racial group with which we are not familiar. Such an encounter becomes a source of discomfort and momentarily a crisis of racial meaning. Without a racial identity, one is in danger of having no identity.

Our compass for navigating race relations depends on preconceived notions of what each specific racial group looks like. Comments such as, "Funny, you don't look black," betray an underlying image of what black should be. We also become disoriented when people do not act "black," "Latino," or indeed "white." The content of such stereotypes reveals a series of unsubstantiated beliefs about who these groups are and what "they" are like.[14]

In US society, then, a kind of "racial etiquette" exists, a set of interpretative codes and racial meanings which operate in the interactions of daily life. Rules shaped by our perception of race in a comprehensively racial society determine the "presentation of self,"[15] distinctions of status, and appropriate modes of conduct. "Etiquette" is not mere universal adherence to the dominant group's rules, but a more dynamic combination of these rules with the values and beliefs of subordinated groupings. This racial "subjection" is quintessentially ideological. Everybody learns some combination, some version, of the rules of racial classification, and of their own racial identity, often without obvious teaching or conscious inculcation. Race becomes "common sense" — a way of comprehending, explaining and acting in the world.

Racial beliefs operate as an "amateur biology," a way of explaining the variations in "human nature."[16] Differences in skin color and other obvious physical characteristics supposedly provide visible clues to differences lurking underneath. Temperament, sexuality, intelligence, athletic ability, aesthetic preferences and so on are presumed to be fixed and discernible from the palpable mark of race. Such diverse questions as our confidence and trust in others (for example, clerks or salespeople, media figures, neighbors), our sexual preferences and romantic images, our tastes in music, films, dance, or sports, and our very ways of talking, walking, eating and dreaming are ineluctably shaped by notions of race. Skin color "differences" are thought to explain perceived differences in intellectual, physical and artistic temperaments, and to justify distinct treatment of racially identified individuals and groups.

The continuing persistence of racial ideology suggests that these racial myths and stereotypes cannot be exposed as such in the popular imagination. They are, we think, too essential, too integral, to the maintenance of the US social order. Of course, particular meanings, stereotypes and myths can change, but the presence of a *system* of racial meanings and stereotypes, of racial ideology, seems to be a permanent feature of US culture.

Film and television, for example, have been notorious in disseminating images of racial minorities which establish for audiences what people from these groups look like, how they behave, and "who they are."[17] The power of the media lies not only in their ability to reflect the dominant racial ideology, but in their capacity to shape that ideology in the first place. D. W. Griffith's epic *Birth of a Nation*, a sympathetic treatment of the rise of the Ku Klux Klan during Reconstruction, helped to generate, consolidate and "nationalize" images of blacks which had been more disparate (more regionally specific, for example) prior to the film's appearance.[18] In US television, the necessity to define characters in the briefest and most condensed manner has led to the perpetuation of racial caricatures, as racial stereotypes serve as shorthand for scriptwriters, directors and actors, in commercials, etc. Television's tendency to address the "lowest common denominator" in order to render programs "familiar" to an enormous and diverse audience leads it regularly to assign and reassign racial characteristics to particular groups, both minority and majority.

These and innumerable other examples show that we tend to view race as something fixed and immutable—something rooted in "nature." Thus we mask the historical construction of racial categories, the shifting meaning of race, and the crucial role of politics and ideology in shaping race relations. Races do not emerge full-blown. They are the results of diverse historical practices and are continually subject to challenge over their definition and meaning.

Racialization: The Historical Development of Race

In the United States, the racial category of "black" evolved with the consolidation of racial slavery. By the end of the seventeenth century, Africans whose specific identity was Ibo, Yoruba, Fulani, etc., were rendered "black" by an ideology of exploitation based on racial logic—the establishment and maintenance of a "color line." This of course did not occur overnight. A period of indentured servitude which was not rooted in racial logic preceded the consolidation of racial slavery. With slavery, however, a racially based understanding of society was set in motion which resulted in the shaping of a specific *racial* identity not only for the slaves but for the European settlers as well. Winthrop Jordan has observed: "From the initially common term *Christian*, at mid-century there was a marked shift toward the terms *English* and *free*. After about 1680, taking the colonies as a whole, a new term of self-identification appeared—*white*."[19]

We employ the term *racialization* to signify the extension of racial meaning to a previously racially unclassified relationship, social practice or group. Racialization is an ideological process, an historically specific one. Racial ideology is constructed from pre-existing conceptual (or, if one prefers, "discursive") elements and emerges from the struggles of competing political projects and ideas seeking to articulate similar elements differently. An account of racialization processes that avoids the pitfalls of US ethnic history[20] remains to be written.

Particularly during the nineteenth century, the category of "white" was subject to challenges brought about by the influx of diverse groups who were not of the same Anglo-Saxon stock as the founding immigrants. In the nineteenth century, political and ideological struggles emerged over the classification of Southern Europeans, the Irish and Jews, among other "non-white" categories.[21] Nativism was only effectively curbed by the institutionalization of a racial order that drew the color line *around*, rather than *within*, Europe.

By stopping short of racializing immigrants from Europe after the Civil War, and by subsequently allowing their assimilation, the American racial order was reconsolidated in the wake of the tremendous challenge placed before it by the abolition of racial slavery.[22] With the end of Reconstruction in 1877, an effective program for limiting the emergent class struggles of the later nineteenth century was forged: the definition of the working class *in racial terms*—as "white." This was not accomplished by any legislative decree or capitalist maneuvering to divide the working class, but rather by white workers themselves. Many of them were recent immigrants, who organized on racial lines as much as on traditionally defined class lines.[23] The Irish on the West Coast, for example, engaged in vicious anti-Chinese race-baiting and committed many pogrom-type assaults on Chinese in the course of consolidating the trade union movement in California.

Thus the very political organization of the working class was in important ways a racial project. The legacy of racial conflicts and arrangements shaped the definition of interests and in turn led to the consolidation of institutional patterns (e.g., segregated unions, dual labor markets, exclusionary legislation) which perpetuated the color line *within* the working class. Selig Perlman, whose study of the development of the labor movement is fairly sympathetic to this process, notes that:

> The political issue after 1877 was racial, not financial, and the weapon was not merely the ballot, but also "direct action"—violence. The anti-Chinese agitation in

California, culminating as it did in the Exclusion Law passed by Congress in 1882, was doubtless the most important single factor in the history of American labor, for without it the entire country might have been overrun by Mongolian [sic] labor and *the labor movement might have become a conflict of races instead of one of classes.*[24]

More recent economic transformations in the US have also altered interpretations of racial identities and meanings. The automation of southern agriculture and the augmented labor demand of the postwar boom transformed blacks from a largely rural, impoverished labor force to a largely urban, working-class group by 1970.[25] When boom became bust and liberal welfare statism moved rightwards, the majority of blacks came to be seen, increasingly, as part of the "underclass," as state "dependents." Thus the particularly deleterious effects on blacks of global and national economic shifts (generally rising unemployment rates, changes in the employment structure away from reliance on labor intensive work, etc.) were explained once again in the late 1970s and 1980s (as they had been in the 1940s and mid-1960s) as the result of defective black cultural norms, of familial disorganization, etc.[26] In this way new racial attributions, new racial myths, are affixed to "blacks."[27] Similar changes in racial identity are presently affecting Asians and Latinos, as such economic forces as increasing Third World impoverishment and indebtedness fuel immigration and high interest rates, Japanese competition spurs resentments, and US jobs seem to fly away to Korea and Singapore.[28]...

Once we understand that race overflows the boundaries of skin color, super-exploitation, social stratification, discrimination and prejudice, cultural domination and cultural resistance, state policy (or of any other particular social relationship we list), once we recognize the racial dimension present to some degree in *every* identity, institution and social practice in the United States—once we have done this, it becomes possible to speak of *racial formation.* This recognition is hard-won; there is a continuous temptation to think of race as an *essence*, as something fixed, concrete and objective, as (for example) one of the categories just enumerated. And there is also an opposite temptation: to see it as a mere illusion, which an ideal social order would eliminate.

In our view it is crucial to break with these habits of thought. The effort must be made to understand race as *an unstable and "decentered" complex of social meanings constantly being transformed by political struggle....*

NOTES

1. *San Francisco Chronicle*, 14 September 1982, 19 May 1983. Ironically, the 1970 Louisiana law was enacted to supersede an old Jim Crow statute which relied on the idea of "common report" in determining an infant's race. Following Phipps's unsuccessful attempt to change her classification and have the law declared unconstitutional, a legislative effort arose which culminated in the repeal of the law. See *San Francisco Chronicle*, 23 June 1983.

2. The Mormon church, for example, has been heavily criticized for its doctrine of black inferiority.

3. Thomas F. Gossett notes:

> Race theory . . . had up until fairly modern times no firm hold on European thought. On the other hand, race theory and race prejudice were by no means unknown at the time when the English colonists came to North America. Undoubtedly, the age of exploration led many to speculate on race differences at a period when neither Europeans nor Englishmen were prepared to make allowances for vast cultural diversities. Even though race theories had not then secured wide acceptance or even sophisticate formulation, the first contacts of the Spanish with the Indians in the Americas can now be recognized as the beginning of a struggle between conceptions of the nature of primitive peoples which has not yet been wholly settled. (Thomas F. Gossett, *Race: The History of an Idea in America* (New York: Schocken Books, 1965), p. 16).

Winthrop Jordan provides a detailed account of early European colonialists' attitudes about color and race in *White Over Black: American Attitudes Toward the Negro, 1550–1812* (New York: Norton, 1977 [1968]), pp. 3–43.

4. Pro-slavery physician Samuel George Morton (1799–1851) compiled a collection of 800 crania from all parts of the world which formed the sample for his studies of race. Assuming that the larger the size of the cranium translated into greater intelligence, Morton established a relationship between race and skull capacity. Gossett reports that:

> In 1849, one of his studies included the following results: The English skulls in his collection proved to be the largest, with an average cranial capacity of 96 cubic inches. The Americans and Germans were rather poor seconds, both with cranial capacities of 90 cubic inches. At the bottom of the list were the Negroes with 83 cubic inches, the Chinese with 82, and the Indians with 79. (Ibid., p. 74).

On Morton's methods, see Stephen J. Gould, "The Finagle Factor," *Human Nature* (July 1978).

5. Definitions of race founded upon a common pool of genes have not held up when confronted by scientific research which suggests that the differences *within* a given human population are greater than those *between* populations. See L. L. Cavalli-Sforza, "The Genetics of Human Populations," *Scientific American* (September 1974), pp. 81–9.

6. Arthur Jensen, "How Much Can We Boost IQ and Scholastic Achievement?", *Harvard Educational Review*, vol. 39 (1969), pp. 1–123.

7. Ernst Moritz Manasse, "Max Weber on Race," *Social Research*, vol. 14 (1947), pp. 191–221.

8. Quoted in Edward D.C. Campbell, Jr, *The Celluloid South: Hollywood and the Southern Myth* (Knoxville: University of Tennessee Press, 1981), pp. 168–70.

9. Marvin Harris, *Patterns of Race in the Americas* (New York: Norton, 1964), p. 56.

10. Ibid., p. 57.

11. After James Meredith had been admitted as the first black student at the University of Mississippi, Harry S. Murphy announced that he, and not Meredith, was the first black student to attend "Ole Miss." Murphy described himself as black but was able to pass for white and spent nine months at the institution without attracting any notice (ibid., p. 56).

12. A. Sivanandan, "From Resistance to Rebellion: Asian and Afro-Caribbean Struggles in Britain," *Race and Class*, vol. 23, nos. 2–3 (Autumn-Winter 1981).

13. Consider the contradictions in racial status which abound in the country with the most rigidly defined racial categories—South Africa. There a race classification agency is employed to adjudicate claims for upgrading of official racial identity. This is particularly necessary for the "coloured" category. The apartheid system considers Chinese as "Asians" while the Japanese are accorded the status of "honorary whites." This logic nearly detaches race from any grounding in skin color and other physical attributes and nakedly exposes race as a juridicial category subject to economic, social and political influences. (We are indebted to Steve Talbot for clarification of some of these points.)

14. Gordon W. Allport, *The Nature of Prejudice* (Garden City, New York: Doubleday, 1958), pp. 184–200.

15. We wish to use this phrase loosely, without committing ourselves to a particular position on such social psychological approaches as symbolic interactionism, which are outside the scope of this study. An interesting study on this subject is S.M. Lyman and W.A. Douglass, "Ethnicity: Strategies of Individual and Collective Impression Management," *Social Research*, vol. 40, no. 2 (1973).

16. Michael Billig, "Patterns of Racism: Interviews with National Front Members," *Race and Class*, vol. 20, no. 2 (Autumn 1978), pp. 161–79.

17. "Miss San Antonio USA Lisa Fernandez and other Hispanics auditioning for a role in a television soap opera did not fit the Hollywood image of real Mexicans and had to darken their faces before filming." Model Aurora Garza said that their faces were bronzed with powder because they looked too white. "'I'm a real Mexican [Garza said] and very dark anyway. I'm even darker right now because I have a tan. But they kept wanting me to make my face darker and darker'" (*San Francisco Chronicle*, 21 September 1984). A similar dilemma faces Asian American actors who feel that Asian character lead roles inevitably go to white actors who make themselves up to be Asian. Scores of Charlie Chan films, for example, have been made with white leads (the last one was the 1981 *Charlie Chan and the Curse of the Dragon Queen*). Roland Winters, who played in six Chan features, was asked by playwright Frank Chin to explain the logic of casting a white man in the role of Charlie Chan: "'The only thing I can think of is, if you want to cast a homosexual in a show, and you get a homosexual, it'll be awful. It won't be funny . . . and maybe there's something there . . .'" (Frank Chin, "Confessions of the Chinatown Cowboy," *Bulletin of Concerned Asian Scholars*, vol. 4, no. 3 (Fall 1972)).

18. Melanie Martindale-Sikes, "Nationalizing 'Nigger' Imagery Through 'Birth of a Nation'," paper prepared for the 73rd Annual Meeting of the American Sociological Association, 4–8 September 1978 in San Francisco.

19. Winthrop D. Jordan, op. cit., p. 95; emphasis added.

20. Historical focus has been placed either on particular racially defined groups or on immigration and the "incorporation" of ethnic groups. In the former case the characteristic ethnicity theory pitfalls and apologetics such as functionalism and cultural pluralism may be avoided, but only by sacrificing much of the focus on race. In the latter case, race is considered a manifestation of ethnicity. See Chapter 1 above.

21. The degree of antipathy for these groups should not be minimized. A northern commentator observed in the 1850s: "An Irish Catholic seldom attempts to rise to a higher condition than that in which he is placed, while the Negro often makes the attempt with success." Quoted in Gossett, op. cit., p. 288.

22. This analysis, as will perhaps be obvious, is essentially DuBoisian. Its main source will be found in the monumental (and still largely unappreciated) *Black Reconstruction in the United States, 1860–1880* (New York: Atheneum, 1977 [1935]).

23. Alexander Saxton argues that:

North Americans of European background have experienced three great racial confrontations: with the Indian, with the African, and with the Oriental. Central to each transaction has been a totally one-sided preponderance of power, exerted for the exploitation of nonwhites by the dominant white society. In each case (but especially in the two that began with systems of enforced labor), white workingmen have played a crucial, yet ambivalent, role. They have been both exploited and exploiters. On the one hand, thrown into competition with nonwhites as enslaved or "cheap" labor, they suffered economically; on the other hand, being white, they benefited by that very exploitation which was compelling the nonwhites to work for low wages or for nothing. Ideologically they were drawn in opposite directions. *Racial identification cut at right angles to class consciousness.* (Alexander Saxton, *The Indispensable Enemy: Labor and the Anti-Chinese Movement in California* (Berkeley and Los Angeles: University of California Press, 1971), p. 1, emphasis added.)

24. Selig Perlman, *The History of Trade Unionism in the United States* (New York: Augustus Kelley, 1950), p. 52; emphasis added.

25. Whether southern blacks were "peasants" or rural workers is unimportant in this context. Some time during the 1960s blacks attained a higher degree of urbanization than whites. Before World War II most blacks had been rural dwellers and nearly 80 percent lived in the South.

26. See George Gilder, *Wealth and Poverty* (New York: Basic Books, 1981); Charles Murray, *Losing Ground* (New York: Basic Books, 1984) See Chapter 7 below.

27. A brilliant study of the racialization process in Britain, focused on the rise of "mugging" as a popular fear in the 1970s, is Stuart Hall *et al.*, *Policing the Crisis* (London: Macmillan, 1978).

28. The case of Vincent Chin, a Chinese American man beaten to death in 1982 by a laid-off Detroit auto worker and his stepson who mistook him for Japanese and blamed him for the loss of their jobs, has been widely publicized in Asian American communities. On immigration conflicts and pressures, see Michael Omi, "New Wave Dread: Immigration and Intra-Third World Conflict," *Socialist Review*, no. 60 (November–December 1981).

2

The Ethics of Living Jim Crow:
An Autobiographical Sketch

Richard Wright

I

My first lesson in how to live as a Negro came when I was quite small. We were living in Arkansas. Our house stood behind the railroad tracks. Its skimpy yard was paved with black cinders. Nothing green ever grew in that yard. The only touch of green we could see was far away, beyond the tracks, over where the white folks lived. But cinders were good enough for me and I never missed the green growing things. And anyhow cinders were fine weapons. You could always have a nice hot war with huge black cinders. All you had to do was crouch behind the brick pillars of a house with your hands full of gritty ammunition. And the first woolly black head you saw pop out from behind another row of pillars was your target. You tried your very best to knock it off. It was great fun.

I never fully realized the appalling disadvantages of a cinder environment till one day the gang to which I belonged found itself engaged in a war with the white boys who lived beyond the tracks. As usual we laid down our cinder barrage, thinking that this would wipe the white boys out. But they replied with a steady bombardment of broken bottles. We doubled our cinder barrage, but they hid behind trees, hedges, and the sloping embankments of their lawns. Having no such fortifications, we retreated to the brick pillars of our homes. During the retreat a broken milk bottle caught me behind the ear, opening a deep gash which bled profusely. The sight of blood pouring over my face completely demoralized our ranks. My fellow-combatants left me standing paralyzed in the center of the yard, and scurried for their homes. A kind neighbor saw me and rushed me to a doctor, who took three stitches in my neck.

I sat brooding on my front steps, nursing my wound and waiting for my mother to come from work. I felt that a grave injustice had been done me. It was all right to throw cinders. The greatest harm a cinder could do was leave a bruise. But broken bottles were dangerous; they left you cut, bleeding, and helpless.

When night fell, my mother came from the white folks' kitchen. I raced down the street to meet her. I could just feel in my bones that she would understand. I knew she would tell me exactly what to do next time. I grabbed her hand and babbled out the whole story. She examined my wound, then slapped me.

"How come yuh didn't hide?" she asked me. "How come yuh awways fightin'?"

I was outraged, and bawled. Between sobs I told her that I didn't have any trees or hedges to hide behind. There wasn't a thing I could have used as a trench. And you couldn't throw very far when you were hiding behind the brick pillars of a house. She grabbed a barrel stave, dragged me home, stripped me naked, and beat me till I had a fever of one hundred and two. She would smack my rump with the stave, and, while the skin was still smarting, impart to me gems of Jim Crow wisdom. I was never to throw cinders any more. I was never to fight any more wars. I was never, never, under any conditions, to fight *white* folks again. And they were absolutely right in clouting me with the broken milk bottle. Didn't I know she was working hard every day in the hot kitchens of the white folks to make money to take care of me? When was I ever going to learn to be a good boy? She couldn't be bothered with my fights. She finished by telling me that I ought to be thankful to God as long as I lived that they didn't kill me.

All that night I was delirious and could not sleep. Each time I closed my eyes I saw monstrous white faces suspended from the ceiling, leering at me.

From that time on, the charm of my cinder yard was gone. The green trees, the trimmed hedges, the cropped lawns grew very meaningful, became a symbol. Even today when I think of white folks, the hard, sharp outlines of white houses surrounded by trees, lawns, and hedges are present somewhere in the background of my mind. Through the years they grew into an overreaching symbol of fear.

It was a long time before I came in close contact with white folks again. We moved from Arkansas to Mississippi. Here we had the good fortune not to live behind the railroad tracks, or close to white neighborhoods. We lived in the very heart of the local Black Belt. There were black churches and black preachers; there were black schools and black teachers; black groceries and black clerks. In fact, everything was so solidly black that for a long time I did not even think of white folks, save in remote and vague terms. But this could not last forever. As one grows older one eats more. One's clothing costs more. When I finished grammar school I had to go to work. My mother could no longer feed and clothe me on her cooking job.

There is but one place where a black boy who knows no trade can get a job, and that's where the houses and faces are white, where the trees, lawns, and hedges are green. My first job was with an optical company in Jackson, Mississippi. The morning I applied I stood straight and neat before the boss, answering all his questions with sharp yessirs and nosirs. I was very careful to pronounce my *sirs* distinctly, in order that he might know that I was polite, that I knew where I was, and that I knew he was a *white* man. I wanted that job badly.

He looked me over as though he were examining a prize poodle. He questioned me closely about my schooling, being particularly insistent about how much mathematics I had had. He seemed very pleased when I told him I had had two years of algebra.

"Boy, how would you like to try to learn something around here?" he asked me.

"I'd like it fine, sir," I said, happy. I had visions of "working my way up." Even Negroes have those visions.

"All right," he said. "Come on."

I followed him to the small factory.

"Pease," he said to a white man of about thirty-five, "this is Richard. He's going to work for us."

Pease looked at me and nodded.

I was then taken to a white boy of about seventeen.

"Morrie, this is Richard, who's going to work for us."

"Whut yuh sayin' there, boy!" Morrie boomed at me.

"Fine!" I answered.

The boss instructed these two to help me, teach me, give me jobs to do, and let me learn what I could in my spare time.

My wages were five dollars a week.

I worked hard, trying to please. For the first month I got along O.K. Both Pease and Morrie seemed to like me. But one thing was missing. And I kept thinking about it. I was not learning anything and nobody was volunteering to help me. Thinking they had forgotten that I was to learn something about the mechanics of grinding lenses, I asked Morrie one day to tell me about the work. He grew red.

"Whut yuh tryin' t' do, nigger, get smart?" he asked.

"Naw; I ain' tryin' t' git smart," I said.

"Well, don't, if yuh know whut's good for yuh!"

I was puzzled. Maybe he just doesn't want to help me, I thought. I went to Pease.

"Say, are yuh crazy, you black bastard?" Pease asked me, his gray eyes growing hard.

I spoke out, reminding him that the boss had said I was to be given a chance to learn something.

"Nigger, you think you're *white*, don't you?"

"Naw, sir!"

"Well, you're acting mighty like it!"

"But, Mr. Pease, the boss said. . . ."

Pease shook his fist in my face.

"This is a *white* man's work around here, and you better watch yourself!"

From then on they changed toward me. They said good-morning no more. When I was just a bit slow in performing some duty, I was called a lazy black son-of-a-bitch.

Once I thought of reporting all this to the boss. But the mere idea of what would happen to me if Pease and Morrie should learn that I had "snitched" stopped me. And after all the boss was a white man, too. What was the use?

The climax came at noon one summer day. Pease called me to his work-bench. To get to him I had to go between two narrow benches and stand with my back against a wall.

"Yes, sir," I said.

"Richard, I want to ask you something," Pease began pleasantly, not looking up from his work.

"Yes, sir," I said again.

Morrie came over, blocking the narrow passage between the benches. He folded his arms, staring at me solemnly.

I looked from one to the other, sensing that something was coming.

"Yes, sir," I said for the third time.

Pease looked up and spoke very slowly.

"Richard, *Mr.* Morrie here tells me you called me *Pease.*"

I stiffened. A void seemed to open up in me. I knew this was the show-down.

He meant that I had failed to call him Mr. Pease. I looked at Morrie. He was gripping a steel bar in his hands. I opened my mouth to speak, to protest, to assure Pease that I had never called him simply *Pease,* and that I had never had any intentions of doing so, when Morrie grabbed me by the collar, ramming my head against the wall.

"Now, be careful, nigger!" snarled Morrie, baring his teeth. "*I* heard yuh call 'im *Pease!* 'N' if yuh say yuh didn't, yuh're callin' me a *lie,* see?" He waved the steel bar threateningly.

If I had said: No, sir Mr. Pease, I never called you *Pease,* I would have been automatically calling Morrie a liar. And if I had said: Yes, sir, Mr. Pease, I called you *Pease,* I would have been pleading guilty to having uttered the worst insult that a Negro can utter to a southern white man. I stood hesitating, trying to frame a neutral reply.

"Richard, I asked you a question!" said Pease. Anger was creeping into his voice.

"I don't remember calling you *Pease,* Mr. Pease," I said cautiously. "And if I did, I sure didn't mean. . . ."

"You black son-of-a-bitch! You called me *Pease,* then!" he spat, slapping me till I bent sideways over a bench. Morrie was on top of me, demanding:

"Didn't yuh call 'im *Pease?* If yuh say yuh didn't, I'll rip yo' gut string loose with this bar, yuh black granny dodger! Yuh can't call a white man a lie 'n' git erway with it, you black son-of-a-bitch!"

I wilted. I begged them not to bother me. I knew what they wanted. They wanted me to leave.

"I'll leave," I promised. "I'll leave right *now.*"

They gave me a minute to get out of the factory. I was warned not to show up again, or tell the boss.

I went.

When I told the folks at home what had happened, they called me a fool. They told me that I must never again attempt to exceed my boundaries. When you are working for white folks, they said, you got to "stay in your place" if you want to keep working.

II

My Jim Crow education continued on my next job, which was portering in a clothing store. One morning, while polishing brass out front, the boss and his twenty-year-old son got out of their car and half dragged and half kicked a Negro woman into the store. A policeman standing at the corner looked on, twirling his night-stick. I watched out of the corner of my eye, never slackening the strokes of my chamois upon the brass. After a few minutes, I heard shrill screams coming from the rear of the store. Later the woman stumbled out, bleeding, crying, and holding her stomach. When she reached the end of the block, the policeman grabbed her and accused her of being drunk. Silently, I watched him throw her into a patrol wagon.

When I went to the rear of the store, the boss and his son were washing their hands at the sink. They were chuckling. The floor was bloody and strewn with wisps of hair and clothing. No doubt I must have appeared pretty shocked, for the boss slapped me reassuringly on the back.

"Boy, that's what we do to niggers when they don't want to pay their bills," he said, laughing.

His son looked at me and grinned.

"Here, hava cigarette," he said.

Not knowing what to do, I took it. He lit his and held the match for me. This was a gesture of kindness, indicating that even if they had beaten the poor old woman, they would not beat me if I knew enough to keep my mouth shut.

"Yes, sir," I said, and asked no questions.

After they had gone, I sat on the edge of a packing box and stared at the bloody floor till the cigarette went out.

That day at noon, while eating in a hamburger joint, I told my fellow Negro porters what had happened. No one seemed surprised. One fellow, after swallowing a huge bite, turned to me and asked:

"Huh! Is tha' all they did t' her?"

"Yeah. Wasn't tha' enough?" I asked.

"Shucks! Man, she's a lucky bitch!" he said, burying his lips deep into a juicy hamburger. "Hell, it's a wonder they didn't lay her when they got through."

III

I was learning fast, but not quite fast enough. One day, while I was delivering packages in the suburbs, my bicycle tire was punctured. I walked along the hot, dusty road, sweating and leading my bicycle by the handle-bars.

A car slowed at my side.

"What's the matter, boy?" a white man called.

I told him my bicycle was broken and I was walking back to town.

"That's too bad," he said, "Hop on the running board."

He stopped the car. I clutched hard at my bicycle with one hand and clung to the side of the car with the other.

"All set?"

"Yes, sir," I answered. The car started.

It was full of young white men. They were drinking. I watched the flask pass from mouth to mouth.

"Wanna drink, boy?" one asked.

I laughed as the wind whipped my face. Instinctively obeying the freshly planted precepts of my mother, I said:

"Oh, no!"

The words were hardly out of my mouth before I felt something hard and cold smash me between the eyes. It was an empty whisky bottle. I saw stars, and fell backwards from the speeding car into the dust of the road, my feet becoming entangled in the steel spokes of my bicycle. The white men piled out and stood over me.

"Nigger, ain' yuh learned no better sense'n tha' yet?" asked the man who hit me. "Ain't yuh learned t' say *sir* t' a white man yet?"

Dazed, I pulled to my feet. My elbows and legs were bleeding. Fists doubled, the white man advanced, kicking my bicycle out of the way.

"Aw, leave the bastard alone. He's got enough," said one.

They stood looking at me. I rubbed my shins, trying to stop the flow of blood. No doubt they felt a sort of contemptuous pity, for one asked:

"Yuh wanna ride t' town now, nigger? Yuh reckon yuh know enough t' ride now?"

"I wanna walk," I said, simply.

Maybe it sounded funny. They laughed.

"Well, walk, yuh black son-of-a-bitch!"

When they left they comforted me with:

"Nigger, yuh sho better be damn glad it wuz us yuh talked t' tha' way. Yuh're a lucky bastard, 'cause if yuh'd said tha' t' somebody else, yuh might've been a dead nigger now."

IV

Negroes who have lived South know the dread of being caught alone upon the streets in white neighborhoods after the sun has set. In such a simple situation as this the plight of the Negro in America is graphically symbolized. While white strangers may be in these neighborhoods trying to get home, they can pass unmolested. But the color of a Negro's skin makes him easily recognizable, makes him suspect, converts him into a defenseless target.

Late one Saturday night I made some deliveries in a white neighborhood. I was pedaling my bicycle back to the store as fast as I could, when a police car, swerving toward me, jammed me into the curbing.

"Get down and put up your hands!" the policemen ordered.

I did. They climbed out of the car, guns drawn, faces set, and advanced slowly. "Keep still!" they ordered.

I reached my hands higher. They searched my pockets and packages. They seemed dissatisfied when they could find nothing incriminating. Finally, one of them said:

"Boy, tell your boss not to send you out in white neighborhoods after sundown."

As usual, I said:

"Yes, sir."

V

My next job was a hall-boy in a hotel. Here my Jim Crow education broadened and deepened. When the bell-boys were busy, I was often called to assist them. As many of the rooms in the hotel were occupied by prostitutes, I was constantly called to carry them liquor and cigarettes. These women were nude most of the time. They did not bother about clothing, even for bell-boys. When you went into their rooms, you were supposed to take their nakedness for granted, as though it startled you no more than a blue vase or a red rug. Your presence awoke in them no sense of shame, for you were not regarded as human. If they were alone, you cold steal sidelong glimpses at them. But if they were receiving men, not a flicker of your eyelids could show. I remember one incident vividly. A new woman, a huge, snowy-skinned blonde, took a room on my floor. I was sent to wait upon her. She was in bed with a thick-set man; both were nude and uncovered. She said she wanted some liquor and slid out of bed and waddled across the floor to get her money from a dresser drawer. I watched her.

"Nigger, what in hell you looking at?" the white man asked me, raising himself upon his elbows.

"Nothing," I answered, looking miles deep into the blank wall of the room.

"Keep your eyes where they belong, if you want to be healthy!" he said.

"Yes, sir."

VI

One of the bell-boys I knew in this hotel was keeping steady company with one of the Negro maids. Out of a clear sky the police descended upon his home and arrested him, accusing him of bastardy. The poor boy swore he had had no intimate relations with the girl. Nevertheless, they forced him to marry her. When the child arrived, it was found to be much lighter in complexion than either of the two supposedly legal parents. The white men around the hotel made a great joke of it. They spread the rumor that some white cow must have scared the poor girl while she was carrying the baby. If you were in their presence when this explanation was offered, you were supposed to laugh.

VII

One of the bell-boys was caught in bed with a white prostitute. He was castrated and run out of town. Immediately after this all the bell-boys and hall-boys were called together and warned. We were given to understand that the boy who had been castrated was a "mighty, mighty lucky bastard." We were impressed with the fact that next time the management of the hotel would not be responsible for the lives of "trouble-makin' niggers." We were silent.

VIII

One night, just as I was about to go home, I met one of the Negro maids. She lived in my direction, and we fell in to walk part of the way home together. As we passed the white night-watchman, he slapped the maid on her buttock. I turned around, amazed. The watchman looked at me with a long, hard, fixed-under stare. Suddenly he pulled his gun and asked:
"Nigger, don't yuh like it?"
I hesitated.
"I asked yuh don't yuh like it?" he asked again, stepping forward.
"Yes, sir," I mumbled.
"Talk like it, then!"
"Oh, yes sir!" I said with as much heartiness as I could muster.
Outside, I walked ahead of the girl, ashamed to face her. She caught up with me and said:
"Don't be a fool! Yuh couldn't help it!"
This watchman boasted of having killed two Negroes in self-defense.
Yet, in spite of all this, the life of the hotel ran with an amazing smoothness. It would have been impossible for a stranger to detect anything. The maids, the hall-boys, and the bell-boys were all smiles. They had to be.

IX

I had learned my Jim Crow lessons so thoroughly that I kept the hotel job till I left Jackson for Memphis. It so happened that while in Memphis I applied for a job at a branch of the optical company. I was hired. And for some reason, as long as I worked there, they never brought my past against me.
Here my Jim Crow education assumed quite a different form. It was no longer brutally cruel, but subtly cruel. Here I learned to lie, to steal, to dissemble. I learned to play that dual role which every Negro must play if he wants to eat and live.
For example, it was almost impossible to get a book to read. It was assumed that after a Negro had imbibed what scanty schooling the state furnished he had no

further need for books. I was always borrowing books from men on the job. One day I mustered enough courage to ask one of the men to let me get books from the library in his name. Surprisingly, he consented. I cannot help but think that he consented because he was a Roman Catholic and felt a vague sympathy for Negroes, being himself an object of hatred. Armed with a library card, I obtained books in the following manner: I would write a note to the librarian, saying: "Please let this nigger boy have the following books." I would then sign it with the white man's name.

When I went to the library, I would stand at the desk, hat in hand, looking as unbookish as possible. When I received the books desired I would take them home. If the books listed in the note happened to be out, I would sneak into the lobby and forge a new one. I never took any chances guessing with the white librarian about what the fictitious white man would want to read. No doubt if any of the white patrons had suspected that some of the volumes they enjoyed had been in the home of a Negro, they would not have tolerated it for an instant.

The factory force of the optical company in Memphis was much larger than that in Jackson, and more urbanized. At least they liked to talk, and would engage the Negro help in conversation whenever possible. By this means I found that many subjects were taboo from the white man's point of view. Among the topics they did not like to discuss with Negroes were the following: American white women; the Ku Klux Klan; France, and how Negro soldiers fared while there; French women; Jack Johnson; the entire northern part of the United States; the Civil War; Abraham Lincoln; U. S. Grant; General Sherman; Catholics; the Pope; Jews; the Republican Party; slavery; social equality; Communism; Socialism; the 13th and 14th Amendments to the Constitution; or any topic calling for positive knowledge or manly self-assertion on the part of the Negro. The most accepted topics were sex and religion.

There were many times when I had to exercise a great deal of ingenuity to keep out of trouble. It is a southern custom that all men must take off their hats when they enter an elevator. And especially did this apply to us blacks with rigid force. One day I stepped into an elevator with my arms full of packages. I was forced to ride with my hat on. Two white men stared at me coldly. Then one of them very kindly lifted my hat and placed it upon my armful of packages. Now the most accepted response for a Negro to make under such circumstances is to look at the white man out of the corner of his eye and grin. To have said: "Thank you!" would have made the white man *think* that you *thought* you were receiving from him a personal service. For such an act I have seen Negroes take a blow in the mouth. Finding the first alternative distasteful, and the second dangerous, I hit upon an acceptable course of action which fell safely between these two poles. I immediately—no sooner than my hat was lifted—pretended that my packages were about to spill, and appeared deeply distressed with keeping them in my arms. In this fashion I evaded having to acknowledge his service, and, in spite of adverse circumstances, salvaged a slender shred of personal pride.

How do Negroes feel about the way they have to live? How do they discuss it when alone amongst themselves? I think this question can be answered in a single sentence. A friend of mine who ran an elevator once told me:

"Lawd, man! Ef it wuzn't fer them polices 'n' them ol' lynch-mobs, there wouldn't be nothin' but uproar down here!"

3

Rethinking Women's Biology

Ruth Hubbard

Women's biology is a social construct and a political concept, not a scientific one, and I mean that in at least three ways. The first can be summed up in Simone de Beauvoir's (1953) dictum "One isn't born a woman, one becomes a woman." This does not mean that the environment shapes us, but that the concept, woman (or man), is a socially constructed one that little girls (or boys) try to fit as we grow up. Some of us are better at it than others, but we all try, and our efforts have biological as well as social consequences (a false dichotomy because our biological and social attributes are related dialectically). How active we are, what clothes we wear, what games we play, what we eat and how much, what kinds of schools we go to, what work we do, all affect our biology as well as our social being in ways we cannot sort out. So, one isn't born a woman (or man), one becomes one.

The concept of women's biology is socially constructed, and political, in a second way because it is not simply women's description of our experience of our biology. Women's biology has been described by physicians and scientists who, for historical reasons, have been mostly economically privileged, university-educated men with strong personal and political interests in describing women in ways that make it appear "natural" for us to fulfill roles that are important for their well-being, personally and as a group. Self-serving descriptions of women's biology date back at least to Aristotle. But if we dismiss the early descriptions as ideological, so are the descriptions scientists have offered that characterize women as weak, over-emotional, and at the mercy of our raging hormones, and that construct our entire being around the functions of our reproductive organs. No one has suggested that men are just walking testicles, but again and again women have been looked on as though they were walking ovaries and wombs.

In the nineteenth century, when women tried to get access to higher education, scientists initially claimed we could not be educated because our brains are too small. When that claim became untenable, they granted that we could be educated the same as men but questioned whether we should be, whether it was good for us. They based their concerns on the claim that girls need to devote much energy to establishing the proper functioning of their ovaries and womb and that if they divert this energy to their brains by studying, their reproductive organs will shrivel, they will become sterile, and the race will die out.

This logic was steeped in race and class prejudice. The notion that women's reproductive organs need careful nurturing was used to justify excluding upper-class girls and young women from higher education but not to spare the working-class, poor, or black women who were laboring in the factories and homes of the upper class. If anything, these women were said to breed too much. In fact, their ability to have many children despite the fact that they worked so hard was taken as evidence that they were less highly evolved than upper-class women; for them breeding was "natural," as for animals.

Finally, and perhaps most importantly, our concept of ourselves is socially constructed and political because our society's interpretation of what is and is not normal and natural affects what we do. It therefore affects our biological structure and functioning because, as I have said before, what we do and how our bodies and minds function are connected dialectically. Thus norms are self-fulfilling prophecies that do not merely describe how we are but prescribe how we should be.

4

The Social Construction of Gender

Judith Lorber

Until the eighteenth century, Western philosophers and scientists thought that there was one sex and that women's internal genitalia were the inverse of men's external genitalia: the womb and vagina were the penis and scrotum turned inside out (Laqueur 1990). Current Western thinking sees women and men as so different physically as to sometimes seem two species. The bodies, which have been mapped inside and out for hundreds of years, have not changed. What has changed are the justifications for gender inequality. When the social position of all human beings was believed to be set by natural law or was considered God-given, biology was irrelevant; women and men of different classes all had their assigned places. When scientists began to question the divine basis of social order and replaced faith with empirical knowledge, what they saw was that women were very different from men in that they had wombs and menstruated. Such anatomical differences destined them for an entirely different social life from men.

In actuality, the basic bodily material *is* the same for females and males, and except for procreative hormones and organs, female and male human beings have similar bodies (Naftolin and Butz 1981). Furthermore, as has been known since the middle of the nineteenth century, male and female genitalia develop from the same fetal tissue, and so infants can be born with ambiguous genitalia (Money and Ehrhardt 1972). When they are, biology is used quite arbitrarily in sex assignment. Suzanne Kessler (1990) interviewed six medical specialists in pediatric intersexuality and found that whether an infant with XY chromosomes and anomalous genitalia was categorized as a boy or a girl depended on the size of the penis—if a penis was very small, the child was categorized as a girl, and sex-change surgery was used to make an artificial vagina. In the late nineteenth century, the presence or absence of ovaries was the determining criterion of gender assignment for hermaphrodites because a woman who could not procreate was not a complete woman (Kessler 1990, 20).

Yet in Western societies, we see two discrete sexes and two distinguishable genders because our society is built on two classes of people, "women" and "men." Once the gender category is given, the attributes of the person are also gendered: Whatever a "woman" is has to be "female"; whatever a "man" is has to be "male." Analyzing the social processes that construct the categories we call "female and male," "women and men," and "homosexual and heterosexual" uncovers the ideology and power differentials congealed in these categories (Foucault 1978). This article will use two familiar areas of social life—sports and technological competence—to show how myriad physiological differences are transformed into similar-appearing, gendered social bodies. My perspective goes beyond accepted feminist views that gender is a cultural overlay that modifies physiological sex differences. That perspective assumes either that there are two fairly similar sexes distorted by social practices into two genders with purposefully different characteristics or that there are two sexes whose essential differences are rendered unequal by social practices. I am arguing that bodies differ in many ways physiologically, but they are completely transformed by social practices to fit into the salient categories of a society, the most pervasive of which are "female" and "male" and "women" and "men."

Neither sex nor gender are pure categories. Combinations of incongruous genes, genitalia, and hormonal input are ignored in sex categorization, just as combinations of incongruous physiology, identity, sexuality, appearance, and behavior are ignored in the social construction of gender statuses. Menstruation, lactation, and gestation do not demarcate women from men. Only some women are pregnant and then only some of the time; some women do not have a uterus or ovaries. Some women have stopped menstruating temporarily, others have reached menopause, and some have had hysterectomies. Some women breastfeed some of the time, but some men lactate (Jaggar 1983, 165fn). Menstruation, lactation, and gestation are individual experiences of womanhood (Levesque-Lopman 1988), but not determinants of the social category "woman," or even "female." Similarly, "men are not always sperm-producers, and in fact, not all sperm producers are men. A male-to-female transsexual, prior to surgery, can be socially a woman, though still potentially (or actually) capable of spermatogenesis" (Kessler and McKenna [1978] 1985, 2).

When gender assignment is contested in sports, where the categories of competitors are rigidly divided into women and men, chromosomes are now used to determine in which category the athlete is to compete. However, an anomaly common enough to be found in several women at every major international sports competition are XY chromosomes that have not produced male anatomy or physiology because of a genetic defect. Because these women are women in every way significant for sports competition, the prestigious International Amateur Athletic Federation has urged that sex be determined by simple genital inspection (Kolata 1992). Transsexuals would pass this test, but it took a lawsuit for Renée Richards, a male-to-female transsexual, to be able to play tournament tennis as a woman, despite his male sex chromosomes (Richards 1983). Oddly, neither basis for gender categorization—chromosomes nor genitalia—has anything to do with sports prowess (Birrell and Cole 1990).

In the Olympics, in cases of chromosomal ambiguity, women must undergo "a battery of gynecological and physical exams to see if she is 'female enough' to compete. Men are not tested" (Carlson 1991, 26). The purpose is not to categorize women and men accurately, but to make sure men don't enter women's competitions, where, it is felt, they will have the advantage of size and strength. This practice sounds fair only because it is assumed that all men are similar in size and strength and different from all women. Yet in Olympics boxing and wrestling matches, men are matched within weight classes. Some women might similarly successfully compete with some men in many sports. Women did not run in marathons until about twenty years ago. In twenty years of marathon competition, women have reduced their finish times by more than one-and-one-half hours; they are expected to run as fast as men in that race by 1998 and might catch up with men's running times in races of other lengths within the next 50 years because they are increasing their fastest speeds more rapidly than are men (Fausto-Sterling 1985, 213–18).

The reliance on only two sex and gender categories in the biological and social sciences is as epistemologically spurious as the reliance on chromosomal or genital tests to group athletes. Most research designs do not investigate whether physical skills or physical abilities are really more or less common in women and men (Epstein 1988). They start out with two social categories ("women," "men"), assume they are biologically different ("female," "male"), look for similarities among them and differences between them, and attribute what they have found for the social categories to sex differences (Gelman, Collman, and Maccoby 1986). These designs rarely question the categorization of their subjects into two and only two groups, even though they often find more significant within-group differences than between-group differences (Hyde 1990). The social construction perspective on sex and gender suggests that instead of starting with the two presumed dichotomies in each category—female, male; woman, man—it might be more useful in gender studies to group patterns of behavior and only then look for identifying markers of the people likely to enact such behaviors.

What Sports Illustrate

Competitive sports have become, for boys and men, as players and as spectators, a way of constructing a masculine identity, a legitimated outlet for violence and aggression, and an avenue for upward mobility (Dunning 1986; Kemper 1990, 167–206; Messner 1992). For men in Western societies, physical competence is an important marker of masculinity (Fine 1987; Glassner 1992; Majors 1990). In professional and collegiate sports, physiological differences are invoked to justify women's secondary status, despite the clear evidence that gender status overrides physiological capabilities. Assumptions about women's physiology have influenced rules of competition; subsequent sports performances then validate how women and men are treated in sports competitions.

Gymnastic equipment is geared to slim, wiry, prepubescent girls and not to mature women; conversely, men's gymnastic equipment is tailored for muscular, mature men, not slim, wiry prepubescent boys. Boys could compete with girls, but are not allowed to; women gymnasts are left out entirely. Girl gymnasts are just that—little girls who will be disqualified as soon as they grow up (Vecsey 1990). Men gymnasts have men's status. In women's basketball, the size of the ball and rules for handling the ball change the style of play to "a slower, less intense, and less exciting modification of the 'regular' or men's game" (Watson 1987, 441). In the 1992 Winter Olympics, men figure skaters were required to complete three triple jumps in their required program; women figure skaters were forbidden to do more than *one*. These rules penalized artistic men skaters and athletic women skaters (Janofsky 1992). For the most part, Western sports are built on physically trained men's bodies:

> Speed, size, and strength seem to be the essence of sports. Women *are* naturally inferior at "sports" so conceived.
>
> But if women had been the historically dominant sex, our concept of sport would no doubt have evolved differently. Competitions emphasizing flexibility, balance, strength, timing, and small size might dominate Sunday afternoon television and offer salaries in six figures. (English 1982, 266, emphasis in original)

Organized sports are big businesses and, thus, who has access and at what level is a distributive or equity issue. The overall status of women and men athletes is an economic, political, and ideological issue that has less to do with individual physiological capabilities than with their cultural and social meaning and who defines and profits from them (Messner and Sabo 1990; Slatton and Birrell 1984). Twenty years after the passage of Title IX of the U.S. Civil Rights Act, which forbade gender inequality in any school receiving federal funds, the *goal* for collegiate sports in the next five years is 60 percent men, 40 percent women in sports participation, scholarships, and funding (Moran 1992).

How access and distribution of rewards (prestigious and financial) are justified is an ideological, even moral, issue (Birrell 1988, 473–76; Hargreaves 1982). One way is that men athletes are glorified and women athletes ignored in the mass media. Messner and his colleagues found that in 1989, in TV sports news in the United States, men's sports got 92 percent of the coverage and women's sports 5 percent, with the rest mixed or gender-neutral (Messner, Duncan, and Jensen 1993). In 1990, in four of the top-selling newspapers in the United States, stories on men's sports outnumbered those on women's sports 23 to 1. Messner and his colleagues also found an implicit hierarchy in naming, with women athletes most likely to be called by first names, followed by Black men athletes, and only white men athletes routinely referred to by their last names. Similarly, women's collegiate sports teams are named or marked in ways that symbolically feminize and trivialize them—the men's team is called Tigers, the women's Kittens (Eitzen and Baca Zinn 1989).

Assumptions about men's and women's bodies and their capacities are crafted in ways that make unequal access and distribution of rewards acceptable (Hudson 1978; Messner 1988). Media images of modern men athletes glorify their strength and power, even their violence (Hargreaves 1986). Media images of modern women athletes tend to focus on feminine beauty and grace (so they are not really athletes) or on their thin, small, wiry androgynous bodies (so they are not really women). In coverage of the Olympics,

> loving and detailed attention is paid to pixie-like gymnasts; special and extended coverage is given to graceful and dazzling figure skaters; the camera painstakingly records the fluid movements of swimmers and divers. And then, in a blinding flash of fragmented images, viewers see a few minutes of volleyball, basketball, speed skating, track and field, and alpine skiing, as television gives its nod to the mere existence of these events. (Boutilier and SanGiovanni 1983, 190)

Extraordinary feats by women athletes who were presented as mature adults might force sports organizers and audiences to rethink their stereotypes of women's capabilities, the way elves, mermaids, and ice queens do not. Sports, therefore, construct men's bodies to be powerful; women's bodies to be sexual. As Connell says,

> The meanings in the bodily sense of masculinity concern, above all else, the superiority of men to women, and the exaltation of hegemonic masculinity over other groups of men which is essential for the domination of women. (1987, 85)

In the late 1970s, as women entered more and more athletic competitions, supposedly good scientific studies showed that women who exercised intensely would cease menstruating because they would not have enough body fat to sustain ovulation (Brozan 1978). When one set of researchers did a yearlong study that compared 66 women—21 who were training for a marathon, 22 who ran more than an hour a week, and 23 who did less than an hour of aerobic exercise a week—they discovered that only 20 percent of the women in any of these groups had "normal" menstrual cycles every month (Prior et al. 1990). The dangers of intensive training for women's fertility therefore were exaggerated as women began to compete successfully in arenas formerly closed to them.

Given the association of sports with masculinity in the United States, women athletes have to manage a contradictory status. One study of women college basketball players found that although they "did athlete" on the court—"pushing, shoving, fouling, hard running, fast breaks, defense, obscenities and sweat" (Watson 1987, 441), they "did woman" off the court, using the locker room as their staging area:

> While it typically took fifteen minutes to prepare for the game, it took approximately fifteen minutes after the game to shower and remove the sweat of an athlete, *and* it took another thirty minutes to dress, apply make-up and style hair. It did not seem to matter whether the players were going out into the public or getting on a van for a long ride home. Average dressing time and rituals did not change. (Watson 1987, 443)

Another way women manage these status dilemmas is to redefine the activity or its result as feminine or womanly (Mangan and Park 1987). Thus women bodybuilders claim that "flex appeal is sex appeal" (Duff and Hong 1984, 378).

Such a redefinition of women's physicality affirms the ideological subtext of sports that physical strength is men's prerogative and justifies men's physical and sexual domination of women (Hargreaves 1986; Messner 1992, 164–72; Olson 1990; Theberge 1987; Willis 1982). When women demonstrate physical strength, they are labeled unfeminine:

> It's threatening to one's takeability, one's rapeability, one's femininity, to be strong and physically self-possessed. To be able to resist rape, not to communicate rapeability with one's body, to hold one's body for uses and meanings other than that can transform what *being a woman means*. (MacKinnon 1987, 122, emphasis in original)

Resistance to that transformation, ironically, was evident in the policies of American women physical education professionals throughout most of the twentieth century. They minimized exertion, maximized a feminine appearance and manner, and left organized sports competition to men (Birrell 1988, 461–62; Mangan and Park 1987).

Dirty Little Secrets

As sports construct gendered bodies, technology constructs gendered skills. Meta-analysis of studies of gender differences in spatial and mathematical ability have found that men have a large advantage in ability to mentally rotate an image, a moderate advantage in a visual perception of horizontality and verticality and in mathematical performance, and a small advantage in ability to pick a figure out of a field (Hyde 1990). It could be argued that these advantages explain why, within the short space of time that computers have become ubiquitous in offices, schools, and homes, work on them and with them has become gendered: Men create, program, and market computers, make war and produce science and art with them; women microwire them in computer factories and enter data in computerized offices; boys play games, socialize, and commit crimes with computers; girls are rarely seen in computer clubs, camps, and classrooms. But women were hired as computer programmers in the 1940s because

> the work seemed to resemble simple clerical tasks. In fact, however, programming demanded complex skills in abstract logic, mathematics, electrical circuitry, and machinery, all of which . . . women used to perform in their work. Once programming was recognized as "intellectually demanding," it became attractive to men. (Donato 1990, 170)

A woman mathematician and pioneer in data processing, Grace M. Hopper, was famous for her work on programming language (Perry and Greber 1990, 86). By the 1960s, programming was split into more and less skilled specialties, and the entry of women into the computer field in the 1970s and 1980s was confined to the lower-paid specialties. At each stage, employers invoked women's and men's purportedly natural capabilities for the jobs for which they were hired (Cockburn 1983, 1985; Donato 1990; Hartmann 1987; Hartmann, Kraut, and Tilly 1986; Kramer and Lehman 1990; Wright et al. 1987; Zimmerman 1983).

It is the taken-for-grantedness of such everyday gendered behavior that gives credence to the belief that the widespread differences in what women and men do must come from biology. To take one ordinarily unremarked scenario: In modern societies, if a man and woman who are a couple are in a car together, he is much more likely to take the wheel than she is, even if she is the more competent driver. Molly Haskell calls this taken-for-granted phenomenon "the dirty little secret of marriage: the husband-lousy-driver syndrome" (1989, 26). Men drive cars whether they are good drivers or not because men and machines are a "natural" combination (Scharff 1991). But the ability to drive gives one mobility; it is a form of social power.

In the early days of the automobile, feminists co-opted the symbolism of mobility as emancipation: "Donning goggles and dusters, wielding tire irons and tool kits, taking the wheel, they announced their intention to move beyond the bounds of women's place" (Scharff 1991, 68). Driving enabled them to campaign for women's suffrage in parts of the United States not served by public transportation, and they effectively used motorcades and speaking from cars as campaign tactics (Scharff 1991, 67–88). Sandra Gilbert also notes that during World War I, women's ability to drive was physically, mentally, and even sensually liberating:

For nurses and ambulance drivers, women doctors and women messengers, the phenomenon of modern battle was very different from that experienced by entrenched combatants. Finally given a chance to take the wheel, these post-Victorian girls raced motorcars along foreign roads like adventurers exploring new lands, while their brothers dug deeper into the mud of France. . . . Retrieving the wounded and the dead from deadly positions, these once-decorous daughters had at last been allowed to prove their valor, and they swooped over the wastelands of the war with the energetic love of Wagnerian Valkyries, their mobility alone transporting countless immobilized heroes to safe havens. (1983, 438–39)

Not incidentally, women in the United States and England got the vote for their war efforts in World War I.

Social Bodies and the Bathroom Problem

People of the same racial ethnic group and social class are roughly the same size and shape—but there are many varieties of bodies. People have different genitalia, different secondary sex characteristics, different contributions to procreation, different orgasmic experiences, different patterns of illness and aging. Each of us experiences our bodies differently, and these experiences change as we grow, age, sicken, and die. The bodies of pregnant and nonpregnant women, short and tall people, those with intact and functioning limbs and those whose bodies are physically challenged are all different. But the salient categories of a society group these attributes in ways that ride roughshod over individual experiences and more meaningful clusters of people.

I am not saying that physical differences between male and female bodies don't exist, but that these differences are socially meaningless until social practices transform them into social facts. West Point Military Academy's curriculum is designed to produce leaders, and physical competence is used as a significant measure of leadership ability (Yoder 1989). When women were accepted as West Point cadets, it became clear that the tests of physical competence, such as rapidly scaling an eight-foot wall, had been constructed for male physiques—pulling oneself up and over using upper-body strength. Rather than devise tests of physical competence for women, West Point provided boosters that mostly women used—but that lost them test points—in the case of the wall, a platform. Finally, the women themselves figured out how to use their bodies successfully. Janice Yoder describes this situation:

I was observing this obstacle one day, when a woman approached the wall in the old prescribed way, got her fingertips grip, and did an unusual thing: she walked her dangling legs up the wall until she was in a position where both her hands and feet were atop the wall. She then simply pulled up her sagging bottom and went over. She solved the problem by capitalizing on one of women's physical assets: lower-body strength. (1989, 530)

In short, if West Point is going to measure leadership capability by physical strength, women's pelvises will do just as well as men's shoulders.

The social transformation of female and male physiology into a condition of inequality is well illustrated by the bathroom problem. Most buildings that have gender-segregated bathrooms have an equal number for women and for men. Where there are crowds, there are always long lines in front of women's bathrooms but rarely in front of men's bathrooms. The cultural, physiological, and demographic combinations of clothing, frequency of urination, menstruation, and child care add up to generally greater bathroom use by women than men. Thus, although an equal number of bathrooms seems fair, equity would mean more women's bathrooms or allowing women to use men's bathrooms for a certain amount of time (Molotch 1988).

The bathroom problem is the outcome of the way gendered bodies are differentially evaluated in Western cultures: Men's social bodies are the measure of what is "human." Gray's *Anatomy*, in use for 100 years, well into the twentieth century, presented the human body as male. The female body was shown only where it differed from the male (Laqueur 1990, 166–67). Denise Riley says that if we envisage women's bodies, men's bodies, and human bodies "as a triangle of identifications, then it is rarely an equilateral triangle in which both sexes are pitched at matching distances from the apex of the human" (1988, 197). Catharine MacKinnon also contends that in Western society, universal "humanness" is male because

> virtually every quality that distinguishes men from women is already affirmatively compensated in this society. Men's physiology defines most sports, their needs define auto and health insurance coverage, their socially defined biographies define workplace expectations and successful career patterns, their perspectives and concerns define quality in scholarship, their experiences and obsessions define merit, their objectification of life defines art, their military service defines citizenship, their presence defines family, their inability to get along with each other—their wars and rulerships—define history, their image defines god, and their genitals define sex. For each of their differences from women, what amounts to an affirmative action plan is in effect, otherwise known as the structure and values of American society. (1987, 36)

The Paradox of Human Nature

Gendered people do not emerge from physiology or hormones but from the exigencies of the social order, mostly, from the need for a reliable division of the work of food production and the social (not physical) reproduction of new members. The moral imperatives of religion and cultural representations reinforce the boundary lines among genders and ensure that what is demanded, what is permitted, and what is tabooed for the people in each gender is well-known and followed by most. Political power, control of scarce resources, and, if necessary, violence uphold the gendered social order in the face of resistance and rebellion.

Most people, however, voluntarily go along with their society's prescriptions for those of their gender status because the norms and expectations get built into their sense of worth and identity as a certain kind of human being and because they believe their society's way is the natural way. These beliefs emerge from the imagery that pervades the way we think, the way we see and hear and speak, the way we fantasize, and the way we feel. There is no core or bedrock human nature below these endlessly looping processes of the social production of sex and gender, self and other, identity and psyche, each of which is a "complex cultural construction" (Butler 1990, 36). The paradox of "human nature" is that it is *always* a manifestation of cultural meanings, social relationships, and power politics—"not biology, but culture, becomes destiny" (Butler 1990, 8).

Feminist inquiry has long questioned the conventional categories of social science, but much of the current work in feminist sociology has not gone beyond adding the universal category "women" to the universal category "men." Our current debates over the global assumptions of only two categories and the insistence that they must be nuanced to include race and class are steps in the direction I would like to see feminist research go, but race and class are *also* global categories (Collins 1990; Spelman 1988). Deconstructing sex, sexuality, and gender reveals many possible categories embedded in the social experiences and social practices of what Dorothy Smith calls the "everyday/everynight world" (1990, 31–57). These emergent categories group some people together for comparison with other people without prior assumptions about who is like whom. Categories can be broken up and people regrouped differently into new categories for comparison. This process of discovering categories from similarities and differences in people's behavior or responses can be more meaningful for feminist research than discovering similarities and differences between "females" and "males" or "women" and "men" because the social construction of the conventional sex and gender categories already assumes differences between them and similarities among them. When we rely only on the conventional categories of sex and gender, we end up finding what we looked for—we see what we believe, whether it is that "females" and "males" are essentially different or that "women" and "men" are essentially the same.

REFERENCES

Birrell, Susan J. 1988. Discourses on the gender/sport relationship: From women in sport to gender relations. In *Exercise and sport science reviews.* Vol. 16, edited by Kent Pandolf. New York: Macmillan.

Birrell, Susan J., and Sheryl L. Cole. 1990. Double fault: Renée Richards and the construction and naturalization of difference. *Sociology of Sport Journal* 7:1–21.

Boutilier, Mary A., and Lucinda SanGiovanni. 1983. *The sporting woman.* Champaign, IL: Human Kinetics.

Brozan, Nadine. 1978. Training linked to disruption of female reproductive cycle. *New York Times,* 17 April.

Butler, Judith. 1990. *Gender trouble: Feminism and the subversion of identity.* New York and London: Routledge & Kegan Paul.

Carlson, Alison. 1991. When is a woman not a woman? *Women's Sport and Fitness* March:24–29.

Cockburn, Cynthia. 1983. *Brothers: Male dominance and technological change.* London: Pluto.

———. 1985. *Machinery of dominance: Women, men and technical know-how.* London: Pluto.

Collins, Patricia Hill. 1990. *Black feminist thought: Knowledge, consciousness, and the politics of empowerment.* Boston: Unwin Hyman.

Connell, R. W. 1987. *Gender and power.* Stanford, CA: Stanford University Press.

Donato, Katharine M. 1990. Programming for change? The growing demand for women systems analysts. In *Job queues, gender queues: Explaining women's inroads into male occupations,* written and edited by Barbara F. Reskin and Patricia A. Roos. Philadelphia: Temple University Press.

Duff, Robert W., and Lawrence K. Hong, 1984. Self-images of women bodybuilders. *Sociology of Sport Journal* 2:374–80.

Dunning, Eric. 1986. Sport as a male preserve: Notes on the social sources of masculine identity and its transformations. *Theory, Culture and Society* 3:79–90.

Eitzen, D. Stanley, and Maxine Baca Zinn. 1989. The deathleticization of women: The naming and gender marking of collegiate sport teams. *Sociology of Sport Journal* 6:362–70.

English, Jane. 1982. Sex equality in sports. In *Femininity, masculinity, and androgyny,* edited by Mary Vetterling-Braggin. Boston: Littlefield, Adams.

Epstein, Cynthia Fuchs. 1988. *Deceptive distinctions: Sex, gender and the social order.* New Haven, CT: Yale University Press.

Fausto-Sterling, Anne. 1985. *Myths of gender: Biological theories about women and men.* New York: Basic Books.

Fine, Gary Alan. 1987. *With the boys: Little League baseball and preadolescent culture.* Chicago: University of Chicago Press.

Foucault, Michel. 1978. *The history of sexuality: An introduction.* Translated by Robert Hurley. New York: Pantheon.

Gelman, Susan A., Pamela Collman, and Eleanor E. Maccoby. 1986. Inferring properties from categories versus inferring categories from properties: The case of gender. *Child Development* 57:396–404.

Gilbert, Sandra M. 1983. Soldier's heart: Literary men, literary women, and the Great War. *Signs: Journal of Women in Culture and Society* 8:422–50.

Glassner, Barry. 1992. Men and muscles. In *Men's lives,* edited by Michael S. Kimmel and Michael A. Messner. New York: Macmillan.

Hargreaves, Jennifer A., ed. 1982. *Sport, culture, and ideology.* London: Routledge & Kegan Paul.

———. 1986. Where's the virtue? Where's the grace? A discussion of the social production of gender relations in and through sport. *Theory, Culture, and Society* 3:109–21.

Hartmann, Heidi I., ed. 1987. *Computer chips and paper clips: Technology and women's employment.* Vol. 2. Washington, DC: National Academy Press.

Hartmann, Heidi I., Robert E. Kraut, and Louise A. Tilly, eds. 1986. *Computer chips and paper clips: Technology and women's employment.* Vol. 1. Washington, DC: National Academy Press.

Haskell, Molly. 1989. Hers: He drives me crazy. *New York Times Magazine,* 24 September, 26, 28.

Hudson, Jackie. 1978. Physical parameters used for female exclusion from law enforcement and athletics. In *Women and sport: From myth to reality,* edited by Carole A. Oglesby. Philadelphia: Lea and Febiger.

Hyde, Janet Shibley. 1990. Meta-analysis and the psychology of gender differences. *Signs: Journal of Women in Culture and Society* 16:55–73.

Jaggar, Alison M. 1983. *Feminist politics and human nature.* Totowa, NJ: Rowman & Allanheld.

Janofsky, Michael. 1992. Yamaguchi has the delicate and golden touch. *New York Times,* 22 February.

Kemper, Theodore D. 1990. *Social structure and testosterone: Explorations of the sociobiosocial chain.* Brunswick, NJ: Rutgers University Press.

Kessler, Suzanne J. 1990. The medical construction of gender: Case management of intersexed infants. *Signs: Journal of Women in Culture and Society* 16:3–26.

Kessler, Suzanne J., and Wendy McKenna. [1978] 1985. *Gender: An ethnomethodological approach.* Chicago: University of Chicago Press.

Kolata, Gina. 1992. Track federation urges end to gene test for femaleness. *New York Times,* 12 February.

Kramer, Pamela E., and Sheila Lehman. 1990. Mismeasuring women: A critique of research on computer ability and avoidance. *Signs: Journal of Women in Culture and Society* 16:158–72.

Laqueur, Thomas. 1990. *Making sex: Body and gender from the Greeks to Freud.* Cambridge, MA: Harvard University Press.

Levesque-Lopman, Louise. 1988. *Claiming reality: Phenomenology and women's experience.* Totowa, NJ: Rowman & Littlefield.

MacKinnon, Catharine. 1987. *Feminism unmodified.* Cambridge, MA: Harvard University Press.

Majors, Richard. 1990. Cool pose: Black masculinity in sports. In *Sport, men, and the gender order: Critical feminist perspectives,* edited by Michael A. Messner and Donald F. Sabo. Champaign, IL: Human Kinetics.

Mangan, J. A., and Roberta J. Park. 1987. *From fair sex to feminism: Sport and the socialization of women in the industrial and post-industrial eras.* London: Frank Cass.

Messner, Michael A. 1988. Sports and male domination: The female athlete as contested ideological terrain. *Sociology of Sport Journal* 5:197–211.

———. 1992. *Power at play: Sports and the problem of masculinity.* Boston: Beacon Press.

Messner, Michael A., Margaret Carlisle Duncan, and Kerry Jensen. 1993. Separating the men from the girls: The gendered language of televised sports. *Gender & Society* 7:121–37.

Messner, Michael A., and Donald F. Sabo, eds. 1990. *Sport, men, and the gender order: Critical feminist perspectives.* Champaign, IL: Human Kinetics.

Molotch, Harvey. 1988. The restroom and equal opportunity. *Sociological Forum* 3: 128–32.

Money, John, and Anke A. Ehrhardt. 1972. *Man & woman, boy & girl.* Baltimore, MD: Johns Hopkins University Press.

Moran, Malcolm. 1992. Title IX: A 20-year search for equity. *New York Times* Sports Section, 21, 22, 23 June.

Naftolin, F., and E. Butz, eds. 1981. Sexual dimorphism. *Science* 211:1263–1324.

Olson, Wendy. 1990. Beyond Title IX: Toward an agenda for women and sports in the 1990s. *Yale Journal of Law and Feminism* 3:105–51.

Perry, Ruth, and Lisa Greber. 1990. Women and computers: An introduction. *Signs: Journal of Women in Culture and Society* 16:74–101.

Prior, Jerilynn C., Yvette M. Yigna, Martin T. Shechter, and Arthur E. Burgess. 1990. Spinal bone loss and ovulatory disturbances. *New England Journal of Medicine* 323:1221–27.

Richards, Renée, with Jack Ames. 1983. *Second serve.* New York: Stein and Day.

Riley, Denise. 1988. *Am I that name? Feminism and the category of women in history.* Minneapolis: University of Minnesota Press.

Scharff, Virginia. 1991. *Taking the wheel: Women and the coming of the motor age.* New York: Free Press.

Slatton, Bonnie, and Susan Birrell. 1984. The politics of women's sport. *Arena Review* 8.

Smith, Dorothy E. 1990. *The conceptual practices of power: A feminist sociology of knowledge.* Toronto: University of Toronto Press.

Spelman, Elizabeth. 1988. *Inessential woman: Problems of exclusion in feminist thought.* Boston: Beacon Press.

Theberge, Nancy. 1987. Sport and women's empowerment. *Women's Studies International Forum* 10:387–93.

Vecsey, George. 1990. Cathy Rigby, unlike Peter, did grow up. *New York Times* Sports Section, 19 December.

Watson, Tracey. 1987. Women athletes and athletic women: The dilemmas and contradictions of managing incongruent identities. *Sociological Inquiry* 57:431–46.

Willis, Paul. 1982. Women in sport in ideology. In *Sport, culture, and ideology,* edited by Jennifer A. Hargreaves. London: Routledge & Kegan Paul.

Wright, Barbara Drygulski et al., eds. 1987. *Women, work, and technology: Transformations.* Ann Arbor: University of Michigan Press.

Yoder, Janice D. 1989. Women at West Point: Lessons for token women in male-dominated occupations. In *Women: A feminist perspective,* edited by Jo Freeman, 4th ed. Palo Alto, CA: Mayfield.

Zimmerman, Jan, ed. 1983. *The technological woman: Interfacing with tomorrow.* New York: Praeger.

5

Ah, Ya Throw like a Girl!

Mike Messner

Although the sociology department at U.C. Berkeley is situated on the fourth floor of a very ugly post-war building, the place does have one thing going for it: the fourth floor balcony overlooks the women's softball field. There I have spent not a few fine afternoons in the past few years basking in the sunshine and watching some of the most talented softball players in the nation.

When I am joined on the balcony (usually only briefly) by my hard-working friends and colleagues who kid me about "taking the day off in the sun," I retort that I am actually doing *research* at this very moment. After all, I *am* doing my dissertation on "sports and male identity" (great thing about sociology: everything is data).

One spring day I was enjoying a beautifully played pitchers' duel between Cal's women and another top-ranked team. It was late in the game, with the score tied 1–1 when I was joined in my personal left field pavillion by a friendly and gentle man who is nearing the end of a very successful career as a sociologist at U.C.B. Suddenly, with a runner on first via a rare base-on-balls from the Cal pitcher, the batter drove the ball on a line into left-center field. The left fielder managed to run the ball down, turn, and fire a strike to the shortstop just at the edge of the infield, who in turn spun and threw perfectly, laser-like, to the plate, nailing the lead runner. What precision teamwork and execution! And the game was still tied!

My fellow fan smiled, as did I, and shook his head. "You know, it amazes me to see a woman throw like that. I always thought that there was something about the female arm that made it impossible to throw like a man."

I'm 8 years old and I'm playing Little League Baseball for the first time and my dad's the coach! It's my first tryout/practice and it's an exciting, confusing, scary affair, with what seems like hundreds of boys, all with identical green caps and leather mitts facing each other in two long lines, throwing balls back and forth as fathers furiously race around coaching, criticizing, encouraging, demonstrating, and scrawling mysterious things on clipboards.

Later at home, my father informs me that there are two boys on the team who throw like girls, and that I, unfortunately, am one of them! By the next practice, he tells me, we will have corrected that problem. That evening, with glove and cap securely in place, I anxiously face my father on the front lawn. And we play catch. For quite a while. I am concentrating, working hard to throw correctly ("like a *man*"), pulling my arm back as far as I can and snapping the ball overhand, just past my ear. When I do this, it feels very strange—I really have very little control over the flight of the ball, and it hurts my shoulder a bit—but I am rewarded with the knowledge that *this is how men throw the ball.* If I learn this, I won't embarrass either myself or my father. When at times I inadvertently revert to what feels like a more natural and more easily controllable throwing style (more of a shot-put style, with hand and ball starting just behind the ear, and elbow leading the way), I immediately am rewarded with a return throw that sails far over my head and lands two or three houses down. "Run! *Run* after that ball! You won't have to chase it anymore when you quit throwing like a girl!"

Simple behavior-modification, actually. And it worked—I learned very rapidly how to throw properly. But it wasn't really the having to run after the ball that taught me: it was the threat to my very fragile sense of maleness. The *fear*—oh, the fear of being thought a sissy—a *girl!*

I was momentarily taken aback that a renowned sociologist would have such a "biological" explanation for gender differences between women and men. I explained to him that, indeed, "throwing like a girl" is actually a more anatomically natural motion for the human arm. "Throwing like a man" is a learned action which can, repeated over time, actually seriously damage the arm.

A few years ago, a sportswriter did an informal survey of major league pitchers, asking of those who had played Little League as youngsters just how many of them had been pitchers in their youth. The astounding answer: *zero.* Stories of Little Leaguers burning their arms out for life are common. The destruction of young shoulders and elbows has led to some Little Leagues outlawing curve balls. Others have even instituted systems in which adults do all the pitching for 8- and 9-year-olds.

"Throwing like a man" is an unnatural act, an act that (like most aspects of "masculinity") must be learned. Indeed, I learned it at a very young age, as did most of my male peers. And while I was on the front lawn with Dad, my older sister Linda was God-knows-where, but certainly not playing ball. Only this past summer did she join a softball team and learn how to throw a ball. She's a natural athlete who had to wait until the age of 31 to get some simple coaching.

Things change far too slowly for most of us, but it is a fact that things are changing. People are changing. As we men begin to question the traditional meaning of "maleness" and reject those aspects of the traditional male role which have been oppressive to others and destructive to ourselves, we discover new ways to be men. After a 15-year break, I, for one, have taken up pitching a baseball to a friend who used to be a catcher. I throw exclusively submarine-style (almost underhand) which does not hurt my shoulder like overhand throwing always has. And we do it just for the simple joy of throwing and catching the ball.

As women become more and more visible and competent at tasks (including sports) that are traditionally "male territory," our conceptions of masculinity and femininity are being challenged. While watching women play softball, my professor friend learned something about the social basis for traditional differences between men and women. My sister not only plays softball, but coaches her 9-year-old daughter Jennifer's team, where she is determined to teach the girls how to throw a ball accurately and safely, among other things. And with this kind of role model and a changing social context, Jennifer is a girl who plays with a sense of enjoyment and confidence that was never allowed her mother. She loves to play. And she even loves to be the "bat-girl" for her father's city-league softball team. The first time she went to clear a bat away from home plate, she was confronted by a boy about her age who said to her derisively, "There's no such *thing* as a bat-*girl!*"

"Watch me," she replied.

6

The Social Construction of Sexuality

Ruth Hubbard

There is no "natural" human sexuality. This is not to say that our sexual feelings are "unnatural" but that whatever feelings and activities our society interprets as sexual are channeled from birth into socially acceptable forms of expression.

Western thinking about sexuality is based on the Christian equation of sexuality with sin, which must be redeemed through making babies. To fulfill the Christian mandate, sexuality must be intended for procreation, and thus all forms of sexual expression and enjoyment other than heterosexuality are invalidated. Actually, for most Christians nowadays just plain heterosexuality will do, irrespective of whether it is intended to generate offspring.

These ideas about sexuality set up a major contradiction in what we tell children about sex and procreation. We teach them that sex and sexuality are about becoming mommies and daddies and warn them not to explore sex by themselves or with playmates of either sex until they are old enough to have babies. Then, when they reach adolescence and the entire culture pressures them into hetero-sexual activity, whether they themselves feel ready for it or not, the more "enlight-ened" among us tell them how to be sexually (meaning heterosexually) active without having babies. Surprise: It doesn't work very well. Teenagers do not act "responsibly"—teenage pregnancies and abortions are on the rise and teenage fathers do not acknowledge and support their partners and babies. Somewhere we forget that we have been telling lies. Sexuality and procreation are not linked in societies like ours. On the contrary, we expect youngsters to be heterosexually active from their teens on but to put off having children until they are economically independent and married, and even then to have only two or, at most, three children.

Other contradictions: This society, on the whole, accepts Freud's assumption that children are sexual beings from birth and that society channels their polymorphously perverse childhood sexuality into the accepted forms. Yet we expect our children to be asexual. We raise girls and boys together more than is done in many societies while insisting that they must not explore their own or each other's sexual parts or feelings.

What if we acknowledged the separation of sexuality from procreation and encouraged our children to express themselves sexually if they were so inclined? What if we, further, encouraged them to explore their own bodies as well as those of friends of the same and the other sex when they felt like it? They might then be able to feel at home with their sexuality, have some sense of their own and other people's sexual needs, and know how to talk about sexuality and procreation with their friends and sexual partners before their ability to procreate becomes an issue for them. In this age of AIDS and other serious sexually transmitted infections, such a course of action seems like essential preventive hygiene. Without the embarrassment of unexplored and unacknowledged sexual needs, contraceptive needs would be much easier to confront when they arise. So, of course, would same-sex love relationships.

Such a more open and accepting approach to sexuality would make life easier for children and adolescents of either sex, but it would be especially advantageous for girls. When a boy discovers his penis as an organ of pleasure, it is the same organ he is taught about as his organ of procreation. A girl exploring her pleasurable sensations finds her clitoris, but when she is taught about making babies, she hears about the functions of the vagina in sex and birthing. Usually, the clitoris goes unmentioned, and she doesn't even learn its name until much later. Therefore for boys there is an obvious link between procreation and their own pleasurable, erotic explorations; for most girls, there isn't.

Individual Sexual Scripts

Each of us writes our own sexual script out of the range of our experiences. None of this script is inborn or biologically given. We construct it out of our diverse life situations, limited by what we are taught or what we can imagine to be permissible and correct. There is no unique female sexual experience, no male sexual experience, no unique heterosexual, lesbian, or gay male experience. We take the experiences of different people and sort and lump them according to socially significant categories. When I hear generalizations about *the* sexual experience of some particular group, exceptions immediately come to mind. Except that I refuse to call them exceptions: They are part of the range of our sexual experiences. Of course, the similar circumstances in which members of a particular group find themselves will give rise to group similarities. But we tend to exaggerate them when we go looking for similarities within groups or differences between them.

This exaggeration is easy to see when we look at the dichotomy between "the heterosexual" and "the homosexual." The concept of "the homosexual", along with many other human typologies, originated toward the end of the nineteenth century. Certain kinds of behavior stopped being attributed to particular persons and came to define them. A person who had sexual relations with someone of the same sex became a certain kind of person, a "homosexual;" a person who had sexual relations with people of the other sex, a different kind, a "heterosexual."

This way of categorizing people obscured the hitherto accepted fact that many people do not have sexual relations exclusively with persons of one or the other sex. (None of us has sex with a kind of person; we have sex with a person.) This categorization created the stereotypes that were popularized by the sex reformers, such as Havelock Ellis and Edward Carpenter, who biologized the "difference." "The homosexual" became a person who is different by nature and therefore should not be made responsible for his or her so-called deviance. This definition served the purpose of the reformers (although the laws have been slow to change), but it turned same-sex love into a medical problem to be treated by doctors rather than punished by judges—an improvement, perhaps, but not acceptance or liberation. . . .

Toward a Nondeterministic Model of Sexuality

. . . Some gay men and lesbians feel that they were born "different" and have always been homosexual. They recall feeling strongly attracted to members of their own sex when they were children and adolescents. But many women who live with men and think of themselves as heterosexual also had strong affective and erotic ties to girls and women while they were growing up. If they were now in loving relationships with women, they might look back on their earlier loves as proof that they were always lesbians. But if they are now involved with men, they may be tempted to devalue their former feelings as "puppy love" or "crushes."

Even within the preferred sex, most of us feel a greater affinity for certain "types" than for others. Not any man or woman will do. No one has seriously suggested that something in our innate makeup makes us light up in the presence of only certain women or men. We would think it absurd to look to hormone levels or any other simplistic biological cause for our preference for a specific "type" within a sex. In fact, scientists rarely bother to ask what in our psychosocial experience shapes these kinds of tastes and preferences. We assume it must have something to do with our relationship to our parents or with other experiences, but we do not probe deeply unless people prefer the "wrong" sex. Then, suddenly, scientists begin to look for specific causes.

Because of our recent history and political experiences, feminists tend to reject simplistic, causal models of how our sexuality develops. Many women who have thought of themselves as heterosexual for much of their life and who have been married and have had children have fallen in love with a woman (or women) when they have had the opportunity to rethink, refeel, and restructure their lives.

The society in which we live channels, guides, and limits our imagination in sexual as well as other matters. Why some of us give ourselves permission to love people of our own sex whereas others cannot even imagine doing so is an interesting question. But I do not think it will be answered by measuring our hormone levels or by trying to unearth our earliest affectional ties. As women begin to speak freely about our sexual experiences, we are getting a varied range of information with which we can reexamine, reevaluate, and change ourselves. Lately, increasing numbers of women have begun to acknowledge their "bisexuality"—the fact that they can love women and men in succession or simultaneously. People fall in love with individuals, not with a sex. Gender need not be a significant factor in our choice, although for some of us it may be.

7

Deconstructing the Underclass

Herbert Gans

A Matter of Definition?

Buzzwords for the undeserving poor are hardly new, for in the past the poor have been termed paupers, rabble, white trash, and the dangerous classes. Today, however, Americans do not use such harsh terms in their public discourse, whatever people may say to each other in private. Where possible, euphemisms are employed, and if they are from the academy, so much the better. A string of these became popular in the 1960s; the most famous is Oscar Lewis's anthropological concept *culture of poverty*, a term that became his generation's equivalent of underclass.

When Gunnar Myrdal invented or reinvented the term underclass in his 1962 book *Challenge to Affluence*, he used the word as a purely economic concept, to describe the chronically unemployed, underemployed, and underemployables being created by what we now call the post-industrial economy. He was thinking of people being driven to the margins, or entirely out, of the modern economy, here and elsewhere; but his intellectual and policy concern was with reforming that economy, not with changing or punishing the people who were its victims.

Some other academics, this author included, used the term with Myrdal's definition in the 1960s and 1970s. However, gradually the users shifted from Myrdal's concern with unemployment to poverty, so that by the late 1970s social scientists had begun to identify the underclass with acute or persistent poverty rather than joblessness. Around the same time a very different definition of the underclass also emerged that has become the most widely used, and is also the most dangerous.

That definition has two novel elements. The first is racial, for users of this definition see the underclass as being almost entirely black and Hispanic. Second, it adds a number of behavioral patterns to an economic definition—and almost always these patterns involve behavior thought to be undeserving by the definers.

Different definers concentrate on somewhat different behavior patterns, but most include antisocial or otherwise harmful behavior, such as crime. Many definers also focus on various patterns that are *deviant* or aberrant from what they consider middle class norms, but that in fact are not automatically or always harmful, such as common law marriage. Some definers even measure membership in the underclass by deviant answers to public opinion poll questions. . . .

In the past five years the term's diverse definitions have remained basically unchanged, although the defining attempt itself has occasioned a very lively, often angry, debate among scholars. Many researchers have accepted much or all of the now-dominant behavioral definition; some have argued for a purely economic one, like Myrdal's; and some—this author included—have felt that the term has taken on so many connotations of undeservingness and blameworthiness that it has become hopelessly polluted in meaning, ideological overtone and implications, and should be dropped—with the issues involved studied via other concepts. Basically the debate has involved positions usually associated with the Right and the Left, partisans of the former arguing that the underclass is the product of the unwillingness of the black poor to adhere to the American work ethic, among other cultural deficiencies, and the latter claiming that the underclass is a consequence of the development of the post-industrial economy, which no longer needs the unskilled poor.

The debate has swirled in part around William J. Wilson, the University of Chicago sociologist and author of *The Truly Disadvantaged* (1987), who is arguably the most prominent analyst of the underclass in the 1980s. He focuses entirely on the black underclass and insists that this underclass exists mainly because of large-scale and harmful changes in the labor market, and its resulting spatial concentration as well as the isolation of such areas from the more affluent parts of the black community. One of his early definitions also included a reference to aberrant behavior patterns, although his most recent one, offered in November 1989, centers around the notion of "weak attachment to the labor force," an idea that seems nearly to coincide with Myrdal's, especially since Wilson attributes that weakness to faults in the economy rather than in the jobless.

Wilson's work has inspired a lot of new research, not only about the underclass but about poverty in general, and has made poverty research funding, public and private, available again after a long drought. Meanwhile, various scholars have tried to resolve or reorient the political debate, but without much luck, for eventually the issue always boils down to whether the fault for being poor and the responsibility for change should be assigned more to poor people or more to the economy and the state. At the same time, journalistic use of the so-called behavioral definition of the underclass has increased—and so much so that there is a danger of researchers and policy analysts being carried along by the popularity of this definition of the term in the public discourse. . . .

The Power of Buzzwords and Labels

The behavioral definition of the underclass, which in essence proposes that some very poor people are somehow to be selected for separation from the rest of society and henceforth treated as especially undeserving, harbors many dangers—for their civil liberties and ours, for example, for democracy, and for the integration of society. But the rest of this essay will concentrate on what seem to me to be the major dangers for planners. The *first* danger of the term is its unusual power as a buzzword. It is a handy euphemism; while it seems inoffensively technical on the surface, it hides within it all the moral opprobrium Americans have long felt toward those poor people who have been judged to be undeserving. Even when it is being used by journalists, scholars, and others as a technical term, it carries with it this judgmental baggage. . . .

A *second* and related danger of the term is its use as a racial codeword that subtly hides anti-black and anti-Hispanic feelings. A codeword of this kind fits in with the tolerant public discourse of our time, but it also submerges and may further repress racial—and class—antagonisms that continue to exist, yet are sometimes not expressed until socio-political boiling points are reached. Racial and class codewords—and codewords of any kind—get in the way of planners, however, because the citizenry may read codewords even though planners are writing analytical concepts.

A *third* danger of the term is its flexible character. Given the freedom of definition available in a democracy, anyone can decide, or try to persuade others, that yet additional people should be included in the underclass. For example, it is conceivable that in a city, region, or country with a high unemployment rate, powerless competitors for jobs, such as illegal immigrants or even legal but recently arrived workers, might be added to the list of undeserving people. . . .

The *fourth* danger of the term, a particularly serious one, is that it is a synthesizing notion—or what William Kornblum has more aptly called a lumping one—that covers a number of different people. Like other synthesizing notions that have moved far beyond the researchers' journals, it has also become a stereotype.

Stereotypes are lay generalizations that are necessary in a very diversified society, and are useful when they are more or less accurate. When they are not, however, or when they are also judgmental terms, they turn into *labels*, to be used by some people to judge, and usually to stigmatize, other people, often those with less power or prestige. . . .

Insofar as poor people keep up with the labels the rest of society sticks on them, they are aware of the latest one. We do not all know the "street-level" consequences of stigmatizing labels, but they cannot be good. One of the likely, and most dangerous, consequences of labels is that they can become self-fulfilling prophecies. People publicly described as members of the underclass may begin to feel that they *are* members of such a class and are therefore unworthy in a new way. At the least, they now have to fight against yet another threat to their self-respect, not to mention another reason for feeling that society would just as soon have them disappear.

More important perhaps, people included in the underclass are quickly treated accordingly in their relations with the private and public agencies in which, like the rest of us, they are embedded—from workplaces, welfare agencies, and schools to the police and the courts. We know from social research that teachers with negative images of their pupils do not expect them to succeed and thus make sure, often unconsciously, that they do not; likewise, boys from single parent families who are picked up by the police are often thought to be wild and therefore guilty because they are assumed to lack male parental control. We know also that areas associated with the underclass do not get the same level of services as more affluent areas. After all, these populations are not likely to protest. . . .

Social Policy Implications

The remaining dangers are more directly relevant for planners, other policy researchers, and policy makers. The most general one, and the *fifth* on my list, is the term's interference with antipoverty policy and other kinds of planning. This results in part from the fact that underclass is a quite distinctive synthesizing term that lumps together a variety of highly diverse people who need different kinds of help. Categorizing them all with one term, and a buzzword at that, can be disastrous, especially if the political climate should demand that planners formulate a single "underclass policy." Whether one thinks of the poorest of the poor as having problems or as making problems for others, or both, they cannot be planned for with a single policy. For example, educational policies to prevent young people from dropping out of school, especially the few good ones in poor areas, have nothing to do with housing policies for dealing with various kinds of homelessness and the lack of affordable dwellings. Such policies are in turn different from programs to reduce street crime, and from methods of discouraging the very poor from escaping into the addictions of drugs, alcohol, mental illness, or pentecostal religion—which has its own harmful side effects. To be sure, policies relevant to one problem may have positive overlaps for another, but no single policy works for all the problems of the different poverty-stricken populations. Experts who claim one policy can do it all, like education, are simply wrong.

This conclusion applies even to jobs and income grant policies. Although it is certain that all of the problems blamed on the people assigned to the underclass would be helped considerably by policies to reduce sharply persistent joblessness and poverty, *and generally before other programs are implemented*, these policies also have limits. While all poor people need economic help, such help will not alone solve other problems some of them have or make for others. Although the middle class does not mug, neither do *the* poor; only a small number of poor male young-sters and young adults do so. Other causal factors are also involved, and effective antipoverty planning has to be based on some understanding of these factors and how to overcome them. Lumping concepts like the underclass can only hurt this effort.

A related or *sixth* danger stems from the persuasive capacity of concepts or buzzwords. These terms may become so *reified* through their use that people think they represent actual groups or aggregates, and may also begin to believe that being in what is, after all, an imaginary group is a *cause* of the characteristics included in its definition. Sometimes journalists and even scholars—especially those of con-servative bent—appear to think that becoming very poor and acting in antisocial or deviant ways is an *effect* of being in the underclass. When the underclass becomes a causal term, however, especially on a widespread basis, planners, as well as poli-ticians and citizens, are in trouble; sooner or later, someone will argue that the only policy solution is to lock up everyone described as an underclass member.

Similar planning problems develop if and when the reification of a term leads to its being assigned *moral* causality. Using notions that blame victims may help the blamers to feel better by blowing off the steam of righteous indignation, but it does not eliminate the problems very poor people have or make. Indeed, those who argue that all people are entirely responsible for what they do sidestep the morally and otherwise crucial issue of determining how much responsibility should be assigned to people who lack resources, who are therefore under unusual stress, and who lack effective choices in many areas of life in which even moderate income people can choose relatively freely. . . .

The *seventh* danger of the term, and one also particularly salient for planners, stems from the way the underclass has been analyzed. As already noted, some re-searchers have tried to identify underclass neighborhoods. Planners must be espe-cially sensitive to the dangers of the underclass neighborhood notion, because, once statistically defined "neighborhoods," or even sets of adjacent census tracts, are marked with the underclass label, the politicians who make the basic land use decisions in the community may propose a variety of harmful policies, such as moving all of a city's homeless into such areas, or declaring them ripe for urban renewal because of the undeservingness of the population. Recall that this is how much of the federal urban renewal of the 1950s and 1960s was justified. In addition, neighborhood policies generally rest on the assumption that people inside the boundaries of such areas are more homogeneous than they in fact are, and that they remain inside boundaries that are more often nothing but lines on a map. Since very poor people tend to suffer more from public policies than they benefit, and since they have fewer defenses than more affluent people against harmful policies, "neighborhood policies" may hurt more often than they will help.

A related danger—and my *eighth*—stems from William J. Wilson's "concentration and isolation" hypotheses. Wilson argues that the economic difficulties of the very poorest blacks are compounded by the fact that as the better-off blacks move out, the poorest are more and more concentrated, having only other very poor people, and the few institutions that minister to them, as neighbors. This concentration causes social isolation, among other things, Wilson suggests, because the very poor are now isolated from access to the people, job networks, role models, institutions, and other connections that might help them escape poverty.

Wilson's hypotheses, summarized all too briefly here, are now being accepted as dogma by many outside the research community. Fortunately, they are also being tested in a number of places, but until they are shown to be valid, planners should probably go slowly with designing action programs—especially programs to reduce concentration. In the minimal-vacancy housing markets in which virtually all poor people live, such a policy might mean having to find a new, and surely more costly, dwelling unit, or having to double up with relatives, or in some cases being driven into shelters or into the streets. Even if working- and middle-class areas were willing to accept relocatees from deconcentrated areas, a response that seems unlikely, the relocatees could not afford to live in such areas—although many would flourish if they had the money to do so. Meanwhile, the dysfunctions of dispersal may be as bad as those of overconcentration, not because the latter has any virtues, but because, until an effective jobs-and-income-grants program has gone into operation, requiring very poor people to move away from the neighborly support structures they *do* have may deprive them of their only resources.

While it may be risky to attempt deconcentration at this stage, it is worth trying to reduce isolation. One form of isolation, the so-called urban-suburban mismatch between jobless workers residing in cities and available suburban jobs, is already being attacked again, which is all to the good. Perhaps something has been learned from the failures of the 1960s to reduce the mismatch. We must bear in mind, however, that in some or perhaps many cases the physical mismatch is only a cover for class and racial discrimination, and the widespread unwillingness of white suburban employers—and white workers—to have black coworkers. . . .

The *ninth* danger is inherent in the concept of an underclass. While it assumes that the people assigned to the underclass are poor, the term itself sidesteps issues of poverty. It also permits analysts to ignore the dramatic recent increases in certain kinds of poverty, or persisting poverty, and hence the need for resuming effective antipoverty programs. For example, terms like underclass make it easier for conservative researchers to look at the homeless mainly as mentally ill or the victims of rent control, and frees them of any need to discuss the disappearance of jobs, SROs, and other low income housing.

Indeed, to the extent that the underclass notion is turned into a synonym for the undeserving poor, the political conditions for reinstituting effective antipoverty policy are removed. If the underclass is undeserving, then the government's responsibility is limited to beefing up the courts and other punitive agencies and institutions that try to isolate the underclass and protect the rest of society from it. Conversely, the moral imperative to help the poor through the provision of jobs and income grants is reduced. Describing the poor as undeserving has long been an effective if immoral short-term approach to tax reduction. . . .

NOTES

I am grateful to Michael Katz for his helpful comments on an earlier draft of this essay.

Kornblum, William. 1984. Lumping the Poor: What *Is* the Underclass. *Dissent.* September: 295–302.

Lewis, Oscar. 1969. The Culture of Poverty. In *On Understanding Poverty*, edited by Daniel P. Moynihan. New York: Basic.

Myrdal, Gunnar. 1962. *The Challenge to Affluence.* New York: Pantheon.

Wilson, William J. 1987. *The Truly Disadvantaged: The Inner City, the Underclass, and Public Policy.* Chicago: University of Chicago Press.

Domination and Subordination

Jean Baker Miller

What do people do to people who are different from them and why? On the individual level, the child grows only via engagement with people very different from her/himself. Thus, the most significant difference is between the adult and the child. At the level of humanity in general, we have seen massive problems around a great variety of differences. But the most basic difference is the one between women and men.

On both levels it is appropriate to pose two questions. When does the engagement of difference stimulate the development and the enhancement of both parties to the engagement? And, conversely, when does such a confrontation with difference have negative effects: when does it lead to great difficulty, deterioration, and distortion and to some of the worst forms of degradation, terror, and violence—both for individuals and for groups—that human beings can experience? It is clear that "mankind" in general, especially in our Western tradition but in some others as well, does not have a very glorious record in this regard.

It is not always clear that in most instances of difference there is also a factor of inequality—inequality of many kinds of resources, but fundamentally of status and power. One useful way to examine the often confusing results of these confrontations with difference is to ask: What happens in situations of inequality? What forces are set in motion? While we will be using the terms "dominant" and "subordinate" in the discussion, it is useful to remember that flesh and blood women and men are involved. Speaking in abstractions sometimes permits us to accept what we might not admit to on a personal level.

Temporary Inequality

Two types of inequality are pertinent for present purposes. The first might be called temporary inequality. Here, the lesser party is *socially* defined as unequal. Major examples are the relationships between parents and children, teachers and students, and, possibly, therapists and clients. There are certain assumptions in these relationships which are often not made explicit, nor, in fact, are they carried through. But they are the social structuring of the relationship.

The "superior" party presumably has more of some ability or valuable quality, which she/he is supposed to impart to the "lesser" person. While these abilities vary with the particular relationship, they include emotional maturity, experience in the world, physical skills, a body of knowledge, or the techniques for acquiring certain kinds of knowledge. The superior person is supposed to engage with the lesser in such a way as to bring the lesser member up to full parity; that is, the child is to be helped to become the adult. Such is the overall task of this relationship. The lesser, the child, is to be given to, by the person who presumably has more to give. Although the lesser party often also gives much to the superior, these relationships are *based in service* to the lesser party. That is their *raison d'être*.

It is clear, then, that the paramount goal is to end the relationship; that is, to end the relationship of inequality. The period of disparity is meant to be temporary. People may continue their association as friends, colleagues, or even competitors, but not as "superior" and "lesser." At least this is the goal.

The reality is that we have trouble enough with this sort of relationship. Parents or professional institutions often tip toward serving the needs of the donor instead of those of the lesser party (for example, schools can come to serve teachers or administrators, rather than students). Or the lesser person learns how to be a good "lesser" rather than how to make the journey from lesser to full stature. Overall, we have not found very good ways to carry out the central task: to foster the movement from unequal to equal. In childrearing and education we do not have an adequate theory and practice. Nor do we have concepts that work well in such other unequal so-called "helping" relationships as healing, penology, and rehabilitation. Officially, we say we want to do these things, but we often fail.

We have a great deal of trouble deciding on how many rights "to allow" to the lesser party. We agonize about how much power the lesser party shall have. How much can the lesser person express or act on her or his perceptions when these definitely differ from those of the superior? Above all, there is great difficulty in maintaining the conception of the lesser person *as a person of as much intrinsic worth as the superior.*

A crucial point is that power is a major factor in all of these relationships. But power alone will not suffice. Power exists and it has to be taken into account, not denied. The superiors hold all the real power, but power will not accomplish *the task.* It will not bring the unequal party up to equality.

Our troubles with these relationships may stem from the fact that they exist within the context of a second type of inequality that tends to overwhelm the ways we learn to operate in the first kind. The second type molds the very ways we perceive and conceptualize what we are doing in the first, most basic kind of relationships.

The second type of inequality teaches us how to enforce inequality, but not how to make the journey from unequal to equal. Most importantly, its consequences are kept amazingly obscure—in fact they are usually denied. . . . However, the underlying notion is that this second type was determined, and still determines, the only ways we can think and feel in the first type.

Permanent Inequality

In these relationships, some people or groups of people are defined as unequal by means of what sociologists call ascription; that is, your birth defines you. Criteria may be race, sex, class, nationality, religion, or other characteristics ascribed at birth. Here, the terms of the relationships are very different from those of temporary inequality. There is, for example, no notion that superiors are present primarily to help inferiors, to impart to them their advantages and "desirable" characteristics. There is no assumption that the goal of the unequal relationship is to end the inequality; in fact, quite the reverse. A series of other governing tendencies are in force, and occur with great regularity. . . . While some of these elements may appear obvious, in fact there is a great deal of disagreement and confusion about psychological characteristics brought about by conditions as obvious as these.

Dominants. Once a group is defined as inferior, the superiors tend to label it as defective or substandard in various ways. These labels accrete rapidly. Thus, blacks are described as less intelligent than whites, women are supposed to be ruled by emotion, and so on. In addition, the actions and words of the dominant group tend to be destructive of the subordinates. All historical evidence confirms this tendency. And, although they are much less obvious, there are destructive effects on the dominants as well. The latter are of a different order and are much more difficult to recognize.

Dominant groups usually define one or more acceptable roles for the subordinate. Acceptable roles typically involve providing services that no dominant group wants to perform for itself (for example, cleaning up the dominant's waste products). Functions that a dominant group prefers to perform, on the other hand, are carefully guarded and closed to subordinates. Out of the total range of human possibilities, the activities most highly valued in any particular culture will tend to be enclosed within the domain of the dominant group; less valued functions are relegated to the subordinates.

Subordinates are usually said to be unable to perform the preferred roles. Their incapacities are ascribed to innate defects or deficiencies of mind or body, therefore immutable and impossible of change or development. It becomes difficult for dominants even to imagine that subordinates are capable of performing the preferred activities. More importantly, subordinates themselves can come to find it difficult to believe in their own ability. The myth of their inability to fulfill wider or more valued roles is challenged only when a drastic event disrupts the usual arrangements. Such disruptions usually arise from outside the relationship itself. For instance, in the emergency situation of World War II, "incompetent" women suddenly "manned" the factories with great skill.

It follows that subordinates are described in terms of, and encouraged to develop, personal psychological characteristics that are pleasing to the dominant group. These characteristics form a certain familiar cluster: submissiveness, passivity, docility, dependency, lack of initiative, inability to act, to decide, to think, and the like. In general, this cluster includes qualities more characteristic of children than adults—immaturity, weakness, and helplessness. If subordinates adopt these characteristics they are considered well-adjusted.

However, when subordinates show the potential for, or even more dangerously have developed other characteristics—let us say intelligence, initiative, assertiveness—there is usually no room available within the dominant framework for acknowledgement of these characteristics. Such people will be defined as at least unusual, if not definitely abnormal. There will be no opportunities for the direct application of their abilities within the social arrangements. (How many women have pretended to be dumb!)

Dominant groups usually impede the development of subordinates and block their freedom of expression and action. They also tend to militate against stirrings of greater rationality or greater humanity in their own members. It was not too long ago that "nigger lover" was a common appellation, and even now men who "allow their women" more than the usual scope are subject to ridicule in many circles.

A dominant group, inevitably, has the greatest influence in determining a culture's overall outlook—its philosophy, morality, social theory, and even its science. The dominant group, thus, legitimizes the unequal relationship and incorporates it into society's guiding concepts. The social outlook, then, obscures the true nature of this relationship—that is, the very existence of inequality. The culture explains the events that take place in terms of other premises, premises that are inevitably false, such as racial or sexual inferiority. While in recent years we have learned about many such falsities on the larger social level, a full analysis of the psychological implications still remains to be developed. In the case of women, for example, despite overwhelming evidence to the contrary, the notion persists that women are meant to be passive, submissive, docile, secondary. From this premise, the outcome of therapy and encounters with psychology and other "sciences" are often determined.

Inevitably, the dominant group is the model for "normal human relationships." It then becomes "normal" to treat others destructively and to derogate them, to obscure the truth of what you are doing, by creating false explanations, and to oppose actions toward equality. In short, if one's identification is with the dominant group, it is "normal" to continue in this pattern. Even though most of us do not like to think of ourselves as either believing in, or engaging in, such dominations, it is, in fact, difficult for a member of a dominant group to do otherwise. But to keep on doing these things, one need only behave "normally."

It follows from this that dominant groups generally do not like to be told about or even quietly reminded of the existence of inequality. "Normally" they can avoid awareness because their explanation of the relationship becomes so well integrated *in other terms;* they can even believe that both they and the subordinate group share the same interests and, to some extent, a common experience. If pressed a bit, the familiar rationalizations are offered: the home is "women's natural place," and we know "what's best for them anyhow."

Dominants prefer to avoid conflict—open conflict that might call into question the whole situation. This is particularly and tragically so, when many members of the dominant group are not having an easy time of it themselves. Members of a dominant group, or at least some segments of it, such as white working-class men (who are themselves also subordinates), often feel unsure of their own narrow toehold on the material and psychological bounties they believe they desperately need. What dominant groups usually cannot act on, or even see, is that the situation of inequality in fact deprives them, particularly on the psychological level.

Clearly, inequality has created a state of conflict. Yet dominant groups will tend to suppress conflict. They will see any questioning of the "normal" situation as threatening; activities by subordinates in this direction will be perceived with alarm. Dominants are usually convinced that the way things are is right and good, not only for them but especially for the subordinates. All morality confirms this view, and all social structure sustains it.

It is perhaps unnecessary to add that the dominant group usually holds all of the open power and authority and determines the ways in which power may be acceptably used.

Subordinates. What of the subordinates' part in this? Since dominants determine what is normal for a culture, it is much more difficult to understand subordinates. Initial expressions of dissatisfaction and early actions by subordinates always come as a surprise; they are usually rejected as atypical. After all, dominants *knew* that all women needed and wanted was a man around whom to organize their lives. Members of the dominant group do not understand why "they"—the first to speak out—are so upset and angry.

The characteristics that typify the subordinates are even more complex. A subordinate group has to concentrate on basic survival. Accordingly, direct, honest reaction to destructive treatment is avoided. Open, self-initiated action in its own self-interest must also be avoided. Such actions can, and still do, literally result in death for some subordinate groups. In our own society, a woman's direct action can result in a combination of economic hardship, social ostracism, and psychological isolation—and even the diagnosis of a personality disorder. Any one of these consequences is bad enough. . . .

It is not surprising then that a subordinate group resorts to disguised and indirect ways of acting and reacting. While these actions are designed to accommodate and please the dominant group, they often, in fact, contain hidden defiance and "put ons." Folk tales, black jokes, and women stories are often based on how the wily peasant or sharecropper outwitted the rich landowner, boss, or husband. The essence of the story rests on the fact that the overlord does not even know that he has been made a fool of.

One important result of this indirect mode of operation is that members of the dominant group are denied an essential part of life—the opportunity to acquire self-understanding through knowing their impact on others. They are thus deprived of "consensual validation," feedback, and a chance to correct their actions and expressions. Put simply, subordinates won't tell. For the same reasons, the dominant group is deprived also of valid knowledge about the subordinates. (It is particularly ironic that the societal "experts" in knowledge about subordinates are usually members of the dominant group.)

Subordinates, then, know much more about the dominants than vice versa. They have to. They become highly attuned to the dominants, able to predict their reactions of pleasure and displeasure. Here, I think, is where the long story of "feminine intuition" and "feminine wiles" begins. It seems clear that these "mysterious" gifts are in fact skills, developed through long practice, in reading many small signals, both verbal and nonverbal.

Another important result is that subordinates often know more about the dominants than they know about themselves. If a large part of your fate depends on accommodating to and pleasing the dominants, you concentrate on them. Indeed, there is little purpose in knowing yourself. Why should you when your knowledge of the dominants determines your life? This tendency is reinforced by many other restrictions. One can know oneself only through action and interaction. To the extent that their range of action or interaction is limited, subordinates will lack a realistic evaluation of their capacities and problems. Unfortunately, this difficulty in gaining self-knowledge is even further compounded.

Tragic confusion arises because subordinates absorb a large part of the untruths created by the dominants; there are a great many blacks who feel inferior to whites, and women who still believe they are less important than men. This internalization of dominant beliefs is more likely to occur if there are few alternative concepts at hand. On the other hand, it is also true that members of the subordinate group have certain experiences and perceptions that accurately reflect the truth about themselves and the injustice of their position. Their own more truthful concepts are bound to come into opposition with the mythology they have absorbed from the dominant group. An inner tension between the two sets of concepts and their derivations is almost inevitable.

From a historical perspective, despite the obstacles, subordinate groups have tended to move toward greater freedom of expression and action, although this progress varies greatly from one circumstance to another. There were always some slaves who revolted; there were some women who sought greater development or self-determination. Most records of these actions are not preserved by the dominant culture, making it difficult for the subordinate group to find a supporting tradition and history.

Within each subordinate group, there are tendencies for some members to imitate the dominants. This imitation can take various forms. Some may try to treat their fellow subordinates as destructively as the dominants treat them. A few may develop enough of the qualities valued by the dominants to be partially accepted into their fellowship. Usually they are not wholly accepted, and even then only if they are willing to forsake their own identification with fellow subordinates. "Uncle Toms" and certain professional women have often been in this position. (There are always a few women who have won the praise presumably embodied in the phrase "she thinks like a man.")

To the extent that subordinates move toward freer expression and action, they will expose the inequality and throw into question the basis for its existence. And they will make the inherent conflict an open conflict. They will then have to bear the burden and take the risks that go with being defined as "troublemakers." Since this role flies in the face of their conditioning, subordinates, especially women, do not come to it with ease.

What is immediately apparent from studying the characteristics of the two groups is that mutually enhancing interaction is not probable between unequals. Indeed, conflict is inevitable. The important questions, then, become: Who defines the conflict? Who sets the terms? When is conflict overt or covert? On what issues is the conflict fought? Can anyone win? Is conflict "bad," by definition? If not, what makes for productive or destructive conflict?

Suggestions for Further Reading

De Beauvoir, Simone. *The Second Sex.* New York: Alfred A. Knopf, 1952.

Doty, William G. *The Myths of Masculinity.* New York: Crossroad, 1993.

Epstein, Cynthia Fuchs. *Deceptive Distinctions: Sex, Gender, and the Social Order.* New Haven: Yale University Press and New York: The Russell Sage Foundation, 1988.

Hubbard, Ruth. *The Politics of Women's Biology.* New Brunswick, N.J.: Rutgers University Press, 1990.

Gould, Stephen. *The Mismeasure of Man.* New York: W.W. Norton, 1984.

Kitano, Harry H. L. *Race Relations*, 3d ed. Englewood Cliffs, N.J.: Prentice-Hall, 1985.

Lipman-Blumen, Jean. *Gender Roles and Power*. Englewood Cliffs, N.J.: Prentice-Hall, 1984.

Lowe, M., and R. Hubbard, eds. *Women's Nature: Rationalizations of Inequality*. New York: Pergamon Press, 1983.

Memmi, Albert. *Dominated Man*. Boston: Beacon Press, 1969.

Montague, M.F. Ashley. *Man's Most Dangerous Myth*. New York: Harper & Row, 1952.

Omni, Michael, and Harold Winant. *Racial Formations in the United States*. New York: Routledge and Kegan Paul, 1986.

Sanday, Peggy R. Female Power and Male Dominance: On the Origins of Sexual Inequality. New York: Cambridge University Press, 1981.

Smith, Dorothy. The Everyday World as Problematic: A Feminist Sociology. Boston: Northeastern Press, 1987.

West, Cornel. *Race Matters*. Boston: Beacon Press, 1993.

Racism, Sexism, and Class Difference

Racism, sexism, class privilege, and homophobia are predicated on difference constructed as deviance or deficiency. We are surrounded by differences everyday, but our society only chooses to place a value on some of them. By valuing the characteristics of certain individuals or groups and devaluing those of others, society constructs some of its members as "Other." Once this happens it is possible to divide wealth, opportunity, and justice unequally without appearing to be unfair. The social construction of race, class, gender, and sexuality as difference, where being white, male, European, heterosexual, and prosperous is the norm and everyone else is understood to be less able and less worthy, has been reinforced and perpetuated by both intentional and unintentional discrimination. In Part II we turn to an examination of how racism, sexism, and class privilege impact on personal and social relations.

Refusing to hire a qualified person because of their race/ethnicity, gender, or sexual orientation, or refusing to rent them an apartment or sell them a home, are fairly straightforward examples of discrimination. Most people would agree that such behavior is unfair or unjust. But once we move beyond these clear-cut cases, it becomes difficult to reach agreement. Is the male gas station attendant just being friendly or is he being sexist when he calls female customers "sweetheart" or "honey"? Does the fact that most major U.S. corporations have few if any women in senior management positions in itself indicate discriminatory hiring policies? Is the underrepresentation of people of color in medical schools in the United States and on college faculties de facto proof of racism in society or does it result from a lack of qualified applicants or candidates? Who determines what it means to be qualified? How do we arrive at the criteria we use to admit students to colleges and professional schools or to hire senior management or faculty? Is it possible that the very criteria we employ already reflect subtle but pervasive racism and sexism? Can individuals and institutions be racist and sexist in the course of their normal everyday functioning quite apart from, even without, their conscious or explicit intent? These are some of the questions that will be raised as we explore the ways in which racism and sexism operate in our society.

Some people are uncomfortable with the words *racism* and *sexism* and prefer to talk about prejudice and discrimination. In Selection 1, the members of the United States Commission on Civil Rights provide us with a survey of race and gender discrimination, past and present. Beginning with examples of discrimination by individuals, they go on to examine organizational and structural discrimination, and conclude with a discussion of the ways in which such treatment forms an interlocking and self-perpetuating *process of discrimination*. Fundamental to this process is the social construction of race, class, and gender as difference, as we have seen in Part I.

Those who wish to emphasize the complex and powerful nature of relations of subordination and domination, as well as the interlocking and self-perpetuating nature of discrimination as a process, find the term *discrimination* too narrow and too limited. They argue that words such as *racism, sexism,* and *oppression* are more appropriate because they capture the comprehensive, systemic nature of the phenomena we are studying. They use these terms to point to a complex and pervasive system of beliefs, policies, practices, and attitudes that interrelate with incredible intricacy, subtlety, and force.

In Selection 2, Marilyn Frye explicitly introduces the concept of *oppression* to describe the pervasive nature of sexism and illustrates how it is possible to participate unintentionally in the continued subordination of women. Frye uses the metaphor of a birdcage to illustrate how sexism imprisons its victims through the interlocking operation of a series of impediments to motion. Taken alone, none of the barriers seems very powerful or threatening; taken together, they construct a cage that appears light and airy, masking the fact that its occupants are trapped as firmly as if they were in a sealed vault. Although Frye focuses on sexism, it is relatively easy to apply the same metaphor and analysis to explicate racism.

Frye follows her discussion of the birdcage metaphor with some examples of seemingly innocent but oppressive practices that will undoubtedly disturb some readers. She takes as her paradigm, or model, the "male door-opening ritual" and argues that its meaning and implications go far beyond the conscious intentions of the man who opens the door. As you think about her example, remember that Frye is analyzing the implications of a social ritual, not looking at any individual's motives for following that ritual. The point is that sexism and racism can and are perpetuated by people who are just trying to be nice.

Gloria Yamato's essay discusses racism as oppression and describes the forms it can take: aware/blatant racism, aware/covert racism, unaware/unintentional racism, and unaware/self-righteous racism, as well as the way in which racism can be internalized by its victims. After exploring the connection between race and class oppression, she concludes her essay with some positive suggestions for all of us who want to come to terms with racism and, by implication, with sexism as well.

Yamato's analysis is carried a step further in Rita Chaudhry Sethi's essay, which focuses on the experiences of Asians in the U.S.. Sethi argues that our understanding of racism in this country has been narrowly derived from the African-American experience and, as a consequence, often fails to recognize and name the racism experienced by Asians and other ethnic groups. Insofar as members of these communities have internalized this narrow paradigm, Sethi maintains they themselves often fail to identify the discrimination they experience as racism. She urges us to broaden our understanding of racism to be more inclusive of the experiences of a variety of ethnic groups.

As these essays suggest, defining racism and sexism is a difficult but essential undertaking. It is made difficult both by the complexity of the phenomena themselves and by the powerful emotional reactions people have to the terms as well as the political consequences of applying them. But wrestling with the problem of definition is essential if we are to come to terms with the reality they denote. Current controversies over whether society should tolerate, protect, or prosecute hate speech; whether we should punish bias crimes more severely than other acts of violence; how we should judge acts of violence carried out by victims of battery and abuse against their victimizers; and similar questions, require that we be able to identify language and actions that are racist, sexist, and homophobic.

Perhaps the most commonly adopted definitions of racism and sexism describe them as any policy, practice, belief, or attitude that attributes characteristics or status to individuals based upon their race or their sex. Many people use the terms in this way, and the universal nature of these definitions gives them obvious appeal. However, in spite of their appeal, there are serious problems with them because they fail to distinguish racism and sexism from a somewhat different phenomenon, *prejudice*.

Prejudice is a general feeling of dislike for people, perhaps even hatred of them, based upon some characteristic they have or are believed to possess. Prejudice may be based on race, sex, or ethnicity, or on hair color, religion, style of dress, or just about any characteristic you can think of. In contrast, racism and sexism require not prejudice alone but *prejudice plus power*. When we use these terms rather than "prejudice" or "discrimination," we highlight the unequal distribution of power in this society and we draw attention to the elaborate interlocking system of rituals, stereotypes, institutions, punishments, and rewards that have functioned historically to reinforce male privilege and white-skin privilege.

Understood in this way *racism involves the subordination of people of color by white people* and *sexism involves the subordination of women by men*. While individual persons of color or women may well discriminate against white people or others because of their color or ethnicity, and while some women may well discriminate against men because of their sex, strictly speaking, this does not qualify as racism or sexism according to our definition. Such discrimination doesn't qualify as racism or sexism because neither the person of color nor the woman can depend upon all the institutions of society to enforce or extend his or her personal dislike. Nor can he or she call upon the force of history to reflect and reinforce that prejudice.

For example, let us assume that the teacher at the front of the room is a person of color who doesn't like white people or a woman who is prejudiced against men. In class he or she can act on this prejudice, but outside the classroom he or she is likely to be the object of institutionalized and comprehensive prejudice, which is what is meant by racism and sexism. If the teacher visits the town where his or her students live, he or she may well be harassed rather than welcomed. If the teacher visits a building on campus where he or she is not known, he or she may be mistaken for a janitor or perhaps be asked to do some photocopying. When white women or women and men of color who are college faculty meet their students in the public world, they are likely to have less status, power, and choices than white students half their age.

For this reason, even if a person of color gives a speech filled with vicious racial hatred or carries out violence against others because of their white skin, it is not, strictly speaking, racism. It may be despicable and it can be condemned and deplored, but it doesn't qualify as racism because the element of power is not present. Failing to call it racism is not a way of excusing, much less, approving of inexcusable hate language or violence. It is simply a way of being consistent and precise in the way we analyze social phenomena. Our definitions of racism and sexism reflect the history of the world that provides us with a long record of white people and men holding power and using that power and privilege over people of color and white women to subordinate and dehumanize them, not the reverse. In the words of Gloria Yamato, "People of color can be prejudiced against one another and whites, but do not have an ice-cube's chance in hell of passing laws that will get whites sent to relocation camps 'for their own protection and the security of the nation.'"

In cases of interethnic-group hostility, as, for example, between or among Koreans, Blacks, or Puerto Ricans, or gender-based prejudice against women expressed by other women, it is appropriate to say that this kind of prejudice *reflects* the racism and/or the sexism of our society. It is a product of our history of oppression—its effect, not its cause. Ironically, racist stereotyping and hatred within and among people of color, like sexism within these groups, divides people who are potential allies. In this way it serves to reinforce rather than challenge the real causes of inequality and violence in our society.

Part II concludes with three newspaper stories that describe different aspects of contemporary life. The first article, "Death of A Teenager Widens a Racial Rift between Two Towns," examines the ways in which white people and people of color literally and metaphorically often live in different worlds, even when they live only a few blocks apart. In the telling of this tragedy from the perspectives of people of different races and classes living in two Michigan towns on either side of a river, we see how differently the same events can appear to people long divided and circumscribed by socially constructed and enforced differences. The second article, "Gang Rape," examines the attitudes of members of a community in the East Bronx toward women, rape, violence, and manhood. It provides a sobering picture of the toll that racism, sexism, and class privilege are taking on the lives of many in our society. This article should be read in conjunction with Peggy Sanday's "Pulling Train," in Part VI, which presents an analysis of gang rape within college fraternity culture, and with June Jordan's "Requiem for the Champ" in Part IV.

The final selection, "No Cure for Sexism in the Medical Profession," describes the sexism encountered by a female medical resident over a period of ten years while on staff at a major urban medical center. As you read this account bear in mind that Dr. Weisman is in some respects highly privileged, able to gather evidence for one of her court cases by flying to China when the authorities are unconvinced by the evidence already presented. The majority of women who experience discrimination in employment have dramatically fewer resources to draw upon in their quest for justice.

The Problem:
Discrimination

U.S. Commission on Civil Rights

Making choices is an essential part of everyday life for individuals and organizations. These choices are shaped in part by social structures that set standards and influence conduct in such areas as education, employment, housing, and government. When these choices limit the opportunities available to people because of their race, sex, or national origin, the problem of discrimination arises.

Historically, discrimination against minorities and women was not only accepted but it was also governmentally required. The doctrine of white supremacy used to support the institution of slavery was so much a part of American custom and policy that the Supreme Court in 1857 approvingly concluded that both the North and the South regarded slaves "as beings of an inferior order, and altogether unfit to associate with the white race, either in social or political relations; and so far inferior, that they had no rights which the white man was bound to respect."[1] White supremacy survived the passage of the Civil War amendments to the Constitution and continued to dominate legal and social institutions in the North as well as the South to disadvantage not only blacks,[2] but other racial and ethnic groups as well—American Indians, Alaskan Natives, Asian and Pacific Islanders and Hispanics.[3]

While minorities were suffering from white supremacy, women were suffering from male supremacy. Mr. Justice Brennan has summed up the legal disabilities imposed on women this way:

> [T]hroughout much of the 19th century the position of women in our society was, in many respects, comparable to that of blacks under the pre-Civil War slave codes. Neither slaves nor women could hold office, serve on juries, or bring suit in their own names, and married women traditionally were denied the legal capacity to hold or convey property or to serve as legal guardians of their own children.[4]

In 1873 a member of the Supreme Court proclaimed, "Man is, or should be, woman's protector and defender. The natural and proper timidity and delicacy which belongs to the female sex evidently unfits it for many of the occupations of civil life."[5] Such romantic paternalism has alternated with fixed notions of male

70

superiority to deny women in law and in practice the most fundamental of rights, including the right to vote, which was not granted until 1920;[6] the Equal Rights Amendment has yet to be ratified.[7]

White and male supremacy are no longer popularly accepted American values.[8] The blatant racial and sexual discrimination that originated in our conveniently forgotten past, however, continues to manifest itself today in a complex interaction of attitudes and actions of individuals, organizations, and the network of social structures that make up our society.

Individual Discrimination

The most common understanding of discrimination rests at the level of prejudiced individual attitudes and behavior. Although open and intentional prejudice persists, individual discriminatory conduct is often hidden and sometimes unintentional.[9] Some of the following are examples of deliberately discriminatory actions by consciously prejudiced individuals. Some are examples of unintentionally discriminatory actions taken by persons who may not believe themselves to be prejudiced but whose decisions continue to be guided by deeply ingrained discriminatory customs.

- Personnel officers whose stereotyped beliefs about women and minorities justify hiring them for low level and low paying jobs exclusively, regardless of their potential experience or qualifications for higher level jobs.[10]
- Administrators, historically white males, who rely on "word-of-mouth" recruiting among their friends and colleagues, so that only their friends and protégés of the same race and sex learn of potential job openings.[11]
- Employers who hire women for their sexual attractiveness or potential sexual availability rather than their competence, and employers who engage in sexual harassment of their female employees.[12]
- Teachers who interpret linguistic and cultural differences as indications of low potential or lack of academic interest on the part of minority students.[13]
- Guidance counselors and teachers whose low expectations lead them to steer female and minority students away from "hard" subjects, such as mathematics and science, toward subjects that do not prepare them for higher paying jobs.[14]
- Real estate agents who show fewer homes to minority buyers and steer them to minority or mixed neighborhoods because they believe white residents would oppose the presence of black neighbors.[15]
- Families who assume that property values inevitably decrease when minorities move in and therefore move out of their neighborhoods if minorities do move in.[16]
- Parole boards that assume minority offenders to be more dangerous or more unreliable than white offenders and consequently more frequently deny parole to minorities than to whites convicted of equally serious crimes.[17]

These contemporary examples of discrimination may not be motivated by conscious prejudice. The personnel manager is likely to deny believing that minorities and women can only perform satisfactorily in low level jobs and at the same time allege that other executives and decisionmakers would not consider them for higher level positions. In some cases, the minority or female applicants may not be aware that they have been discriminated against—the personnel manager may inform them that they are deficient in experience while rejecting their applications because of prejudice; the white male administrator who recruits by word-of-mouth from his friends or white male work force excludes minorities and women who never learn of the available positions. The discriminatory results these activities cause may not even be desired. The guidance counselor may honestly believe there are no other realistic alternatives for minority and female students.

Whether conscious or not, open or hidden, desired or undesired, these acts build on and support prejudicial stereotypes, deny their victims opportunities provided to others, and perpetuate discrimination, regardless of intent.

Organizational Discrimination

Discrimination, though practiced by individuals, is often reinforced by the well-established rules, policies, and practices of organizations. These actions are often regarded simply as part of the organization's way of doing business and are carried out by individuals as just part of their day's work.

Discrimination at the organizational level takes forms that are similar to those on the individual level. For example:

- Height and weight requirements that are unnecessarily geared to the physical proportions of white males and, therefore, exclude females and some minorities from certain jobs.[18]
- Seniority rules, when applied to jobs historically held only by white males, make more recently hired minorities and females more subject to layoff—the "last hired, first fired" employee—and less eligible for advancement.[19]
- Nepotistic membership policies of some referral unions that exclude those who are not relatives of members who, because of past employment practices, are usually white.[20]
- Restrictive employment leave policies, coupled with prohibitions on part-time work or denials of fringe benefits to part-time workers, that make it difficult for the heads of single parent families, most of whom are women, to get and keep jobs and meet the needs of their families.[21]
- The use of standardized academic tests or criteria, geared to the cultural and educational norms of the middle-class or white males, that are not relevant indicators of successful job performance.[22]
- Preferences shown by many law and medical schools in the admission of children of wealthy and influential alumni, nearly all of whom are white.[23]

- Credit policies of banks and lending institutions that prevent the granting of mortgage monies and loans in minority neighborhoods, or prevent the granting of credit to married women and others who have previously been denied the opportunity to build good credit histories in their own names.[24]

Superficially "color blind" or "gender neutral," these organizational practices have an adverse effect on minorities and women. As with individual actions, these organizational actions favor white males, even when taken with no conscious intent to affect minorities and women adversely, by protecting and promoting the status quo arising from the racism and sexism of the past. If, for example, the jobs now protected by "last hired, first fired" provisions had always been integrated, seniority would not operate to disadvantage minorities and women. If educational systems from kindergarten through college had not historically favored white males, many more minorities and women would hold advanced degrees and thereby be included among those involved in deciding what academic tests should test for. If minorities had lived in the same neighborhoods as whites, there would be no minority neighborhoods to which mortgage money could be denied on the basis of their being minority neighborhoods.

In addition, these barriers to minorities and women too often do not fulfill legitimate needs of the organization, or these needs can be met through other means that adequately maintain the organization without discriminating. Instead of excluding all women on the assumption that they are too weak or should be protected from strenuous work, the organization can implement a reasonable test that measures the strength actually needed to perform the job or, where possible, develop ways of doing the work that require less physical effort. Admissions to academic and professional schools can be decided not only on the basis of grades, standardized test scores, and the prestige of the high school or college from which the applicant graduated, but also on the basis of community service, work experience, and letters of recommendation. Lending institutions can look at the individual and his or her financial ability rather than the neighborhood or marital status of the prospective borrower.

Some practices that disadvantage minorities and women are readily accepted aspects of everyday behavior. Consider the "old boy" network in business and education built on years of friendship and social contact among white males, or the exchanges of information and corporate strategies by business acquaintances in racially or sexually exclusive country clubs and locker rooms paid for by the employer.[25] These actions, all of which have a discriminatory impact on minorities and women, are not necessarily acts of conscious prejudice. Because such actions are so often considered part of the "normal" way of doing things, people have difficulty recognizing that they are discriminating and therefore resist abandoning these practices despite the clearly discriminatory results. Consequently, many decision-makers have difficulty considering, much less accepting, nondiscriminatory alternatives that may work just as well or better to advance legitimate organizational interests but without systematically disadvantaging minorities and women.

This is not to suggest that all such discriminatory organizational actions are spurious or arbitrary. Many may serve the actual needs of the organization. Physical size or strength at times may be a legitimate job requirement; sick leave and insurance policies must be reasonably restricted; educational qualifications are needed for many jobs; lending institutions cannot lend to people who cannot reasonably demonstrate an ability to repay loans. Unless carefully examined and then modified or eliminated, however, these apparently neutral rules, policies, and practices will continue to perpetuate age-old discriminatory patterns into the structure of today's society.

Whatever the motivation behind such organizational acts, a process is occurring, the common denominator of which is unequal results on a very large scale.[26] When unequal outcomes are repeated over time and in numerous societal and geographical areas, it is a clear signal that a discriminatory process is at work.

Such discrimination is not a static, one-time phenomenon that has a clearly limited effect. Discrimination can feed on discrimination in self-perpetuating cycles.[27]

- The employer who recruits job applicants by word-of-mouth within a predominantly white male work force reduces the chances of receiving applications from minorities and females for open positions. Since they do not apply, they are not hired. Since they are not hired, they are not present when new jobs become available. Since they are not aware of new jobs, they cannot recruit other minority or female applicants. Because there are no minority or female employees to recruit others, the employer is left to recruit on his own from among his predominantly white and male work force.[28]
- The teacher who expects poor academic performance from minority and female students may not become greatly concerned when their grades are low. The acceptance of their low grades removes incentives to improve. Without incentives to improve, their grades remain low. Their low grades reduce their expectations, and the teacher has no basis for expecting more of them.[29]
- The realtor who assumes that white home owners do not want minority neighbors "steers" minorities to minority neighborhoods. Those steered to minority neighborhoods tend to live in minority neighborhoods. White neighborhoods then remain white, and realtors tend to assume that whites do not want minority neighbors.[30]
- Elected officials appoint voting registrars who impose linguistic, geographic, and other barriers to minority voter registration. Lack of minority registration leads to low voting rates. Lower minority voting rates lead to the election of fewer minorities. Fewer elected minorities leads to the appointment of voting registrars who maintain the same barriers.[31]

Structural Discrimination

Such self-sustaining discriminatory processes occur not only within the fields of employment, education, housing, and government but also between these structural areas. There is a classic cycle of structural discrimination that reproduces itself. Discrimination in education denies the credentials to get good jobs. Discrimination in employment denies the economic resources to buy good housing. Discrimination in housing confines minorities to school districts providing inferior education, closing the cycle in a classic form.[32]

With regard to white women, the cycle is not as tightly closed. To the extent they are raised in families headed by white males, and are married to or live with white males, white women will enjoy the advantages in housing and other areas that such relationships to white men can confer. White women lacking the sponsorship of white men, however, will be unable to avoid gender-based discrimination in housing, education, and employment. White women can thus be the victims of discrimination produced by social structures that is comparable in form to that experienced by minorities.

This perspective is not intended to imply that either the dynamics of discrimination or its nature and degree are identical for women and minorities. But when a woman of any background seeks to compete with men of any group, she finds herself the victim of a discriminatory process. Regarding the similarities and differences between the discrimination experienced by women and minorities, one author has aptly stated:

> [W]hen two groups exist in a situation of inequality, it may be self-defeating to become embroiled in a quarrel over which is more unequal or the victim of greater oppression. The more salient question is how a condition of inequality for both is maintained and perpetuated—through what means is it reinforced?[33]

The following are additional examples of the interaction between social structures that affect minorities and women:

- The absence of minorities and women from executive, writing, directing, news reporting, and acting positions in television contributes to unfavorable stereotyping on the screen, which in turn reinforces existing stereotypes among the public and creates psychological roadblocks to progress in employment, education, and housing.[34]
- Living in inner-city high crime areas in disproportionate numbers, minorities, particularly minority youth, are more likely to be arrested and are more likely to go to jail than whites accused of similar offenses, and their arrest and conviction records are then often used as bars to employment.[35]
- Because of past discrimination against minorities and women, female and minority-headed businesses are often small and relatively new. Further disadvantaged by contemporary credit and lending practices, they are more likely than white male-owned businesses to remain small and be less able to employ full-time specialists in applying for government contracts. Because they cannot monitor the availability of government contracts, they do not receive such contracts. Because they cannot demonstrate success with gov-

ernment contracts, contracting officers tend to favor other firms that have more experience with government contracts.[36]

Discriminatory actions by individuals and organizations are not only pervasive, occurring in every sector of society, but also cumulative with effects limited neither to the time nor the particular structural area in which they occur. This process of discrimination, therefore, extends across generations, across organizations, and across social structures in self-reinforcing cycles, passing the disadvantages incurred by one generation in one area to future generations in many related areas.[37]

These interrelated components of the discriminatory process share one basic result: the persistent gaps seen in the status of women and minorities relative to that of white males. These unequal results themselves have real consequences. The employer who wishes to hire more minorities and women may be bewildered by charges of racism and sexism when confronted by what appears to be a genuine shortage of qualified minority and female applicants. The guidance counselor who sees one promising minority student after another drop out of school or give up in despair may be resentful of allegations of racism when there is little he or she alone can do for the student. The banker who denies a loan to a female single parent may wish to do differently, but believes that prudent fiscal judgment requires taking into account her lack of financial history and inability to prove that she is a good credit risk. These and other decisionmakers see the results of a discriminatory process repeated over and over again, and those results provide a basis for rationalizing their own actions, which then feed into that same process.

When seen outside the context of the interlocking and intertwined effects of discrimination, complaints that many women and minorities are absent from the ranks of qualified job applicants, academically inferior and unmotivated, poor credit risks, and so forth, may appear to be justified. Decisionmakers like those described above are reacting to real social problems stemming from the process of discrimination. But many too easily fall prey to stereotyping and consequently disregard those minorities and women who have the necessary skills or qualifications. And they erroneously "blame the victims" of discrimination,[38] instead of examining the past and present context in which their own actions are taken and the multiple consequences of these actions on the lives of minorities and women.

The Process of Discrimination

Although discrimination is maintained through individual actions, neither individual prejudices nor random chance can fully explain the persistent national patterns of inequality and underrepresentation. Nor can these patterns be blamed on the persons who are at the bottom of our economic, political, and social order. Overt racism and sexism as embodied in popular notions of white and male supremacy have been widely repudiated, but our history of discrimination based on race, sex, and national origin has not been readily put aside. Past discrimination continues to have present effects. The task today is to identify those effects and the forms and dynamics of the discrimination that produced them.

Discrimination against minorities and women must now be viewed as an interlocking process involving the attitudes and actions of individuals and the organizations and social structures that guide individual behavior. That process, started by past events, now routinely bestows privileges, favors, and advantages on white males and imposes disadvantages and penalties on minorities and women. This process is also self-perpetuating. Many normal, seemingly neutral, operations of our society create stereotyped expectations that justify unequal results; unequal results in one area foster inequalities in opportunity and accomplishment in others; the lack of opportunity and accomplishment confirm the original prejudices or engender new ones that fuel the normal operations generating unequal results.

As we have shown, the process of discrimination involves many aspects of our society. No single factor sufficiently explains it, and no single means will suffice to eliminate it. Such elements of our society as our history of *de jure* discrimination, deeply ingrained prejudices,[39] inequities based on economic and social class,[40] and the structure and function of all our economic, social, and political institutions[41] must be continually examined in order to understand their part in shaping today's decisions that will either maintain or counter the current process of discrimination.

It may be difficult to identify precisely all aspects of the discriminatory process and assign those parts their appropriate importance. But understanding discrimination starts with an awareness that such a process exists and that to avoid perpetuating it, we must carefully assess the context and consequences of our everyday actions. . . .

NOTES

1. Dred Scott v. Sanford, 60 U.S. (19 How.) 393, 408 (1857).

2. For a concise summary of this history, see U.S., Commission on Civil Rights, *Twenty Years After Brown*, pp. 4–29 (1975); *Freedom to the Free: 1863, Century of Emancipation* (1963).

3. The discriminatory conditions experienced by these minority groups have been documented in the following publications by the U.S. Commission on Civil Rights: *The Navajo Nation: An American Colony* (1975); *The Southwest Indian Report* (1973); *The Forgotten Minority: Asian Americans in New York City* (State Advisory Committee Report 1977); *Success of Asian Americans: Fact or Fiction?* (1980); *Stranger in One's Land* (1970); *Toward Quality Education for Mexican Americans* (1974); *Puerto Ricans in the Continental United States: An Uncertain Future* (1976).

4. Frontiero v. Richardson, 411 U.S. 677, 684–86 (1973), citing L. Kanowitz, *Women and the Law: The Unfinished Revolution*, pp. 5–6 (1970), and G. Myrdal, *An American Dilemma* 1073 (20th Anniversary Ed., 1962). Justice Brennan wrote the opinion of the Court, joined by Justices Douglas, White, and Marshall. Justice Stewart concurred in the judgment. Justice Powell, joined by Chief Justice Burger and Justice Blackmun, wrote a separate concurring opinion. Justice Rehnquist dissented. See also H. M. Hacker, "Women

as a Minority Group," *Social Forces*, vol. 30 (1951), pp. 60–69; W. Chafe, *Women and Equality: Changing Patterns in American Culture* (New York: Oxford University Press, 1977).

5. Bradwell v. State, 83 U.S. (16 Wall) 130, 141 (1873) (Bradley, J., concurring), quoted in *Frontiero, supra* note 4.

6. U.S. Const. amend. XIX.

7. See U.S., Commission on Civil Rights, *Statement on the Equal Rights Amendment* (December 1978).

8. See note 4, Introduction.

9. See, e.g., R. K. Merton, "Discrimination and the American Creed," in R. K. Merton, *Sociological Ambivalence and Other Essays* (New York: The Free Press, 1976), pp. 189–216. In this essay on racism, published for the first time more than 30 years ago, Merton presented a typology which introduced the notion that discriminatory actions are not always directly related to individual attitudes of prejudice. Merton's typology consisted of the following: Type 1—the unprejudiced nondiscriminator; Type II—the unprejudiced discriminator; Type III—the prejudiced nondiscriminator; Type IV—the prejudiced discriminator. In the present context, Type II is crucial in its observation that discrimination is often practiced by persons who are not themselves prejudiced, but who respond to, or do not oppose, the actions of those who discriminate because of prejudiced attitudes (Type IV). See also D. C. Reitzes, "Prejudice and Discrimination: A Study in Contradictions," in *Racial and Ethnic Relations*, ed. H. M. Hughes (Boston: Allyn and Bacon, 1970), pp. 56–65.

10. See R. M. Kanter and B. A. Stein, "Making a Life at the Bottom," in *Life in Organizations, Workplaces as People Experience Them*, ed. Kanter and Stein (New York: Basic Books, 1976), pp. 176–90; also L. K. Howe, "Retail Sales Worker," ibid., pp. 248–51; also R. M. Kanter, *Men and Women of the Corporation* (New York: Basic Books, 1977).

11. See M. S. Granovetter, *Getting A Job: A Study of Contract and Careers* (Cambridge: Harvard University Press, 1974), pp. 6–11; also A. W. Blumrosen, *Black Employment and the Law* (New Brunswick, N.J.: Rutgers University Press, 1971), p. 232.

12. See U.S., Equal Employment Opportunity Commission, "Guidelines on Discrimination Because of Sex," 29 C.F.R. §1604.4 (1979); L. Farley, *Sexual Shakedown: The Sexual Harassment of Women on the Job* (New York: McGraw-Hill, 1978), pp. 92–96, 176–79; C. A. Mackinnon, *Sexual Harassment of Working Women* (New Haven: Yale University Press, 1979), pp. 25–55.

13. See R. Rosenthal and L. F. Jacobson, "Teacher Expectations for the Disadvantaged," *Scientific American*, 1968 (b) 218, 219–23; also D. Bar Tal, "Interactions of Teachers and Pupils," in *New Approaches to Social Problems* ed. I. H. Frieze, D. Bar Tal, and J. S. Carrol (San Francisco: Jossey Bass, 1979), pp. 337–58; also U.S., Commission on Civil Rights, *Teachers and Students, Report V: Mexican American Education Study. Differences in Teacher Interaction With Mexican American and Anglo Students* (1973), pp. 22–23.

14. Ibid.

15. U.S., Department of Housing and Urban Development, "Measuring Racial Discrimination in American Housing Markets: The Housing Market Practices Survey" (1979); D. M. Pearce, "Gatekeepers and Home Seekers: Institutional Patterns in Racial Steering," in *Social Problems*, vol. 26 (1979) pp. 325–42; "Benign Steering and Benign Quotas: The Validity of Race Conscious Government Policies to Promote Residential Integration," 93 *Harv. L. Rev.* 938, 944 (1980).

16. See M. N. Danielson, *The Politics of Exclusion* (New York: Columbia University Press, 1976), pp. 11–12; U.S., Commission on Civil Rights, *Equal Opportunity in Suburbia* (1974).

17. See L. L. Knowles and K. Prewitt, eds., *Institutional Racism in America* (Englewood Cliffs, N.J.: Prentice Hall, 1969) pp. 58–77, and E. D. Wright, *The Politics of Punishment* (New York: Harper and Row, 1973). Also, S. V. Brown, "Race and Parole Hearing Outcomes," in *Discrimination in Organizations*, ed. R. Alvarez and K. G. Lutterman (San Francisco: Jossey Bass, 1979), pp. 355–74.

18. Height and weight minimums that disproportionately exclude women without a showing of legitimate job requirement constitute unlawful sex discrimination. See Dothard v. Rawlinson, 433 U.S. 321 (1977); Bowe v. Colgate Palmolive Co., 416 F.2d 711 (7th Cir. 1969). Minimum height requirements used in screening applicants for employment have also been held to be unlawful where such a requirement excludes a significantly higher percentage of Hispanics than other national origin groups in the labor market and no job relatedness is shown. See Smith v. City of East Cleveland, 520 F.2d 492 (6th Cir. 1975).

19. U.S., Commission on Civil Rights, *Last Hired, First Fired* (1976); Tangren v. Wackenhut Servs., Inc., 480 F. Supp. 539 (D. Nev. 1979).

20. U.S., Commission on Civil Rights, *The Challenge Ahead, Equal Opportunity in Referral Unions* (1977), pp. 84–89.

21. A. Pifer, "Women Working: Toward a New Society," pp. 13–34, and D. Pearce, "Women, Work and Welfare: The Feminization of Poverty," pp. 103–24, both in K. A. Fernstein, ed., *Working Women and Families* (Beverly Hills: Sage Publications, 1979). Disproportionate numbers of single-parent families are minorities.

22. See Griggs v. Duke Power Company, 401 U.S. 424 (1971); U.S., Commission on Civil Rights, *Toward Equal Educational Opportunity: Affirmative Admissions Programs at Law and Medical Schools* (1978), pp. 10–12; I. Berg, *Education and Jobs: The Great Training Robbery* (Boston: Beacon Press, 1971), pp. 58–60.

23. See U.S., Commission on Civil Rights, *Toward Equal Educational Opportunity: Affirmative Admissions Programs at Law and Medical Schools* (1978), pp. 14–15.

24. See U.S., Commission on Civil Rights, *Mortgage Money: Who Gets It? A Case Study in Mortgage Lending Discrimination in Hartford, Conn.* (1974); J. Feagin and C. B. Feagin, *Discrimination American Style, Institutional Racism and Sexism* (Englewood Cliffs, N.J.: Prentice Hall, 1976), pp. 78–79.

25. See *Club Membership Practices by Financial Institutions: Hearing Before the Comm. on Banking, Housing and Urban Affairs, United States Senate*, 96th Cong., 1st Sess. (1979). The Office of Federal Contract Compliance Programs of the Department of Labor has proposed a rule that would make the payment or reimbursement of membership fees in a private club that accepts or rejects persons on the basis of race, color, sex, religion, or national origin a prohibited discriminatory practice. 45 Fed. Reg. 4954 (1980) (to be codified in 41 C.F.R. §60–1.11).

26. See discussion of the courts' use of numerical evidence of unequal results in the text accompanying notes 4–21 in Part B of this statement.

27. See U.S., Commission on Civil Rights, *For All The People . . . By All the People* (1969), pp. 122–23.

28. See note 11.

29. See note 13.

30. See notes 15 and 16.

31. See Statement of Arthur S. Flemming, Chairman, U.S., Commission of Civil Rights, before the Subcommittee on Constitutional Rights of the Committee on the Judiciary of the U.S. Senate on S.407, S.903, and S.1279, Apr. 9, 1975, pp. 15–18, based on U.S., Commission on Civil Rights, *The Voting Rights Act: Ten Years After* (January 1975).

32. See, e.g., U.S., Commission on Civil Rights, *Equal Opportunity in Suburbia* (1974).

33. Chafe, *Women and Equality*, p. 78.

34. U.S., Commission on Civil Rights, *Window Dressing on the Set* (1977).

35. See note 17; Gregory v. Litton Systems, Inc., 472 F.2d 631 (9th Cir. 1972); Green v. Mo.-Pac. R.R., 523 F.2d 1290 (8th Cir. 1975).

36. See U.S., Commission on Civil Rights, *Minorities and Women as Government Contractors*, pp. 20, 27, 125 (1975).

37. See, e.g., A. Downs, *Racism in America and How to Combat It* (U.S., Commission on Civil Rights, 1970); "The Web of Urban Racism," in *Institutional Racism in America*, ed. Knowles and Prewitt (Englewood Cliffs, N.J.: Prentice Hall, 1969) pp. 134–76. Other factors in addition to race, sex, and national origin may contribute to these interlocking institutional patterns. In *Equal Opportunity in Suburbia* (1974), this Commission documented what it termed "the cycle of urban poverty" that confines minorities in central cities with declining tax bases, soaring educational and other public needs, and dwindling employment opportunities, surrounded by largely white, affluent suburbs. This cycle of poverty, however, started with and is fueled by discrimination against minorities. *See also* W. Taylor, *Hanging Together, Equality in an Urban Nation* (New York: Simon & Schuster, 1971).

38. The "self-fulfilling prophecy" is a well known phenomenon. "Blaming the victim" occurs when responses to discrimination are treated as though they were the causes rather than the results of discrimination. *See* Chafe, *Women and Equality* (New York: Oxford University Press, 1977) pp. 76–78; W. Ryan. *Blaming the Victim* (New York: Pantheon Books, 1971).

39. See, e.g., J. E. Simpson and J. M. Yinger, *Racial and Cultural Minorities* (New York: Harper and Row, 1965) pp. 49–79; J. M. Jones, *Prejudice and Racism* (Reading, Mass.: Addison Wesley, 1972) pp. 60–111; M. M. Tumin, "Who Is Against Desegregation?" in *Racial and Ethnic Relations*, ed. H. Hughes (Boston: Allyn and Bacon, 1970) pp. 76–85; D. M. Wellman, *Portraits of White Racism* (Cambridge: Cambridge University Press, 1977).

40. See, e.g., D. C. Cox, *Caste, Class and Race: A Study In Social Dynamics* (Garden City, N.Y.: Doubleday, 1948); W. J. Wilson, *Power, Racism and Privilege* (New York: Macmillan, 1973).

41. H. Hacker, "Women as a Minority Group," *Social Forces*, vol. 30 (1951) pp. 60–69; J. Feagin and C. B. Feagin, *Discrimination American Style*; Chafe, *Women and Equality*; J. Feagin, "Indirect Institutionalized Discrimination," *American Politics Quarterly*, vol. 5 (1977) pp. 177–200; M. A. Chesler, "Contemporary Sociological Theories of Racism," in *Towards the Elimination of Racism*, ed. P. Katz (New York: Pergamon Press, 1976); P. Van den Berghe, *Race and Racism: A Comparative Perspective* (New York: Wiley, 1967); S. Carmichael and C. Hamilton, *Black Power* (New York: Random House, 1967); Knowles and Prewitt, *Institutional Racism in America*; Downs, *Racism in America and How To Combat It* (1970).

2

Oppression

Marilyn Frye

It is a fundamental claim of feminism that women are oppressed. The word "oppression" is a strong word. It repels and attracts. It is dangerous and dangerously fashionable and endangered. It is much misused, and sometimes not innocently.

The statement that women are oppressed is frequently met with the claim that men are oppressed too. We hear that oppressing is oppressive to those who oppress as well as to those they oppress. Some men cite as evidence of their oppression their much-advertised inability to cry. It is tough, we are told, to be masculine. When the stresses and frustrations of being a man are cited as evidence that oppressors are oppressed by their oppressing, the word "oppression" is being stretched to meaninglessness; it is treated as though its scope includes any and all human experience of limitation or suffering, no matter the cause, degree or consequence. Once such usage has been put over on us, then if ever we deny that any person or group is oppressed, we seem to imply that we think they never suffer and have no feelings. We are accused of insensitivity, even of bigotry. For women, such accusation is particularly intimidating, since sensitivity is one of the few virtues that has been assigned to us. If we are found insensitive, we may fear we have no redeeming traits at all and perhaps are not real women. Thus are we silenced before we begin: the name of our situation drained of meaning and our guilt mechanisms tripped.

But this is nonsense. Human beings can be miserable without being oppressed, and it is perfectly consistent to deny that a person or group is oppressed without denying that they have feelings or that they suffer.

We need to think clearly about oppression, and there is much that mitigates against this. I do not want to undertake to prove that women are oppressed (or that men are not), but I want to make clear what is being said when we say it. We need this word, this concept, and we need it to be sharp and sure.

The root of the word "oppression" is the element "press." *The press of the crowd; pressed into military service; to press a pair of pants; printing press; press the button.* Presses are used to mold things or flatten them or reduce them in bulk, sometimes to reduce them by squeezing out the gasses or liquids in them. Something pressed is something caught between or among forces and barriers which are so related to each other that jointly they restrain, restrict or prevent the thing's motion or mobility. Mold. Immobilize. Reduce.

The mundane experience of the oppressed provides another clue. One of the most characteristic and ubiquitous features of the world as experienced by oppressed people is the double bind—situations in which options are reduced to a very few and all of them expose one to penalty, censure or deprivation. For example, it is often a requirement upon oppressed people that we smile and be cheerful. If we comply, we signal our docility and our acquiescence in our situation. We need not, then, be taken note of. We acquiesce in being made invisible, in our occupying no space. We participate in our own erasure. On the other hand, anything but the sunniest countenance exposes us to being perceived as mean, bitter, angry or dangerous. This means, at the least, that we may be found "difficult" or unpleasant to work with, which is enough to cost one one's livelihood; at worst, being seen as mean, bitter, angry or dangerous has been known to result in rape, arrest, beating and murder. One can only choose to risk one's preferred form and rate of annihilation.

Another example: It is common in the United States that women, especially younger women, are in a bind where neither sexual activity nor sexual inactivity is all right. If she is heterosexually active, a woman is open to censure and punishment for being loose, unprincipled or a whore. The "punishment" comes in the form of criticism, snide and embarrassing remarks, being treated as an easy lay by men, scorn from her more restrained female friends. She may have to lie and hide her behavior from her parents. She must juggle the risks of unwanted pregnancy and dangerous contraceptives. On the other hand, if she refrains from heterosexual activity, she is fairly constantly harassed by men who try to persuade her into it and pressure her to "relax" and "let her hair down"; she is threatened with labels like "frigid," "uptight," "man-hater," "bitch" and "cocktease." The same parents who would be disapproving of her sexual activity may be worried by her inactivity because it suggests she is not or will not be popular, or is not sexually normal. She may be charged with lesbianism. If a woman is raped, then if she has been heterosexually active she is subject to the presumption that she liked it (since her activity is presumed to show that she likes sex), and if she has not been heterosexually active, she is subject to the presumption that she liked it (since she is supposedly "repressed and frustrated"). Both heterosexual activity and heterosexual nonactivity are likely to be taken as proof that you wanted to be raped, and hence, of course, weren't *really* raped at all. You can't win. You are caught in a bind, caught between systematically related pressures.

Women are caught like this, too, by networks of forces and barriers that expose one to penalty, loss or contempt whether one works outside the home or not, is on welfare or not, bears children or not, raises children or not, marries or not, stays married or not, is heterosexual, lesbian, both or neither. Economic necessity; confinement to racial and/or sexual job ghettos; sexual harassment; sex discrimination; pressures of competing expectations and judgments about *women*, *wives* and *mothers* (in the society at large, in racial and ethnic subcultures and in one's own mind); dependence (full or partial) on husbands, parents or the state; commitment to political ideas; loyalties to racial or ethnic or other "minority" groups; the demands of self-respect and responsibilities to others. Each of these factors exists in complex tension with every other, penalizing or prohibiting all of the apparently available options. And nipping at one's heels, always, is the endless pack of little things. If one dresses one way, one is subject to the assumption that one is advertising one's sexual availability; if one dresses another way, one appears to "not care about oneself" or to be "unfeminine." If one uses "strong language," one invites categorization as a whore or slut; if one does not, one invites categorization as a "lady" — one too delicately constituted to cope with robust speech or the realities to which it presumably refers.

The experience of oppressed people is that the living of one's life is confined and shaped by forces and barriers which are not accidental or occasional and hence avoidable, but are systematically related to each other in such a way as to catch one between and among them and restrict or penalize motion in any direction. It is the experience of being caged in: all avenues, in every direction, are blocked or booby-trapped.

Cages. Consider a birdcage. If you look very closely at just one wire in the cage, you cannot see the other wires. If your conception of what is before you is determined by this myopic focus, you could look at that one wire, up and down the length of it, and be unable to see why a bird would not just fly around the wire any time it wanted to go somewhere. Furthermore, even if, one day at a time, you myopically inspected each wire, you still could not see why a bird would have trouble going past the wires to get anywhere. There is no physical property of any one wire, *nothing* that the closest scrutiny could discover, that will reveal how a bird could be inhibited or harmed by it except in the most accidental way. It is only when you step back, stop looking at the wires one by one, microscopically, and take a macroscopic view of the whole cage, that you can see why the bird does not go anywhere; and then you will see it in a moment. It will require no great subtlety of mental powers. It is perfectly *obvious* that the bird is surrounded by a network of systematically related barriers, no one of which would be the least hindrance to its flight, but which, by their relations to each other, are as confining as the solid walls of a dungeon.

It is now possible to grasp one of the reasons why oppression can be hard to see and recognize: one can study the elements of an oppressive structure with great care and some good will without seeing the structure as a whole, and hence without seeing or being able to understand that one is looking at a cage and that there are people there who are caged, whose motion and mobility are restricted, whose lives are shaped and reduced.

The arresting of vision at a microscopic level yields such common confusion as that about the male door-opening ritual. This ritual, which is remarkably widespread across classes and races, puzzles many people, some of whom do and some of whom do not find it offensive. Look at the scene of the two people approaching a door. The male steps slightly ahead and opens the door. The male holds the door open while the female glides through. Then the male goes through. The door closes after them. "Now how," one innocently asks, "can those crazy womenslibbers say that is oppressive? The guy *removed* a barrier to the lady's smooth and unruffled progress." But each repetition of this ritual has a place in a pattern, in fact in several patterns. One has to shift the level of one's perception in order to see the whole picture.

The door-opening pretends to be a helpful service, but the helpfulness is false. This can be seen by noting that it will be done whether or not it makes any practical sense. Infirm men and men burdened with packages will open doors for able-bodied women who are free of physical burdens. Men will impose themselves awkwardly and jostle everyone in order to get to the door first. The act is not determined by convenience or grace. Furthermore, these very numerous acts of unneeded or even noisome "help" occur in counterpoint to a pattern of men not being helpful in many practical ways in which women might welcome help. What *women* experience is a world in which gallant princes charming commonly make a fuss about being helpful and providing small services when help and services are of little or no use, but in which there are rarely ingenious and adroit princes at hand when substantial assistance is really wanted either in mundane affairs or in situations of threat, assault or terror. There is no help with the (his) laundry; no help typing a report at 4:00 A.M.; no help in mediating disputes among relatives or children. There is nothing but advice that women should stay indoors after dark, be chaperoned by a man, or when it comes down to it, "lie back and enjoy it."

The gallant gestures have no practical meaning. Their meaning is symbolic. The door-opening and similar services provided are services which really are needed by people who are for one reason or another incapacitated—unwell, burdened with parcels, etc. So the message is that women are incapable. The detachment of the acts from the concrete realities of what women need and do not need is a vehicle for the message that women's actual needs and interests are unimportant or irrelevant. Finally, these gestures imitate the behavior of servants toward masters and thus mock women, who are in most respects the servants and caretakers of men. The message of the false helpfulness of male gallantry is female dependence, the invisibility or insignificance of women, and contempt for women.

One cannot see the meanings of these rituals if one's focus is riveted upon the individual event in all its particularity, including the particularity of the individual man's present conscious intentions and motives and the individual woman's conscious perception of the event in the moment. It seems sometimes that people take a deliberately myopic view and fill their eyes with things seen microscopically in order not to see macroscopically. At any rate, whether it is deliberate or not, people can and do fail to see the oppression of women because they fail to see macroscopically and hence fail to see the various elements of the situation as systematically related in larger schemes.

As the cageness of the birdcage is a macroscopic phenomenon, the oppressiveness of the situations in which women live our various and different lives is a macroscopic phenomenon. Neither can be *seen* from a microscopic perspective. But when you look macroscopically you can see it—a network of forces and barriers which are systematically related and which conspire to the immobilization, reduction and molding of women and the lives we live.

3

Racism:
Something about the Subject Makes It Hard to Name

Gloria Yamato

Racism—simple enough in structure, yet difficult to eliminate. Racism—pervasive in the U.S. culture to the point that it deeply affects all the local town folk and spills over, negatively influencing the fortunes of folk around the world. Racism is pervasive to the point that we take many of its manifestations for granted, believing "that's life." Many believe that racism can be dealt with effectively in one hellifying workshop, or one hour-long heated discussion. Many actually believe this monster, racism, that has had at least a few hundred years to take root, grow, invade our space and develop subtle variations . . . this mind-funk that distorts thought and action, can be merely wished away. I've run into folks who really think that we can beat this devil, kick this habit, be healed of this disease in a snap. In a sincere blink of a well-intentioned eye, presto—poof—racism disappears. "I've dealt with my racism . . . (envision a laying on of hands) . . . Hallelujah! Now I can go to the beach." Well, fine. Go to the beach. In fact, why don't we all go to the beach and continue to work on the sucker over there? Cuz you can't even shave a little piece off this thing called racism in a day, or a weekend, or a workshop.

When I speak of *oppression*, I'm talking about the systematic, institutionalized mistreatment of one group of people by another for whatever reason. The oppressors are purported to have an innate ability to access economic resource, information, respect, etc., while the oppressed are believed to have a corresponding negative innate ability. The flip side of oppression is *internalized oppression*. Members of the target group are emotionally, physically, and spiritually battered to the point that they begin to actually believe that their oppression is deserved, is their lot in life, is natural and right, and that it doesn't even exist. The oppression begins to feel comfortable, familiar enough that when mean ol' Massa lay down de whip, we got's to pick up and whack ourselves and each other. Like a virus, it's hard to beat racism, because by the time you come up with a cure, it's mutated to a "new cure-resistant'" form. One shot just won't get it. Racism must be attacked from many angles.

The forms of racism that I pick up on these days are 1) aware/blatant racism, 2) aware/covert racism, 3) unaware/unintentional racism, and 4) unaware/self-righteous racism. I can't say that I prefer any one form of racism over the others, because they all look like an itch needing a scratch. I've heard it said (and under-standably so) that the aware/blatant form of racism is preferable if one must suffer it. Outright racists will, without apology or confusion, tell us that because of our color we don't appeal to them. If we so choose, we can attempt to get the hell out of their way before we get the sweat knocked out of us. Growing up, aware/covert racism is what I heard many of my elders bemoaning "up north," after having escaped the overt racism "down south." Apartments were suddenly no longer vacant or rents were outrageously high, when black, brown, red, or yellow persons went to inquire about them. Job vacancies were suddenly filled, or we were fired for very vague reasons. It still happens, though the perpetrators really take care to cover their tracks these days. They don't want to get gummed to death or slobbered on by the toothless laws that supposedly protect us from such inequities.

Unaware/unintentional racism drives usually tranquil white liberals wild when they get called on it, and confirms the suspicions of many people of color who feel that white folks are just plain crazy. It has led white people to believe that it's just fine to ask if they can touch my hair (while reaching). They then exclaim over how soft it is, how it does not scratch their hand. It has led whites to assume that bending over backwards and speaking to me in high-pitched (terrified), condescending tones would make up for all the racist wrongs that distort our lives. This type of racism has led whites right to my doorstep, talking 'bout, "We're sorry/we love you and want to make things right," which is fine, and further, "We're gonna give you the oppor-tunity to fix it while we sleep. Just tell us what you need. 'Bye!!"—which *ain't* fine. With the best of intentions, the best of educations, and the greatest generosity of heart, whites, operating on the misinformation fed to them from day one, will be-have in ways that are racist, will perpetuate racism by being "nice" the way we're taught to be nice. You can just "nice" somebody to death with naïveté and lack of awareness of privilege. Then there's guilt and the desire to end racism and how the two get all tangled up to the point that people, morbidly fascinated with their guilt, are immobilized. Rather than deal with ending racism, they sit and ponder their guilt and hope nobody notices how awful they are. Meanwhile, racism picks up momentum and keeps on keepin' on.

Now, the newest form of racism that I'm hip to is unaware/self-righteous racism. The "good white" racist attempts to shame Blacks into being blacker, scorns Japanese-Americans who don't speak Japanese, and knows more about the Chi-cano/a community than the folks who make up the community. They assign them-selves as the "good whites," as opposed to the "bad whites," and are often so busy telling people of color what the issues in the Black, Asian, Indian, Latino/a com-munities should be that they don't have time to deal with their errant sisters and brothers in the white community. Which means that people of color are still left to deal with what the "good whites" don't want to . . . racism.

Internalized racism is what really gets in my way as a Black woman. It influences the way I see or don't see myself, limits what I expect of myself or others like me. It results in my acceptance of mistreatment, leads me to believe that being treated with less than absolute respect, at least this once, is to be expected because I am Black, because I am not white. "Because I am (*you fill in the color*)," you think, "Life is going to be hard." The fact is life may be hard, but the color of your skin is not the cause of the hardship. The color of your skin may be used as an excuse to mistreat you, but there is no reason or logic involved in the mistreatment. If it seems that your color is the reason; if it seems that your ethnic heritage is the cause of the woe, it's because you've been deliberately beaten down by agents of a greedy system until you swallowed the garbage. That is the internalization of racism.

Racism is the systematic, institutionalized mistreatment of one group of people by another based on racial heritage. Like every other oppression, racism can be internalized. People of color come to believe misinformation about their particular ethnic group and thus believe that their mistreatment is justified. With that basic vocabulary, let's take a look at how the whole thing works together. Meet "the Ism Family," racism, classism, ageism, adultism, elitism, sexism, heterosexism, physicalism, etc. All these ism's are systematic, that is, not only are these parasites feeding off our lives, they are also dependent on one another for foundation. Racism is supported and reinforced by classism, which is given a foothold and a boost by adultism, which also feeds sexism, which is validated by heterosexism, and so it goes on. You cannot have the "ism" functioning without first effectively installing its flipside, the internalized version of the ism. Like twins, as one particular form of the ism grows in potency, there is a corresponding increasing in its internalized form within the population. Before oppression becomes a specific ism like racism, usually all hell breaks loose. War. People fight attempts to enslave them, or to subvert their will, or to take what they consider theirs, whether that is territory or dignity. It's true that the various elements of racism, while repugnant, would not be able to do very much damage, but for one generally overlooked key piece: power/privilege.

While in one sense we all have power we have to look at the fact that, in our society, people are stratified into various classes and some of these classes have more privilege than others. The owning class has enough power and privilege to not have to give a good whinney what the rest of the folks have on their minds. The power and privilege of the owning class provides the ability to pay off enough of the working class and offer that paid-off group, the middle class, just enough privilege to make it agreeable to do various and sundry oppressive things to other working-class and outright disenfranchised folk, keeping the lid on explosive inequities, at least for a minute. If you're at the bottom of this heap, and you believe the line that says you're there because that's all you're worth, it is at least some small solace to believe that there are others more worthless than you, because of their gender, race, sexual preference . . . whatever. The specific form of power that runs the show here is the power to intimidate. The power to take away the most lives the quickest, and back it up with legal and "divine" sanction, is the very bottom line. It makes the difference between who's holding the racism end of the stick and who's getting beat with it (or beating others as vulnerable as they are) on the internalized racism end of the stick. What I am saying is, while people of color are welcome to tear up their own neighborhoods and each other, everybody knows that you cannot do that to white folks without hell to pay. People of color can be prejudiced against one another and whites, but do not have an ice-cube's chance in hell of passing laws that will get whites sent to relocation camps "for their own protection and the security of the nation." People who have not thought about or refuse to acknowledge this imbalance of power/privilege often want to talk about the racism of people of color. But then that is one of the ways racism is able to continue to function. You look for someone to blame and you blame the victim, who will nine times out of ten accept the blame out of habit.

So, what can we do? Acknowledge racism for a start, even though and especially when we've struggled to be kind and fair, or struggled to rise above it all. It is hard to acknowledge the fact that racism circumscribes and pervades our lives. Racism must be dealt with on two levels, personal and societal, emotional and institutional. It is possible—and most effective—to do both at the same time. We must reclaim whatever delight we have lost in our own ethnic heritage or heritages. This so-called melting pot has only succeeded in turning us into fast food-gobbling "generics" (as in generic "white folks" who were once Irish, Polish, Russian, English, etc. and "black folks," who were once Ashanti, Bambara, Baule, Yoruba, etc). Find or create safe places to actually *feel* what we've been forced to repress each time we were a victim of, witness to or perpetrator of racism, so that we do not continue, like puppets, to act out the past in the present and future. Challenge oppression. Take a stand against it. When you are aware of something oppressive going down, stop the show. At least call it. We become so numbed to racism that we don't even think twice about it, unless it is immediately life-threatening.

Whites who want to be allies to people of color: You can educate yourselves via research and observation rather than rigidly, arrogantly relying solely on interrogating people of color. Do not expect that people of color should teach you how to behave non-oppressively. Do not give into the pull to be lazy. Think, hard. Do not blame people of color for your frustration about racism, but do appreciate the fact that people of color will often help you get in touch with that frustration. Assume that your effort to be a good friend is appreciated, but don't expect or accept gratitude from people of color. Work on racism for your sake, not "their" sake. Assume that you are needed and capable of being a good ally. Know that you'll make mistakes and commit yourself to correcting them and continuing on as an ally, no matter what. Don't give up.

People of color, working through internalized racism: Remember always that you and others like you are completely worthy of respect, completely capable of achieving whatever you take a notion to do. Remember that the term "people of color" refers to a variety of ethnic and cultural backgrounds. These various groups have been oppressed in a variety of ways. Educate yourself about the ways different peoples have been oppressed and how they've resisted that oppression. Expect and insist that whites are capable of being good allies against racism. Don't give up. Resist the pull to give out the "people of color seal of approval" to aspiring white allies. A moment of appreciation is fine, but more than that tends to be less than helpful. Celebrate yourself. Celebrate yourself. Celebrate the inevitable end of racism.

4

Smells like Racism

Rita Chaudhry Sethi

When I started my first job after college, Steve Riley, an African American activist, asked me: "So, how do you feel being black?" I confessed, "I am not black." "In America," Steve responded, "if you're not white, you're black."

U.S. discourse on racism is generally framed in these simplistic terms: the stark polarity of black/white conflict. As it is propagated, it embraces none of the true complexities of racist behavior. Media sensationalism, political expedience, intellectual laziness, and legal constraints conspire to narrow the scope of cognizable racism. What remains is a pared-down image of racism, one that delimits the definition of its forms, its perpetrators, and, especially, its victims. Divergent experiences are only included in the hierarchy of racial crimes when they sufficiently resemble the caricature. Race-based offenses that do not conform to this model are permitted to exist and fester without remedy by legal recourse, collective retribution, or even moral indignation.

Asians' experiences exist in the penumbra of actionable racial affronts. Our cultural, linguistic, religious, national, and color differences do not, as one might imagine, form the basis for a modified paradigm of racism; rather, they exist on the periphery of offensiveness. The racial insults we suffer are usually trivialized; our reactions are dismissed as hypersensitivity or regarded as a source of amusement. The response to a scene where a Korean-owned store is being destroyed with a bat in the 1993 film, *Falling Down* (a xenophobic and racist diatribe on urban life)[1] reflects how mainstream America/American culture responds to the phenomenon of anti-Asian violence:

> There was, in the theater where I saw the film, a good deal of appreciative laughter and a smattering of applause during this scene, which of course flunks the most obvious test of comparative racism: imagine a black or an Orthodox Jew, say, in that Korean's place and you imagine the theater's screen being ripped from the walls. Asians, like Arabs, remain safe targets for the movies' casual racism.[2]

The perpetuation of the caricature of racism is attributable to several complex and symbiotic causes. First, Asians often do not ascribe racist motivation to the discrimination they suffer, or they have felt that they could suffer the injustice of racial intolerance, in return for being later compensated by the fruits of economic success. Second, many Asians do not identify with other people of color. Sucheta Mazumdar posits that South Asians exclude themselves from efforts at political mobilization because of their rigid self-perception as Aryan, not as people of color.[3]

The final and most determinative factor, however, is the perspective that excludes the experiences of Asians (and other people of color) from the rubric of racism. Whites would deny us our right to speak out against majority prejudice, partially because it tarnishes their image of Asians as "model" minorities; other people of color would deny us the same because of monopolistic sentiments that they alone endure real racism.

For example, a poll conducted by *The Wall Street Journal* and NBC News revealed that "most American voters thought that Asian Americans did not suffer discrimination" but in fact received too many "special advantages."[4] Similarly, when crimes against Asians were on the rise in housing projects in San Francisco, the Housing Authority was loathe to label the crimes as racially motivated, despite the clear racial bias involved.[5] The deputy director of the Oakland Housing Authority's response to the issue was: "There may be some issues of race in it, but it's largely an issue of people who don't speak English feeling very isolated and not having a support structure to deal with what's happening to them."[6]

Other minorities reject Asian claims of racial victimization by pointing to economic privilege or perceived whiteness.[7] Such rejections even occur among different Asian groups. Chinese Americans in San Francisco attempted to classify Indians as white for the purposes of the California Minority Business Enterprise Statute: "If you are a white, male buyer in the City, all else being equal, would you buy from another Caucasian [i.e., Indian] or from a person of the Mongolian race?"[8]

The perspective of some people of color that there is a monopoly on oppression is debilitating to an effort at cross-ethnic coalition building. Our experiences are truly distinct, and our battles will in turn be unique; but if we are to achieve a community, we must begin to educate ourselves about our common denominator as well as our different histories and struggles. Ranking and diminishing relative subjugation and discrimination will only subvert our goal of unity. Naheed Islam expresses this sentiment in part of a poem addressed to African American women:

> Ah Sister! What have they done to us! Separated, segregated, unable to love one another, to cross the color line. I am not trying to cash in on your chains. I have my own. The rape, plunder, pain of dislocation is not yours alone. We have different histories, different voices, different ways of expressing our anger, but they used the same bullets to reach us all.[9]

The combination of white America refusing to acknowledge anti-Asian discrimination, and minority America minimizing anti-Asian discrimination foists a formidable burden upon Asians: to combat our own internalized racial alienation, and to fight extrinsic racial classifications by both whites and other minority groups. It also renders overly simplistic those suggestions that if South Asians simply became "sufficiently politicized" they could overcome fragmentation in the struggle by people of color.[10]

As activists, a narrow-minded construct of racism impairs our political initiatives to use racism as a banner that unites all people of color in a common struggle.[11] The mainstream use of the word "racism" does not embrace Asian experiences, and we are not able to include ourselves in a definition that minimizes our encounters with racism. Participation in an antiracism campaign, therefore, is necessarily limited to those involved in a battle against racism that fits within the confines of the black/white paradigm, and conversely relegates anti-Asian racism to a lesser realm in terms of both exposure and horribleness.

We need to be more sophisticated in our analysis of racism, and less equivocal in our condemnation. In doing so, we will expand the base of opposition against anti-Asian racism, and forge an alliance against all its myriad forms. The first step in this process is for Asians to apply a racial analysis to our lives. This involves developing a greater understanding of how racism has operated socially and institutionally in this country against ourselves and other people of color, as well as acknowledging our own complicity; and secondly, accepting ourselves as people of color, with a shared history of being targeted as visibly Other. Only then can we act in solidarity with other efforts at ending racism.

Anti-Asian Racism: Fashioning a More Inclusive Paradigm

Racism takes on manifold creative and insidious expressions. Intra-racism, racism among different racial communities, and internalized racism all complicate an easy understanding of the phenomenon. My project here is to uncover shrouded racism perpetrated against Asians, particularly South Asians, in an attempt to broaden the use of the term.

Accent

It is only since 1992 that the Courts have begun to realize the legitimacy of discrimination based upon accent.[12] Immigrants, primarily those not of European descent,[13] suffer heightened racism because of their accents, including job discrimination and perpetual taunting and caricaturization. This is a severe and pervasive form of racism that is often not acknowledged as racist, or even offensive. Even among Asians there is a high degree of denial about the accent discrimination that is attributable to race. In a letter to the *New York Times*, an Asian man blithely encouraged immigrants to maintain their accents, without acknowledging the potential discrimination that we face, though he personally was "linguistically gifted" with an "American accent." The man wrote, "Fellow immigrants, don't worry about the way you speak until Peter Jennings eliminates his Canadian accent."[14]

Accent discrimination is linked directly to American jingoism, and its accompanying virulently anti-immigrant undertones. In the aforementioned movie *Falling Down,* the protagonist has the following exchange with a Korean grocer:

Mr. Lee: Drink eighty-five cent. You pay or go.

Foster: This "fie," I don't understand a "fie." There's a "v" in the word. It's "fie-vah." You don't got "v's" in China?

Mr. Lee: Not Chinese. I'm Korean.

Foster: Whatever. You come to my country, you take my money, you don't even have the grace to learn my language?[15]

A person's accent is yet another symbol of otherness, but it is one that even U.S.-born minorities do not regard as a target for race-based discrimination. Language is implicitly linked with race, and must be treated as such.

Subversive Stereotyping

The myths that are built based on the commonality of race are meant to depersonalize and simplify people. To many, the Indian persona is that of a greedy, unethical, cheap immigrant. This stereotype is reflected in popular culture, where its appearance gives it credibility, thereby reinforcing the image. In the television comedy, *The Simpsons,* a purportedly politically sensitive program, one of the characters is a South Asian owner of a convenience store. In one episode, in an effort to make a sale, he says, "I'll sell you expired baby food for a nickel off." Similarly, in the program, *Star Trek: Deep Space Nine,* an alien race called the Firengi (Hindi for foreigner) are proprietors and sleazy entrepreneurs who take advantage of any opportunity for wealth, regardless of the moral cost.[16]

These constructs are reified in everyday life as people respond to Indians as if they have certain inherent qualities. Indian physicians, for example, are perceived as shoddy practitioners, who are greedy and disinterested in the health of their patients. In successful medical malpractice suits, Indian doctors are routinely required to pay higher penalties.[17] Similarly, in the now-famous "East Side Butcher" case, where an Indian doctor was convicted of performing illegal abortions, there was no racial analysis despite the fact that no one had been prosecuted for that crime in New York State since the early 1980s despite the fact that hundreds of illegal abortions are performed annually.[18] Another Indian doctor, less than two weeks later, was found guilty of violations in her mammography practice and fined the largest amount in New York State history in such a case. One can not help but wonder if these convictions were, at least in part, motivated by the stereotype of the Indian immigrant.[19]

The Onus

A white, liberal woman once asked my friend Ritu if she wasn't being overly sensitive for taking offense when people put their feet near her face (a high insult in Indian culture), when she could not fairly expect people to understand her culture. The onus is always on us, as outsiders, to explain and justify our culture while also being expected to know and understand majority culture.[20] Constant cultural slights about cows, bindis, and Gandhi are deemed appropriate by the majority while we are expected to subjugate expression of our culture to an understanding and acceptance of American culture. As another example, the swastika is an extremely common, ancient Hindu symbol. However, Hindus cannot wear or display the swastika in America because of Hitler's appropriation of it, and the expectation that we suppress our cultural symbols in an attempt to understand the affront to Jewish Americans. The assumption that it is our normative responsibility to make our culture secondary is racist because it suggests that one culture should be more free to express itself than another.

Religious Fanaticism

Eastern religions are commonly perceived as fraudulent, cultish, and fanatical; they are rarely perceived as equally legitimate as the spiritual doctrines of the Judeo-Christian tradition. The story of immaculate conception is accepted as plausible, while the multiarmed, multiheaded God is an impossible fantasy. Hinduism is portrayed as Hare Krishnas chanting with shaved heads and orange robes; and Islam is characterized as a rigid, violent, military religion. These hyperbolic characterizations are responsible for the fear of religion that causes local communities to refuse to permit places of worship in their neighborhoods.[21]

Western appropriation of Hindu terms reflects the perception of religion as charlatanical; the words have been reshaped through their use in the English language with an edge of irreverence or disbelief.

	Hindi Meaning	**English Use**
1. Guru	Religious teacher	Purported head; self-designated leader
2. Nirvana	Freedom from endless cycle of rebirth	Psychedelic ecstasy; drug-induced high
3. Pundit	Religious scholar	One with claimed knowledge
4. Mantra	A meditative tool; repetition of word or phrase	Mindless chant

Similarly, during times of political crisis (the 1991 Persian Gulf War; the February 1993 World Trade Center bombing), Islam has been the object of derision as a dangerous and destructive religion. After the suspects from the World Trade Center bombing were identified as Muslims, the media, the FBI and mainstream America responded with gross anti-Muslim rhetoric. A Professor in Virginia pointed out the ignorant conflation of the entire Muslim population into one extremist monolith:

> Not all Islamic revivalists are Islamic fundamentalists, and not all Islamic fundamentalists are political activists, and not all Islamic political activists are radical and prone to violence.[22]

Muslims have linked these characterizations of their religion to racial demonization.[23] The *New York Post* carried a headline entitled "The Face of Hate" with the face of a dark-skinned, bearded man of South Asian or Middle Eastern descent (the accused bomber). Similarly, the *New York Times* described the work of courtroom artists: "the defendant's beakish nose, hollow cheeks, cropped beard and the sideways tilt of his head."[24] In an Op-Ed piece in the *New York Times,* one Muslim responded to this description: "Such racial stereotyping serves nothing except to feed an existing hate and fear."[25]

Indicia of Culturalness

Indicia that identify us as Other are generally used as vehicles for discrimination; with East Asians, eye-shape provides the target for racial harassment. South Asians' unique attributes are warped for use as racist artillery: attire (we are towel heads and wear loin cloths and sheets); costume (we are dot-heads); and odor (we are unclean and smelly). Nila Gupta has written about the power of smell, and its identification of South Asians as targets for racist behavior:[26]

> it is spring
> she walks a strong walk
> but they are waiting
> for her in the air
> they can't smell curry and oil poori and dahl for breakfast
> scents they are trained to hate
> confusion
> like hunting dogs after prey
> enraged
> thrown off the scent
> by a river
> enraged
> was she trying to pass?

Gupta's poem recounts a moment of racial discrimination as it is manifested in the degradation of cultural characteristics. When we explore racism, and its effect upon different ethnic and cultural groups, we must also examine the unique ways that specific groups experience racism, and the more neutral proxies and buzzwords used to signify race.

Class Conflicts/Economic Envy

Racism and economic tension are inextricable because race discrimination against Asians has often been manifested as class competition, and vice versa. Since the early 1800s, when Asians became a source of cheap labor for the railroads, we have been an economic threat. As Asians have more recently been portrayed as the prosperous minority, the favored child of America, there has inevitably been sibling rivalry. When auto workers beat up Vincent Chin, was it Japanese competition in the auto industry or unbridled racism that motivated the murderers? When African Americans targeted Korean-owned stores in the riots in Los Angeles after the Rodney King verdict, was it the economic hardship of the inner city and perceived Asian advantages or was it simply racism? The answer is that race and class are inseparable because of the inherent difficulty in identifying the primary or motivating factor; any racial analysis must consider economic scapegoating as an avenue for racial harassment and racial victimization as an excuse for expressing economic tensions.

Conceptual and Perspective Differences

When an immigrant perspective clashes with a white American perspective, the conflict should be considered a racial one. Values such as individuality, privacy, confrontation, competition, and challenging the status quo are considered positive and healthy; however, these components of the liberal state are not necessarily virtues elsewhere. When Hawaiian children do not respond to competitive models of teaching, but thrive in group activities; and when Punjabi children defer to authority, rather than challenge their teachers out of intellectual "curiosity," they are harmed by their inability to function in an essentially and uniquely "American" world. Identifying the differences in perspective and lifestyle between Asian immigrants and Americans will help in recognizing arenas in which we will be at a cultural/racial disadvantage.[27]

A Case Study in Anti-Asian Racism: The Dotbusters of Jersey City

In early fall of 1986, Asian Indians in New Jersey were the targets of racial terrorism. Houses and businesses were vandalized, and graffitied with racial slurs, women had their saris pulled, Indians on the street were harassed and assaulted, and a 28-year-old man was beaten into a coma. The *Jersey Journal* received and printed a letter from a group calling themselves the Dotbusters threatening all Asian Indians in Jersey City, and promising to drive them out of Jersey City. Teenagers in Dickinson High School were found with Dotbuster IDs. In spite of the obvious danger to the community, the police were unresponsive and denied that any Indians should truly be concerned.

The most heinous incident was the murder of Navroze Mody, a 30-year-old Citicorp executive. Navroze was bludgeoned to death with bricks by a group of young Latinos. Long after he had lost consciousness, he was repeatedly propped up and beaten further. His white companion was not touched. Four of the eleven attackers were indicted for manslaughter; two of the indicted were also accused of assaulting two Indian students two weeks before killing Navroze.

Despite the context in which the murder occurred, the incident was not generally perceived as racist in motive by the mainstream, the press, or the Indian community. The ways that Indians were targeted made it convenient to try to find other names for their encounters with racism. Their experiences were unrecognizable as the caricature of racism, and there was a collective refusal to be expansive and open-minded in interpreting what was happening.

The tone for the general characterization of the crime as not racially motivated was set by Hudson County prosecutor, Paul DePascale, assigned to Mody's case. Although he conceded that: "There was no apparent motive for the assault other than the fact that the victim was an Asian American,"[28] he refused to pursue criminal charges for racial bias.[29]

The press, a reflection of mainstream sentiment, was reluctant to label the crime as racial in nature. Even *The Village Voice*, a liberal newspaper, carried a story asking above the headline: "Was his [Navroze Mody's] murder racially motivated?"[30] One newspaper accepted the racial motive by qualifying it as a "new" racism/"new" bigotry. The defendants' supporters saw no racial animus against Indians in the crime, inquiring instead: "Do you think there would be justice if it was the other way around? If the Indian were alive and the Puerto Rican dead?"[31]

Indians-at-large were mystified about the source of the anti-Asian wave of violence and found it difficult to accept as pure racism. People looked for other potential justifications and alternative labels.[32] One community leader remarked, "We pay our taxes," and characterized the Indian community as "faultless immigrants" in an effort to distinguish Asian Indians from African Americans and Latinos.[33] A second-generation Indian lawyer characterized such attacks as "national origin" discrimination, rather than racism.[34] Such denial prevented Asian Indians from making the obvious connection to other groups victimized because of their race.

The uncommonness of the anti-Indian discrimination obfuscated the real racism that rested at its core. Economic envy was the most obvious nonracial analysis proffered for escalating crimes against Asians. One Jersey City resident commented: "I've been in this country all my life and they come here and plop down $200,000 for a house."[35] Part of the infamous Dotbuster letter contained similar comments to journalist Ronald Leir: "You say that Indians are good businessmen. Well I suppose if I had 15 people living in my apartment I'd be able to save money too."[36]

Another major source of attack was traditional Indian attire. According to one community leader: "The number two factor for racism is that we look different."[37] Similarly, the hate group, the Dotbusters, takes its name from the cosmetic dot, or bindi, worn by many Indian women on their foreheads.

Finally, Indian languages and residential clustering create a sense of exclusive cohesiveness that threaten Jersey City's non-Asian communities. Anything that represented the insular-seeming culture was the object of harrassment and hatred. Indian religion and cuisine were mocked, and Indians were repeatedly characterized as smelly (due to the lingering scents of cooking spice).

Despite the heinousness of the crime, the Mody case, and anti-Indian violence, did not receive sufficient public attention or outrage. During the same time that the case was being tried, the Howard Beach case[38] was in the headlines of all major newspapers. Of the four Howard Beach attackers, three received manslaughter convictions; of the eleven attackers in the Mody case, three were convicted of aggravated assault, and one of simple assault. Perhaps it was because Asian Indians did not know how to employ the political system that the verdicts returned did not fit the crimes committed. Perhaps it was because the attackers were also minorities. But the main reason why justice was not served was because the racism that Indians were enduring did not fit the neat, American paradigm for racial violence.

In 1993, we can no longer see the world in black and white, where "those who don't fit the color scheme become shadows."[39] Lessons from our battles with bigotry should convince us that our understanding of it and the machinery we have built to fight it are hopelessly obsolete. Denying the richness of our community of people of color ultimately undermines the objective of unity, and hampers our political work combatting racism. During the late '80s, the left fought to find a common ground for people of color to coalesce; however, it is now the time to refine our collective mission to truly encompass the range of diversity among us. Any movement forged upon the principles of equality and tolerance can only be legitimate if it represents its margins.

NOTES

1. While the film generated much debate about the possible ironic intent of its stereotyping, the reactions of moviegoers showed that the irony was lost on most audiences.

2. Godfrey Cheshire, complete citation for article not available.

3. Mazumdar, Sucheta, "Race and Racism: South Asians in the United States" *Frontiers of Asian American Studies.*

4. Polner, Murray, "Asian-Americans Say They Are Treated Like Foreigners," *The New York Times,* March 7, 1993, Section B, p. 1.

5. Racial slurs were rampant (including "Go home, Chinaman" and accent harassment) and tension between the Asian and African American community was worsening. The fact that the perpetrators were African American might have contributed to the general

reluctance to characterize these crimes as racially motivated. Again, this reflects an inability, or an unwillingness, to intellectually digest racism between non-white races, as it falls outside of the narrow black/white paradigm.

6. Chin, Steven, A. "Asians Terrorized in Housing Projects" *San Francisco Examiner.* January 17, 1993, B1.

7. Witness this morsel of divisiveness: In Miami, where large Latino and African American populations coexist, a Cuban woman was sworn in as State Attorney General. Many in the African American community were dismayed by this decision, and responded by stripping Cubans of their "rank" as a minority. One black lawyer commented: "Cubans are really 'white people whose native language is Spanish' and others agreed that Cuban Americans should be "disqualified because they have higher income levels than other minorities." Certainly there is complexity in this conflict; however, the net result is that people who could be in alliance based on race are divided. Rohter, Larry. "Black-Cuban Rift Extends to Florida Law School" The New York Times; March 19, 1993; B16L.

8. Transcript of San Francisco Board of Supervisors Special Session of Economic and Social Policy Committee April 30, 1991.

9. Islam, Naheed. "Untitled" from *Smell This,* an official publication of The Center for Racial Education, Berkeley, CA 1991.

10. Mazumdar, *supra* at p. 36.

11. Here, and throughout my chapter, I am operating within the constructs of our existing political reality. I am not addressing the normative question of whether people of color should be in coalition against racism, but given that it has been our primary organizing principle, how can we be more effective and inclusive?

12. Interestingly, the case was brought by the EEOC while under the tenure of Joy Cherian, a naturalized Indian. The Commission's 1980 guidelines covering this type of discrimination were written by an Indian, and the case was brought by an Indian plaintiff. Is that what it takes to obtain recognition of the racism that we experience?

13. The Executive Assistant for the Commissioner noted: "If an employer has an applicant who speaks with a French accent . . . or with an English accent, they say, 'How cute.' But if he speaks with a Hispanic accent they say, 'What's wrong with this guy?'"

14. Letter to the editor from Yan Hong Krompacky. "Immigrants, Don't Be In Such a Hurry to Shed Your Accents," *The New York Times* March 4, 1993.

15. Foster then proceeds to demolish Mr. Lee's grocery store with a bat, in much the same way that Japanese cars were hatefully demolished just before Vincent Chin's death.

16. That such stereotypes exist in two programs that are perceived as being among the more progressive on television is itself indicative of the continuing denial that anti-Asian racism exists.

17. According to several medical malpractice attorneys.

18. This was exacerbated further by the fact that Dr. Hayat's sentence was so severe that even the District Attorney's Office had expected less and was "pleasantly surprised." Perez-Pena, Richard, "Prison Term for Doctor Convicted in Abortions" The New York Times, June 15, 1993, p. B1.

19. These stereotypes find expression everywhere. I was haggling for a pair of earrings in Times Square, and the vendor asked me if I was Indian. When I replied that I was, he responded, "Oh, I should have guessed. Indians don't want to take anything out of their pockets."

20. In an effort to better integrate into America culture, and mend relations with ethnic groups in New York City, Korean grocers are taking seminars to learn to smile more frequently, supposedly rare in their culture. *The New York Times,* March 22, 1993

21. "It's the Hindus! Circle the Zoning Laws." Viewpoint by Bob Weiner, *Newsday*, April 26, 1993, p. 40.

22. Steinfeld, Peter. "Many Varieties of Fundamentalism." *The New York Times* no date! An even better response was: [the World Trade bomber suspect's] "variety of fundamentalism was not any more representative of Islam than the people in Waco are representative of [mainstream] Christianity." *Id.*

23. Op Ed Letter to Editor "Don't Let Trade Center Blast Ignite Witch Hunt," March 23, 1993

24. "Surprises In A Crowded Courtroom," Moustafa Bayami March 5, 1993

25. *Ibid.*

26. Gupta, Nila. "So She Could Walk" from *The Best of Fireweed*; Women's Press, Canada (1986).

27. Many Asians find themselves in low-ranking jobs in the corporate world because their skills have little application in the old boy cultural network. This is due in part to different concepts of authority and competition, as much as it is pure racial bigotry. My point is that the two should be viewed together to truly understand the full flourish of racism.

28. Vicente, Raul Jr., "Cops Arrest Two As Dotbusters." *Gold Coast*, March 24–March 31, 1988, p. 4.

29. His failure to label this as a racially-motivated crime may in fact be racially motivated. In March of 1988 there was opposition by Inter Departmental Minority Police Action Council in Jersey City to his appointment as city's acting police director because of alleged discrimination against a black woman officer. "Minority Cops Blast Director," Gold Coast March 31, 1988, p. 7.

30. "Racial Terror on The Gold Coast" *The Village Voice* January 26, 1988.

31. Jersey Journal 3/1/88

32. The collective denial precluded group solutions. Around the same time in Elmhurst 25 African American and Indian families were "preyed" upon in Queens. However, Indians were uninterested in forging an alliance with the African American community to fight ongoing racial harassment. Pais, Arthur, "Long Island Families Were Apathetic and Tearful When Harassed," India Abroad July 31, 1987, p. 1.

33. Walt, Vivienne, "A New Racism Gets Violent in New Jersey," *Newsday*, 4/6/88, p. 5.

34. Spoken at the Strategy Session for the case of Dr. Kaushal Sharan, March 28, 1993, by a representative of the *Indian American Magazine*.

35. Walt, Vivienne, "A New Racism Gets Violent in New Jersey," *Newsday*, 4/6/88, p. 5.

36. Letter to *Jersey Journal* on August 5, 1987.

37. Walt, Vivienne, "A New Racism Gets Violent in New Jersey," *Newsday*, 4/6/88, p. 5.

38. 1986 attack by white youths in Queens where a group of African Americans were stranded; one person died when he was chased onto a highway by the mob.

39. Zia, Helen, "Another American Racism," *The New York Times* letter to the editor.

5

Death of a Teenager Widens a Racial Rift between Two Towns

Alex Kotlowitz

The Michigan towns of St. Joseph and Benton Harbor have little in common other than the river that flows between them and a mystery that began on its banks on May 17, 1991.

That Friday evening, a few blocks from the river in downtown St. Joseph, Deputy Sheriff Stephen Marschke spotted something unusual for the quaint town of 9,200 people: a middle-age white man chasing a black teenager. "He just broke into my car," the man shouted.

The 36-year-old off-duty officer dashed to a restaurant pay phone. Soon, three St. Joseph patrol cars—the town's entire force—were out looking for the black youth, their searchlights scanning alleyways, parks and front yards.

No one seems quite sure what happened next. But five days later, the body of a black youth was discovered floating in the St. Joseph River. The death of Eric McGinnis, a 16-year-old who lived with his divorced mother in Benton Harbor, unleashed a storm of suspicion and hostility between the towns.

Indeed, years of mistrust, misunderstanding and fear—even of the truth—surfaced. In St. Joseph, which is 95% white, people were quick to believe Eric had accidentally drowned. But in Benton Harbor, which is 92% black, residents were certain he had been murdered.

His death sent shock waves through the black community, and Benton Harbor grew even firmer in its convictions as details of the mystery began to unfold. Eric was known to have been a good swimmer, and the current in the river isn't particularly swift.

"He didn't just fall into that river," declares Don Mitchell, a retired postal worker who echoes the thoughts of his neighbors. "Somebody knows what happened."

Accusations of a coverup and conjecture that Eric was the victim of a modern-day lynching persist to this day. The local chapter of the National Association for the Advancement of Colored People has demanded a grand-jury investigation of the case. The controversy has undercut the reputation of local public officials, law-enforcement officers and the media.

Eric's death has become a symbol for the deep rift between the two towns—and in a larger sense a symbol for the wide gulf between blacks and whites nationwide. While the issue of race haunts the nation quietly, it occasionally erupts with jarring urgency, as in the aftermath to Eric's death.

At such moments it becomes clear that individuals respond to a racially charged incident not as objective onlookers but out of their own personal and collective experiences. In the Japanese film "Rashomon," eyewitnesses to a rape all recount the crime differently. Eric's puzzling death has become a kind of Rashomon of the races, with relations between the two communities distorting and coloring the perceptions of what happened on the night he disappeared.

"There are so many misconceptions in both communities," says Ken Overley, an assistant principal at Benton Harbor High School. "In Benton Harbor the misconceptions are grounded in an anger; in St. Joseph they're grounded in a fear. Anytime you have glasses that shade what you're seeing you won't get a true picture."

Like a swollen snake, the St. Joseph River lazily winds its way north from Indiana through the flat cropland of southwestern Michigan, where it rolls into the deep waters of Lake Michigan. It is here that the river is at its widest—170 feet. It is also here that this otherwise undramatic chute of water become formidable, not because of its currents, which are steady and slow, but because of what it separates: Benton Harbor and St. Joseph. The only connections between the towns are two bridges and an undertow of contrasts.

Where in St. Joseph the average family income is $38,504, in Benton Harbor the typical family earns $10,447. Where St. Joseph's downtown mall is a mixture of antique stores, art galleries and clothing boutiques, Benton Harbor's downtown strip is pockmarked by two abandoned movie theaters and rows of vacant stores.

Earlier in the century, Benton Harbor's majestic homes and bustling downtown overshadowed the more working-class crowd of St. Joseph. As industry settled in the area—and nearby farms yielded prodigious fruit crops—Southern blacks migrated to Benton Harbor for work. By the late-1960s, they accounted for 59% of the town's population. Whites, as they did elsewhere, fled. Many settled across the river in St. Joseph. In the years following, industry moved or simply closed down, leaving behind in Benton Harbor a chronically double-digit jobless rate.

Most people in the two towns—called, with unintentional irony, the Twin Cities—rarely cross the two bridges. When Benton Harbor's Mercy Hospital proposed opening a business office in St. Joseph last year, some residents objected on grounds that it would attract blacks to their town.

"If you walk into a store [in St. Joseph] they're going to think you're stealing, so you tell your children, 'I don't want you over there,'" says James Rutter, who until recently was the superintendent of the Benton Harbor school system.

Excell McGinnis, Eric's father, says he felt nervous on the fateful night when Eric had asked to be driven across the bridge to St. Joseph. "I know St. Joseph," he says. "If you're over there after dark, they want to know what you're doing."

It is not an uncomplicated relationship, though. Just last year, St. Joseph Mayor William Gillespie, while riding in a parade in Benton Harbor, was taunted by a spectator: "Honky, go back." Even so, the mayor insists "relations are very good" between the two towns.

There has been some progress in the past few years. A group of business leaders, led by Whirlpool Corp., whose corporate headquarters are in the area, has tried to spur economic development in Benton Harbor, a town of 12,800 people. Whirlpool has also contributed money to the beleaguered Benton Harbor school system. Nonetheless, the gap is still wide. While St. Joseph debates what color to paint the tin roofs of the bathrooms by the lake, Benton Harbor wrestles with one of the highest murder rates in the state.

Despite the divisions between the towns, Eric, who had skirted the dark canyon of drugs and gangs, had been making trips across the river fairly often. Alternately described as shy and outgoing, he joined a gymnastics club on the St. Joseph side of the water, where he quickly won the friendship of students there. "He brightened the gym up," says Leigh Ann Bender, a fellow gymnast. "I looked forward to coming to the gym when he was there."

He also met many white teenagers at a place called the Club, a St. Joseph nightspot for kids 18 years old and younger who liked to dance and hang out with friends. The teenagers could buy juice and soda pop, play video games and scrawl messages on a wall designated for graffiti. With the exception of a few minor scuffles, the Club had a good reputation. The nightspot was unusual. While most of the kids came from St. Joseph, it also attracted a handful from the other side of the river.

The Club was Eric's destination on the night he disappeared. But few people were there, so Eric decided to join four friends from St. Joseph in the Young Women's Christian Association parking lot across the street.

A bit later, Ted Warmbein, the 41-year-old owner of an office-supply store, was leaving the nearby Silver Dollar Cafe with his date when he saw a black youth rifling through his car. Mr. Warmbein ran toward him and the teen fled.

Mr. Warmbein, a stocky man, couldn't keep pace with the fleet youth. As they ran down the town's main street, Mr. Warmbein almost knocked over Mr. Marschke. The deputy sheriff went into the Silver Dollar to phone the St. Joseph police and then walked back outside. When he saw a squad car turn the corner, he says he returned to the restaurant rather than help direct the police.

Mr. Warmbein, meanwhile, says an unidentified man who had witnessed the chase offered to drive him around to see if they could find the youth. They couldn't, though Mr. Warmbein did find his checkbook. Forty-four dollars in cash was missing. So was Eric.

The St. Joseph Police Department, which has handled a total of three murders in the past half century, assigned all three patrol cars to search for the suspect. According to police records, they found no trace of him. Mr. Warmbein filed a police report and then went home to sleep.

When Eric didn't return to his father's house, Mr. McGinnis assumed he had gone to his mother's instead. The next morning Mr. McGinnis called his ex-wife. Eric wasn't there. Ruth McGinnis filed a missing person's report with the police that afternoon. Mr. McGinnis feared the worst. "I went over to St. Joseph. . . . I did it three or four times. I just had a feeling he might have been in the river or laying on the side of the road," he says.

Four days passed. And then, Saul Brignoni, a Coast Guard seaman, received a radio call from the crew of a nearby dredging boat. "We got something out here you might want to take a look at," he was told. As he and his colleagues pushed off in their small boat, they spotted the bloated body of a fully clothed black teen. "You don't forget your first body," says Mr. Brignoni, who remembers even the brand names of the clothes Eric was wearing. He also recalls that Eric's belt was un-buckled, his pants were open and his shoes were untied—all of which would add to the questions surrounding his death.

An autopsy ruled it a drowning, concluding that there were no physical marks on Eric's body to indicate he'd been hit or had been in a fight. Likewise, there weren't any drugs in his system; his alcohol level was at 0.04%, the equivalent of about two beers.

Police investigators concluded that this was the teen they had been searching for. Three of Eric's friends told police they had seen him break into the car. And in his pockets, the police found a set of house keys and $49—the $5 his mother had given him and presumably the $44 taken from Mr. Warmbein's car. The police also noted that his long, heavy Task Force-brand coat was missing.

Benton Harbor nearly exploded after Eric's body was found. Justice for blacks, many felt, had long been elusive in predominantly white and conservative Berrien County. James Turner, a Benton Harbor city commissioner, still seethes when re-calling the time his two sons were pulled over by police after driving through a St. Joseph residential neighborhood.

Eric McGinnis's death fanned the resentment, a residue of small and large slights that pricked and stung even the proudest and strongest of people. Benton Harbor High School virtually emptied out for the funeral, which was attended by about 1,200 people. Eric had many friends. He belonged to the NAACP, his church choir and his school's junior ROTC.

In the week after Eric's burial, black Benton Harbor High School students attacked two white students. A gang threatened to cross the bridge and wreak havoc on St. Joseph. Eric's friends gathered in front of his house, "waiting for me to say, 'Go get them,'" recalls Ms. McGinnis. She urged them not to. Chris Adams, owner of the Club, received death threats. Five blacks, one of whom was believed to be carrying a gun, threatened to disrupt a women's softball practice at Lake Michigan College. And a white couple necking in a lake-side park were beaten by a group of blacks. An anonymous caller warned a St. Joseph police dispatcher: "Next time, someone will get hurt seriously."

People in St. Joseph heard about these incidents. Fearful parents kept their children home from school. One mother prevented her son from leaving the house all summer, worried that he might be the target of an attack because he knew Eric. The police were put on alert after they heard rumors that there might be a drive-by shooting of the Club. Kids stopped frequenting the nightspot; it closed three weeks later for lack of business.

Three or four times a week, Ms. McGinnis, a quality-control supervisor for a local plastics maker, would drive to downtown St. Joseph after work. She would stand by the building that once housed the Club and try to imagine the events of the night her son disappeared. "I just want to know what happened so that I can rest," she says. "I'm not bitter. I'm hurt. I miss my son."

People wanted answers. The NAACP offered a reward for any information that might help resolve the questions about Eric's death. Ms. McGinnis and her brother, Bennie Bowers, a state trooper who had been close to Eric, began questioning people themselves. And the St. Joseph police, who recognized how volatile a case they had, interviewed 91 people and eventually called in the Federal Bureau of Investigation and the Michigan State Police to get their expert opinions as well.

"This was a time bomb ready to go off," says James Reeves Jr., a detective with the St. Joseph police.

When Eric's body was found, it was clear to civic leaders and law-enforcement officials that the death could cause unrest, so they assembled a task force that included police from the surrounding communities, including Benton Harbor. Mr. Reeves, a 22-year veteran of the St. Joseph Police Department, headed the investigation. An earnest, affable 44-year-old, Mr. Reeves, who is white, grew up in Benton Harbor. Unlike others, he stayed—until last year, when his daughter was ready to enter school. He moved to St. Joseph, into a larger home and into a better-financed school district.

Dennis Wiley, the county prosecutor, would deal with the press. Early in the investigation, Mr. Wiley made a decision that eventually led to accusations of incompetence and coverup. He chose not to make public the suspicion that Eric had broken into a car, worried that such a disclosure would inflame racial tensions. Mr. Wiley told the editors of the local newspaper, the Herald-Palladium, who agreed to keep it off the record and not to print it. Bob DeWitt, news director at WSJM radio, had uncovered the information in his reporting but chose not to broadcast it because "we didn't want to fan the flames."

"Everybody's gotten so paranoid about one another," sighs one law-enforcement official who favored releasing the information. "They're worried even about telling someone the truth. It's just crazy. It wasn't malicious. It was just like: 'Oh, my God, if we say this they won't believe us.' People around here are their own worst enemy."

Ms. McGinnis, in a meeting with Mr. Wiley, also agreed to leave the matter private. Now, though, she regrets her acquiescence. "I don't know whether they didn't print that as a favor to me or as a favor to them," she says.

That decision would, in particular, hurt Mr. Reeves: It later led people to raise questions about his investigation. Mr. Reeves says he pursued every lead. Six people took lie-detector tests, including five of Eric's buddies who were questioned about the goings-on the night Eric disappeared. All were found to be telling the truth. Mr. Warmbein, who for a while was the chief suspect, took a polygraph and passed. The police checked out his alibi that he had gone directly home after giving chase. His cousin and niece, both of whom lived with him, confirmed it. The police talked to a St. Joseph girl Eric had dated. Her father was rumored to hate blacks. She was able to prove that she wasn't at or near the Club the night Eric disappeared. And her father had been out of town.

It left Mr. Reeves with only one conclusion: Eric had somehow ended up in the river—either he fell in or tried to swim it—and then drowned. Mr. Reeves devised a number of scenarios. In an effort to get back home after having broken into the car, he speculated, Eric might have attempted to cross the railroad trestle and failed in his effort. Or in an attempt to avoid the police searchlights, maybe he hung over the edge of a retaining wall and slipped. Or perhaps, he suggested, Eric tried to swim across the river and drowned in the chilly, 48-degree water.

Even though the FBI and state police supported Mr. Reeves's conclusion, none of this made sense to the people of Benton Harbor. Why, after all, would Eric try to swim the river? Why wouldn't he simply walk over the bridge, or call his parents and have one of them pick him up? Besides, everyone insisted, Eric was a good swimmer—and because of dredging, the currents weren't strong.

There were other questions, as well. Why was his belt unbuckled and pants open when he was found? Where was his coat? Another persistent question: Why didn't Mr. Marschke, the deputy sheriff who went on to be appointed sheriff, give chase to Eric?

In Benton Harbor, Mr. Marschke had a reputation for being an arrogant officer. In a reelection bid this past summer, he ran newspaper advertisements showing him arresting a young black man. The headline asked rhetorically: "In the war on drugs who knows the enemy best?" Even after the black community expressed alarm over the ad, Mr. Marschke persisted in running it. When people learned that he said he hadn't given chase, it aroused suspicion.

"I can't imagine him not going after that guy," says Mr. Turner, the city commissioner.

When St. Joseph police officer Dale Easton arrived in response to Mr. Marschke's phone call, the deputy sheriff was nowhere to be seen. "It kind of surprised me," Mr. Easton recalls. "If he witnessed something I figured he'd stay around to tell what he saw."

The deputy sheriff met a friend for dinner that night, Mr. Marschke explains. "I saw the guy running, and that was the extent of my involvement," he says. "There was nothing to wait for. [The police] had the description of what I gave them."

Ms. McGinnis and her brother, Mr. Bowers, visited with Mr. Marschke last spring. Didn't he think it odd that a black youth was running in downtown St. Joseph? "It was a little unusual, but I didn't think much of it," he says. "People want to make it a racial situation. Why would I think that was unusual that a black man was running down the street?"

Mr. Reeves says he has never considered Mr. Marschke a suspect. He didn't review the police tape of the emergency call Mr. Marschke made. It has since been erased. The detective concedes it was "an oversight on my part." But Mr. Marschke's decision not to join in the pursuit doesn't appear out of character, say friends and former colleagues. Mr. Marschke, they say, has always been a politically ambitious man with his sights set on becoming sheriff, a position he obtained temporarily, when the reigning sheriff retired in the fall of 1991. (Mr. Marschke failed in an election bid.)

Eric's death hovered like a noxious cloud over the two towns, waiting for answers. Blacks didn't bring it up with whites, nor whites with blacks.

Then the inevitable happened. At a forum last July, Mr. Marschke, who was running to retain his position as sheriff, was asked by a Benton Harbor resident what had happened the night Eric disappeared. Mr. Marschke ran through the story. This time, though, he detonated an emotional bomb. While retelling the tale, he let slip that Eric had broken into a car. All of Benton Harbor wanted to know why this fact had been concealed. "It leads you to wonder what else was withheld and why it was withheld," says Michael Green, the community project officer for Peoples State Bank and a Benton Harbor resident.

"There's either been a coverup or it's the worst investigation I've ever observed," insists Mr. Turner.

Within the next two weeks, the NAACP made its request to the state's attorney general to convene a grand-jury inquiry. The Benton Harbor City Council passed a resolution supporting the request. Protesters then marched to the county building, decrying the police investigation.

In his office, where an aerial photograph of the river hangs on one wall, Mr. Reeves patiently answers a barrage of questions by a reporter from a statewide black newspaper. A cautious and reticent man by nature, he has felt compelled to respond to all queries and to make public the two-inch-thick file on the case so that everything would be out in the open.

After the disclosure that Eric allegedly had committed a crime, Mr. Reeves and his department came under intense criticism, some of which Mr. Reeves took personally. He says that he periodically rereads the now-bulging police report to see if there is anything he missed. He frequently reviews the Polaroid photographs of Eric's mud-splattered body.

"I guess I'm frustrated with not being able to give the family an absolute, definitive replay of what happened," he says. Not far into the probe, Mr. Reeves learned that he and Ms. McGinnis had graduated together from Benton Harbor High School. "It was common ground," he says. But at their 25th-year reunion that same summer, Mr. Reeves says, "it was hard to look at Ruthie and say, 'I just don't know'" exactly what happened to Eric. Since he has nothing new to disclose, he has been reluctant to call Ms. McGinnis. For her part, Ms. McGinnis has complained of not being kept abreast of the police inquiry. "I'm not pointing fingers," she says. "All I want are answers."

Whenever leads come up, Mr. Reeves pursues them. Still, he considers the case solved, ruling it an accidental drowning.

But he doesn't know—and says he may never know—how Eric ended up in the river, whether he fell in or tried to swim. "I have about 105 different possibilities," he says. He is convinced, however, that no foul play was involved.

How about the missing coat? Maybe, suggests Mr. Reeves, the coat is "at the bottom of the river." How about the unbuckled belt? Mr. Reeves says that it was chic for some teenage boys to wear their belts open like that. He also points out that Eric's body was lifted out of the water by a rope attached to his belt. Another law-enforcement official suggests that Eric was frantically trying to disrobe while in the water, though that doesn't explain why his untied shoes would still be on.

The attorney general's office has referred the NAACP's grand-jury request to Mr. Wiley, the local prosecutor. The group is planning another courthouse rally sometime next month urging a further investigation into Eric's death.

The lack of concrete answers leaves those in Benton Harbor unsatisfied. Mr. Green, the bank officer, wrote an op-ed piece for the local newspaper that began and ended with the same assertion: "Someone knows what happened to Eric McGinnis. He didn't just jump into the St. Joseph River and drown."

Says an exasperated Mr. Reeves: "I guess people are going to believe what they want to believe."

"It's classified as an accidental drowning," he says, almost apologetically, "but I don't think we're ever going to convince everybody."

Nearly two years have passed since Eric's body was found in the St. Joseph River. In that time 15 people have been murdered in Benton Harbor, including two children. The only deaths in St. Joseph have been those of natural causes and three by drowning in Lake Michigan.

The Twin Cities also remain worlds apart in their conjecture as to what happened the night of May 17. Most in St. Joseph believe Eric McGinnis accidentally drowned. Those in Benton Harbor, even the most conservative and conciliatory, not only believe, they say they know for certain that Eric McGinnis was murdered. What else would account for the death of a black youth in all-white St. Joseph?

This debate involves more than just differences between Benton Harbor and St. Joseph; it embodies the fault line separating the races. Emotional quakes, like Eric's death, only push the two sides even further apart. The truth of what happened that night may have been buried with Eric, whose body lies at the far end of the Crystal Springs Cemetery under a simple tombstone that reads: "My Beloved Son."

6

Gang Rape

David Gonzalez with Garry Pierre-Pierre

There is little public outrage in East New York, even though it's only days since a 31-year-old woman returning from a store was raped and sodomized by what the police said was a gang of six teen-agers, toting a toy gun, who sauntered away from the attack to shoot baskets and boast of their conquest.

There is no outcry among the residents of the housing projects off Sutter Avenue where the youths live and were arrested, only weary warnings that the woman should have known better than to walk alone through the dark streets. Nor is there surprise that two of those arrested were 13 years old, only an "anything's possible" attitude in a neighborhood where some youths pack more deadly force than the police.

As if to lessen or deny the crime, some even insisted that the victim must have been a prostitute. The police said she was not but may have been mistaken for one by the gang, which is suspected in attacks on prostitutes in the area.

Along the streets of the East Brooklyn Industrial Park, where the woman was forced to have sex in a scraggly lot littered with beer bottles and condom wrappers, streetwalkers still meander and flash wan smiles at passing drivers. As the scars and scabs on their faces show, violence is an occupational hazard that is to be expected as much from an emotionally unhinged john as from packs of teen-agers who make sport of showering them with rocks and bottles.

Unlike the torrent of rage after a jogger was raped and beaten by teen-agers in Central Park several years ago, there are no memorials, no legions of police, no Take Back the Night rallies. The routine reigns in East New York, and the night is best avoided.

"It would be extraordinary if somebody did something about it," said Thomas Johnson, 39, who has lived on Hinsdale Street for three years. "It's going to come and go. There's been too many incidents like this. It's everyday life around here."

The attack itself was brazenly cruel, even by the dizzying standards of violence that have left residents both fearful and jaded. According to the police and criminal complaints filed last week, six youths accosted the woman on Monday evening as she walked near Sheffield and Glenmore Avenues, a desolate stretch of empty lots and squat industrial buildings. The complaint says Daniel Rivera, 17, pulled out a cap pistol and forced her into a lot a few blocks away, where he and the others raped and sodomized her, including inserting a metal pipe into her vagina. The youths then robbed her of cigarettes and food stamps and let her go, the complaint says.

A police officer familiar with the case, who spoke on condition of anonymity, said that after the attack, Mr. Rivera and another youth, Sam Singleton, 15, went to a basketball court near their homes on Georgia Avenue and boasted about how they had robbed the woman.

The police said that the woman, who has been identified only as a school board employee, flagged down a patrol car and began searching the neighborhood for her attackers. She spotted them playing basketball with several other youths, and all were quickly arrested.

In addition to the Rivera and Singleton youths, the police arrested Tyrone Smith, 16, and two 13-year-olds, whose names were not released because of their age. Jermaine Dawson, 15, who was also arrested, was released on Friday, and charges were dropped after investigators said he was arrested by mistake. The police are continuing their search for a sixth suspect.

After his release, Jermaine said the other boys had suggested on Monday night that they rob someone. He refused and continued to play basketball, he said. When his friends returned sometime later, he said, they boasted of having robbed the woman.

Blaming Bad Company

Ramon Rivera, Daniel's grandfather, sat inside his barely furnished apartment a few days after the arrests and insisted that the boy, whom he had reared since birth and who had been his constant companion since his wife died two years ago, could not have committed such a crime. Daniel went to school at Thomas Jefferson High School, where he played baseball, and talked of becoming a police officer, Mr. Rivera said.

"He's not bad," he insisted, sitting among the few possessions that survived an apartment fire several years ago. "What happened is that two months ago he started hanging out with those black kids."

Mr. Rivera said he often warned his grandson that his friends were no good, that they played hooky and started trouble. But Daniel wouldn't listen, he said.

"Sometimes he would look bad at me," Mr. Rivera said. "Or he would say bad things to me. But he wasn't bad."

Taking an occasional sip from a beer bottle wrapped in a brown bag, Mr. Rivera insisted that his grandson's accuser made up her story after having an argument with some other men in the neighborhood.

"She's a whore and a crackhead," he said bluntly, even though the police had said she was not. "She had a problem at the liquor store and came over here to where the kids were playing. The police don't know what happened."

Numerous men who linger outside the liquor store by Sheffield and Sutter Avenues, as well as the store's owner, said they had not seen the woman and said no such argument had happened that night.

Frances Smith, Tyrone's mother, echoed Mr. Rivera's comments that the woman was a prostitute. "I never seen her," she said. "But a lot of people had. I don't think these young boys's lives should be wasted over a prostitute."

She said her son and his friends were playing basketball on Monday night. She said that she could see them from her fourth-floor window and that at one point in the evening he even shouted upstairs to see if anyone had called for him.

She said she had never had any problem with her son, who likes dogs and wants to be a veterinarian, she said. He is not, she insisted, capable of rape.

Where Anything Is Possible

Friends of the arrested youths said that they were not the type to start trouble, that they only liked to play basketball and hang out together. But they had an almost blasé attitude to the possibility that teen-agers, regardless of who they were, could have committed such a crime.

Considering how some youths he knows carry guns, Lamar Sanders, 16, said "anything's possible" in that neighborhood.

That's the problem, said Carol Beck, who retired in June as principal of Thomas Jefferson High School, where in recent years several students have been murdered inside the building.

"The little guys follow the larger guys," Mrs. Beck said. "Everybody wants to be respected and show their peers they are somebody. It's insane. The level of insanity just keeps escalating to where everyone tries to outdo the other. It's almost like we're trying to see how bizarre we can be."

In a way, she added, reality and fantasy have melded in the minds of some youths, allowing situations to veer out of control in the blink of an eye.

"Everybody just keeps escalating, the same behavior that happened in L.A. or wherever you get a group of people anywhere," she said. "There are fewer people with a level of sanity that says: 'Stop. We're going too far.'"

The problem is well known at Jefferson High School, where yesterday about 20 male students attending a workshop on "What It Takes to Be a Young Man in East New York" were urged to reconsider their attitudes toward women. The session, the first of eight, was scheduled before the attack.

"We've been taught that we have to disrespect our women," said Khm Ur Amsu Amen Ra, a member of a fraternal order that sponsored the workshop. "That is wrong. You cannot disrespect that which you come from."

He said that incidents like the attack on the woman showed "a misplaced sense of values." And, he said, "All that causes is genocide."

Earlier in the week, two women who stood outside a variety store, agreed that they could not put anything past some of the youths in the neighborhood.

One woman, who gave her name only as Margie, said there were some "healthy, mature-looking" children barely into their teen years who have little respect for others. Nor did she think parents knew what their children were up to once they left their houses to play in the street.

"I'm a parent, and as a parent you know you have to have an open mind that there are just some things your child is going to do," she said. "You can fantasize and hope for the best, but there are some things you won't know."

She knows that some youths pick on people in the neighborhood, almost as if they could sense who they could bother and whom they should steer clear of.

"I haven't experienced any problems with them," she said, pausing. "Yet."

Lucy Lopez has.

Ms. Lopez, a 38-year-old streetwalker, said she had been chased by packs of youngsters who descended at night on "the stroll," where prostitutes ply their trade in the industrial park for as little as $2 a "date." Last week, she said, a friend was hit in the face by a bottle thrown by teen-agers.

Sometimes, the youngsters are looking for more than a chase.

"They want to pick up girls who are walking, show them cash or crack, and if the girl is feeding, she'll go with them and end up getting hurt," Ms. Lopez said. "It's gotten worse."

Other prostitutes talked of being robbed and threatened with knives by some teen-agers who have cornered them in the past. Few report the crimes to the police.

One prostitute, who would give her name only as Deborah, said the women had to be careful. "If you see four or five boys, they'll pull you into the bushes and rape you," she said.

Last week's attack has not deterred them from walking the street, even if it and other assaults have led some of them to take a friend or relative for protection.

For some teen-agers, harassing prostitutes is a rite of passage born of boredom.

"We'll go down there and say 'Come here, come here,'" said William Bond, 17. "They'll start running, and we'll chase and beat them."

When asked why he used to do that, he replied: "We did not have anything better to do. It was fun."

That idea of fun wore off when they got older.

"I got too mature for that," said James, a 16-year-old who refused to give his last name. "I got to chase girls now, and I don't have time to go to jail for beating crackheads."

Corey Williams, 15, said: "We realized it was wrong. It could be our own sister or mother."

Dubb Johnson, who lives in one of the few houses nestled amid the industrial landscape, simply dismissed the violence as a hazard run by the prostitutes. Similarly, he doubted that parents could counter the influence of their children's friends.

"If you're not down with this, you're not down," he said. "It's a shame they're living that kind of life."

Then again, he said, it's a shame others have to tolerate it.

"Nobody feels safe living in the neighborhood," he said. "It's East New York, the whole deal."

No Cure for Sexism in the Medical Profession

Kathy K. Astor

When Dr. Heidi Weissmann joined the staff of Montefiore Medical Center/Albert Einstein College of Medicine/Yeshiva University in 1977 as a fourth-year student in the Unified Department of Nuclear Medicine, she never dreamed that she would have to spend much of her time fighting a pattern of discriminatory behavior against the female medical staff, and that she would find herself engaged in a series of court battles against her former supervisor and Montefiore/Einstein/Yeshiva that so far has consumed almost seven years of her life.

Weissmann's legal and political struggle is taking place against a background of impressive and uncommon academic and professional achievement. She completed her internship and began her residency at Mt. Sinai School of Medicine, after obtaining an MD from that institution in 1974. Weissmann, who knew she wanted to be a doctor from the time she was a small child, entered college at the age of 15, and began medical school when she was just 19 years old. In 1980, she received the Sol Horowitz Award for Distinguished Alumna of the Year. Endorsed by Dr. Leonard Freeman, her section head, for an award from the Society of Nuclear Medicine, in 1984 she was promoted to Associate Professor of Nuclear Medicine after coming up with a new way to diagnose cholescystitis (acute gall bladder disease), a discovery she made while she was still a resident. According to a September 25, 1990 article in the *Medical Post*, Dr. Harold Jacobson, Chair of Radiology at Montefiore, said in a letter sent to a colleague at the time of her promotion that "Dr. Weissmann's rise in the academic community is little short of phenomenal . . . [her] work is of extreme importance clinically, and has 'turned around' the diagnosis of acute cholescystitis." Jacobson praised Weissmann's work again in a letter he sent her one year later that made note of her national and even international prominence.

All of these personal accomplishments, however, occurred in the context of systemic and pervasive gender discrimination directed at Weissmann and other women at Montefiore. Weissmann was paid less than men in similar positions; she was passed over on at least two occasions for promotion to Chief of Nuclear Medicine in favor of less qualified and less senior men; she was not given the secretarial assistance she required; was reimbursed less than her male colleagues for travel and related expenses; and was repeatedly discouraged from taking part in professional activities that increased her individual recognition, although official departmental policy encouraged such activities.

One especially blatant instance occurred when Weissmann was appointed to a National Institutes of Health (NIH) study section formed to evaluate proposals for funding research in radiology. This particular research area has wide-ranging implications for women's health issues—breast cancer being but one example. In addition, the very fact she was asked to serve in this study section was a testament to the professional respect she had already achieved: "It's a tremendous honor to be asked to serve," Weissmann noted. Nevertheless, she was discouraged from accepting the appointment and not given the support she needed to carry out her responsibilities. The discouragement was subtle at first, such as not being able to get a secretary to type up critiques. When she persisted, she was told straight out that she didn't get the message, that she was just a junior woman in the department; why had she been asked to serve instead of one of the older men who had been there longer?

Weissmann did not remain silent about the unequal treatment she observed and experienced firsthand. She discussed it directly with Freeman and Dr. Donald Blaufox, her department chair. Their response was to stonewall her, although she did not realize it at the time. They told her they were aware of the problems and would see that they were corrected, but it would take time, and she should be patient. So Weissmann took their advice, and tried to be patient—for about three years. "I was a good girl," she wryly remarked. But in that time, the situation did not improve—it got worse.

Weissmann found out how much worse in 1986, when she requested a six-month sabbatical at full pay to write a book about gall bladder nuclear medicine. Sabbaticals at Montefiore/Einstein had to be earned; they were not granted automatically. Indeed, Blaufox told her she was one of only three people to whom he would consider giving a sabbatical, the other two being Freeman and himself. Nevertheless, Blaufox refused to give her the sabbatical on the terms she had requested; he insisted she take a 12-month sabbatical at half instead of full pay, because, according to him, "hers was a second income"; although as Weissmann told *New Directions for Women*, she and her husband, also a doctor, had never considered her career to be secondary to his. In addition, Blaufox told Weissmann she could only use the sabbatical to write a grant proposal; this in spite of the fact that in the past men had been granted sabbaticals to write books. Weissmann notes that this distinction was crucial, since a grant proposal could have bought recognition and funding to Einstein and the Department of Nuclear Medicine, whereas a book would have meant individual recognition only for her. Of course, Einstein would have benefited indirectly from the prestige of having such a distinguished medical professional on staff, but this advantage apparently did not carry as much weight with them.

At about this time, Weissmann arranged a meeting to discuss the continuing problem of unequal treatment based on gender with an associate dean at Einstein,

Dr. Deborah Kligler, Ph.D. Kligler agreed that Weissmann was being discriminated against, but advised her not to become a martyr. Kligler told Weissmann she would be better off biding her time, and moving on when the right opportunity presented itself.

Weissmann decided to take Kligler's advice to heart—"I didn't go to medical school to become a martyr." So Weissmann resigned from the NIH study section and took her sabbatical the way Blaufox wanted her to.

Weissmann's sabbatical began in September of 1986. In January of 1987—about three months after she had met with Dean Kligler to discuss a pattern of discrimination at Einstein—Weissmann received a letter from Blaufox, informing her that her return to the department would be on a "probationary basis." At this point, Weissmann had been on staff at Einstein for ten years. No reasons were given for this extraordinary action, other than "nonsensical, Mickey Mouse" excuses involving failure to adequately perform certain administrative functions such as attending discussion meetings and filling out forms; which, in any case, Weissmann maintains she did. Although she did not know it at the time, Weissmann found out later that the probation was a sham, because such a thing "doesn't exist for someone at my rank and level." And, tellingly, when Weissmann asked Freeman for an explanation for Blaufox's action, she was told that Blaufox wanted to "shake her up and put her back in her place."

But Weissmann refused to return to "her place." She filed a discrimination complaint with the Equal Employment Opportunities Commission (EEOC). Then, in August of 1987 just before she was scheduled to return from her sabbatical, Weissmann discovered that Freeman had removed her name from a chapter she had written and that had been published in a book in 1985, had inserted his own name as author, and was about to present the information from the chapter as his own at a course being sponsored by another medical school. Weissmann got a restraining order to prevent Freeman from using the chapter and on August 20, 1987, filed a copyright infringement suit against him.

The very next day, August 21, Weissmann was met by a security guard when she attempted to return to her office at Einstein. She was informed that she had to leave and could not take anything with her. In addition, the security officer packed her bags for her and searched her before she left. Although it seemed obvious to Weissmann that she had been fired, her former employer maintains that she quit. In a letter from Blaufox, Weissmann was informed that her "failure to return to work constitutes a resignation of employment." On the same day that Blaufox wrote this letter, he wrote another letter to department staff, praising Freeman's work and announcing his promotion to vice-chairman of the Unified Department of Nuclear Medicine.

Subsequent events have brought both victory and defeat to Heidi Weissmann. Although the copyright infringement suit was decided in March 1988 by a judge without a jury in Freeman's favor, the U.S. Court of Appeals for the 2nd Circuit reversed the original decision, and Freeman's petition to the Supreme Court was denied, indicating that the Supreme Court upheld the decision of the Court of

Appeals. The 2nd Circuit court's decision was unusually strong, as well. Weissmann did not simply win the appeal; she won the case on appeal. The distinction, Weissmann notes, is important. If she had just won the appeal, the case would have gone back to the lower court judge for reconsideration of its decision. But that is not what happened. When she won the case on appeal, the lower court judge was ordered to enter a decision in her favor. The language used by the appeals court judge was, in addition, very strong and clear. He stated that the lower court decision "eviscerated copyright law . . . stood copyright law on its head . . . flew in the face of copyright law . . ." and ". . . implausibly overlooked the evidence." One piece of evidence overlooked was the fact that in addition to his attempt to pass off Weissmann's work as his own at that medical school course, Freeman also submitted Weissmann's chapter to a book being published in China. Because chapters for this book had to be in the form of original manuscripts and not reprints, Freeman had the article retyped before sending it. The book was not only published, but subsequently distributed in 30 countries. This all came out during the course of the copyright infringement trial, but Freeman denied under oath that the book existed and that he had submitted the chapter. When confronted with a copy of the book in court, Freeman acknowledged the chapter was there, but still denied knowing how it got there, with Weissmann's name off and Freeman's name shown as author. The judge assisted him in this denial, maintaining there was no proof Freeman had submitted the chapter himself; this, in spite of the fact that a paragraph at the start of the book clearly stated that all chapters had been prepared and submitted by their authors. So Weissmann flew to China, at her own expense, and brought back the evidence that Freeman had submitted the chapter.

Weissmann has had other victories as well. Her plagiarism charges were supported by the Congressional Committee on Government Operations. And Weissmann filed a sex discrimination lawsuit against Freeman and Montefiore/Einstein/Yeshiva in the winter of 1988 (currently in the pretrial discovery stage), wherein she demands reinstatement to her original position and complete back pay.

Clearly, Heidi Weissmann is a woman who cannot be intimidated or easily discouraged. This persistence is especially impressive in view of the fact that Montefiore/Einstein/Yeshiva has chosen to give its considerable legal, financial, and moral support to Leonard Freeman and deny any assistance to Weissmann. Although the original copyright infringement suit was filed only against Freeman, and not against his former employer, Montefiore/Einstein/Yeshiva has paid Freeman's legal fees from the beginning, while Weissmann has had to pay hers—amounting to about $500,000 now—out of her own pocket. Further, Weissmann points out, Freeman has been fully employed, promoted, and made an honorary member of Alpha Omega Alpha, the national medical honor society, all this after being exposed as a plagiarist by a federal court and a Congressional investigation. Weissmann not only lost her job at Einstein, but has been unable to find other work in her field. "This is not a level playing field," Weissmann points out. Indeed, it may not even be legal. A letter prepared by the Rita J. and Stanley H. Kaplan Foundation, Inc., and joined by thirty-nine signatories, which was sent to Montefiore/Einstein/Yeshiva, states that . . . "according to federal regulations, an institution must ensure that the accuser as well as the accused do not suffer professionally."

So why are these institutions continuing to engage in what the Kaplan Foundation letter calls "a legal, financial, and emotional war of attrition against Dr. Weissmann?" The answer may lie in Dr. Freeman's response when Weissmann asked him why Blaufox had recommended her for a "probationary reappointment" and he responded that Blaufox would like to put Weissmann "back in her place." As long as she was content to be a "worker bee" everything was fine, but she stepped out of her place when she began to notice and openly confront a pattern of gender discrimination in her institution. She stepped out of her place when she started to gain individual recognition for her accomplishments, separate and apart from her collaborations with her senior male colleagues. And she stepped out of her place when she refused to fade away and sued to vindicate her rights—the one course of action that Montefiore/Einstein/Yeshiva have always sought to discourage.

Suggestions for Further Reading

Baird, Robert M., and Stuart E. Rosenbaum. *Bigotry, Prejudice, and Hatred.* Buffalo, N.Y.: Prometheus Press, 1992.

Cose, Ellis. *The Rage of a Privileged Class.* New York: Collins, 1994.

Essed, Philomena. *Everyday Racism.* Alameda, Calif.: Hunter House, 1990.

King, Larry L. *Confessions of a White Racist.* New York: Viking Press, 1971.

Knowlees, Louis L., and Kenneth Prewitt, eds. *Institutional Racism in America.* Englewood Cliffs, N.J.: Prentice-Hall, 1969.

Levin, Jack, and William Levin. *The Function of Discrimination and Prejudice,* 2d ed. New York: Harper & Row, 1982.

United States Civil Rights Commission. *Racism in America and How to Combat It.* Washington, D.C.: United States Civil Rights Commission, 1970.

Wellman, David T. *Portraits of White Racism.* New York: Cambridge University Press, 1977.

And watch daily, weekly, and monthly newspapers and magazines for accounts of bias incidents.

Editor's note: In March of 1994, Dr. Weissmann received $900,000 as part of a settlement of her sex discrimination lawsuit against Montifiore Medical Center. Unemployed at the time of the settlement, Dr. Weissmann called it "a bittersweet victory."

PART III

The Economics of Race, Class, and Gender in the United States

The average salary of a Latina or African-American woman who has graduated college and is working in a full-time job is less than that of a white male high-school dropout.[1]

The number of poor people in the United States rose in 1992 for the third straight year, reaching 36.9 million, or 14.5 percent of the population.[2]

Entry level jobs for female business-school graduates paid 12 percent less than entry level jobs for male graduates.[3]

27 percent of Hispanics, 19.3 percent of African Americans, and 12.4 percent of whites in the United States have no health insurance.[4]

In an ideal world, every child born would have the same opportunity to realize his or her potential. In the real world, this is not yet the case. As the statistics in this section indicate, socially constructed differences in race, class, and gender are very costly for some and very profitable for others. They impact directly on the life chances of all of us and they reflect and perpetuate the cycle of racism, sexism, and class inequality that are both their cause and their effect.

While it is fashionable to deny the existence of rich and poor and to proclaim us all "middle class," class divisions are real, and recent economic data show that the gap between rich and poor in this country is growing. Being born into a particular class, racial/ethnic group, and sex has repercussions that affect every aspect of a person's life. In Part III, we attempt to understand their impact by turning our attention from magazine covers and sports stars' salaries to statistics that reveal the economic realities that most ordinary people face in their daily lives. Holly Sklar's essay, "Imagine a Country," provides a dramatic and thought-provoking introduction to this section.

Almost as disturbing as the enormous differences in earnings, life-style, health care, and education that separate us as a people, is the fact that so many of us are completely ignorant of them. Selection 2, Gregory Mantsios's classic and newly revised essay on class in America, explores some of the myths about class that mislead people about their real life chances and documents the impact of class position on daily life. Mantsios is particularly critical of the myth that education functions as a great equalizer, providing all those who work hard and persevere with an opportunity to achieve success. In fact, statistics show that acquiring the same level of education as white, male job applicants or coworkers often fails to ensure that white women or women or men of color will be hired for equivalent positions or paid at the same rate. (See Selections 3 and 4). Currently, the greatest rate of job growth in the economy is in dead-end, low-skilled jobs that do not require education beyond a high-school diploma, suggesting that even the small margin for class mobility provided by education in the past may be vanishing. In fact, Mantsios provides statistics indicating that the class position of one's family is probably the single greatest determinant of future success, quite apart from intelligence, determination, or hard work.

In addition to denying or underestimating the existence and importance of class divisions in the United States, many people are quick to argue that though racism and sexism existed in the past, they have now been replaced by "reverse discrimination," a type of preferential treatment afforded white women and people of color to the detriment of white males. This erroneous belief is created and reinforced by advertising, the media, and even by statements of misinformation from people in high places. Magazine covers and television stories about female and Black and Asian astronauts, female jockeys, and Latin and Black politicians and business executives would have us believe that women and people of color have been fully integrated into society. But is this the case? Do these highly touted "firsts" indicate profound and fundamental changes in the distribution of wealth and opportunity in society, or do they merely serve to distract our attention from the reality of most people's lives?

Selection 3 presents an overview of the way that differences in race and sex affect occupation and earnings in the United States. It shows significant occupational segregation by both race and sex and broad disparities in earnings between women and men. As the charts in this selection show, Hispanic/Latina, African-American, and Native American women, all of whom bear the double burden of race and sex, earn the lowest wages of all. (For an interesting perspective on Asian women's earnings relative to the wages of other women the reader may wish to look ahead to Deborah Woo's article, "The Gap between Striving and Achieving: The Case of Asian American Women," in Part IV.) At the same time that it documents a persistent wage gap based on race and sex over many years, Selection 3 examines the various explanations commonly offered for this discrepancy and concludes that racism and sexism, not ability or qualifications, have determined what jobs women and men do and how much worth is attached to their work.

While there has been general agreement for some time that women professionals often face a glass ceiling in employment, Julie Amparano Lopez suggests that many women may be facing glass walls as well. The term "glass ceiling" was developed to explain why so few women are able to rise above middle management positions in both private corporations and public agencies. "Glass walls" point to the impediments that keep women out of the particular middle- and lower-level jobs that allow them to obtain the kinds of work experience that is then considered a prerequisite for promotion. While professional women confront glass ceilings and glass walls, other workers find themselves locked into part-time or dead-end jobs often without health insurance and other benefits.

In 1990, The Business–Higher Education Forum published a major study of minority life in America entitled *Three Realities*. In its study, this group of corporate and education leaders from around the country paint a disturbing picture of the opportunities and realities that define the lives of so-called minority group members in the United States. While deploring the abysmal conditions that define the lives of the poorest third of this group, the Forum suggests that focusing exclusively on its plight prevents us from acknowledging the strides toward a better life made by the most successful members of minority communities. It analyzes their economic and social success as well as the failure of other African Americans to achieve even a part of the American dream by using the ethnicity paradigm or model that, in contrast to the analysis Mantsios presents, discounts the impact of racism and slavery and assumes that hard work and ability will always be rewarded.

But, as Selection 6 makes clear, even African Americans who qualify for middle-class standing based upon family earnings, face very different realities than many whites with similar status. For example, although many white middle-class families count on two incomes to get by, most middle-class minority-group families owe their middle-class status to the presence of two full-time salaries in the family and, unlike their white counterparts, would not qualify as middle class without both incomes. Further, Blacks and other so-called minority-group families are more likely to be called upon to support a large extended family with their middle-class earnings than are whites and, because of the effects of racism and long-term discrimination, are less likely to have the financial assets that whites, whose families have been middle class for several generations, can count on.

It is clear that statistics provide us with data that are critical for understanding our society, but statistics alone cannot tell the whole story. That is why it is important to place statistics within the context of personal narrative such as the one offered by Theresa Funiciello in "The Poverty Industry." In the course of telling the story of Ameenah Abdus-Salaam and describing her own personal interaction with the poverty industry, Funiciello offers us a first-hand look at the welfare system and raises serious questions about the nature of government and social-agency polices designed to deal with poverty in the United States. She ends her essay reminding us that "poverty is the number one killer of children" in this country and that "children are poor because their mothers are poor."

NOTES

1. Women's Action Coalition. *WAC STATS.* New York: The New Press, 1993, p. 59.
2. Pear, Robert. "Poverty 1993: Bigger, Deeper, Younger, Getting Worse." *New York Times,* October 10, 1993, p. E5.
3. *Ibid.,* p. 61.
4. *Ibid.,* p. 25.

Imagine a Country

Holly Sklar

Imagine a country where one out of four children is born into poverty, while the top 1 percent of families have a financial net worth greater than that of the entire bottom 90 percent.

Imagine a country where budget deficits are the flip side of greed surpluses. Where the poor and middle class are told to tighten their belts to pay off the debts, bloated salaries, and tax breaks of the rich.

It's not Mexico.

Imagine a country where the average inflation-adjusted earnings of nonsupervisory workers crashed 19 percent between 1973 and 1990, while corporate executives enriched themselves enormously. The average chief executive officer (CEO) of a large corporation was paid as much as 41 factory workers in 1960, 42 factory workers in 1980, 104 factory workers in 1991, and 157 factory workers in 1992.

It's not Japan. There, CEOs are paid less than 32 factory workers.

Imagine a country where income inequality has grown so much that by 1989 the top 4 percent "earned" as much in wages and salaries as the entire bottom 51 percent—in 1959, the top 4 percent earned as much as the bottom 35 percent. The top 1 percent of families hold over one-third of the nation's total private wealth.

It's not the Philippines.

Imagine a country where living standards are falling for younger generations despite the fact that many households have two wage earners, fewer children, and better education than their parents. The inflation-adjusted median income for families with children headed by persons younger than thirty plunged 32 percent between 1973 and 1990. Forty percent of all children in families headed by someone younger than thirty were *officially* living in poverty in 1990—up from 20 percent in 1973. (The official poverty line is set well below the actual cost of minimally adequate housing, health care, food, and other necessities.)

Imagine a country whose official unemployment rate averaged 4.5 percent in the 1950s, 4.7 percent in the 1960s, 6.2 percent in the 1970s, and 7.3 percent in the 1980s—not counting workers so discouraged by a fruitless job search that they have stopped actively looking or those involuntarily working part-time. The 1990s began with another official recession followed by a so-called "jobless recovery"—that's like declaring recovery for a patient resuscitated into a coma. The government acknowledged in late 1993 that it had substantially underestimated unemployment, especially among women. Government interviewers typically asked men, "What were you doing most of last week, working or something else?" Women were typically asked whether they were "keeping house or something else." If they answered keeping house, the interviewer didn't bother to find out if they were laid off or looking for work; so even if they were laid off or looking for work, the government counted them as homemakers, not unemployed members of the work force.

Imagine a country where a leading news weekly has observed: Downsizing and other "trends have created an 'industrial reserve army' so large that a quite extraordinary and prolonged surge in output would be required to put all its members to full-time, well-paid work. Two indications of the yawning chasm between job supply and demand, in [one major city the post office] handed out 20,000 applications for such jobs as clerk, sorter and letter carrier, even though it announced it would have at most a few hundred openings and that some of them would not be filled for three to five years. [Later that city] was again the scene of a sort of job panic: thousands of unemployed workers began lining up at 7 A.M. to apply for jobs that might never exist in a gambling casino" that might never be built.

It's not Poland.

Imagine a country where for more and more people a job is not a ticket out of poverty, but into the ranks of the working poor. The official poverty rate for families with children in which the householder works jumped one-third between 1979 and 1990. In that same period, the proportion of full-time workers paid low wages increased to nearly one in every five workers. Among young full-time workers (ages eighteen to twenty-four), the percentage earning low wages nearly doubled from 23 percent in 1979 to over 43 percent in 1990.

Imagine a country where, according to a government study, 30 percent of each new class of college graduates between 1992 and 2005 will be jobless or underemployed. Still, government rhetoric promises a future of high-paid jobs in high-tech industries, as if the occupations with high growth rates were the same as those creating the largest number of jobs. A congressional report observes, "Those who look at occupational employment growth rates have concluded that faster-growing occupations generally require higher levels of education or training" and are generally higher paid. As projected for the years 1990–2005, "eight of the ten occupations projected to experience the largest absolute increase in employment . . . typically require high school graduation or less education" and are generally low paid. The ten occupations producing the most new jobs are: retail salespersons; registered nurses; cashiers; general office clerks; truck drivers; general managers and top executives; janitors and cleaners; nursing aides, orderlies, and attendants; food counter, fountain, and related workers; and waiters and waitresses.

It's not England.

Imagine a country where more workers are going back to the future of sweatshops. Corporations are rapidly replacing full-time jobs with variations on day labor and piece work performed by disposable "contingent workers"—temporary employees, contract workers, "leased" employees, and part-time workers, many of whom want permanent full-time work. Contingent workers—some of them fired and then hired or "leased" back at a large discount by the same company—made up one-third of the nation's work force in 1993, up significantly from one-fourth in 1988.

Imagine a country where contingent workers are expected to outnumber permanent full-time employees by the end of the decade. In 1992, the average weekly income was $445 for full-time workers, $259 for temporary workers, and $132 for part-time workers. How do workers increasingly forced to migrate from job to job, at low and inconsistent wage rates, without paid vacation, much less a pension, care for themselves and their families, own a home, pay for college, save for retirement, and build a future?

Imagine a country where after mass layoffs and union-busting, only 11 percent of private sector jobs were unionized as of 1993.

Imagine a country whose corporations are rewarded with government subsidies to freely trade on cheap labor at home and abroad. One ad financed by the country's agency for international development shows a Salvadoran woman in front of a sewing machine. It tells corporations, "You can hire her for 33 cents an hour. Rosa is more than just colorful. She and her co-workers are known for their industriousness, reliability and quick learning. They make El Salvador one of the best buys." The country that financed the ad intervened militarily to make sure El Salvador would stay a "best buy" for corporations.

Imagine a country whose commerce department encourages runaway corporations, inviting them to "evaluate and take advantage of pre-screened business opportunities in the developing world's two leading offshore centers for information processing. . . . Barbados and Jamaica offer a unique combination of educated, low-cost workers; highly developed telecommunications services; and geographic proximity; which together equal profitability and productivity."

It's not Canada.

Imagine a country where the cycle of unequal opportunity has been reinforced by tax cuts rewarding wealthy people and corporations and ballooning the national debt. According to the country's secretary of labor, "were the tax code as progressive as it was even as late as 1977," the top 10 percent of income earners "would have paid approximately $93 billion more in taxes" than they paid in 1989. How much is $93 billion? About the same amount as the combined 1989 government budget for all these programs for low-income persons: aid to families with dependent children, supplemental security income, general assistance, food and nutrition benefits, housing, jobs and employment training, and education aid from preschool to college loans.

Imagine a country where lower-income citizens not only pay for the debt with harsh cutbacks, but also with less talked about tax hikes. Payroll taxes, which are regressive because they tax the poor proportionately more than the rich, are up; the Social Security payroll tax increased 30 percent between 1978 and 1990. Up also are regressive state and local sales, excise, and property taxes. Tax reforms passed in 1993 did not restore the tax system's earlier progressivity, and the top personal income tax bracket remains far below the average top rate of 47 percent charged by other countries with an income tax. Making things worse, state and local governments are rushing to expand lotteries, video poker, and other government-promoted gambling to raise revenues, again disproportionately from the poor, which they should be raising from a fair tax system.

Imagine a country where more than half of all women with children under age six (and three-fourths of women with children ages six to seventeen) are in the paid work force, but there is no national day care. Women working year-round, full-time in 1992 earned 71 cents for every dollar men earned. Women don't pay 71 cents on a man's dollar for their college degrees or 71 percent as much to feed their children. Since single mothers of color experience both race and gender discrimination, their families are the most impoverished. Instead of rooting out discrimination, many policymakers are busily blaming women for their disproportionate poverty.

The fact that many female-headed households are poorer because women are generally paid less than men is taken as a given in much poverty policy discussion, as if pay equity was a pipe dream not even worth mentioning. A 1977 government study found that if working women were paid what similarly qualified men earn, the number of poor families would decrease by half. A 1991 government study found that even "if all poor single mothers obtained [full-time] jobs at their potential wage rates," given their educational and employment background and prevailing wages, "the percentage not earning enough to escape from poverty would be 35 percent." Two out of three workers who earn minimum wage are women. Full-time work at minimum wage earns below the official poverty line for a family of two.

Imagine a country where discrimination against women is pervasive from the bottom to the top of the pay scale and it's not because women are on the "mommy track." In the words of a leading business magazine, "at the same level of management, the typical woman's pay is lower than her male colleague's—even when she has the exact same qualifications, works just as many years, relocates just as often, provides the main financial support for her family, takes no time off for personal reasons, and wins the same number of promotions to comparable jobs."

Imagine a country where violence against women is so epidemic it is women's leading cause of injury. So-called "domestic violence" accounts for more visits to hospital emergency departments than car crashes, muggings, and rapes combined. About one-third of all murdered women are killed by husbands, boyfriends, and ex-partners. The country has no equal rights amendment.

It's not Saudi Arabia.

Imagine a country where homicide is now the second-largest killer of young people, ages fifteen to twenty-four; "accidents," many of them drunk driving fatalities, are first. Increasingly lethal weapons designed for hunting people are produced for profit by major manufacturers and proudly defended by a politically powerful national rifle association. In many places, you can legally possess firearms before you can legally drink and it's easier to buy a gun than to register to vote. Half the homes in the country contain firearms, and guns in the home greatly increase the risk of murder and suicide for family members and close acquaintances.

The nation's federal bureau of investigation reports an escalation of juvenile violence, "evident in all races, social classes, and life-styles." Children are being taught violence is the way to resolve conflict through popular wars and media "entertainment" at a time when military-style weapons have become commonplace. "In the media world, brutality is portrayed as ordinary and amusing" and often merged with sex, observes a prominent public health educator in her book *Deadly Consequences.* The screen "good guys" not only use violence as a first resort, but total war is the only response to the dehumanized "bad guys" who often speak with foreign accents. Between 1982 and 1988—a period when children's TV was deregulated and networks defended programs like *G.I. Joe* as "educational"—television time devoted to war cartoons jumped from 90 minutes to 27 hours a week. By age eighteen, the average child will have seen 40,000 murders on television. Violent "superhero" shows are created expressly to sell toys to children. Virtual reality video games are bringing even more graphic and participatory "virtual" violence. The strong consensus of private and government research is that on-screen violence contributes to off-screen violence.

It's not the former Yugoslavia.

Imagine a country whose school system is rigged in favor of the already privileged with lower-caste children tracked by race and income into the most deficient and demoralizing schools and classrooms. Public-school budgets are heavily determined by private property taxes, allowing higher-income districts to spend much more than poor ones. In one large state in 1991–1992, spending per pupil ranged from $2,337 in the poorest district to $56,791 in the wealthiest.

In rich districts kids take well-stocked libraries, laboratories, and state-of-the-art computers for granted. In poor schools they are rationing out-of-date textbooks and toilet paper. Rich schools often look like country clubs—with manicured sports fields and swimming pools. Poor schools often look more like jails—with concrete grounds and grated windows. Art, music, physical education, field trips, foreign languages, and advanced courses are often considered necessities for the affluent, luxuries for the poor. Wealthier citizens argue that lack of money isn't the problem in poorer schools—family values are—until proposals are made to make school spending more even. Then money matters greatly for those who already have more.

It's not India.

Imagine a country where Black unemployment and infant mortality is more than twice that of whites and Black life expectancy is seven years less. A 1991 study documented that discrimination against Black job seekers is "entrenched and widespread." An earlier study documented discrimination against Latinos.

Imagine a country whose constitution once defined Black slaves as worth three-fifths of a human being. Today, median Black per capita income is three-fifths of whites. That's an economic measure of racism. The Latino-White ratio is similar.

Imagine a country that subsidized decades of segregated suburbanization for whites while the inner cities left to people of color were treated as outsider cities—separate, unequal, and disposable. Inner-city neighborhoods are slanderously stereotyped as full of hoodlums and not neighborly. Terms like "underclass" are used to stigmatize those most systematically undervalued, underpaid, underemployed, underfinanced, underinsured, underrated, and otherwise underserved and undermined—as undeserving, impoverished in moral and social values, and lacking the proper "work ethic."

Imagine a country that imprisons Black men at a rate nearly five times more than apartheid South Africa. One out of four Black men between the ages of twenty and twenty-nine are either in jail, on probation, or on parole. A 1990 justice department report observed, "The fact that the legal order not only countenanced but sustained slavery, segregation, and discrimination for most of our nation's history—and the fact that the police were bound to uphold that order—set a pattern for police behavior and attitudes toward minority communities that has persisted until the present day." A 1992 newspaper article is titled, "GUILTY . . . of being black: Black men say success doesn't save them from being suspected, harassed and detained." A bank CEO says he hesitates to shop in neighboring suburbs where suspicious shopkeepers don't know him. A prominent law professor says he has "encounters with police almost annually" and "worries about his son . . . 'It scares the hell out of me when I think that there is little I can do to ensure his safety, because the police don't see him as a person. They see him as a statistic, one they equate with crime.'"

Imagine a country waging a racially biased "War on Drugs." More than three out of four drug users are white (not of Hispanic origin), but Blacks are much more likely to be arrested and convicted for drug offenses and receive much harsher sentences (even so-called mandatory minimum sentences are racially biased). The nation's leading lawyer's association found that between 1986 and 1991, drug arrests skyrocketed by 78 percent for juveniles of color, while *decreasing* by one-third for other juveniles, though government studies show that youth of color are not more likely to use drugs. A study in a prominent medical journal found that drug and alcohol rates were slightly higher for pregnant white women than pregnant Black women, but Black women were about ten times more likely to be reported to authorities by private doctors and public health clinics—under a mandatory reporting law. Poor women were also more likely to be reported.

The same country is number four in the world in alcohol consumption, the drug most associated with violence and death, and number one in drunk-driving fatalities per capita—those arrested for drunk driving are overwhelmingly white and male and typically treated much more leniently than illicit drug offenders. It intervenes in other countries in the name of the "War on Drugs," while it is the number one exporter of addictive, cancer-causing tobacco.

It's not France.

Imagine a country that puts a far higher portion of its people behind bars than any other country. The prison population has more than doubled since 1980, a time of rollbacks in social programs and rising economic inequality. The country has been criticized by human rights organizations for expanding rather than abolishing use of the death penalty—despite documented racial bias and numerous cases of innocents being put to death.

It's not China.

Imagine a country where descendants of its first inhabitants live on reservations strip-mined of resources and opportunity. Life expectancy averages in the forties— not the seventies. Infant mortality is seven times higher than the national average, and a higher proportion of people live in poverty than any other ethnic group. An Indian leader is the country's best known political prisoner.

Imagine a country where Indian names are used as labels for sports teams, cars, and beer. Where a popular children's toy catalog advertises cowboy and Indian gear with lines such as "It's heap big fun to wear this Indian Brave costume" and "Hunt for game and defend your homestead with these Wild West toy firearms." Where 500 years of plunder and lies are masked in expressions like "Indian giver." Where the military still dubs enemy territory, "Indian country."

Imagine a country that has only 5 percent of the world's population, but uses 25 percent of the world's oil resources. Only 3 percent of the public's trips are made by public transportation. It has no national conservation policy. It is the number 1 contributor to global warming. It has felled more trees since 1978 than any other country.

It's not Brazil.

Imagine a country that is first by far in military might, but twenty-first in the world in infant mortality and twelfth in school-age population per teacher. First in military spending, but every day, in cities and suburbs and farm country, one out of eight children under the age of twelve goes hungry.

Imagine a country spending almost as much on the military as it did when the superpower enemy, which used to justify that spending, still existed. It leads the world in arms exports and has no national plan for military-civilian conversion though its people need jobs and homes, its schools are in crisis, and its public works infrastructure is crumbling.

Imagine a country where corrupt banks are bailed out while farmers and un-employed homeowners are foreclosed.

Imagine a country where the majority—workers, women, people of color—are dismissed as "special interests" and the profit-making interests of transnational corporations substitute for the "national interest." A national survey of senior exec-utives found that in the 1980s, Blacks increased their minuscule share of top corporate positions from .2 to .6 percent; Latinos from .1 to .4 percent; and women from .5 to 3 percent. The nation's house of representatives is overwhelmingly white and male. The senate is even more unrepresentative of the citizenry.

Imagine a country where on top of discrimination comes insult. It's common for people of color to get none of the credit when they succeed—portrayed as unde-serving beneficiaries of affirmative action and "reverse discrimination"—and all of the blame when they fail. A study of the views of fifteen-to-twenty-four-year-olds found that 49 percent of whites believe that it is more likely that "qualified whites lose out on scholarships, jobs, and promotions because minorities get special pref-erences" than "qualified minorities are denied scholarships, jobs, and promotions because of racial prejudice." Only 34 percent believed that minorities are more likely to lose out.

Imagine a country where the shrinking middle class is misled into thinking that those below them on the economic ladder are pulling them down, when in reality those on the top rungs of the ladder are rising at the expense of everyone else. The oft-heard stereotype of deadbeat poor people masks the growing reality of dead-end jobs and disposable workers. The false charge of "reverse discrimination" provides scapegoats for the economic distress being felt by more people of all races.

It's not Germany.

Imagine a country where a former presidential press secretary boasted to reporters: "You can say anything you want in a debate, and 80 million people hear it. If reporters then document that a candidate spoke untruthfully, so what? Maybe 200 people read it, or 2,000 or 20,000."

Imagine a country where a far-right television commentator-turned-presidential candidate—whose heroes include Senator Joe McCarthy, Spanish dictator Franco and Chilean dictator Pinochet—told the national convention of one of the two major parties: "There is a religious war going on in this country. It is a cultural war." Delegates waved signs saying "Gay Rights Never"—the '90s version of segregation forever. Referring to recent rioting in a major city, following the acquittal of police officers who had severely beaten a Black man, the once and future candidate said: "I met the troopers of the 18th Cavalry, who had come to save the city . . . And as those boys took back the streets of [that city], block by block, my friends, we must take back our cities and take back our culture and take back our country."

It's not Russia.

It's the *dis*United States.

Decades ago Martin Luther King Jr. warned, in *Where Do We Go from Here: Chaos or Community*. "History is cluttered with the wreckage of nations and individuals who pursued [the] self-defeating path of hate." King declared:

> A true revolution of values will soon cause us to question the fairness and justice of many of our past and present policies. We are called to play the good samaritan on life's roadside; but . . . One day the whole Jericho road must be transformed so that men and women will not be beaten and robbed as they make their journey through life. . . .
>
> There is nothing but a lack of social vision to prevent us from paying an adequate wage to every American citizen whether he be a hospital worker, laundry worker, maid or day laborer. There is nothing except shortsightedness to prevent us from guaranteeing an annual minimum—and *livable*—income for every American family. There is nothing, except a tragic death wish, to prevent us from reordering our priorities, so that the pursuit of peace will take precedence over the pursuit of war.

SELECTED SOURCES

American Bar Association, *The State of Criminal Justice: An Annual Report* (Chicago: ABA, February 1993).

Donald L. Barlett and James B. Steele, *America: What Went Wrong* (Kansas City: Andrews and McMeel, 1992).

David Barry, "Screen Violence: It's Killing Us," *Harvard Magazine*, November–December 1993.

Business Week, "Executive Pay: It Doesn't Add Up," editorial, and "Executive Pay: The Party Ain't Over Yet," April 26, 1993; "What, Me Overpaid? CEOs Fight Back," May 4, 1992.

Janice Castro, "Disposable Workers" and Lance Morrow, "The Temping of America, *Time*, March 29, 1993.

Children's Defense Fund and Northeastern University's Center for Labor Market Studies, *Vanishing Dreams: The Economic Plight of America's Young Families* (Washington, DC: Children's Defense Fund, 1992).

Community Childhood Hunger Identification Project, *A Survey of Childhood Hunger in the United States* (Washington, DC: Food Research and Action Center, 1991).

Ira J. Chasnoff, et al., "The Prevalence of Illicit-Drug or Alcohol Use During Pregnancy and Discrepancies in Mandatory Reporting in Pinellas County, Florida," *New England Journal of Medicine*, April 26, 1990.

George J. Church, "Jobs in an Age of Insecurity" and John Greenwald, "Bellboys with B.A.s," *Time*, November 22, 1993.

Ellis Cose, "To the Victors, Few Spoils," *Newsweek*, March 29, 1993, p. 54; also see David Gates, "White Male Paranoia," in the same issue.

Economic Policy Institute, Lawrence Mishel and Jared Bernstein, "Declining Wages For High School AND College Graduates: Pay and Benefits Trends by Education, Gender, Occupation, and State, 1979–1991," *Briefing Paper* (May 1992) and Edward N. Wolff, "The Rich Get Increasingly Richer: Latest Data on Household Wealth During the 1980s," *Briefing Paper* (1992).

FBI, *Crime in the United States 1991: Uniform Crime Reports and Crime in the United States 1992.*

Anne B. Fisher, "When Will Women Get To The Top?" *Fortune*, September 21, 1992.

S. C. Gwynne, "The Long Haul," *Time*, September 28, 1992.

Arthur L. Kellermann, et al., "Gun Ownership as a Risk Factor For Homicide in the Home" and Jerome P. Kassirer, "Guns in the Household," editorial, *New England Journal of Medicine*, October 7, 1993.

Arthur L. Kellermann and James A. Mercy, "Men, Women, and Murder: Gender-Specific Differences in Rates of Fatal Violence and Victimization," *The Journal of Trauma* 33:1, July 1992.

Jonathan Kozol, *Savage Inequalities: Children in America's Schools* (New York: Crown Publishers, 1991).

Iris J. Lav, et al., *The States and the Poor: How Budget Decisions Affected Low Income People in 1992* (Washington, DC: Center on Budget and Policy Priorities and Albany, NY: Center for the Study of the States, 1993).

Coramae Richey Mann, *Unequal Justice: A Question of Color* (Bloomington, Indiana: Indiana University Press, 1993).

The Sentencing Project, Marc Mauer, *Americans Behind Bars: One Year Later* (Washington, DC: February 1992); Cathy Shine and Marc Mauer, *Does the Punishment Fit the Crime? Drug Users and Drunk Drivers: Questions of Race and Class* (March 1993).

John Miller, "The Clinton Budget: New Voodoo and Old Snake Oil," *Dollars & Sense*, November/December 1993.

National Labor Committee Education Fund in Support of Worker and Human Rights in Central America (New York), *Free Trade's Hidden Secrets: Why We Are Losing Our Shirts* (November 1993) and *Paying to Lose Our Jobs* (September 1992).

People for the American Way, *Democracy's Next Generation II: A Study of American Youth on Race* (Washington, DC: 1992).

Deborah Prothrow-Stith, *Deadly Consequences: How Violence is Destroying Our Teenage Population and a Plan to Begin Solving the Problem* (New York: Harper Perennial, 1991/1993).

Albert J. Reiss, Jr. and Jeffrey A. Roth, eds., National Research Council, *Understanding and Preventing Violence* (Washington, D.C.: National Academy Press, 1993).

Margery Austin Turner, et al., *Opportunities Denied, Opportunities Diminished: Racial Discrimination in Hiring,* (Washington, DC: Urban Institute Press, 1991).

Robert B. Reich, *The Work of Nations* (New York: Alfred A. Knopf, 1991).

John E. Schwarz and Thomas J. Volgy, *The Forgotten Americans: Thirty Million Working Poor in the Land of Opportunity* (New York: W.W. Norton, 1992).

Ruth Leger Sivard, World Military and Social Expenditures 1993 (Washington, DC: World Priorities, 1993).

Karin Stallard, Barbara Ehrenreich and Holly Sklar, *Poverty in the American Dream: Women and Children First* (Boston: South End Press, 1983).

Carol Stocker and Barbara Carton, "GUILTY . . . of being black," *Boston Globe*, May 7, 1992.

USA Today, Special Series, "Is the Drug War Racist?" including Sam Vincent Meddis, "Disparities suggest the answer is yes," July 23–25, 1993.

U.S. Senate Judiciary Committee, *Violence Against Women: A Week in the Life of America*, report prepared by the Majority Staff, October 1992.

U.S. Bureau of the Census, *Statistical Abstract of the United States 1993; Money Income of Households, Families, and Persons in the United States: 1992; Poverty in the United States: 1992; Workers With Low Earnings: 1964 to 1990; Trends in Relative Income: 1964 to 1989.*

U.S. Department of Health and Human Services, National Institute on Drug Abuse (NIDA), *National Household Survey on Drug Abuse,* various reports.

U.S. General Accounting Office, *Mother-Only Families: Low Earnings Will Keep Many Children in Poverty* (April 1991); *Workers At Risk: Increased Numbers in Contingent Employment Lack Insurance, Other Benefits* (March 1991).

U.S. House of Representatives, Committee on Ways and Means, Subcommittee on Human Resources, *Background Material on Family Income and Benefit Changes* (December 19, 1991).

U.S. House of Representatives, Committee on Ways and Means, *1993 Green Book: Overview of Entitlement Programs* (July 7, 1993).

U.S Sentencing Commission, Special Report to the Congress, *Mandatory Minimum Penalties in the Federal Criminal Justice System*, Washington, DC, August 1991.

Hubert Williams and Patrick V. Murphy, "The Evolving Strategy of Police: A Minority View," *Perspectives on Policing*, U.S. Department of Justice (January 1990).

Class in America:
Myths and Realities

Gregory Mantsios

People in the United States don't like to talk about class. Or so it would seem. We don't speak about class privileges, or class oppression, or the class nature of society. These terms are not part of our everyday vocabulary, and in most circles they are associated with the language of the rhetorical fringe. Unlike people in most other parts of the world, we shrink from using words that classify along economic lines or that point to class distinctions: phrases like "working class," "upper class," and "ruling class" are rarely uttered by Americans.

For the most part, avoidance of class-laden vocabulary crosses class boundaries. There are few among the poor who speak of themselves as lower class; they identify, rather, with their race, ethnic group, or geographic location. Workers are more likely to identify with their employer, industry, or occupational group than with other workers, or with the working class.[1]

Neither are those at the other end of the economic spectrum likely to identify with the word "class." In her study of thirty-eight wealthy and socially prominent women, Susan Ostrander asked participants if they considered themselves members of the upper class. One participant responded, "I hate to use the word 'class.' We are responsible, fortunate people, old families, the people who have something." Another said, "I hate [the term] upper class. It is so non-upper class to use it. I just call it 'all of us,' those who are wellborn."[2]

It is not that Americans, rich or poor, aren't keenly aware of class differences— those quoted above obviously are—it is that class is not in the domain of public discourse. Class is not discussed or debated in public because class identity has been stripped from popular culture. The institutions that shape mass culture and define the parameters of public debate have avoided class issues. In politics, in primary and secondary education, and in the mass media, formulating issues in terms of class is unacceptable, perhaps even un-American.

There are, however, two notable exceptions to this phenomenon. First, it is acceptable in the United States to talk about "the middle class." Interestingly enough, such references appear to be acceptable precisely because they mute class differences. References to the middle class by politicians, for example, are designed to encompass and attract the broadest possible constituency. Not only do references to the middle class gloss over differences, these references also avoid any suggestion of conflict or exploitation.

This leads us to the second exception to the class-avoidance phenomenon. We are, on occasion, presented with glimpses of the upper class and the lower class (the language used is "the wealthy" and "the poor"). In the media, these presentations are designed to satisfy some real or imagined voyeuristic need of "the ordinary person." As curiosities, the ground-level view of street life and the inside look at the rich and the famous serve as unique models, one to avoid and one to aspire to. In either case, the two models are presented without causal relation to each other: One is not rich because the other is poor. Similarly, when social commentators or liberal politicians draw attention to the plight of the poor, they do so in a manner that obscures the class structure and denies class exploitation. Wealth and poverty are viewed as one of several natural and inevitable states of being: Differences are only differences. One may even say differences are the American way, a reflection of American social diversity.

We are left with one of two possibilities: Either talking about class and recognizing class distinctions are not relevant to U.S. society, or we mistakenly hold a set of beliefs that obscure the reality of class differences and their impact on people's lives.

Let us look at four common, albeit contradictory, beliefs about the United States.

Myth 1: The United States is fundamentally a classless society. Class distinctions are largely irrelevant today, and whatever differences do exist in economic standing are, for the most part, insignificant. Rich or poor, we are all equal in the eyes of the law, and such basic needs as health care and education are provided to all regardless of economic standing.

Myth 2: We are, essentially, a middle-class nation. Despite some variations in economic status, most Americans have achieved relative affluence in what is widely recognized as a consumer society.

Myth 3: We are all getting richer. The American public as a whole is steadily moving up the economic ladder, and each generation propels itself to greater economic well-being. Despite some fluctuations, the U.S. position in the global economy has brought previously unknown prosperity to most, if not all, North Americans.

Myth 4: Everyone has an equal chance to succeed. Success in the United States requires no more than hard work, sacrifice, and perseverance: "In America, anyone can become a millionaire; it's just a matter of being in the right place at the right time."

In trying to assess the legitimacy of these beliefs, we want to ask several important questions. Are there significant class differences among Americans? If these differences do exist, are they getting bigger or smaller, and do these differences have a significant impact on the way we live? Finally, does everyone in the United States really have an equal opportunity to succeed?

The Economic Spectrum

We will begin by looking at differences. An examination of official census materials reveals that variations in economic well-being are in fact immense. Consider the following:

- The wealthiest 20 percent of the American population holds 79 percent of the total household wealth in the country. That is, they own more than three-quarters of all the consumer durables (such as houses, cars, and stereos) and financial assets (such as stocks, bonds, property, and savings accounts).[3]
- Approximately 17,000 Americans declare more than $1 million of *annual* income on their tax returns; that is more money than most Americans expect to earn in an entire lifetime.[4]

Affluence and prosperity are clearly alive and well in certain segments of the U.S. population. However, this abundance is in contrast to the poverty and despair that is also prevalent in the United States. At the other end of the spectrum:

- A total of 15 percent of the American population—that is, one of every seven—live below the government's official poverty line (calculated in 1992 at $7,143 for an individual and $14,335 for a family of four).[5] These poor include a significant number of homeless people—approximately three million Americans.
- Nearly a quarter of all the children in the United States under the age of six live in poverty.[6]

The contrast between rich and poor is sharp, and with nearly one-third of the American population living at one extreme or the other, it is difficult to argue that we live in a classless society. The income gap between rich and poor in the United States (measured as the percentage of total income held by the wealthiest 20 percent of the population versus the poorest 20 percent) is approximately 9 to 1, one of the highest ratios in the industrialized world. The ratio in Japan, by contrast is 4 to 1.[7]

Reality 1: There are enormous differences in the economic status of American citizens. A sizeable proportion of the U.S. population occupies opposite ends of the economic spectrum. And it cannot be said that the majority of the American population fairs very well. In the middle range of the economic spectrum:

- Fifty percent of the American population hold less than 3.5 percent of the nation's wealth.[8]
- While the real income of the top 1 percent of U.S. families skyrocketed by 78 percent during the economic growth period leading up to the 1990s, the income of the middle fifth of the population actually declined by 5.3 percent. This led one prominent economist to describe economic growth as a "spectator sport for the majority of American families".[9]

The level of inequality is sometimes difficult to comprehend fully with dollar figures and percentages. To help his students visualize the distribution of income, the well-known economist Paul Samuelson asked them to picture an income pyramid made of children's blocks, with each layer of blocks representing $1,000. If we were to construct Samuelson's pyramid today, the peak of the pyramid would be much higher than the Eiffel Tower, yet almost all of us would be within six feet of the ground.[10] In other words, the distribution of income is heavily skewed; a small minority of families take the lion's share of national income, and the remaining income is distributed among the vast majority of middle-income and low-income families. Keep in mind that Samuelson's pyramid represents the distribution of income, not wealth. The distribution of wealth is skewed even further.

Reality 2: The middle class in the United States holds a very small share of the nation's wealth.

Lottery millionaires and Horatio Alger stories notwithstanding, evidence suggests that the level of inequality in the United States is getting higher. Statistically, it is getting harder to make it big and more difficult to even stay in the middle-income level. Census data show the gap between the rich and the poor to be the widest since the government began collecting information in 1947. Furthermore, the percentage of households earnings at a middle-income level (the middle quintile) has been falling steadily since 1968.[11] Most of those who disappeared from the middle-income level moved downward, not upward. And economic polarization is expected to increase over the next several decades.[12]

Reality 3: The middle class is shrinking in size, and most of those leaving the ranks of the middle class are falling to a lower economic standing.

American Life-Styles

At last count, nearly 40 million Americans across the nation lived in unrelenting poverty. Yet, as political scientist Michael Harrington once commented, "America has the best dressed poverty the world has ever known."[13] Clothing disguises much of the poverty in the United States, and this may explain, in part, its middle-class image. With increased mass marketing of "designer" clothing and with shifts in the nation's economy from blue-collar (and often better-paying) manufacturing jobs to white-collar and pink-collar jobs in the service sector, it is becoming increasingly difficult to distinguish class differences based on appearance.[14]

Beneath the surface, there is another reality. Let us look at some "typical" and not-so-typical life-styles

---

American Profile: Harold S. Browning

Father: manufacturer, industrialist.

Mother: prominent social figure in the community.

Principal child-rearer: governess.

Primary education: exclusive private school in Manhattan's Upper East Side. *Note:* a small, well-respected primary school where teachers and administrators have a reputation for nurturing student creativity and for providing the finest educational preparation. *Ambition:* "to become president."

Supplemental tutoring: tutors in French and mathematics.

Summer camp: sleep-away camp in northern Connecticut. *Note:* camp provides instruction in the creative arts, athletics, and the natural sciences.

Secondary education: prestigious preparatory school in Westchester County. Classmates included the sons of ambassadors, doctors, attorneys, television personalities, and well-known business leaders. *After-school activities:* private riding lessons. *Ambition:* "to take over my father's business." *High-school graduation gift:* BMW.

Family activities: theater, recitals, museums, summer vacations in Europe, occasional winter trips to the Caribbean. *Note:* as members and donors of the local art museum, the Browning's and their children attend private receptions and exhibit openings at the invitation of the museum director.

Higher education: Ivy League liberal arts college in Massachusetts. *Major:* economics and political science. *After-class activities:* debating club, college newspaper, swim team. *Ambition:* "to become a leader in business."

First full-time job (age 23): assistant manager of operations, Browning Tool and Die, Inc. (family enterprise).

Subsequent employment: 3 years—executive assistant to the president, Browning Tool and Die. *Responsibilities included:* purchasing (materials and equipment), personnel, and distribution networks.
4 years—advertising manager, Lackheed Manufacturing (home appliances).
3 years—director of marketing and sales, Comerex Inc. (business machines).

Present employment (age 38): executive vice president, SmithBond and Co. (digital instruments). *Typical daily activities:* review financial reports and computer printouts, dictate memoranda, lunch with clients, initiate conference calls, meet with assistants, plan business trips, meet with associates.

	Transportation to and from work: chauffeured company limousine. *Annual salary:* $315,000. *Ambition:* "to become chief executive officer of the firm, or one like it, within the next five to ten years."
Present residence:	Eighteenth floor condominium in Manhattan's Upper West Side, eleven rooms, including five spacious bedrooms and terrace overlooking river. *Interior:* professionally designed and accented with elegant furnishings, valuable antiques, and expensive artwork. *Note:* building management provides doorman and elevator attendant. Family employs au pair for children and maid for other domestic chores.
Second residence:	Farm in northwestern Connecticut, used for weekend retreats and for horse breeding (investment/hobby). *Note:* to maintain the farm and cater to their needs when they are there, the Browning's employ a part-time maid, groundskeeper, and horse breeder.

Harold S. Browning was born into a world of nurses, maids, and governesses. His world today is one of airplanes and limousines, five-star restaurants, and luxurious living accommodations. The life and life-style of Harold Browning is in sharp contrast to that of Bob Farrell.

	American Profile: Bob Farrell
Father:	machinist.
Mother:	retail clerk.
Principal child-rearer:	mother and sitter.
Primary education:	medium-sized public school in Queens, New York, characterized by large class size, outmoded physical facilities, and an educational philosophy emphasizing basic skills and student discipline. *Ambition:* "to become president."
Supplemental tutoring:	none.
Summer camp:	YMCA day camp emphasizing team sports, and arts and crafts.
Secondary education:	large regional high school in Queens. Classmates included the sons and daughters of carpenters, postal clerks, teachers, nurses, shopkeepers, mechanics, bus

	drivers, police officers, and salespersons. *After-school activities:* basketball and handball in school park. *Ambition:* "to make it through college." *High-school graduation gift:* $500 savings bond.
Family activities:	family gatherings around the television set, bowling, an occasional trip to the movie theater, summer Sundays at the public beach.
Higher education:	two-year community college with a technical orientation. *Major:* electrical technology. *After-class activities:* employed as a part-time bagger in local supermarket. *Ambition:* "to become an electrical engineer."
First full-time job (age 19):	service-station attendant. *Note:* continued to take college classes in the evening.
Subsequent employment:	Mail clerk at large insurance firm. Manager trainee, large retail chain.
Present employment (age ??):	assistant sales manager, building supply firm. *Typical daily activities:* demonstrate products, write up product orders, handle customer complaints, check inventory. *Transportation to and from work:* city subway. *Annual salary:* $32,000. *Additional income:* $6,100 in commissions from evening and weekend work as salesman in local men's clothing store. *Ambition:* "to open up my own business."
Present residence:	the Farrell's own their own home in a working-class suburb in Queens.
Second residence:	none.

Bob Farrell and Harold Browning live very differently: the life-style of one is privileged; the other is not so privileged. The differences are class differences, and these differences have a profound impact on the way they live. They are differences between playing a game of handball in the park and taking riding lessons at a private stable, watching a movie on television and going to the theater, and taking the subway to work and being driven in a limousine. More important, the difference in class determines where they live, who their friends are, how well they are educated, what they do for a living, and what they come to expect from life.

Yet, as dissimilar as their life-styles are, Harold Browning and Bob Farrell have some things in common. They live in the same city, they work long hours, and they are highly motivated. More important, they are both white males.

Let us look at someone else who works long and hard and is highly motivated. This person, however, is Black and female.

American Profile: Cheryl Mitchell

Father: janitor.

Mother: waitress.

Principal child-rearer: grandmother.

Primary education: large public school in Ocean Hill-Brownsville, Brooklyn, New York. *Notes:* rote teaching of basic skills and emphasis on conveying the importance of good attendance, good manners, and good work habits. School patrolled by security guards. *Ambition:* "to be a teacher."

Supplemental tutoring: none.

Summer camp: none.

Secondary education: large public school in Ocean Hill-Brownsville. Classmates included sons and daughters of hairdressers, groundskeepers, painters, dressmakers, dishwashers, domestics. *After-school activities:* domestic chores, part-time employment as a babysitter and housekeeper. *Ambition:* "to be a social worker." *High-school graduation gift:* corsage.

Family activities: church-sponsored socials.

Higher education: one semester of local community college. *Note:* dropped out of school for financial reasons.

First full-time job (age 17): counter clerk at a local bakery.

Subsequent employment: file clerk with a temporary service agency, supermarket checker.

Present employment (age ??): nurse's aide at a municipal hospital. *Typical daily activities:* make up hospital beds, clean out bedpans, weigh patients and assist them to the bathroom, take temperature readings, pass out and collect food trays, feed patients who need help, bathe patients, and change dressings. *Transportation to and from work:* city bus. *Annual salary:* $16,000. *Ambition:* "to get out of the ghetto."

Present residence: three-room apartment in the South Bronx, needs painting, has poor ventilation, is in a high-crime area. *Note:* Cheryl Mitchell lives with her two children and her elderly mother.

Second residence: none.

When we look at the lives of Cheryl Mitchell, Bob Farrell, and Harold Browning, we see life-styles that are very different. We are not looking, however, at economic extremes. Cheryl Mitchell's income as a nurse's aide puts her above the government's official poverty line. Below her on the income pyramid are 40 million poverty-stricken Americans. Far from being poor, Bob Farrell's annual income as an assistant sales manager puts him, in the fifty-first percentile of the income distribution. More than 50 percent of the U.S. population earns less money than Bob Farrell. And while Harold Browning's income puts him in a high-income bracket, he stands only a fraction of the way up Samuelson's income pyramid. Well above him are the 17,000 individuals whose annual salary exceeds $1 million. Yet, Harold S. Browning spends more money on his horses than Cheryl Mitchell earns in a year.

Reality 4: Even ignoring the extreme poles of the economic spectrum, we find enormous class differences in the life-styles among the haves, the have-nots, and the have-littles.

Class affects more than life-style and material well-being. It has a significant impact on our physical and mental well-being as well.

Researchers have found an inverse relation between social class and health. Lower-class standing is correlated to higher rates of infant mortality, eye and ear disease, arthritis, physical disability, diabetes, nutritional deficiency, respiratory disease, mental illness, and heart disease.[15] In all areas of health, poor people do not share the same life chances as those in the social class above them. Furthermore, lower-class standing is correlated to a lower quality of treatment for illness and disease. The results of poor health and poor treatment are born out in the life expectancy rates within each class. Researchers have found that the higher your class standing, the higher your life expectancy. Conversely, they have also found that within each age group, the lower one's class standing, the higher the death rate; in some age groups, the figures are as much as two and three times as high.[16]

Reality 5: From cradle to grave, class standing has a significant impact on our chances for survival.

The lower one's class standing, the more difficult it is to secure appropriate housing, the more time is spent on the routine tasks of everyday life, the greater is the percentage of income that goes to pay for food and other basic necessities, and the greater is the likelihood of crime victimization.[17] Class can predict chances for both survival and success.

Class and Educational Attainment

School performance (grades and test scores) and educational attainment (level of schooling completed) also correlate strongly with economic class. Furthermore, despite some efforts to make testing fairer and schooling more accessible, current data suggest that the level of inequity is staying the same or getting worse.

In his study for the Carnegie Council on Children fifteen years ago, Richard de Lone examined the test scores of over half a million students who took the College Board exams (SAT's). His findings were consistent with earlier studies that showed a relationship between class and scores on standardized tests; his conclusion, "the higher the student's social status, the higher the probability that he or she will get higher grades."[18] Fifteen years after the release of the Carnegie report, College Board surveys reveal data that are no different: test scores still correlate strongly with family income.

TABLE 1
Average Combined Scores by Income (400 to 1600 scale)[19]

Family Income	Median Score
$70,000 or more	1005
$60,000 to $70,000	953
$50,000 to $60,000	933
$40,000 to $50,000	914
$30,000 to $40,000	887
$20,000 to $30,000	857
$10,000 to $20,000	813
less than $10,000	768

Based on the test results of 879,909 SAT takers

A little more than twenty years ago, researcher William Sewell showed a positive correlation between class and overall educational achievement. In comparing the top quartile (25 percent) of his sample to the bottom quartile, he found that students from upper-class families were: twice as likely to obtain training beyond high school and four times as likely to attain a postgraduate degree. Sewell concluded, "Socio-economic background . . . operates independently of academic ability at every stage in the process of educational attainment."[20]

Today, the pattern persists. There are however, two significant changes. On the one hand, the odds of getting into college have improved for the bottom quartile of the population, although they still remain relatively low compared to the top. On the other hand, the chances of completing a college degree have deteriorated markedly for the bottom. Researchers estimate the chances of completing a four-year college degree (by age twenty-four) to be nineteen times as great for the top 25 percent of the population as it is for the bottom 25 percent. "Those from the bottom quartile of family income . . . are faring worse than they have at any time in the 23 years of published Current Population Survey data."[21]

Reality 6: Class standing has a significant impact on chances for educational attainment.

Class standing, and consequently life chances, are largely determined at birth. Although examples of individuals who have gone from rags to riches abound in the mass media, statistics on class mobility show these leaps to be extremely rare. In fact, dramatic advances in class standing are relatively few. One study showed that fewer than one in five men surpass the economic status of their fathers.[22] For those whose annual income is in six figures, economic success is due in large part to the wealth and privileges bestowed upon them at birth. Over 66 percent of the consumer units with incomes of $100,000 or more have some inherited assets. Of these units, over 86 percent reported that inheritances constituted a substantial portion of their total assets.[23]

Economist Harold Wachtel likens inheritance to a series of Monopoly games in which the winner of the first game refuses to relinquish his or her cash and commercial property for the second game. "After all," argues the winner, "I accumulated my wealth and income by my own wits." With such an arrangement, it is not difficult to predict the outcome of subsequent games.[24]

Reality 7: All Americans do not have an equal opportunity to succeed. Inheritance laws assure a greater likelihood of success for the offspring of the wealthy.

Spheres of Power and Oppression

When we look at society and try to determine what it is that keeps most people down—what holds them back from realizing their potential as healthy, creative, productive individuals—we find institutionally oppressive forces that are largely beyond their individual control. Class domination is one of these forces. People do not choose to be poor or working class; instead, they are limited and confined by the opportunities afforded or denied them by a social system. The class structure in the United States is a function of its economic system—capitalism, a system that is based on private rather than public ownership and control of commercial enterprises, and on the class division between those who own and control and those who do not. Under capitalism, these enterprises are governed by the need to produce a profit for the owners, rather than to fulfill collective needs.

Racial and gender domination are other forces that hold people down. Although there are significant differences in the way capitalism, racism, and sexism affect our lives, there are also a multitude of parallels. And although race, class, and gender act independently of each other, they are at the same time very much interrelated.

On the one hand, issues of race and gender oppression cut across class lines. Women experience the effects of sexism whether they are well-paid professionals or poorly paid clerks. As women, they face discrimination and male domination, as well as catcalls and stereotyping. Similarly, a Black man faces racial oppression, is subjected to racial slurs, and is denied opportunities because of his color. Regardless of their class standing, women and members of minority races are confronted with oppressive forces precisely because of their gender, color, or both.

On the other hand, class oppression permeates other spheres of power and oppression, so that the oppression experienced by women and minorities is also differentiated along class lines. Although women and minorities find themselves in subordinate positions vis-à-vis white men, the particular issues they confront may be quite different depending on their position in the class structure. Inequalities in the class structure distinguish social functions and individual power, and these distinctions carry over to race and gender categories.

Power is incremental, and class privileges can accrue to individual women and to individual members of a racial minority. At the same time, class-oppressed men, whether they are white or Black, have privileges afforded them as men in a sexist society. Similarly, class-oppressed whites, whether they are men or women, have privileges afforded them as whites in a racist society. Spheres of power and oppression divide us deeply in our society, and the schisms between us are often difficult to bridge.

Whereas power is incremental, oppression is cumulative, and those who are poor, Black, and female have all of the forces of classism, racism, and sexism bearing down on them. This cumulative oppression is what is meant by the double and triple jeopardy of women and minorities.

Furthermore, oppression in one sphere is related to the likelihood of oppression in another. If you are Black and female, for example, you are much more likely to be poor or working class than you would be as a white male. Census figures show that the incidence of poverty varies greatly by race and gender.

TABLE 2
Chances of Being Poor in America[25]

White male/female	White female head*	Hispanic male/female	Hispanic female head	Black male/female	Black female head
1 in 10	1 in 3	1 in 3	1 in 2	1 in 3	1 in 2

*Persons in families with female householder, no husband present.

In other words, being female and being nonwhite are attributes in our society that increase the chances of poverty and of lower-class standing.

Reality 8: Racism and sexism compound the effects of classism in society.

NOTES

1. See Benjamin DeMott, *The Imperial Middle*, New York, William Morrow and Company, 1990; Ira Katznelson, *City Trenches: Urban Politics and Patterning of Class in the United States*, New York, Pantheon Books, 1981; Charles W. Tucker, "A Comparative Analysis of Subjective Social Class: 1945–1963," *Social Forces*, no.46, June 1968, pp. 508–514; Robert Nisbet, "The Decline and Fall of Social Class," *Pacific Sociological Review*, vol. 2, Spring 1959, pp. 11–17; and Oscar Glantz, "Class Consciousness and Political Solidarity," *American Sociological Review*, vol. 23, August 1958, pp. 375–382.

2. Susan Ostander, "Upper-Class Women: Class Consciousness as Conduct and Meaning," in *Power Structure Research* by G. William Domhoff, Beverly Hills, Calif., Sage Productions, 1980, pp. 78–79.

3. U.S. Bureau of the Census, 1989 Current Population Reports, series P-60, no. 146.

4. Barbara Kallen, "Getting By on $1 Million a Year," *Forbes*, October 27, 1986, p.48

5. "Poverty in the United States: 1992" from Current Population Reports: Consumer Income 1993, Series P-60, no. 185, Department of Commerce, Bureau of the Census, Washington, D.C., p. A8.

6. Ibid., p. 11.

7. Derived from U.S. Department of Commerce, Current Population Reports: Consumer Income: 1992, Washington, D.C., 1993, and The World Bank, "World Development Report: 1992," International Bank for Reconstruction and Development, Washington, D.C., 1992.

8. See U.S. Bureau of the Census Current Population Reports," series P-60, no. 146, 1989, and Steven Rose, *The American Profile Poster*, New York, Pantheon Books, 1986, page 31.

9. Paul Krugman, quoting Alan Blinder in "Disparity and Dispare," *U.S. News and World Report*, March 23, 1992, p. 54.

10. Paul Samuelson, *Economics*, 10th ed., New York, McGraw Hill, 1976, p. 84.

11. "Money Income of Households, Families, and Persons in the United States: 1992," U.S. Department of Commerce, Current Population Reports: Consumer Income, Series P-60, no. 184, Washington, D.C., 1993, p. B6.

12. Paul Blumberg, *Inequality in an Age of Decline*, New York, Oxford University Press, 1980.

13. Michael Harrington, *The Other America*, New York, Macmillan, 1962, p. 12–13.

14. Stuart Ewen and Elizabeth Ewen, *Channels of Desire: Mass Images and the Shaping of American Consciousness*, New York, McGraw-Hill, 1982.

15. Melvin Krasner, *Poverty and Health in New York City*, United Hospital Fund of New York, 1989. See also, U.S. Department of Health and Human Services, *Health Status of Minorities and Low Income Groups, 1985*; and Dan Hughes, Kay Johnson, Sara Rosenbaum, Elizabeth Butler, Janet Simons, *The Health of America's Children*, The Children's Defense Fund, 1988.

16. Aaron Antonovsky, "Social Class, Life Expectancy, and Overall Mortality," *The Impact of Social Class*, New York, Thomas Crowell, 1972, pp. 467–491. See also, Harriet Duleep, "Measuring the Effect of Income on Adult Mortality Using Longitudinal Administrative Record Data," *Journal of Human Resources*, vol. 21, no. 2, Spring 1986.

17. Dennis W. Roncek, "Dangerous Places: Crime and Residential Environment," *Social Forces*, 60:1, September 1981, pp. 74–96.

18. Richard De Lone, *Small Futures*, New York, Harcourt Brace Jovanovich, 1978, pp 14–19.

19. Derived from, The College Entrance Examination Board, "College-Bound Seniors: 1993 Profile of SAT and Achievement Test Takers," Princeton, N.J., 1993, p. 7.

20. William H. Sewell, "Inequality of Opportunity for Higher Education," *American Sociological Review*, vol. 36, no. 5, 1971, pp. 793–809.

21. The Mortenson Report on Public Policy Analysis of Opportunity for Postsecondary Education, "Postsecondary Education Opportunity", no. 16, Iowa City, Iowa, September 1993.

22. De Lone, Ibid., pp. 14–19.

23. Howard Tuchman, *Economics of the Rich*, New York, Random House, 1973, p. 15.

24. Howard Wachtel, *Labor and the Economy*, Orlando, Fla., Academic Press, 1984, pp. 161–162.

25. Derived from "Poverty in the United States: 1992," U.S. Department of Commerce, Current Population Reports: Consumer Income, Series P-60, no. 185, Washington, D.C., 1993, pp. 2–3.

The Wage Gap:
Myths and Facts

National Committee on Pay Equity

1. The United States Labor Force Is Occupationally Segregated by Race and Sex.

- In 1992, women constituted 45.7 percent of all workers in the civilian labor force (over 57 million women).[1]
- People of color constituted 14.5 percent of all workers.[2]
- Labor force participation is almost equal among white women, Black women, and women of Hispanic origin. In 1992, 57.2 percent (7.1 million) of Black women, 61.3 percent (52.7 million) of white women, and 52.8 percent (4.2 million) of Hispanic women were in the paid labor force.[3]
- In 1992, women were:
  99.0 percent of all secretaries
  93.5 percent of all registered nurses
  98.8 percent of all pre-school and kindergarten teachers
  89.0 percent of all telephone operators
  73.2 percent of all teachers (excluding colleges and universities)
  86.6 percent of all data entry keyers
  Women were only:
  8.7 percent of all engineers
  30.3 percent of all lawyers and judges
  15.1 percent of all police and detectives
  8.2 percent of all precision, production, craft, and repair workers
  26.2 percent of all physicians[4]

The U.S. labor force is segregated by sex and race.

Occupations with the Highest Concentration by Race/Ethnicity/Sex[5]

Black women:	Social workers; postal clerks; dieticians; child-care workers and teacher's aides; private household cooks and cleaners; nursing aides, orderlies, and attendants

Black men:	Vehicle washers and equipment cleaners; bus drivers; concrete and terrazzo workers; guards; sheriffs, bailiffs, and other law enforcement
Hispanic women:	Private household cleaners and servants; child-care workers; janitors and cleaners; health service occupations; sewing machine operators; graders and sorters
Hispanic men:	Janitors and cleaners; construction trades; machine operators and tenders; cooks; drivers-sales workers; handlers, laborers, and helpers; roofers; groundskeepers, gardeners, farm and agricultural workers
White women:	Physical therapists; dental hygienists; secretaries and stenographers; bookkeepers, accounting and auditing clerks
White men:	Marketing, advertising, and public relations managers; engineers, architects, and surveyors; dentists; firefighters; construction supervisors; tool and die makers
Asian women:	Marine life workers; electrical assemblers; dressmakers; launderers
Asian men:	Physicians; engineers; professors; technicians; baggage porters; cooks; launderers; longshore equipment operators
Native American women:	Welfare aides; child-care workers; teacher's aides; forestry (except logging)
Native American men:	Marine life workers; hunters; forestry (except logging); fishers

2. Economic Status.

- In 1992, 58 percent of all women were either the sole supporter of their families or their husbands earned less than $15,000.[6]
- Over 8.8 million women work full time in jobs that pay wages below the poverty line (in 1992 for a family of three the poverty line was $11,186 per year). They work in jobs such as day care, food counter, and many service jobs. Many more women than men are part of the working poor (125 percent of the poverty level) and work in jobs such as clerical, blue collar, and sales.[7]
- In 1992, married couple families with two children present had a median income of $43,818 while female headed households with two children present had a median income of only $11,591.[8]
- Women of color are in the lowest paid jobs.
- The majority of women, just as the majority of men, work out of economic necessity to support their families. Women do not work for "pin money."

Occupations and Average Salaries of Occupations with a High Percentage of Women of Color[9]

Occupation	Annual Weekly Salary	Percentage of Women of Color
Social workers	$489	16
Health aides	309	22
Nursing aides	266	31
Food preparation workers	236	10
Sewing machine operators	217	28
Cleaners and servants	191	26
Child-care workers	154	14

In 1992, median weekly salaries for all men were $505 and $381 for all women. Women of color represented approximately 7 percent of all workers.

3. The Wage Gap Is One of the Major Causes of Economic Inequality in the United States Today.

- In 1992, all men, working year-round full-time, were paid a median salary of $30,358.
- All women, working year-round full-time, were paid a median salary of $21,440.
- Therefore, women were paid 70.6 cents compared to each dollar paid to men.

The breakdown by race shows the double burden that women of color face because of race and sex discrimination.

Year-Round Full-Time Earnings for 1992[10]

Race/Sex	Earnings	Earnings as a Percentage of White Men's
White men	$31,012	100.0
Black men	22,369	72.1
Hispanic men	20,049	64.6
White women	21,659	69.8
Black women	19,819	63.9
Hispanic women	17,138	55.3

Data for Asian/Pacific Islanders and Native Americans is not available.

4. The Wage Gap Has Fluctuated, But Has Not Disappeared in the Last Several Decades.

Over the last decade, the wage gap has narrowed by about ten cents, from 60.2 percent in 1980 to 70.6 percent in 1992. However, a significant portion of the change is due to the fact that man's real earnings have fallen over the last several years. 38 percent of the change in the wage ratio can be attributed to the drop in men's earnings, while 62 percent is due to the increase in women's earnings over the decade.

Comparison of Median Earnings of Year-Round Full-Time Workers, by Sex, Selected Years

Year	Median Earnings		Women's Earnings as a Percent of Men's	Year	Median Earnings		Women's Earnings as a Percent of Men's
	WOMEN	MEN			WOMEN	MEN	
1992	$21,440	$30,358	70.6	1973	$6,335	$11,186	56.6
1991	20,553	29,421	69.8	1972	5,903	10,202	57.9
1990	20,656	28,843	71.6	1971	5,593	9,399	59.5
1989	18,780	27,430	68.5	1970	5,323	8,966	59.4
1988	17,606	26,656	66.0	1969	4,977	8,227	60.5
1987	16,909	26,008	65.0	1966	3,973	6,848	58.0
1986	16,232	25,256	64.3	1965	3,823	6,375	60.0
1985	15,624	24,195	64.5	1964	3,690	6,195	59.6
1984	14,780	23,218	63.7	1963	3,561	5,978	59.6
1983	13,915	21,881	63.6	1962	3,446	5,974	59.5
1982	13,014	21,077	61.7	1961	3,351	5,644	59.4
1981	12,001	20,260	59.2	1960	3,293	5,317	60.8
1980	11,197	18,612	60.2	1959	3,193	5,209	61.3
1979	10,151	17,014	59.7	1958	3,102	4,927	63.0
1978	9,350	15,730	59.4	1957	3,008	4,713	63.8
1977	8,618	14,626	58.9	1956	2,827	4,466	63.3
1976	8,099	13,455	60.2	1955	2,719	4,252	63.9
1975	7,504	12,758	58.8	1946	1,710	2,588	66.1
1974	6,772	11,835	57.2				

5. The Cause of the Wage Gap Is Discrimination.

Differences in education, labor force experience, and commitment (years in the labor force) do not account for the entire wage gap.

- In 1992, women with college degrees earned $11,721 less per year than their white male colleagues, and only $1,916 more per year than white men with only a high-school diploma.

- College educated Hispanic women actually earned less than white men who had never taken a college course.[12]
- The National Academy of Sciences (NAS) found in 1981 that usually less than a quarter (25 percent) of the wage gap is due to differences in education, labor force experience, and commitment.
- According to the 1986 NAS study, *Women's Work, Men's Work,* "each additional percentage point female in an occupation was associated with $42 less in median annual earnings."
- According to the 1987 National Committee on Pay Equity (NCPE) study, in New York State, for every 5 to 6 percent increase in Black and Hispanic representation in a job there is one salary grade decrease. (One salary grade decrease amounts to a 5 percent salary decrease.)
- A 1985 U.S. Census Bureau study reported that differences in education, labor force experience, and commitment account for only 14.6 percent of the wage gap between men and women.

White Vs. Minority Wage Inequity By Education for Entry Level Jobs

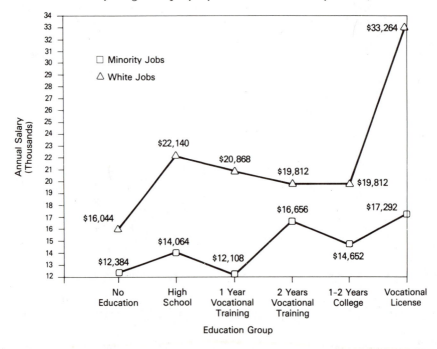

6. Employers Are Always Comparing Different Jobs in Order to Set Wages.

- Two-thirds of employees are paid according to a formal job evaluation system

7. The Cost of Implementing Pay Equity.

- Achieving pay equity usually costs about 2 to 5 percent of an employer's payroll budget.

For example, in the State of Minnesota, after conducting a job evaluation study, it was determined that there was a 20 percent gap between comparable male-dominated and female-dominated jobs. It cost the state 3.7 percent of the payroll budget to eliminate this inequity. The adjustments were phased-in over a four-year period and have resulted in a narrowing of the wage gap by nine percentage points, without affecting overall employment for women in the state.

8. Pay Equity Is Being Addressed All Over the Country.

- All but five states (Alaska, Arkansas, Delaware, Georgia, and Idaho) have addressed the issue of pay equity.
- Twenty-four states and the District of Columbia have conducted job evaluation studies to determine if their wage setting systems are discriminatory.
- Twenty states have actually adjusted wages for women in jobs that have been found to be underpaid because of wage bias.
- Four states (New York, New Jersey, Florida, and Wisconsin) and Washington, D.C., have addressed race in addition to sex discrimination.[13]

9. Everyone in Society Benefits from Pay Equity.

A. **Men's wages will not be lowered.** Employers cannot remedy discrimination by penalizing another group. Men who are working in predominantly female jobs will also be paid more if pay equity adjustments are made. Everyone benefits from women and people of color being paid fairly. Whether it is your mother, sister, wife, or daughter, wage discrimination hurts the entire family. Men of color will benefit in additional ways to those listed for all men: elimination of race from the wage setting system will boost their wages and men of color are more likely to be found in undervalued "women's" occupations.

B. Employers benefit because the employees' productivity will increase if there is a sense of fairness in how wages are set. Also, pay equity helps employers recruit and retain the best workers.

C. Society benefits because if wage discrimination is eliminated, the need for government subsidies for food stamps, health care, etc., will not be as great. In addition, when workers whose wages were lowered by discrimination are paid fairly, their pensions will be greater upon retirement and they will need less government assistance in their senior years.

Where We Get the Statistics

The U.S. Department of Commerce, Census Bureau, collects wage data every ten years. This data provides in-depth information for Blacks, whites, Hispanics, Asian/ Pacific Islanders, and Native Americans. The 1990 decennial census figures of the national work force and occupational data sorted by gender and race had not been released as of January 1994.

The Census Bureau also provides annual salary data for Blacks, whites, and Hispanics. They gather this information in March of the following year and release it in September. Therefore, the annual salary data for 1993 will not have been released until September of 1994.

The U.S. Department of Labor, Bureau of Labor Statistics (BLS), provides quarterly reports each year on weekly salaries for Blacks, whites, and Hispanics. They also provide an annual average of weekly wages.

NOTES

1. U. S. Department of Labor, Bureau of Labor Statistics, 1992 Annual Average Tables from *Employment and Earnings*, Jan., 1993.

2. Ibid.

3. U. S. Department of Commerce, Census Bureau, Current Population Reports, Consumer Income, Series P–60, No. 184, Table No. 31.

4. U. S. Department of Labor, Bureau of Labor Statistics, 1992 Annual Average Tables, Table 5.

5. Data for Black, Hispanic, and white men and women from the U. S. Department of Labor, Bureau of Labor Statistics, 1992 Annual Averages, unpublished tables. Data for Asian and Native American men and women from U. S. Department of Commerce, 1980 Decennial Census.

6. U. S. Department of Commerce, Census Bureau, Current Population Reports, Consumer Income, Series P–60, No. 184, Table No. 28.

7. U. S. Department of Commerce, Census Bureau, Current Population Reports, Consumer Income, Series P–60, No. 185, Table A.

8. U. S. Department of Commerce, Census Bureau, Current Population Reports, Consumer Income, Series P–60, No. 184, Table No. 18.

9. U. S. Department of Labor, Bureau of Labor Statistics, 1992 Annual Averages, unpublished data.

10. U. S. Department of Commerce, Census Bureau, Current Population Reports, Consumer Income, Series P–60, No. 184, Table No. 31.

11. *Background on the Wage Gap*, National Committee on Pay Equity, 1126 Sixteenth Street, NW, Suite 411, Washington, D.C., 20036.

12. U. S. Department of Commerce, Census Bureau, Current Population Reports, Consumer Income, Series P–60, No. 184, Table No. 30.

13. *Pay Equity in the Public Sector*, 1993 Addendum, National Committee on Pay Equity, 1126 Sixteenth Street, NW, Suite 411, Washington, D.C., 20036.

Women Face Glass Walls as well as Ceilings

Julie Amparano Lopez

If the ceiling doesn't stop today's working woman, the walls will, a new study suggests.

For a long time, invisible barriers called "glass ceilings" were viewed as the big obstacle facing women trying to climb the corporate ladder. But the new survey has found that the problem starts before that, with "glass walls" that keep women from moving laterally.

Lack of lateral movement deprives women of the experience, especially in line supervision, that they need to advance vertically, concludes the study conducted by Catalyst, a nonprofit research organization here that focuses on women's issues in the workplace.

The new study is based on interviews with senior managers and focus groups with middle managers from large corporations. It will be released today at a Catalyst conference on strategies for women's advancement.

According to the report, women tend to be placed in staff or support positions in areas such as public relations and human resources and are often steered away from jobs in core areas such as marketing, production and sales.

Catalyst President Felice Schwartz says women get trapped in these kinds of jobs because of unintentional stereotyping that labels them as people who can provide support. Support functions such as human resources, law or finance typically don't offer the critical experience expected of those advancing to senior levels.

"Women are being inadvertently separated," Ms. Schwartz says. "Women go one way, and men go another."

The study says women account for as many as half of the professional employees in the largest industrial and service companies, yet they hold fewer than 5% of the senior management positions. And most of the senior jobs they do hold are in areas such as human resources, finance or public relations.

Among the reasons that few women are assigned to line jobs: Many men still feel uncomfortable dealing with women, and many doubt that the women can balance career and family, says Mary Mattis, Catalyst vice president of research. "Furthermore," she says, "60% of human resources managers who participated in the study reported that putting women in line jobs is perceived as risky."

Several outside experts say that the glass wall has been a longstanding problem but is gaining new importance. As companies pare layers of specialized management, it has become more critical than ever to gain broader management expertise, they add.

"The glass wall is just a new name for an old phenomenon called occupational segregation," says Myra H. Strober, a labor economist at Stanford University who is researching issues women face at major corporations. "Jobs get segregated when women begin to move through them," Dr. Strober says. "That's just a way of maintaining old types of discrimination."

Dr. Strober urges women to express their concerns to employers. But she says that corporations bear the ultimate responsibility for breaking down the walls. "If companies are serious about moving women to the top, they have to make sure that women don't get stuck in certain dead-end areas," Dr. Strober says.

Other executives say women need to become more assertive to break through the walls. Eunice Salton, a vice president in a division of Simon & Schuster, recommends that women request transfers and go after important line positions. "The walls are still there," she says, but they're getting weaker. . . .

Three Realities:
Minority Life in America

Business—Higher Education Forum

As measured by virtually all statistical measures of income, opportunity, education, access to health care, and personal security, it is clear that the *typical* minority American does not begin to enjoy anything close to parity with the life experiences of the average white American.

The general picture is deeply disturbing: the statistics chart a wide gulf between the races. For example, life expectancy figures for whites and blacks are heading in opposite directions. After narrowing for decades, the gap in life expectancy between blacks and whites has grown for the last three years in a row, according to the most recent data from the National Center for Health Statistics—increasing between 1984 and 1987 from 5.6 years to 6.2 years.

In 1986, poverty rates for all black individuals, from infancy through old age, were nearly three times the rate for whites (31 percent and 11 percent, respectively). Poverty rates for other minority groups are also extraordinarily high. American Indians living on reservations experience the highest rates of poverty in the United States, followed by Puerto Ricans. The median wealth (assets less liabilities) of black households is 9 percent of the white household median.

In any given month, Hispanic unemployment is about 50 percent higher than the rate for whites, and black unemployment is 2.5 times as high. In a 45-year work career, a white man, on average, can expect to work for 36 years, to be unemployed for 2, and to be "out of the labor force" for 7. Comparable figures for a black man are 29 years of work, 5 years of unemployment, and 11 years out of the labor force.

Less money, on average, is spent on public education for minority group members, who are frequently isolated in cities or in rural areas where the tax base cannot adequately support the public schools. The National Assessment of Educational Progress reveals that despite progress in recent years the average performance of young blacks and Hispanics in reading, mathematics, and science still lags far behind that of their white peers.

But useful though these statistics may be, they conceal as much as they reveal about the nation's 30 million black and 18 million Hispanic citizens. Just as understanding the average daily temperature in the continental United States does not prepare the visitor for August heat or January frost, so, too, understanding the average situation for members of minority groups does not illuminate the diversity of minority life in this country.

That diversity, as a recent exhaustive analysis by the National Research Council points out, reflects the confluence of two major developments in the status of all Americans. First, between 1940 and 1973, real earnings for all, including members of minority groups, appreciated steadily, after which they stagnated. Second, since 1973, inequality among all Americans increased as the least skilled were the most damaged by economic change. These two developments are reflected in minority communities as well, including, in the words of the National Research Council, pronounced differences in the "material well-being and opportunities among blacks."

As a result, three separate realities exist for minority Americans.

The first reality is that a significant number of minority group members—black and Hispanic—are succeeding in the American society, economy, and culture. They are repeating the successes of ethnic immigrants and doing it in much the same way: by insisting they be treated with the dignity to which every human being is entitled; by demanding the equal treatment that is every citizen's due; by diligence and education; by seizing each new opportunity; and by sacrificing today for the tomorrow of their children. More than a third of *all* blacks and Hispanics are included in this group. The proportion of the *working-age* minority population is even larger, probably exceeding 40 percent.

The second reality is more troublesome. It involves, overwhelmingly, working minority Americans who are at the margin of making it in American life. Despite their best efforts, limited educational opportunities, low levels of literacy, and the lack of marketable skills prevent them from keeping pace with the rising demands of the workplace. They are falling behind economically and receive little attention from policymakers. About a third of all blacks and Hispanics are included in this precarious position. For the working-age minority population, the figure appears to be slightly lower, between 25 and 30 percent.

The third reality—severe minority poverty—confounds America's fundamental concept of itself. The persistence of severe minority poverty in the United States remains a paradox in a just and compassionate society.

In any given year, three out of 10 minority Americans live below the poverty line. We estimate that roughly 25 percent of working-age minority Americans are poor.

What's more, of all those Americans living in poverty in one year, about three-quarters are still living in poverty the next year. Analysts refer to this group as the "persistently poor." The persistently poor include a group frequently referred to as the underclass, a group that is largely black and Hispanic, and most readily apparent in the nation's cities. But the underclass also exists in isolated rural areas where large numbers of people, majority *and* minority, live in poverty. The underclass is defined in various ways, but is generally said to include individuals who are chronically jobless, who are living in communities that have very high rates of poverty, or who do not embrace mainstream norms.

The underclass has endured for nearly two generations. Despite the piecemeal strategies developed since the 1960s, this human tragedy in the midst of plenty threatens to become permanent. A new pathology is overwhelming many communities. Hope for the future, dreams for one's children, and aspirations for a better life are being replaced by the anesthetic of drugs, dependency on public assistance, and the destructiveness of violence.

Middle Class Blacks Try to Grip a Ladder While Lending a Hand

Isabel Wilkerson

Joyce Ford, the daughter of laborers, fled the hand-to-mouth world of Washington's black housing projects and now has amenities of the middle class: a good job in the Government, an office across the street from the White House, a merit raise and an American Express card. But she still has the bone-deep worries of the poor.

Sitting at her desk the other day, she got yet another call from a frantic relative with bad news and high expectations. "Your brother's sick," the caller said. "He needs to see somebody. What are you going to do?"

What else could she do? She spent the better part of the day trying to figure out where her out-of-work brother should go for treatment, and how to pay for it.

Mrs. Ford, 44 years old, is among tens of thousands of black people who are the first in their families to break out of poverty and take a tenuous place in the American middle class. Many are scaling the economic ladder with one hand on the middle rung and the other still outstretched to the relatives who need them.

The Peril of Falling Back

To the outside world, Mrs. Ford and those like her are examples of how far this nation has come since the civil rights movement opened up legions of professional jobs previously closed to black people. To their families, they are the American dream come true, showpieces to brag about.

But even in the best of times, these newly arrived blacks have a loose grasp on prosperity. And as a faltering economy tumbles toward recession, they may slip out of the middle class altogether, many economists and sociologists fear, creating an even deeper well of need among impoverished blacks to whom they now lend support.

Two main things tend to distinguish black middle-class people from middle-class whites. One is the likelihood that many more of their relatives will come to

155

them for help. The other is that they tend to lack the resources of people who started life in the middle class.

There is no clear-cut definition of "middle-class," a concept that can embrace not just how much money people make but the way they make it: usually not with their hands. Most economists and sociologists agree that the middle class includes mainly professionals, skilled service and clerical workers and entrepreneurs, each one earning $25,000 to about $50,000 a year, or more if the person lives in an expensive city or has a lot of children.

Under those criteria, about 40 percent of blacks fall into the category of middle class or above while 30 percent are blue-collar working class and 30 percent are the unskilled poor.

But unlike the white middle and upper classes, which include nearly 70 percent of all white households and have been a fixture for three or four generations, the vast majority of the black middle class is starting from scratch.

Census Bureau figures for 1989 show that in median annual income, the households of black college graduates trailed those of white college graduates by more than a third: $37,958 for blacks as against $48,862 for whites.

And while all couples earn more if both husband and wife work, a second income for black families is usually what allows them to be middle class.

When both spouses work, the median income of black couples is $37,787, according to 1989 census figures. But when one spouse did not bring home a paycheck, the black couple's median income dropped to $18,727—out of the middle class. White couples, by contrast, tend to keep their middle-class status even when one spouse does not work. Last year, white couples earned a median figure of $45,803 with two paychecks and $29,689 with one.

Perhaps equally important, economists say, black people often enter the middle class with a slight fraction of the financial assets of middle-class whites whose parents and grandparents were middle class. So blacks lack the reserve of money and property needed to buy a house, to finance a college education, to weather a personal catastrophe or a national recession.

"Middle-class blacks are much more vulnerable than whites because they tend to be new to their positions and don't have the seniority of accumulated wealth," said William Julius Wilson, a professor of sociology at the University of Chicago.

Reminders of Desperation

Unlike most middle-class whites, they live with daily, personal reminders of the poverty and desperation they are trying to put behind them, as the loved ones back home who have not fared so well turn to them for help with the rent, use of a car, a place to stay.

"We're all tied together because upward mobility is recent for us," said Dr. Andrew Billingsly, chairman of the Department of Family and Community Development at the University of Maryland and a leading researcher on the black middle class.

The topic can be painful. Many middle-class black people were reluctant to talk to a reporter about their experiences out of a sense of duty and protectiveness toward their loved ones. Some did not want to take credit or appear to be holding themselves above the people they once played stickball with.

And in a society that in many ways judges people not only by where they are but by where they came from, many feared that their backgrounds and family responsibilities would subject them to unwanted scrutiny at work, or even be held against them.

In dozens of interviews, middle-class black people said they were proud to be the ones able to help their families, but were frustrated by their inability to get ahead.

"You can never accomplish anything," said Mrs. Ford, the Government worker in Washington. "As soon as you get anything, there's something there to take it away. I often wonder what will happen if something happens to me. Who'll be there for me?"

Some Dependents Aren't Declared

Donald Sheppard, an assistant professor of social work at Texas Southern University in Houston, has a wife and five children, but they are just the dependents the Internal Revenue Service gives him credit for.

When a brother needs a loan, when a sister needs a job, when a nephew needs a car, when a cousin needs a credit card or a friend needs a place to stay, they come to him.

"I know that when I get paid on the first of the month, I'm going to get a call," Mr. Sheppard, 40, said. "It's expected that I have it and that I'm going to give it. I feel I'm working for the whole extended family. It's not a question of *if* they're going to need it. I know they're going to need it."

His relatives have looked to him for help since he was in grade school. "When the television would get those horizontal lines, they would always call on me," Mr. Sheppard recalled. "I didn't know what to do any more than they did. But I'd turn some screw and it would work. Even as a child, people expected me to do everything."

By the time he was 11, he was catching the bus to go pay the family's utility bills. His father, a wool presser at a Houston dry cleaners with not a day of high school, could not dare ask for the time off; his mother, a maid, had suffered a stroke and was too sick. So she kept him out of school to pay the bills. He remembers being stopped by a truant officer and telling him, "Sir, my mama's sick. I'm going to go to school as soon as I pay the bills."

Mr. Sheppard became the only one of eight children to get a college degree and carry a briefcase to work. A sister once told him, "You're almost like a god in our family."

He and his wife, Jina, both social workers, earned their master's degrees at the University of Chicago in the mid-1980's by packing their five children in their 1971 station wagon and all their belongings in a U-Haul truck, driving north and feeding seven mouths on what was left of their scholarship money.

Sometimes He Gets Burned

They returned to Houston to an extended family of relatives and friends who needed them. Mr. Sheppard has gone into the refrigerator to get chicken broilers and T-bone steaks for them; he has had to choose between helping a relative out with the rent or fixing the boiler at his house. The family always wins.

Lately, he has been trying to provide services rather than money. He recently got one of his nephews a maintenance job at the university. "I have to do it for me," Mr. Sheppard said. "If I get them a job, they won't have to be asking me for something."

Last August, a childhood friend of Mr. Sheppard's who was down on his luck and recently evicted asked if he could move his family in with Mr. Sheppard and his family. The answer was yes, and Mr. Sheppard's children slept on the floor to make room. They stayed for five weeks.

"Every day, I had to buy milk and bread and cereal," Mr. Sheppard said. "I had 12 people in the house, and I was the provider."

Some of his investments have begun to pay off. For instance, he saw promise in the young son of one of his sisters, who was raising the boy as a single parent. Mr. Sheppard signed the boy up for Little League Baseball, coached him and counseled him as a surrogate father. The boy is now a senior in high school, at the top of his class and a drum major in the band.

Mr. Sheppard is still paying for the help he has given. His credit cards are up to their limit and the car needs fixing. Even on his and his wife's combined income of $60,000 a year, they have only a $5,000 cushion for their retirement and have not been able to save for their children's college education.

"In my family's eyesight, we've made it," Mr. Sheppard said. "But we're living paycheck to paycheck. To lavish and wallow in the status of the middle class, we can't do it. And I can't give like I used to. But it doesn't seem to register. People still come up to me and say, 'I know it's rough on you, but it's rougher on me, so can you give me this?'"

His goal is to build up reserves so he can provide for relatives without depleting his own money. But he is a long way from that. "When I think about it, it really kind of frightens me," he said. "Sometimes I find myself frustrated and depressed. I'm called on by my children, my wife, family members, students, colleagues, friends, needing, asking, wanting. The cycle never ends."

An Easier Road for Immigrants?

The role of family pathfinder is not new. Immigrants who flocked here from Europe early in this century typically relied on the first child who got an education and a foothold to serve as ambassador and teacher for the rest of the family.

But there are key differences for today's black people. For one, while many unskilled immigrants were able to get relatively good-paying factory jobs or make connections with local political machines to vault their children into the middle class, discrimination prohibited the parents and grandparents of most of today's black middle class from nearly all but menial positions in industry or politics. That meant black families had far less than white families to pass on.

Soon after civil rights measures created a more even playing field, the economy changed: once-dependable, relatively lucrative factory jobs started to vanish just as they began opening up to blacks.

Sociologists, however, point to the effects of lingering racial discrimination as the main difference. Dr. Joe R. Feagin, a professor of sociology at the University of Florida who is completing a book on racial discrimination and the black middle class, contrasts his experiences as an Irish-American with those of black Americans.

"My great-great-grandparents saw signs that said, 'No Irish or dogs allowed,'" Dr. Feagin said. "But once we lost the brogue and the look of the Irish, we could pass. People couldn't single us out for discrimination anymore. That has not been the case for blacks, no matter what their status."

Indeed, the civil rights gains of the last 20 years have done little to even out the huge gaps in white and black wealth. Census figures from 1984, the most recent available for this category, showed that for black households, the median net worth, or total value of what they own (cars, houses, stocks, equity in a business, for example) minus what they owe, such as an outstanding mortgage or education loan, was $3,397. For white households, it was $39,135.

More disturbing, perhaps, nearly a third of blacks have zero or negative net worth, meaning they owe more than they own. Only 8 percent of whites are in that category.

Giving Help, Giving Space

When Marjorie Ellis, 38, is not punching blueprint data into a computer as a drafting clerk at the Southern Bell Telephone Company, she runs a boarding-house—for her own family. Her two-bedroom ranch house just south of Atlanta bustles with the banter and footsteps of her sister, her sister's children, her elderly aunt and her mother.

They are all in transition. Her sister has a job as a civilian worker in the military and is trying to get on her feet, one of the nephews is in college, the aunt is recovering from hip surgery and her mother is struggling on a pension. They all turned to Miss Ellis when they needed help and now share space in the house, chipping in whenever they can.

Their fortune is tied to her fortune. "If there's a middle class, I'm in the poor section," said Miss Ellis, who earns about $30,000 a year.

In the months since her relatives moved in, she has depleted her savings and fallen behind on her house payments.

She doesn't have the $2,500 she needs to get the engine fixed for her 1984 Thunderbird. The car sits cold and idle in her driveway as she leaves to catch the 5:30 bus each dark morning to get to work by 7.

"I'm behind and it's hard to catch up," Miss Ellis said. "I pay one bill one week, the others when I can. I might be late a month. That doesn't mess your credit up too bad. Sometimes I sit and pray and cry. Then I figure it'll be all right somehow. I'm not going to let any of my relatives go wanting if I can help them."

A Wreck Is Disastrous

A few years ago, when her nephew needed a car to get to school, for instance, she bought a car, for which he agreed to make the payments if she covered the down payment and insurance. He never got the money. Worse, the car was in an accident and she ended up owing $1,300 on it. She is still paying for the car, which neither of them can use.

Miss Ellis's father was a cement finisher who died when she was in grade school; her mother was a maid. She and her sister were the first to graduate from high school and work behind a desk.

She remembers her minister's words when she got her house: "You're coming up in the world. You're coming up slow, but you're coming up in the world."

Between the economy and her family responsibilities, she doesn't feel that way anymore. She sleeps on the speckled beige sofa in the den, beneath pictures of the assorted relatives who rely on her. There is also a dog-eared picture of her grandmother, posing not with any of the 25 children she bore but with one of the white children she tended to for a living.

Under the strain, Miss Ellis has developed a bleeding ulcer, diabetes and chronic depression for which she takes regular medication. Her nightmares are not of ghosts and gremlins but of becoming homeless.

Her mother has begun to catch on. She has seen the somber-looking letters from the Department of Housing and Urban Development, which backed her mortgage. But Miss Ellis doesn't want to let on to her situation. Her relatives look up to her. She wouldn't want to let them down.

"What are you studying about?" her mother will ask in rural Georgiaspeak when she sees her daughter thinking of the weight on her shoulders.

"Nothing," Miss Ellis will answer, and smile not very convincingly. "I'm fine."

Saying "No" to Relatives

Glen Giles of Atlanta doesn't go out for lunch or take his family on trips to Florida anymore. And for the first time in his life, he must sometimes say no when relatives need money. It is not easy for a man who, after he got his degree, sent $25 every week to the next sibling in line to go to college.

But he is an insurance account agent with an office to run and a commission to earn at a time when people are not buying houses or cars, two of the biggest things people insure.

Since the first of the year, his business has been off 50 percent as the housing market in Atlanta has slowed. Last summer he had to lay off his entire office staff: a secretary and two other agents.

Now the shiny new desks sit empty in his gray-carpeted office, and he answers the phone, takes orders and messages himself.

So when relatives need help with the electric bill or the rent, he can't help them as he used to. One brother-in-law spent several nights in jail on a traffic violation because no one in the family could bail him out.

"I don't have it to give," said Mr. Giles, 43. "It takes everything we make to pay the bills. I have to dip into my own money to pay the office bills. Some bills go lacking as long as they can. We're borrowed out."

He is the third of 10 children born to textile workers in South Carolina, and even though his siblings are all college graduates and all working, they have limited resources just as he does. So he has no place to turn. "It's just me and whatever financial institution that will help me," Mr. Giles said.

Decades Behind in Prosperity

Jared Samples presumably went from working poor to middle class overnight when he won a seat on the Atlanta City Council last year. One of the first things he did when he got his first paycheck was to move out of the Perry Homes housing project where he grew up. The next thing he wants to do is get his mother out.

He is saving for the house he wants to buy for her, but he is finding that the $25,000 he makes as a full-time public servant doesn't go very far, especially when he still tries to give money to his nephew in college or a sister to pay her car insurance when he can.

He drives a 1975 Dodge. "My family knows I'm still poor," he said. "I might be able to loan somebody a little money, but I need my money back. We're four generations out of slavery and one generation out of the projects."

He knows he is starting from a deficit. "I'm working for my nephews and nieces," he said. "My life is pretty much set. I can work every day but I can't get but so far."

Waiting for the Century?

Many economists say it will take much of the next century to close the gap between the security levels of the black and white middle class. "Blacks can try to do better than in the past and save up, but the best they can do is to try to provide an education for their children so that by the second or third generation, perhaps there will be parity," said William D. Bradford, a professor of finance at the University of Maryland who has written extensively on race and wealth. "I don't see anything in the next 20 years. We're looking at 40 to 60 years."

And many public policy analysts say that such an outcome will require continuing Government intervention. "Blacks are dependent on the Government opening doors and keeping those doors open," said Dr. Walter Allen, a professor of sociology at the University of California at Los Angeles.

Much is at stake for the entire country, sociologists say. "If the black middle class is not stable and secure, they will fall into the lower classes and not be able to pay their bills, their fair share of taxes, and will use a larger share of public services," Dr. Billingsly of the University of Maryland said.

Black people say they are doing what they can to help themselves. Betty Brown Chappell, a social worker and a doctoral candidate at the University of Chicago, remembers her tough freshman year at the University of Michigan, when she arrived on campus with not even enough money for books and food. She remembers how her father, a factory worker, sent what he had—a $10 bill. She gave $5 of it to one sister in college, who then sent $2.50 to another sister in college.

Mrs. Chappell wanted things to be different for the next generation. So when her niece, Alea, was born 18 years ago, she bought $150 in savings bonds for her. Last September, Alea enrolled at the University of Michigan. The savings bonds had doubled in value. She used the money to buy her books.

7

The Poverty Industry

Theresa Funiciello

Firefighters returning from a false alarm in Queens, New York, one beautiful October day in 1989 were gazing into the sky when they passed an apartment complex. Ten stories up, a body was dangling from the window. Hector Faberlle and his co-workers yelled up front to get the rig turned around. Just as it arrived back at the building, a little girl, naked, hit the ground. Faberlle ran to resuscitate her as two other firefighters dashed into the building.

According to Faberlle, "We tried to stabilize her. Just as she was breathing on her own, I heard people screaming. I looked up and saw another small child spinning down." Witnesses said a woman had seemed to dangle him before she let go of him. Hussein, age three, fell on his seven-year-old sister. "After that we couldn't get a pulse from her and blood was spilling from her mouth."

Ameenah Abdus-Salaam, a 32-year-old black middle-class Muslim housewife, was trying to send all five of her children back to Allah, through their apartment window. Her daughter Zainab was pronounced dead at the hospital. Hussein survived and a year later is still in rehabilitation. Just as Ms. Abdus-Salaam was about to toss out her one-year-old, firefighters burst in. As they were overtaking her, she urged the children to go quickly, as if they would go on their own. All were naked. According to one news report, she said, "We came into this world with nothing and that's how we're going to leave." Three children and their mother, who intended to jump when she completed the task, were rescued.

Ms. Abdus-Salaam was charged with murder, attempted murder, first- and second-degree assault, reckless endangerment, and endangering the welfare of a child. Neighbors said the mother was loving and the children were always polite and clean, as if that rendered the occurrence more mysterious. And then Ameenah Abdus-Salaam and her children vanished from our collective memory.

When I was young I could not possibly have understood or forgiven (as if it were mine to forgive) the acts of Ameenah Abdus-Salaam on October 5, 1989. Some of that youth I spent as a Muslim—drapes for clothes, virtually nonstop prayers, my two feet of hair cordoned with a bolt of white cloth bound so tightly I could never forget it was there. I took this religion as seriously as those that preceded it, starting with Catholicism (I went to *that* church every day until I was 18). My religion was as solid as a rock mountain pervious only to centuries of dripping water. (Latent feminism finally crept up on me.)

In Islam, everything is ritualized, from sex to eating. That's how I know what Ameenah Abdus-Salaam was doing calmly while she held Hussein out of the window before letting go. She was praying.

In form and function, as in other patriarchal religions, Muslim women are buried alive in contradictions. They are equal; no, superior; no, inferior—to men, to snakes, to witches. Make no mistake: an Islamic woman without a man, especially a woman with children, isn't remotely like a fish without a bicycle.

This woman had five children, aged one to eight years, and was recently separated from her husband. She had trouble making her last month's rent. She surely feared a descent into poverty and probably homelessness. (As of this writing she is not granting interviews.) Ahead lay the streets. Welfare. Welfare hotels. Drugs, prostitution, guns, knives, gambling, drunkenness, and all manner of spiritual death. But for a woman with the option of deliverance, it wasn't inevitable.

Some years after shedding my Muslim garb, I had a baby and ended up homeless and on welfare myself. Not long after, I organized a welfare rights center, where we (the mothers trapped in this system) tried, among other things, to sort out the differences between "us" and "them" (mothers not on welfare). One subject was the stereotype of child abuse. It was something each of us understood at some terribly private gut level, but never articulated outside our circle; even then, we were cautious.

My own revelation came when my daughter was about a year old. At one point, she was sick and cried almost nonstop for a week. I was experiencing severe sleep deprivation coupled with the trauma of being unable to comfort her. For one horrible moment, I felt like hurling her against the wall. Fortunately, my mother came by unexpectedly and held the baby for a couple of hours, giving me time to gather composure. My daughter's fever broke and we both survived. But ever since, I have understood child abuse. And any parent who claims not to understand it in that context, ain't hardly trying.

I had been very close to where Ameenah Abdus-Salaam was. On another level, our circumstances were very different. A homeless mother of five (I had only one) has virtually no chance of being taken in by friends or family for more than a night or two. A homeless mother of four or more has only a 16 percent chance of keeping her children together. If she stays in an abandoned building with them and gets caught, they'll be taken away for "neglect." Still, there are commonalities shared by women of all races and religions, from rural to urban poverty. The merciless anxiety, the humiliation of being shuttled back and forth like herded animals, the stress of keeping kids in school, are constant. Only the details vary.

In New York City, if she were able to keep them together, at some point they would approach an Emergency Assistance Unit (EAU), which is obligated to shelter them in some way. This would mean waiting for hours, sometimes even days, on plastic chairs or the bare floor. If the family didn't eat pork, they'd eat nothing, since baloney sandwiches are about all they'd get for several meals. Some nights they might be moved (often after midnight) to a roach, lice, and rat infested welfare hotel for a few hours. In the morning the family would be shuttled back to wait again.

If they were lucky, after some days they would finally be placed in a welfare hotel or "transitional" shelter. These often provide less space per family member than that required for jail cells. Because the family was large, they wouldn't even get apartment referrals from city workers until after they'd been in this hell for months. (One rural homeless mother told me her family was placed in a motel with bars instead of windows and not one store or school within walking distance. She was at the mercy of a barely functional shuttle system for the homeless.)

At first, many mothers try to continue taking children to their previous schools. In New York City, this usually means traveling with them (other babies in tow) to another borough in the morning and returning for them in the afternoon. When one child is too sick to travel, none go to school. After a while, the mother might try to place the children in a school closer to the shelter. Legal, yes. Easy, no. If the mother does accomplish this, other kids in the new school will soon realize her children are "untouchables." School life will become anathema to her kids. They'll begin to adopt the coping mechanisms of other homeless kids who *will* associate with them.

Night brings scant respite. Police sirens. Gunshots from outside or down the hall. Families fighting. Too many people and too few beds, often with neither sheets nor blankets, much less pillows. The mattresses have long since burst like pastry puffs. Bedbugs pinch.

Those of us who are lucky have a little stove in the room. I'll never forget the first time I used one in a welfare hotel. I had just added eggs to the frying pan when swarms of roaches scrambled out of the lit burner in every direction—including into the frying pan. It was days before I could bring myself to try it again. All the things most people take for granted become little horrors.

If the Abdus-Salaam family emerged from the "temporary" shelter intact and were placed in an apartment, the world would think their problems solved. But now they would be a welfare family. Overnight she would switch from homeless victim to society's victimizer. Her living conditions would not improve nor her stress diminish, but she would join the larger class of poor women—despised abusers of the system—welfare mothers. To have come this far would have been a heroic feat, but what would be said of her is that she's a drain on national resources, has too many children she shouldn't have had if she couldn't afford to, and she doesn't "work."

On welfare, the chances of having enough money to live in a remotely decent neighborhood and pay for basic human needs are laughable—even in New York, where welfare benefits are "high." On the day when the Abdus-Salaam family almost came to total halt, the *maximum* monthly grant in New York City for a mother and five children was $814.20—or *less than three fifths of the federal poverty threshold for the same size family.* The *average* New York grant for six was $655 per month. (In January 1990 there was a slight, almost negligible increase in aggregate benefits.) Assuming the family received the maximum, the rent allotment would have been $349. Assuming the absurd—that they could find habitable housing for that price in New York or most any other U.S. city—they would be left with $465.20, or about $2.50 per person, per day, for most of their food. (Food stamps would provide less than two weeks of nutritionally adequate food for the month.) That same $2.50 must cover some of their medical expenses, and *all* their utilities, toothpaste, toilet paper, furniture, soap, baby bottles, diapers, laundry, transportation, kitchen utensils, and clothing. If Ms. Abdus-Salaam lived in South Dakota, she'd have had just about $1.88 for all those things. If she were a single mother living in California aged 25 or less, she'd have a 98 percent chance of landing on welfare. In New York, if she took one subway ride in search of an elusive job, she'd use up over 90 percent of her daily ration. If she's menstruating and needs to buy a box of sanitary napkins, she'd have to dip into her children's share. Like millions of women, she has at her disposal only one commodity guaranteed to produce sufficient income to keep her family together: her body. For some women that's unthinkable; for example, to a devout Muslim, even survival does not justify such a damning act. Yet to kill herself—only herself—would be to act irresponsibly to her children. Had Mr. Abdus-Salaam died instead of leaving the family, everything would have been different.

Ameenah would have been the recipient of sympathy and support. As a widow with minor children, she would become a Social Security recipient instead of a welfare mother. (The maximum family benefit for survivor families on Social Security in 1989—$1,898.90 per month—could be enough to continue living modestly where she was. While this sum is hardly lavish, the family would remain above poverty.) No social policy experts would go nuts because she didn't have a "job." In fact, she would be thought a good mother for taking care of her children full-time, "at least while they're small." If and when she did get a paying job, she could earn thousands of dollars without a reduction in her Social Security check. (On welfare, a job would be taxed at 100 percent. Outside of minimal work-related expenses, for the most part her welfare check would be reduced one dollar for every dollar she was paid.) The message: the needs and rights of women and children are determined by the nature of their prior relationship to a man; the only difference between "survivor" families and "welfare" families is the imprimatur of the father. How did such a cruel policy come to be?

Whose Welfare?

The Social Security Act of 1935 was the legislative blast-off point. From the start it had the aim of protecting men—and only incidentally their families—from the vagaries of the marketplace. It insured most citizens, but *not* mothers separated from living husbands. The elderly—men, by more than two to one because of their laborforce participation rates back then—were designated beneficiaries of old age insurance. It was also this bill that created unemployment insurance, intended primarily to cover males temporarily disjointed from the waged labor market. Widows (the *good* single mothers/wives) and their children were to receive survivors' benefits. (Early on, if the father divorced his wife two minutes before he died, she was not eligible for "his" Social Security benefits.) Children with living but absent fathers were almost left out, but Frances Perkins and others fought to cover them through what came to be called Aid to Dependent Children (ADC). ADC kids were presumed to live with their mothers, as in fact almost all did. But *no sum of money was designated for the women*; Perkins lost that one. It wasn't until the 1950s that the caretaker parent (mother) was added to the beneficiary unit, and ADC was changed to AFDC, or Aid to *Families* with Dependent Children.

   AFDC is the program most frequently thought of today as "welfare"; 94 percent of its recipients are single mothers and their children. Conservatives, especially during the Reagan era, argued recipients opted out of the job market in favor of plentiful dollars on the dole, offered by Lyndon Johnson's Great Society legacy. In fact, for most of the post 1960s, the purchasing power of cash assistance to poor families plummeted, though aggregate social spending soared. The Great Society was a culprit—but for different reasons than those given by Reaganites. *It emphasized a service strategy to the near exclusion of income security*—with the long-term effect of eroding the income security of millions of people, thousands of whom became homeless. The conceptual framework that supported this disaster held into the 1990s, long after the nation had surrendered in the War on Poverty.

War (Games) on Poverty

The foundation for the Great Society was laid in the Kennedy administration. Income maintenance had been ruled out; it was thought to breed a degenerative social disease—dependency. (There was no rigorous examination of this notion, although income maintenance was really the same as Social Security payments to survivor families, and "dependency" didn't destroy *them*.)

President Johnson declared War on Poverty not only because he felt the political necessity to carry on where Kennedy left off, but because big spending programs aimed at reducing the effects of poverty had been his turf as far back as the New Deal. He liked programs that doled out contracts across the country. Although income maintenance strategy was discussed during (and after) his administration, he too rejected it. But he did appoint an investigatory Commission on Income Maintenance Programs, which continued into the Nixon administration. Barbara Jordan, then a Texas state senator, was one of the few commission members not from the business community; still, even dominated by such stalwart capitalists as IBM's Thomas Watson and the Rand Corporation's Henry Rowen, the commission ultimately endorsed the "creation of a universal income supplement program . . . to all members of the population in need."

Why did Johnson reject income redistribution? The decline in the industrial base had limited certain jobs, and Democratic reform movements had put a stranglehold on party machines accustomed to wielding power through the jobs *they* controlled. Johnson's War on Poverty must have seemed an excellent chance to rebuild the party machine. So services emerged with regularity, each new "need" defined by the helping industry and by elected officials shagging dollars or votes. (When it works to their advantage, Republicans have shown they can also use service money to control allegiances. But generally, Republican conservatives, while railing about "big government," hand out their patronage through the military. Government spending is rarely about social remedies *or* defense; it's a contemporary form of patronage.)

The Great Society programs were the perfect vehicle for distributing patronage on a grand scale: Community Action, Vista, Model Cities. The service (plus economic development) strategy was to achieve a marriage of otherwise feuding factions: mayors, poor people (who at first had cause for optimism), civil rights leaders, liberals, and the press. Were it not for the Vietnam war, Johnson had every reason to believe reelection in the bag. His programs were shoring up a deteriorating political machine while providing the rhetorical posture for an end to poverty.

Among the War on Poverty designers was Kennedy administration holdover Richard Boone, who repeatedly urged citizen participation in the Office of Economic Opportunity (OEO) programs, believing institutional change possible only with the "maximum feasible participation" of community (poor) people. Community Action Agencies (CAAs) were hatched to do the job.

But with the exception of a few highly publicized locations, input by poor people was nonexistent. In *Betrayal of the Poor*, Stephen Rose wrote that no poor people or neighborhood representatives were involved in any of the 20 cities, although — *after* programs were designed and money budgeted — some members of groups to be served appeared on the agencies' boards of directors. In *The Great Society's Poor Law*, Sar Levitan concurred, noting that "affluent citizens who happened to live in a 'target area' could represent the poor. The law could therefore be observed without having a single low-income person on the CAA board."

CAAs genuinely committed to citizen participation were either swiftly defunded or never got out of the planning stages. Participation of poor people never took place; only the appearance of it occurred.

The mirage of participation had value, though. The impact of the civil rights, women's, and welfare rights movements was felt strongly through the 1970s, so that it was politically uncouth for advantaged parties to act in the absence of input from the disadvantaged. By manipulating the input, the social welfare establishment could appear to address poverty with the imprimatur of poor people (most commonly, women on welfare). The resulting aura of equality made it easier to get and maintain government and private foundation grants. The pretense of poor people's participation thus legitimized the social welfare institutions. The Great Society *did* offer a guaranteed income—to the social welfare establishment. By the 1980s, genuflecting to "participation" was dispensed with altogether.

Meanwhile, various other legislative events also displaced income needs in favor of "service." The 1962 and 1967 Amendments to Social Security Law set the stage. First, the federal government moved to increase the states' revenue share for family services from 50 to 75 percent. Second, states were allowed to contract these services out to *nongovernmental agencies* (previously, local welfare departments were the sole service providers using federal dollars).

Those states that previously and systematically had denied welfare benefits to millions of needy families (especially black families) were now eager to qualify for the windfall revenue sharing. But first they had to find people categorically eligible for welfare. Furthermore, in order to capture services dollars from the feds, states would actually have to pay the families welfare benefits (which were also federally subsidized, but not so liberally). Not to worry. Cash assistance levels were set *by* the states, so it was (1) possible to find families eligible for welfare (to get the federal funding for services) and (2) *set AFDC levels so low that families would stay poor.*

The welfare rolls climbed so fast the phenomenon was characterized as an "explosion." This legislated windfall to states (combined with the War on Poverty strategy of delivering megabucks to state and local governments for "services" to the poor) set off a spending spree—that was peaking just when purchasing power of cash assistance began to decline.

The decrease was coupled with an increase in rhetoric about "dependency" and the necessity for women to "work." Never mind that the jobs didn't (and still don't) exist that would pay enough to lift them out of poverty. Never mind that single parenting under any circumstances *is* "work," and even harder work in poverty.

The Birth of an Industry

What became the professionalization of being human took off, bloating under government contracts. For every poverty problem, a self-perpetuating profession proposed to ameliorate the situation without altering the poverty. In *The Politics of a Guaranteed Income,* published in 1973, Daniel Patrick Moynihan noted the "astonishing consistency" with which middle-class professionals "improved" the condition of lower-class groups by devising schemes that would first improve their *own* condition. It doesn't take a genius to figure out that paying the administrators of a homeless shelter two or three thousand dollars a month for each family instead of providing a permanent apartment is ludicrous. Yet the most massive growth in AFDC spending in the 1980s has been for just that purpose. Furthermore, to keep the "service" engine stoked, every manner of failure has been ascribed to the families themselves. Laziness. Cheating. Dependency. The families lack resources to defend themselves, though the "helping" institutions always have government and/or foundation funds to lobby (ostensibly on the families' behalf) for *more* funding.

What has happened over the last quarter century *has* been an income redistribution scheme, the most disturbing one this country has ever seen: a redistribution from poor women and children to middle-class professionals — with men at the top calling the shots.

This has been done not only with government tax dollars but also with private charitable (and tax deductible) dollars. The United Way. The American Red Cross. The Children's Aid Society. The independent federations of Protestant, Jewish, and Catholic charities. Hands Across America. . . . Each year, the New York *Times* begs its readers daily, from Thanksgiving to February, for its "Neediest Cases Fund." For nearly a century the *Times* has reported that all the money goes to the poor through eight social service agencies who distribute it, with no funds spent on "administration or fundraising." This is a wild exaggeration from the venerable newspaper; most of the money pays workers' salaries in the agencies, and has for years. Not to mention that the male directors of several of these already obese agencies are paid salaries in excess of $100,000 annually. Not bad for social work.

The "Workfare" Myth

In the great welfare reform debates of the late 1980s, social welfare professionals fell all over each other running after more funding (for themselves) through the jobs, training, and child care provisions of the so-called welfare reform bill, ironically presided over by Moynihan. Forgotten were the words of the President's Commission on Income Maintenance two decades earlier: "Services cannot be a substitute for adequate incomes; they cannot pay rent or buy food for a poor family." (The few surviving organizations of poor women put guaranteed income at the top of their lists, but they are rarely listened to. After all, they have no money.)

What stalled the "reform" debates for months was the issue of how much money would be allocated for those running the "reform" programs, and a turf war over whether the programs would be run by welfare departments or contracted out to private charities. (Everybody knew getting the women to "work" didn't mean getting them out of poverty.) Welfare rolls dipped slightly and briefly, but are now on the rise again nationwide. And the number and percent of single-parent female families living in profound poverty continues to climb. The relentless theme, from both the right and the left, still is to get those "nonworking" mothers to work.

In fact, the key to the tragedy of U.S. welfare policies is the notion of work—specifically, the unpaid and uncounted labor of women outside the waged labor market. About the only time the word labor is applied to women outside the wage system is in reference to the birthing process.

If any woman reading this were penniless today and went to apply for welfare to feed her children, she would not receive her first welfare check for about a month. Not because the welfare is prohibited from giving her money sooner, but because they are allowed to take 30 days to determine the obvious: that she is poor. The 30-day deadline might come and go with no relief. Or destructive policies plus bureaucratic bungling might prevent a check from ever coming. If she did make it onto the rolls, she might—like at least one million needy U.S. citizens every year—be cut off despite being still legally entitled to welfare. This process has been given the name "churning" by the welfare department, as needy people are routinely cut off and sometimes put back on months later.

One ghastly result of such U.S. social policy is that far more children die from poverty than slip away at the hands of mothers like Ameenah Abdus-Salaam. Twelve times as many poor children die in fires than do nonpoor children. Eight times as many die of disease, according to a study done by the state of Maine—where, by the way, 98 percent of the population is white. Thirty times as many low birth weight babies die as do normal weight babies. In 1987, one in two homeless mothers in New York reported *losing* weight during pregnancy. Even at the bottom, luck plays a role: whose kid is hit by a stray bullet, whose kitchen stove explodes because it was used nonstop as the only source of heat in a frozen apartment, whose infant dies of pneumonia. Poverty is the number one killer of children in the U.S.A. Murder by malfeasance.

Children are poor because their mothers are poor.

Ameenah Abdus-Salaam's tragic acts may not be so mysterious, after all. The miracle is that more women, facing similar anguish, don't do the same.

On September 19, 1990, I attended a court hearing. Ameenah Abdus-Salaam's male attorney had pleaded her "not responsible by reason of mental disease or defect." Two court-appointed phychiatrists agreed, and recommended she be released—no longer a danger to herself or anyone else. District Attorney John Santucci's office refused to accept the recommendation until another psychiatrist, of the D.A.'s choosing, can evaluate her. The case could drag on indefinitely. The male judge has consistently refused to set bail. Ameenah herself was not "produced" for the proceedings. All four walls of the courtroom are of elaborately carved wood. Above the judge's throne, in raised gold letters, gleam the words *In God We Trust.* However misguided it may seem to outsiders, that was the one thing Ameenah Abdus-Salaam intended to do.

Suggestions for Further Reading

Amott, Teresa, and Dorothy Amott. *Caught in the Crisis: Women and the U.S. Economy.* New York: Monthly Review Press, June 1993.

Amott, Theresa L., and Julie Atthaei. *Race, Gender, and Work: A Multicultural History of Women in the U.S.* Boston: South End Press, 1991.

Bartlett, Donald L., and James B. Steele. *America: What Went Wrong.* Kansas City: Andrews and McMeel, 1992.

Blumberg, Paul. *Inequality in an Age of Decline.* Oxford, England: Oxford University Press, 1980.

Children's Defense Fund: *The State of America's Children.* Children's Defense Fund, 25 E Street NW, Washington, D.C. 20001. Published annually.

Children's Defense Fund and Northeastern University's Center for Labor Market Studies. *Vanishing Dreams: The Economic Plight of America's Young Families.* Washington, D.C.: Children's Defense Fund, 1992.

Danziger, Sheldon, and Peter Gottschalk, eds. *Uneven Tides Rising: Inequality in America.* New York: Russell Sage Foundation, 1993.

De Lone, Richard. *Small Futures.* New York: Harcourt Brace Jovanovich, 1978.

DeMott, Benjamin. *The Imperial Middle.* New York: William Morrow, 1990.

Domhoff, G. William. *Who Rules America Now?* New York: Simon and Schuster, 1983.

Hacker, Andrew. *Two Nations.* New York: Scribner's, 1992.

Hacker, Andrew. *US: A Statistical Portrait of the American People.* New York: Viking Press, 1983.

Horwitz, Lucy, and Lou Ferleger. *Statistics for Social Change.* Boston: South End Press, 1980.

Jaynes, Gerald David, and Robin M. Williams, Jr., eds. *A Common Destiny: Blacks and American Society.* Washington, D.C.: National Academy Press, 1989.

Kozol, Jonathan. *Savage Inequalities: Children in America's Schools.* New York: Crown Publishers, 1991.

Lav, Iris J., et al. *The States and the Poor: How Budget Decisions Affected Low Income People in 1992.* Washington, D.C.: Center on Budget and Policy Priorities and Albany, N.Y.: Center for the Study of the States, 1993.

Newman, Katherine S. *Falling from Grace: The Experience of Downward Mobility in the American Middle Class.* New York: Vintage Books, 1989.

Phillips, Kevin. *The Politics of the Rich and the Poor.* New York: Random House 1990.

Polakrow, Valerie. *Lives on the Edge: Single Women and Their Children in Other America.* Chicago: University of Chicago Press, 1993.

Rix, Sara E. for the Women's Research and Education Institute. *The American Woman, 1993–94 Status Report.* New York: W. W. Norton, 1994.

Schwarz, John E., and Thomas J. Volgy. *The Forgotten Americans: Thirty Million Working Poor in the Land of Opportunity.* New York: W. W. Norton, 1992.

Sennet, Richard, and Jonathan Cobb. *The Hidden Injuries of Class.* New York: Vintage Books, 1973.

Stallard, Karin, Barbara Ehrenreich, and Holly Sklar. *Poverty in the American Dream: Women and Children First.* Boston: South End Press, 1983.

Turner, Margery Austin, et al. *Opportunities Denied, Opportunities Diminished: Racial Discrimination in Hiring.* Washington, D.C.: Urban Institute Press, 1991.

Women's Action Coalition. *WAC States the Facts about Women.* New York: The New Press, 1993.

Yates, Michael. *Longer Hours, Fewer Jobs: Employment and Unemployment in the United States.* New York: Monthly Review Press, 1993.

In addition to these books, the following organizations are good sources for obtaining current statistics analyzed in terms of race, class, and gender:

The Association for American Indian Affairs, 432 Park Avenue South, New York, NY 10016.
The Council on Interracial Books for Children, 1841 Broadway, New York, NY 10023.
Institute for Women's Policy Research, 1400 20th Street, NW, Suite 104, Washington, DC.
The National Urban League, Inc., 500 East 62nd Street, New York, NY 10021.
The National Committee on Pay Equity, 1201 Sixteenth Street, NW, Room 422, Washington, DC 20036.
Southern Regional Council, Inc., 60 Walton, NW, Atlanta, GA 30303.

PART IV

Many Voices, Many Lives

Statistics can tell us a great deal about living conditions in a given society, but they paint only part of the picture. They can tell us that more and more women and children are living in poverty, but they cannot make that poverty real to us. They can tell us that a woman is raped in the United States at least as often as every two minutes, but they cannot help us share her pain, anger, or terror.[1] They can tell us that one-third of the adult population in this country cannot read well enough to get through the front page of a daily newspaper, but they cannot translate those numbers into lived experience.[2] For that, we must turn to stories about people's lives.

Who will tell these stories? For many years, it was difficult to find books about the experiences of women and minorities. Even books about breast-feeding and childbirth were authored almost exclusively by male "experts," who described and defined a reality that they had never known. White sociologists and anthropologists set themselves up as experts on Black, Hispanic, and American Indian experiences and offered elaborate, critical accounts of the family structure and life-style of each. Novels chronicling the growth to manhood of young white males from the upper or upper-middle class were routinely assigned in high-school and college English courses and examined for "universal themes," while novels about women's lives or the experiences of minorities or working people were relegated to "special-interest"

173

courses and treated as marginal. In short, by definition serious scholarship, real science, and great literature has been that which was produced by well-to-do white males and most often focused exclusively on their experiences; accounts of the lives of other groups, if available at all, were rarely written by members of these groups.

During the recent past, more accounts of the lives of ordinary people have become available, thus bridging some of the gaps in the limited experience each of us brings to our study of race, class, and gender. The selections in Part IV are offered as a way of putting flesh and blood around the bare-bones facts provided in Part III. Some of the selections are excerpts from novels; others are nonfiction pieces drawn from magazines and books. All of them are offered as a vehicle for shedding our own particular identity, at least for a few minutes, and finding out what it is like to live as someone who is different from us. They can begin to suggest to us something of the price that is paid in the destruction of human lives by the racism, sexism, homophobia, and class differences that define our world, at the same time that they reflect and celebrate the richness of a variety of cultures and life-styles.

While race, class, and gender are the primary factors that define opportunity and limit possibility for people in the United States at this time, other factors can also have a significant impact on life choices: among them are religion, age, sexual orientation or preference, physical condition, and whether one lives in a rural or an urban area. Some of these factors are touched upon or highlighted in the selections included in Part IV. In some contexts, these factors play a major role in shaping the way others treat us, in how much we are paid, in what kinds of educational opportunities are available to us, and in where and how we live. In other contexts, these variables may well be irrelevant. Reading about them adds another dimension to our understanding of the complex set of additional factors that interact with issues of race, class, and gender.

But even as we acknowledge how much there is to learn from looking at the lives and experiences of many different people, there is also a danger in this project—the danger of overgeneralizing. It is easy to take the particular experience of one member of a group and attribute it to all members of that group. Many students who are members of a religious, racial, or ethnic minority have had the uncomfortable experience of being asked to speak for all Asians or all Latinas or all Jews at some point in their college experience. Failing to see members of minority groups as individuals is typical of a society where stereotyping flourishes. On the other hand, for the purposes of studying race, class, and gender, it is often necessary to look beyond individual differences and generalize about "Native Americans" or "Chicanas" or "men" in order to highlight aspects of their experience that are more typical of that group's experience than of others. As we have already seen, it would be naive to think that the individual exists in a vacuum, untouched by the racism, sexism, and class bias of society. Unless we understand something about the ways different *groups* experience life in the United States, we will never adequately understand the particular experiences of individual people.

The articles in this Part have been selected because they give us some sense of the diversity of life in the United States at the same time that they reflect some of the consequences of the racial, gender, and class inequalities documented in Part III. For the most part, these stories, articles, poems, and essays need no introduction. They speak for themselves.

NOTES

1. The statistic on rape is drawn from the FBI's Uniform Crime Report.

2. The statistic on literacy is drawn from an article Jonathan Kozol wrote for the *New York Times* Book Review Section, March 3, 1985. There he writes: "Among adults, 16 percent of whites, 44 percent of blacks and 56 percent of Hispanic people are either total, functional or marginal nonreaders."

Racial and Ethnic Minorities:
An Overview

*Beth B. Hess, Elizabeth W. Markson,
and Peter J. Stein*

Native Americans

The Native American tribes that populated North America before the arrival of Europeans were quickly defined as biologically and morally "inferior" to the more "civilized" newcomers who were only doing God's will in conquering the natives and taking their land. All Native Americans were categorized as "Indians" and their widely varying cultures treated with equal contempt. In addition to their losses in battle with the settlers, the tribes were also ravaged by diseases brought by the Europeans, against which they had no biological defenses (Thornton, 1987).

These ethnocentric assumptions followed the westward flow of white settlers, continually displacing the native tribes and absorbing their lands on the basis of treaties that were not intended to be taken seriously. During the late 1800s, entire tribes were forcibly relocated to reservations in sparsely populated areas with few natural resources—certainly not the farming or grazing lands that had been the basis of their traditional way of life. Here, too, disease and economic hardship followed, and the Native American population fell from several million to roughly 250,000 in 1900 (Thornton, 1987). By this time, also, an unknown number of Native Americans had joined the industrial labor force, intermarried, and disappeared into the multicultural urban population. In the 1950s and 1960s, many more left the reservations to live and work in cities, but rather than melt into the urban masses, these newcomers often formed cohesive communities in which diverse Native American traditions were maintained but also modified to fit the city environment (Weibel-Orlando, 1991).

Today, there are about two million Americans of native ancestry, including Eskimo and Aluet populations in Alaska. Slightly over one-third live on reservations or other designated areas held in trust by the federal government and administered by the Bureau of Indian Affairs (BIA) as part of the nineteenth-century treaties whereby tribal land was exchanged for protection of Indian rights. Although the treaties promised adequate housing, education, and health care, the history of the BIA has been one of almost total neglect and goal displacement, in which the billions allocated to the tribes have gone mostly to maintaining the bureaucracy that administers the funds. Not one of the more than 300 treaties between the tribes and the government of the United States has been honored (Richardson, 1993).

As a consequence of this pattern of *internal colonialism,* whereby native populations are treated as if they were foreign colonies, life on the reservation remains grim, marked by high rates of poverty and its consequences: homicide, suicide, family violence, school failure, infant mortality, alcohol-related diseases, diabetes, and tuberculosis (Bachman, 1992). Because relative poverty also characterizes Native Americans outside the reservations, their life expectancy is the lowest of all subpopulations in the United States.

Yet, the past decade has also been one of great hope for Native Americans. Court cases requiring compliance with the treaties have resulted in favorable judgments for many tribes, including 300,000 acres of prime land in Maine returned to the Penobscot and Passamaquoddy, and fishing rights restored to Great Lakes tribes. College graduation rates are inching upward, although they remain much lower than for Asian and white students (Cage, 1993). And changes at the federal level have encouraged self-determination in spending priorities on the reservations, bypassing the BIA (Richardson, 1993).

The major factor in the improving economic status of American Indians, however, has been the introduction of gambling casinos on the reservations. The original treaties guaranteed tribal rights to local resources as well as freedom from control by the state governments. These conditions brought great wealth to the Oklahoma reservations, where oil deposits had been discovered earlier. More recently, the tribes have invoked the same treaty rights to exempt the reservations from state-level prohibitions against gambling establishments. As a result, casinos have been opened on several Indian reservations, bringing jobs and millions of dollars in profits to formerly poverty stricken tribes. For example, the Pequot Indian casino in Connecticut has been so successful that tribal leaders are negotiating to acquire thousands of additional acres from local landowners. The casino is one of the largest employers in the state and its proposed expansion will make the facility one of the largest in the world (Johnson, 1993). This has prompted Donald Trump to file a lawsuit arguing that the Indians are taking unfair advantage of honest businesspersons such as himself.

There has also been a revival of Indian cultural pride and an increasing interest in preserving the diversity of tribal history, customs, and crafts. Perhaps all these trends together will finally bring hope and help to the tens of thousands of Native Americans still trapped in the cycle of poverty and violence.

African Americans

The history of slavery in America raises many important questions about the construction of difference. How can one group of humans treat another as if they were not human? Only by defining "the other" as so very different as to be "non-human." Obviously, this process is easiest when the "other" has little resemblance to "us," as in the case of black African tribal peoples compared to the European Christians on this continent who bought and sold them. Within the overall system of dehumanization and degradation, the actual conditions of slave life varied greatly from colony to colony, by the type of agriculture involved, and over time as the black population increased and the mix between African- and American-born slave changed (Kolchin, 1993).

Of all enslaved Africans brought to the Americas, only about 10 percent or 650,000 were sold to owners in the North American colonies, the remainder going to South America. But because the living and working conditions for slaves in the colonies were somewhat better than elsewhere, this relatively small population expanded rapidly, so that the number of native-born Blacks made further trade with Africa unnecessary (Kolchin, 1993). Thus, by 1860, most of the three million Blacks in the United States were American-born and racial stereotypes changed to reflect the paternalistic view of slaves as children rather than as untamed savages.

Over time, African-American slaves developed a unique culture, blended from native elements and those imposed by their owners, within which some degree of *autonomy* (self-direction) could be exercised. The subculture of slavery, as with any other, provided a supportive environment, alternative definitions of reality, a basis for positive self-image, and a strength necessary for survival. Although whites were of two minds about introducing Christianity to the slaves, the idea of converting "heathen" won out over the definitions of Blacks as unredeemable. Not only did Christianity spread rapidly among the slaves, but it was reworked in such a way as to become a force for ultimately challenging the system of slavery itself.

Not all African Americans lived as slaves in the South; many made their way to the North and West where they also met with prejudice and discrimination, but were at least free from everyday controls. Similarly, the formal end of slavery in 1865 brought one kind of freedom but left former slaves under the control of a range of "Jim Crow" laws designed to limit their choices of jobs, residential location, right to vote, and so forth. It was these limitations, written into law, that created the system of de jure segregation that was dismantled only in the 1960s.

Today, African Americans compose about 12 percent of the U.S. population, but remain disadvantaged along many dimensions of social stratification. Blacks are overrepresented at the lower end of the income and occupation hierarchies, and underrepresented in positions of political and economic power. In addition, the employment and income gaps that had been narrowing between 1965 and 1980 began to widen once again, as the Reagan and Bush administrations cut programs that assisted racial minorities and failed to enforce regulations designed to reduce discrimination in housing and jobs. The result has been labeled *American apart-*

heid to refer to the systematic residential segregation of African Americans in areas where employment opportunities are almost nonexistent (Massey and Denton, 1993). Unlike the experience of other urban minorities, the isolation of Blacks has been more intense over a longer period of time while the kinds of jobs available to earlier waves of immigrants have been moved to where the labor force is whiter (Neckerman and Kirschenman, 1991). Even Atlanta, Georgia, once thought to be a symbol of Black political and economic progress, is experiencing the effects of the new apartheid (Orfield and Ashkinaze, 1991).

Institutionalized racism remains a powerful determinant of the life chances of African Americans. In 1992, for example, rejection rates for mortgage and home improvement loans were twice as high for Blacks as for whites *at the same income level* (Quint, 1992). Employers continue to prefer hiring immigrant workers who do not speak English rather than American-born Blacks willing to work for lower wages (Massey and Denton, 1993). Social Security disability benefits are refused more often to African Americans than to whites at similar levels of physical impairment (Labaton, 1992). Blacks are twice as likely as whites to be fired from the U.S. Postal Service, even when their work records and educational backgrounds are identical (Zwerling and Silver, 1992). Even middle-class African Americans continue to face hostile treatment in restaurants and stores (Feagin, 1991).

The employment and income gulf between whites and Blacks will grow even larger as Americans demand that the federal government cut its own labor force as a deficit reduction measure. This is so because minority groups have always found the government a more willing employer than private businesses. Thus, any reduction in public employment will have its most negative impact on African Americans. As a consequence, the proportion of blacks attaining middle-class occupational status will also decline, reversing one of the more favorable statistical trends of the past three decades.

What happens when immigrants are also Black? Their fate depends on the skills they bring, their family structure, and whether or not they speak English. Thus, French-speaking unskilled Black Haitians are intercepted at sea and turned back. In contrast, English-speaking, relatively well-educated Blacks from the Carribean region have enjoyed unusual economic and political success in New York City, but only within the limits to upward mobility set by race as a "master status" (Kasinitz, 1992). Despite the obvious influence of skin color, most white Americans continue to interpret racial inequality in terms of personal variables—less ability, less willingness to learn—rather than situational factors such as discrimination (Sigelman and Welch, 1993).

Asian Americans

Asian Americans represent at least a dozen distinct cultures and language groups, yet a tendency to classify all Asians together has dominated immigration policy and popular attitudes. In fact, the Pan-Asian (*pan,* or *all*) community is not only increasingly varied, but its composition has changed dramatically between 1970 and 1990, as shown in Figure 1. Whereas Americans of Japanese origin were the largest Asian subgroup in 1970, today they rank below Americans of Chinese and Philippine ancestry. The recent wave of immigrants from Southeast Asia has added diversity and numbers to the Pan-Asian population.

In general, Asian Americans are considered to be examples of a *model minority* for having fulfilled the American Dream of upward mobility as a result of hard work. And indeed, poverty rates for most Asian subgroups are lower than for the nation as a whole; average family incomes are even slightly above that of non-Hispanic whites; and educational achievement the highest of any race/ethnic subgroup (Lott and Felt, 1991). These global numbers, however, hide great variation between and within various Asian populations.

Chinese Americans

In both the United States and Canada, in the mid nineteenth century, young Chinese men were imported (often forcibly put on ships in the Chinese city of Shanghai—hence, "shanghaied") to work on the transcontinental railroad. Not allowed to become citizens and forbidden to send for a wife or marry an American, those who remained formed an almost exclusively male community in West Coast cities in the United States and Canada. The gambling, opium smoking, and prostitution that characterized these segregated all-male communities only reinforced the socially constructed image of Chinese as anti-family and immoral (Anderson, 1991).

Chinese neighborhoods were targets of white mob violence as racial fears were periodically fanned by politicians up until the outbreak of World War II in 1941, when the Chinese suddenly became the "good" Asians in contrast to the "evil Japs."

Restrictive immigration laws were greatly revised in 1965, by which time many Chinese were finally granted citizenship and allowed to bring family members to North America. Over the past three decades, the Chinese American community has grown in size and wealth. The educational success of Chinese American youth has been exceptional, in part due to the traditional high value placed on learning in Chinese culture. The more important influence, however, appears to be the achievement motivation derived from their parents' involvement in family-owned small businesses such as restaurants, laundries, garment manufacturing, and tourist stores in Chinatowns (Sanchirico, 1991).

Studies of the assimilation patterns of minority groups often focus on the degree to which the group has carved out a special place in the urban economy—an *ethnic/racial enclave*—in which they control local businesses and establish a protective subculture, often reinforced by discrimination and other segregating forces. The enclave nurtures economic stability and serves as a springboard to upward mobility. In the case of Chinese Americans, various Chinatowns have served this purpose well, thanks in large part to an influx of money from Hong Kong, Taiwan,

FIGURE 1
Distribution of Asian American Population, 1970–1990.

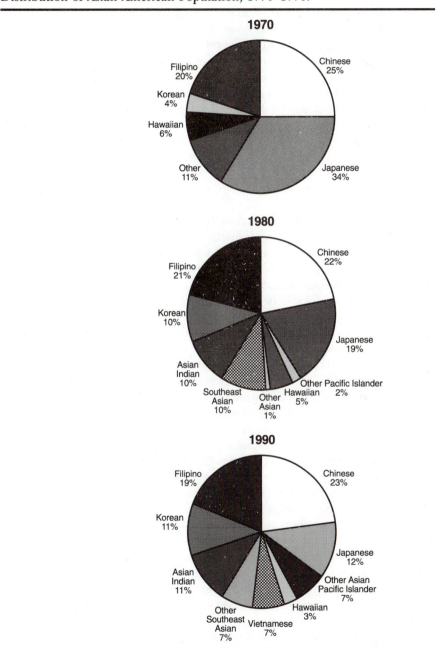

Source: U.S. Bureau of the Census, *We, the Asian Americans* (Washington, D.C.: GPO, 1973) p. 2; U.S. Bureau of the Census, *We, the Asian and Pacific Islander Americans* (Washington, D.C.: GPO, 1988) p. 2; *Statistical Abstract of the United States, 1992*, p. 21.

and other "offshore" territories. As a result, banks and mortgage companies are able to provide loans for new businesses and homes, ultimately encouraging assimilation among the children and grandchildren of immigrants who move up and out to the suburbs (Zhou and Logan, 1991; Zhou, 1992).

Despite the general prosperity of the community, many Chinese who remain in the enclave and most new immigrants live in poverty and are exploited at work. In addition, with so much offshore money entering the enclave, the line between legitimate and illegitimate business is often blurred.

Local merchants today are targets for gangs of young Asians involved in the protection racket, as well as drugs, gambling, and prostitution—in the grand tradition of organized crime in America.

Japanese Americans

The path to structural assimilation for Japanese Americans has also been marked by discrimination, prejudice, segregation, and official violence. Lacking the numbers and resources to form an enclave of the size and influence of a Chinatown, Japanese communities on the West Coast were located in areas where members enjoyed great success as farmers and gardeners. Like all Asians, Japanese immigrants were forbidden to own land or become citizens; they had, however, been able to emigrate as husband and wife, and because their children were born in the United States, the second generation, which soon outnumbered the first, were American citizens.

Nonetheless, following the Japanese attack on Pearl Harbor and the outbreak of World War II in 1941, all Japanese Americans living on the West Coast were forcibly rounded up and sent to detention camps for the duration of the war. Although the reason given for this forced evacuation was "national security," the more powerful motives were economic and emotional. Japanese agricultural successes had long been envied by their white neighbors, who eagerly took over the property that had been confiscated without compensation. Emotionally, the social construction of the Japanese as untrustworthy Asians could go unchallenged because of their relative isolation. In contrast, in Hawaii, where national security really was at stake, the Japanese had become so integrated into mainstream institutions that they were able to avoid such fear and mistrust (Parrillo, 1994).

The experience of the detention camps had several long-term effects on the Japanese American community, primarily through the erosion of power of men over women and of elders over juniors (Fugita and O'Brien, 1991). Many of the younger detainees were able to leave the camps to attend school elsewhere in the United States or to serve in the armed forces. This weakening of traditional authority speeded up the process of assimilation once the war ended and the camps were emptied.

No longer tied to agricultural occupations or to an ethnic enclave, native-born Japanese Americans were both geographically and socially mobile, attending college in large numbers, moving into white collar jobs in electronics and engineering, and marrying outside the Asian community. Few are left who remember the camps, and only in 1988 did Congress approve legislation that officially apologized for the forced detention and that offered a tax-free payment of $20,000 to surviving victims—very little and extremely late.

Other Asians

Policy changes in the 1980s led to the lifting of other restrictions on immigration from various parts of Asia. The outcome, as shown in Figure 1 has been a large influx of people from Southeast Asia: Cambodia, Thailand, Laos, and Vietnam, representing dozens of ethnic groups, each with its unique language and culture. Many of these new immigrants are from rural areas, with minimal education and job skills, and little knowledge of English—traits likely to arouse fear and hostility as well as inhibit economic integration. In addition, the most recent arrivals have faced greater than usual resentment because of growing competition for jobs among workers at the lower end of the occupational system. It does not take a crystal ball to predict that their assimilation will be slower and more problematic than that of earlier Asian immigrants.

In contrast, Asians from the Indian subcontinent entered the United States with educational credentials and technical skills, and have found their economic foothold in the pharmaceutical industry and health-care facilities. Although they, too, have experienced discrimination, their economic success allows greater choice of where to live. Recent arrivals from the Philippine Islands are also relatively well educated, with professional degrees in medicine, law, and engineering, even though most have had to settle for less prestigious jobs. Immigrants from Korea lack the educational background of the Asian Indians and Philippinos, but compensate with a powerful commitment to self-employment for the entire family. Koreans have been successful in operating small grocery stores in urban neighborhoods, although this often brings them into conflict with other minority groups resentful of the Korean's presence.

The New Ethnics

The "old ethnics" refers to the waves of immigrants from Europe. The "new ethnics," and fastest growing subgroups, come from South and Central America and from the Middle East.

Latinos

The Census categories of "Hispanic," "Spanish Origin," and the more recently preferred "Latino/a," are umbrella terms that cover a diverse although largely Catholic population. The four major subgroups of Spanish origin Americans,

FIGURE 2
Subgroups within the Hispanic Population of the United States, 1991

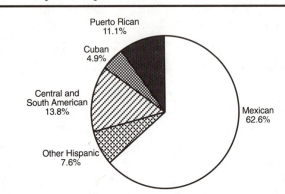

Source: U.S. Bureau of the Census, Series P20–455, "The Hispanic Population of the United States: March 1991," 1991: 2.

shown in Figure 2, are very different from one another in racial/ethnic ancestry, immigrant history, and current status. Together, however, they currently compose 10 percent of the population of the United States and are expected to outnumber African Americans as the nation's largest minority group by 2010. Their political influence, however, is diluted by the many divisions within this population, which is also stratified by socioeconomic status and skin color (Knouse et al., 1992).

MEXICAN AMERICANS (CHICANO/AS)   The largest Latino subgroup (62 percent) is of Mexican origin. Some are descendents of people who had settled in the Southwest territories before that area was annexed by the United States in 1848; others have lived in the United States for several generations; and many have entered more recently in response to employment opportunities in American factories close to the border.

Most Mexican Americans continue to live in the Southwest and in distinctly Mexican neighborhoods, or *barrios*. While language and culture set the Chicano community apart from the world of European Americans ("Anglos"), appearance also has an impact on their employment and earnings. Mexican American men with dark skin and/or Native American features receive significantly lower earnings than their more Anglo-looking peers, all other characteristics being equal. Although the stereotype of the Mexican farmhand persists, about 90 percent live in urban areas where the men typically find work as laborers and machine operators and the women as domestic servants or office cleaners.

Despite the fact that the great majority are legal residents, the social construction of "illegal alien" is often applied to all Chicanos (and even to all Latinos). As a consequence of economic discrimination and social isolation, upward mobility has been severely limited. Family income and educational attainment remain below the U.S. average, while family size is higher. Although the traditional extended family network continues to be a major source of economic and emotional support, many aspects of family life have undergone change, particularly with respect to the power of men and of elders. As Mexican American women become acculturated, educated, and part of the labor force, their power in the family and marriage is enhanced (Segura, 1993). Similarly, the children who are educated in America often have an advantage over their parents.

PUERTO RICANS   American citizens since 1917, Puerto Ricans arrived on the North American mainland in large numbers in the 1950s because of the collapse of the sugar industry on their island. The majority have settled in the Northeast, especially the New York/New Jersey/Connecticut area, where they have found employment in low-skill, low-pay service jobs. The ethnic enclave has not yet generated the kind of resources or opportunities for self-employment of many Asian communities. Nor has the overall economy produced the type of jobs that could serve as a springboard to upward mobility.

Puerto Ricans are characterized by a mixture of Spanish, Indian, and African ancestry, which subjects them to racial as well as ethnic barriers to upward mobility. Although the poverty rate for Puerto Rican Americans is close to 60 percent, and labor force participation rates for both men and women are below those for the population as a whole, their expectations of success are higher than are those of persons remaining on the Island.

There are some signs of positive upward movement in high school and college graduation rates, political influence, representation in the arts, and community control. On the negative side, dropout and unemployment rates remain high, and four in ten families are headed by a single parent (U.S. Bureau of the Census, P20–455, 1991).

CUBAN AMERICANS   The first wave of Cuban immigrants consisted of relatively well-educated and affluent people fleeing the revolution that brought Fidel Castro to power in the mid-1950s. This cultural and social elite, many of whom were descended from European Spaniards, settled in Miami, Florida, where a very successful ethnic enclave was established, which has gradually accumulated great political influence. Cuban Americans are better educated, wealthier, and more assimilated than the other subgroups. In contrast to other Latinos, this is an extremely conservative population, highly favored under the Reagan and Bush administrations that openly encouraged the Cubans' desire to overthrow the Castro regime and reestablish their power on the island.

Nonetheless, Miami Anglos remain mistrustful of their spanish-speaking neighbors, especially after Castro expelled another wave of immigrants in 1980 who were much poorer and less educated, and included former prisoners and inmates. Various attempts by Anglos to impose "English only" rules on the city government have ultimately failed in the courts. The primary opposition to Cuban American power today comes from local African Americans who feel that authorities have favored Latino immigrants over native-born Blacks.

In general, the success of the Cuban immigrants was largely due to the resources with which they entered, and later to the degree to which their conservative politics fit the spirit of the 1980s.

Middle Easterners

In recent years, a new group of immigrants has emerged as a visible urban minority: newcomers from the Middle Eastern countries of Egypt, Syria, Jordan, Lebanon, Iran, and Iraq. Relatively light-skinned, they bring many diverse cultures, languages, and religions to America. Some are ethnic Arabs, others not; most are Moslem, but not all; many are from affluent families, but others are working class youth; some are political refugees, but the majority seek economic opportunities (Parrillo, 1994). Their common denominator is the geographic area from which they come, and up until the 1990s their presence had not been a matter of public concern. The best estimates are that between three and four million Middle Easterners, primarily Moslem, currently reside in the United States. But because this is primarily a young adult population from countries with traditionally high fertility, the number could soon exceed six million, surpassing the size of the American Jewish population (Bernstein, 1993).

Assimilation has been made difficult by the demands of the Moslem religion, particularly the need to stop other activity and pray at particular hours during the day, and to observe many dietary (eating) rules. Family relationships and the role of women are also very different from those of the surrounding culture. But these typical problems of any new minority in America have been compounded in the 1990s by international events such as the war against Iraq and the emergence of terrorist groups on American soil. All "Arabs" have become objects of fear and hostility, although very few are a danger to public safety. This reaction is similar to the "yellow menace" scares that led to anti-Asian riots in California in the 1920s and to detention camps for Japanese Americans in the 1940s.

In reality, the Middle Eastern populations have in many ways fit the pattern of "model minorities," establishing ethnic/religious enclaves that provide employment and funding for businesses within the community. Middle Eastern communities depart from the model, however, in that their goal may not be assimilation but, rather, maintaining a unique heritage in the face of modernizing influences. The key institution here is the religious center, called a mosque, which serves as a unifying element and source of shared identity, reinforcing traditional customs and power relationships. It remains to be seen whether exposure to the modernizing influences of American culture, especially on the part of youth and women, will produce a major challenge to these traditions.

REFERENCES

Anderson, Kay J. *Vancouver's Chinatown: Racial Discourse in Canada, 1875–1980.* Montreal: McGill–Queen's University Press, 1991.

Bachman, Ronet. *Death and Violence on the Reservation: Homicide, Family Violence, and Suicide in American Indian Populations.* New York: Auburn House, 1992.

Bernstein, Richard. "A Growing Islamic Presence: Balancing Sacred and Secular." *New York Times*, May 2, 1993: 1 ff.

Cage, Mary Crystal. "Graduation Rates of American Indians and Blacks Improve, Lag behind Others'." *Chronicle of Higher Education*, May 26, 1993: A29.

Feagin, Joe R. "The Continuing Significance of Race: Anti-Black Discrimination in Public Places." *American Sociological Review* 56 (1991): 101–116.

Fugita, Stephen S., and David J. O'Brien. *Japanese American Ethnicity: The Persistence of Community.* Seattle: University of Washington Press, 1991.

Johnson, Kirk. "Indians' Casino Money Pumps Up the Volume." *New York Times*, September 1, 1993: B1.

Kasinitz, Philip. *Caribbean New York: Black Immigrants and the Politics of Race.* Ithaca, N.Y.: Cornell University Press, 1992.

Knouse, Stephen P., Paul Rosenfeld, and Amy L. Culbertson, (Eds.) *Hispanics in the Workplace.* Newbury Park, Calif.: Sage, 1992.

Kolchin, Peter. *American Slavery, 1619–1877.* New York: Hill & Wang, 1993.

Labaton, Stephen. "Benefits Are Refused More Often to Disabled Blacks, Study Finds." *New York Times*, May 11, 1992: 1 ff.

Lott, Juanita Tamayo, and Judy C. Felt. "Studying the Pan-Asian Community." *Population Today* 19 (2) (1991): 6–8.

Massey, Douglas S., and Nancy A. Denton. *American Apartheid: Segregation and the Making of the Underclass.* Cambridge, Mass: Harvard University Press, 1993.

Neckerman, Kathryn M., and Joleen Kirschenman. "Hiring Strategies, Racial Bias, and Inner-City Workers." *Social Problems* 38 (1991): 433–452.

Orfield, Gary, and Carole Ashkinaze. *The Closing Door: Conservative Policy and Black Opportunity.* Chicago: University of Chicago Press, 1991.

Parrillo, Vincent N. *Strangers to These Shores: Race and Ethnic Relations in the United States,* 4th ed. New York: Macmillan, 1994.

Quint, Michael. "Anti-Black Bias Still Found in Mortgage Applications." *New York Times*, October 2, 1992: D1.

Richardson, Bill. "More Power to the Tribes." *New York Times*, July 7, 1993: A15.

Sanchirico, Andrew. "The Importance of Small-Business Ownership in Chinese American Educational Achievement." *Sociology of Education* 64 (1991): 293–304.

Segura, Denise A. "Chicanas in White Collar Jobs: Gender/Race-Ethnic Dilemmas and Affirmations." Paper presented at the annual meeting of the American Sociological Association, Miami, Fla., August 1993.

Sigelman, Lee, and Susan Welch. "The Contact Hypothesis Revisited: Black-White Interaction and Positive Racial Attitudes." *Social Forces* 71 (1993): 781–795.

Telles, Edward E. "Residential Segregation by Skin Color in Brazil," *American Sociological Review* 57 (1992): 186–197.

Thornton, Russell. *American Indian Holocaust and Survival: A Population History Since 1492.* Norman: University of Oklahoma Press, 1987.

U.S. Bureau of the Census. "The Hispanic Population of the United States: March 1991." *Current Population Reports*, P20–455. Washington, D.C.: U.S. Government Printing Office, 1991.

Weibel-Orlando, Joan. *Indian Country, L.A.: Maintaining Ethnic Community in Complex Society.* Urbana: University of Illinois Press, 1991.

Zhou, Min. *Chinatown: The Socioeconomic Potential of an Urban Enclave.* Philadelphia: Temple University Press, 1992.

Zhou, Min, and John R. Logan. "In and Out of Chinatown: Residential Mobility and Segregation of New York City's Chinese." *Social Forces* 70 (1991): 387–407.

Zwerling, Craig, and Hilary Silver. "Race and Job Dismissals in a Federal Bureaucracy." *American Sociological Review* 57 (1992): 651–660.

Sun Chief:
Autobiography of a Hopi Indian

Leo W. Simmons, Editor

I grew up believing that Whites are wicked, deceitful people. It seemed that most of them were soldiers, government agents, or missionaries, and that quite a few were Two-Hearts. The old people said that the Whites were tough, possessed dangerous weapons, and were better protected than we were from evil spirits and poison arrows. They were known to be big liars too. They sent Negro soldiers against us with cannons, tricked our war chiefs to surrender without fighting, and then broke their promises. Like Navahos, they were proud and domineering—and needed to be reminded daily to tell the truth. I was taught to mistrust them and to give warning whenever I saw one coming.

Our chief had to show respect to them and pretend to obey their orders, but we knew that he did it halfheartedly and that he put his trust in our Hopi gods. Our ancestors had predicted the coming of these Whites and said that they would cause us much trouble. But it was understood that we had to put up with them until our gods saw fit to recall our Great White Brother from the East to deliver us. Most people in Oraibi argued that we should have nothing to do with them, accept none of their gifts, and make no use of their building materials, medicine, food, tools, or clothing—but we did want their guns. Those who would have nothing to do with Whites were called "Hostiles" and those who would cooperate a little were called "Friendlies." These two groups were quarreling over the subject from my earliest memories and sometimes their arguments spoiled the ceremonies and offended the Six-Point-Cloud-People, our ancestral spirits, who held back the rain and sent droughts and disease. Finally the old chief, with my grandfather and a few others, became friendly with the Whites and accepted gifts, but warned that we would never give up our ceremonies or forsake our gods. But it seemed that fear of Whites, especially of what the United States Government could do, was one of the strongest powers that controlled us, and one of our greatest worries.

A few years before my birth the United States Government had built a boarding school at the Keams Canyon Agency. At first our chief, Lolulomai, had not wanted to send Oraibi children, but chiefs from other villages came and persuaded him to accept clothes, tools, and other supplies, and to let them go. Most of the people disliked this and refused to cooperate. Troops came to Oraibi several times to take the children by force and carry them off in wagons. The people said that it was a terrible sight to see Negro soldiers come and tear children from their parents. Some boys later escaped from Keams Canyon and returned home on foot, a distance of forty miles.

Some years later a day school was opened at the foot of the mesa in New Oraibi, where there were a trading post, a post office, and a few government buildings. Some parents were permitted to send their children to this school. When my sister started, the teacher cut her hair, burned all her clothes, and gave her a new outfit and a new name, Nellie. She did not like school, stopped going after a few weeks, and tried to keep out of sight of the Whites who might force her to return. About a year later she was sent to the New Oraibi spring to fetch water in a ceremonial gourd for the Ooqol society and was captured by the school principal who permitted her to take the water up to the village, but compelled her to return to school after the ceremony was over. The teachers had then forgotten her old name, Nellie, and called her Gladys. Although my brother was two years older than I, he had managed to keep out of school until about a year after I started, but he had to be careful not to be seen by Whites. When finally he did enter the day school at New Oraibi, they cut his hair, burned his clothes, and named him Ira. . . .

3

Then Came the War

Yuri Kochiyama

I was red, white, and blue when I was growing up. I taught Sunday school, and was very, very American. But I was also very provincial. We were just kids rooting for our high school.

My father owned a fish market. Terminal Island was nearby, and that was where many Japanese families lived. It was a fishing town. My family lived in the city proper. San Pedro was very mixed, predominantly white, but there were blacks also.

I was nineteen at the time of the evacuation. I had just finished junior college. I was looking for a job, and didn't realize how different the school world was from the work world. In the school world, I never felt racism. But when you got into the work world, it was very difficult. This was 1941, just before the war. I finally did get a job at a department store. But for us back then, it was a big thing, because I don't think they had ever hired an Asian in a department store before. I tried, because I saw a Mexican friend who got a job there. Even then they didn't hire me on a regular basis, just on Saturdays, summer vacation, Easter vacation, and Christmas vacation. Other than that, I was working like the others—at a vegetable stand, or doing part-time domestic work. Back then, I only knew of two Japanese American girl friends who got jobs as secretaries—but these were in Japanese companies. But generally you almost never saw a Japanese American working in a white place. It was hard for Asians. Even for Japanese, the best jobs they felt they could get were in Chinatowns, such as in Los Angeles. Most Japanese were either in some aspect of fishing, such as in the canneries, or went right from school to work on the farms. That was what it was like in the town of San Pedro. I loved working in the department store, because it was a small town, and you got to know and see everyone. The town itself was wonderful. People were very friendly. I didn't see my job as work—it was like a community job.

Everything changed for me on the day Pearl Harbor was bombed. On that very day—December 7—the FBI came and they took my father. He had just come home from the hospital the day before. For several days we didn't know where they had taken him. Then we found out that he was taken to the federal prison at Terminal Island. Overnight, things changed for us. They took all men who lived near the Pacific waters, and had nothing to do with fishing. A month later, they took every fisherman from Terminal Island, sixteen and over, to places—not the regular concentration camps—but to detention centers in places like South Dakota, Montana, and New Mexico. They said that all Japanese who had given money to any kind of Japanese organization would have to be taken away. At that time, many people were giving to the Japanese Red Cross. The first group was thirteen hundred Isseis—my parent's generation. They took those who were leaders of the community, or Japanese school teachers, or were teaching martial arts, or who were Buddhist priests. Those categories which would make them very "Japanesey," were picked up. This really made a tremendous impact on our lives. My twin brother was going to the University at Berkeley. He came rushing back. All of our classmates were joining up, so he volunteered to go into the service. And it seemed strange that here they had my father in prison, and there the draft board okayed my brother. He went right into the army. My other brother, who was two years older, was trying to run my father's fish market. But business was already going down, so he had to close it. He had finished college at the University of California a couple of years before.

They took my father on December 7th. The day before, he had just come home from the hospital. He had surgery for an ulcer. We only saw him once, on December 13. On December 20th they said he could come home. By the time they brought him back, he couldn't talk. He made guttural sounds and we didn't know if he could hear. He was home for twelve hours. He was dying. The next morning, when we got up, they told us that he was gone. He was very sick. And I think the interrogation was very rough. My mother kept begging the authorities to let him go to the hospital until he was well, then put him back in the prison. They did finally put him there, a week or so later. But they put him in a hospital where they were bringing back all these American Merchant Marines who were hit on Wake Island. So he was the only Japanese in that hospital, so they hung a sheet around him that said, Prisoner of War. The feeling where he was was very bad.

You could see the hysteria of war. There was a sense that war could actually come to American shores. Everybody was yelling to get the "Japs" out of California. In Congress, people were speaking out. Organizations such as the Sons and Daughters of the Golden West were screaming "Get the 'Japs' out." So were the real estate people, who wanted to get the land from the Japanese farmers. The war had whipped up such a hysteria that if there was anyone for the Japanese, you didn't hear about it. I'm sure they were afraid to speak out, because they would be considered not only just "Jap" lovers, but unpatriotic.

Just the fact that my father was taken made us suspect to people. But on the whole, the neighbors were quite nice, especially the ones adjacent to us. There was already a six AM to six PM curfew and a five mile limit on where we could go from our homes. So they offered to do our shopping for us, if we needed.

Most Japanese Americans had to give up their jobs, whatever they did, and were told they had to leave. The edict for 9066—President Roosevelt's edict* for evacuation—was in February 1942. We were moved to a detention center that April. By then the Japanese on Terminal Island were just helter skelter, looking for anywhere they could go. They opened up the Japanese school and Buddhist churches, and families just crowded in. Even farmers brought along their chickens and chicken coops. They just opened up the places for people to stay until they could figure out what to do. Some people left for Colorado and Utah. Those who had relatives could do so. The idea was to evacuate all the Japanese from the coast. But all the money was frozen, so even if you knew where you wanted to go, it wasn't that simple. By then, people knew they would be going into camps, so they were selling what they could, even though they got next to nothing for it.

We were fortunate, in that our neighbors, who were white, were kind enough to look after our house, and they said they would find people to rent it, and look after it till we got back. But these neighbors were very, very unusual.

We were sent to an assembly center in Arcadia, California, in April. It was the largest assembly center on the West Coast, having nearly twenty thousand people. There were some smaller centers with about six hundred people. All along the West Coast—Washington, Oregon, California—there were many, many assembly centers, but ours was the largest. Most of the assembly centers were either fairgrounds,

*Executive Order No. 9066 does not mention detention of Japanese specifically, but was used exclusively against the Japanese. Over 120,000 Japanese were evacuated from the West Coast.

or race tracks. So many of us lived in stables, and they said you could take what you could carry. We were there until October.

Even though we stayed in a horse stable, everything was well organized. Every unit would hold four to six people. So in some cases, families had to split up, or join others. We slept on army cots, and for mattresses they gave us muslin bags, and told us to fill them with straw. And for chairs, everybody scrounged around for carton boxes, because they could serve as chairs. You could put two together and it could be a little table. So it was just makeshift. But I was amazed how, in a few months, some of those units really looked nice. Japanese women fixed them up. Some people had the foresight to bring material and needles and thread. But they didn't let us bring anything that could be used as weapons. They let us have spoons, but no knives. For those who had small children or babies, it was rough. They said you could take what you could carry. Well, they could only take their babies in their arms, and maybe the little children could carry something, but it was pretty limited.

I was so red, white, and blue, I couldn't believe this was happening to us. America would never do a thing like this to us. This is the greatest country in the world. So I thought this is only going to be for a short while, maybe a few weeks or something, and they will let us go back. At the beginning no one realized how long this would go on. I didn't feel the anger that much because I thought maybe this was the way we could show our love for our country, and we should not make too much fuss or noise, we should abide by what they asked of us. I'm a totally different person now than I was back then. I was naïve about so many things. The more I think about it, the more I realize how little you learn about American history. It's just what they want you to know.

At the beginning, we didn't have any idea how temporary or permanent the situation was. We thought we would be able to leave shortly. But after several months they told us this was just temporary quarters, and they were building more permanent quarters elsewhere in the United States. All this was so unbelievable. A year before we would never have thought anything like this could have happened to us—not in this country. As time went by, the sense of frustration grew. Many families were already divided. The fathers, the heads of the households, were taken to other camps. In the beginning, there was no way for the sons to get in touch with their families. Before our group left for the detention camp, we were saying good-bye almost every day to other groups who were going to places like Arizona and Utah. Here we finally had made so many new friends—people who we met, lived with, shared the time, and got to know. So it was even sad on that note and the goodbyes were difficult. Here we had gotten close to these people, and now we had to separate again. I don't think we even thought about where they were going to take us, or how long we would have to stay there. When we got on the trains to leave for the camps, we didn't know where we were going. None of the groups knew. It was later on that we learned so and so ended up in Arizona, or Colorado, or some other place. We were all at these assembly centers for about seven months. Once they started pushing people out, it was done very quickly. By October, our group headed out for Jerome, Arkansas, which is on the Texarkana corner.

We were on the train for five days. The blinds were down, so we couldn't look out, and other people couldn't look in to see who was in the train. We stopped in Nebraska, and everybody pulled the blinds to see what Nebraska looked like. The interesting thing was, there was a troop train stopped at the station too. These American soldiers looked out, and saw all these Asians, and they wondered what we were doing on the train. So the Japanese raised the windows, and so did the soldiers. It wasn't a bad feeling at all. There was none of that "you Japs" kind of thing. The women were about the same age as the soldiers—eighteen to twenty-five, and we had the same thing on our minds. In camps, there wasn't much to do, so the fun thing was to receive letters, so on our train, all the girls who were my age, were yelling to the guys, "Hey, give us your address where you're going, we'll write you." And they said, "Are you sure you're going to write?" We exchanged addresses and for a long time I wrote to some of those soldiers. On the other side of the train, I'll never forget there was this old guy, about sixty, who came to our window and said, "We have some Japanese living here. This is Omaha, Nebraska." This guy was very nice, and didn't seem to have any ill feelings for Japanese. He had calling cards, and he said "Will any of you people write to me?" We said, "Sure," so he threw in a bunch of calling cards, and I got one, and I wrote to him for years. I wrote to him about what camp was like, because he said, "Let me know what it's like wherever you end up." And he wrote back, and told me what was happening in Omaha, Nebraska. There were many, many interesting experiences too. Our mail was generally not censored, but all the mail from the soldiers was. Letters meant everything.

When we got to Jerome, Arkansas, we were shocked because we had never seen an area like it. There was forest all around us. And they told us to wait till the rains hit. This would not only turn into mud, but Arkansas swamp lands. That's where they put us—in swamp lands, surrounded by forests. It was nothing like California.

I'm speaking as a person of twenty who had good health. Up until then, I had lived a fairly comfortable life. But there were many others who didn't see the whole experience the same way. Especially those who were older and in poor health and had experienced racism. One more thing like this could break them. I was at an age where transitions were not hard—the point where anything new could even be considered exciting. But for people in poor health, it was hell.

There were army-type barracks, with two hundred to two hundred and five people to each block and every block had its own mess hall, facility for washing clothes, showering. It was all surrounded by barbed wire, and armed soldiers. I think they said only seven people were killed in total, though thirty were shot, because they went too close to the fence. Where we were, nobody thought of escaping because you'd be more scared of the swamps—the poisonous snakes, the bayous. Climatic conditions were very harsh. Although Arkansas is in the South, the winters were very, very cold. We had a pot bellied stove in every room and we burned wood. Everything was very organized. We got there in October, and were warned to prepare ourselves. So on our block, for instance, males eighteen and over could go out in the forest to chop down trees for wood for the winter. The men would bring back the trees, and the women sawed the trees. Everybody worked. The children would pile up the wood for each unit.

They told us when it rained, it would be very wet, so we would have to build our own drainage system. One of the barracks was to hold meetings, so block heads would call meetings. There was a block council to represent the people from different areas.

When we first arrived, there were some things that weren't completely fixed. For instance, the roofers would come by, and everyone would hunger for information from the outside world. We wanted to know what was happening with the war. We weren't allowed to bring radios; that was contraband. And there were no televisions then. So we would ask the workers to bring us back some papers, and they would give us papers from Texas or Arkansas, so for the first time we would find out about news from the outside.

Just before we went in to the camps, we saw that being a Japanese wasn't such a good thing, because everybody was turning against the Japanese, thinking we were saboteurs, or linking us with Pearl Harbor. But when I saw the kind of work they did at camp, I felt so proud of the Japanese, and proud to be Japanese, and wondered why I was so white, white when I was outside, because I was always with white folks. Many people had brothers or sons who were in the military and Japanese American servicemen would come into the camp to visit the families, and we felt so proud of them when they came in their uniforms. We knew that it would only be a matter of time before they would be shipped overseas. Also what made us feel proud was the forming of the 442 unit.*

I was one of these real American patriots then. I've changed now. But back then, I was all American. Growing up, my mother would say we're Japanese. But I'd say, "No, I'm American." I think a lot of Japanese grew up that way. People would say to them, "You're Japanese," and they would say, "No, we're Americans." I don't even think they used the hyphenated term "Japanese-American" back then. At the time, I was ashamed of being Japanese. I think many Japanese Americans felt the same way. Pearl Harbor was a shameful act, and being Japanese Americans, even though we had nothing to do with it, we still somehow felt we were blamed for it. I hated Japan at that point. So I saw myself at that part of my history as an American, and not as a Japanese or Japanese American. That sort of changed while I was in the camp.

I hated the war, because it wasn't just between the governments. It went down to the people, and it nurtured hate. What was happening during the war were many things I didn't like. I hoped that one day when the war was over there could be a way that people could come together in their relationships.

Now I can relate to Japan in a more mature way, where I see its faults and its very, very negative history. But I also see its potential. Scientifically and techno-

---

*American soldiers of Japanese ancestry were assembled in two units: the 442 Regimental Combat Team and the 100th Infantry Battalion. The two groups were sent to battle in Europe. The 100th Battalion had over 900 casualties and was known as the Purple Heart Battalion. Combined, the units received 9,486 purple hearts and 18,143 individual decorations.

logically it has really gone far. But I'm disappointed that when it comes to human rights she hasn't grown. The Japan of today—I feel there are still things lacking. For instance, I don't think the students have the opportunity to have more leeway in developing their lives.

We always called the camps "relocation centers" while we were there. Now we feel it is apropos to call them concentration camps. It is not the same as the concentration camps of Europe; those we feel were death camps. Concentration camps were a concentration of people placed in an area, and disempowered and disenfranchised. So it is apropos to call what I was in a concentration camp. After two years in the camp, I was released.

Going home wasn't much of a problem for us because our neighbors had looked after our place. But for most of our Japanese friends, starting over again was very difficult after the war.

I returned in October of 1945. It was very hard to find work, at least for me. I wasn't expecting to find anything good, just something to tide me over until my boyfriend came back from New York. The only thing I was looking for was to work in a restaurant as a waitress. But I couldn't find anything. I would walk from one end of the town to the other, and down every main avenue. But as soon as they found out I was Japanese, they would say no. Or they would ask me if I was in the union, and of course I couldn't be in the union because I had just gotten there. Anyway, no Japanese could be in the union, so if the answer was no I'm not in the union, they would say no. So finally what I did was go into the rough area of San Pedro—there's a strip near the wharf—and I went down there. I was determined to keep the jobs as long as I could. But for a while, I could last maybe two hours, and somebody would say "Is that a 'Jap'?" And as soon as someone would ask that, the boss would say, "Sorry, you gotta go. We don't want trouble here." The strip wasn't that big, so after I'd go the whole length of it, I'd have to keep coming back to the same restaurants, and say, "Gee, will you give me another chance." I figure, all these servicemen were coming back and the restaurants didn't have enough waitresses to come in and take these jobs. And so, they'd say "Okay. But soon as somebody asks who you are, or if you're a 'Jap,' or any problem about being a 'Jap,' you go." So I said, "Okay, sure. How about keeping me until that happens?" So sometimes I'd last a night, sometimes a couple of nights that no one would say anything. Sometimes people threw cups at me or hot coffee. At first they didn't know what I was. They thought I was Chinese. Then someone would say, "I bet she's a 'Jap'." And I wasn't going to say I wasn't. So as soon as I said "Yeah," then it was like an uproar. Rather than have them say, "Get out," I just walked out. I mean, there was no point in fighting it. If you just walked out, there was less chance of getting hurt. But one place I lasted two weeks. These owners didn't want to have to let me go. But they didn't want to have problems with the people.

And so I did this until I left for New York, which was about three months later. I would work the dinner shift, from six at night to three in the morning. When you are young you tend not to take things as strongly. Everything is like an adventure. Looking back, I felt the people who were the kindest to me were those who went out and fought, those who just got back from Japan or the Far East. I think the worst ones were the ones who stayed here and worked in defense plants, who felt they had to be so patriotic. On the West Coast, there wasn't hysteria anymore, but there were hostile feelings towards the Japanese, because they were coming back. It took a while, but my mother said that things were getting back to normal, and that the Japanese were slowly being accepted again. At the time, I didn't go through the bitterness that many others went through, because it's not just what they went through, but it is also what they experienced before that. I mean, I happened to have a much more comfortable life before, so you sort of see things in a different light. You see that there are all kinds of Americans, and that they're not all people who hate Japs. You know too that it was hysteria that had a lot to do with it.

All Japanese, before they left camp, were told not to congregate among Japanese, and not to speak Japanese. They were told by the authorities. There was even a piece of paper that gave you instructions. But then people went on to places like Chicago where there were churches, so they did congregate in churches. But they did ask people not to. I think psychologically the Japanese, having gone through a period where they were so hated by everyone, didn't even want to admit they were Japanese, or accept the fact that they were Japanese. Of course, they would say they were Japanese Americans. But I think the psychological damage of the wartime period, and of racism itself, has left its mark. There is a stigma to being Japanese. I think that is why such a large number of Japanese, in particular Japanese American women, have married out of the race. On the West Coast I've heard people say that sixty to seventy percent of the Japanese women have married, I guess, mostly whites. Japanese men are doing it too, but not to that degree. I guess Japanese Americans just didn't want to have that Japanese identity, or that Japanese part. There is definitely some self-hate, and part of that has to do with the racism that's so deeply a part of this society.

Historically, Americans have always been putting people behind walls. First there were the American Indians who were put on reservations, Africans in slavery, their lives on the plantations, Chicanos doing migratory work, and the kinds of camps they lived in, and even, too, the Chinese when they worked on the railroad camps where they were almost isolated, dispossessed people—disempowered. And I feel those are the things we should fight against so they won't happen again. It wasn't so long ago—in 1979—that the feeling against the Iranians was so strong because of the takeover of the U.S. embassy in Iran, where they wanted to deport Iranian students. And that is when a group called Concerned Japanese Americans organized, and that was the first issue we took up, and then we connected it with what the Japanese had gone through. This whole period of what the Japanese went through is important. If we can see the connections of how often this happens in history, we can stem the tide of these things happening again by speaking out against them.

Most Japanese Americans who worked years and years for redress never thought it would happen the way it did. The papers have been signed, we will be given reparation, and there was an apology from the government. I think the redress movement itself was very good because it was a learning experience for the Japanese people; we could get out into our communities and speak about what happened to us and link it with experiences of other people. In that sense, though, it wasn't done as much as it should have been. Some Japanese Americans didn't even learn that part. They just started the movement as a reaction to the bad experience they had. They don't even see other ethnic groups who have gone through it. It showed us, too, how vulnerable everybody is. It showed us that even though there is a Constitution, that constitutional rights could be taken away very easily.

TV Arabs

Jack G. Shaheen

America's bogyman is the Arab. Until the nightly news brought us TV pictures of Palestinian boys being punched and beaten, almost all portraits of Arabs seen in America were dangerously threatening. Arabs were either billionaires or bombers—rarely victims. They were hardly ever seen as ordinary people practicing law, driving taxis, singing lullabies or healing the sick. Though TV news may portray them more sympathetically now, the absence of positive media images nurtures suspicion and stereotype. As an Arab-American, I have found that ugly caricatures have had an enduring impact on my family.

I was sheltered from prejudicial portraits at first. My parents came from Lebanon in the 1920s; they met and married in America. Our home in the steel city of Clairton, Pa., was a center for ethnic sharing—black, white, Jew and gentile. There was only one major source of media images then, at the State movie theater where I was lucky enough to get a part-time job as an usher. But in the late 1940s, Westerns and war movies were popular, not Middle Eastern dramas. Memories of World War II were fresh, and the screen heavies were the Japanese and the Germans. True to the cliché of the times, the only good Indian was a dead Indian. But when I mimicked or mocked the bad guys, my mother cautioned me. She explained that stereotypes blur our vision and corrupt the imagination. "Have compassion for all people, Jackie," she said. "This way, you'll learn to experience the joy of accepting people as they are, and not as they appear in films. Stereotypes hurt."

Mother was right. I can remember the Saturday afternoon when my son, Michael, who was seven, and my daughter, Michele, six, suddenly called out: "Daddy, Daddy, they've got some bad Arabs on TV." They were watching that great

American morality play, TV wrestling. Akbar the Great, who liked to hear the cracking of bones, and Abdullah the Butcher, a dirty fighter who liked to inflict pain, were pinning their foes with "camel locks." From that day on, I knew I had to try to neutralize the media caricatures.

It hasn't been easy. With my children, I have watched animated heroes Heckle and Jeckle pull the rug from under "Ali Boo-Boo, the Desert Rat," and Laverne and Shirley stop "Sheik Ha-Mean-Ie" from conquering "the U.S. and the world." I have read comic books like the "Fantastic Four" and "G.I. Combat" whose characters have sketched Arabs as "lowlifes" and "human hyenas." Negative stereotypes were everywhere. A dictionary informed my youngsters that an Arab is a "vagabond, drifter, hobo and vagrant." Whatever happened, my wife wondered, to Aladdin's good genie?

To a child, the world is simple: good versus evil. But my children and others with Arab roots grew up without ever having seen a humane Arab on the silver screen, someone to pattern their lives after. Is it easier for a camel to go through the eye of a needle than for a screen Arab to appear as a genuine human being?

Hollywood producers must have an instant Ali Baba kit that contains scimitars, veils, sunglasses and such Arab clothing as *chadors* and *kufiyahs*. In the mythical "Ay-rabland," oil wells, tents, mosques, goats and shepherds prevail. Between the sand dunes, the camera focuses on a mock-up of a palace from "Arabian Nights"—or a military air base. Recent movies suggest that Americans are at war with Arabs, forgetting the fact that out of 21 Arab nations, America is friendly with 19 of them. And in "Wanted Dead or Alive," a movie that starred Gene Simmons, the leader of the rock group Kiss, the war comes home when an Arab terrorist comes to the United States dressed as a rabbi and, among other things, conspires with Arab-Americans to poison the people of Los Angeles. The movie was released last year.

The Arab remains American culture's favorite whipping boy. In his memoirs, Terrel Bell, Ronald Reagan's first secretary of education, writes about an "apparent bias among mid-level, right-wing staffers at the White House" who dismissed Arabs as "sand niggers." Sadly, the racial slurs continue. At a recent teacher's conference, I met a woman from Sioux Falls, S.D., who told me about the persistence of discrimination. She was in the process of adopting a baby when an agency staffer warned her that the infant had a problem. When she asked whether the child was mentally ill, or physically handicapped, there was silence. Finally, the worker said: "The baby is Jordanian."

To me, the Arab demon of today is much like the Jewish demon of yesterday. We deplore the false portrait of Jews as a swarthy menace. Yet a similar portrait has been accepted and transferred to another group of Semites—the Arabs. Print and broadcast journalists have started to challenge this stereotype. They are now revealing more humane images of Palestinian Arabs, a people who traditionally suffered from the myth that Palestinian equals terrorist. Others could follow that lead and retire the stereotypical Arab to a media Valhalla.

It would be a step in the right direction if movie and TV producers developed characters modeled after real-life Arab-Americans. We could then see a White

House correspondent like Helen Thomas, whose father came from Lebanon, in "The Golden Girls," a heart surgeon patterned after Dr. Michael DeBakey on "St. Elsewhere," or a Syrian-American playing tournament chess like Yasser Seirawan, the Seattle grandmaster.

Politicians, too, should speak out against the cardboard caricatures. They should refer to Arabs as friends, not just as moderates. And religious leaders could state that Islam, like Christianity and Judaism, maintains that all mankind is one family in the care of God. When all image makers rightfully begin to treat Arabs and all other minorities with respect and dignity, we may begin to unlearn our prejudices.

The Circuit

Francisco Jiménez

It was that time of year again. Ito, the strawberry sharecropper, did not smile. It was natural. The peak of the strawberry season was over and the last few days the workers, most of them braceros, were not picking as many boxes as they had during the months of June and July.

As the last days of August disappeared, so did the number of braceros. Sunday, only one—the best picker—came to work. I liked him. Sometimes we talked during our half-hour lunch break. That is how I found out he was from Jalisco, the same state in Mexico my family was from. That Sunday was the last time I saw him.

When the sun had tired and sunk behind the mountains, Ito signaled us that it was time to go home. "Ya esora," he yelled in his broken Spanish. Those were the words I waited for twelve hours a day, every day, seven days a week, week after week. And the thought of not hearing them again saddened me.

As we drove home Papá did not say a word. With both hands on the wheel, he stared at the dirt road. My older brother, Roberto, was also silent. He leaned his head back and closed his eyes. Once in a while he cleared from his throat the dust that blew in from outside.

Yes, it was that time of year. When I opened the front door to the shack, I stopped. Everything we owned was neatly packed in cardboard boxes. Suddenly I felt even more the weight of hours, days, weeks, and months of work. I sat down on a box. The thought of having to move to Fresno and knowing what was in store for me there brought tears to my eyes.

That night I could not sleep. I lay in bed thinking about how much I hated this move.

A little before five o'clock in the morning, Papá woke everyone up. A few minutes later, the yelling and screaming of my little brothers and sisters, for whom the move was a great adventure, broke the silence of dawn. Shortly, the barking of the dogs accompanied them.

While we packed the breakfast dishes, Papá went outside to start the "Carcanchita." That was the name Papá gave his old '38 black Plymouth. He bought it in a used-car lot in Santa Rosa in the winter of 1949. Papá was very proud of his little jalopy. He had a right to be proud of it. He spent a lot of time looking at other cars before buying this one. When he finally chose the "Carcanchita," he checked it thoroughly before driving it out of the car lot. He examined every inch of the car. He listened to the motor, tilting his head from side to side like a parrot, trying to detect any noises that spelled car trouble. After being satisfied with the looks and sounds of the car, Papá then insisted on knowing who the original owner was. He never did find out from the car salesman, but he bought the car anyway. Papá figured the original owner must have been an important man because behind the rear seat of the car he found a blue necktie.

Papá parked the car out in front and left the motor running. "Listo," he yelled. Without saying a word, Roberto and I began to carry the boxes out to the car. Roberto carried the two big boxes and I carried the two smaller ones. Papá then threw the mattress on top of the car roof and tied it with ropes to the front and rear bumpers.

Everything was packed except Mamá's pot. It was an old large galvanized pot she had picked up at an army surplus store in Santa Maria the year I was born. The pot had many dents and nicks, and the more dents and nicks it acquired the more Mamá liked it. "Mi olla," she used to say proudly.

I held the front door open as Mamá carefully carried out her pot by both handles, making sure not to spill the cooked beans. When she got to the car, Papá reached out to help her with it. Roberto opened the rear car door and Papá gently placed it on the floor behind the front seat. All of us then climbed in. Papá sighed, wiped the sweat off his forehead with his sleeve, and said wearily: "Es todo."

As we drove away, I felt a lump in my throat. I turned around and looked at our little shack for the last time.

At sunset we drove into a labor camp near Fresno. Since Papá did not speak English, Mamá asked the camp foreman if he needed any more workers. "We don't need no more," said the foreman, scratching his head. "Check with Sullivan down the road. Can't miss him. He lives in a big white house with a fence around it."

When we got there, Mamá walked up to the house. She went through a white gate, past a row of rose bushes, up the stairs to the front door. She rang the doorbell. The porch light went on and a tall husky man came out. They exchanged a few words. After the man went in, Mamá clasped her hands and hurried back to the car. "We have work! Mr. Sullivan said we can stay there the whole season," she said, gasping and pointing to an old garage near the stables.

The garage was worn out by the years. It had no windows. The walls, eaten by termites, strained to support the roof full of holes. The dirt floor, populated by earth worms, looked like a gray road map.

That night, by the light of a kerosene lamp, we unpacked and cleaned our new home. Roberto swept away the loose dirt, leaving the hard ground. Papá plugged the holes in the walls with old newspapers and tin can tops. Mamá fed my little brothers and sisters. Papá and Roberto then brought in the mattress and placed it on the far corner of the garage. "Mamá, you and the little ones sleep on the mattress. Roberto, Panchito, and I will sleep outside under the trees," Papá said.

Early next morning Mr. Sullivan showed us where his crop was, and after breakfast, Papá, Roberto, and I headed for the vineyard to pick.

Around nine o'clock the temperature had risen to almost one hundred degrees. I was completely soaked in sweat and my mouth felt as if I had been chewing on a handkerchief. I walked over to the end of the row, picked up the jug of water we had brought, and began drinking. "Don't drink too much; you'll get sick," Roberto shouted. No sooner had he said that than I felt sick to my stomach. I dropped to my knees and let the jug roll off my hands. I remained motionless with my eyes glued on the hot sandy ground. All I could hear was the drone of insects. Slowly I began to recover. I poured water over my face and neck and watched the dirty water run down my arms to the ground.

I still felt a little dizzy when we took a break to eat lunch. It was past two o'clock and we sat underneath a large walnut tree that was on the side of the road. While we ate, Papá jotted down the number of boxes we had picked. Roberto drew designs on the ground with a stick. Suddenly I noticed Papá's face turn pale as he looked down the road. "Here comes the school bus," he whispered loudly in alarm. Instinctively, Roberto and I ran and hid in the vineyards. We did not want to get in trouble for not going to school. The neatly dressed boys about my age got off. They carried books under their arms. After they crossed the street, the bus drove away. Roberto and I came out from hiding and joined Papá. "Tienen que tener cuidado," he warned us.

After lunch we went back to work. The sun kept beating down. The buzzing insects, the wet sweat, and the hot dry dust made the afternoon seem to last forever. Finally the mountains around the valley reached out and swallowed the sun. Within an hour it was too dark to continue picking. The vines blanketed the grapes, making it difficult to see the bunches. "Vámonos," said Papá, signaling to us that it was time to quit work. Papá then took out a pencil and began to figure out how much we had earned our first day. He wrote down numbers, crossed some out, wrote down some more. "Quince," he murmured.

When we arrived home, we took a cold shower underneath a water-hose. We then sat down to eat dinner around some wooden crates that served as a table. Mamá had cooked a special meal for us. We had rice and tortillas with "carne con chile," my favorite dish.

The next morning I could hardly move. My body ached all over. I felt little control over my arms and legs. This feeling went on every morning for days until my muscles finally got used to the work.

It was Monday, the first week of November. The grape season was over and I could now go to school. I woke up early that morning and lay in bed, looking at the stars and savoring the thought of not going to work and of starting sixth grade for the first time that year. Since I could not sleep, I decided to get up and join Papá and Roberto at breakfast. I sat at the table across from Roberto, but I kept my head down. I did not want to look up and face him. I knew he was sad. He was not going to school today. He was not going tomorrow, or next week, or next month. He would not go until the cotton season was over, and that was sometime in February. I rubbed my hands together and watched the dry, acid stained skin fall to the floor in little rolls.

When Papá and Roberto left for work, I felt relief. I walked to the top of a small grade next to the shack and watched the "Carcanchita" disappear in the distance in a cloud of dust.

Two hours later, around eight o'clock, I stood by the side of the road waiting for school bus number twenty. When it arrived I climbed in. Everyone was busy either talking or yelling. I sat in an empty seat in the back.

When the bus stopped in front of the school, I felt very nervous. I looked out the bus window and saw boys and girls carrying books under their arms. I put my hands in my pant pockets and walked to the principal's office. When I entered I heard a woman's voice say: "May I help you?" I was startled. I had not heard English for months. For a few seconds I remained speechless. I looked at the lady who waited for an answer. My first instinct was to answer her in Spanish, but I held back. Finally, after struggling for English words, I managed to tell her that I wanted to enroll in the sixth grade. After answering many questions, I was led to the classroom.

Mr. Lema, the sixth grade teacher, greeted me and assigned me a desk. He then introduced me to the class. I was so nervous and scared at that moment when everyone's eyes were on me that I wished I were with Papá and Roberto picking cotton. After taking roll, Mr. Lema gave the class the assignment for the first hour. "The first thing we have to do this morning is finish reading the story we began yesterday," he said enthusiastically. He walked up to me, handed me an English book, and asked me to read. "We are on page 125," he said politely. When I heard this, I felt my blood rush to my head; I felt dizzy. "Would you like to read?" he asked hesitantly. I opened the book to pate 125. My mouth was dry. My eyes began to water. I could not begin. "You can read later," Mr. Lema said understandingly.

For the rest of the reading period I kept getting angrier and angrier with myself. I should have read, I thought to myself.

During recess I went into the restroom and opened my English book to page 125. I began to read in a low voice, pretending I was in class. There were many words I did not know. I closed the book and headed back to the classroom.

Mr. Lema was sitting at his desk correcting papers. When I entered he looked up at me and smiled. I felt better. I walked up to him and asked if he could help me with the new words. "Gladly," he said.

The rest of the month I spent my lunch hours working on English with Mr. Lema, my best friend at school.

One Friday during lunch hour Mr. Lema asked me to take a walk with him to the music room. "Do you like music?" he asked me as we entered the building.

"Yes, I like corridos," I answered. He then picked up a trumpet, blew on it and handed it to me. The sound gave me goose bumps. I knew that sound. I had heard it in many corridos. "How would you like to learn how to play it?" he asked. He must have read my face because before I could answer, he added: "I'll teach you how to play it during our lunch hours."

That day I could hardly wait to tell Papá and Mamá the great news. As I got off the bus, my little brothers and sisters ran up to meet me. They were yelling and screaming. I thought they were happy to see me, but when I opened the door to our shack, I saw that everything we owned was neatly packed in cardboard boxes.

The Myth of the Latin Woman:
I Just Met a Girl Named María

Judith Ortiz Cofer

On a bus trip to London from Oxford University where I was earning some graduate credits one summer, a young man, obviously fresh from a pub, spotted me and as if struck by inspiration went down on his knees in the aisle. With both hands over his heart he broke into an Irish tenor's rendition of "María" from *West Side Story*. My politely amused fellow passengers gave his lovely voice the round of gentle applause it deserved. Though I was not quite as amused, I managed my version of an English smile: no show of teeth, no extreme contortions of the facial muscles—I was at this time of my life practicing reserve and cool. Oh, that British control, how I coveted it. But María had followed me to London, reminding me of a prime fact of my life: you can leave the Island, master the English language, and travel as far as you can, but if you are a Latina, especially one like me who so obviously belongs to Rita Moreno's gene pool, the Island travels with you.

This is sometimes a very good thing—it may win you that extra minute of someone's attention. But with some people, the same things can make *you* an island—not so much a tropical paradise as an Alcatraz, a place nobody wants to visit. As a Puerto Rican girl growing up in the United States and wanting like most children to "belong," I resented the stereotype that my Hispanic appearance called forth from many people I met.

Our family lived in a large urban center in New Jersey during the sixties, where life was designed as a microcosm of my parents' casas on the island. We spoke in Spanish, we ate Puerto Rican food bought at the bodega, and we practiced strict Catholicism complete with Saturday confession and Sunday mass at a church where our parents were accommodated into a one-hour Spanish mass slot, performed by a Chinese priest trained as a missionary for Latin America.

As a girl I was kept under strict surveillance, since virtue and modesty were, by cultural equation, the same as family honor. As a teenager I was instructed on how to behave as a proper señorita. But it was a conflicting message girls got, since the Puerto Rican mothers also encouraged their daughters to look and act like women and to dress in clothes our Anglo friends and their mothers found too "mature" for our age. It was, and is, cultural, yet I often felt humiliated when I appeared at an American friend's party wearing a dress more suitable to a semiformal than to a playroom birthday celebration. At Puerto Rican festivities, neither the music nor the colors we wore could be too loud. I still experience a vague sense of letdown when I'm invited to a "party" and it turns out to be a marathon conversation in hushed tones rather than a fiesta with salsa, laughter, and dancing—the kind of celebration I remember from my childhood.

I remember Career Day in our high school, when teachers told us to come dressed as if for a job interview. It quickly became obvious that to the barrio girls, "dressing up" sometimes meant wearing ornate jewelry and clothing that would be more appropriate (by mainstream standards) for the company Christmas party than as daily office attire. That morning I had agonized in front of my closet, trying to figure out what a "career girl" would wear because, essentially, except for Marlo Thomas on TV, I had no models on which to base my decision. I knew how to dress for school: at the Catholic school I attended we all wore uniforms; I knew how to dress for Sunday mass, and I knew what dresses to wear for parties at my relatives' homes. Though I do not recall the precise details of my Career Day outfit, it must have been a composite of the above choices. But I remember a comment my friend (an Italian-American) made in later years that coalesced my impressions of that day. She said that at the business school she was attending the Puerto Rican girls always stood out for wearing "everything at once." She meant, of course, too much jewelry, too many accessories. On that day at school, we were simply made the negative models by the nuns who were themselves not credible fashion experts to any of us. But it was painfully obvious to me that to the others, in their tailored skirts and silk blouses, we must have seemed "hopeless" and "vulgar." Though I now know that most adolescents feel out of step much of the time, I also know that for the Puerto Rican girls of my generation that sense was intensified. The way our teachers and classmates looked at us that day in school was just a taste of the culture clash that awaited us in the real world, where prospective employers and men on the street would often misinterpret our tight skirts and jingling bracelets as a come-on.

Mixed cultural signals have perpetuated certain stereotypes—for example, that of the Hispanic woman as the "Hot Tamale" or sexual firebrand. It is a one-dimensional view that the media have found easy to promote. In their special vocabulary, advertisers have designated "sizzling" and "smoldering" as the adjectives of choice for describing not only the foods but also the women of Latin America. From conversations in my house I recall hearing about the harassment that Puerto Rican women endured in factories where the "boss men" talked to them as if sexual innuendo was all they understood and, worse, often gave them the choice of submitting to advances or being fired.

It is custom, however, not chromosomes, that leads us to choose scarlet over pale pink. As young girls, we were influenced in our decisions about clothes and colors by the women—older sisters and mothers who had grown up on a tropical island where the natural environment was a riot of primary colors, where showing your skin was one way to keep cool as well as to look sexy. Most important of all, on the island, women perhaps felt freer to dress and move more provocatively, since, in most cases, they were protected by the traditions, mores, and laws of a Spanish/Catholic system of morality and machismo whose main rule was: *You may look at my sister, but if you touch her I will kill you.* The extended family and church structure could provide a young woman with a circle of safety in her small pueblo on the island; if a man "wronged" a girl, everyone would close in to save her family honor.

This is what I have gleaned from my discussions as an adult with older Puerto Rican women. They have told me about dressing in their best party clothes on Saturday nights and going to the town's plaza to promenade with their girlfriends in front of the boys they liked. The males were thus given an opportunity to admire the women and to express their admiration in the form of *piropos*: erotically charged street poems they composed on the spot. I have been subjected to a few piropos while visiting the Island, and they can be outrageous, although custom dictates that they must never cross into obscenity. This ritual, as I understand it, also entails a show of studied indifference on the woman's part; if she is "decent," she must not acknowledge the man's impassioned words. So I do understand how things can be lost in translation. When a Puerto Rican girl dressed in her idea of what is attractive meets a man from the mainstream culture who has been trained to react to certain types of clothing as a sexual signal, a clash is likely to take place. The line I first heard based on this aspect of the myth happened when the boy who took me to my first formal dance leaned over to plant a sloppy overeager kiss painfully on my mouth, and when I didn't respond with sufficient passion said in a resentful tone: "I thought you Latin girls were supposed to mature early"—my first instance of being thought of as a fruit or vegetable—I was supposed to *ripen*, not just grow into womanhood like other girls.

It is surprising to some of my professional friends that some people, including those who should know better, still put others "in their place." Though rarer, these incidents are still commonplace in my life. It happened to me most recently during a stay at a very classy metropolitan hotel favored by young professional couples for their weddings. Late one evening after the theater, as I walked toward my room with my new colleague (a woman with whom I was coordinating an arts program), a middle-aged man in a tuxedo, a young girl in satin and lace on his arm, stepped directly into our path. With his champagne glass extended toward me, he exclaimed, "Evita!"

Our way blocked, my companion and I listened as the man half-recited, half-bellowed "Don't Cry for Me, Argentina." When he finished, the young girl said: "How about a round of applause for my daddy?" We complied, hoping this would bring the silly spectacle to a close. I was becoming aware that our little group was attracting the attention of the other guests. "Daddy" must have perceived this too, and he once more barred the way as we tried to walk past him. He began to shout-sing a ditty to the tune of "La Bamba"—except the lyrics were about a girl named María whose exploits all rhymed with her name and gonorrhea. The girl kept saying "Oh, Daddy" and looking at me with pleading eyes. She wanted me to laugh along with the others. My companion and I stood silently waiting for the man to end his offensive song. When he finished, I looked not at him but at his daughter. I advised her calmly never to ask her father what he had done in the army. Then I walked between them and to my room. My friend complimented me on my cool handling of the situation. I confessed to her that I really had wanted to push the jerk into the swimming pool. I knew that this same man—probably a corporate executive, well educated, even worldly by most standards—would not have been likely to regale a white woman with a dirty song in public. He would perhaps have checked his impulse by assuming that she could be somebody's wife or mother, or at least *somebody* who might take offense. But to him, I was just an Evita or a María: merely a character in his cartoon-populated universe.

Because of my education and my proficiency with the English language, I have acquired many mechanisms for dealing with the anger I experience. This was not true for my parents, nor is it true for the many Latin women working at menial jobs who must put up with stereotypes about our ethnic group such as: "They make good domestics." This is another facet of the myth of the Latin woman in the United States. Its origin is simple to deduce. Work as domestics, waitressing, and factory jobs are all that's available to women with little English and few skills. The myth of the Hispanic menial has been sustained by the same media phenomenon that made "Mammy" from *Gone with the Wind* America's idea of the black woman for generations; María, the housemaid or counter girl, is now indelibly etched into the national psyche. The big and the little screens have presented us with the picture of the funny Hispanic maid, mispronouncing words and cooking up a spicy storm in a shiny California kitchen.

This media-engendered image of the Latina in the United States has been documented by feminist Hispanic scholars, who claim that such portrayals are partially responsible for the denial of opportunities for upward mobility among Latinas in the professions. I have a Chicana friend working on a Ph.D. in philosophy at a major university. She says her doctor still shakes his head in puzzled amazement at all the "big words" she uses. Since I do not wear my diplomas around my neck for all to see, I too have on occasion been sent to that "kitchen," where some think I obviously belong.

One such incident that has stayed with me, though I recognize it as a minor offense, happened on the day of my first public poetry reading. It took place in Miami in a boat-restaurant where we were having lunch before the event. I was nervous and excited as I walked in with my notebook in my hand. An older woman motioned me to her table. Thinking (foolish me) that she wanted me to autograph a copy of my brand new slender volume of verse, I went over. She ordered a cup of coffee from me, assuming that I was the waitress. Easy enough to mistake my poems for menus, I suppose. I know that it wasn't an intentional act of cruelty, yet of all the good things that happened that day, I remember that scene most clearly, because it reminded me of what I had to overcome before anyone would take me seriously. In retrospect I understand that my anger gave my reading fire, that I have almost always taken doubts in my abilities as a challenge—and that the result is, most times, a feeling of satisfaction at having won a covert when I see the cold, appraising eyes warm to my words, the body language change, the smile that indicates that I have opened some avenue for communication. That day I read to that woman and her lowered eyes told me that she was embarrassed at her little faux pas, and when I willed her to look up at me, it was my victory, and she graciously allowed me to punish her with my full attention. We shook hands at the end of the reading, and I never saw her again. She has probably forgotten the whole thing but maybe not.

Yet I am one of the lucky ones. My parents made it possible for me to acquire a stronger footing in the mainstream culture by giving me the chance at an education. And books and art have saved me from the harsher forms of ethnic and racial prejudice that many of my Hispanic *compañeras* have had to endure. I travel a lot around the United States, reading from my books of poetry and my novel, and the reception I most often receive is one of positive interest by people who want to know more about my culture. There are, however, thousands of Latinas without the privilege of an education or the entrée into society that I have. For them life is a struggle against the misconceptions perpetuated by the myth of the Latina as whore, domestic, or criminal. We cannot change this by legislating the way people look at us. The transformation, as I see it, has to occur at a much more individual level. My personal goal in my public life is to try to replace the old pervasive stereotypes and myths about Latinas with a much more interesting set of realities. Every time I give a reading, I hope the stories I tell, the dreams and fears I examine in my work, can achieve some universal truth which will get my audience past the particulars of my skin color, my accent, or my clothes.

I once wrote a poem in which I called us Latinas "God's brown daughters." This poem is really a prayer of sorts, offered upward, but also, through the human-to-human channel of art, outward. It is a prayer for communication, and for respect. In it, Latin women pray "in Spanish to an Anglo God/with a Jewish heritage," and they are "fervently hoping/that if not omnipotent,/at least He be bilingual."

Suicide Note

Janice Mirikitani

. . . An Asian American college student was reported to have jumped to her death
from her dormitory window. Her body was found two days later under a deep
cover of snow. Her suicide note contained an apology to her parents for having
received less than a perfect four point grade average . . .

How many notes written . . .
ink smeared like birdprints in snow.

not good enough   not pretty enough   not smart enough
dear mother and father.
I apologize
for disappointing you.
I've worked very hard,
not good enough
harder, perhaps to please you.
If only I were a son, shoulders broad
as the sunset threading through pine,
I would see the light in my mother's
eyes, or the golden pride reflected
in my father's dream
of my wide, male hands worthy of work
and comfort.
I would swagger through life
muscled and bold and assured,
drawing praises to me
like currents in the bed of wind, virile
with confidence.
not good enough   not strong enough   not good enough

I apologize.
Tasks do not come easily.
Each failure, a glacier.

Each disapproval, a bootprint.
Each disappointment,
ice above my river.
So I have worked hard.
        not good enough
My sacrifice I will drop
bone by bone, perched
on the ledge of my womanhood,
fragile as wings.
        not strong enough
It is snowing steadily
surely not good weather
for flying—this sparrow
sillied and dizzied by the wind
on the edge.
        not smart enough
I make this ledge my altar
to offer penance.
This air will not hold me,
the snow burdens my crippled wings,
my tears drop like bitter cloth
softly into the gutter below.
    not good enough   not strong enough   not smart enough

       Choices thin as shaved
       ice. Notes shredded
       drift like snow

on my broken body,
covers me like whispers
of sorries
sorries.
Perhaps when they find me
they will bury
my bird bones beneath
a sturdy pine
and scatter my feathers like
unspoken song
over this white and cold and silent
breast of earth.

8

The Gap between Striving and Achieving:
The Case of Asian American Women

Deborah Woo

Much academic research on Asian Americans tends to underscore their success, a success which is attributed almost always to a cultural emphasis on education, hard work, and thrift. Less familiar is the story of potential not fully realized. For example, despite the appearance of being successful and highly educated, Asian American women do not necessarily gain the kind of recognition or rewards they deserve.

The story of unfulfilled dreams remains unwritten for many Asian Americans. It is specifically this story about the gap between striving and achieving that I am concerned with here. Conventional wisdom obscures the discrepancy by looking primarily at whether society is adequately rewarding individuals. By comparing how minorities as disadvantaged groups are doing relative to each other, the tendency is to view Asian Americans as a "model minority." This practice programs us to ignore structural barriers and inequities and to insist that any problems are simply due to different cultural values or failure of individual effort.

Myths about the Asian American community derive from many sources. All ethnic groups develop their own cultural myths. Sometimes, however, they create myths out of historical necessity, as a matter of subterfuge and survival. Chinese Americans, for example, were motivated to create new myths because institutional opportunities were closed off to them. Succeeding in America meant they had to invent fake aspects of an "Oriental culture," which became the beginning of the Chinatown tourist industry.

What has been referred to as the "model minority myth," however, essentially originated from without. The idea that Asian Americans have been a successful group has been a popular news media theme for the last twenty years. It has become a basis for cutbacks in governmental support for all ethnic minorities—for Asian Americans because they apparently are already successful as a group; for other ethnic minorities because they are presumably not working as hard as Asian Americans or they would not need assistance. Critics of this view argue that the portrayal of Asian Americans as socially and economically successful ignores fundamental inequities. That is, the question "Why have Asians been successful vis-à-vis other minorities?" has been asked at the expense of another equally important question: "What has kept Asians from *fully* reaping the fruits of their education and hard work?"

The achievements of Asian Americans are part reality, part myth. Part of the reality is that a highly visible group of Asian Americans are college-educated, occupationally well-situated, and earning relatively high incomes. The myth, however, is that hard work reaps commensurate rewards. This essay documents the gap between the level of education and subsequent occupational or income gains.

The Roots and Contours of the "Model Minority" Concept

Since World War II, social researchers and news media personnel have been quick to assert that Asian Americans excel over other ethnic groups in terms of earnings, education, and occupation. Asian Americans are said to save more, study more, work more, and so achieve more. The reason given: a cultural emphasis on education and hard work. Implicit in this view is a social judgment and moral injunction: if Asian Americans can make it on their own, why can't other minorities?

While the story of Asian American women workers is only beginning to be pieced together, the success theme is already being sung. The image prevails that despite cultural and racial oppression, they are somehow rapidly assimilating into the mainstream. As workers, they participate in the labor force at rates higher than all others, including Anglo women. Those Asian American women who pursue higher education surpass other women, and even men, in this respect. Moreover, they have acquired a reputation for not only being conscientious and industrious but docile, compliant, and uncomplaining as well.

In the last few decades American women in general have been demanding "equal pay for equal work," the legitimation of housework as work that needs to be recompensed, and greater representation in the professional fields. These demands, however, have not usually come from Asian American women. From the perspective of those in power, this reluctance to complain is another feature of the "model minority." But for those who seek to uncover employment abuses, the unwillingness to talk about problems on the job is itself a problem. The garment industry, for example, is a major area of exploitation, yet it is also one that is difficult to investigate and control. In a 1983 report on the Concentrated Employment Program of the California Department of Industrial Relations, it was noted:

> The major problem for investigators in San Francisco is that the Chinese community is very close-knit, and employers and employees cooperate in refusing to speak to investigators. In two years of enforcing the Garment Registration Act, the

CEP has never received a complaint from an Asian employee. The few complaints received have been from Anglo or Latin workers.[1]

While many have argued vociferously either for or against the model minority concept, Asian Americans in general have been ambivalent in this regard. Asian Americans experience pride in achievement born of hard work and self-sacrifice, but at the same time, they resist the implication that all is well. Data provided here indicate that Asian Americans have not been successful in terms of benefitting fully, (i.e., monetarily), from their education. It is a myth that Asian Americans have proven the American Dream. How does this myth develop?

The working consumer: income and cost of living. One striking feature about Asian Americans is that they are geographically concentrated in areas where both income and cost of living are very high. In 1970, 80 percent of the total Asian American population resided in five states—California, Hawaii, Illinois, New York, and Washington. Furthermore, 59 percent of Chinese, Filipino, and Japanese Americans were concentrated in only 5 of the 243 Standard Metropolitan Statistical Areas (SMSA) in the United States—Chicago, Honolulu, Los Angeles/Long Beach, New York, and San Francisco/Oakland.[2] The 1980 census shows that immigration during the intervening decade has not only produced dramatic increases, especially in the Filipino and Chinese populations, but has also continued the overwhelming tendency for these groups to concentrate in the same geographical areas, especially those in California.[3] Interestingly enough, the very existence of large Asian communities in the West has stimulated among more recent refugee populations what is now officially referred to as "secondary migration," that is, the movement of refugees away from their sponsoring communities (usually places where there was no sizable Asian population prior to their own arrival) to those areas where there are well-established Asian communities.[4]

This residential pattern means that while Asian Americans may earn more by living in high-income areas, they also pay more as consumers. The additional earning power gained from living in San Francisco or Los Angeles, say, is absorbed by the high cost of living in such cities. National income averages which compare the income of Asian American women with that of the more broadly dispersed Anglo women systematically distort the picture. Indeed, if we compare women within the same area, Asian American women are frequently less well-off than Anglo American females, and the difference between women pales when compared with Anglo males, whose mean income is much higher than that of any group of women.[5]

When we consider the large immigrant Asian population and the language barriers that restrict women to menial or entry-level jobs, we are talking about a group that not only earns minimum wage or less, but one whose purchasing power is substantially undermined by living in metropolitan areas of states where the cost of living is unusually high.

Another striking pattern about Asian American female employment is the high rate of labor force participation. Asian American women are more likely than Anglo American women to work full time and year round. The model minority interpretation tends to assume that mere high labor force participation is a sign of successful employment. One important factor motivating minority women to enter the work force, however, is the need to supplement family resources. For Anglo American women some of the necessity for working is partly offset by the fact that they often share in the higher incomes of Anglo males, who tend not only to earn more than all other groups but, as noted earlier, also tend to receive higher returns on their education. Moreover, once regional variation is adjusted for, Filipino and Chinese Americans had a median annual income equivalent to black males in four mainland SMSAs—Chicago, Los Angeles/Long Beach, New York, San Francisco/Oakland.[6] Census statistics point to the relatively lower earning capacity of Asian males compared to Anglo males, suggesting that Asian American women enter the work force to help compensate for this inequality. Thus, the mere fact of high employment must be read cautiously and analyzed within a larger context.

The different faces of immigration. Over the last decade immigration has expanded the Chinese population by 85.3 percent, making it the largest Asian group in the country at 806,027, and has swelled the Filipino population by 125.8 percent, making it the second largest at 774,640. Hence at present the majority of Chinese American and Filipino American women are foreign-born. In addition the Asian American "success story" is misleading in part because of a select group of these immigrants: foreign-educated professionals.

Since 1965 U.S. immigration laws have given priority to seven categories of individuals. Two of the seven allow admittance of people with special occupational skills or services needed in the United States. Four categories facilitate family reunification, and the last applies only to refugees. While occupation is estimated to account for no more than 20 percent of all visas, professionals are not precluded from entering under other preference categories. Yet this select group is frequently offered as evidence of the upward mobility possible in America when Asian Americans who are born and raised in the United States are far less likely to reach the doctoral level in their education. Over two-thirds of Asians with doctorates in the United States are trained and educated abroad.[7]

Also overlooked in some analyses is a great deal of downward mobility among the foreign-born. For example, while foreign-educated health professionals are given preferential status for entry into this country, restrictive licensing requirements deny them the opportunity to practice or utilize their special skills. They are told that their educational credentials, experience, and certifications are inadequate. Consequently, for many the only alternatives are menial labor or unemployment.[8] Other highly educated immigrants become owner/managers of Asian businesses, which also suggests downward mobility and an inability to find jobs in their field of expertise.

"Professional" obscures more than it reveals. Another major reason for the perception of "model minority" is that the census categories implying success, "professional-managerial" or "executive, administrative, managerial," frequently camouflage important inconsistencies with this image of success. As managers, Asian Americans, usually male, are concentrated in certain occupations. They tend to be self-employed in small-scale wholesale and retail trade and manufacturing. They are rarely buyers, sales managers, administrators, or salaried managers in large-scale retail trade, communications, or public utilities. Among foreign-born Asian women, executive-managerial status is limited primarily to auditors and accountants.[9]

In general, Asian American women with a college education are concentrated in narrow and select, usually less prestigious, rungs of the "professional-managerial" class. In 1970, 27 percent of native-born Japanese women were either elementary or secondary school teachers. Registered nurses made up the next largest group. Foreign-born Filipino women found this to be their single most important area of employment, with 19 percent being nurses. They were least represented in the more prestigious professions—physicians, judges, dentists, law professors, and lawyers.[10] In 1980 foreign-born Asian women with four or more years of college were most likely to find jobs in administrative support or clerical occupations.

Self-help through "taking care of one's own." Much of what is considered ideal or model behavior in American society is based on Anglo-Saxon, Protestant values. Chief among them is an ethic of individual self-help, of doing without outside assistance or governmental support. On the other hand, Asian Americans have historically relied to a large extent on family or community resources. Their tightly-knit communities tend to be fairly closed to the outside world, even when under economic hardship. Many below the poverty level do not receive any form of public assistance.[11] Even if we include social security benefits as a form of supplementary income, the proportion of Asian Americans who use them is again very low, much lower than that for Anglo Americans.[12] Asian American families, in fact, are more likely than Anglo American families to bear economic hardships on their own.

While Asian Americans appear to have been self-sufficient as communities, we need to ask, at what personal cost? Moreover, have they as a group reaped rewards commensurate with their efforts? The following section presents data which document that while Asian American women may be motivated to achieve through education, monetary returns for them are less than for other groups.

The Nature of Inequality

The decision to use white males as the predominant reference group within the United States is a politically charged issue. When women raise and push the issue of "comparable worth," of "equal pay for equal work," they argue that women frequently do work equivalent to men's, but are paid far less for it.

The same argument can be made for Asian American women, and the evidence of inequality is staggering. For example, after adjustments are made for occupational prestige, age, education, weeks worked, hours worked each week, and state of residence in 1975, Chinese American women could be expected to earn only 70 percent of the majority male income. Even among the college-educated, Chinese American women fared least well, making only 42 percent of what majority males earned. As we noted earlier, the mean income of all women, Anglo and

Asian, was far below that of Anglo males in 1970 and 1980. This was true for both native-born and foreign-born Asians. In 1970 Anglo women earned only 54 percent of what their male counterparts did. Native-born Asian American women, depending on the particular ethnic group, earned anywhere from 49 to 57 percent of what Anglo males earned. In 1980, this inequity persisted.

Another way of thinking about comparable worth is not to focus only on what individuals do on the job, but on what they bring to the job as well. Because formal education is one measure of merit in American society and because it is most frequently perceived as the means to upward mobility, we would expect greater education to have greater payoffs.

Asian American women tend to be extraordinarily successful in terms of attaining higher education. Filipino American women have the highest college completion rate of all women and graduate at a rate 50 percent greater than that of majority males. Chinese American and Japanese American women follow closely behind, exceeding both the majority male and female rate of college completion.[13] Higher levels of education, however, bring lower returns for Asian American women than they do for other groups.

While education enhances earnings capability, the return on education for Asian American women is not as great as that for other women, and is well below parity with white males. Data on Asian American women in the five SMSAs where they are concentrated bear this out.[14] In 1980 all these women fell far behind Anglo males in what they earned in relation to their college education. Between 8 and 16 percent of native-born women earned $21,200 compared to 50 percent of Anglo males. Similar patterns were found among college-educated foreign-born women.

The fact that Asian American women do not reap the income benefits one might expect given their high levels of educational achievement raises questions about the reasons for such inequality. To what extent is this discrepancy based on outright discrimination? On self-imposed limitations related to cultural modesty? The absence of certain social or interpersonal skills required for upper managerial positions? Or institutional factors beyond their control? It is beyond the scope of this paper to address such concerns. However, the fact of inequality is itself noteworthy and poorly appreciated.

In general, Asian American women usually are overrepresented in clerical or administrative support jobs. While there is a somewhat greater tendency for foreign-born college-educated Asian women to find clerical-related jobs, both native- and foreign-born women have learned that clerical work is the area where they are most easily employed. In fact, in 1970 a third of native-born Chinese women were doing clerical work. A decade later Filipino women were concentrated there. In addition Asian American women tend to be overrepresented as cashiers, file clerks, office machine operators, and typists. They are less likely to get jobs as secretaries or receptionists. The former occupations not only carry less prestige but generally have "little or no decision-making authority, low mobility and low public contact."[15]

In short, education may improve one's chances for success, but it cannot promise the American Dream. For Asian American women education seems to serve less as an opportunity for upward mobility than as protection against jobs as service or assembly workers, or as machine operatives—all areas where foreign-born Asian women are far more likely to find themselves.

Conclusion

In this essay I have attempted to direct our attention on the gap between achievement and reward, specifically the failure to reward monetarily those who have demonstrated competence. Asian American women, like Asian American men, have been touted as "model minorities," praised for their outstanding achievements. The concept of model minority, however, obscures the fact that one's accomplishments are not adequately recognized in terms of commensurate income or choice of occupation. By focusing on the achievements of one minority in relation to another, our attention is diverted from larger institutional and historical factors which influence a group's success. Each ethnic group has a different history, and a simplistic method of modeling which assumes the experience of all immigrants is the same ignores the sociostructural context in which a certain kind of achievement occurred. For example, World War II enabled many Asian Americans who were technically trained and highly educated to move into lucrative war-related industries.[16] More recently, Korean immigrants during the 1960s were able to capitalize on the fast-growing demand for wigs in the United States. It was not simply cultural ingenuity or individual hard work which made them successful in this enterprise, but the fact that Korean immigrants were in the unique position of being able to import cheap hair products from their mother country.[17]

Just as there are structural opportunities, so there are structural barriers. However, the persistent emphasis in American society on individual effort deflects attention away from such barriers and creates self-doubt among those who have not "made it." The myth that Asian Americans have succeeded as a group, when in actuality there are serious discrepancies between effort and achievement, and between achievement and reward, adds still further to this self-doubt.

While others have also pointed out the myth of the model minority, I want to add that myths do have social functions. It would be a mistake to dismiss the model minority concept as merely a myth. Asian Americans are—however inappropriately—thrust into the role of being models for other minorities.

A closer look at the images associated with Asians as a model minority group suggests competing or contradictory themes. One image is that Asian Americans exemplify a competitive spirit enabling them to overcome structural barriers through perseverance and ingenuity. On the other hand, they are also seen as complacent, content with their social lot, and expecting little in the way of outside help. A third image is that Asian Americans are experts at assimilation, demonstrating that this society still functions as a melting pot. Their values are sometimes equated with white, middle-class, Protestant values of hard work, determination, and thrift. Opposing this image, however, is still another, namely that Asian Americans have succeeded because they possess cultural values unique to them as a group—their family-centeredness and long tradition of reverence for scholarly achievement, for example.

Perhaps, then, this is why so many readily accept the myth, whose tenacity is due to its being vague and broad enough to appeal to a variety of different groups. Yet to the extent that the myth is based on misconceptions, we are called upon to reexamine it more closely in an effort to narrow the gap between striving and achieving.[18]

NOTES

1. Ted Bell, "Quiet Loyalty Keeps Shops Running," *Sacramento Bee*, 11 February 1985.

2. Amado Y. Cabezas and Pauline L. Fong, "Employment Status of Asian-Pacific Women" (Background paper; San Francisco: ASIAN, Inc., 1976).

3. U.S. Bureau of the Census, *Race of the Population by States* (Washington, D.C., 1980). According to the census, 40 percent of all Chinese in America live in California, as well as 46 percent of all Filipinos, and 37 percent of all Japanese. New York ranks second for the number of Chinese residing there, and Hawaii is the second most populated state for Filipinos and Japanese.

4. Tricia Knoll, *Becoming Americans: Asian Sojourners, Immigrants, and Refugees in the Western United States* (Portland, Oreg.: Coast to Coast Books, 1982), 152.

5. U.S. Commission on Civil Rights, *Social Indicators of Equality for Minorities and Women* (Washington, D.C., 1978), 24, 50, 54, 58, 62.

6. David M. Moulton, "The Socioeconomic Status of Asian American Families in Five Major SMSAs" (Paper prepared for the Conference of Pacific and Asian American Families and HEW-related Issues, San Francisco, 1978). No comparative data were available on blacks for the fifth SMSA, Honolulu.

7. James E. Blackwell, *Mainstreaming Outsiders* (New York: General Hall, Inc., 1981), 306; and Commission on Civil Rights, *Social Indicators*, 9.

8. California Advisory Committee, "A Dream Unfulfilled: Korean and Filipino Health Professionals in California" (Report prepared for submission to U.S. Commission on Civil Right, May 1975), iii.

9. See Amado Y. Cabezas, "A View of Poor Linkages between Education, Occupation and Earnings for Asian Americans" (Paper presented at the Third National Forum on Education and Work, San Francisco, 1977), 17; and Census of Population, PUS, 1980.

10. Census of the Population, PUS, 1970, 1980.

11. A 1977 report on California families showed that an average of 9.3 percent of Japanese, Chinese, and Filipino families were below the poverty level, but that only 5.4 percent of these families received public assistance. The corresponding figures for Anglos were 6.3 percent and 5.9 percent. From Harold T. Yee, "The General Level of Well-Being of Asian Americans" (Paper presented to U.S. government officials in partial response to Justice Department amicus).

12. Moulton, "Socioeconomic Status," 70–71.

13. Commission on Civil Rights, *Social Indicators*, 54.

14. The few exceptions occur in Honolulu with women who had more than a high school education and in Chicago with women who had a high school education or three years of college. Even these women fared poorly when compared to men, however.

15. Bob H. Suzuki, "Education and the Socialization of Asian Americans: A Revisionist Analysis of the 'Model Minority' Thesis," *Amerasia Journal* 4:2 (1977): 43. See also Fong and Cabezas, "Economic and Employment Status," 48–49; and Commission on Civil Rights, *Social Indicators*, 97–98.

16. U.S. Commission on Civil Rights, "Education Issues" in *Civil Rights Issues of Asian and Pacific Americans: Myths and Realities* (Washington, D.C., 1979), 370–376. This material was presented by Ling-chi Wang, University of California, Berkeley.

17. Illsoo Kim, *New Urban Immigrants: The Korean Community in New York* (Princeton, N.J.: Princeton University Press, 1981).

18. For further discussion of the model minority myth and interpretation of census data, see Deborah Woo, "The Socioeconomic Status of Asian American Women in the Labor Force: An Alternative View," *Sociological Perspectives* 28:3 (July 1985):307–338.

Black Hispanics:
The Ties That Bind

Vivian Brady

At the bottom of the Spring semester course selection sheet is an optional question: students are requested to supply the college with their ethnicity for federal reporting requirements. Six categories are provided: White non-Hispanic, Black non-Hispanic, Puerto Rican, Hispanic other, Asian/Pacific Islander and Native American/Alaskan. Students must choose only one category, the one that best describes them.

I have always found the restriction to only one choice incredibly frustrating. As someone who describes herself as Black-Puerto Rican, there never seems to be any category that acknowledges the strong African heritage of Hispanic people in the Caribbean and Latin America. We, as Hispanics, are isolated as if we were a separate race unto ourselves. Unlike English and French-speaking people of the Caribbean, the kinship ties of Puerto Ricans to the Black American community are often ignored or denied. Our common bond of African heritage, as people of color in this hemisphere and our implicit sisterhood and brotherhood are often left unrecognized, even on my course selection sheet.

My recognition of myself as a Black-Puerto Rican may be facilitated by the fact that my parents come from two different islands. My mother is from Puerto Rico and my father from St. Thomas VI, but I have met many Hispanics who do not have mixed parentage who see themselves as I do. My mother emigrated to this country from Puerto Rico when she was three years old. The economic situation in Puerto Rico during the War was harsh and her family came to find a better life, settling in *El Barrio*, East Harlem. She has always viewed herself as a Black woman, a brave and independent stance to take in the 1940s and 50s. To my mother, separating the communities was a dangerous thing. She believes that it strengthens us to find our commonalities and stand united because the price of separation can be great in the face of racist oppression.

The "West Side Story" of my mother's time was more the relationship between the newly arrived Puerto Ricans and American Blacks than the romanticized tensions between the Italians and the Puerto Ricans of that musical's fame. An imaginary line was drawn on Lenox Avenue creating two insular communities, one Black and one Puerto Rican, and even though their lives and experiences were startlingly similar there was ambivalence. This ambivalence still survives today and divides us. Both groups fell into the trap of believing what the racist dogma of the day heralded. Many Puerto Ricans accepted on face value that Black was synonymous with inferiority. They believed the stereotypes about Blacks being "bad" and shied away from building a relationship with them, not wanting to be tainted by their status. Black Americans also fell into the mire of white racism; Puerto Ricans were loud, heavy drinkers and the men were womanizing Latinos. It seems funny to list these ridiculous images, yet they live on. I know because I have lived on both sides of the issue, red faced and embarrassed at how glibly we apply these stereotypes to each other; the multitudes of accusatory general statements not based on direct knowledge. Underneath it all is a wealth of strength that can help us discard the pervasive racism that our country is shackled to, but it must be a combined effort.

Our shared experience is not just the oppression that we have had to survive in this country, although it is of crucial importance and should serve to bind us together politically in order to create change and support each other's self determination. We live together in some of the poorest communities, are racked by a drug epidemic, inadequate housing, and an educational system that leaves us unqualified and intellectually stifled. We ride the subways together every day, feeling much the same anger and despair, yet there is uncertainty between us. We are determined to see our cultural differences as insurmountable even though we have a shared heritage. The core of this uncertainty and divisiveness is ignorance.

My grandmother lives in Ceiba, a sleepy town near the Navy base in Puerto Rico where all the houses are painted in tropical pastels and one can hear the war games being executed along the coast. I see in her brown face my African heritage. Slaves were imported into Puerto Rico like the other neighboring islands for their cheap labor. They were exploited in the sugar cane fields under the hot sun. They brought with them their music, spirit and culture, enriching Puerto Rico. Black people in the Spanish-speaking Caribbean and in Latin America have left us with great legacies: The quilombo leader Ganga Zambi in Brazil, the African rhythms of the *merengue* and the spiritual influences in our religions. My grandmother would never call herself Black though; she is firstly and lastly Puerto Rican. Most Puerto Ricans describe their country like a rainbow, a mixture and blend of African, European and Indian. The manner in which they view their "blackness" is directly related to their environment and culture.

I have often heard Black Americans alienated by this concept; they see a woman as dark as my grandmother not identifying herself as Black and conclude that "Puerto Ricans don't know what they are" or that they seek to deny their blackness. Sadly enough this is true for some. I certainly don't wish to obscure the issues of race, color and class among Puerto Ricans. We are afflicted by these prejudices, much like Black Americans. It is Puerto Rican to recognize our mixed heritage. It is a mulatto country, not the stark Black and White of the United States.

When I learn about Afro-American history I treat it as my own, as part of my identity as a Black woman. I see the accomplishments and survival as a testimony to all people of color. I hope that Black Americans can find pride and strength in Puerto Rican and other Afro-Latin histories, but I know that it will take time for people to see this global Pan-Africanist view.

Things are not simple though, and viewing the situation perched on the edge of both communities I see that though we may socialize, form committees and lobby together, we must learn more about each other to see the merits of standing nonjudgmentally side by side. A good place to begin is to examine our histories.

I recently asked some of my Black American friends, "What if Michael Griffith were Puerto Rican? Would you fight racist aggression in Howard Beach if the lynch mob were out to kill "dirty spics" with bats and pipes?" Most said their response would have been tempered by the fact that the victim was Hispanic and that they would not be as passionate. By the same token I would have liked to see a stronger voice made by the Hispanic community during the case. We do not yet see that the enemy and the issue are the same: we must both be energized to see the struggle.

I have been told that it is impossible for me to continue being both Puerto Rican and Black and that I will inevitably need to choose sides, perhaps as a way to show my allegiance to my chosen community. But I, like many other Hispanics, know that the blood I share with Afro-Americans links me to the survival and work necessary in both communities equally.

10

Blacks and Hispanics:
A Fragile Alliance

Jacqueline Conciatore and
Roberto Rodriguez

On the stone steps of City Hall, a leader of Latino workers makes a decision. Standing above an assemblage of microphones and tape recorders, he angrily tells reporters that African Americans are making gains at the expense of his people. "Blacks had their turn in the fight for equality," he says. "Now it's our turn." The next day on the same steps, a Black labor leader hosts the same audience. "Latinos," he says, "are pimping off the civil rights struggle. They didn't sacrifice their lives 25 years ago—or get beat with their own picket signs. They can't benefit from our fight." Both leaders take to the airwaves. People listen as they accuse each other of being racially motivated and of taking each other's jobs. In a number of inner-city schools, fights between Black and Latino students break out. Gang wars, already a problem, escalate into racial battles. Newspapers begin to report a killing a day. The leaders of the Latino and African American employees associations call for a truce. It is a show of unity. Restore peace to this city, they say. But the wrong people are talking. Nobody's listening. In a racially mixed community, tension is palpable. The possibility of violence is a hair trigger away . . . Sound familiar? Los Angeles? New York? Chicago? Houston? Philadelphia? Washington, DC? Miami? Oakland? Denver? Phoenix?

Some cities have already witnessed Black-Latino conflicts such as the one just described. Typically, tensions between the two groups arise from a perception that they must compete for scant educational and economic opportunities. "Any time communities of color have been locked out of the American dream," says Antonio Villaraigoza, past co-chair of the Los Angeles Black/Latino Agenda, "they have had to fight over the same limited resources—jobs, education."

As the above scenario illustrates, what leaders do and say are crucial to the state of Black-Latino relations. Many leaders recognize the potential revolutionary impact of a real alliance and are calling on Blacks and Hispanics to mobilize around a host of common concerns.

They stress that for people of color, alliance is not a luxury, not a utopian ideal, but a necessity. Creative and forceful initiatives are needed to confront the problems of the '90s, they say, to lift both communities out of the bottom of the barrel they share. If Blacks and Latinos do it together, the climb will be all the faster.

Demographic Changes: Impacting Race Relations

In a working class neighborhood in Washington, DC, a priest has a dilemma.

His 12:30 Spanish-language Mass is getting to be overcrowded. Standing shoulder to shoulder, patrons fill the pews, then take scattered positions at the back of the church.

The 9:30 Mass must become a Spanish service as well. But to accomplish this will take a doctorate in diplomacy, says Father Robert McCrary. People from the neighborhood—African Americans, Vietnamese, some whites—have been going to that Mass in English for years and years. When the transition happens, McCrary predicts, "the fur will fly."

The population changes that require solutions in McCrary's Mount Pleasant parish are also occurring in nearby Northern Virginia, in suburban Maryland, throughout the metropolitan area. With a wider lens, one can see the same demographic tides in Florida, Chicago and on the West Coast. The nation as a whole, in fact, has seen a 39 percent increase in Hispanic members—both immigrants and those born here—since 1980. This compares to a total population growth of 9.5 percent.

For a nation that likes to call itself a melting pot, shifts in the demographic makeup of its citizenry are nothing new. Never before, however, has the emergence of a population promised to so significantly alter the racial balance of the nation, as is happening with the current influx of Latinos (and Asian Americans as well).

The change forces Black Americans to alter their conception of race relations, to make room for new players. Says Dr. Manning Marable of the Center for Studies of Ethnicity and Race in America: "Black Americans are still accustomed to thinking of race relations in Black and white terms." But that conceptual framework, he says, has not been appropriate for 50 years at least.

Ben Benavidez, director of the Fresno-based Mexican American Political Association (MAPA), agrees: "Black people have to remember they're not the only minority. And they're not the only oppressed minority."

In Fresno and its San Joaquin Valley, there is some tension between Blacks and Mexican-Americans as they struggle for a share of power in the educational system. Local board members are apt to see "minority progress" as putting one or two Blacks in high administrative posts, Benavidez says. But Mexican-American children are the majority school-age population.

"We're not fighting to see who's the most oppressed," Benavidez says. But, he adds, "there are going to be some struggles, and the powers that be love that."

Economic Competition

In Miami's Black community, says Guillermo Grenier, director of the Center for Labor Research, everyone knows that you can't get a job if you can't speak Spanish.

"In the Black community, you have common knowledge that Blacks were displaced by Latins," he says.

Although Blacks in many urban areas say they are losing economic ground to immigrants and their offspring, nowhere is that plaint heard more clearly than in Miami. Since Cuban exiles laid stakes there 30 years ago, the city has erupted into periodic race-related violence.

The Black sense of displacement, along with Cuban-Black political differences and a police force that many say is racist, combine to create tensions that lead to riots, says Marvin Dunn, author of a book on the Miami riots of 1980.

But Dunn says objective evidence does not bear out the perception that Miami's Blacks have been displaced by Hispanics. In the last decade, the number of Blacks earning $35,000 or more has doubled. Black median family incomes have also improved, while they held steady for whites and dropped for Hispanics he says.

These upward trends, however, do not hold true for low-income Blacks, who comprise 30 percent of the city's Black population. This group has indeed lost access to housing, health care and early intervention programs such as Head Start, Dunn says. "In the competition for basic services, lower income Blacks have definitely lost out," he says. Dunn attributes this economic decline to an influx of "new poor," many of them Cubans who came in the Mariel exodus of 1980, when Fidel Castro packed American-bound boats with convicts and those diagnosed as mentally ill.

Grenier counters that the Cuban presence impacts more affluent Blacks in less measurable ways. "The managers and city mothers and fathers, when they look at, 'Should we include minorities in our doings?,' They say, 'Yes,' but they will include mostly Latinos." Middle-class Blacks are not being displaced in the upper levels of business and government, he says, because "they were never there to begin with."

The belief that the success of Hispanics means the failure of Blacks, and vice versa, is not unique to Miami. But a recent study by Paula McClain of Arizona State University and Albert Karnig of the University of Wyoming indicates that Blacks and Latinos have reason to celebrate each other's success. McClain and Karnig analyzed the distribution of power and resources in 49 U.S. cities with populations exceeding 25,000 and at least 10 percent Black and 10 percent Hispanic populations. They found that where Blacks are succeeding in some measure with respect to education, income, and employment, Hispanics are likely to be successful as well.

In the end, it is a waste of energy to focus on the deprivation of one's group relative to another, Marable says. "The whole approach is wrong. It's like battling for crumbs." The correct approach, he says, is to determine "how race and ethnicity are used to perpetuate the inferior status for people of color across the board."

Political Differences

When Miami officials did not give Nelson Mandela a celebratory welcome this past summer because the Cuban community objected to Mandela's stated affiliation with Fidel Castro, Black residents were outraged and chagrined.

While the incident was an illustration of how diverse the Latino community is (Cubans shunned Mandela, while Mexican Americans, Central Americans, South Americans and Latinos from the Caribbean welcomed him with open arms), it also illustrated how political differences work to separate Blacks and Latinos. In Miami, many Blacks feel Cuban Americans care only about Castro and have no appreciation of their experience of oppression in the United States, said Dunn.

That perception in some cases is well founded, said Max Castro, head of Greater Miami United, a multicultural coalition of activists. When Cuban Americans first arrived, the civil rights struggle was flowering. "It was like watching the person that threw the second punch and not seeing all the punches that were thrown before that," he said. Because Cubans were relatively well-treated here, "they kind of overestimate the benevolence of the system and may not be sufficiently critical of the way [it] treats other minorities—and even ourselves on some occasions," he said.

The two groups have a gap in their world views as well, Max Castro said. Cubans see the world in terms of "communist or noncommunist," he said. Blacks tend to see the world in terms of race. "Cubans see Nelson Mandela as someone allied with the African Nationalist party. . . . African Americans see Mandela as a liberator in the struggle for equality. Cubans attack Mandela for ideological reasons. African Americans see that as a racial attack."

Racism

Racism occupies a place in the Black-Hispanic dynamic as well. Blacks have been known to question the right of Hispanics to empowerment because some do not have legal status as citizens. Hispanics have been known to argue that many Blacks cannot beat the system because they are unwilling to work.

Says Ona Alston, a former Howard University student body president who works as project manager for the Committee in Solidarity with the People of El Salvador in Washington, DC: "Even when African Americans and Latinos live in close proximity, which is generally not the case, there is a tremendous amount of ignorance and misunderstanding."

But, she says, proximity improves the chances for understanding. "Where there is proximity, African Americans and Latinos can see they have a lot more in common than, say, African Americans and European Americans do, or Latinos and European Americans do.

"But if there's one thing that America is good at . . . it's letting people know, when you come to these shores, whatever you are, you aren't Black. We are at the bottom of the totem pole—'These are the people to be dumped on.' And that's very real."

11

Blacks and Jews:
Commonalities and Conflicts

Cornel West

The period of genuine empathy and principled alliances between Jews and blacks constitutes a major pillar of American progressive politics in this century. These supportive links begin with W. E. B. DuBois's The Crisis and Abraham Cahan's Jewish Daily Forward and are seen clearly between Jewish leftists and A. Philip Randolph's numerous organizations, between Elliot Cohen's Commentary and the early career of James Baldwin, between prophets like Abraham Joshua Heschel and Martin Luther King Jr., between the predominantly Jewish Students for a Democratic Society and the Student Nonviolent Coordinating Committee, and are now seen in Tikkun magazine.

Presently, this inspiring period of cooperation is often downplayed by blacks and romanticized by Jews. It is downplayed by blacks because they focus on the astonishing entree of most Jews into the middle and upper-middle classes—an entree that has spawned an intense conflict with the slower growing black middle class and a social resentment from a fast-growing black impoverished class. Jews tend to romanticize this period because their present status as upper-middle and top dogs unsettles their historical self-image as progressives with a compassion for the underdog.

There are two major issues over which blacks and Jews contend. The first is the question of what constitutes the most effective means for black progress. With more than half of all black professionals and managers employed in the public sphere, and those in the private sphere often gaining entree owing to regulatory checks by the Equal Employment Opportunity Commission, attacks by Jews on affirmative action are perceived as assaults on black livelihood. And since a disproportionate percentage of poor blacks depend on Government support to survive, attempts to dismantle public programs are viewed by blacks as opposition to black survival.

Visible Jewish resistance to affirmative action and Government spending on social programs pits some Jews against black progress. This opposition is all the more visible to black people because of past Jewish support for black progress. It also seems to reek of naked group interest as well as a willingness to abandon compassion for the underdogs. The second major area of contention is the meaning

225

and practice of Zionism as embodied in Israel. Without a sympathetic understanding of the historical sources of Jewish fears and anxieties about group survival, blacks will not grasp the visceral attachment of most Jews to Israel. Similarly, without a candid acknowledgment of blacks' status as permanent underdogs in American society, Jews will not comprehend what the plight of Palestinians in Israel means to blacks symbolically and literally.

Jews rightly pointed out that the atrocities of Africa's elites on oppressed Africans in Kenya, Uganda and Ethiopia are just as bad as or worse than those perpetrated on Palestinians by Israeli elites. Some also point out—rightly—that deals and treaties between Israel and South Africa are not so radically different from those between some black African countries and South Africa.

Still, these and other Jewish charges of black double standards with regard to Israel do not take us to the heart of the matter. Blacks often perceive Jewish defense of Israel as a second instance of naked group interest and, again, an abandonment of substantive moral deliberation.

Jews tend to view black critiques of Israel as black rejection of their right to group survival, hence a betrayal of the precondition for a black-Jewish alliance. What is at stake is not simply black-Jewish relations, but, more important, the moral content of Jewish and black identities and their political consequences.

The ascendancy of the Likud Party in 1977 and the prominence of narrow black nationalists' voices in the 80's aggravated this impasse. When mainstream American Jewish organizations supported the inhumane policies of Menachem Begin and Yitzhak Shamir, they tipped their hats toward cold-hearted interest-group calculations.

When black nationalist spokesmen like Louis Farrakhan and Leonard Jeffries excessively targeted Jewish power as subordinating black and brown peoples, they played the same mean-spirited game. (The nationalists' anti-Semitic rhetoric, however, rarely degenerates into anti-Semitic violence.) In turning their heads from the ugly truth of Palestinian subjugation and in refusing to admit the falsity of the Jewish conspiracies, both sides failed to define the *moral* character of their identities.

The impasse in black-Jewish relations will be overcome only when self-critical exchanges take place within and across black and Jewish communities, not simply about their own group interest but also, and more important, about what being black or Jewish means in *ethical* terms.

This reflection should not be so naïve as to ignore group interest, but it should take us to a higher moral ground where discussions about democracy and justice determine how we define ourselves and our politics and help us formulate strategies and tactics to sidestep the traps of tribalism and chauvinism.

Pigskin, Patriarchy, and Pain

Don Sabo

I am sitting down to write as I've done thousands of times over the last decade. But today there's something very different. I'm not in pain.

A half-year ago I underwent back surgery. My physician removed two disks from the lumbar region of my spine and fused three vertebrae using bone scrapings from my right hip. The surgery is called a "spinal fusion." For seventy-two hours I was completely immobilized. On the fifth day, I took a few faltering first steps with one of those aluminum walkers that are usually associated with the elderly in nursing homes. I progressed rapidly and left the hospital after nine days completely free of pain for the first time in years.

How did I, a well-intending and reasonably gentle boy from western Pennsylvania ever get into so much pain? At a simple level, I ended up in pain because I played a sport that brutalizes men's (and now sometimes women's) bodies. *Why* I played football and bit the bullet of pain, however, is more complicated. Like a young child who learns to dance or sing for a piece of candy, I played for rewards and payoffs. Winning at sport meant winning friends and carving a place for myself within the male pecking order. Success at the "game" would make me less like myself and more like the older boys and my hero, Dick Butkus. Pictures of his hulking and snarling form filled my head and hung over my bed, beckoning me forward like a mythic Siren. If I could be like Butkus, I told myself, people would adore me as much as I adored him. I might even adore myself. As an adolescent I hoped sport would get me attention from the girls. Later, I became more practical-minded and I worried more about my future. What kind of work would I do for a living? Football became my ticket to a college scholarship which, in western Pennsylvania during the early 'sixties, meant a career instead of getting stuck in the steelmills.

The Road to Surgery

My bout with pain and spinal "pathology" began with a decision I made in 1955 when I was 8 years old. I "went out" for football. At the time, I felt uncomfortable

227

inside my body—too fat, too short, too weak. Freckles and glasses, too! I wanted to change my image, and I felt that changing my body was one place to begin. My parents bought me a set of weights, and one of the older boys in the neighborhood was solicited to demonstrate their use. I can still remember the ease with which he lifted the barbell, the veins popping through his bulging biceps in the summer sun, and the sated look of strength and accomplishment on his face. This was to be the image of my future.

That Fall I made a dinner-table announcement that I was going out for football. What followed was a rather inauspicious beginning. First, the initiation rites. Pricking the flesh with thorns until blood was drawn and having hot peppers rubbed in my eyes. Getting punched in the gut again and again. Being forced to wear a jockstrap around my nose and not knowing what was funny. Then came what was to be an endless series of proving myself: calisthenics until my arms ached; hitting hard and fast and knocking the other guy down; getting hit in the groin and not crying. I learned that pain and injury are "part of the game."

I "played" through grade school, co-captained my high school team, and went on to become an inside linebacker and defensive captain at the NCAA Division I level. I learned to be an animal. Coaches took notice of animals. Animals made first team. Being an animal meant being fanatically aggressive and ruthlessly competitive. If I saw an arm in front of me, I trampled it. Whenever blood was spilled, I nodded approval. Broken bones (not mine of course) were secretly seen as little victories within the bigger struggle. The coaches taught me to "punish the other man," but little did I suspect that I was devastating my own body at the same time. There were broken noses, ribs, fingers, toes and teeth, torn muscles and ligaments, bruises, bad knees, and busted lips, and the gradual pulverizing of my spinal column that, by the time my jock career was long over at age 30, had resulted in seven years of near-constant pain. It was a long road to the surgeon's office.

Now surgically freed from its grip, my understanding of pain has changed. Pain had gnawed away at my insides. Pain turned my awareness inward. I blamed myself for my predicament; I thought that I was solely responsible for every twinge and sleepless night. But this view was an illusion. My pain, each individual's pain, is really an expression of a linkage to an outer world of people, events, and forces. The origins of our pain are rooted *outside*, not inside, our skins.

The Pain Principle

Sport is just one of the many areas in our culture where pain is more important than pleasure. Boys are taught that to endure pain is courageous, to survive pain is manly. The principle that pain is "good" and pleasure is "bad" is crudely evident in the "no pain, no gain" philosophy of so many coaches and athletes. The "pain principle" weaves its way into the lives and psyches of male athletes in two fundamental ways. It stifles men's awareness of their bodies and limits our emotional expression. We learn to ignore personal hurts and injuries because they interfere with the "efficiency" and "goals" of the "team." We become adept at taking the feelings that boil up inside us—feelings of insecurity and stress from striving so hard for success—and channeling them in a bundle of rage which is directed at opponents and enemies. This posture toward oneself and the world is not limited to "jocks." It is evident in the lives of many nonathletic men who, as tough guys, deny their authentic physical or emotional needs and develop health problems as a result.

Today, I no longer perceive myself as an *individual* ripped off by athletic injury. Rather, I see myself as just *one more man among many men* who got swallowed up by a social system predicated on male domination. Patriarchy has two structural aspects. First, it is an hierarchical system in which men dominate women in crude and debased, slick and subtle ways. Feminists have made great progress exposing and analyzing this dimension of the edifice of sexism. But it is also a system of *intermale dominance,* in which a minority of men dominates the masses of men. This intermale dominance hierarchy exploits the majority of those it beckons to climb its heights. Patriarchy's mythos of heroism and its morality of power-worship implant visions of ecstasy and masculine excellence in the minds of the boys who ultimately will defend its inequities and ridicule its victims. It is inside this institutional framework that I have begun to explore the essence and scope of "the pain principle."

Taking It

Patriarchy is a form of social hierarchy. Hierarchy breeds inequity and inequity breeds pain. To remain stable, the hierarchy must either justify the pain or explain it away. In a patriarchy, women and the masses of men are fed the cultural message that pain is inevitable and that pain enhances one's character and moral worth. This principle is expressed in Judeo-Christian beliefs. The Judeo-Christian god inflicts or permits pain, yet "the Father" is still revered and loved. Likewise, a chief disciplinarian in the patriarchal family, the father has the right to inflict pain. The "pain principle" also echoes throughout traditional western sexual morality; it is better to experience the pain of *not* having sexual pleasure than it is to have sexual pleasure.

Most men learn to heed these cultural messages and take their "cues for survival" from the patriarchy. The Willie Lomans of the economy pander to the profit and the American Dream. Soldiers, young and old, salute their neo-Hun generals. Right-wing Christians genuflect before the idols of righteousness, affluence, and conformity. And male athletes adopt the visions and values that coaches are offering: to take orders, to take pain, to "take out" opponents, to take the game seriously, to take women, and to take their place on the team. And if they can't "take it," then the rewards of athletic camaraderie, prestige, scholarship, pro contracts, and community recognition are not forthcoming.

Becoming a football player fosters conformity to male-chauvinistic values and self-abusing lifestyles. It contributes to the legitimacy of a social structure based on patriarchal power. Male competition for prestige and status in sport and elsewhere leads to identification with the relatively few males who control resources and are able to bestow rewards and inflict punishment. Male supremacists are not born, they are made, and traditional athletic socialization is a fundamental contribution to this complex social-psychological and political process. Through sport, many males, indeed, learn to "take it"—that is, to internalize patriarchal values which, in turn, become part of their gender identity and conception of women and society.

My high school coach once evoked the pain principle during a pregame pep talk. For what seemed an eternity, he paced frenetically and silently before us with fists clenched and head bowed. He suddenly stopped and faced us with a smile. It was as though he had approached a podium to begin a long-awaited lecture. "Boys," he began, "people who say that football is a 'contact sport' are dead wrong. Dancing is a contact sport. Football is a game of pain and violence! Now get the hell out of here and kick some ass." We practically ran through the wall of the locker room, surging in unison to fight the coach's war. I see now that the coach was right but for all the wrong reasons. I should have taken him at his word and never played the game!

He Defies You Still:
The Memoirs of a Sissy

Tommi Avicolli

You're just a faggot
No history faces you this morning
A faggot's dreams are scarlet
Bad blood bled from words that scarred[1]

Scene One

A homeroom in a Catholic high school in South Philadelphia. The boy sits quietly in the first aisle, third desk, reading a book. He does not look up, not even for a moment. He is hoping no one will remember he is sitting there. He wishes he were invisible. The teacher is not yet in the classroom so the other boys are talking and laughing loudly.

Suddenly, a voice from beside him:

"Hey, you're a faggot, ain't you?"

The boy does not answer. He goes on reading his book, or rather pretending he is reading his book. It is impossible to actually read the book now.

"Hey, I'm talking to you!"

The boy still does not look up. He is so scared his heart is thumping madly; it feels like it is leaping out of his chest and into his throat. But he can't look up.

"Faggot, I'm talking to you!"

To look up is to meet the eyes of the tormentor.

Suddenly, a sharpened pencil point is thrust into the boy's arm. He jolts, shaking off the pencil, aware that there is blood seeping from the wound.

"What did you do that for?" he asks timidly.

"Cause I hate faggots," the other boy says, laughing. Some other boys begin to laugh, too. A symphony of laughter. The boy feels as if he's going to cry. But he must not cry. Must not cry. So he holds back the tears and tries to read the book again. He must read the book. Read the book.

When the teacher arrives a few minutes later, the class quiets down. The boy does not tell the teacher what has happened. He spits on the wound to clean it, dabbing it with a tissue until the bleeding stops. For weeks he fears some dreadful infection from the lead in the pencil point.

Scene Two

The boy is walking home from school. A group of boys (two, maybe three, he is not certain) grab him from behind, drag him into an alley and beat him up. When he gets home, he races up to his room, refusing dinner ("I don't feel well," he tells his mother through the locked door) and spends the night alone in the dark wishing he would die. . . .

These are not fictitious accounts—I *was* that boy. Having been branded a sissy by neighborhood children because I preferred jump rope to baseball and dolls to playing soldiers, I was often taunted with "hey sissy" or "hey faggot" or "yoo hoo honey" (in a mocking voice) when I left the house.

To avoid harassment, I spent many summers alone in my room. I went out on rainy days when the street was empty.

I came to like being alone. I didn't need anyone, I told myself over and over again. I was an island. Contact with others meant pain. Alone, I was protected. I began writing poems, then short stories. There was no reason to go outside anymore. I had a world of my own.

In the schoolyard today
they'll single you out
Their laughter will leave your ears ringing
like the church bells
which once awed you. . . .[2]

School was one of the more painful experiences of my youth. The neighborhood bullies could be avoided. The taunts of the children living in those endless repetitive row houses could be evaded by staying in my room. But school was something I had to face day after day for some two hundred mornings a year.

I had few friends in school. I was a pariah. Some kids would talk to me, but few wanted to be known as my close friend. Afraid of labels. If I was a sissy, then he had to be a sissy, too. I was condemned to loneliness.

Fortunately, a new boy moved into our neighborhood and befriended me; he wasn't afraid of the labels. He protected me when the other guys threatened to beat me up. He walked me home from school; he broke through the terrible loneliness. We were in third or fourth grade at the time.

We spent a summer or two together. Then his parents sent him to camp and I was once again confined to my room.

Scene Three

High school lunchroom. The boy sits at a table near the back of the room. Without warning, his lunch bag is grabbed and tossed to another table. Someone opens it and confiscates a package of Tastykakes; another boy takes the sandwich. The empty bag is tossed back to the boy who stares at it, dumbfounded. He should be used to this; it has happened before.

Someone screams, "faggot," laughing. There is always laughter. It does not annoy him anymore.

There is no teacher nearby. There is never a teacher around. And what would he say if there were? Could he report the crime? He would be jumped after school if he did. Besides, it would be his word against theirs. Teachers never noticed anything. They never heard the taunts. Never heard the word, "faggot." They were the great deaf mutes, pillars of indifference; a sissy's pain was not relevant to history and geography and god made me to love honor and obey him, amen.

Scene Four

High school Religion class. Someone has a copy of *Playboy*. Father N. is not in the room yet; he's late, as usual. Someone taps the boy roughly on the shoulder. He turns. A finger points to the centerfold model, pink fleshy body, thin and sleek. Almost painted. Not real. The other asks, mocking voice, "Hey, does she turn you on? Look at those tits!"

The boy smiles, nodding meekly; turns away.

The other jabs him harder on the shoulder, "Hey, whatsamatter, don't you like girls?"

Laughter. Thousands of mouths; unbearable din of laughter. In the Arena: thumbs down. Don't spare the queer.

"Wanna suck my dick? Huh? That turn you on, faggot!"
The laughter seems to go on forever. . . .

Behind you, the sound of their laughter
echoes a million times
in a soundless place
They watch how you walk/sit/stand/breathe. . . .[3]

What did being a sissy really mean? It was a way of walking (from the hips rather than the shoulders); it was a way of talking (often with a lisp or in a high-pitched voice); it was a way of relating to others (gently, not wanting to fight, or hurt anyone's feelings). It was being intelligent ("an egghead" they called it sometimes); getting good grades. It means not being interested in sports, not playing football in the street after school; not discussing teams and scores and playoffs. And it involved not showing fervent interest in girls, not talking about scoring with tits or *Playboy* centerfolds. Not concealing naked women in your history book; or porno books in your locker.

On the other hand, anyone could be a "faggot." It was a catch-all. If you did something that didn't conform to what was the acceptable behavior of the group, then you risked being called a faggot. If you didn't get along with the "in" crowd, you were a faggot. It was the most commonly used put-down. It kept guys in line. They became angry when somebody called them a faggot. More fights started over someone calling someone else a faggot than anything else. The word had power. It toppled the male ego, shattered his delicate facade, violated the image he projected. He was tough. Without feeling. Faggot cut through all this. It made him vulnerable. Feminine. And feminine was the worst thing he could possibly be. Girls were fine for fucking, but no boy in his right mind wanted to be like them. A boy was the opposite of girl. He was not feminine. He was not feeling. He was not weak.

Just look at the gym teacher who growled like a dog; or the priest with the black belt who threw kids against the wall in rage when they didn't know their Latin. They were men, they got respect.

But not the physics teacher who preached pacifism during lectures on the nature of atoms. Everybody knew what he was—and why he believed in the anti-war movement.

My parents only knew that the neighborhood kids called me names. They begged me to act more like the other boys. My brothers were ashamed of me. They never said it, but I knew. Just as I knew that my parents were embarrassed by my behavior.

At times, they tried to get me to act differently. Once my father lectured me on how to walk right. I'm still not clear on what that means. Not from the hips, I guess, don't "swish" like faggots do.

A nun in elementary school told my mother at Open House that there was "something wrong with me." I had draped my sweater over my shoulders like a girl, she said. I was a smart kid, but I should know better than to wear my sweater like a girl!

My mother stood there, mute. I wanted her to say something, to chastise the nun; to defend me. But how could she? This was a nun talking—representative of Jesus, protector of all that was good and decent.

An uncle once told me I should start "acting like a boy" instead of like a girl. Everybody seemed ashamed of me. And I guess I was ashamed of myself, too. It was hard not to be.

Scene Five

Priest: Do you like girls, Mark?
Mark: Uh-huh.
Priest: I mean *really* like them?
Mark: Yeah—they're okay.
Priest: There's a role they play in your salvation. Do you understand it, Mark?
Mark: Yeah.
Priest: You've got to like girls. Even if you should decide to enter the seminary, it's
    important to keep in mind God's plan for a man and a woman. . . .[4]

Catholicism of course condemned homosexuality. Effeminacy was tolerated as long as the effeminate person did not admit to being gay. Thus, priests could be effeminate because they weren't gay.

As a sissy, I could count on no support from the church. A male's sole purpose in life was to father children—souls for the church to save. The only hope a homosexual had of attaining salvation was by remaining totally celibate. Don't even think of touching another boy. To think of a sin was a sin. And to sin was to put a mark upon the soul. Sin—if it was a serious offense against god—led to hell. There was no way around it. If you sinned, you were doomed.

Realizing I was gay was not an easy task. Although I knew I was attracted to boys by the time I was about eleven, I didn't connect this attraction to homosexuality. I was not queer. Not I. I was merely appreciating a boy's good looks, his fine features, his proportions. It didn't seem to matter that I didn't appreciate a girl's looks in the same way. There was no twitching in my thighs when I gazed upon a beautiful girl. But I wasn't queer.

I resisted that label—queer—for the longest time. Even when everything pointed to it, I refused to see it. I was certainly not queer. Not I.

We sat through endless English classes, and History courses about the wars between men who were not allowed to love each other. No gay history was ever taught. No history faces you this morning. You're just a faggot. Homosexuals had never contributed to the human race. God destroyed the queers in Sodom and Gomorrah.

We learned about Michelangelo, Oscar Wilde, Gertrude Stein—but never that they were queer. They were not queer. Walt Whitman, the "father of American poetry," was not queer. No one was queer. I was alone, totally unique. One of a kind. Were there others like me somewhere? Another planet, perhaps?

In school, they never talked of the queers. They did not exist. The only hint we got of this other species was in religion class. And even then it was clouded in mystery—never spelled out. It was sin. Like masturbation. Like looking at *Playboy* and getting a hard-on. A sin.

Once a progressive priest in senior year religion class actually mentioned homosexuals—he said the word—but was into Erich Fromm, into homosexuals as pathetic and sick. Fixated at some early stage; penis, anal, whatever. Only hetero-sexuals passed on to the nirvana of sexual development.

No other images from the halls of the Catholic high school except those the other boys knew: swishy faggot sucking cock in an alley somewhere, grabbing asses in the bathroom. Never mentioning how much straight boys craved blowjobs, it was part of the secret.

It was all a secret. You were not supposed to talk about the queers. Whisper maybe. Laugh about them, yes. But don't be open, honest; don't try to understand. Don't cite their accomplishments. No history faces you this morning. You're just a faggot   faggot   no history   just a faggot

Epilogue

The boy marching down the Parkway. Hundreds of queers. Signs proclaiming gay pride. Speakers. Tables with literature from gay groups. A miracle, he is thinking. Tears are coming loose now. Someone hugs him.

> *You could not control*
> *the sissy in me*
> *nor could you exorcise him*
> *nor electrocute him*
> *You declared him illegal illegitimate*
> *insane and immature*
> *But he defies you still.*[5]

NOTES

1. From the poem "Faggot" by Tommi Avicolli, published in *GPU News*, Sept. 1979.
2. Ibid.
3. Ibid.
4. From the play *Judgment of the Roaches* by Tommi Avicolli, produced in Philadelphia at the Gay Community Center, the Painted Bride Arts Center and the University of Penn-sylvania; aired over WXPN-FM, in four parts; and presented at the Lesbian/Gay Conference in Norfolk, VA, July, 1980.
5. From the poem "Sissy Poem," published in *Magic Doesn't Live Here Anymore* (Philadelphia: Spruce Street Press, 1976).

With No Immediate Cause

Ntozake Shange

every 3 minutes a woman is beaten
every five minutes a
woman is raped/every ten minutes
a lil girl is molested
yet i rode the subway today
i sat next to an old man who
may have beaten his old wife
3 minutes ago or 3 days/30 years ago
he might have sodomized his
daughter but i sat there
cuz the young men on the train
might beat some young women
later in the day or tomorrow
i might not shut my door fast
enuf/push hard enuf
every 3 minutes it happens
some woman's innocence
rushes to her cheeks/pours from her mouth
like the betsy wetsy dolls have been torn
apart/their mouths
menses red & split/every
three minutes a shoulder
is jammed through plaster and the oven door/
chairs push thru the rib cage/hot water or
boiling sperm decorate her body
i rode the subway today
& bought a paper from a
man who might
have held his old lady onto
a hot pressing iron/i dont know
maybe he catches lil girls in the
park & rips open their behinds

with steel rods/i can't decide
what he might have done i only
know every 3 minutes
every 5 minutes every 10 minutes/so
i bought the paper
looking for the announcement
the discovery/of the dismembered
woman's body/the
victims have not all been
identified/today they are
naked and dead/refuse to
testify/one girl out of 10's not
coherent/i took the coffee
& spit it up/i found an
announcement/not the woman's
bloated body in the river/floating
not the child bleeding in the
59th street corridor/not the baby
broken on the floor/
    "there is some concern
      that alleged battered women
      might start to murder their
      husbands & lovers with no
      immediate cause"
i spit up i vomit i am screaming
we all have immediate cause
every 3 minutes
every 5 minutes
every 10 minutes
every day
women's bodies are found
in alleys & bedrooms/at the top of the stairs
before i ride the subway/buy a paper/drink
coffee/i must know/
have you hurt a woman today
did you beat a woman today
throw a child across a room
    are the lil girl's panties
    in yr pocket
did you hurt a woman today

i have to ask these obscene questions
the authorities require me to

establish
immediate cause

every three minutes
every five minutes
every ten minutes
every day.

The Tyranny of Slenderness

Kim Chernin

A woman should never give the impression that she is so capable, so self-sufficient, that she doesn't need him at all. Men are enchanted by minor, even amusing frailties. This quality of vulnerability, of needing a man, is something that the mature woman should study very carefully. Because it's that quality that she loses most easily. Years of dealing with home and family, of making decisions, of coping, can turn the woman of forty-plus into a brusque, cold-eyed, and somewhat frightening figure.
GLORIA HEIDI

Is it a conspiracy, unknown even to those who participate in it?

A whole culture busily spinning out images and warnings intended to keep women from developing their bodies, their appetites, and their powers?

Maybe, when we see another calorie counter on the stand, or read of another miracle diet in a women's magazine, or pick up another container of low-calorie cottage cheese, we must begin to understand these trivial items symbolically and realize that what we are purchasing is the covert advice not to grow too large and too powerful for our culture.

Maybe, indeed, this whole question of the body's reduction is analogous to the binding of women's feet in prerevolutionary China?*

"My mother buys me a girdle when I am fifteen years old," says Louise Bernikow, "because she doesn't like the jiggle. . . . Tighter. I hold myself tighter, as

*Alice Walker, in a conversation about women and their body, suggested this analogy to me.

my mother has taught me to do. . . . Is the impulse to cripple a girl peculiar to China between the eleventh and twentieth centuries? The lotus foot was the size of a doll's and the woman could not walk without support. Her foot was four inches long and two inches wide. A doll. A girl-child. Crippled, indolent, and bound." [1]

There is a relationship between the standards set for women's beauty and the desire to limit their development. In the name of a beautiful foot, the women of China were deprived of autonomy and made incapable of work. A part of the body was forced to remain in a childish condition. They did not walk, they hobbled. In the name of beauty they were crippled.

What happens to women today in the name of beauty?

> I'd never wear a girdle, she said,
> just medieval throwbacks
> to whale baleen brassieres 'n
> laced-up waist confiner corsets.
> We burned em in the sixties,
> girdles, she said walking
> into Bloomingdales, grabbing
> a pair of cigarette-legged
> tight denim jeans off the rack.
> Hoisting them up to her hips,
> how do ya get em on, she said,
> have surgery, take steam baths,
> slimnastic classes'n Dr. Nazi's
> diet clinic fatshots for a month?
> These aren't jeans for going
> to lunch in, she said trying
> to do the snap, these
> aren't even jeans
> for eating an hour
> before ya put em on, just
> for standin up in without
> your hands in the pockets,
> there's not even room
> in here for my underpants.
> One hour later she returns
> to the store for a new zipper,
> front snap, and the side seams
> re-stitched. These're jeans
> for washing in cold water only
> then wearin round the house
> til they dry on yr shape,
> put em in a clothes dryer,
> she said, and you'll get
> all pinch bruised
> round the crotch'n
> your stomach covered

with red streak marks
cross the front.

We burned em in the sixties,
girdles, she said.[2]

We must not imagine that it is only the fashion industry that is upset about the large size of our bodies. Fashion creates and it reflects. Creates, as we have seen, an image few women in this culture are able to realize for themselves. Creates longing—and we all know this longing to win the approval of our culture even at cost to our health, our identity as women, our experience of pleasure in our bodies. But fashion also reflects hidden cultural intentions, as it did in China with the binding of women's feet. As it does in our own day, with pants so tight they serve as an adequate replacement for the girdles that used to bind us. Fashion, for all its appearance of superficiality, is a mirror in which we can read the responses of conventional culture to what is occurring, at the deepest levels of cultural change, among its people.

For instance: if the problem of body and mind is as old in this culture as I have suggested, why is anorexia a new disease and bulmarexia a condition first named during the 1970s? Why for that matter is Christine Olman a model now and not twenty years ago when Marilyn Monroe inspired our admiration?

These questions may help us to understand that something has happened in our culture during the last twenty years that has made us particularly uneasy about the abundance of our flesh. Something, unnamed as yet, which fashion expresses as a shift from the voluptuous to the ascetic.

I wish to place before us a cluster of related facts that constitutes an important cultural synchronicity.

FACT: During the 1960s Marilyn Monroe stood for the ideal in feminine beauty. Now Christine Olman represents that ideal.

FACT: During the 1960s anorexia nervosa began to be a widespread social disease among women.

FACT: During the late 1960s and early 1970s bulmarexia began to be observed as a condition among women.

FACT: During the 1960s Weight Watchers opened their doors. In 1965 Diet Workshop appeared, in 1960s Over-Eaters Anonymous, in 1966 Why Weight, in 1968 Weight Losers Institute, in 1969 Lean Line.

FACT: During the 1960s the Feminist Movement began to emerge, asserting woman's right to authority, development, dignity, liberation and above all, power.

What am I driving at here? I am suggesting that the changing awareness among women of our position in this society has divided itself into two divergent movements, one of which is a movement toward feminine power, the other a retreat from it, supported by the fashion and diet industries, which share a fear of women's power.

In this light it is significant that one of the first feminist activities in our time was an organized protest against the Miss America Contest and the idea of feminine beauty promulgated by the dominant culture through this pageant, in which women strut and display their bodies, as men sit passively, judging them. It is interesting, further, that as a significant portion of the female population in the last two decades began to go to consciousness-raising groups and to question the role and subservience of women in this society, other women hastened to groups where the large size of their bodies was deplored. The same era gave birth to these two contradictory movements among women.

Yet we sense that there is an underlying similarity of motive in both movements. In both, women are driven to gather together and make confessions and find sisterly support for the new resolutions they are taking. In both, women have created new forms of social organization, apart from the established institutions of the dominant culture.

There is, however, also a fundamental divergence here. The groups that arise among feminists are dedicated to the enlargement of women. Confessions made in these groups reveal anger over rape and the shame women have been taught to feel about their bodies; there is interest in the longing to develop the self, concern for the boredom and limitations of motherhood, acknowledgement of the need for sisterly support in the resolution to return to work, go back to school, become more of oneself, grow larger. But in the other groups, confessions are voiced about indulgence in the pleasures of eating, and resolutions are made to control the amount of food consumed, and sisterly support is given for a renewed warfare against the appetite and the body.

Listen to the spontaneous metaphor that finds its way into the discussions of these two groups. In the feminist group it is *largeness* in a woman that is sought, the *power* and *abundance* of the feminine, the assertion of a woman's right to be taken seriously, to *acquire weight*, to *widen* her *frame* of reference, to be *expansive, enlarge* her views, *acquire gravity, fill out*, and *gain* a sense of self-esteem. It is always a question of *widening, enlarging, developing* and *growing*. But in the weight-watching groups the women are trying to *reduce* themselves; and the metaphoric consistency of this is significant: they are trying to make themselves *smaller*, to *narrow* themselves, to become *lightweight*, to lose *gravity*, to be-*little* themselves. Here, emphasis is placed upon *shrinking* and *diminution, confinement* and *contraction*, a *loss* of pounds, a *losing* of flesh, a *falling* of weight, a *lessening*.

These metaphoric consistencies reveal a struggle that goes beyond concern for the body. Thus, in the feminist groups the emphasis is significantly upon liberation—upon release of power, the unfettering of long-suppressed ability, the freeing of one's potential, a woman shaking off restraints and delivering herself from limitations. But in the appetite control groups the emphasis is upon restraint and prohibition, the keeping of watch over appetites and urges, the confining of impulses, the control of the hungers of the self.

When all other personal motives for losing weight are stripped away—the desire to be popular, to be loved, to be successful, to be acceptable, to be in control, to be admired, to admire one's self—what unites the women who seek to reduce their weight is the fact that they look for an answer to their life's problems in the control of their bodies and appetites. A woman who walks through the doors of a weight-watching organization and enters the women's reduction movement has allowed her culture to persuade her that significant relief from her personal and cultural dilemma is to be found in the reduction of her body. Thus, her decision, although she may not be aware of it, enters the domain of the body politic and becomes symbolically a political act.

It is essential to interpret anorexia nervosa, that other significant movement among women during the last decades so that it, too, can be understood as part of women's struggle for liberation during the last decades. Indeed, Hilde Bruch calls it a new disease because in the last fifteen or twenty years it has occurred at a "rapidly increasing rate." From 1960 on, she writes, "reports on larger patient groups have been published in countries as far apart as Russia and Australia, Sweden and Italy, England and the United States."[3]

The fact that these are highly developed industrial countries, and that anorexia occurs primarily among girls of the upper-middle class, should remind us that anorexia is a symbolic illness. Where hunger is imposed by external circumstances, the act of starvation remains literal, a tragic biological event that does not serve metaphoric or symbolic purposes. It is only in a country where one is able to choose hunger that elective starvation may come to express cultural conflict or even social protest.

"You go over to the high school today and it's like walking into a concentration camp," says the mother of an anorexic girl, in a telephone conversation with a friend, whose daughter has just lost fifty pounds in five months. "Betty Talbot has the same problem, I understand. . . . And of course you know about Kimmy Sanders, don't you? That absolutely gorgeous girl. What a tragedy."[4]

This conversation between mothers, about their anorexic daughters, would not have been heard during the 1950s, or only in rare and isolated cases. Today, however, we may expect to find this conversation in most affluent communities, where families raise daughters who are not able to express their angers and rebellions directly, yet who feel a distinct reluctance to become the conventional people their mothers are.

"Ugh, wretched curves," says the daughter of the mother whose telephone conversation we have just overheard. "I grab my breasts, pinching them until they hurt. If only I could eliminate them, cut them off if need be to become as flat-chested as a child again. It is better now than before I started dieting. To think that I needed a size B bra! Now I don't even need to wear one, but the womanly outline still remains, and I'm afraid that if I should gain again they'll blow up like zeppelins. I would probably start having periods again as well. I would probably look and function just like my mother."[5]

Anorexia nervosa speaks exactly the same protest being spoken by the women's liberation movement. Feminists, it is true, in an outspoken gesture of refusal to comply with the conventional expectations for a woman in this culture, take off their bras. The anorexic girl starves herself instead, so that she does not develop the breasts that would require the bra. The underlying emotional attitude of anorexia is clear: "I don't want to be an imitation," says the anorexic girl. "I don't want to be a victim of fate. . . . I want to make my own name, cut my own image, set my own trend. I want to surpass [my mother], not follow her lead."

This rebellious attitude toward the mother seems to be directed less against the personal mother, more against the limitations of woman's social destiny. Indeed, the mothers of anorexic girls "had often been career women, who felt they had sacrificed their aspirations for the good of the family. In spite of superior intelligence and education, practically all had given up their careers when they married." Their daughters feel impatience with their mothers, dreading that they will share their mothers' fate, which one anorexic girl characterizes in the following way: "to be a nothing, to be devoted to a husband, to be devoted to her children, but without a life of her own."[6] . . .

Anorexic girls continue to get good grades, they graduate with honors from their high schools, but they sit on the stage in all the terrible, mute eloquence of their rebellion. This is how an anorexic girl, looking at her high school graduating class, describes them: "Nan, so frail these days, looks as though she's ready to pass out"; Candy, who has been "released from the hospital on the condition that she gain ten pounds by the end of the month"; Kim, "wraithlike and miserable, her ghostly eyes staring vacantly toward the speaker's podium."[7]

In America . . . no woman can possibly remain unaware of the fact that significant numbers of her sisters are asserting their rights to autonomy, to power, to the development of their full emotional and creative capacities. This movement of women into their enlargement is likely to affect her in a number of ways. She may grow depressed with the life she is living and rebel against it. She may refuse to recognize that her life depresses her and fail to develop a meaningful analysis of her condition as a woman. Or she may feel the force of these contradictory tendencies and enact her entire response to them through her body.

Let us imagine then that a woman comes to awareness of her condition one day in 1969. She is, let us say, forty-five years old, she wears old, dreary clothes, and she is seriously depressed. She is a woman who has tried to diet and failed and who has exhausted her tolerance for weight-watching groups. For her the anorexic solution is simply not a possibility. And so she decides to join a women's consciousness-raising group. There, she tells the other women that her husband has just left her after twenty-five years. She tells how she is stuck in a job with a poverty wage in an insurance company, how she feels a thousand years old. She blames herself, she says, and the fatness in her body, for everything that has gone wrong with her life. But now, because she is encouraged to talk and because no one here believes her rounded belly is the cause of these complex failures, she speaks about a dream she had once as a young girl when she wished to become a writer. She tells how absurd this old dream seems now and how she is afraid. But because the women listen to her fears and encourage her to speak further, she goes home and she begins to dream that she might want to dream of becoming a writer.

Let us also imagine that another similar woman comes to a group intended to help women change their lives. But here, in fact, we do not have to provide the script, for the story of a middle-aged woman named Faye has been written for us by Gloria Heidi, in her unintentionally revealing book:

> She was about forty-five years old when she enrolled in my class—a gray, doughy woman in a dreary maroon, half-size dress—a woman who had obviously come to me as a last resort. "Look, my husband Harry has just walked out after twenty-five years. I'm stuck in a poverty-wage, nowhere job at the insurance company. I feel a thousand years old—and look sixty. But I'm determined to be a new me . . . and I want to start by losing this excess weight. After all, now that I've lost Harry"—her eyes filled with tears—"what else have I got to lose?"[8]

In this group, where the woman comes with a complex social and personal situation, her terrible despair is attributed to the fact that she is fat. She is therefore encouraged to lose weight; a chart is kept of the weight she loses. When the magical transformation finally takes place we are told that the horror of her personal and social position has miraculously altered. A moral is drawn. We are assured that we, too, if only we will lose weight, can be "filled with energy, go aggressively after a better job and with a new figure, a revitalized personality, and an exciting new social life, [like] formerly dowdy and half-sized Faye, [soon] be sitting on top of the world."

The hidden message in this story is profoundly disturbing. Implicitly, we are asked to believe that if every woman lost twenty-five or thirty pounds she would be able to overcome the misogyny in our land; her social problems would be solved, the business world would suddenly fling wide its gates and welcome her into its privileges. Isn't it incredible? We, as women, need only lose weight and all of us will find jobs equal in authority and status and salary to those of men? The need for the Equal Rights Amendment will vanish? Unemployment figures will dissolve and the very structure of our society will be transformed?

There is a profound untruth here and a subversion of the radical discontent women feel. In a class of this sort, women are directed to turn their dissatisfaction and depression toward their own bodies. They are encouraged to look at their large size as the cause of the failure they sustain in their lives. Consider what it means to persuade a woman who is depressed and sorrowful and disheartened by her entire life, that if only she succeeds in reducing herself, in becoming even less than she already is, she will be acceptable to this culture which cannot tolerate her if she is any larger or more developed than an adolescent girl. The radical protest she might utter, if she correctly understood the source of her despair and depression, has been directed toward herself and away from her culture and society. Now, she will not seek to change her culture so that it might accept her body; instead, she will spend the rest of her life in anguished failure at the effort to change her body so that it will be acceptable to her culture.*

We should not be misled by the fact that we feel more at home in our culture when we lose weight. It may indeed happen that a woman becomes more attractive to men, finds it easier to get a job, experiences less discrimination, receives fewer gibes from strangers, and endures far less humiliation in her own family. Culture rewards those who comply with its standards. But we have to wonder what cost the woman is paying when she sacrifices her body in this way for the approval of her culture. . . .

NOTES

1. Louise Bernikow, *Among Women*, New York, 1980.
2. Jana Harris, *Manhattan as a Second Language*, Harper & Row, forthcoming.
3. Bruch, *The Golden Cage*.
4. Liu, *Solitaire*.
5. Ibid.
6. Bruch, *The Golden Cage*.
7. Liu, *Solitaire*.
8. Heidi, *Winning the Age Game*.

The Triangular Tube of Pink Lipstick

Gail Watnick

I lay in bed with my eyes closed. I visualize the make-up sitting on my dresser, and my mother lying in her bed visualizing the make-up and wishing it were on my face instead of the dresser. I open my eyes and see the square blue eyeshadow box and the triangular tube of pink lipstick. My parents! They buy me a pink lipstick and think it will hide my sexual feelings toward other women if I put it on my lips.

*Adapted from a very similar utterance by Louise Wolfe, "The Politics of Body Size," Pacifica Tape Library.

I lay on my back glancing occasionally at the ceiling and the make-up. I really thought it would make my life easier if I told them how I was feeling. So instead of hiding my true self, I announced that I thought I might be a lesbian. I was grappling with this issue for four years and was wondering what my future would be like as a homosexual. What is life like when you are thirty, or forty? And what will my neighbors think? I hope they are not as hostile as my parents are; if so, I had better continue suppressing my feelings, I thought.

The decision to be open and honest with my parents followed much soul searching. I no longer wanted to act or wear a mask and I believed they could offer me some support. Unhappily, however, they were not understanding at all, making me feel worthless and as if all of my prior achievements meant nothing.

I lay in bed staring at the make-up. Putting it on would make my distraught mother happy. To them, it would mean I was no longer gay—as simple as that. They tried their hardest to change me. They felt that letting my hair grow would somehow change my feelings and no longer make me feel sexually attracted to women. Wearing fancy shoes would change that too. Well, the only things that wearing fancy shoes would change was getting me blisters.

Then they tried some really crazy things (I was not that calm myself). They went out and bought me a beautiful flower print bedcover with matching sheets. They would have looked wonderful on someone else's bed but not on mine. It just was not me to have flowered sheets. My mother ripped off my favorite red, yellow, blue, and green striped sheets and put these on. In turn, I ripped off the flowered sheets and replaced it with my favorite stripes. We took turns and created this pointless action two more times. We were struggling to fit me in, just as we were trying to fit the bed with the "right" pattern. My mother's pattern consisted of marriage and kids.

I lay on my flowered sheets looking at the make-up thinking, "I wonder if I am going to be a lesbian all of my life and if so, will my parents every accept me?"

Yesterday, my father refused to talk to me. Mother said he felt that he gave me so much love and opportunity, and he feels like I let him down. She then insisted that the children I could have were going to be fabulous and that the world would be a lesser place without them. How could I argue with that! When it came right down to it, however, they admitted they did not want the neighbors discriminating against me—and them.

I lay in bed thinking about Robert Frost's poem, "The Road Not Taken". Reciting the last two lines, "I took the road less traveled by,/And that has made all the difference," I realized the confrontation with my family has changed my view of the poem. I used to think the difference referred to individuality and following one's own heart; that in itself would create positive effects.

I lay in bed. I think about the unrealistic options my family created for me—women or men, pink lipstick or not.

"We Are Who You Are":
Feminism and Disability

Bonnie Sherr Klein

It all begins in 1987. I am 46 years old, and enjoying an athletic and sexy vacation with my husband, Michael. On a hot day, we bicycle ten miles to the town tennis courts. I feel weak and nauseated, and play badly. We think it must be junk-food poisoning.

Within several hours, I am staggering and slurring my speech. I have double vision. Michael, a family physician, recognizes the signs of central nervous system damage. At midnight, he speeds me home to Montreal, to the emergency room of the hospital where he works.

Diagnostic tests are inconclusive. We are shocked and scared, but I begin to stabilize. Within a few days, I am released from the intensive care unit, and take a few steps with a walker. After two weeks, we celebrate our twentieth anniversary in the hospital with our children. I feel blessed and happy to be alive.

The next day I become totally paralyzed. Semiconscious, I am "locked in" and unable to speak. A respirator breathes for me. A magnetic resonance test (MRI) reveals that a congenital malformation at the base of my brain stem has bled, resulting in several strokes. It is like a time bomb waiting to explode again. Local specialists declare it inoperable because of its inaccessible location. Close family and friends come to say goodbye.

Michael refuses to accept this fatal verdict. He locates a surgeon who is prepared to remove the malformation.

I am jet-ambulanced on a respirator to London, Ontario. By my bed, the surgeon posts a newspaper clipping: a picture of me with Kate Millett from my documentary *Not a Love Story*. I overhear a staff remark: "She used to be a filmmaker." I remain in intensive care for several months. Michael stays with me, acting as husband, family doctor, nurse, and advocate. He will not resume work for several months.

As I come back to life but cannot move, speak, or breathe, I have frequent panic attacks. Only Michael can talk me down. He breathes with me until I fall asleep. The literal meaning of "conspire" is to breathe together. We are in a conspiracy for my life. This becomes the metaphor of our partnership. This *is* a love story.

Recovery

Back in Montreal, I spend more months in the hospital, and then in a rehabilitation institute. Like a helpless baby, I learn how to swallow, speak, sit upright, use the toilet, stand.

(Memory Journal: When I am sufficiently recovered, I get bathing privileges twice a week. A male orderly transfers me to a gurney and wheels me down the hall. I am "wrapped" diaper-fashion in a rubber sling, and with a horrible-sounding grind, winched into a tub where a nurse bathes and shampoos me. The soothing warm water is one of the few nice body sensations I have. But it is frightening to be winched. I can hear older women screaming and moaning, and all I can think of—as in my nightmares—is a concentration camp.)

But I am never abandoned to institutional care. I am supported and nursed every day by Michael and our daughter, Naomi—then 17. Our son, Seth, 19, begins attending the University of Toronto shortly after my surgery. He studies on the five-hour train commute each way; his enthusiastic comments about my dramatic changes since the previous weekend are like a transfusion. Naomi is just emerging from a difficult adolescence. Conflicted by her mother's highly visible feminism, she has asserted her individuality by learning the skills of femininity. Now she does the intimate niceties for me—shaving the underarms; bleaching the facial hairs darkened by steroids mistakenly prescribed. My skin is blotched, my features lopsided, but my daughter makes me feel pretty. Not surprisingly, Naomi also fails her semester at school.

Several months after the stroke, as soon as I can use a pencil, the occupational therapist helps me to copy circles and squares like a schoolgirl. My first communication is an illegible letter to Naomi, in which I share my fear about how slow recovery may be, an admission I make to no one else. Once I can write, I begin my journal, which becomes a tool for my survival. I use it to process the strange and troubling events happening in my body, to record thoughts I cannot trust my damaged mind to remember, to remind myself how far I have come.

The Long Haul: Rehabilitation

After seven months in the hospital, I am at home over the next two and a half years, in the long process of rehabilitation. I have conventional physical, occupational, and speech therapy. As I gradually improve, I remember my old feminist wisdom that I know my body better than anyone else. I take control. I experiment with so-called alternative approaches like acupuncture. Michael and I dance and play, in whatever motivating ways we can invent to push my physical limits. And I learn to rest. In my prestroke life, this was never easy for me, juggling the three F's: family, filmmaking, and feminism. Now I have no choice. My body's messages are nonnegotiable.

The anguish is profound when I let it emerge, and it comes out at the slightest invitation.

(Journal, March 1, 1989: This evening, when Michael and I dance, I am weepy. Because he's been outside playing basketball, my girlhood sport, while I am curled up

inside in bed. And because I can hardly dance, and dancing was one of the things we did together, starting the day we met 22 years ago. I want to kick up my heels, and they won't go, dammit! But strange as it may sound, I also experience the euphoria of just being alive. It is not a cover-up, it is real. I laugh out loud when the leaves riot with autumn colors. I am living on the edge, with no script guides or maps, inventing every moment as I live it.)

The stroke hit me in the middle of editing a film. The producer and editor bring the film to the hospital and my home so we can work on it together. *Mile Zero* is the story of four teenagers—one of whom is Seth—who are organizing against nuclear arms. The premiere, 16 months after my stroke, is the most triumphant moment in my rehabilitation. I have reclaimed the important piece of myself that was a filmmaker.

Yet I still do not accept myself as disabled; disability is "a stage I am just passing through." For the premiere, I reject a fully accessible educational institution and choose a glamorous cinema with inaccessible bathrooms—even though I am in a wheelchair.

I long to hold on to the acute appreciation of life engendered by survival and rebirth, but euphoria does not last indefinitely. My mother dies after a long struggle with Alzheimer's disease. This loss is compounded by Naomi's departure for the University of Toronto. I want to be generous about letting her go, but losses are interconnected: I mourn my mother, my daughter, myself.

In June 1989, almost two years poststroke, I receive a last-minute invitation to participate in a festival of Canadian women's films abroad. Two of my films are featured. My immediate response is "Impossible! I can't travel without personal assistance." The travel money is quickly offered to another filmmaker. When Naomi discovers me crying, she offers to quit work to accompany me. We go off together at great personal expense, and greater trepidation.

The women who had organized the festival—also Canadian filmmakers—had promised to "accommodate" me, but they make no provision for my needs. I am expected to fit in and keep up. They schedule my films late at night when I am too tired; they do not include me in panel discussions or press conferences; they arrange social events in inaccessible places. I miss the informal personal exchanges catalyzed by the shared film experience.

I can no longer move in what had been my world. I feel I have been used for my films, but neglected and made invisible as a person. I feel as if my colleagues are ashamed of me because I am no longer the image of strength, competence, and independence that feminists, including myself, are so eager to project. There is clearly a conflict between feminism's rhetoric of inclusion and failure to include disability. My journals reveal that this is the only moment in which I think of suicide.

I am coming up against multiple barriers, personal and social. I cannot return to my former life, and I do not know what my life will be now. Even feminism has betrayed me. It seems too narrow a lens for the new realities of my life. I also feel an unresolved conflict between feminism and my increased dependence on—and appreciation for—Michael.

About two and a half years poststroke, I have an experience that begins to clarify my thinking about feminism. We spend the winter in Beersheba, Israel, where

Michael is working to help me escape Montreal's ice and snow. A woman from the local chapter of the Israel Women's Network phones: as a visiting feminist, would I speak on any "women's issue" of my choosing at their next meeting? Again my first reaction is negative: "I am no longer engaged with women's issues; I have been so self-obsessed with my stroke that's all I could possibly talk about." Her response is quick: "That's exactly what we want to hear about, but were too shy to ask!"

I have forgotten how wonderful it is to share intimately with a group of women! I read bits from my journal, and my story prompts theirs. One woman says, "My relationship with my husband is fine as long as I'm healthy, capable, and available sexually, but I don't know what would happen if I were incapacitated." She hadn't read the United Nations statistic that disabled women are twice as likely to get divorced or separated as disabled men. We realize that we rarely talk about illness, disability, and dying, though we will all confront these realities.

Every issue is a woman's issue; relationships, dependence, and autonomy are as much a part of feminism as day care and violence. I have undersold feminism. I slowly recognize that the way I am living my stroke has everything to do with myself as a feminist—as well as with implications for feminism itself.

"Coming Out" Disabled

I feel comfortable and stimulated in this group of Israeli women; they are middle-class, middle-aged, married Jewish women like me. But no one else there is disabled. I am "other." I desperately need company.

I had first heard of DAWN (the DisAbled Women's Network, Canada) years earlier when it approached Studio D to make our screenings more accessible. We appreciated being sensitized, favored wheelchair-accessible venues, and enjoyed the aesthetics of sign language interpretation with our movies. But sometimes DAWN's demands seemed "excessive"; our meager resources were already exhausted by items on our agenda that seemed to affect *most* women. But in retrospect, I know that as a not-yet-disabled woman I was afraid of disability.

As soon as I return to Canada, I dig DAWN's phone number out of a feminist newsletter. I realize that its agenda is identical to mine (and feminism's): dependence and autonomy, image and self-esteem, powerlessness, isolation, violence, and vulnerability; equality and access; sexuality. Three years after my stroke, I go to my first DAWN meeting at the local YWCA.

I feel apologetic, illegitimate, because I was not born disabled, and am not as severely disabled as many other people. I feel guilty about my privileges of class, profession (including my disability pension), and family. I am a newcomer to the disability movement; I have not paid my dues. (Doesn't this litany sound "just like a woman"?)

Our talk keeps moving between the personal and the political, because disability—like gender, race, age, and sexuality—is a social as well as a biological construct. The DAWN members, typical of disabled women, are mostly unemployed, poor, and living alone. It is like the early days of consciousness-raising in the women's movement: sharing painful (and funny) experiences, "clicks!" of recognition; swapping tips for coping with social service bureaucracies and choosing the least uncomfortable tampons for prolonged sitting. It is exhilarating to cry and laugh with other women again.

Here I am not other, because everyone is other. It is the sisterhood of disability. The stroke has connected me with women who were not part of my world before—working-class women with little education, women with intellectual and psychiatric disabilities, women with physical "abnormalities" from whom I would have averted my eyes in polite embarrassment. All women like me.

"We are women. We are women with disabilities. We are women who are abused. We are your sisters. . . . Your issues are our issues, and each of our issues is also your issue. We are who you are." (From "Meeting Our Needs: An Access Manual for Transition Houses," DAWN, June 1991.)

I discover it is easier for me to be a disabled feminist than a disabled person. Feminism means loving myself as I am. After three long years, I am finally ready to accept myself as permanently, irrevocably disabled: acceptance is not an event but an ongoing process. I learn more about the disability rights movement. I meet other women with disabilities, who become my buddies, sisters, teachers, and "rolling" models. I learn, not surprisingly, that women are leaders in the disability movement.

(Journal, October 1990: Boston's first Disability Pride Day. I usually dislike the rhetoric of rallies, the solicited mass response. But today I want my tape recorder. A gutsy, nervous young woman with the thick drawl of cerebral palsy is emcee. Not only is her speech different, but there is a new language being spoken here. I feel like a privileged eavesdropper at first, but she is speaking for me and about me. Or is she? She cues us for a chant: "Disabled and . . ." The crowd responds: PROUD! My throat jams on the word mid-chant. Is this honest? Who am I trying to fool? It's one thing to accept, but another to be proud. I'm proud of surviving and adapting maybe, but am I proud of being disabled? But it feels good to be shouting with hundreds of other bodies, looking happy despite—because of?—their "deformities." Or is the word "differences"? Or is it "our"?)

Happily, the timing of my personal journey is synchronous with the women's movement. The Canadian Research Institute for the Advancement of Women (CRIAW) announces the theme for its 1990 national conference: "The More We Get Together . . ." on women and disability. I decide to go, alone, to Prince Edward Island. Thanks to the joint efforts of CRIAW and DAWN, this historic event is not only totally accessible but empowering—for both the women with disabilities and those without. Every woman with disability is paired with a "sister" who gives us whatever assistance we need—and who learns firsthand about disability.

It is a coming-out experience for many of us. For me, it is the first time I identify myself publicly as a woman with disability, and revel in the company of so many others. Because women with disabilities are often isolated, for many this is their first conference. They learn from the experience of longtime feminists.

Many of the so-called nondisabled women come out as well. Kay Macpherson, 79, and Muriel Duckworth, 83, are well-known Canadian peace activists and feminists. But we have never considered them "disabled." Now, for the first time, Kay talks about what it means to be losing her sight. She talks loudly because her close friend Muriel has learned to be assertive about her increasing deafness. Muriel and Kay describe their support networks of friends who look after each other by sharing meals, and house keys in case of falls. Our stories lead us to discover the continuum from "ability" to "disability." My stroke has given me a telescope on aging. We are all disabled under the skin—each of us has vulnerabilities, visible or not, and they are part of us. We are interdependent. Feminism is strongest when it includes its "weakest."

I leave CRIAW with a new sense of purpose and continuity. No longer illegitimate among either feminists or people with disabilities, I feel I have a particular contribution to make: perhaps I can help to bridge the gap between our two cultures. After all, my life's work has been about telling each other our stories.

Where Am I Now?

After five years, my physical condition is still evolving—but almost imperceptibly. I feel constantly imbalanced. I stand and walk with two canes, slowly and unsteadily. For longer distances, I drive my electric three-wheeled scooter, Gladys, but she can only be transported in a lift-equipped van, and furthermore is stopped by the smallest step. I am often dependent on someone to push Manny, my portable manual wheelchair. I do not drive a car alone—yet.

I need to exercise and nap every day, and I get weekly massages, acupuncture, and chiropractic to maximize my fluidity and minimize my pain. With only one functioning vocal chord, I choke frequently, but my speech is intelligible (and my voice as breathlessly sexy as I always wanted). I tire easily and tolerate stress badly.

Being forced to slow down is not all negative. The rhythm of my life has changed dramatically. Before, it was governed by the calendar and the clock. Now I follow the natural pace of my body. The tasks of everyday living take me much longer. I have become patient, as have those around me. I have to ration my limited energy and choose carefully who I see and what I do. I have no time to waste on bullshit, but I do have time to smell the flowers. I cherish my solitude, and enjoy the fullness of the company of intimate friends and family.

But I need to be useful and connected, to feel once again that I am contributing to making this a better world. I don't know if I will ever make films again, but I am writing a book about my experience, and spending time with other people with disabilities. As with my walking, it all comes to balance. Some people look at me suspiciously when I hint at the gifts of the stroke. I would never deny the pain of dependence, the grieving for lost freedoms, the fear for the future. Would I take an immediate cure if offered? Probably. But would I want to undo it, as if it never happened? Absolutely not. It has become part of my identity. It is who I am now.

In retrospect, the "clicks!" in my consciousness about disability paralleled my coming to feminist consciousness two decades earlier. For a long time, I denied I was disabled, and kept my distance from other "cripples" in the hospital gym because I was an exception to the rule. Later, I was sure I could "overcome" it; I would be supercrip (superwoman); I would support the rights of other people with disabilities, but *I* was not oppressed. As time passed, I experienced with great pain the ways in which other people's attitudes and societal barriers disempowered me. At first, I internalized the oppression and lost all self-esteem. Then, as I reconnected with feminism and discovered my commonality with other women (and men) with disabilities, I began to see more clearly. With solidarity came strength.

Between writing this piece and correcting the galleys, I have taken a giant step in my journey. I went to Independence 92 in Vancouver, an international conference on disability—more than 2,000 of us from more than 100 countries! For one week, I had the heady feeling that we were taking over the world. Even better—we were remaking it, creating a world in which difference is not the problem but part of the solution.

It is a feast for this disabled filmmaker's eyes: a gridlock of wheelchairs on a freight elevator, a shoulder chain of the blind leading the blind, signing singing, nursing babies in wheelchairs—images we have not seen because we disabled are invisible, even to each other; images so rare and precious they have not yet been co-opted or trivialized.

Somehow, I think I will be making films again.

The Case of Sharon Kowalski and Karen Thompson: *Ableism, Heterosexism, and Sexism*

Joan L. Griscom

In November, 1983, in Minnesota, Sharon Kowalski was in a head-on collision with a drunk driver. Her four-year old niece died soon after; her seven-year old nephew survived; and she suffered a severe brain-stem injury. As a result, she was paralyzed and lost the ability to speak. Kowalski was living in a committed partnership with Karen Thompson, although only their closest friends knew. Soon after the accident, serious conflict developed between Thompson and Kowalski's parents, which erupted in a series of law-suits that still continue. Thompson has been fighting in the courts of Minnesota to secure adequate rehabilitation for her as well as access to friends and family of her choice. In July, 1985, acting under Minnesota guardianship laws, her father placed Kowalski in a nursing home that lacked adequate rehabilitation facilities and prohibited Thompson and other friends from visiting her. If Thompson had not continued the struggle in the courts, Kowalski would probably still be locked away in this home. While in January, 1989, she was finally transferred to an appropriate rehabilitation center and reunited with lover and friends, she still is not free to make her own choices.[1]

In this article I tell the story of Sharon Kowalski and Karen Thompson and show how prejudices deeply entrenched in our medical and legal systems intertwined to deny Kowalski the fullest quality of life. Among these modes of oppression are ableism, discrimination against disabled persons; heterosexism, the belief structured into our institutions that only heterosexual relationships are legitimate; and sexism, discrimination against women.

A History of the Events

By November of 1983, Sharon Kowalski and Karen Thompson had lived in partnership for almost four years. Karen was thirty-six years old, an assistant professor of physical education at St. Cloud State University in Minnesota. Devoutly religious, conservative in social outlook, three years earlier she had refused to join a class action sex discrimination suit at her university since it seemed irrelevant to her. Sharon was twenty-seven years old, an outstanding athlete who had graduated from St. Cloud in physical education and had just accepted a job coaching golf at St. Cloud for the next spring. She had grown up in the Iron Mine area of northern Minnesota, a conservative world where women are expected to marry young and have children. Defying such expectations, she became the first member of her family to attend college and earned her own tuition by working part-time in the mines. After she and Karen fell in love, they exchanged rings, bought a house together, and vowed a lifetime commitment to each other.

After the accident, it was unclear if Sharon would live. For weeks she lay in a coma, and Karen spent as many as eight or ten hours a day talking to her, reading the Bible, massaging and stretching her neck, shoulders, and hands. As medical staff explained, it is essential to massage and stretch brain-injured patients in a coma, for they tend to curl up tightly and permanently damage their muscles in the process. The next concern was the degree to which she would recover. Doctors were pessimistic. However, in January, 1984, Karen noticed that Sharon was moving her right index finger, and discovered that Sharon could indicate yes-and-no answers to questions by moving her finger. Later she began to tap her fingers, and then slowly learned to write letters and words.

The Kowalski parents became increasingly suspicious of the long hours Karen was spending with their daughter. Increasingly Karen feared they would take steps to prevent her from participating in medical decisions and to exclude her from Sharon's life. Initially the parents stayed at Karen's and Sharon's home, but one day, they moved out, without telling her; and in the evening, Donald Kowalski told her she was visiting too often, that only family could really love Sharon. After consulting a hospital psychologist, Karen wrote the parents a letter explaining their love, in hopes they would understand her need to be with Sharon and her importance to Sharon. They reacted with shock, denial, and rage. As the nightmare deepened, Karen consulted an attorney and learned she had no legal rights, unless she won guardianship. In March, 1984, she therefore filed for guardianship, and Donald Kowalski immediately counterfiled.

The results of the hearing at first appeared positive. In an out-of-court settlement, guardianship was awarded to Donald Kowalski, but Karen was granted equal access to medical and financial information and full visitation rights. She participated in both the physical and occupational therapy. Sharon continued to improve slowly, responding more often than before and more fully. Karen made her an alphabet board, and Sharon began to spell out answers to questions. Subsequently she began to communicate by using a typewriter, and in August she spoke a few words. However, conflicts continued. The day after the hearing, Donald Kowalski incorrectly told Karen she did not have visitation rights. Later, when it became necessary to move Sharon to another institution, he tried to cancel Karen's arrangements to work with Sharon and her therapists. When Karen and other friends took Sharon out on day passes, to church and other events, he objected, and subsequently testified in court that he did not want her out in public. In October, 1984, by court order, Sharon was moved further away to Duluth, and Kowalski filed a motion to gain full power as guardian and deny Karen visitation. Karen counterfiled to remove him as guardian.

The hearings on these motions took months to complete. During this period Sharon was moved several times, regressed in her skills, and became clinically depressed. By this time the Minnesota Civil Liberties Union had entered the case, arguing that Sharon's rights of free speech and free association, under the First Amendment, were being violated. The Handicap Services Program of Tri-County Action Programs, Inc., submitted lengthy testimony of Sharon's capacity to communicate, including a long conversation with her in which she stated that she was gay and Karen was her lover. At Sharon's request, the MCLU asked for the right to represent her and suggested she might eventually testify for herself. Ultimately the court refused both requests. They found that Sharon lacked sufficient understanding to make decisions for herself, and wrote that the elimination of the conflict between the Kowalski's and Karen was in her best interest. Accordingly, on July 23, 1985, the court awarded Donald Kowalski full guardianship, including the right to determine visitation. Within a day he denied visitation to Karen, other friends of Sharon, the MCLU, various disability rights groups, and others. In two days, he transferred her to a nursing home hear his home with only minimal rehabilitation facilities. In August, 1985, Karen saw Sharon for what would be the last time for over three years.

As this summary indicates, the medical system had failed Sharon in at least three respects. First, they failed to supply her with necessary rehabilitation in the years when it was vital to her recovery. Following brain-stem injury, the initial months and years are crucial in rehabilitation; the longer the incapacity lasts, the more permanent the damage. As the legal battles protracted themselves, her chances of rehabilitation diminished. Stark in the medical record is the fact that this woman who was starting to stand and starting to feed herself was locked away for over three years with an implanted feeding tube, insufficiently stretched and exercised so that muscles that were starting to work curled back on themselves again. Second, she was deprived of the bombardment of emotional and physical stimulation needed to regenerate her cognitive faculties. For example, once she was in the nursing home, the regenerative outside excursions were forbidden. Third, although medical staff often recognized Sharon's unusual response to Karen, they failed to explain to her parents the importance of maintaining the connection. There was an urgent need for counseling to assist the parents, but except for one court-mandated session, there was none.

The failure of the medical system was consistently supported by the legal system. Initially the court ruled that Sharon must be in a nursing home with a young adult rehabilitation ward. But once Donald Kowalski was awarded full guardianship, he was able to move her to a nursing home without such a ward. Another contradiction occurred in late 1985 when the Minnesota Office of Health Facility Complaints investigated Sharon's right to visitors of her choice, a right guaranteed under the Minnesota Patient Bill of Rights. They found that indeed her right was being violated. However, the state appeals court held that visitation rights under the Patient Bill of Rights were inapplicable to this case, since the healthcare facility was not restricting the right of visitation, the guardian was.

The deficiencies of guardianship law are a key problem throughout this case. First, a guardian can restrict a patient's rights and there is no legal recourse. As is often said, under present laws a guardian can lock a person up and throw away the key. This is a national problem, affecting disabled people, elderly people, and others who are presumed incompetent for whatever reason. Second, guardians are inadequately supervised. Under Minnesota statutes, a guardian is required to have the ward tested annually for competency. Donald Kowalski never did so, and for over three years the courts did not require him to do so. As early as December, 1985, Karen filed a motion in district court to hold the guardian in contempt for failure to arrange competency testing and for failure to heed Sharon's "reliably expressed" wishes for visitation. The courts routinely rejected such motions until 1988.

Between 1985 and 1988 Karen and the Minnesota Civil Liberties Union pursued repeated appeals to various Minnesota courts, and all were denied. By now, since the legal system had failed her, Karen had begun to speak publicly and to seek help from the media, disability rights groups, gay and lesbian groups, and women's groups. She recognized that the legal precedents set in this case could be devastating for others, whether gay/lesbian couples, unmarried heterosexual people, or people living in communities of choice. The reserved, closeted, conservative professor slowly transformed into a passionate speaker in her quest to secure freedom and adequate rehabilitation for Sharon; and slowly she gained national attention. The alternative press, in particular, responded: national groups such as the National Organization for Women passed resolutions of support; the National Committee to Free Sharon Kowalski, a coalition of activists, formed with regional chapters. Finally the mainstream media, initially hostile, began publishing supportive articles; Karen appeared on national T.V. programs; and significant politicians, including Jesse Jackson, began to express concern and support. Meanwhile Sharon remained in the nursing home, cut off from many former friends, physically regressing and psychologically depressed.

In September, 1987, Karen filed a new request to have Sharon tested for competency. February, 1988, brought the first break in the case; the judge ruled the testing should be done, and finally, in July, ordered it. In January, 1989, Sharon was moved to the Miller-Dwan Medical Center in Duluth for a 60-day evaluation. Through his attorney, Donald Kowalski unsuccessfully argued against both the move and the testing. At Miller-Dwan, Sharon immediately expressed her wish to see Karen, as well as her awareness that her father would disapprove. On February 2, 1989, Karen visited her for the first time in three and a half years, an event which made banner headlines in the alternative press across the nation. She was, however, highly depressed, and there were numerous physical changes: for example, her feet had curled up so tightly that she was no longer able to stand. A more significant issue was her cognitive ability, her short-term memory loss remains considerable.

The competency evaluation nevertheless demonstrated that she could communicate on an adult level and that she had significant potential for rehabilitation. As a long-term goal Miller-Dwan recommended "her return to pre-morbid home environment" and added,

> We believe Sharon has shown areas of potential and ability to make rational choices
> in many areas of her life. She has consistently indicated a desire to return home and,
> by that, means to St. Cloud to live with Karen Thompson again.

Soon after the release of this report, Donald Kowalski resigned as guardian, for both financial and health reasons, and the parents stopped attending medical conferences. In June, 1989, Sharon was transferred to Travilla, a long-term rehabilitation center in Minneapolis for brain-injured young adults. Here she has continued to have extensive occupational, physical, and speech therapy. Karen again has been able to spend many hours with her, taking her out on passes. She had surgery on her legs, feet, toes, left shoulder and arm to reverse the results of three years of inadequate care. She uses both a speech synthesizer and a motorized wheel chair. However, major issues remain unsettled.

Karen subsequently filed for guardianship, and Sharon's court-appointed attorney and medical staff from Miller-Dwan and Travilla testified positively in favor of their relationship. The medical personnel testified unanimously that Sharon is capable of deciding for herself what kinds of relationships she wants and with whom, and that she responds more to Karen than to anyone else. Further, they testified that Sharon is capable of living outside an institution, that returning home to St. Cloud would be best for her, and that Karen is best qualified to care for her in a home environment. However, witnesses for the Kowalski's strenuously opposed the petition. According to one report, they stated they would not continue to see Sharon if Karen became her guardian. The judge appeared increasingly uncomfortable with the national publicity generated by the case. While in August, 1990, he allowed Sharon and Karen to fly out to San Francisco for the national convention of the National Organization for Women, where they each received a Woman of Courage award, in October he denied permission for Sharon to attend the first Disability Pride Day in Boston. He issued a gag order against Karen, which was overturned on appeal. Finally, in April, 1991, in a lengthy decision, he denied guardianship to Karen and awarded it to a supposedly "neutral third party," a former classmate of Sharon who lives near the Kowalski parents and testified against Karen in a 1984 hearing. He based his decision in part on the Kowalskis' opposition, in part on his belief that while Sharon is capable of expressing wishes for visitation, her expressed wish to live with Karen in St. Cloud is "not tantamount to a preference of who should be her guardian." Karen will appeal this decision.[1]

The Three Modes of Oppression

Sharon Kowalski has been denied the fullest quality of life by three interacting systems of oppression: ableism, heterosexism, and sexism. These are not simply prejudices held by individuals; they also pervade social structures such as the medical and legal systems and thus become modes of oppression. Originally Karen believed that their difficulties were merely personal problems. She had believed all her life that the institutions of our society are basically fair and reasonable and support the rights of individuals. In the book[4] she co-authored with her St. Cloud colleague Julie Andrzejewski, she documented the development of her awareness that wide social and political forces were involved in their supposedly personal problems and that the oppression they have experienced is systemic.

Ableism has been rampant throughout this case. Sharon's inability to speak has often been construed as a lack of competence, and her particular kinds of communication have not been recognized. Quite early Karen noticed that some people did not speak to Sharon, some raised their voices as if she was deaf, and others spoke to her as if she was a child. A doctor spoke about Sharon in her presence as if she was not there. When Karen later asked her how she felt about this, Sharon typed out, "Shitty." Probably one reason Sharon has responded to Karen more than anyone else is that from the start Karen has talked directly to her, at length, has read to her, has played music for her, and has consulted her wishes at every point. Although the MCLU and the Handicap Services Program submitted extensive transcripts of conversations with Sharon, the courts did not accept these as evidence of competence, relying instead on the testimony of people who had much less inter-action with her. In a major article in the St. Paul *Pioneer Press* (1987), the reporter described the Kowalskis' visiting the room "where their eerily silent daughter lies trapped in her twisted body." Eerily silent? This is the person who typed out "columbine" when asked what her favorite flower is, answered arithmetical ques-tions correctly, and responded to numerous questions about her life, her feelings, and her wishes. She also communicates nonverbally in many ways: gestures, facial expressions, smiles, tears, and laughter.

Thanks to ableism, Sharon has often been stereotyped as helpless. The pre-sumption of helplessness "traps" her far more severely than her "twisted body." Once a person is stereotyped as helpless, then there is no need to consult her wishes; her testimony is unnecessary; her written communications can be ignored. When Sharon was transferred to Miller-Dwan in 1989 for competency testing, Karen re-ported with joy that the staff was giving her full information and allowing her to make choices, even if her choice was to do nothing. Most seriously, if a person is seen as helpless, then there is no potential for rehabilitation. As Ellen Bilofsky[2] has written, Sharon was presumed "incompetent until proven competent." If the courts had not accepted Karen's 1987 motion for competency testing, Sharon could have remained in the nursing home indefinitely, presumed incompetent.

Finally, ableism can lead to keeping disabled people invisible and hidden, lit-erally out of sight. This is clearly illustrated in Donald Kowalski's responses to his daughter. He argued strenuously against day passes and resented Karen's efforts to take her out. He testified that he would not take her to a shopping center or to church because he did not wish to put her "on display . . . . in her condition." Although it was clear to medical staff that outside excursions provided Sharon with important pleasure and stimulation, both vital for rehabilitation, they often co-operated with the father in denying her the possibility. According to an article in the *Washington Post*, Kowalski once said, "What the hell difference does it make if she's gay or lesbian or straight or anything because she's laying there in diapers? . . . let the poor kid rest in peace." Invisible in the nursing home to which he had moved her, cut off from lover and friends, there was little chance for Sharon to demon-strate competence. The wonder is that after three and a half years of loss, loneliness, and lack of proper physical care, she was able to emerge from her depression and respond to her examiners. To retain her capacity for response, through such an experience, suggests a strong spirit.

The second mode of oppression infusing this case is homophobia, the fear and dislike of homosexuality, and heterosexism, the structuring of our institutions so that only heterosexual relationships are legitimated. Glaringly apparent throughout is the failure to recognize committed gay/lesbian partnerships. Donald Kowalski has consistently denied the possibility. When Karen first arrived at the hospital after the accident, the first on the scene, she was not allowed access to Sharon or even to any information because she was not "family." Seeing her anguish, a Roman Catholic priest interceded, brought information, and arranged for a doctor to speak with her. Although the two women considered themselves married, in law they were not, and therefore lacked any social or legal rights as a couple. If recognized as a couple, there would have been no question of denying visitation, and the long nightmare of the three-and-a-half year separation would have been impossible. While unmarried heterosexual partners might still have trouble securing guardianship, there would be little or no problem for a married partner.

Because of heterosexism, it was not important to honor Sharon's obvious emotional need for her partner and Karen's rehabilitative effect on her. Since it was clear that Sharon responded actively to Karen, she was often included in the therapeutic work. Yet, prior to 1989, medical staff often were unwilling to testify to this positive effect, even when they had privately noted it to Karen. Perhaps they feared condoning the same-sex relationship if they reported positively about it; perhaps they did not wish to be involved in the conflict. One neurologist, Dr. Keith Larson, did testify, although he stipulated that he spoke as a friend of the court, not as one of Karen's witnesses. His testimony is worth looking at in detail.

> The reason I'm here today is . . . to deliver an observation that I have agonized over, and thought a great deal about, and prayed a little bit . . . I cannot help but say that Sharon's friend, Karen, can get out of Sharon physical actions, attempts at vocalization, and longer periods of alertness and attention than can really any of our professional therapists.

Why was it necessary to "agonize" over this testimony? To pray about it? Why such a tremendous effort? Clearly, had one of the partners been male, Larson would have had no such difficulty. He simply would have reported the obvious fact: that the patient responded far more to her partner than to anyone else. Some medical staff did testify to Karen's positive effects: psychologists, nurses, occupational therapists. And since 1989 the testimony of medical personnel from Miller-Dwan and Travilla has been consistent, strong, and unanimous. However, in repeated decisions, including the most recent (1991), the courts have chosen to ignore this testimony.

Finally, heterosexism is evident in a consistent tendency to exaggerate the role of sex in same-sex relationships. In general our society believes that the lives of gay/lesbian people revolve around sex, although evidence from all social-psychological research is that homosexual people are no more sexually active than heterosexual people. Further, gay/lesbian sex is often perceived as sexual exploitation rather than an appropriate expression of mutual caring. The final denial of Karen's visitation rights was based on the charge that she might sexually abuse Sharon. A physician hired by the Kowalskis, Dr. William L. Wilson, levelled this charge as follows:

> It has come to my attention that Karen Thompson has been involved in bathing Sharon Kowalski behind a closed door for a prolonged period of time. It has also come to my attention that Ms. Thompson has alleged a sexual relationship with Sharon Kowalski that existed prior to the accident. Based on this knowledge and my best medical judgment concerning Sharon and her welfare, I feel that visits by Karen Thompson at this time would expose Sharon Kowalski to a high risk of sexual abuse.

Accordingly, as Sharon's physician, Wilson directed the nursing home staff not to permit Karen to visit. Even though under legal statute Karen could have continued her visits while the various decisions were under appeal, the nursing home was obliged to obey the doctor's order.

In this instance, ableism and heterosexism merge. Had Sharon and Karen been unmarried heterosexual partners, sexual abuse probably would have not been a significant argument. Had they been married, the issue would not exist. Ableism often denies disabled persons their sexuality. However, a person does not lose her sexuality simply because she becomes disabled. Furthermore, a person who loses the capacity to speak has a special need for touching. What are Sharon's sexual rights? Karen has written that when Sharon was starting to emerge from the coma, she once reached out and touched Karen's breast, and later placed Karen's hand on her breast. At the time Karen did not dare to ask medical advice, for fear of revealing their relationship, and she recognized that if they were a heterosexual couple, she would have been free to ask advice. Even to raise such questions could have exposed her to further charges of sexual abuse. Thus ableism and heterosexism combined to deny both Sharon and Karen the chance to explore such questions.

Heterosexism dictates that only heterosexual partnership can form the basis for a family. While same-sex partnerships are often called "anti-family" in our homophobic society, actually such relationships create family, in that they create stable emotional and economic units. *Family*, in this sense, may be defined as a kin-like unit of two or more persons who are related by blood, marriage, adoption, or primary commitment, and who usually share the same household. Sharon and Karen considered themselves married. Karen's long pilgrimage over almost nine years is testimony to an extraordinary depth of commitment; she would not permit her loved one to be locked away without rehabilitation. Sharon, similarly, has consistently said that she is gay, Karen is her lover, and she wishes to live again with her in St. Cloud. While marriage has historically occurred between two sexes, we cannot determine our definition from history. In United States history, for example, marriage between black and white persons was forbidden for centuries. In 1967, when the Supreme Court finally declared miscegenation laws unconstitutional, there were still such laws on the books in sixteen states.

Sexism is sufficiently interfused with heterosexism that it is difficult to separate them. Heterosexism often enforces a social role on women in which they are subordinated to men. For example, women in the social world of the area in Minnesota where Sharon grew up were expected to marry young and submit to the authority of their husbands, a model that is intrinsically sexist. From the perspective of this model, Sharon's partnership with Karen was illegitimate. Sexism is also apparent in the awarding of full guardianship to the father. In a sexist society, it is appropriate to assign a woman to her male parent; had Sharon been a man rather than a twenty-eight year old "girl," such a decision might have been less possible. In a sexist society, women are not encouraged to take responsibility for their sexuality, just as society denies sexual rights to the disabled and the elderly. Finally, our society devalues friendship, especially friendship between women. Soon after the accident, a doctor advised Karen to go away and forget Sharon. The gist of his remarks were that "Sharon's parents will always be her parents. They have to deal with this, but you don't. Maybe you should go back to leading your own life." Friendship between two women was unimportant. Ableism as well as sexism is apparent in this advice.

It is sometimes impossible to separate the modes of oppression even for the purpose of analysis. It is tempting to ask which mode was the most significant in denying Sharon her rights. However, this case makes clear that all the issues work simultaneously and dealing with any one of them in isolation from the others is mistaken. Like Audre Lorde[3], I argue that "there is no hierarchy of oppressions." Admittedly, any individual's perspective on the case is likely to reflect the issue most central to their life: e.g., the gay press emphasizes heterosexism, and the disability rights press emphasizes ableism. Unfortunately, however, each all too often slights or omits the other. While working in coalition on the case, some women were ill at ease with disability rights activists, and some disability rights groups were anxious about associating themselves with gay/lesbian issues. But the fact is that there are lesbians and gays in the disabled community, and disabled folks in the women's community. Karen experienced the inseparability of the issues on one occasion when she was invited to speak to a Presbyterian disability rights concerns group. They asked her to speak only about ableism, since they had already "done" gay concerns. She tried, but found it nearly impossible; she had to censor her material, ignore basic facts, and leave out crucial connections.

What the three modes of oppression have in common is that in each case one group of people take power over another. Disabled people, women, gays and lesbians are all to some degree denied their full personhood by the structures of our society. Their self-determination is limited; their choices can be denied. Their sexuality is controlled. On the basis of ableism, heterosexism, and sexism, Sharon Kowalski's opportunity for the fullest quality of life was permanently taken from her. She was denied proper medical care, legal counsel of her choice, and access to the people she wished to see. As the Minnesota Civil Liberties Union put it, "The convicted criminal loses only his or her liberty; Sharon Kowalski has lost the right to choose who she may see, who she may like, and who she may love." Even her right to be tested for competency was denied for years. Since that right was restored, she now has access to good medical treatment and the people she loves, but she is still denied the right to live where she chooses.

Conclusion

Many activists and coalition groups have become involved nationally in the struggle to provide rehabilitation for Sharon Kowalski and bring her home. These include disability rights activists, gays and lesbians, feminists and their male supporters, and civil rights workers. In addition there have been many hundreds, perhaps by now thousands, of people who are not involved in activist work but are drawn to this case by the dimension of human rights. After all, any of us could be hit by a drunk driver, become disabled, and in the process lose our legal and medical rights in comparable ways. The Kowalski/Thompson case stands as a warning that in our deeply divided society, freedom is still a privilege and rights are fragile.

People living in nontraditional families—whether gay/lesbian, unmarried heterosexuals, or communities of choice—need legal protection to secure their legal and medical rights. Karen Thompson has suggested the importance of making your relationships known to your family of birth, if possible, and informing them of your wishes in case of accident. Also, it is essential to execute a durable power of attorney, a document in which you stipulate a person to make medical and financial decisions for you in case you are incapacitated. Copies should be given to your physicians. While requirements vary from state to state and such powers of attorney are not always enforceable, they may serve to protect your rights. Information about how to execute them may be found in your public library, in consultation with a competent lawyer, or in Appendix B of the book *Why Can't Sharon Kowalski Come Home?*[4]

NOTES

1. In December 1991, the Minnesota appeals court granted guardianship of Sharon to Karen. Their decision was based primarily on two factors: the medical testimony that Sharon is capable of making her own choices, and the fact that the two women are "a family of affinity" that deserves respect. Sharon now lives with Karen.

2. Ellen Bilofsky. "The Fragile Rights of Sharon Kowalski." *Health/PAC Bulletin*, 1989, 19, 4–16.

3. Audre Lorde. "There Is No Hierarchy of Oppressions." *Interracial Books for Children Bulletin*, 1983, 14, 9. See also "Age, Race, Class, and Sex: Women Redefining Difference"' in *Sister Outsider*. Trumansburg, New York: The Crossing Press, 1984.

4. Karen Thompson and Julie Andrzejewski. *Why Can't Sharon Kowalski Come Home?* San Francisco: Spinster/Aunt Lute, 1988.

Silent Scream

Carole R. Simmons

My late Uncle Harold was an effervescent man. Just give him an audience and he'd bubble over with stories of growing up black in the South. A sudden increase in the day's temperature would remind him of having to work for endless hours under the hot Georgia sun in Mr. John's fields. A newscaster's mention of racial rebellion would prompt Uncle Harold to retell the story about his left eyebrow's three-inch scar, a souvenir from a 1966 trip to Jackson, Mississippi, where he was clubbed by a state patrolman who was unsatisfied with the volume of Uncle Harold's "sir."

He lived through a lot of unpleasant situations, my uncle, and each one made him stronger and wiser. But I never really believed him when he'd say, "Baby girl, as long as dey call you nigga to yo face, you ain't got nothin' to worry 'bout. When dey don't call you nothin', you bettuh look out." Now I understand completely what Uncle Harold meant because at the University of Georgia at Athens, where I'm a journalism graduate student, they ain't callin' me nothin'.

When I was in high school, there was no question that I'd go to college. And like most of my classmates, both black and white, I'd heard that those four years would be the best of my life. I daydreamed about debating the issues of the day. I looked forward to bundling up against winter winds to cheer the football team. I thought I might join a few clubs. I sure never thought that the color of my skin could prevent me from achieving those simple dreams. I was wrong.

Despite federally mandated desegregation, affirmative action, and a succession of intelligent black UG graduates, racism thrives at this predominantly white Southern institution of 25,000. It's as alive as the azalea bushes in the spring, as plentiful as beer on a football weekend, and as much a part of college as the overcrowded bookstore on the first day of class or the lack of student parking spaces.

But to expedite buying books, people discussed the problem and enlarged the bookstore. To make more parking spaces available to students, administrators admitted the problem and approved the construction of several lots.

Meanwhile, not many people want to hear about how I feel when I get on a campus bus and watch the seats around me fill up while the one next to me remains empty until some other minority student takes it or a white student is left with no other choice.

Few nonblacks here are willing to talk about how I lost my first roommate. I never actually met her. When I checked in, her belongings were already in the room. She's written a chatty note introducing herself and informing me that she was eating dinner with her family and would meet me later. I unpacked my bags, set a few family photos on my desk, and went to dinner. When I returned a few hours later, a picture of my mother was facedown on my bed. My roommate's things were gone.

I remember starting a journal when I first arrived in 1981. I was so excited; everything was new and promising. But I stopped writing the journal at the end of my first term. The last entry reads, "I feel as if I've been invited to dinner and everybody's eating, but there's no seat at the table for me." Five years later I've returned to attend graduate school, and I could write that same line again.

I've often asked myself why I returned to UG. I knew it hadn't changed. I told myself that I returned to get my master's degree and that nothing would alter that goal. My resolve was unshakable until the first day of orientation, when I overheard one white professor tell another that he had two blacks in his class that quarter. He was anxious, he said, to see how they'd do. I was one of those students.

To an outsider it could very easily look as though black students don't attend UG. I know that for some, owning up to the fact that there are more than 1,000 black students on this campus would be inconvenient. It would mean giving up things like the annual Old South Ball, at which the women dress up in crinolines and hoop skirts, the men don Confederate uniforms, and everyone frolics on the lawn while little black boys serve mint juleps.

And the university would have to relinquish the acts of bias it appears to sanction. Black students are never featured in the pages of the student newspaper unless it's football or basketball season. Of the scores of lecturers, entertainers, and special events brought to campus, few programs reflect that there's any ethnic diversity here.

But by far the most troublesome act of omission is repeated in the classroom every day. During my enrollment the only time that a professor mentioned the name of any ethnic person, group, or publication was in an American history class. We spent a week on the Civil War; we barely covered slavery.

When I tell my friends at other schools about feeling isolated here, they say that at least I haven't experienced the overt racial acts many of them have recently lived through. When my friend Donna attended Carleton College in Minnesota, she was often told that the coursework was too tough for her and was repeatedly encouraged to leave. She now attends graduate school. While at Yale, my friend Terry attended an antiapartheid rally she helped organize, then returned to her car to find its tires slashed and a dead bird hanging from the antenna. Around the bird's neck was a note that read, SOUTH AFRICA HAS THE RIGHT IDEA.

I guess I've been lucky as I've rarely been the recipient of such open hostility. Still the frustration I experience on a daily basis, just dealing with an ongoing succession of insensitivities, makes me angry.

Educated people at UG believe that not making "special provisions" for minority students is a cause for celebration. But what they seem to have made is an institution that resists change and rationalizes insensitivity. In failing to understand that black students have their own culture that should be incorporated into the academic structure, UG appears to subscribe to "the notion that one ethnic stock is superior"—which, according to my dictionary, is the definition of racism.

As far back as I can remember, I'd always heard that education is the great equalizer of people. That philosophy was taught in my family, in my secondary schools, and in my church. And despite what I've experienced at UG, I believe education has that potential; I believe that college campuses should be among the most civil places on earth. Places where we learn to appreciate one another's differences. Places where we're not afraid to admit our transgressions and to work to change them. Places where the only name we call one another is friend.

Poem for the Young White Man Who Asked Me How I, an Intelligent, Well-read Person Could Believe in the War between Races

Lorna Dee Cervantes

In my land there are no distinctions.
The barbed wire politics of oppression
have been torn down long ago. The only reminder
of past battles, lost or won, is a slight
rutting in the fertile fields.

In my land
people write poems about love,
full of nothing but contented childlike syllables.
Everyone reads Russian short stories and weeps.
There are no boundaries.
There is no hunger, no
complicated famine or greed.
I am not a revolutionary.
I don't even like political poems.
Do you think I can believe in a war between races?
I can deny it. I can forget about it
when I'm safe,
living on my own continent of harmony
and home, but I am not
there.

I believe in revolution
because everywhere the crosses are burning,
sharp-shooting goose-steppers round every corner,
there are snipers in the schools . . .
(I know you don't believe this.
You think this in nothing
but faddish exaggeration. But they
are not shooting at you.)

I'm marked by the color of my skin.
The bullets are discrete and designed to kill slowly.
They are aiming at my children.
These are facts.
Let me show you my wounds: my stumbling mind, my
"excuse me" tongue, and this
nagging preoccupation
with the feeling of not being good enough.

These bullets bury deeper than logic.
Racism is not intellectual.
I can not reason these scars away.

Outside my door
there is a real enemy
who hates me.

I am a poet
who yearns to dance on rooftops,
to whisper delicate lines about joy
and the blessings of human understanding.
I try. I go to my land, my tower of words and
bolt the door, but the typewriter doesn't fade out
the sounds of blasting and muffled outrage.
My own days bring me slaps on the face.
Every day I am deluged with reminders
that this is not
my land

and this is my land.

I do not believe in the war between races

but in this country
there is war.

Requiem for the Champ

June Jordan

Mike Tyson comes from Brooklyn. And so do I. Where he grew up was about a twenty-minute bus ride from my house. I always thought his neighborhood looked like a war zone. It reminded me of Berlin—immediately after World War II. I had never seen Berlin except for black-and-white photos in *Life* magazine, but that was bad enough: Rubble. Barren. Blasted. Everywhere you turned your eyes recoiled from the jagged edges of an office building or a cathedral, shattered, or the tops of apartment houses torn off, and nothing alive even intimated, anywhere. I used to think, "This is what it means to fight and really win or really lose. War means you hurt somebody, or something, until there's nothing soft or sensible left."

For sure I never had a boyfriend who came out of Mike Tyson's territory. Yes, I enjoyed my share of tough guys and/or gang members who walked and talked and fought and loved in quintessential Brooklyn ways: cool, tough, and deadly serious. But there was a code as rigid and as romantic as anything that ever made the pages of traditional English literature. A guy would beat up another guy or, if appropriate, he'd kill him. But a guy talked different to a girl. A guy made other guys clean up their language around "his girl." A guy brought ribbons and candies and earrings and tulips to a girl. He took care of her. He walked her home. And if he got serious about that girl, and even if she was only twelve years old, then she became his "lady." And woe betide any other guy stupid enough to disrespect that particular young Black female.

But none of the boys—none of the young men—none of the young Black male inhabitants of my universe and my heart ever came from Mike Tyson's streets or avenues. We didn't live someplace fancy or middle-class, but at least there were ten-cent gardens, front and back, and coin Laundromats, and grocery stores, and soda parlors, and barber shops, and Holy Roller churchfronts, and chicken shacks, and dry cleaners, and bars-and-grills, and a takeout Chinese restaurant, and all of that usable detail that does not survive a war. That kind of seasonal green turf and daily-life supporting pattern of establishments to meet your needs did not exist inside the gelid urban cemetery where Mike Tyson learned what he thought he needed to know.

I remember when the City of New York decided to construct a senior housing project there, in the childhood world of former heavyweight boxing champion Mike Tyson. I remember wondering, "Where in the hell will those old people have to go in order to find food? And how will they get there?"

I'm talking godforsaken. And much of living in Brooklyn was like that. But then it might rain or it might snow and, for example, I could look at the rain forcing forsythia into bloom or watch how snowflakes can tease bare tree limbs into temporary blossoms of snow dissolving into diadems of sunlight. And what did Mike Tyson ever see besides brick walls and garbage in the gutter and disintegrating concrete steps and boarded-up windows and broken car parts blocking the sidewalk and men, bitter, with their hands in their pockets, and women, bitter, with their heads down and their eyes almost closed?

In his neighborhood, where could you buy ribbons for a girl, or tulips?

Mike Tyson comes from Brooklyn. And so do I. In the big picture of America, I never had much going for me. And he had less. I only learned, last year, that I can stop whatever violence starts with me. I only learned, last year, that love is infinitely more interesting, and more exciting, and more powerful, than really winning or really losing a fight. I only learned, last year, that all war leads to death and that all love leads you away from death. I am more than twice Mike Tyson's age. And I'm not stupid. Or slow. But I'm Black. And I come from Brooklyn. And I grew up fighting. And I grew up and I got out of Brooklyn because I got pretty good at fighting. And winning. Or else, intimidating my would-be adversaries with my fists, my feet, and my mouth. And I never wanted to fight. I never wanted anybody to hit me. And I never wanted to hit anybody. But the bell would ring at the end of another dumb day in school and I'd head out with dread and a nervous sweat because I knew some jackass more or less my age and more or less my height would be waiting for me because she or he had nothing better to do than to wait for me and hope to kick my butt or tear up my books or break my pencils or pull hair out of my head.

This is the meaning of poverty: when you have nothing better to do than to hate somebody who, just exactly like yourself, has nothing better to do than to pick on you instead of trying to figure out how come there's nothing better to do. How come there's no gym/no swimming pool/no dirt track/no soccer field/no ice-skating rink/ no bike/no bike path/no tennis courts/no language arts workshop/no computer science center/no band practice/no choir rehearsal/no music lessons/no basketball or baseball team? How come neither one of you has his or her own room in a house where you can hang out and dance and make out or get on the telephone or eat and drink up everything in the kitchen that can move? How come nobody on your block and nobody in your class has any of these things?

I'm Black. Mike Tyson is Black. And neither one of us was ever supposed to win anything more than a fight between the two of us. And if you check out the mass-media material on "us," and if you check out the emergency-room reports on "us," you might well believe we're losing the fight to be more than our enemies have decreed. Our enemies would deprive us of everything except each other: hungry and furious and drug-addicted and rejected and ever convinced we can never be beautiful or right or true or different from the beggarly monsters our enemies envision and insist upon, and how should we then stand, Black man and Black woman, face to face?

Way back when I was born, Richard Wright had just published *Native Son* and, thereby, introduced white America to the monstrous produce of its racist hatred.

Poverty does not beautify. Poverty does not teach generosity or allow for sucker attributes of tenderness and restraint. In white America, hatred of Blackfolks has imposed horrible poverty upon us.

And so, back in the thirties, Richard Wright's Native Son, Bigger Thomas, did what he thought he had to do: he hideously murdered a white woman and he viciously murdered his Black girlfriend in what he conceived as self-defense. He did not perceive any options to these psychopathic, horrifying deeds. I do not believe he, Bigger Thomas, had any other choices open to him. Not to him, he who was meant to die like the rat he, Bigger Thomas, cornered and smashed to death in his mother's beggarly clean space.

I never thought Bigger Thomas was okay. I never thought he should skate back into my, or anyone's community. But I did and I do think he is my brother. The choices available to us dehumanize. And any single one of us, Black in this white country, we may be defeated, we may become dehumanized, by the monstrous hatred arrayed against us and our needy dreams.

And so I write this requiem for Mike Tyson: international celebrity, millionaire, former heavyweight boxing champion of the world, a big-time winner, a big-time loser, an African-American male in his twenties, and, now, a convicted rapist.

Do I believe he is guilty of rape?

Yes I do.

And what would I propose as appropriate punishment?

Whatever will force him to fear the justice of exact retribution, and whatever will force him, for the rest of his damned life, to regret and to detest the fact that he defiled, he subjugated, and he wounded somebody helpless to his power.

And do I therefore rejoice in the jury's finding?

I do not.

Well, would I like to see Mike Tyson a free man again?

He was never free!

And I do not excuse or condone or forget or minimize or forgive the crime of his violation of the young Black woman he raped!

But did anybody ever tell Mike Tyson that you talk different to a girl? Where would he learn that? Would he learn that from U.S. Senator Ted Kennedy? Or from hotshot/scot-free movie director Roman Polanski? Or from rap recording star Ice Cube? Or from Ronald Reagan and the Grenada escapade? Or from George Bush in Panama? Or from George Bush and Colin Powell in the Persian Gulf? Or from the military hero flyboys who returned from bombing the shit out of civilian cities in Iraq and then said, laughing and proud, on international TV: "All I need, now, is a woman"? Or from the hundreds of thousands of American football fans? Or from the millions of Americans who would, if they could, pay surrealistic amounts of money just to witness, up close, somebody like Mike Tyson beat the brains out of somebody?

And what could which university teach Mike Tyson about the difference between violence and love? Is there any citadel of higher education in the country that does not pay its football coach at least three times as much as the chancellor and six times as much as its professors and ten times as much as its social and psychological counselors?

In this America where Mike Tyson and I live together and bitterly, bitterly, apart, I say he became what he felt. He felt the stigma of a priori hatred and intentional poverty. He was given the choice of violence or violence: the violence of defeat or the violence of victory. Who would pay him to rehabilitate innercity housing or to refurbish a bridge? Who would pay him what to study the facts of our collective history? Who would pay him what to plant and nurture the trees of a forest? And who will write and who will play the songs that tell a guy like Mike Tyson how to talk to a girl?

What was America willing to love about Mike Tyson? Or any Black man? Or any man's man?

Tyson's neighborhood and my own have become the same no-win battleground. And he has fallen there. And I do not rejoice. I do not.

C. P. Ellis

Studs Terkel

We're in his office in Durham, North Carolina. He is the business manager of the International Union of Operating Engineers. On the wall is a plaque: "Certificate of Service, in recognition to C. P. Ellis, for your faithful service to the city in having served as a member of the Durham Human Relations Council. February 1977."

At one time, he had been president (exalted cyclops) of the Durham chapter of the Ku Klux Klan . . .

He is fifty-three years old.

My father worked in a textile mill in Durham. He died at forty-eight years old. It was probably from cotton dust. Back then, we never heard of brown lung. I was about seventeen years old and had a mother and sister depending on somebody to make a livin'. It was just barely enough insurance to cover his burial. I had to quit school and go to work. I was about eighth grade when I quit.

My father worked hard but never had enough money to buy decent clothes. When I went to school, I never seemed to have adequate clothes to wear. I always left school late afternoon with a sense of inferiority. The other kids had nice clothes, and I just had what Daddy could buy. I still got some of those inferiority feelin's now that I have to overcome once in a while.

I loved my father. He would go with me to ball games. We'd go fishin' together. I was really ashamed of the way he'd dress. He would take this money and give it to me instead of putting it on himself. I always had the feeling about somebody looking at him and makin' fun of him and makin' fun of me. I think it had to do somethin' with my life.

My father and I were very close, but we didn't talk about too many intimate things. He did have a drinking problem. During the week, he would work every day, but weekend he was ready to get plastered. I can understand when a guy looks at his paycheck and looks at his bills, and he's worried hard all the week, and his bills are larger than his paycheck. He'd done the best he could the entire week, and there seemed to be no hope. It's an illness thing. Finally you just say: "The heck with it. I'll just get drunk and forget it."

My father was out of work during the depression, and I remember going with him to the finance company uptown, and he was turned down. That's something that's always stuck.

My father never seemed to be happy. It was a constant struggle with him just like it was for me. It's very seldom I'd see him laugh. He was just tryin' to figure out what he could do from one day to the next.

After several years pumping gas at a service station, I got married. We had to have children. Four. One child was born blind and retarded, which was a real additional expense to us. He's never spoken a word. He doesn't know me when I go to see him. But I see him, I hug his neck. I talk to him, tell him I love him. I don't know whether he knows me or not, but I know he's well taken care of. All my life, I had work, never a day without work, worked all the overtime I could get and still could not survive financially. I began to say there's somethin' wrong with this country. I worked my butt off and just never seemed to break even.

I had some real great ideas about this great nation. (Laughs.) They say to abide by the law, go to church, do right and live for the Lord, and everything'll work out. But it didn't work out. It just kept gettin' worse and worse.

I was workin' a bread route. The highest I made one week was seventy-five dollars. The rent on our house was about twelve dollars a week. I will never forget: outside of this house was a 265-gallon oil drum, and I never did get enough money to fill up that oil drum. What I would do every night, I would run up to the store and buy five gallons of oil and climb up the ladder and pour it in that 265-gallon drum. I could hear that five gallons when it hits the bottom of that oil drum, splatters, and it sounds like it's nothin' in there. But it would keep the house warm for the night. Next day you'd have to do the same thing.

I left the bread route with fifty dollars in my pocket. I went to the bank and I borrowed four thousand dollars to buy the service station. I worked seven days a week, open and close, and finally had a heart attack. Just about two months before the last payments of that loan. My wife had done the best she could to keep it runnin'. Tryin' to come out of that hole, I just couldn't do it.

I really began to get bitter. I didn't know who to blame. I tried to find somebody. I began to blame it on black people. I had to hate somebody. Hatin' America is hard to do because you can't see it to hate it. You gotta have somethin' to look at to hate. (Laughs.) The natural person for me to hate would be black people, because my father before me was a member of the Klan. As far as he was concerned, it was the savior of the white people. It was the only organization in the world that would take care of the white people. So I began to admire the Klan.

I got active in the Klan while I was at the service station. Every Monday night, a group of men would come by and buy a Coca-Cola, go back to the car, take a few drinks, and come back and stand around talkin'. I couldn't help but wonder: Why are these dudes comin' out every Monday? They said they were with the Klan and have meetings close-by. Would I be interested? Boy, that was an opportunity I really looked forward to! To be part of somethin'. I joined the Klan, went from member to chaplain, from chaplain to vice-president, from vice-president to president. The title is exalted cyclops.

The first night I went with the fellas, they knocked on the door and gave the signal. They sent some robed Klansmen to talk to me and give me some instructions. I was led into a large meeting room, and this was the time of my life! It was thrilling. Here's a guy who's worked all his life and struggled all his life to be something, and here's the moment to be something. I will never forget it. Four robed Klansmen led me into the hall. The lights were dim, and the only thing you could see was an illuminated cross. I knelt before the cross. I had to make certain vows and promises. We promised to uphold the purity of the white race, fight communism, and protect white womanhood.

After I had taken my oath, there was loud applause goin' throughout the buildin', musta been at least four hundred people. For this one little ol' person. It was a thrilling moment for C. P. Ellis.

It disturbs me when people who do not really know what it's all about are so very critical of individual Klansmen. The majority of 'em are low-income whites, people who really don't have a part in something. They have been shut out as well as the blacks. Some are not very well educated either. Just like myself. We had a lot of support from doctors and lawyers and police officers.

Maybe they've had bitter experiences in this life and they had to hate somebody. So the natural person to hate would be the black person. He's beginnin' to come up, he's beginnin' to learn to read and start votin' and run for political office. Here are white people who are supposed to be superior to them, and we're shut out.

I can understand why people join extreme right-wing or left-wing groups. They're in the same boat I was. Shut out. Deep down inside, we want to be part of this great society. Nobody listens, so we join these groups.

At one time, I was state organizer of the National Rights party. I organized a youth group for the Klan. I felt we were getting old and our generation's gonna die. So I contacted certain kids in schools. They were havin' racial problems. On the first night, we had a hundred high school students. When they came in the door, we had "Dixie" playin'. These kids were just thrilled to death. I begin to hold weekly meetin's with 'em, teachin' the principles of the Klan. At that time, I believed

Martin Luther King had Communist connections. I began to teach that Andy Young was affiliated with the Communist party.

I had a call one night from one of our kids. He was about twelve. He said: "I just been robbed downtown by two niggers." I'd had a couple of drinks and that really teed me off. I go downtown and couldn't find the kid. I got worried. I saw two young black people. I had the .32 revolver with me. I said: "Nigger, you seen a little young white boy up here? I just got a call from him and was told that some niggers robbed him of fifteen cents." I pulled my pistol out and put it right at his head. I said: "I've always wanted to kill a nigger and I think I'll make you the first one." I nearly scared the kid to death, and he struck off.

This was the time when the civil rights movement was really beginnin' to peak. The blacks were beginnin' to demonstrate and picket downtown stores. I never will forget some black lady I hated with a purple passion. Ann Atwater. Every time I'd go downtown, she'd be leadin' a boycott. How I hated—pardon the expression, I don't use it much now—how I just hated that black nigger. (Laughs.) Big, fat, heavy woman. She'd pull about eight demonstrations, and first thing you know they had two, three blacks at the checkout counter. Her and I have had some pretty close confrontations.

I felt very big, yeah. (Laughs.) We're more or less a secret organization. We didn't want anybody to know who we were, and I began to do some thinkin'. What am I hidin' for? I've never been convicted of anything in my life. I don't have any court record. What am I, C. P. Ellis, as a citizen and a member of the United Klansmen of America? Why can't I go the city council meeting and say: "This is the way we feel about the matter? We don't want you to purchase mobile units to set in our schoolyards. We don't want niggers in our schools."

We began to come out in the open. We would go to the meetings, and the blacks would be there and we'd be there. It was a confrontation every time. I didn't hold back anything. We began to make some inroads with the city councilmen and county commissioners. They began to call us friend. Call us at night on the telephone: "C. P., glad you came to that meeting last night." They didn't want integration either, but they did it secretively, in order to get elected. They couldn't stand up openly and say it, but they were glad somebody was sayin' it. We visited some of the city leaders in their home and talk to 'em privately. It wasn't long before councilmen would call me up: "The blacks are comin' up tonight and makin' outrageous demands. How about some of you people showin' up and have a little balance?" I'd get on the telephone: "The niggers is comin' to the council meeting tonight. Persons in the city's called me and asked us to be there."

We'd load up our cars and we'd fill up half the council chambers, and the blacks the other half. During these times, I carried weapons to the meetings, outside my belt. We'd go there armed. We would wind up just hollerin' and fussin' at each other. What happened? As a result of our fightin' one another, the city council still had their way. They didn't want to give up control to the blacks nor the Klan. They were usin' us.

I began to realize this later down the road. One day I was walkin' downtown and a certain city council member saw me comin'. I expected him to shake my hand because he was talkin' to me at night on the telephone. I had been in his home and visited with him. He crossed the street. Oh shit, I began to think, somethin's wrong here. Most of 'em are merchants or maybe an attorney, an insurance agent, people like that. As long as they kept low-income whites and low-income blacks fightin', they're gonna maintain control.

I began to get that feeling after I was ignored in public. I thought: Bullshit, you're not gonna use me any more. That's when I began to do some real serious thinkin'.

The same thing is happening in this country today. People are being used by those in control, those who have all the wealth. I'm not espousing communism. We got the greatest system of government in the world. But those who have it simply don't want those who don't have it to have any part of it. Black and white. When it comes to money, the green, the other colors make no difference. (Laughs.)

I spent a lot of sleepless nights. I still didn't like blacks. I didn't want to associate with 'em. Blacks, Jews, or Catholics. My father said: "Don't have anything to do with 'em." I didn't until I met a black person and talked with him, eyeball to eyeball, and met a Jewish person and talked to him, eyeball to eyeball. I found out they're people just like me. They cried, they cussed, they prayed, they had desires. Just like myself. Thank God, I got to the point where I can look past labels. But at that time, my mind was closed.

I remember one Monday night Klan meeting. I said something was wrong. Our city fathers were using us. And I didn't like to be used. The reactions of the others was not too pleasant: "Let's just keep fightin' them niggers."

I'd go home at night and I'd have to wrestle with myself. I'd look at a black person walkin' down the street, and the guy'd have ragged shoes or his clothes would be worn. That began to do somethin' to me inside. I went through this for about six months. I felt I just had to get out of the Klan. But I wouldn't get out.

Then something happened. The state AFL-CIO received a grant from the Department of HEW, a $78,000 grant: how to solve racial problems in the school system. I got a telephone call from the president of the state AFL-CIO. "We'd like to get some people together from all walks of life." I said: "All walks of life? Who you talkin' about?" He said: "Blacks, whites, liberals, conservatives, Klansmen, NAACP people."

I said: "No way am I comin' with all those niggers. I'm not gonna be associated with those type of people." A White Citizens Council guy said: "Let's go up there and see what's goin' on. It's tax money bein' spent." I walk in the door, and there was a large number of blacks and white liberals. I knew most of 'em by face 'cause I seen 'em demonstratin' around town. Ann Atwater was there. (Laughs.) I just forced myself to go in and sit down.

The meeting was moderated by a great big black guy who was bushy-headed. (Laughs.) That turned me off. He acted very nice. He said: "I want you all to feel free to say anything you want to say." Some of the blacks stand up and say it's white racism. I took all I could take. I asked for the floor and I cut loose. I said: "No, sir, it's black racism. If we didn't have niggers in the schools, we wouldn't have the problems we got today."

I will never forget. Howard Clements, a black guy, stood up. He said: "I'm certainly glad C. P. Ellis come because he's the most honest man here tonight." I said: "What's that nigger tryin' to do?" (Laughs.) At the end of that meeting, some blacks tried to come up shake my hand, but I wouldn't do it. I walked off.

Second night, same group was there. I felt a little more easy because I got some things off my chest. The third night, after they elected all the committees, they want to elect a chairman. Howard Clements stood up and said: "I suggest we elect two co-chairpersons." Joe Beckton, executive director of the Human Relations Commission, just as black as he can be, he nominated me. There was a reaction from some blacks. Nooo. And, of all things, they nominated Ann Atwater, that big old fat black gal that I had just hated with a purple passion, as co-chairman. I thought to myself: Hey, ain't no way I can work with that gal. Finally, I agreed to accept it, 'cause at this point, I was tired of fightin', either for survival or against black people or against Jews or against Catholics.

A Klansman and a militant black woman, co-chairmen of the school committee. It was impossible. How could I work with her? But after about two or three days, it was in our hands. We had to make it a success. This gave me another sense of belongin', a sense of pride. This helped this inferiority feelin' I had. A man who has stood up publicly and said he despised black people, all of a sudden he was willin' to work with 'em. Here's a chance for a low-income white man to be somethin'. In spite of all my hatred for blacks and Jews and liberals, I accepted the job. Her and I began to reluctantly work together. (Laughs.) She had as many problems workin' with me as I had workin' with her.

One night, I called her: "Ann, you and I should have a lot of differences and we got 'em now. But there's somethin' laid out here before us, and if it's gonna be a success, you and I are gonna have to make it one. Can we lay aside some of these feelin's?" She said: "I'm willing if you are." I said: "Let's do it."

My old friends would call me at night: "C. P., what the hell is wrong with you? You're sellin' out the white race." This begin to make me have guilt feelin's. Am I doin' right? Am I doin' wrong? Here I am all of a sudden makin' an about-face and tryin' to deal with my feelin's, my heart. My mind was beginnin' to open up. I was beginnin' to see what was right and what was wrong. I don't want the kids to fight forever.

We were gonna go ten nights. By this time, I had went to work at Duke University, in maintenance. Makin' very little money. Terry Sanford give me this ten days off with pay. He was president of Duke at the time. He knew I was a Klansman and realized the importance of blacks and whites getting along.

I said: "If we're gonna make this thing a success, I've got to get to my kind of people." The low-income whites. We walked the streets of Durham, and we knocked on doors and invited people. Ann was goin' into the black community. They just wasn't respondin' to us when we made these house calls. Some of 'em were cussin' us out. "You're sellin' us out, Ellis, get out of my door. I don't want to talk to you." Ann was gettin' the same response from blacks: "What are you doin' messin' with that Klansman?"

One day, Ann and I went back to the school and we sat down. We began to talk and just reflect. Ann said: "My daughter came home cryin' every day. She said her teacher was makin' fun of me in front of the other kids." I said: "Boy, the same thing happened to my kid. White liberal teacher was makin' fun of Tim Ellis's father, the Klansman. In front of other peoples. He came home cryin'." At this point—(he pauses, swallows hard, stifles a sob)—I begin to see, here we are, two people from the far ends of the fence, havin' identical problems, except hers bein' black and me bein' white. From that moment on, I tell ya, that gal and I worked together good. I begin to love the girl, really. (He weeps.)

The amazing thing about it, her and I, up to that point, had cussed each other, bawled each other, we hated each other. Up to that point, we didn't know each other. We didn't know we had things in common.

We worked at it, with the people who came to these meetings. They talked about racism, sex education, about teachers not bein' qualified. After seven, eight nights of real intense discussion, these people, who'd never talked to each other before, all of a sudden came up with resolutions. It was really somethin', you had to be there to get the tone and feelin' of it.

At that point, I didn't like integration, but the law says you do this and I've got to do what the law says, okay? We said: "'Let's take these resolutions to the school board." The most disheartening thing I've ever faced was the school system refused to implement any one of these resolutions. These were recommendations from the people who pay taxes and pay their salaries. (Laughs.)

I thought they were good answers. Some of 'em I didn't agree with, but I been in this thing from the beginning, and whatever comes of it, I'm gonna support it. Okay, since the school board refused, I decided I'd just run for the school board.

I spent eighty-five dollars on the campaign. The guy runnin' against me spent several thousand. I really had nobody on my side. The Klan turned against me. The low-income whites turned against me. The liberals didn't particularly like me. The blacks were suspicious of me. The blacks wanted to support me, but they couldn't muster up enough to support a Klansman on the school board. (Laughs.) But I made up my mind that what I was doin' was right, and I was gonna do it regardless what anybody said.

It bothered me when people would call and worry my wife. She's always supported me in anything I wanted to do. She was changing, and my boys were too. I got some of my youth corps kids involved. They still followed me.

I was invited to the Democratic women's social hour as a candidate. Didn't have but one suit to my name. Had it six, seven, eight years. I had it cleaned, put on the best shirt I had and a tie. Here were all this high-class wealthy candidates shakin' hands. I walked up to the mayor and stuck out my hand. He give me that handshake with that rag type of hand. He said: "C. P., I'm glad to see you." But I could tell by his handshake he was lyin' to me. This was botherin' me. I know I'm a low-income person. I know I'm not wealthy. I know they were sayin': "What's this little ol' dude runnin' for school board?" Yet they had to smile and make like they're glad to see me. I begin to spot some black people in that room. I automatically went to 'em and that was a firm handshake. They said: "I'm glad to see you, C. P." I knew they meant it—you can tell about a handshake.

Every place I appeared, I said I will listen to the voice of the people. I will not make a major decision until I first contacted all the organizations in the city. I got 4,640 votes. The guy beat me by two thousand. Not bad for eighty-five bucks and no constituency.

The whole world was openin' up, and I was learnin' new truths that I had never learned before. I was beginnin' to look at a black person, shake hands with him, and see him as a human bein'. I hadn't got rid of all this stuff. I've still got a little bit of it. But somethin' was happenin' to me.

It was almost like bein' born again. It was a new life. I didn't have these sleepless nights I used to have when I was active in the Klan and slippin' around at night. I could sleep at night and feel good about it. I'd rather live now than at any other time in history. It's a challenge.

Back at Duke, doin' maintenance, I'd pick up my tools, fix the commode, unstop the drains. But this got in my blood. Things weren't right in this country, and what we done in Durham needs to be told. I was so miserable at Duke, I could hardly stand it. I'd go to work every mornin' just hatin' to go.

My whole life had changed. I got an eighth-grade education, and I wanted to complete high school. Went to high school in the afternoons on a program called PEP—Past Employment Progress. I was about the only white in class, and the oldest. I begin to read about biology. I'd take my books home at night, 'cause I was determined to get through. Sure enough, I graduated. I got the diploma at home.

I come to work one mornin' and some guy says: "We need a union." At this time I wasn't pro-union. My daddy was anti-labor, too. We're not gettin' paid much, we're havin' to work seven days in a row. We're all starvin' to death. The next day, I meet the international representative of the Operating Engineers. He give me authorization cards. "Get these cards out and we'll have an election." There was eighty-eight for the union and seventeen no's. I was elected chief steward for the union.

Shortly after, a union man come down from Charlotte and says we need a full-time rep. We've got only two hundred people at the two plants here. It's just barely enough money comin' in to pay your salary. You'll have to get out and organize more people. I didn't know nothin' about organizin' unions, but I knew how to organize people, stir people up. (Laughs.) That's how I got to be business agent for the union.

When I began to organize, I began to see far deeper. I began to see people again bein' used. Blacks against whites. I say this without any hesitancy: management is vicious. There's two things they want to keep: all the money and all the say-so. They don't want these poor workin' folks to have none of that. I begin to see management fightin' me with everything they had. Hire anti-union law firms, badmouth unions. The people were makin' a dollar ninety-five an hour, barely able to get through weekends. I worked as a business rep for five years and was seein' all this.

Last year, I ran for business manager of the union. He's elected by the workers. The guy that ran against me was black, and our membership is seventy-five percent black. I thought: Claiborne, there's no way you can beat that black guy. People know your background. Even though you've made tremendous strides, those black people are not gonna vote for you. You know how much I beat him? Four to one. (Laughs.)

The company used my past against me. They put out letters with a picture of a robe and a cap: Would you vote for a Klansman? They wouldn't deal with the issues. I immediately called for a mass meeting. I met with the ladies at an electric component plant. I said: "Okay, this is Claiborne Ellis. This is where I come from. I want you to know right now, you black ladies here, I was at one time a member of the Klan. I want you to know, because they'll tell you about it."

I invited some of my old black friends. I said: "Brother Joe, Brother Howard, be honest now and tell these people how you feel about me." They done it. (Laughs.) Howard Clements kidded me a little bit. He said: "I don't know what I'm doin' here, supportin' an ex-Klansman." (Laughs.) He said: "I know what C. P. Ellis come from. I knew him when he was. I knew him as he grew, and growed with him. I'm tellin' you now: follow, follow this Klansman." (He pauses, swallows hard.) "Any questions?" "No," the black ladies said. "Let's get on with the meeting, we need Ellis." (He laughs and weeps.) Boy, black people sayin' that about me. I won one thirty-four to forty-one. Four to one.

It makes you feel good to go into a plant and butt heads with professional union busters. You see black people and white people join hands to defeat the racist issues they use against people. They're tryin' the same things with the Klan. It's still happenin' today. Can you imagine a guy who's got an adult high school diploma runnin' into professional college graduates who are union busters? I gotta compete with 'em. I work seven days a week, nights, and on Saturday and Sunday. The salary's not that great, and if I didn't care, I'd quit. But I care and I can't quit. I got a taste of it. (Laughs.)

I tell people there's a tremendous possibility in this country to stop wars, the battles, the struggles, the fights between people. People say: "That's an impossible dream. You sound like Martin Luther King." An ex-Klansman who sounds like Martin Luther King. (Laughs.) I don't think it's an impossible dream. It's happened in my life. It's happened in other people's lives in America.

I don't know what's ahead of me. I have no desire to be a big union official. I want to be right out here in the field with the workers. I want to walk through their factory and shake hands with that man whose hands are dirty. I'm gonna do all that one little ol' man can do. I'm fifty-two years old, and I ain't got many years left, but I want to make the best of 'em.

When the news came over the radio that Martin Luther King was assassinated, I got on the telephone and begin to call other Klansmen. We just had a real party at the service station. Really rejoicin' 'cause that son of a bitch was dead. Our troubles are over with. They say the older you get, the harder it is for you to change. That's not necessarily true. Since I changed, I've set down and listened to tapes of Martin Luther King. I listen to it and tears come to my eyes 'cause I know what he's sayin' now. I know what's happenin'.

POSTSCRIPT: *The phone rings. A conversation. . . .*

"*This was a black guy who's director of Operation Breakthrough in Durham. I had called his office. I'm interested in employin' some young black person who's interested in learnin' the labor movement. I want somebody who's never had an opportunity, just like myself. Just so he can read and write, that's all.*"

Suggestions for Further Reading

Abbott, Franklin, ed. *New Men, New Minds.* Freedom, Calif.: The Crossing Press, 1993.

Aguilar-San Juan, Karin. *The State of Asian America.* Boston: South End Press, 1994.

Anzaldua, Gloria, ed. *Making Faces, Making Soul: Creative and Critical Perspectives by Women of Color.* San Francisco: Aunt Lute Books, 1990.

Bean, Joseph. *In the Life: A Black Gay Anthology.* Boston: Alyson Publishers, 1986.

Chinese Historical Society of Southern California: *Linking Our Lives: Chinese American Women of Los Angeles.* Los Angeles: Chinese Historical Society of Southern California, 1984.

Brown, R. M. *RubyFruit Jungle.* New York: Bantam, 1977.

Browne, Susan E. *With the Power of Each Breath.* Pittsburgh: Cleis Press, 1985.

Brumberg, Joan Jacobs. *Fasting Girls: The Emergence of Anorexia Nervosa as a Modern Disease.* Cambridge, Mass.: Harvard University Press, 1988.

Cofer, Judith Ortiz. *The Latin Deli.* Athens, Ga.: University of Georgia Press, 1993.

David, J., ed. *The American Indian: The First Victim.* New York: William Morrow, 1972.

Native Americans 500 Years After. Photographs by Joseph C. Farner, text by Michael Dorris. New York: Thomas Crowell, 1975.

Flores, Angel, and Kate Flores. *The Defiant Muse: Hispanic Feminist Poems from the Middle Ages to the Present.* New York: The Feminist Press, 1986.

Geary, Hobson, ed. *The Remembered Earth: An Anthology of Contemporary Native American Literature.* Albuquerque: University of New Mexico Press, 1981.

Gwaltney, J. *Drylongso: A Self-Portrait of Black America.* New York: Vintage Books, 1981.

Haley, Alex. *The Autobiography of Malcolm X.* New York: Grove Press, 1964.

James, M. Annette. *The State of Native Americans.* Boston: South End Press, 1993.

Kimmel, Michael S., and Michael A. Messner, eds. *Men's Lives, 2d ed.* New York: Macmillan, 1992.

Kingston, M. H. *The Woman Warrior.* New York: Vintage Books, 1981.

Lee, Joann Faung Jean, ed. *Asian Americans.* New York: The New Press, 1991.

Moody, A. *Coming of Age in Mississippi.* New York: Dell, 1968.

Moore, Joan, and Harry Pachon. *Hispanics in the U.S.* Englewood Cliffs, N.J.: Prentice-Hall, 1985.

Naylor, G. *The Women of Brewster Place.* New York: Penguin, 1983.

Ng, Fae Myenne. *Bone.* New York: Harper Perennial, 1994.

Pemberton, Gayle. *The Hottest Water in Chicago.* New York: Doubleday/Anchor, 1992.

Reid, John. *The Best Little Boy in the World.* New York: G. P. Putnam's Sons, 1973.

Rebollendo, Tey Diana, and Eliana S. Rivero, eds. *Infinite Divisions: An Anthology of Chicana Literature.* Tucson: University of Arizona Press, 1993.

Rivera, E. *Family Installments: Memories of Growing Up Hispanic.* New York: Penguin, 1983.

Rubin, L. B. *Worlds of Pain: Life in the Working Class Family.* New York: Basic Books, 1976.

Shulman, A. K. *Memoirs of an Ex-Prom Queen.* New York: Knopf, 1972.

Silko, L. M. *Ceremony.* New York: New American Library, 1972.

Smith, B., ed. *Home Girls: A Black Feminist Anthology.* New York: Kitchen Table/Women of Color Press, 1983.

Tan, Amy. *The Joy Luck Club.* New York: Ivy Books, 1990.

Tatum, Charles, ed. *New Chicana/Chicano Writing 2.* Tucson: University of Arizona Press, 1992.

Thompson, Karen, and Julie Andrzejewski. *Why Can't Sharon Kowalski Come Home?* San Francisco: Spinsters/Aunt Lute, 1988.

Turkel, Studs. *Working.* New York: Avon Books, 1972.

Warshaw, Robin. *I Never Called It Rape.* New York: Harper & Row, 1988.

Winged Words: American Indian Writers Speak. Lincoln, Neb.: University of Nebraska Press, 1990.

Zahava, Irene, ed. *Speaking for Ourselves: Short Stories by Jewish Lesbians.* Freedom, Calif.: The Crossing Press, 1990.

How It Happened:
Race and Gender
Issues in U.S. Law

It is clear that being born a woman, a person of color, or both, in addition to being poor, makes it far more likely that an individual will have less education, inferior health care, a lower standard of living, and a diminished set of aspirations compared with those who are born white, wealthy, and male. How does this happen? Is the lack of equality of opportunity and condition documented in the first four parts of this book accidental and aberrant? Or is it the inevitable result of a system designed to perpetuate the privileges of those who are wealthy, white, and male? To answer these questions, we must turn to history.

But whose history shall we study? History can be written from many perspectives. The lives of "great men" will vary greatly depending upon whether their biographers are their mothers, their peers, their wives, their lovers, their children, or their servants. And there is no basis for singling out one point of view as more correct or appropriate than any other, for each tells us part of the history of the person. Furthermore, we might ask why history should be the history of "great men" exclusively. What about the lives of valets, dancers, carpenters, teachers, and mothers? Aren't their experiences essential to reconstructing the past? Can history omit the lives of the majority of people in a society and still claim to give us an accurate account of the past?

We can even question who decides what counts as history. In the past, the war diaries of generals were kept as prized historical documents, whereas diaries written by women giving an account of their daily lives were ignored or discounted. What makes one invaluable and the other irrelevant? Many historians have chosen to call one particular point of view history and have used it to evaluate the relevance and worth of all else—this point of view being that of white men of property. It is this point of view that has permeated our American history texts and classes. The greatest secret kept by many traditional history texts was that women and people of color and working people created the wealth and culture of this country.

History, we are told, involves collecting and studying facts. But what counts as a "fact," and who decides which facts are important? Whose interests are served or furthered by these decisions? For many years, one of the first "facts" that grade-school children learned was that Christopher Columbus discovered America. And yet this "history" is neither clear nor incontrovertible. It is a piece of the past examined from the point of view of white Europeans; it is to their interest to persuade others to believe it, since this "fact" undermines the claims of others. American Indians might well ask how Columbus could have discovered America in 1492 if they had already been living here for thousands of years. Teaching children that bit of fiction about Columbus served to render Native Americans invisible and thus tacitly excused or denied the genocide carried out by European settlers.

During the contemporary period, many new approaches to history have arisen to remedy the omissions and distortions of the past. Women's history, Black history, lesbian and gay history, ethnic history, labor history, and others all propose to transform traditional history so that it more accurately reflects the reality of people's lives past and present.

Part V does not attempt to provide a comprehensive history of the American Republic since its beginning. Rather it is designed to trace the legal status of people of color and women since the first Europeans came to this land. After two preliminary readings that present an overview of legal issues as they apply to Native Americans and African Americans in particular, this Part V proceeds by reproducing legal documents that highlight developments in legal status. In a few cases, these legal documents are supplemented with materials that help paint a clearer picture of the issues involved or their implications.

Much is left out by adopting this framework for our study. Most significantly, the actual political and social movements that brought about the changes in the legal realm are omitted. For this reason, students are urged to supplement their study of the legal documents with the rich accounts of social history from the "Suggested Readings" listed at the end of Part V.

However, the legal documents themselves are fascinating. They make it possible for us to reduce hundreds of years of history to a manageable size. We can thus form a picture of the rights and status of many so-called minority groups in this country, a picture that contrasts sharply with the one usually offered in high-school social-studies classes. Most importantly, the documents can help us answer the question raised by material in the first four parts of this text: how did it happen that all women and all people of color came to have such limited access to power and opportunity?

The readings here show that, from the country's inception, the laws and institutions of the United States were designed to create and maintain the privileges of wealthy white males. The discrimination documented in the early parts of this book is no accident. It has a long and deliberate history. Understanding this history is essential if we are to create a more just and democratic society.

On July 4, 1776, the thirteen colonies set forth a declaration of independence from Great Britain. In that famous document, the founders of the Republic explained their reasons for separating from the homeland and expressed their hopes for the new republic. In lines that are rightly famous and often quoted, the signatories proclaimed that "all Men are created equal, that they are endowed by their Creator with certain unalienable Rights, that among these are Life, Liberty and the Pursuit of Happiness." They went on to assert that "to secure these Rights, Governments are instituted among Men, deriving their just Powers from the Consent of the Governed." When these words were written, however, a large portion of the population of the United States had no legal rights whatsoever. American Indians, women, indentured servants, poor white men who did not own property, and, of course, African Americans held as slaves could not vote, nor were they free to exercise their liberty or pursue their happiness in the same way that white men with property could. When the authors of the Declaration of Independence proclaimed that all men were created equal and endowed with unalienable rights, they meant "men" quite literally and white men specifically. Negro slaves, as it turned out, were worth "three fifths of all other Persons," a figure stipulated in Article 1, Section 2, of the United States Constitution. This section of the Constitution, which is often referred to as the "three-fifths compromise," undertook to establish how slaves would be counted for the purposes of determining taxes as well as for calculating representation of the states in Congress.

Faced with the need for an enormous work force to cultivate the land, the European settlers first tried to enslave the American Indian population. Later, the settlers brought over large numbers of "indentured workers" from Europe. These workers were poor white men, women, and children, some serving prison sentences at home, who were expected to work in the colonies for a certain period of time and then receive their freedom. When neither of these populations proved suitable, the settlers began importing African Negroes to serve their purposes.

Records show that the first African Negroes were brought to this country as early as 1526. Initially, the Negroes appear to have had the same status as indentured servants, but the laws reflect a fairly rapid distinction between the two groups. Maryland law made this distinction as early as 1640; Massachusetts legally recognized slavery in 1641; Virginia passed a law making Negroes slaves for life in 1661; and so it went until the number of slaves grew to roughly 600,000 at the time of the signing of the Declaration of Independence.[1] Numerous legal documents, such as An Act for the Better Ordering and Governing of Negroes and Slaves passed in

South Carolina in 1712 and excerpted in Selection 3, prescribed the existence of the slaves, as did the acts modeled on An Act Prohibiting the Teaching of Slaves to Read, a North Carolina statute reprinted here in Selection 5.

When the early European settlers came to this country, there were approximately 2.5 million Native Americans living on the land that was to become the United States. These Indian peoples were divided among numerous separate and autonomous tribes, each with its own highly developed culture and history. The white man quickly lumped these diverse peoples into a single and inferior category, "Indians," and set about destroying their culture and seizing their lands. The Indian Removal Act of 1830 was fairly typical of the kinds of laws that were passed to carry out the appropriation of Indian lands. Believing the Indians to be inherently inferior to whites, the United States government had no hesitation about legislating the removal of the Indians from valuable ancestral lands to ever more remote and barren reservations. The dissolution of the Indian tribal system was further advanced by the General Allotment Act (Dawes Act) of 1887, which divided tribal landholdings among individual Indians and thereby successfully undermined the tribal system and the culture of which it was a part. In addition, this act opened up lands within the reservation area for purchase by the United States government, which then made those lands available to white settlers for homesteading. Many supporters of the allotment policy, who were considered "friends" of the Indians, argued that the benefits of individual ownership would have a "civilizing effect" on them.[2] Instead, it ensured a life of unrelenting poverty for most because it was usually impossible for a family to derive subsistence from the use of a single plot of land and without the support of the tribal community.

While John Adams was involved in writing the Declaration of Independence, his wife, Abigail Adams, took him to task for failing to accord women the same rights and privileges as men. "I cannot say that you are very generous to the ladies; for whilst you are proclaiming peace and good will to men, emancipating all nations, you insist upon retaining an absolute power over wives."[3] Although law and custom consistently treated women as if they were physically and mentally inferior to men, the reality of women's lives was very different. Black female slaves were forced to perform the same inhuman fieldwork as Black male slaves and were expected to do so even in the final weeks of pregnancy. They were routinely beaten and abused without regard for the supposed biological fragility of the female sex. White women settlers gave birth to large numbers of children, ten and twelve being quite common and as many as twenty births not being unusual. And they did so in addition to working side by side with men to perform all those duties necessary to survival in a new and unfamiliar environment. When her husband died, a woman often assumed his responsibilities as well. It was not until well into the 1800s, primarily as a result of changes brought about by the Industrial Revolution, that significant class differences began to affect the lives and work of white women.

As women, both Black and white, became increasingly active in the antislavery movement during the 1800s, many noticed certain similarities between the legal status of women and the legal status of people held as slaves. Participants at the first women's rights convention held at Seneca Falls, New York, in 1848 listed women's grievances and specified their demands. At this time, married women were regarded as property of their husbands and had no direct legal control over their own wages, their property, or even their children. The Declaration of Sentiments issued at Seneca Falls was modeled on the Declaration of Independence in the hope that men would extend the declaration's rights to women. Similar emotional attacks are still used today to ridicule and then dismiss contemporary feminist demands.

The abysmal legal status of women and people of color in the United States during the nineteenth century is graphically documented in a series of court decisions reproduced in this part. In *People v. Hall*, 1854, the California Supreme Court decided that a California statute barring Indians and Negroes from testifying in court cases involving whites also applied to Chinese Americans. The judges asserted that the Chinese are "a race of people whom nature has marked as inferior, and who are incapable of progress or intellectual development beyond a certain point." The extent of anti-Chinese feeling in parts of the United States can be further inferred from portions of the California Constitution adopted in 1876 and included in this part.

In a more famous case, *Dred Scott v. Sanford*, 1857, the United States Supreme Court was asked to decide whether Dred Scott, a Negro, was a citizen of the United States with the rights that that implied. Scott, a slave who had been taken from Missouri, a slave state, into the free state of Illinois for a period of time, argued that because he was free and had been born in the United States, he was therefore a citizen. The Court ruled that this was not the case and, using reasoning that strongly parallels *People v. Hall*, offered a survey of United States law and custom to show that Negroes were never considered a part of the people of the United States. In *Bradwell v. Illinois*, 1873, the Supreme Court ruled that women could not practice law and used the opportunity to carefully distinguish the rights and prerogatives of women from those of men. The Court maintained that "civil law, as well as nature herself, has always recognized a wide difference in the respective spheres and destinies of man and woman" and went on to argue that women belong in the "domestic sphere."

During the period in which these and other court cases were brought, the United States moved toward and ultimately fought a bloody civil war. Allegedly fought "to free the slaves," much more was at stake. The Civil War reflected a struggle to the death between the Southern aristocracy, whose wealth was based on land and whose power rested on a kind of feudal economic-political order, and the Northern capitalists, who came into being by virtue of the Industrial Revolution and who wished to restructure the nation's economic-political institutions to better serve the needs of the new industrial order. Chief among these needs was a large and mobile work force for the factories in the North. Hundreds of thousands of soldiers died in the bloody conflict, while other men purchased army deferments and used the war years to amass tremendous personal wealth. On the Confederate side, men who owned fifty or more slaves were exempted from serving in the army, while wealthy Northern men were able to purchase deferments from the Union for the sum of $300. Among those who purchased deferments and went on to become millionaires as a result of war profiteering were John D. Rockefeller, Andrew Carnegie, J. Pierpont Morgan, Philip Armour, James Mellon, and Jay Gould.[4]

In September 1862, President Abraham Lincoln signed the Emancipation Proclamation (Selection 10) as part of his efforts to bring the Civil War to an end by forcing the Southern states to concede. It did not free all slaves; it freed only those in states or parts of states in rebellion against the federal government. Only in September 1865, after the conclusion of the war, were all people held as slaves freed by the Thirteenth Amendment (Selection 11). However, Southern whites did not yield their privileges easily. Immediately after the war, the Southern states began to pass laws known as "The Black Codes," which attempted to reestablish the relations of slavery. Some of these codes are described in this part in a selection written by the distinguished historian W. E. B. Du Bois.

In the face of such efforts to deny the rights of citizenship to Black men, Congress passed the Fourteenth Amendment (Selection 11) in July 1868. This amendment, which continues to play a major role in contemporary legal battles over discrimination, includes a number of important provisions. It explicitly extended citizenship to all those born or naturalized in the United States and guarantees all citizens "due process" and "equal protection" of the law. In addition, it canceled all debts incurred by the Confederacy in its unsuccessful rebellion while recognizing the validity of the debts incurred by the federal government. This meant that wealthy Southerners who had extended large sums of money or credit to the Confederacy would lose it, while wealthy Northern industrialists would be paid.

Southern resistance to extending the rights and privileges of citizenship to Black men persisted, and the Southern states used all their powers, including unbridled terror and violence, to subvert the intent of the Thirteenth and Fourteenth Amendments. The Fifteenth Amendment (Selection 11), which explicitly granted the vote to Black men, was passed in 1870 but it was received by the Southern states with as little enthusiasm as had greeted the Thirteenth and Fourteenth Amendments.

As the abolitionist movement grew and the Civil War became inevitable, many women's rights activists, also active in the struggle to end slavery, argued that the push for women's rights should temporarily defer to the issue of slavery. In fact, after February 1861, no women's rights conventions were held until the end of the war. Although Black and white women had long worked together in both movements, the question of which struggle took precedence created serious splits among women's rights activists, including such strong Black allies as Frederick Douglass and Sojourner Truth. Some argued that the evils of slavery were so great that they took precedence over the legal discrimination experienced by middle-class white women. They resented attempts by Elizabeth Cady Stanton and others to equate the condition of white women with that of Negro slaves and argued, moreover, that the women's rights movement had never been concerned with the extraordinary suffering of Black women or the special needs of working women. The explicitly racist appeals made by some white women activists as they sought white men's support for women's suffrage did nothing to bridge this schism. While Black men received the vote in 1868, at least on paper, women would have to continue their fight until the passage of the Nineteenth Amendment (Selection 18) in 1920. As a result, many women and Blacks saw each other as adversaries or obstacles in their struggle for legal equality, deflecting their attention from the privileged white men who provoked the conflict and whose power was reinforced by it.

One special cause for bitterness was the Fourteenth Amendment's reference to male inhabitants and the right to vote. This was the first time that voting rights had explicitly been rendered gender-specific. The Fourteenth Amendment was tested in 1874 by *Minor* v. *Happersett* (Selection 14), in which the court was asked to rule directly on the question of whether women had the vote by virtue of their being citizens of the United States. The Court ruled unanimously that women did not have the vote, arguing that women, like criminals and mental defectives, could legitimately be denied the vote by the states.[5] In a somewhat similar case, *Elk* v. *Wilkens*, 1884 (Selection 16), John Elk, an American Indian who had left his tribe and lived among whites, argued that he was a citizen by virtue of the Fourteenth Amendment and should not be denied the right to vote by the state of Nebraska. The Supreme Court ruled that neither the Fourteenth nor Fifteenth Amendments applied to Elk. Native Americans became citizens of the United States three years later, under one of the provisions of the Dawes Act of 1887.

Unsuccessful in their attempts to reinstate some form of forced servitude by passage of "The Black Codes," Southern states began to legalize the separation of the races in all aspects of public and private life. In *Plessy* v. *Ferguson*, 1896, (Selection 17), the Supreme Court was asked to rule on whether segregation by race in public facilities violated the Thirteenth and Fourteenth Amendments. In a ruling that was to cruelly affect several generations of Black Americans, the Supreme Court decided that restricting Negroes to the use of "separate but equal" public accommodations did not deny them equal protection of the law. This decision remained in effect for almost sixty years until *Brown* v. *Board of Education of Topeka*, 1954 (Selection 20). In the historic *Brown* decision, the Court ruled, in effect, that "separate" could not possibly be "equal." Nonetheless, abolishing segregation on paper was one thing; actually bringing about the integration of public facilities was another. The integration of public schools, housing, and employment in both the North and the South has been a long and often bloody struggle that continues to this day.

The racist attitudes toward Chinese Americans, reflected in the nineteenth-century California statutes and constitution as we have already seen, extended toward Japanese Americans as well. This racism erupted during the twentieth century after the bombing of Pearl Harbor by Japan on December 7, 1941. Anti-Japanese feelings ran so high that President Franklin Roosevelt issued an executive order allowing the military to designate "military areas" from which it could then exclude any persons it chose. On March 2, 1942, the entire West Coast was designated as such an area, and within a few months, everyone of Japanese ancestry (defined as those having as little as one-eighth Japanese blood) was evacuated. More than 110,000 people of Japanese descent, most of them American citizens, were forced to leave their homes and jobs and to spend the war years in so-called relocation camps behind barbed wire.[6] Although the United States was also at war with Germany, no such barbaric treatment was afforded German Americans. The military evacuation of Japanese Americans was challenged in *Korematsu* v. *United States*, 1944. In its decision, excerpted in Selection 19, the Supreme Court upheld the forced evacuation.

The twentieth century has seen the growth of large and diverse movements for race and gender justice. These movements precipitated the creation of a number of commissions and government agencies, which were to research and enforce equal treatment for people of color and women; the passage of a number of statutes to this end; and a series of Supreme Court decisions in the area. For women, one of the most significant Court decisions of the recent past was *Roe* v. *Wade*, 1973 (Selection 21), which, for the first time, give women the right to terminate pregnancy by abortion. Rather than affirming a woman's right to control her body, however, the *Roe* decision is based upon the right to privacy. The impact of *Roe* was significantly blunted by *Harris* v. *McRae*, 1980, in which the Court ruled that the right to privacy did not require public funding of medically necessary abortions for women who could not afford them. In practice, this meant that white middle-class women who chose abortion could exercise their right but that many poor white women and women of color could not. The single biggest defeat for the Women's Movement of this period was the failure to pass the much misunderstood Equal Rights Amendment, which is reproduced in Selection 22.

More recently, the Supreme Court was asked to rule on the constitutionality of homosexual intercourse when Michael Hardwick, a practicing homosexual, brought suit challenging the constitutionality of Georgia's sodomy law. In *Bowers* v. *Hardwick* (Selection 23), the Court upheld that law. In a broad decision that could have disturbing implications for many different kinds of private sexual conduct between consenting adults, the Supreme Court ruled that it is not unconstitutional to legislate against certain forms of sexual activity. The prohibition against sodomy as well as other legal issues that might impact directly on lesbian and gay people are surveyed in Selection 24, "The Law and the Lesbian and Gay Community."

NOTES

1. W. Z. Foster: *The Negro People in American History*, International Publishers, New York, 1954, p. 37.

2. United States Commission on Civil Rights: *Indian Tribes: A Continuing Quest for Survival*, a report of the United States Commission on Civil Rights, June 1981, p. 34.

3. Letter to John Adams, May 7, 1776.

4. H. Wasserman: *Harvey Wasserman's History of the United States*, Harper & Row, New York, 1975. p. 3.

5. E. Flexner: *Century of Struggle*, Harvard University Press, Cambridge, Massachusetts, 1976, p. 172.

6. R. E. Cushman and R. F. Cushman: *Cases in Constitutional Law*, Appleton-Century-Crofts, New York, 1958, p. 127.

Indian Tribes:
A Continuing Quest for Survival

U.S. Commission on Human Rights

Traditional civil rights, as the phrase is used here, includes those rights that are secured to individuals and are basic to the United States system of government. They include the right to vote and the right to equal treatment without discrimination on the basis of race, religion, or national origin, among others, in such areas as education, housing, employment, public accommodations, and the administration of justice.

In order to understand where American Indians stand today with respect to these rights, it is important to look at historical developments of the concept of Indian rights along with the civil rights movement in this country. The consideration given to these factors here will not be exhaustive, but rather a brief look at some of the events that are most necessary to a background understanding of this area.

A basic and essential factor concerning American Indians is that the development of civil rights issues for them is in reverse order from other minorities in this country. Politically, other minorities started with nothing and attempted to obtain a voice in the existing economic and political structure. Indians started with everything and have gradually lost much of what they had to an advancing alien civilization. Other minorities have had no separate governmental institutions. Their goal primarily has been and continues to be to make the existing system involve them and work for them. Indian tribes have always been separate political entities interested in maintaining their own institutions and beliefs. Their goal has been to prevent the dismantling of their own systems. So while other minorities have sought integration into the larger society, much of Indian society is motivated to retain its political and cultural separateness.

Although at the beginning of the colonization process Indian nations were more numerous and better adapted to survival on this continent than the European settlers, these advantages were quickly lost. The colonization period saw the rapid expansion of non-Indian communities in numbers and territory covered and a shift in the balance of strength from Indian to non-Indian communities and governments. The extent to which Indians intermingled with non-Indian society varied by time period, geographical location, and the ability of natives and newcomers to get along with one another. As a general matter, however, Indians were viewed and treated as members of political entities that were not part of the United States. The Constitution acknowledges this by its separate provision regarding trade with the Indian tribes.[1] Indian tribes today that have not been forcibly assimilated, extinguished, or legally terminated still consider themselves to be, and are viewed in American law, as separate political units.

The Racial Factor

An important element in the development of civil rights for American Indians today goes beyond their legal and political status to include the way they have been viewed racially. Since colonial times Indians have been viewed as an "inferior race"; sometimes this view is condescendingly positive—the romanticized noble savage— at other times this view is hostile—the vicious savage—at all times the view is racist. All things Indian are viewed as inherently inferior to their counterparts in the white European tradition. Strong racist statements have appeared in congressional debates, Presidential policy announcements, court decisions, and other authoritative public utterances. This racism has served to justify a view now repudiated, but which still lingers in the public mind, that Indians are not entitled to the same legal rights as others in this country. In some cases, racism has been coupled with apparently benevolent motives, to "civilize" the "savages," to teach them Christian principles. In other cases, the racism has been coupled with greed; Indians were "removed" to distant locations to prevent them from standing in the way of the development of the new Western civilization. At one extreme the concept of inferior status of Indians was used to justify genocide; at the other, apparently benevolent side, the attempt was to assimilate them into the dominant society. Whatever the rationale or motive, whether rooted in voluntary efforts or coercion, the common denominator has been the belief that Indian society is an inferior lifestyle.

> It sprang from a conviction that native people were a lower grade of humanity for whom the accepted cannons of respect need not apply; one did not debase oneself by ruining a native person. At times, this conviction was stated explicitly by men in public office, but whether expressed or not, it generated decision and action.[2]

Early assimilationists like Thomas Jefferson proceeded from this assumption with benevolent designs.

> Thus, even as they acknowledged a degree of political autonomy in the tribes, their conviction of the natives' cultural inferiority led them to interfere in their social, religious, and economic practices. Federal agents to the tribes not only negotiated

treaties and tendered payments; they pressured husbands to take up the plow and wives to learn to spin. The more conscientious agents offered gratuitous lectures on the virtues of monogamy, industry, and temperance.

The same underlying assumption provided the basis for Andrew Jackson's attitude. "I have long viewed treaties with the Indians an absurdity not to be reconciled to the principles of our government," he said. As President he refused to enforce the decisions of the U. S. Supreme Court upholding Cherokee tribal autonomy, and he had a prominent role in the forced removal of the Cherokees from Georgia and the appropriation of their land by white settlers. Other eastern tribes met a similar fate under the Indian Removal Act of 1830.[3]

Another Federal Indian land policy, enacted at the end of the 19th century and followed until 1934, that shows the virulent effect of racist assumptions was the allotment of land parcels to individual Indians as a replacement for tribal ownership. Many proponents of the policy were considered "friends of the Indians," and they argued that the attributes of individual land ownership would have a great civilizing and assimilating effect on American Indians. This action, undertaken for the benefit of the Indians, was accomplished without consulting them. Had Congress heeded the views of the purported beneficiaries of this policy, allotment might not have been adopted. Representatives of 19 tribes met in Oklahoma and unanimously opposed the legislation, recognizing the destructive effect it would have upon Indian culture and the land base itself, which was reduced by 90 million acres in 45 years.

An important principle established by the allotment policy was that the Indian form of land ownership was not "civilized," and so it was the right of the Government to invalidate that form. It is curious that the principle of the right to own property in conglomerate form for the benefit of those with a shareholder's undivided interest in the whole was a basis of the American corporate system, then developing in strength. Yet a similar form of ownership when practiced by Indians was viewed as a hallmark of savagery. Whatever the explanation for this double standard, the allotment policy reinforced the notion that Indians were somehow inferior, that non-Indians in power knew what was best for them, and that these suppositions justified the assertion that non-Indians had the power and authority to interfere with the basic right to own property.

Religion is another area in which non-Indians have felt justified in interfering with Indian beliefs. The intent to civilize the natives of this continent included a determined effort to Christianize them. Despite the constitutional prohibition, Congress, beginning in 1819, regularly appropriated funds for Christian missionary efforts. Christian goals were visibly aligned with Federal Indian policy in 1869 when a Board of Indian Commissioners was established by Congress under President Grant's administration. Representative of the spectrum of Christian denominations, the independently wealthy members of the Board were charged by the Commissioner of Indian Affairs to work for the "humanization, civilization and Christianization of the Indians." Officials of the Federal Indian Service were supposed to cooperate with this Board.

The benevolent support of Christian missionary efforts stood in stark contrast to the Federal policy of suppressing tribal religions. Indian ceremonial behavior was misunderstood and suppressed by Indian agents. In 1892 the Commissioner of Indian Affairs established a regulation making it a criminal offense to engage in such ceremonies as the sun dance. The spread of the Ghost Dance religion, which promised salvation from the white man, was so frightening to the Federal Government that troops were called in to prevent it, even though the practice posed no threat to white settlers.

The judiciary of the United States, though it has in many instances forthrightly interpreted the law to support Indian legal claims in the face of strong, sometimes violent opposition, has also lent support to the myth of Indian inferiority. For example, the United States Supreme Court in 1883, in recognizing the right of tribes to govern themselves, held that they had the exclusive authority to try Indians for criminal offenses committed against Indians. In describing its reasons for refusing to find jurisdiction in a non-Indian court in such cases, the Supreme Court said:

> It [the non-Indian court] tries them, not by their peers, nor by the customs of their people, nor the law of their land, but by *superiors* of a different race, according to the law of a social state of which they have an imperfect conception, and which is opposed to the traditions of their history, to the habits of their lives, to the strongest prejudices of their *savage nature*; one which measures the red man's revenge by the maxims of the white man's morality.[4] (emphasis added)

In recognizing the power of the United States Government to determine the right of Indians to occupy their lands, the Supreme Court expressed the good faith of the country in such matters with these words: "the United States will be governed by such considerations of justice as will control a Christian people in their treatment of an ignorant and dependent race."[5]

Another example of racist stereotyping to be found in the courts is this example from the Supreme Court of Washington State:

> The Indian was a child, and a dangerous child, of nature, to be both protected and restrained. . . . True, arrangements took the form of treaty and of terms like "cede," "relinquish," "reserve." But never were these agreements between equals . . . [but rather] that "between a superior and an inferior."[6]

This reasoning, based on racism, has supported the view that Indians are wards of the Government who need the protection and assistance of Federal agencies and it is the Government's obligation to recreate their governments, conforming them to a non-Indian model, to establish their priorities, and to make or approve their decisions for them.

Indian education policies have often been examples of the Federal Government having determined with is "best" for Indians. Having judged that assimilation could be promoted through the indoctrination process of white schools, the Federal Government began investing in Indian education. Following the model established by army officer Richard Pratt in 1879, boarding schools were established where Indian children were separated from the influences of tribal and home life. The boarding schools tried to teach Indians skills and trades that would be useful in white society, utilizing stern disciplinary measures to force assimilation. The tactics used are within memory of today's generation of tribal leaders who recall the policy of deterring communication in native languages. "I remember being punished many times for . . . singing one Navajo song, or a Navajo word slipping out of my tongue just in an unplanned way, but I was punished for it."

Federal education was made compulsory, and the policy was applied to tribes that had sophisticated school systems of their own as well as to tribes that really needed assistance to establish educational systems. The ability of the tribal school to educate was not relevant, given that the overriding goal was assimilation rather than education.

Racism in Indian affairs has not been sanctioned recently by political or religious leaders or other leaders in American society. In fact, public pronouncements over the last several decades have lamented past evils and poor treatment of Indians.[7] The virulent public expressions of other eras characterizing Indians as "children" or "savages" are not now acceptable modes of public expression. Public policy today is a commitment to Indian self-determination. Numerous actions of Congress and the executive branch give evidence of a more positive era for Indian policy.[8] Beneath the surface, however, the effects of centuries of racism still persist. The attitudes of the public, of State and local officials, and of Federal policymakers do not always live up to the positive pronouncements of official policy. Some decisions today are perceived as being made on the basis of precedents mired in the racism and greed of another era. Perhaps more important, the legacy of racism permeates behavior and that behavior creates classic civil rights violations. . . .

NOTES

1. U.S. Const. Art. 1, §8.

2. D'Arcy McNickel, *Native American Tribalism* (New York: Oxford University Press, 1973), p. 56.

3. Act of May 28, 1830, ch. 148, 4 Stat. 411.

4. Ex Parte Crow Dog, 109 U.S. 556, 571 (1883).

5. Missouri, Kansas, and Texas Railway Co. v. Roberts, 152 U.S. 114, 117 (1894).

6. State v. Towessnute, 154 P. 805, 807 (Wash. Sup. Ct. 1916), quoting Choctaw Nation v. United States, 119 U.S. 1, 27 (1886).

7. See, e.g., President Nixon's July 8, 1970, Message to the Congress, Recommendations for Indian Policy, H. Doc. No. 91–363, 91st Cong., 2d sess. (hereafter cited as *Recommendations for Indian Policy*).

8. Ibid; Indian Self-Determination and Education Assistance Act, Pub. L. No. 93–638, 88 Stat. 2203 (1975); Indian Child Welfare Act of 1978, Pub. L. No. 95–608, 92 Stat. 3096; U.S., Department of the Interior, *Report on the Implementation of the Helsinki Final Act* (1979).

2

Race and the American Legal Process

A. Leon Higginbotham, Jr.

"Why of all of the multitudinous groups of people in this country [do] you have to single out Negroes and give them this separate treatment."
—*Oral argument before the United States Supreme Court by Thurgood Marshall, then Chief Counsel for the Plaintiffs in* Brown v. Board of Education.

At approximately 7:17 P.M., April 4, 1968, an assassin fired a shot mortally wounding Martin Luther King. Late that evening I received a call from the President, Lyndon Johnson, who had appointed me four years earlier to the United States District Court, asking me to come to the White House early the next morning to discuss with others who were being called the national significance of Dr. King's death. Though the President acted quickly in collecting his counselors for a meeting the next morning, another section of the nation would not wait the night to express its own response to this national tragedy. Ten blocks from the White House, buildings in the largely black ghettoes of Washington, D.C. were already in flames. As the painful night lingered on, news reports indicated that more and more people had taken to the streets, many striking out irrationally and in anger, in city after city, in response to the senseless death of the prophet of nonviolence.

President Johnson opened the meeting at the White House the next morning with the question, "What can we do now?"

There were many thoughtful responses. Some talked of strengthening civil rights legislation, others spoke of further improving manpower programs, still others argued for additional condemnations of racism. The idea for appointing yet another presidential commission was also introduced. Although the discussion was calm and dispassionate, a deep sense of shared pain was apparent. Most of us present had known Dr. King intimately and had worked with him in the attempt to obliterate racism from American life.

As I listened and reflected on the various suggestions made from such thoughtful and well-meaning people, I kept thinking of the question Thurgood Marshall had asked the Supreme Court thirteen years earlier: "Why," he had asked, "of all the multitudinous groups of people in this country, do you have to single out

295

Negroes and give them this separate treatment." That morning, sitting in the White House, I knew there was an indisputable nexus between the dark shadow of repression under which, historically, most American blacks have lived and the rioting occurring within ten blocks of the White House. Why, I thought to myself, in the land of the free and the home of the brave, had even brave blacks so often failed to get free? Why had that very legal process that had been devised to protect the rights of individuals against the will of the government and the whim of the majority been often employed so malevolently against blacks? What were the options that ought to have been exercised years ago, even centuries ago, to narrow those disparities in meted-out justice that had periodically—and had now once more— kindled black hatred and white fear?

In the company of the great lawyers present at the President's meeting— Supreme Court Associate Justice Thurgood Marshall and Attorney General Ramsey Clark—as well as the other notable government and public officials—Cabinet officer Robert C. Weaver, Civil Rights leaders Roy Wilkins, Whitney Young, Clarence Mitchell, Reverend Leon Sullivan, and Vice President Humphrey—it was inevitable that I would ponder how the legal process had contributed to this malaise. For in 1968, in this nation's 192nd year, things could have been different. If the legal process had been racially just, the nation in the 1960s would not have been torn asunder as it was by the unrelenting demands by blacks for dignity and equal justice under the law pulling against the stubborn resistance of those who had been conditioned to believe in the status quo as the ultimate expression of "liberty and justice for all." The institutionalized injustice of racial apartness had first brought Martin Luther King to the forefront and now, ultimately, had brought him to his death.

Particularly during this Bicentennial era, it is appropriate to assess the interrelationship of race and the American legal process. This nation has just celebrated its 200th birthday in a most grandiose fashion. Conventions have been held in almost every town to reaffirm those "self-evident truths," and the oratory will continue to 1987, the 200th anniversary of the United States Constitution. As praise is heaped on the great leaders of yesterday, and as some laud 1776 as the Golden Era of liberty, it is often suggested that if only today's leaders had the integrity and character of Jefferson, Franklin, John Adams, Washington, and Madison, today's racial difficulties might be quickly resolved. Few have had the temerity to contradict this general but misdirected consensus, for it is bad bicentennial form to refer to the fact that many of America's founding fathers owned slaves and that most, either directly or indirectly, profited from the evil institution that enslaved black human beings only.

The bicentennial drum roll of revolutionary heroes and events, then, symbolizes one thing to white Americans but quite another to blacks. From a predominantly white perspective, the Declaration of Independence is viewed as former President Nixon described it: "the greatest achievement in the history of man. We are the beneficiaries of that achievement." But who, until recently, did the "we" describe? Not black America. Frederick Douglass, a leading abolitionist who was born a slave, described Independence Day in 1852 from the perspective of blacks and slaves rather than whites and slaveholders:

> This Fourth of July is *yours*, not mine. You may rejoice, I must mourn. To drag a man in fetters to the grand illuminated temple of liberty, and call upon him to join you in joyous anthems, were inhuman mockery and sacrilegious irony. . . . I say it with a sad sense of the disparity between us. I am not included within the pale of this glorious anniversary. . . . The blessings in which you, this day, rejoice, are not enjoyed in common. The rich inheritance of justice, liberty, prosperity and independence, bequeathed by your fathers, is shared by you, not by me. The sunlight that brought light and healing to you, has brought stripes and death to me.

Likewise, from a predominantly white perspective, the pledges of the Preamble to the Constitution honestly set out the largest principles for which the new American legal process would strive.

> We the people . . . in order to form a more perfect union, establish justice, . . . promote the general welfare, and secure the blessings of liberty to ourselves and our posterity. . . .

From a black perspective, however, the Constitution's references to justice, welfare, and liberty were mocked by the treatment meted out daily to blacks from the seventeenth to nineteenth centuries through the courts, in legislative statutes, and in those provisions of the Constitution that sanctioned slavery for the majority of black Americans and allowed disparate treatment for those few blacks legally "free."

Further, whatever opening there might have been for one day peacefully redefining "We the people" to include, as it should have in the first place, black Americans, was abruptly closed with the 1857 U.S. Supreme Court decision *Dred Scott v. Sanford*. When asked if the phrase "We the people" included black people and whether blacks were embraced in the egalitarian language of the Declaration of Independence, Chief Justice Roger Taney, speaking for the majority, wrote:

> [A]t the time of the Declaration of Independence, and when the Constitution of the United States was framed and adopted . . . [blacks] had no rights which the white man was bound to respect.

In effect, Taney had not answered the question. Rather, he had gone back in time in an attempt to determine what the founding fathers had intended, and in so doing, had argued from the untenable position that the Constitution might never be any larger than the restrictive vision of eighteenth-century America.

Thus, for black Americans today—the children of all the hundreds of Kunta Kintes unjustly chained in bondage—the early failure of the nation's founders and their constitutional heirs to share the legacy of freedom with black Americans is at least one factor in America's perpetual racial tensions. Twenty years after the Civil War, over one hundred years after the Declaration of Independence, two hundred fifty years after the first black man set foot in America, in *Huckleberry Finn,* Mark Twain, in a parody of white attitudes, suggested that as late as 1884 many white Americans still failed to perceive blacks as human beings. He writes:

> "Good gracious. Anybody hurt?"
> "No'm. Killed a nigger."
> "Well, it's lucky because sometimes people do get hurt." . . .

This book will treat from a legal standpoint this historically persistent failure of perception. What should have been on the minds of all in power during the seventeenth and eighteenth centuries was the question James Otis raised in his provocative paper of 1764:

> Does it follow that, tis right to enslave a man because he is black?

. . . I am aware that an analysis of cases, statutes, and legal edicts does not tell the whole story as to why and how this sordid legal tradition managed to establish itself. Nevertheless, there is merit in abolitionist William Goodell's statement: "No people were ever yet found who were better than their laws, though many have been known to be worse."

While I recognize that a view of slavery from the perspective of the law does not make a complete picture, I join in the conclusions of Winthrop D. Jordan when writing on the Colonial period and C. Vann Woodward when writing on the Reconstruction period. Jordan has advised us:

> while statutes usually speak falsely as to actual behavior, they afford probably the best single means of ascertaining what a society thinks behavior ought to be; they sweep up the felt necessities of the day and indirectly expound the social norm of the legislators.

And C. Vann Woodward has stated:

> I am convinced that law has a special importance in the history of segregation, more importance than some sociologists would allow, and that the emphasis on legal history is justified.

While I do not represent what I put forward here as a complete picture of the practices of the society, that canvas will never be painted unless someone first treats adequately the interrelationship of race and the American legal process.

Obviously, there were several factors that contributed to the inclination of the legal process to treat blacks so differently from all others. Many have written in great detail on some of these factors. For instance, in so many legal decisions, there was the powerful presence of the economics of slavery. The key question for many a righteous and learned community leader was whether it was cheaper to have blacks as slaves or to have blacks as "free" labor. Or, possibly, instead of black slaves would it have been cheaper to have had white indentured servants or white free labor.

The issue of safety and the natural fear of slave revolts was also intertwined in the chain of legal judgments. While never reluctant to protect and maximize their property rights in the slaves, many judges and legislators were reluctant to recognize that slaves had, in their own right, any basic human rights. Many feared that any judicial protection of the slave would trigger further challenges to the legitimacy of the dehumanized status of blacks and slaves. Since the plantations were often in isolated settings and there was an ever threatening possibility that the slaves might rise up and slay their oppressors, any judge whose decision criticized racial injustice might be accused of weakening the master-slave system. For instance, in a famous North Carolina decision *State* v. *Mann* involving the issue of whether or not it was a criminal offense to subject a slave woman to "a cruel and unreasonable battery," the court stated that a slave was to "labor upon a principle of natural duty," to disregard "his own personal happiness," and that the purpose of the legal system was to convince each slave that he had

> no will of his own [and that he must surrender] his will in implicit obedience to that of another. Such obedience is the consequence only of uncontrolled authority over the body. There is nothing else that can operate to produce the effect. The power of the master must be absolute to render the submission of the slave perfect.

The court emphasized that for the slave "there is no remedy," that "[w]e cannot allow the right of the master to be brought into discussion in the courts of justice. The slave, to remain a slave, must be made sensible that there is no appeal from his master; that his power is in no instance usurped; but is conferred by the laws of man at least, if not by the law of God." The court noted that this unlimited "dominion is essential to the value of slaves as property, and to the security of the master, and the public tranquility."

The control the court sought was the *total* submission of blacks. It had incorporated into its law-made morality the psychological conceptions Frederick Douglass subsequently described:

> Beat and cuff the slave, keep him hungry and spiritless, and he will follow the chain of his master like a dog, but feed and clothe him well, work him moderately and surround him with physical comfort, and dreams of freedom will intrude. . . . You may hurl a man so low beneath the level of his kind, that he loses all just ideas of his natural position, but elevate him a little, and the clear conception of rights rises to life and power, and leads him onward.

With only slightly less paranoia, white society feared that slaves and free blacks would form an alliance with either indentured servants or poor whites to topple the plantation aristocracy, which exploited both blacks and poor whites. As the percentage of blacks, slave or free, increased, the probability of successful rebellions and revolts became greater. Thus, in examining degrees of repression one can almost correlate a rise in the black population with an increased level of legal repression.

In terms of moral and religious issues, there was the underlying question of whether or not America had the right to treat differently and more malevolently people whose skins were darker. From this perspective it became necessary to determine whether blacks were part of the human family and whether, after they had adopted your "religion," they were then entitled to be treated as equals, or at least less harshly. In a nation "under God" the moral or religious rationale that justified or rejected the institution of slavery had to have been an important factor. But what tortuous moral or religious rationale had to have been devised for a religious people to have tolerated treating black human beings more like horses or dogs than white human beings?

Finally, there was always the issue of whether or not blacks were inherently inferior to whites. If blacks could be perceived as inferior, basically uneducable and inherently venal, it might be intellectually less self-condemnatory to relegate them because of their "lower status" to a subordinate role — either for "their own good" or, as one judge had the audacity to express it, for the good of the total society, whites and blacks alike.

Thus it was that even the man many Americans see as one of the major forces for liberty and equality, Thomas Jefferson, found blacks to be "inferior to whites in the endowments both of body and mind." After comparing the characteristics of the three major races in America, white, black, and red, Jefferson concluded that although the condition of slavery imposed great misery on blacks, the inferiority of the black race was caused by more than mere environmental factors:

> The improvement of the blacks in body and mind, in the first instance of their mixture with the whites, has been observed by everyone, and proves that their inferiority is not the effect merely of their condition of life. . . . This unfortunate difference of color, and perhaps of faculty, is a powerful obstacle to the emancipation of these people.

Yet even during the seventeenth and eighteenth centuries, there were voices that challenged the morality and legality of slavery. . . . As early as February, 1688 the Germantown Mennonites of Philadelphia had issued a proclamation against slavery, having found it inconsistent with Christian principles. . . . In 1772, four years prior to our Declaration of Independence and fifteen years prior to the Constitution, Lord Mansfield, Chief Justice of the King's Bench, said that "the state of slavery is of such a nature that it is incapable of being introduced on any reasons moral or political, . . . It is so odious that nothing can be suffered to support it, but positive law." And with that statement, Lord Mansfield freed the slave, Sommersett, demonstrating that there was no universal view on slavery among the civilized nations of the world.

As we survey . . . legislative and judicial doctrines, it will be difficult to isolate one and only one factor as the sole explanation for the legislated, adjudicated, and upheld racial deprivation that gained the official approval of the American legal establishment. As in most things, the causal factors were multifaceted. On some occasions the economic concerns seemed the dominating influence, while in other instances a moral or religious aspect appeared to be more significant. But however tightly woven into the history of their country is the legalization of black suppression, many Americans still find it too traumatic to study the true story of racism as it has existed under their "rule of law." For many, the primary conclusion of the National Commission on Civil Disorders is still too painful to hear:

> What white Americans have never fully understood—but what the Negro can never forget—is that white society is deeply implicated in the ghetto. White institutions created it, white institutions maintain it, and white society condones it.

Since the language of the law shields one's consciousness from direct involvement with the stark plight of its victims, the human tragedy of the slavery system does not surface from the mere reading of cases, statutes, and constitutional provisions. Rather it takes a skeptical reading of most of the early cases and statutes to avoid having one's surprise and anger dulled by the casualness with which the legal process dealt with human beings who happened to be slaves. Generally neither the courts nor the legislatures seemed to have been any more sensitive about commercial transactions involving slaves than they were about sales of corn, lumber, horses, or dogs. This casualness is reflected in a perfectly legal and acceptable advertisement of that era:

> One hundred and twenty Negroes for sale—The subscriber has just arrived from Petersburg, Virginia, with one hundred and twenty likely young Negroes of both sexes and every description, which he offers for sale on the most reasonable terms. The lot now on hand consists of plough-boys, several likely and well-qualified house servants of both sexes, several women and children, small girls suitable for nurses, and *several small boys without their mothers.* Planters and traders are earnestly requested to give the subscriber a call previously to making purchases elsewhere, as he is enabled to sell as cheap or cheaper than can be sold by any other person in the trade.
>
> —Hamburg, South Carolina, Benjamin Davis

The advertisement of Benjamin Davis was not unique; it was typical of thousands of advertisements posted in newspapers and bulletin boards throughout our land. In the *New Orleans Bee* an advertisement noted:

> Negroes for sale—a Negro woman, 24 years of age, and her two children, one eight and the other three years old. Said Negroes will be sold separately or together, as desired. The woman is a good seamstress. She will be sold low for cash, or exchange for groceries. For terms apply to Matthew Bliss and Company, 1 Front Levee.

How could a legal system encourage and sanction such cruelty—cruelty that permitted the sale, as Benjamin Davis bragged, of "several small boys without their mothers?" Was there any justice in a legal process that permitted a mother, twenty-four years of age, to be sold in exchange for groceries and separated from her children, only eight and three years old? Looking past the commercial façade, one sees the advertisement as stating that American laws encouraged the destruction of black families and the selling of human beings. The only criterion was the demand of the marketplace.

. . . For example, we cite several statutes that offered rewards to bounty hunters bringing in the scalp and ears of runaway slaves. These statutes, subtly cast in the language of lawyers, can make one oblivious to the fact that the lives of human beings were involved. From one perspective, it appears that these two legislatures were merely defining penalties and granting rewards—just as they would do upon the recovery of an individual's lost property or as a reward for the slaying of a bear or wild coyote. Yet the scalps and the ears referred to in the Georgia and South Carolina statutes were *not* those of wild animals. They were not those of murderers or traitors. They were the scalps and ears of human beings, persons who had committed no crime other than that of seeking that same freedom the colonists declared to be the birthright of all whites.

As I reflect on these statutes, I think of my experiences as a youngster forty years ago viewing the local cowboy and Indian movies. The bad guys—the Indians, naturally—would occasionally scalp some white adult. Always as my friends and I left the movies, we were angry because of the cruelty the Indians had inflicted on those innocent pioneers, who were merely traveling over Indian land. Thus, it was a matter of astonishment to learn as an adult that the legislatures of Georgia, South Carolina and many of the other colonies actually legalized acts as inhumane as those dreamt up by movie producers. Perhaps the movies were fictionalized accounts representing Hollywood screenwriters' vivid imagination. But the colonial statutes were not bits of fiction; they were the reality of the colonial legal process, a process that rewarded those who were willing to scalp and cut off the ears of blacks who dared to seek freedom.

While we recognize today how inhumane and how immoral this legal process was, it seems that Americans would rather distort their history than face the extraordinary brutality to which these advertisements attest and the inadequacy of a system of laws that promoted and sanctioned such brutality.

The legal process has never been devoid of values, preferences, or policy positions. By the very nature of its pronouncements, when the legal process establishes a right of one particular person, group, or institution, it simultaneously imposes a restraint on those whose preferences impinge on the right established. Ultimately, the legal process has always acted as an expression of social control. Professor Vilhelm Aubert has argued that "beneath the veneer of consensus on legal principles, a struggle of interest is going on, and the law is seen as a weapon in the hands of those who possess the power to use it for their own ends."

The mechanisms of control through judicial decisions and statutes span the sanctioning of slavery and the special limitations imposed on free blacks, to the prohibitions against interracial marriage and sexual activity, to the eliminating of the legal significance of blacks' "conversions to Christianity," to generally restricting any activities or aspirations of blacks that might threaten the groups in control. The law is usually perceived as a normative system, founded on a society's custom and convention.

Charles Warren, one of the most distinguished scholars on the history of the Supreme Court, observed:

> The Court is not an organism dissociated from the conditions and history of the times in which it exists. It does not formulate and deliver its opinions in a legal vacuum. Its Judges are not abstract and impersonal oracles, but are men whose views are necessarily, though by no conscious intent, affected by inheritance, education and environment and by the impact of history past and present. . . .

Oliver Wendell Holmes shared this perception:

> The life of the law has not been logic: it has been experience. The felt necessities of the time, the prevalent moral and political theories, intuitions of public policy, avowed or unconscious, even the prejudices which judges share with their fellow-men, have had a good deal more to do than the syllogism in determining the rules by which men should be governed.

An Act for the Better Ordering and Governing of Negroes and Slaves, South Carolina, 1712

Colonial America had a role for the Negro. But the presence of a servile population, presumably of inferior stock, made it necessary to adopt measures of control. As might be expected, the southern colonies had the most highly developed codes governing Negroes. In 1712 South Carolina passed "An Act for the better ordering and governing of Negroes and Slaves." This comprehensive measure served as a model for slave codes in the South during the colonial and national periods. Eight of its thirty-five sections are reproduced below.

Whereas, the plantations and estates of this province cannot be well and sufficiently managed and brought into use, without the labor and service of negroes and other slaves; and forasmuch as the said negroes and other slaves brought unto the people of this Province for that purpose, are of barbarous, wild, savage natures, and such as renders them wholly unqualified to be governed by the laws, customs, and practices of this Province; but that it is absolutely necessary, that such other constitutions, laws and orders, should in this Province be made and enacted, for the good regulating and ordering of them, as may restrain the disorders, rapines and inhumanity, to which they are naturally prone and inclined, and may also tend to the safety and security of the people of this Province and their estates; to which purpose,

I. *Be it therefore enacted,* by his Excellency William, Lord Craven, Palatine, and the rest of the true and absolute Lords and Proprietors of this Province, by and with the advice and consent of the rest of the members of the General Assembly, now met at Charlestown, for the South-west part of this Province, and by the authority of the same, That all negroes, mulatoes, mustizoes or Indians, which at any time heretofore have been sold, or now are held or taken to be, or hereafter shall be bought and sold for slaves, are hereby declared slaves; and they, and their children, are hereby made and declared slaves, to all intents and purposes; excepting all such negroes, mulatoes, mustizoes or Indians, which heretofore have been, or hereafter shall be, for some particular merit, made and declared free, either by the Governor and council of this Province, pursuant to any Act or law of this Province, or by their respective owners or masters; and also, excepting all such negroes, mulatoes, mustizoes or Indians, as can prove they ought not to be sold for slaves. And in case any negro, mulatoe, mustizoe or Indian, doth lay claim to his or her freedom, upon all or any of the said accounts, the same shall be finally heard and determined by the Governor and council of this Province.

II. And for the better ordering and governing of negroes and all other slaves in this Province, *Be it enacted* by the authority aforesaid, That no master, mistress, overseer, or other person whatsoever, that hath the care and charge of any negro or slave, shall give their negroes and other slaves leave, on Sundays, hollidays, or any other time, to go out of their plantations, except such negro or other slave as usually wait upon them at home or abroad, or wearing a livery; and every other negro or slave that shall be taken hereafter out of his master's plantation, without a ticket, or leave in writing, from his master or mistress, or some other person by his or her appointment, or some white person in the company of such slave, to give an account of his business, shall be whipped; and every person who shall not (when in his power) apprehend every negro or other slave which he shall see out of his master's plantation, without leave as aforesaid, and after apprehended, shall neglect to punish him by moderate whipping, shall forfeit twenty shillings, the one half to the poor, to be paid to the church wardens of the Parish where such forfeiture shall become due, and the other half to him that will inform for the same, within one week after such neglect; and that no slave may make further or other use of any one ticket than was intended by him that granted the same, every ticket shall particularly mention the name of every slave employed in the particular business, and to what place they are sent, and what time they return; and if any person shall presume to give any negro or slave a ticket in the name of his master or mistress, without his or her consent, such person so doing shall forfeit the sum of twenty shillings; one half to the poor, to be disposed of as aforesaid, the other half to the person injured, that will complain against the person offending, within one week after the offence committed. And for the better security of all such persons that shall endeavor to take any runaway, or shall examine any slave for his ticket, passing to and from his master's plantation, it is hereby declared lawful for any white person to beat, maim or assult, and if such negro or slave cannot otherwise be taken, to kill him, who small refuse to shew his ticket, or, by running away or resistance, shall endeavor to avoid being apprehended or taken.

III. *And be it further enacted* by the authority aforesaid, That every master, mistress or overseer of a family in this Province, shall cause all his negro houses to be searched diligently and effectually, once every fourteen days, for fugitive and runaway slaves, guns, swords, clubs, and any other mischievous weapons, and finding any, to take them away, and cause them to be secured; as also, for clothes, goods, and any other things and commodities that are not given them by their master, mistress, commander or overseer, and honestly come by; and in whose custody they find any thing of that kind, and suspect or know to be stolen goods, the same they shall seize and take into their custody, and a full and ample description of the particulars thereof, in writing, within ten days after the discovery thereof, either to the provost marshall, or to the clerk of the parish for the time being, who is hereby required to receive the same, and to enter upon it the day of its receipt, and the particulars to file and keep to himself; and the clerk shall set upon the posts of the church door, and the provost marshall upon the usual public places, or places of notice, a short brief, that such lost goods are found; whereby, any person that hath lost his goods may the better come to the knowledge where they are; and the owner going to the marshall or clerk, and proving, by marks or otherwise, that the goods lost belong to him, and paying twelve pence for the entry and declaration of the same, if the marshall or clerk be convinced that any part of the goods certified by him to be found, appertains to the party inquiring, he is to direct the said party inquiring to the place and party where the goods be, who is hereby required to make restitution of what is in being to the true owner; and every master, mistress or overseer, as also the provost marshall or clerk, neglecting his duty in any the particulars aforesaid, for every neglect shall forfeit twenty shillings.

IV. And for the more effectual detecting and punishing such persons that trade with any slave for stolen goods, *Be it further enacted* by the authority aforesaid, That where any person shall be suspected to trade as aforesaid, any justice of the peace shall have power to take from him suspected, sufficient recognizance, not to trade with any slave contrary to the laws of this Province; and if it shall afterwards appear to any of the justices of the peace, that such person hath, or hath had, or shipped off, any goods, suspected to be unlawfully come by, it shall be lawful for such justice of the peace to oblige the person to appear at the next general sessions, who shall there be obliged to make reasonable proof, of whom he brought, or how he came by, the said goods, and unless he do it, his recognizance shall be forfeited. . . .

VII. And *whereas*, great numbers of slaves which do not dwell in Charlestown, on Sundays and holidays resort thither, to drink, quarrel, fight, curse and swear, and profane the Sabbath, and using and carrying of clubs and other mischievous weapons, resorting in great companies together, which may give them an opportunity of executing any wicked designs and purposes, to the damage and prejudice of the inhabitants of this Province; for the prevention whereof, *Be it enacted* by the authority aforesaid, That all and every the constables of Charlestown, separately on every Sunday, and the holidays at Christmas, Easter and Whitsonside, together with so many men as each constable shall think necessary to accompany him, which he is hereby empowered for that end to press, under the penalty of twenty shillings to the person that shall disobey him, shall, together with such persons, go through all or any the streets, and also, round about Charlestown, and as much further on the neck as they shall be informed or have reason to suspect any meeting or concourse of any such negroes or slaves to be at that time, and to enter into any house, at Charlestown, or elsewhere, to search for such slaves, and as many of them as they can apprehend, shall cause to be publicly whipped in Charlestown, and then to be delivered to the marshall, who for every slave so whipped and delivered to him by the constable, shall pay the constable five shillings, which five shillings shall be repaid the said marshall by the owner or head of that family to which the said negro or slave, doth belong, together with such other charges as shall become due to him for keeping runaway slaves; and the marshall shall in all respects keep and dispose of such slave as if the same was delivered to him as a runaway, under the same penalties and forfeiture as hereafter in that case is provided; and every constable of Charlestown which shall neglect or refuse to make search as aforesaid, for every such neglect shall forfeit the sum of twenty shillings. . . .

IX. *And be it further enacted* by the authority aforesaid, That upon complaint made to any justice of the peace, of any heinous or grievous crime, committed by any slave or slaves, as murder, burglary, robbery, burning of houses, or any lesser crimes, as killing or stealing any meat or other cattle, maiming one the other, stealing of fowls, provisions, or such like trespasses or injuries, the said justice shall issue out his warrant for apprehending the offender or offenders, and for all persons to come before him that can give evidence; and if upon examination, it probably appeareth, that the apprehended person is guilty, he shall commit him or them to prison, or immediately proceed to tryal of the said slave or slaves, according to the form hereafter specified, or take security for his or their forthcoming, as the case shall require, and also to certify to the justice next to him, the said cause, and to require him, by virtue of this Act, to associate himself to him, which said justice is hereby required to do, and they so associated, are to issue their summons to three sufficient freeholders, acquainting them with the matter, and appointing them a day, hour and place, when and where the same shall be heard and determined, at which day, hour and place, the said justices and freeholders shall cause the offenders and evidences to come before them, and if they, on hearing the matter, the said freeholders being by the said justices first sworn to judge uprightly and according to evidence, and diligently weighing and examining all evidences, proofs and testimonies (and in case of murder only, if on violent presumption and circumstances), they shall find such negro or other slave or slaves guilty thereof, they shall give sentence of death, if the crime by law deserve the same, and forthwith by their warrant cause immediate execution to be done, by the common or any other executioner, in such manner as they shall think fit, the kind of death to be inflicted to be left to their judgment and discretion; and if the crime committed shall not deserve death, they shall then condemn and adjudge the criminal or criminals to any other punishment, but not extending to limb or disabling him, without a particular law directing such punishment, and shall forthwith order execution to be done accordingly.

X. And in regard great mischiefs daily happen by petty larcenies committed by negroes and slaves of this Province, *Be it further enacted* by the authority aforesaid, That if any negro or other slave shall hereafter steal or destroy any goods, chattels, or provisions whatsoever, of any other person than his master or mistress, being under the value of twelve pence, every negro or other slave so offending, and being brought before some justice of the peace of this Province, upon complaint of the party injured, and shall be adjudged guilty by confession, proof, or probable circumstances, such negro or slave so offending, excepting children, whose punishment is left wholly to the discretion of the said justice, shall be adjudged by such justice to be publicly and severely whipped, not exceeding forty lashes; and if such negro or other slave punished as aforesaid, be afterwards, by two justices of the peace, found guilty of the like crimes, he or they, for such his or their second offence, shall either have one of his ears cut off, or be branded in the forehead with a hot iron, that the mark thereof may remain; and if after such punishment, such negro or slave for his third offence, shall have his nose slit; and if such negro or other slave, after the third time as aforesaid, be accused of petty larceny, or of any of the offences before mentioned, such negro or other slave shall be tried in such manner as those accused of murder, burglary, *etc.* are before by this Act provided for to be tried, and in case they shall be found guilty a fourth time, of any the offences before mentioned, then such negro or other slave shall be adjudged to suffer death, or other punishment, as the said justices shall think fitting; and any judgment given for the first offence, shall be a sufficient conviction for the first offence; and any after judgment after the first judgment, shall be a sufficient conviction to bring the offender within the penalty of the second offence, and so for inflicting the rest of the punishments; and in case the said justices and freeholders, and any or either of them, shall neglect or refuse to perform the duties by this Act required of them, they shall severally, for such their defaults, forfeit the sum of twenty-five pounds. . . .

XII. *And it is further enacted* by the authority aforesaid, That if any negroes or other slaves shall make mutiny or insurrection, or rise in rebellion against the authority and government of this Province, or shall make preparation of arms, powder, bullets or offensive weapons, in order to carry on such mutiny or insurrection, or

· shall hold any counsel or conspiracy for raising such mutiny, insurrection or rebellion, the offenders shall be tried by two justices of the peace and three freeholders, associated together as before expressed in case of murder, burglary, *etc.*, who are hereby empowered and required to try the said slaves so offending, and inflict death, or any other punishment, upon the offenders, and forthwith by their warrant cause execution to be done, by the common or any other executioner, in such manner as they shall think fitting; and if any person shall make away or conceal any negro or negroes, or other slave or slaves, suspected to be guilty of the beforementioned crimes, and not upon demand bring forth the suspected offender or offenders, such person shall forfeit for every negro or slave so concealed or made away, the sum of fifty pounds; *Provided, nevertheless,* that when and as often as any of the beforementioned crimes shall be committed by more than one negro, that shall deserve death, that then and in all such cases, if the Governor and council of this Province shall think fitting, and accordingly shall order, that only one or more of the said criminals should suffer death as exemplary, and the rest to be returned to the owners, that then, the owners of the negroes so offending, shall bear proportionably the loss of the said negro or negroes so put to death, as shall be allotted them by the said justices and freeholders; and if any person shall refuse his part so allotted him, that then, and in all such cases, the said justices and freeholders are hereby required to issue out their warrant of distress upon the goods and chattels of the person so refusing, and shall cause the same to be sold by public outcry, to satisfy the said money so allotted him to pay, and to return the overplus, if any be, to the owner; *Provided, nevertheless,* that the part allotted for any person to pay for his part or proportion of the negro or negroes so put to death, shall not exceed one sixth part of his negro or negroes so excused and pardoned; and in case that shall not be sufficient to satisfy for the negro or negroes that shall be put to death, that the remaining sum shall be paid out of the public treasury of this Province.*

*Thomas Cooper and David J. McCord, eds., *Statutes at Large of South Carolina* (10 vols., Columbia, 1836–1841), VII, 352–357.

The "Three-Fifths Compromise":
The U.S. Constitution, Article I, Section 2

One of the major debates in the Constitutional Convention hinged on the use of slaves in computing taxes and fixing representation. Southern delegates held that slaves should be computed in determining representation in the House, but that they should not be counted in determining a state's share of the direct tax burden. The northern delegates' point of view was exactly the opposite. A compromise was reached whereby three fifths of the slaves were to be counted in apportionment of representation and in direct taxes among the states. Thus the South was victorious in obtaining representation for her slaves, even though delegate Luther Martin might rail that the Constitution was an insult to the Deity "who views with equal eye the poor African slave and his American master." The "three-fifths compromise" appears in Article I, Section 2.

Representatives and direct Taxes shall be apportioned among the several States which may be included within this Union, according to their respective Numbers, which shall be determined by adding to the whole Number of free Persons, including those bound to Service for a Term of Years, and excluding Indians not taxed, three fifths of all other Persons.

5

An Act Prohibiting the Teaching of Slaves to Read*

To keep the slaves in hand it was deemed necessary to keep them innocent of the printed page. Otherwise they might read abolitionist newspapers that were smuggled in, become dissatisfied, forge passes, or simply know too much. Hence most states passed laws prohibiting anyone from teaching slaves to read or write. The North Carolina statute was typical.

An Act to Prevent All Persons from Teaching Slaves to Read or Write, the Use of Figures Excepted

Whereas the teaching of slaves to read and write, has a tendency to excite dissatisfaction in their minds, and to produce insurrection and rebellion, to the manifest injury of the citizens of this State:

Therefore,

Be it enacted by the General Assembly of the State of North Carolina, and it is hereby enacted by the authority of the same, That any free person, who shall hereafter teach, or attempt to teach, any slave within the State to read or write, the use of figures excepted, or shall give or sell to such slave or slaves any books or pamphlets, shall be liable to indictment in any court of record in this State having jurisdiction thereof, and upon conviction, shall, at the discretion of the court, if a white man or woman, be fined not less than one hundred dollars, nor more than two hundred dollars, or imprisoned; and if a free person of color, shall be fined, imprisoned, or whipped, at the discretion of the court, not exceeding thirty-nine lashes, nor less than twenty lashes.

II. *Be it further enacted,* That if any slave shall hereafter teach, or attempt to teach, any other slave to read or write, the use of figures excepted, he or she may

*Acts Passed by the General Assembly of the State of North Carolina at the Session of 1830–1831 (Raleigh, 1831), 11.

310

be carried before any justice of the peace, and on conviction thereof, shall be sentenced to receive thirty-nine lashes on his or her bare back.

III. *Be it further enacted,* That the judges of the Superior Courts and the justices of the County Courts shall give this act in charge to the grand juries of their respective counties.

6

Declaration of Sentiments and Resolutions, Seneca Falls Convention, 1848

The Declaration of Sentiments, adopted in July 1848 at Seneca Falls, New York, at the first woman's-rights convention, is the most famous document in the history of feminism. Like its model, the Declaration of Independence, it contains a bill of particulars. Some people at the meeting thought the inclusion of disfranchisement in the list of grievances would discredit the entire movement, and when the resolutions accompanying the Declaration were put to a vote, the one calling for the suffrage was the only one that did not pass unanimously. But it did pass and thus inaugurated the woman-suffrage movement in the United States.

Declaration of Sentiments

When, in the course of human events, it becomes necessary for one portion of the family of man to assume among the people of the earth a position different from that which they have hitherto occupied, but one to which the laws of nature and of nature's God entitle them, a decent respect to the opinions of mankind requires that they should declare the causes that impel them to such a course.

We hold these truths to be self-evident: that all men and women are created equal; that they are endowed by their Creator with certain inalienable rights; that among these are life, liberty, and the pursuit of happiness; that to secure these rights governments are instituted, deriving their just powers from the consent of the governed. Whenever any form of government becomes destructive of these ends, it is the right of those who suffer from it to refuse allegiance to it, and to insist upon the institution of a new government, laying its foundation on such principles, and organizing its powers in such form, as to them shall seem most likely to effect their safety and happiness. Prudence, indeed, will dictate that governments long established should not be changed for light and transient causes; and accordingly all experience hath shown that mankind are more disposed to suffer, while evils are sufferable, than to right themselves by abolishing the forms to which they were accustomed. But when a long train of abuses and usurpations, pursuing invariably the same object, evinces a design to reduce them under absolute depotism, it is their duty to throw off such government, and to provide new guards for their future security. Such has been the patient sufferance of the women under this government, and such is now the necessity which constrains them to demand the equal station to which they are entitled.

The history of mankind is a history of repeated injuries and usurpations on the part of man toward woman, having in direct object the establishment of an absolute tyranny over her. To prove this, let facts be submitted to a candid world.

He has never permitted her to exercise her inalienable right to the elective franchise.

He has compelled her to submit to laws, in the formation of which she had no voice.

He has withheld from her rights which are given to the most ignorant and degraded men—both natives and foreigners.

Having deprived her of this first right of a citizen, the elective franchise, thereby leaving her without representation in the halls of legislation, he has oppressed her on all sides.

He has made her, if married, in the eye of the law, civilly dead.

He has taken from her all right in property, even to the wages she earns.

He has made her, morally, an irresponsible being, as she can commit many crimes with impunity, provided they be done in the presence of her husband. In the covenant of marriage, she is compelled to promise obedience to her husband, he becoming, to all intents and purposes, her master—the law giving him power to deprive her of her liberty, and to administer chastisement.

He has so framed the laws of divorce, as to what shall be the proper causes, and in case of separation, to whom the guardianship of the children shall be given, as to be wholly regardless of the happiness of women—the law, in all cases, going upon the false supposition of the supremacy of man, and giving all power into his hands.

After depriving her of all rights as a married woman, if single, and the owner of property, he has taxed her to support a government which recognizes her only when her property can be made profitable to it.

He has monopolized nearly all the profitable employments, and from those she is permitted to follow, she receives but a scanty remuneration. He closes against her all the avenues to wealth and distinction which he considers most honorable to himself. As a teacher of theology, medicine, or law, she is not known.

He has denied her the facilities for obtaining a thorough education, all colleges being closed against her.

He allows her in Church, as well as State, but a subordinate position, claiming Apostolic authority for her exclusion from the ministry, and, with some exceptions, from any public participation in the affairs of the Church.

He has created a false public sentiment by giving to the world a different code of morals for men and women, by which moral delinquencies which exclude women from society, are not only tolerated, but deemed of little account in man.

He has usurped the prerogative of Jehovah himself, claiming it as his right to assign for her a sphere of action, when that belongs to her conscience and to her God.

He has endeavored, in every way that he could, to destroy her confidence in her own powers, to lessen her self-respect, and to make her willing to lead a dependent and abject life.

Now, in view of this entire disfranchisement of one-half the people of this country, their social and religious degradation—in view of the unjust laws above mentioned, and because women do feel themselves aggrieved, oppressed, and fraudulently deprived of their most sacred rights, we insist that they have immediate admission to all the rights and privileges which belong to them as citizens of the United States.

In entering upon the great work before us, we anticipate no small amount of misconception, misrepresentation, and ridicule; but we shall use every instrumentality within our power to effect our object. We shall employ agents, circulate tracts, petition the State and National legislatures, and endeavor to enlist the pulpit and the press in our behalf. We hope this Convention will be followed by a series of Conventions embracing every part of the country.

Resolutions

WHEREAS, The great precept of nature is conceded to be, that "man shall pursue his own true and substantial happiness." Blackstone in his Commentaries remarks, that this law of Nature being coeval with mankind, and dictated by God himself, is of course superior in obligation to any other. It is binding over all the globe, in all countries and at all times; no human laws are of any validity if contrary to this, and such of them as are valid, derive all their force, and all their validity, and all their authority, mediately and immediately, from this original; therefore,

Resolved, That such laws as conflict, in any way, with the true and substantial happiness of woman, are contrary to the great precept of nature and of no validity, for this is "superior in obligation to any other."

Resolved, That all laws which prevent woman from occupying such a station in society as her conscience shall dictate, or which place her in a position inferior to that of man, are contrary to the great precept of nature, and therefore of no force or authority.

Resolved, That woman is man's equal—was intended to be so by the Creator, and the highest good of the race demands that she should be recognized as such.

Resolved, That the women of this country ought to be enlightened in regard to the laws under which they live, that they may no longer publish their degradation by declaring themselves satisfied with their present position, nor their ignorance, by asserting that they have all the rights they want.

Resolved, That inasmuch as man, while claiming for himself intellectual superiority, does accord to woman moral superiority, it is pre-eminently his duty to encourage her to speak and teach, as she has an opportunity, in all religious assemblies.

Resolved, That the same amount of virtue, delicacy, and refinement of behavior that is required of woman in the social state, should also be required of man, and the same transgressions should be visited with equal severity on both man and woman.

Resolved, That the objection of indelicacy and impropriety, which is so often brought against woman when she addresses a public audience, comes with a very ill-grace from those who encourage, by their attendance, her appearance on the stage, in the concert, or in feats of the circus.

Resolved, That woman has too long rested satisfied in the circumscribed limits which corrupt customs and a perverted application of the Scriptures have marked out for her, and that it is time she should move in the enlarged sphere which her great Creator has assigned her.

Resolved, That it is the duty of the women of this country to secure to themselves their sacred right to the elective franchise.

Resolved, That the equality of human rights results necessarily from the fact of the identity of the race in capabilities and responsibilities.

Resolved, therefore, That, being invested by the Creator with the same capabilities, and the same consciousness of responsibility for their exercise, it is demonstrably the right and duty of woman, equally with man, to promote every righteous cause by every righteous means; and especially in regard to the great subjects of morals and religion, it is self-evidently her right to participate with her brother in teaching them, both in private and in public, by writing and by speaking, by any instrumentalities proper to be used, and in any assemblies proper to be held; and this being a self-evident truth growing out of the divinely implanted principles of human nature, any custom or authority adverse to it, whether modern or wearing the hoary sanction of antiquity, is to be regarded as a self-evident falsehood, and at war with mankind.

[All the above resolutions had been drafted by Elizabeth Cady Stanton. At the last session of the convention Lucretia Mott offered the following, which, along with all the other resolutions except the ninth, was adopted unanimously.—*Ed.*]

Resolved, That the speedy success of our cause depends upon the zealous and untiring efforts of both men and women, for the overthrow of the monopoly of the pulpit, and for the securing to woman an equal participation with men in the various trades, professions, and commerce.

7

The Antisuffragists:
Selected Papers, 1852–1887

Editorial, New York Herald (1852)*

The farce at Syracuse has been played out. . . .

Who are these women? What do they want? What are the motives that impel them to this course of action? The *dramatis personae* of the farce enacted at Syracuse present a curious conglomeration of both sexes. Some of them are old maids, whose personal charms were never very attractive, and who have been sadly slighted by the masculine gender in general; some of them women who have been badly mated, whose own temper, or their husbands', has made life anything but agreeable to them, and they are therefore down upon the whole of the opposite sex; some, having so much of the virago in their disposition, that nature appears to have made a mistake in their gender—mannish women, like hens that crow; some of boundless vanity and egotism, who believe that they are superior in intellectual ability to "all the world and the rest of mankind," and delight to see their speeches and addresses in print; and man shall be consigned to his proper sphere—nursing the babies, washing the dishes, mending stockings, and sweeping the house. This is "the good time coming." Besides the classes we have enumerated, there is a class of wild enthusiasts and visionaries—very sincere, but very mad—having the same vein as the fanatical Abolitionists, and the majority, if not all of them, being, in point of fact, deeply imbued with the anti-slavery sentiment. Of the male sex who attend these Conventions for the purpose of taking part in them, the majority are hen-pecked husbands, and all of them ought to wear petticoats. . . .

*"The Woman's Rights Convention—The Last Act of the Drama," editorial, New York *Herald*, September 12, 1852.

How did woman first become subject to man as she now is all over the world? By her nature, her sex, just as the negro is and always will be, to the end of time, inferior to the white race, and, therefore, doomed to subjection; but happier than she would be in any other condition, just because it is the law of her nature. The women themselves would not have this law reversed. . . .

What do the leaders of the Woman's Rights Convention want? They want to vote, and to hustle with the rowdies at the polls. They want to be members of Congress, and in the heat of debate to subject themselves to coarse jests and indecent language. . . . They want to fill all other posts which men are ambitious to occupy— to be lawyers, doctors, captains of vessels, and generals in the field. How funny it would sound in the newspapers, that Lucy Stone, pleading a cause, took suddenly ill in the pains of parturition, and perhaps gave birth to a fine bouncing boy in court! Or that Rev. Antionette Brown was arrested in the middle of her sermon in the pulpit from the same cause, and presented a "pledge" to her husband and the congregation; or, that Dr. Harriot K. Hunt, while attending a gentleman patient for a fit of the gout or *fistula in ano*, found it necessary to send for a doctor, there and then, and to be delivered of a man or woman child—perhaps twins. A similar event might happen on the floor of Congress, in a storm at sea, or in the raging tempest of battle, and then what is to become of the woman legislator?

New York State Legislative Report (1856)*

Mr. Foote, from the Judiciary Committee, made a report on Women's rights that set the whole House in roars of laughter:

"The Committee is composed of married and single gentlemen. The bachelors on the Committee, with becoming diffidence, having left the subject pretty much to the married gentlemen, they have considered it with the aid of the light they have before them and the experience married life has given them. Thus aided, they are enabled to state that the ladies always have the best place and choicest titbit at the table. They have the best seat in the cars, carriages, and sleighs; the warmest place in the winter, and the coolest place in the summer. They have their choice on which side of the bed they will lie, front or back. A lady's dress costs three times as much as that of a gentleman; and, at the present time, with the prevailing fashion, one lady occupies three times as much space in the world as a gentleman.

"It has thus appeared to the married gentlemen of your Committee, being a majority (the bachelors being silent for the reason mentioned, and also probably for the further reason that they are still suitors for the favors of the gentler sex), that, if there is any inequality or oppression in the case, the gentlemen are the sufferers. They, however, have presented no petitions for redress; having, doubtless, made up their minds to yield to an inevitable destiny. . . ."

*This Report on Woman's Rights, made to the New York State Legislature and concerning a petition for political equality for women, was printed in an Albany paper in March 1856.

Orestes A. Brownson, The Woman Question (1869 and 1873)*

The conclusive objection to the political enfranchisement of women is, that it would weaken and finally break up and destroy the Christian family. The social unit is the family, not the individual; and the greatest danger to American society is, that we are rapidly becoming a nation of isolated individuals, without family ties or affections. The family has already been much weakened, and is fast disappearing. We have broken away from the old homestead, have lost the restraining and purifying associations that gathered around it, and live away from home in hotels and boarding-houses. We are daily losing the faith, the virtues, the habits, and the manners without which the family cannot be sustained; and when the family goes, the nation goes too, or ceases to be worth preserving. . . .

Extend now to women suffrage and eligibility; give them the political right to vote and to be voted for; render it feasible for them to enter the arena of political strife, to become canvassers in elections and candidates for office, and what remains of family union will soon be dissolved. The wife may espouse one political party, and the husband another, and it may well happen that the husband and wife may be rival candidates for the same office, and one or the other doomed to the mortification of defeat. Will the husband like to see his wife enter the lists against him, and triumph over him? Will the wife, fired with political ambition for place or power, be pleased to see her own husband enter the lists against her, and succeed at her expense? Will political rivalry and the passions it never fails to engender increase the mutual affection of husband and wife for each other, and promote domestic union and peace, or will it not carry into the bosom of the family all the strife, discord, anger, and division of the political canvass? . . .

Woman was created to be a wife and a mother; that is her destiny. To that destiny all her instincts point, and for it nature has specially qualified her. Her proper sphere is home, and her proper function is the care of the household, to manage a family, to take care of children, and attend to their early training. For this she is endowed with patience, endurance, passive courage, quick sensibilities, a sympathetic nature, and great executive and administrative ability. She was born to be a queen in her own household, and to make home cheerful, bright, and happy.

We do not believe women, unless we acknowledge individual exceptions, are fit to have their own head. The most degraded of the savage tribes are those in which women rule, and descent is reckoned from the mother instead of the father. Revelation asserts, and universal experience proves that the man is the head of the

*The following document consists of two articles by Orestes A. Brownson: "The Woman Question. Article I [from the *Catholic World*, May 1869]," in Henry F. Brownson, ed., *The Works of Orestes A. Brownson*, XVIII (Detroit, 1885), 388–89; and "The Woman Question. Article II [a review of Horace Bushnell, *Women's Suffrage: The Reform against Nature* (New York, 1869), from *Brownson's Quarterly Review* for October 1873]," in Henry F. Brownson, *op. cit.*, p. 403.

woman, and that the woman is for the man, not the man for the woman; and his greatest error, as well as the primal curse of society is that he abdicates his headship, and allows himself to be governed, we might almost say, deprived of his reason, by woman. It was through the seductions of the woman, herself seduced by the serpent, that man fell, and brought sin and all our woe into the world. She has all the qualities that fit her to be a help-meet of man, to be the mother of his children, to be their nurse, their early instructress, their guardian, their life-long friend; to be his companion, his comforter, his consoler in sorrow, his friend in trouble, his ministering angel in sickness; but as an independent existence, free to follow her own fancies and vague longings, her own ambition and natural love of power, without masculine direction or control, she is out of her element, and a social anomaly, sometimes a hideous monster, which men seldom are, excepting through a woman's influence. This is no excuse for men, but it proves that women need a head, and the restraint of father, husband, or the priest of God.

Remarks of Senator George G. Vest
in Congress (1887)*

MR. VEST. . . . If this Government, which is based on the intelligence of the people, shall ever be destroyed it will be by injudicious, immature, or corrupt suffrage. If the ship of state launched by our fathers shall ever be destroyed, it will be by striking the rock of universal, unprepared suffrage. . . .

The Senator who last spoke on this question refers to the successful experiment in regard to woman suffrage in the Territories of Wyoming and Washington. Mr. President, it is not upon the plains of the sparsely settled Territories of the West that woman suffrage can be tested. Suffrage in the rural districts and sparsely settled regions of this country must from the very nature of things remain pure when corrupt everywhere else. The danger of corrupt suffrage is in the cities, and those masses of population to which civilization tends everywhere in all history. Whilst the country has been pure and patriotic, cities have been the first cancers to appear upon the body-politic in all ages of the world.

Wyoming Territory! Washington Territory! Where are their large cities? Where are the localities in those Territories where the strain upon popular government must come? The Senator from New Hampshire [Henry W. Blair—*Ed.*], who is so conspicuous in this movement, appalled the country some months since by his ghastly array of illiteracy in the Southern States. . . . That Senator proposes now to double, and more than double, that illiteracy. He proposes now to give the negro women of the South this right of suffrage, utterly unprepared as they are for it.

In a convention some two years and a half ago in the city of Louisville an intelligent negro from the South said the negro men could not vote the Democratic

*The following remarks of Senator George G. Vest (Democrat, Missouri) may be found in the *Congressional Record*, 49th Congress, 2d Session, January 25, 1887, p. 986.

ticket because the women would not live with them if they did. The negro men go out in the hotels and upon the railroad cars. They go to the cities and by attrition they wear away the prejudice of race; but the women remain at home, and their emotional natures aggregate and compound the race-prejudice, and when suffrage is given them what must be the result? . . .

I pity the man who can consider any question affecting the influence of woman with the cold, dry logic of business. What man can, without aversion, turn from the blessed memory of that dear old grandmother, or the gentle words and caressing hand of that dear blessed mother gone to the unknown world, to face in its stead the idea of a female justice of the peace or township constable? For my part I want when I go to my home—when I turn from the arena where man contends with man for what we call the prizes of this paltry world—I want to go back, not to be received in the masculine embrace of some female ward politician, but to the earnest, loving look and touch of a true woman. I want to go back to the jurisdiction of the wife, the mother; and instead of a lecture upon finance or the tariff, or upon the construction of the Constitution, I want those blessed, loving details of domestic life and domestic love.

. . . I speak now respecting women as a sex. I believe that they are better than men, but I do not believe they are adapted to the political work of this world. I do not believe that the Great Intelligence ever intended them to invade the sphere of work given to men, tearing down and destroying all the best influences for which God has intended them.

The great evil in this country to-day is in emotional suffrage. The great danger to-day is in excitable suffrage. If the voters of this country could think always coolly, and if they could deliberate, if they could go by judgment and not by passion, our institutions would survive forever, eternal as the foundations of the continent itself; but massed together, subject to the excitements of mobs and of these terrible political contests that come upon us from year to year under the autonomy of our Government, what would be the result if suffrage were given to the women of the United States?

Women are essentially emotional. It is no disparagement to them they are so. It is no more insulting to say that women are emotional than to say that they are delicately constructed physically and unfitted to become soldiers or workmen under the sterner, harder pursuits of life.

What we want in this country is to avoid emotional suffrage, and what we need is to put more logic into public affairs and less feeling. There are spheres in which feeling should be paramount. There are kingdoms in which the heart should reign supreme. That kingdom belongs to woman. The realm of sentiment, the realm of love, the realm of the gentler and the holier and kindlier attributes that make the name of wife, mother, and sister next to that of God himself.

I would not, and I say it deliberately, degrade woman by giving her the right of suffrage. I mean the word in its full signification, because I believe that woman as she is to-day, the queen of the home and of hearts, is above the political collisions of this world, and should always be kept above them. . . .

It is said that the suffrage is to be given to enlarge the sphere of woman's influence. Mr. President, it would destroy her influence. It would take her down from that pedestal where she is to-day, influencing as a mother the minds of her offspring, influencing by her gentle and kindly caress the action of her husband toward the good and pure.

People v. *Hall,* 1854

Bias against Chinese and other colored "races" was endemic in Nineteenth Century California, but perhaps no single document so well demonstrates that bias as this majority opinion handed down by the Chief Justice of the California Supreme Court. Since Chinese miners lived in small, segregated groups, the practical effect of this decision was to declare "open season" on Chinese, since crimes against them were likely to be witnessed only by other Chinese.

The People, Respondent, v. George W. Hall, Appellant

The appellant, a free white citizen of this State, was convicted of murder upon the testimony of Chinese witnesses.

The point involved in this case, is the admissibility of such evidence.

The 394th section of the Act Concerning Civil Cases, provides that no Indian or Negro shall be allowed to testify as a witness in any action or proceeding in which a White person is a party.

The 14th section of the Act of April 16th, 1850, regulating Criminal Proceedings, provides that "No Black, or Mulatto person, or Indian, shall be allowed to give evidence in favor of, or against a white man."

The true point at which we are anxious to arrive, is the legal signification of the words, "Black, Mulatto, Indian and White person," and whether the Legislature adopted them as generic terms, or intended to limit their application to specific types of the human species.

Before considering this question, it is proper to remark the difference between the two sections of our Statute, already quoted, the latter being more broad and comprehensive in its exclusion, by use of the word "Black," instead of Negro.

Conceding, however, for the present, that the word "Black," as used in the 14th section, and "Negro," in 394th, are convertible terms, and that the former was intended to include the latter, let us proceed to inquire who are excluded from testifying as witnesses under the term "Indian."

When Columbus first landed upon the shores of this continent, in his attempt to discover a western passage to the Indies, he imagined that he had accomplished the object of his expedition, and that the Island of San Salvador was one of those Islands of the Chinese sea, lying near the extremity of India, which had been described by navigators.

Acting upon this hypothesis, and also perhaps from the similarity of features and physical conformation, he gave to the Islanders the name of Indians, which appellation was universally adopted, and extended to the aboriginals of the New World, as well as of Asia.

From that time, down to a very recent period, the American Indians and the Mongolian, or Asiatic, were regarded as the same type of human species. . . .

. . . That this was the common opinion in the early history of American legislation, cannot be disputed, and, therefore, all legislation upon the subject must have borne relation to that opinion. . . .

. . . In using the words, "No Black, or Mulatto person, or Indian shall be allowed to give evidence for or against a White person," the Legislature, if any intention can be ascribed to it, adopted the most comprehensive terms to embrace every known class or shade of color, as the apparent design was to protect the White person from the influence of all testimony other than that of persons of the same caste. The use of these terms must, by every sound rule of construction, exclude every one who is not of white blood. . . .

. . . We have carefully considered all the consequences resulting from a different rule of construction, and are satisfied that even in a doubtful case we would be impelled to this decision on grounds of public policy.

The same rule which would admit them to testify, would admit them to all the equal rights of citizenship, and we might soon see them at the polls, in the jury box, upon the bench, and in our legislative halls.

This is not a speculation which exists in the excited and overheated imagination of the patriot and statesman, but it is an actual and present danger.

The anomalous spectacle of a distinct people, living in our community, recognizing no laws of this State except through necessity, bringing with them their prejudices and national feuds, in which they indulge in open violation of law; whose mendacity is proverbial; a race of people whom nature has marked as inferior, and who are incapable of progress or intellectual development beyond a certain point, as their history has shown; differing in language, opinions, color, and physical conformation; between whom and ourselves nature has placed an impassible difference, is now presented, and for them is claimed, not only the right to swear away the life of a citizen, but the further privilege of participating with us in administering the affairs of our Government. . . .

. . . For these reasons, we are of opinion that the testimony was inadmissible. . . .

Dred Scott v. Sanford, 1857

The question is simply this: Can a negro, whose ancestors were imported into this country, and sold as slaves, become a member of the political community formed and brought into existence by the Constitution of the United States, and as such become entitled to all the rights, and privileges, and immunities, guarantied by that instrument to the citizen? One of which rights is the privilege of suing in a court of the United States in the cases specified in the Constitution.

It will be observed, that the plea applies to that class of persons only whose ancestors were negroes of the African race, and imported into this country, and sold and held as slaves. The only matter in issue before this court, therefore, is whether the descendants of such slaves, when they shall be emancipated, or who are born of parents who had become free before their birth, are citizens of a State, in the sense in which the word citizen is used in the Constitution of the United States. And this being the only matter in dispute on the pleadings, the court must be understood as speaking in his opinion of that class only, that is, of those persons who are the descendants of Africans who were imported into this country, and sold as slaves.

It becomes necessary, therefore, to determine who were citizens of the several States when the Constitution was adopted. And in order to do this, we must recur to the Governments and institutions of the thirteen colonies, when they separated from Great Britain and formed new sovereignties, and took their places in the family of independent nations. We must inquire who, at that time, were recognised as the people or citizens of a State, whose rights and liberties had been outraged by the English Government; and who declared their independence, and assumed the powers of Government to defend their rights by force of arms.

In the opinion of the court, the legislation and histories of the times, and the language used in the Declaration of Independence, show, that neither the class of persons who had been imported as slaves, nor their descendants, whether they had become free or not, were then acknowledged as a part of the people, nor intended to be included in the general words used in that memorable instrument.

It is difficult at this day to realize the state of public opinion in relation to that unfortunate race, which prevailed in the civilized and enlightened portions of the world at the time of the Declaration of Independence, and when the Constitution of the United States was formed and adopted. But the public history of every European nation displays it in a manner too plain to be mistaken.

They had for more than a century before been regarded as beings of an inferior order, and altogether unfit to associate with the white race, either in social or political relations; and so far inferior, that they had no rights which the white man was bound to respect; and that the negro might justly and lawfully be reduced to slavery for his benefit. He was bought and sold, and treated as an ordinary article of merchandise and traffic, whenever a profit could be made by it. This opinion was at that time fixed and universal in the civilized portion of the white race. It was regarded as an axiom in morals as well as in politics, which no one thought of disputing, or supposed to be open to dispute; and men in every grade and position in society daily and habitually acted upon it in their private pursuits, as well as in matters of public concern, without doubting for a moment the correctness of this opinion.

And in no nation was this opinion more firmly fixed or more uniformly acted upon than by the English Government and English people. They not only seized them on the coast of Africa, and sold them or held them in slavery for their own use, but they took them as ordinary articles of merchandise to every country where they could make a profit on them, and were far more extensively engaged in this commerce than any other nation in the world.

The opinion thus entertained and acted upon in England was naturally impressed upon the colonies they founded on this side of the Atlantic. And, accordingly, a negro of the African race was regarded by them as an article of property, and held, and bought and sold as such, in every one of the thirteen colonies which united in the Declaration of Independence, and afterwards formed the Constitution of the United States. The slaves were more or less numerous in the different colonies, as slave labor was found more or less profitable. But no one seems to have doubted the correctness of the prevailing opinion of the time.

The legislation of the different colonies furnishes positive and indisputable proof of this fact.

The language of the Declaration of Independence is equally conclusive:

It begins by declaring that, "when in the course of human events it becomes necessary for one people to dissolve the political bands which have connected them with another, and to assume among the powers of the earth the separate and equal station to which the laws of nature and nature's God entitle them, a decent respect for the opinions of mankind requires that they should declare the causes which impel them to the separation."

It then proceeds to say: "We hold these truths to be self-evident: that all men are created equal; that they are endowed by their Creator with certain unalienable rights; that among them is life, liberty, and the pursuit of happiness; that to secure these rights, Governments are instituted, deriving their just powers from the consent of the governed."

The general words above quoted would seem to embrace the whole human family, and if they were used in a similar instrument at this day would be so understood. But it is too clear for dispute, that the enslaved African race were not intended to be included, and formed no part of the people who framed and adopted this declaration; for if the language, as understood in that day, would embrace them, the conduct of the distinguished men who framed the Declaration of Independence would have been utterly and flagrantly inconsistent with the principles they asserted; and instead of the sympathy of mankind, to which they so confidently appealed, they would have deserved and received universal rebuke and reprobation.

Yet the men who framed this declaration were great men—high in literary acquirements—high in their sense of honor, and incapable of asserting principles inconsistent with those on which they were acting. They perfectly understood the meaning of the language they used, and how it would be understood by others; and they knew that it would not in any part of the civilized world be supposed to embrace the negro race, which, by common consent, had been excluded from civilized Governments and the family of nations, and doomed to slavery. They spoke and acted according to the then established doctrines and principles, and in the ordinary language of the day, and no one misunderstood them. The unhappy black race were separated from the white by indelible marks, and laws long before established, and were never thought of or spoken of except as property, and when the claims of the owner or the profit of the trader were supposed to need protection.

The state of public opinion had undergone no change when the Constitution was adopted, as is equally evident from its provisions and language.

This brief preamble sets forth by whom it was formed, for what purposes, and for whose benefit and protection. It declares that it is formed by the *people* of the United States; that is to say, by those who were members of the different political communities in the several States; and its great object is declared to be to secure the blessings of liberty to themselves and their posterity. It speaks in general terms of the *people* of the United States, and of *citizens* of the several States, when it is providing for the exercise of the powers granted or the privileges secured to the citizen. It does not define what description of persons are intended to be included under these terms, or who shall be regarded as a citizen and one of the people. It uses them as terms so well understood, that no further description or definition was necessary.

But there are two clauses in the Constitution which point directly and specifically to the negro race as a separate class of persons, and show clearly that they were not regarded as a portion of the people or citizens of the Government then formed.

One of these clauses reserves to each of the thirteen States the right to import slaves until the year 1808, if it thinks proper. And the importation which it thus sanctions was unquestionably of persons of the race of which we are speaking, as the traffic in slaves in the United States had always been confined to them. And by the other provision the States pledge themselves to each other to maintain the right of property of the master, by delivering up to him any slave who may have escaped from his service, and be found within their respective territories. By the first above-mentioned clause, therefore, the right to purchase and hold this property is directly sanctioned and authorized for twenty years by the people who framed the Constitution. And by the second, they pledge themselves to maintain and uphold the right of the master in the manner specified, as long as the Government they then formed should endure. And these two provisions show, conclusively, that neither the description of persons therein referred to, nor their descendants, were embraced in any of the other provisions of the Constitution, for certainly these two clauses were not intended to confer on them or their posterity the blessings of liberty, or any of the personal rights so carefully provided for the citizen.

Upon the whole, therefore, it is the judgment of this court, that it appears by the record before us that the plaintiff in error is not a citizen of Missouri, in the sense in which that word is used in the Constitution; and that the Circuit Court of the United States, for that reason, had no jurisdiction in the case, and could give no judgment in it. Its judgment for the defendant must, consequently, be reversed, and a mandate issued, directing the suit to be dismissed for want of jurisdiction.*

The Emancipation Proclamation

Abraham Lincoln

Emancipation Proclamation by the President of the United States of America: A Proclamation

January 1, 1863

Whereas, on the twenty-second day of September, in the year of our Lord one thousand eight hundred and sixty two, a proclamation was issued by the President of the United States, containing, among other things, the following, to wit:

*Benjamin C. Howard, *Report of the Decision of the Supreme Court of the United States in the Case Dred Scott.* . . (Washington, 1857), 9, 13–14, 15–17, 60.

"That on the first day of January, in the year of our Lord one thousand eight hundred and sixty-three, all persons held as slaves within any State or designated part of a State, the people whereof shall then be in rebellion against the United States, shall be then, thenceforward, and forever free; and the Executive Government of the United States, including the military and naval authority thereof, will recognize and maintain the freedom of such persons, and will do no act or acts to repress such persons, or any of them, in any efforts they may make for their actual freedom.

"That the Executive will, on the first day of January aforesaid, by proclamation, designate the States and parts of States, if any, in which the people thereof, respectively, shall then be in rebellion against the United States; and the fact that any State, or the people thereof, shall on that day be, in good faith, represented in the Congress of the United States by members chosen thereto at elections wherein a majority of the qualified voters of such State shall have participated, shall, in the absence of strong countervailing testimony, be deemed conclusive evidence that such State, and the people thereof, are not then in rebellion against the United States."

Now, therefore I, Abraham Lincoln, President of the United States, by virtue of the power in me vested as Commander-in-Chief, of the Army and Navy of the United States in time of actual armed rebellion against authority and government of the United States, and as a fit and necessary war measure for suppressing said rebellion, do, on this first day of January, in the year of our Lord one thousand eight hundred and sixty-three, and in accordance with my purpose so to do publicly proclaimed for the full period of one hundred days, from the day first above mentioned, order and designate as the States and parts of States wherein the people thereof respectively, are this day in rebellion against the United States, the following, to wit:

Arkansas, Texas, Louisiana, (except the Parishes of St. Bernard, Plaquemines, Jefferson, St. Johns, St. Charles, St. James[,] Ascension, Assumption, Terrebonne, Lafourche, St. Mary, St. Martin, and Orleans, including the City of New-Orleans) Mississippi, Alabama, Florida, Georgia, South-Carolina, North-Carolina, and Virginia (except the forty-eight counties designated as West Virginia, and also the counties of Berkley, Accomac, Northampton, Elizabeth-City, York, Princess Ann, and Norfolk, including the cities of Norfolk & Portsmouth [)]; and which excepted parts are, for the present, left precisely as if this proclamation were not issued.

And by virtue of the power, and for the purpose aforesaid, I do order and declare that all persons held as slaves within said designated States, and parts of States, are, and henceforward shall be free; and that the Executive government of the United States, including the military and naval authorities thereof, will recognize and maintain the freedom of said persons.

And I hereby enjoin upon the people so declared to be free to abstain from all violence, unless in necessary self-defence; and I recommend to them that, in all cases when allowed, they labor faithfully for reasonable wages.

And I further declare and make known, that such persons of suitable condition, will be received into the armed service of the United States to garrison forts, positions, stations, and other places, and to man vessels of all sorts in said service.

And upon this act, sincerely believed to be an act of justice, warranted by the Constitution, upon military necessity, I invoke the considerate judgment of mankind, and the gracious favor of Almighty God.

In witness whereof, I have hereunto set my hand and caused the seal of the United States to be affixed.

Done at the City of Washington, this first day of January, in the year of our Lord one thousand eight hundred and sixty-three, and of the Independence of the United States of America the eighty-seventh.

By the President:
Abraham Lincoln

William H. Steward,
Secretary of State*

11

United States Constitution: *Thirteenth (1865), Fourteenth (1868), and Fifteenth (1870) Amendments*

Amendment XIII (Ratified December 6, 1865). *Section 1.* Neither slavery nor involuntary servitude, except as a punishment for crime whereof the party shall have been duly convicted, shall exist within the United States, or any place subject to their jurisdiction.

Section 2. Congress shall have power to enforce this article by appropriate legislation.

Amendment XIV (Ratified July 9, 1868). *Section 1.* All persons born or naturalized in the United States, and subject to the jurisdiction thereof, are citizens of

*Basler, *op. cit.*, VI, 28–30.

the United States and of the state wherein they reside. No State shall make or enforce any law which shall abridge the privileges or immunities of citizens of the United States; nor shall any State deprive any person of life, liberty, or property, without due process of law; nor deny to any person within its jurisdiction the equal protection of the laws.

Section 2. Representatives shall be apportioned among the several states according to their respective numbers, counting the whole number of persons in each state, excluding Indians not taxed. But when the right to vote at any election for the choice of Electors for President and Vice-President of the United States, Representatives in Congress, the executive and judicial officers of a State, or the members of the Legislature thereof, is denied to any of the male inhabitants of such State, being twenty-one years of age, and, citizens of the United States, or in any way abridged, except for participation in rebellion, or other crime, the basis of representation therein shall be reduced in the proportion which the number of such male citizens shall bear to the whole number of male citizens twenty-one years of age in such State.

Section 3. No person shall be a Senator or Representative in Congress, or elector of President and Vice-President, or hold any office, civil or military, under the United States, or under any State, who, having previously taken an oath, as a member of Congress, or as an officer of the United States, or as an executive or judicial officer of any State, to support the Constitution of the United States, shall have engaged in insurrection or rebellion against the same, or given aid or comfort to the enemies thereof. But Congress may by a vote of two-thirds of each House, remove such disability.

Section 4. The validity of the public debt of the United States, authorized by law, including debts incurred for payment of pensions and bounties for services in suppressing insurrection or rebellion, shall not be questioned. But neither the United States nor any State shall assume or pay any debt or obligation incurred in aid of insurrection or rebellion against the United States, or any claim for the loss or emancipation of any slave; but all such debts, obligations, and claims, shall be held illegal and void.

Section 5. The Congress shall have power to enforce, by appropriate legislation, the provisions of this article.

Amendment XV (Ratified February 3, 1870). *Section 1.* The right of citizens of the United States to vote shall not be denied or abridged by the United States or by any State on account of race, color, or previous condition of servitude.

Section 2. The Congress shall have power to enforce this article by appropriate legislation.

12

The Black Codes

W. E. B. Du Bois

The whole proof of what the South proposed to do to the emancipated Negro, unless restrained by the nation, was shown in the Black Codes passed after Johnson's accession, but representing the logical result of attitudes of mind existing when Lincoln still lived. Some of these were passed and enforced. Some were passed and afterward repealed or modified when the reaction of the North was realized. In other cases, as for instance, in Louisiana, it is not clear just which laws were retained and which were repealed. In Alabama, the Governor induced the legislature not to enact some parts of the proposed code which they overwhelmingly favored.

The original codes favored by the Southern legislatures were an astonishing affront to emancipation and dealt with vagrancy, apprenticeship, labor contracts, migration, civil and legal rights. In all cases, there was plain and indisputable attempt on the part of the Southern states to make Negroes slaves in everything but name. They were given certain civil rights: the right to hold property, to sue and be sued. The family relations for the first time were legally recognized. Negroes were no longer real estate.

Yet, in the face of this, the Black Codes were deliberately designed to take advantage of every misfortune of the Negro. Negroes were liable to a slave trade under the guise of vagrancy and apprenticeship laws; to make the best labor contracts, Negroes must leave the old plantations and seek better terms; but if caught wandering in search of work, and thus unemployed and without a home, this was vagrancy, and the victim could be whipped and sold into slavery. In the turmoil of war, children were separated from parents, or parents unable to support them properly. These children could be sold into slavery, and "the former owner of said minors shall have the preference." Negroes could come into court as witnesses only in cases in which Negroes were involved. And even then, they must make their appeal to a jury and judge who would believe the word of any white man in preference to that of any Negro on pain of losing office and caste.

The Negro's access to the land was hindered and limited; his right to work was curtailed; his right of self-defense was taken away, when his right to bear arms was stopped; and his employment was virtually reduced to contract labor with penal servitude as a punishment for leaving his job. And in all cases, the judges of the Negro's guilt or innocence, rights and obligations were men who believed firmly, for the most part, that he had "no rights which a white man was bound to respect."

Making every allowance for the excitement and turmoil of war, and the mentality of a defeated people, the Black Codes were infamous pieces of legislation.

Let us examine these codes in detail.[1] They covered, naturally, a wide range of subjects. First, there was the question of allowing Negroes to come into the state. In South Carolina the constitution of 1865 permitted the Legislature to regulate immigration, and the consequent law declared "that no person of color shall migrate into and reside in this State, unless, within twenty days after his arrival within the same, he shall enter into a bond, with two freeholders as sureties . . . in a penalty of one thousand dollars, conditioned for his good behavior, and for his support."

Especially in the matter of work was the Negro narrowly restricted. In South Carolina, he must be especially licensed if he was to follow on his own account any employment, except that of farmer or servant. Those licensed must not only prove their fitness, but pay an annual tax ranging from $10–$100. Under no circumstances could they manufacture or sell liquor. Licenses for work were to be granted by a judge and were revokable on complaint. The penalty was a fine double the amount of the license, one-half of which went to the informer.

Mississippi provided that "every freedman, free Negro, and mulatto shall on the second Monday of January, one thousand eight hundred and sixty-six, and annually thereafter, have a lawful home or employment, and shall have written evidence thereof . . . from the Mayor . . . or from a member of the board of police . . . which licenses may be revoked for cause at any time by the authority granting the same."

Detailed regulation of labor was provided for in nearly all these states.

Louisiana passed an elaborate law in 1865, to "regulate labor contracts for agricultural pursuits." Later, it was denied that this legislation was actually enacted but the law was published at the time and the constitutional convention of 1868 certainly regarded this statute as law, for they formally repealed it. The law required all agricultural laborers to make labor contracts for the next year within the first ten days of January, the contracts to be in writing, to be with heads of families, to embrace the labor of all the members, and to be "binding on all minors thereof." Each laborer, after choosing his employer, "shall not be allowed to leave his place of employment, until the fulfillment of his contract, unless by consent of his employer, or on account of harsh treatment, or breach of contract on the part of the employer; and if they do so leave, without cause or permission, they shall forfeit all wages earned to the time of abandonment. . . .

"In case of sickness of the laborer, wages for the time lost shall be deducted, and where the sickness is feigned for purposes of idleness, . . . and also should refusal to work be continued beyond three days, the offender shall be reported to a justice of the peace, and shall be forced to labor on roads, levees, and other public works, without pay, until the offender consents to return to his labor. . . .

"When in health, the laborer shall work ten hours during the day in summer, and nine hours during the day in winter, unless otherwise stipulated in the labor contract; he shall obey all proper orders of his employer or his agent; take proper care of his work mules, horses, oxen, stock; also of all agricultural implements; and employers shall have the right to make a reasonable deduction from the laborer's wages for injuries done to animals or agricultural implements committed to his care, or for bad or negligent work. Bad work shall not be allowed. Failing to obey reasonable orders, neglect of duty and leaving home without permission, will be deemed disobedience. . . . For any disobedience a fine of one dollar shall be imposed on the offender. For all lost time from work hours, unless in case of sickness, the laborer shall be fined twenty-five cents per hour. For all absence from home without leave, the laborer will be fined at the rate of two dollars per day. Laborers will not be required to labor on the Sabbath except to take the necessary care of stock and other property on plantations and do the necessary cooking and household duties, unless by special contract. For all thefts of the laborers from the employer of agricultural products, hogs, sheep, poultry or any other property of the employer, or willful destruction of property or injury, the laborer shall pay the employer double the amount of the value of the property stolen, destroyed or injured, one half to be paid to the employer, and the other half to be placed in the general fund provided for in this section. No live stock shall be allowed to laborers without the permission of the employer. Laborers shall not receive visitors during work hours. All difficulties arising between the employers and laborers, under this section, shall be settled, and all fines be imposed, by the former; if not satisfactory to the laborers, an appeal may be had to the nearest justice of the peace and two freeholders, citizens, one of said citizens to be selected by the employer and the other by the laborer; and all fines imposed and collected under this section shall be deducted from the wages due, and shall be placed in a common fund, to be divided among the other laborers employed on the plantation at the time when their full wages fall due, except as provided for above."

Similar detailed regulations of work were in the South Carolina law. Elaborate provision was made for contracting colored "servants" to white "masters." Their masters were given the right to whip "moderately" servants under eighteen. Others were to be whipped on authority of judicial officers. These officers were given authority to return runaway servants to their masters. The servants, on the other hand, were given certain rights. Their wages and period of service must be specified in writing, and they were protected against "unreasonable" tasks, Sunday and night work, unauthorized attacks on their persons, and inadequate food.

Contracting Negroes were to be known as "servants" and contractors as "masters." Wages were to be fixed by the judge, unless stipulated. Negroes of ten years of age or more without a parent living in the district might make a valid contract for a year or less. Failure to make written contracts was a misdemeanor, punishable by a fine of $5 to $50; farm labor to be from sunrise to sunset, with intervals for meals; servants to rise at dawn, to be careful of master's property and answerable for property lost or injured. Lost time was to be deducted from wages. Food and clothes might be deducted. Servants were to be quiet and orderly and to go to bed at reasonable hours. No night work or outdoor work in bad weather was to be asked, except in cases of necessity, visitors not allowed without the master's consent. Servants leaving employment without good reason must forfeit wages. Masters might discharge servants for disobedience, drunkenness, disease, absence, etc. Enticing away the services of a servant was punishable by a fine of $20 to $100. A master could command a servant to aid him in defense of his own person, family or property. House servants at all hours of the day and night, and at all days of the weeks, "must answer promptly all calls and execute all lawful orders. . . ."

Mississippi provided "that every civil officer shall, and every person may, arrest and carry back to his or her legal employer any freedman, free Negro, or mulatto who shall have quit the service of his or her employer before the expiration of his or her term of service without good cause; and said officer and person shall be entitled to receive for arresting and carrying back every deserting employee afore-said the sum of five dollars, and ten cents per mile from the place of arrest to the place of delivery, and the same shall be paid by the employer and held as a set-off for so much against the wages of said deserting employee."

It was provided in some states, like South Carolina, that any white man, whether an officer or not, could arrest a Negro. "Upon view of a misdemeanor committed by a person of color, any person present may arrest the offender and take him before a magistrate, to be dealt with as the case may require. In case of a misdemeanor committed by a white person toward a person of color, any person may complain to a magistrate, who shall cause the offender to be arrested, and according to the nature of the case, to be brought before himself, or be taken for trial in the district court."

On the other hand, in Mississippi, it was dangerous for a Negro to try to bring a white person to court on any charge. "In every case where any white person has been arrested and brought to trial, by virtue of the provisions of the tenth section of the above recited act, in any court in this State, upon sufficient proof being made to the court or jury, upon the trial before said court, that any freedman, free Negro or mulatto has falsely and maliciously caused the arrest and trial of said white person or persons, the court shall render up a judgment against said freedman, free Negro or mulatto for all costs of the case, and impose a fine not to exceed fifty dollars, and imprisonment in the county jail not to exceed twenty days; and for a failure of said freedman, free Negro or mulatto to pay, or cause to be paid, all costs, fines and jail fees, the sheriff of the county is hereby authorized and required, after giving ten days' public notice, to proceed to hire out at public outcry, at the court-house of the county, said freedman, free Negro or mulatto, for the shortest time to raise the amount necessary to discharge said freedman, free Negro or mulatto from all costs, fines, and jail fees aforesaid."

Mississippi declared that: "Any freedman, free Negro, or mulatto, committing riots, routs, affrays, trespasses, malicious mischief and cruel treatment to animals, seditious speeches, insulting gestures, language or acts, or assaults on any person, disturbance of the peace, exercising the functions of a minister of the gospel with-out a license from some regularly organized church, vending spirituous or intoxicat-ing liquors, or committing any other misdemeanor, the punishment of which is not specifically provided for by law, shall, upon conviction thereof, in the county court, be fined not less than ten dollars, and not more than one hundred dollars, and may be imprisoned, at the discretion of the court, not exceeding thirty days. . . ."

The most important and oppressive laws were those with regard to vagrancy and apprenticeship. Sometimes they especially applied to Negroes; in other cases, they were drawn in general terms but evidently designed to fit the Negro's condition and to be enforced particularly with regard to Negroes.

The Virginia Vagrant Act enacted that "any justice of the peace, upon the complaint of any one of certain officers therein named, may issue his warrant for the apprehension of any person alleged to be a vagrant and cause such person to be apprehended and brought before him; and that if upon due examination said justice of the peace shall find that such person is a vagrant within the definition of vagrancy contained in said statute, he shall issue his warrant, directing such person to be employed for a term not exceeding three months, and by any constable of the county wherein the proceedings are had, be hired out for the best wages which can be procured, his wages to be applied to the support of himself and his family. The said statute further provides, that in case any vagrant so hired shall, during his term of service, run away from his employer without sufficient cause, he shall be apprehended on the warrant of a justice of the peace and returned to the custody of his employer, who shall then have, free from any other hire, the services of such vagrant for one month in addition to the original term of hiring, and that the employer shall then have power, if authorized by a justice of the peace, to work such vagrant with ball and chain. The said statute specified the persons who shall be considered vagrants and liable to the penalties imposed by it. Among those declared to be vagrants are all persons who, not having the wherewith to support their families, live idly and without employment, and refuse to work for the usual and common wages given to other laborers in the like work in the place where they are."

In Florida, January 12, 1866: "It is provided that when any person of color shall enter into a contract as aforesaid, to serve as a laborer for a year, or any other specified term, on any farm or plantation in this State, if he shall refuse or neglect to perform the stipulations of his contract by willful disobedience of orders, wanton impudence or disrespect to his employer, or his authorized agent, failure or refusal to perform the work assigned to him, idleness, or abandonment of the premises or the employment of the party with whom the contract was made, he or she shall be liable, upon the complaint of his employer or his agent, made under oath before any justice of the peace of the county, to be arrested and tried before the criminal court of the county, and upon conviction shall be subject to all the pains and penalties prescribed for the punishment of vagrancy."

In Georgia, it was ruled that "All persons wandering or strolling about in idleness, who are able to work, and who have no property to support them; all persons leading an idle, immoral, or profligate life, who have no property to support them and are able to work and do not work; all persons able to work having no visible and known means of a fair, honest, and respectable livelihood; all persons having a fixed abode, who have no visible property to support them, and who live by stealing or by trading in, bartering for, or buying stolen property; and all professional gamblers living in idleness, shall be deemed and considered vagrants, and shall be indicted as such, and it shall be lawful for any person to arrest said vagrants and have them bound over for trial to the next term of the country court, and upon conviction, they shall be fined and imprisoned or sentenced to work on the public works, for not longer than a year, or shall, in the discretion of the court, be bound over for trial to the next term of the country court, and upon conviction, they shall be fined and imprisoned or sentenced to work on the public works, for not longer than a year, or shall, in the discretion of the court, be bound out to some person for a time not longer than one year, upon such valuable consideration as the court may prescribe."

Mississippi provided "That all freedmen, free Negroes, and mulattoes in this state over the age of eighteen years, found on the second Monday in January, 1866, or thereafter, with no lawful employment or business, or found unlawfully assembling themselves together, either in the day or night time, and all white persons so assembling with freedmen, free Negroes or mulattoes, or usually associating with freedmen, free Negroes or mulattoes on terms of equality, or living in adultery or fornication with a freedwoman, free Negro or mulatto, shall be deemed vagrants, and on conviction thereof shall be fined in the sum of not exceeding, in the case of a freedman, free Negro or mulatto, fifty dollars, and a white man two hundred dollars and imprisoned, at the discretion of the court, the free Negro not exceeding ten days, and the white men not exceeding six months."

Sec. 5 provides that "all fines and forfeitures collected under the provisions of this act shall be paid into the county treasury for general county purposes, and in case any freedman, free Negro or mulatto, shall fail for five days after the imposition of any fine or forfeiture upon him or her, for violation of any of the provisions of this act to pay the same, that it shall be, and is hereby made, the duty of the Sheriff of the proper county to hire out said freedman, free Negro or mulatto, to any person who will, for the shortest period of service, pay said fine or forfeiture and all costs; *Provided*, a preference shall be given to the employer, if there be one, in which case the employer shall be entitled to deduct and retain the amount so paid from the wages of such freedman, free Negro or mulatto, then due or to become due; and in case such freedman, free Negro or mulatto cannot be hired out, he or she may be dealt with as a pauper. . . ."

In Alabama, the "former owner" was to have preference in the apprenticing of a child. This was true in Kentucky and Mississippi.

Mississippi "provides that it shall be the duty of all sheriffs, justices of the peace, and other civil officers of the several counties in this state to report to the probate courts of their respective counties semi-annually, at the January and July terms of said courts, all freedmen, free Negroes and mulattoes, under the age of eighteen, within their respective counties, beats, or districts, who are orphans, or whose parent or parents have not the means, or who refuse to provide for and support said minors, and thereupon it shall be the duty of said probate court to order the clerk of said court to apprentice said minors to some competent and suitable person, on such terms as the court may direct, having a particular care to the interest of said minors; *Provided*, that the former owner of said minors shall have the preference when, in the opinion of the court, he or she shall be a suitable person for that purpose. . . ."

"Capital punishment was provided for colored persons guilty of willful homicide, assault upon a white woman, impersonating her husband for carnal purposes, raising an insurrection, stealing a horse, a mule, or baled cotton, and house-breaking. For crimes not demanding death Negroes might be confined at hard labor, whipped, or transported; 'but punishments more degrading than imprisonment shall not be imposed upon a white person for a crime not infamous.'"[2]

In most states Negroes were allowed to testify in courts but the testimony was usually confined to cases where colored persons were involved, although in some states, by consent of the parties, they could testify in cases where only white people were involved. . . .

Mississippi simply reenacted her slave code and made it operative so far as punishments were concerned. "That all the penal and criminal laws now in force in this State, defining offenses, and prescribing the mode of punishment for crimes and misdemeanors committed by slaves, free Negroes or mulattoes, be and the same are hereby reenacted, and declared to be in full force and effect, against freedmen, free Negroes, and mulattoes, except so far as the mode and manner of trial and punishment have been changed or altered by law."

North Carolina, on the other hand, abolished her slave code, making difference of punishment only in the case of Negroes convicted of rape. Georgia placed the fines and costs of a servant upon the master. "Where such cases shall go against the servant, the judgment for costs upon written notice to the master shall operate as a garnishment against him, and he shall retain a sufficient amount for the payment thereof, out of any wages due to said servant, or to become due during the period of service, and may be cited at any time by the collecting officer to make answer thereto."

The celebrated ordinance of Opelousas, Louisiana, shows the local ordinances regulating Negroes. "No Negro or freedman shall be allowed to come within the limits of the town of Opelousas without special permission from his employer, specifying the object of his visit and the time necessary for the accomplishment of the same.

"Every Negro freedman who shall be found on the streets of Opelousas after ten o'clock at night without a written pass or permit from his employer, shall be imprisoned and compelled to work five days on the public streets, or pay a fine of five dollars.

"No Negro or freedman shall be permitted to rent or keep a house within the limits of the town under any circumstances, and anyone thus offending shall be ejected, and compelled to find an employer or leave the town within twenty-four hours.

"No Negro or freedman shall reside within the limits of the town of Opelousas who is not in the regular service of some white person or former owner, who shall be held responsible for the conduct of said freedman.

"No Negro or freedman shall be permitted to preach, exhort, or otherwise declaim to congregations of colored people without a special permission from the Mayor or President of the Board of Police, under the penalty of a fine of ten dollars or twenty days' work on the public streets.

"No freedman who is not in the military service shall be allowed to carry fire-arms, or any kind of weapons within the limits of the town of Opelousas without the special permission of his employer, in writing, and approved by the Mayor or President of the Board.

"Any freedmen not residing in Opelousas, who shall be found within its cor-·porate limits after the hour of 3 o'clock, on Sunday, without a special permission from his employer or the Mayor, shall be arrested and imprisoned and made to work two days on the public streets, or pay two dollars in lieu of said work."[3]

Of Louisiana, Thomas Conway testified February 22, 1866: "Some of the lead-ing officers of the state down there—men who do much to form and control the opinions of the masses—instead of doing as they promised, and quietly submitting to the authority of the government, engaged in issuing slave codes and in promul-gating them to their subordinates, ordering them to carry them into execution, and this to the knowledge of state officials of a higher character, the governor and others. And the men who issued them were not punished except as the military authorities punished them. The governor inflicted no punishment on them while I was there, and I don't know that, up to this day, he has ever punished one of them. These codes were simply the old black code of the state, with the word 'slave' expunged, and 'Negro' substituted. The most odious features of slavery were preserved in them. . . ."[4]

NOTES

1. Quotations from McPherson, *History of United States During Reconstruction,* pp. 29–44.

2. Simkins and Woody, *South Carolina During Reconstruction,* pp. 49, 50.

3. Warmoth, *War, Politics and Reconstruction,* p. 274.

4. *Report on the Joint Committee on Reconstruction,* 1866, Part IV, pp. 78–79.

13

Bradwell v. *Illinois*, 1873

Mid-nineteenth century feminists, many of them diligent workers in the cause of abolition, looked to Congress after the Civil War for an express guarantee of equal rights for men and women. Viewed in historical perspective, their expectations appear unrealistic. A problem of far greater immediacy faced the nation. Moreover, the common law heritage, ranking the married woman in relationship to her husband as "something better than his dog, a little dearer than his horse,"[1] was just beginning to erode. Nonetheless, the text of the fourteenth amendment appalled the proponents of a sex equality guarantee. Their concern centered on the abortive second section of the amendment, which placed in the Constitution for the first time the word "male." Threefold use of the word "male," always in conjunction with the term "citizens," caused concern that the grand phrases of the first section of the fourteenth amendment would have, at best, qualified application to women.[2]

For more than a century after the adoption of the fourteenth amendment, the judiciary, with rare exceptions, demonstrated utmost deference to sex lines drawn by the legislature. . . .

The Court's initial examination of a woman's claim to full participation in society through entry into a profession traditionally reserved to men came in 1873 in Bradwell v. Illinois.[3] Myra Bradwell's application for a license to practice law had been denied by the Illinois Supreme Court solely because she was a female. The Supreme Court affirmed this judgment with only one dissent, recorded but not explained, by Chief Justice Chase. Justice Miller's opinion for the majority was placed on two grounds: (1) since petitioner was a citizen of Illinois, the privileges and immunities clause of article IV, section 2 of the Federal Constitution[4] was inapplicable to her claim; and (2) since admission to the bar of a state is not one of the privileges and immunities of United States citizenship, the fourteenth amendment did not secure the asserted right. Justice Bradley, speaking for himself and Justices Swayne and Field, chose to place his concurrence in the judgment on broader grounds. He wrote[5]:

> [T]he civil law, as well as nature herself, has always recognized a wide difference in the respective spheres and destinies of man and woman. Man is, or should be, woman's protector and defender. The natural and proper timidity and delicacy which belongs to the female sex evidently unfits it for many of the occupations of civil life. The constitution of the family organization, which is founded in the divine ordinance, as well as in the nature of things, indicates the domestic sphere as that which properly belongs to the domain and functions of womanhood. The harmony, not to say identity, of interests and views which belong, or should belong, to the family institution is repugnant to the idea of a woman adopting a distinct and independent career from that of her husband. So firmly fixed was this sentiment in the founders of the common law that it became a maxim of that system of jurisprudence that a woman had no legal existence separate from her husband, who was regarded as her head and representative in the social state and, notwithstanding some recent modifications of this civil status, many of the special rules of law flowing from and dependent upon this cardinal principle still exist in full force in most States. One of these is, that a married woman is incapable, without her husband's consent, of making contracts which shall be binding on her or him. This very incapacity was one circumstance which the Supreme Court of Illinois deemed important in rendering a married woman incompetent fully to perform the duties and trusts that belong to the office of an attorney and counsellor.

It is true that many women are unmarried and not affected by any of the duties, complications, and incapacities arising out of the married state, but these are exceptions to the general rule. The paramount destiny and mission of woman are to fulfil the noble and benign offices of wife and mother. This is the law of the Creator. And the rules of civil society must be adapted to the general constitution of things, and cannot be based upon exceptional cases.

The humane movements of modern society, which have for their object the multiplication of avenues for woman's advancement, and of occupations adapted to her condition and sex, have my heartiest concurrence. But I am not prepared to say that it is one of her fundamental rights and privileges to be admitted into every office and position, including those which require highly special qualifications and demanding special responsibilities. In the nature of things it is not every citizen of every age, sex, and condition that is qualified for every calling and position. It is the prerogative of the legislator to prescribe regulations founded on nature, reason, and experience for the due admission of qualified persons to professions and callings demanding special skill and confidence. This fairly belongs to the police power of the State; and, in my opinion, in view of the peculiar characteristics, destiny, and mission of woman, it is within the province of the legislature to ordain what offices, positions, and callings shall be filled and discharged by men, and shall receive the benefit of those energies and responsibilities, and that decision and firmness which are presumed to predominate in the sterner sex.

Although the method of communication between the Creator and the judge is never disclosed, "divine ordinance" has been a dominant theme in decisions justifying laws establishing sex-based classifications.[6] Well past the middle of the twentieth century laws delineating "a sharp line between the sexes"[7] were sanctioned by the judiciary on the basis of lofty inspiration as well as restrained constitutional interpretation. . . .

NOTES

1. Alfred Lord Tennyson, Locksley Hall (1842); see Johnston, Sex and Property: The Common Law Tradition, The Law School Curriculum, and Developments Toward Equality, 47 N.Y.U.L. Rev. 1033, 1044–1070 (1972); pp. 163–183 infra.

2. E. Flexner, Century of Struggle 142–55 (1959).

3. 83 U.S. (16 Wall.) 130, 21 L. Ed. 442 (1873).

4. Article IV, section 2 reads: "The Citizens of each State shall be entitled to all Privileges and Immunities of Citizens in the several States."

5. 83 U.S. (16 Wall.) at 141–42.

6. E.g., State v. Heitman, 105 Kan. 139, 146–47, 181 P. 630. 633–34 (1919); State v. Bearcub, 1 Or. App. 579, 580, 465 P. 2d 252, 253 (1970).

7. Goesaert v. Cleary, 335 U.S. 464, 466, 69 S. Ct. 198, 199, 93 L. Ed. 163, 165 (1948). *Goesaert* was disapproved in Craig v. Boren, 429 U.S. 190, 210 n. 23, 97 S. Ct. 451, 463, 50 L. Ed. 2d 397, 414 (1976).

Minor v. Happersett, 1875

"In this case the court held that although women were citizens, the right to vote was not a privilege or immunity of national citizenship before adoption of the 14th Amendment, nor did the amendment add suffrage to the privileges and immunities of national citizenship. Therefore, the national government could not require states to permit women to vote."*

California Constitution, 1876

In 1876, at the height of the anti-Chinese movement, California adopted a new constitution. Its anti-Chinese provisions, largely unenforceable, represent an accurate measure of public feeling.

Article XIX

Section 1. The Legislature shall prescribe all necessary regulations for the protection of the State, and the counties, cities, and towns thereof, from the burdens and evils arising from the presence of aliens, who are or may become vagrants, paupers, mendicants, criminals, or invalids afflicted with contagious or infectious diseases, and from aliens otherwise dangerous or detrimental to the well-being or peace of the State, and to impose conditions upon which such persons may reside

*From *Congressional Quarterly's Guide to the U.S. Supreme Court*, 1979, p. 631.

in the State, and to provide means and mode of their removal from the State upon failure or refusal to comply with such conditions; provided, that nothing contained in this section shall be construed to impair or limit the power of the Legislature to pass such police laws or other regulations as it may deem necessary.

Section 2. No corporation now existing or hereafter formed under the laws of this State, shall, after the adoption of this Constitution, employ, directly or indirectly, in any capacity, any Chinese or Mongolian. The Legislature shall pass such laws as may be necessary to enforce this provision.

Section 3. No Chinese shall be employed on any State, county, municipal, or other public work, except in punishment for crime.

Section 4. The presence of foreigners ineligible to become citizens of the United States is declared to be dangerous to the well-being of the State, and the Legislature shall discourage their immigration by all the means within its power. Asiatic coolie-ism is a form of human slavery, and is forever prohibited in this State; and all contracts for coolie labor shall be void. All companies or corporations, whether formed in this country or any foreign country, for the importation of such labor, shall be subject to such penalties as the Legislature may prescribe. The Legislature shall delegate all necessary power to the incorporated cities and towns of this State for the removal of Chinese without the limits of such cities and towns, or for their location within prescribed portions of those limits; and it shall also provide the necessary legislation to prohibit the introduction into this State of Chinese after the adoption of this Constitution. This section shall be enforced by appropriate legislation.

16

Elk v. *Wilkins,* November 3, 1884

John Elk, an Indian who had voluntarily separated himself from his tribe and taken up residence among the whites, was denied the right to vote in Omaha, Nebraska, on the ground that he was not a citizen. The Supreme Court considered the question of whether Elk had been made a citizen by the Fourteenth Amendment and decided against him.

. . . The plaintiff, in support of his action, relies on the first clause of the first section of the Fourteenth Article of Amendment of the Constitution of the United States, by which "all persons born or naturalized in the United States, and subject to the jurisdiction thereof, are citizens of the United States and of the State wherein they reside;" and on the Fifteenth Article of Amendment, which provides that "the right of citizens of the United States to vote shall not be denied or abridged by the United States or by any State on account of race, color, or previous condition of servitude." . . .

The petition, while it does not show of what Indian tribe the plaintiff was a member, yet, by the allegations that he "is an Indian, and was born within the United States," and that "he had severed his tribal relation to the Indian tribes," clearly implies that he was born a member of one of the Indian tribes within the limits of the United States, which still exists and is recognized as a tribe by the government of the United States. Though the plaintiff alleges that he "had fully and completely surrendered himself to the jurisdiction of the United States," he does not allege that the United States accepted his surrender, or that he has ever been naturalized, or taxed, or in any way recognized or treated as a citizen, by the State or by the United States. Nor is it contended by his counsel that there is any statute or treaty that makes him a citizen.

The question then is, whether an Indian, born a member of one of the Indian tribes within the United States, is, merely by reason of his birth within the United States, and of his afterwards voluntarily separating himself from his tribe and taking up his residence among white citizens, a citizen of the United States, within the meaning of the first section of the Fourteenth Amendment of the Constitution. . . .

Indians born within the territorial limits of the United States, members of, and owing immediate allegiance to, one of the Indian tribes (an alien, though dependent, power), although in a geographical sense born in the United States, are no more "born in the United States and subject to the jurisdiction thereof," within the meaning of the first section of the Fourteenth Amendment, than the children of subjects of any foreign government born within the domain of that government, or the children born within the United States, of ambassadors or other public ministers of foreign nations.

This view is confirmed by the second section of the Fourteenth Amendment, which provides that "representatives shall be apportioned among the several States according to their respective numbers, counting the whole number of persons in each State, excluding Indians not taxed." Slavery having been abolished, and the persons formerly held as slaves made citizens, this clause fixing the apportionment of representatives has abrogated so much of the corresponding clause of the original Constitution as counted only three-fifths of such persons. But Indians not taxed are still excluded from the count, for the reason that they are not citizens. Their absolute exclusion from the basis of representation, in which all other persons are now included, is wholly inconsistent with their being considered citizens. . . .

The plaintiff, not being a citizen of the United States under the Fourteenth Amendment of the Constitution, has been deprived of no right secured by the Fifteenth Amendment, and cannot maintain this action.*

*112 *United States Reports: Cases Adjudged in the Supreme Court*, Banks & Brothers, New York.

17

Plessy v. Ferguson, 1896

After the collapse of Reconstruction governments, southern whites began gradually to legalize the informal practices of segregation which obtained in the South. One such law was passed by the Louisiana legislature in 1890 and provided that "all railway companies carrying passengers . . . in this State shall provide separate but equal accommodations for the white and colored races."

Plessy vs. Ferguson tested the constitutionality of this recent trend in southern legislation. Plessy was a mulatto who, on June 7, 1892, bought a first-class ticket on the East Louisiana Railway for a trip from New Orleans to Covington, La., and sought to be seated in the "white" coach. Upon conviction of a violation of the 1890 statute, he appealed to the Supreme Court of Louisiana, which upheld his conviction, and finally to the U.S. Supreme Court, which pronounced the Louisiana law constitutional, on May 18, 1896. The defense of Plessy and attack on the Louisiana statute was in the hands of four men, the most famous of whom was Albion W. Tourgée. M. J. Cunningham, Attorney General of Louisiana, was assisted by two other lawyers in defending the statute. The majority opinion of the Court was delivered by Justice Henry B. Brown. John Marshall Harlan dissented and Justice David J. Brewer did not participate, making it a 7–1 decision.

In his dissent to this decision Harlan asserted that "Our Constitution is color-blind, and neither knows nor tolerates classes among citizens. In respect of civil rights, all citizens are equal before the law." He offered the prophecy that "the judgment rendered this day will, in time, prove to be quite as pernicious as the decision made by this tribunal in the Dred Scott case."

The constitutionality of this act is attacked upon the ground that it conflicts both with the Thirteenth Amendment of the Constitution, abolishing slavery, and the Fourteenth Amendment, which prohibits certain restrictive legislation on the part of the States.

1. That it does not conflict with the Thirteenth Amendment, which abolished slavery and involuntary servitude, except as a punishment for crime, is too clear for argument. Slavery implies involuntary servitude—a state of bondage: the owner-ship of mankind as a chattel, or at least the control of the labor and services of one man for the benefit of another, and the absence of a legal right to the disposal of his own person, property and services. . . .

A statute which implies merely a legal distinction between the white and colored races—a distinction which is founded in the color of the two races, and which must always exist so long as white men are distinguished from the other race by color—has no tendency to destroy the legal equality of the two races, or re-establish a state of involuntary servitude. Indeed, we do not understand that the Thirteenth Amendment is strenuously relied upon by the plaintiff in error in this connection.

2. By the Fourteenth Amendment, all persons born or naturalized in the United States, and subject to the jurisdiction thereof, are made citizens of the United States and of the State wherein they reside; and the States are forbidden from making or enforcing any law which shall abridge the privileges or immunities of citizens of the United States, or shall deprive any person of life, liberty or property without due process of law, or deny to any person within their jurisdiction the equal protection of the laws. . . .

The object of the amendment was undoubtedly to enforce the absolute equality of the two races before the law, but in the nature of things it could not have been intended to abolish distinctions based upon color, or to enforce social, as distin-guished from political equality, or a commingling of the two races upon terms un-satisfactory to either. Laws permitting, and even requiring, their separation in places where they are liable to be brought into contact do not necessarily imply the infe-riority of either race to the other, and have been generally, if not universally, rec-ognized as within the competency of the state legislatures in the exercise of their police power. The most common instance of this is connected with the establish-ment of separate schools for white and colored children, which has been held to be a valid exercise of the legislative power even by courts of States where the political rights of the colored race have been longest and most earnestly enforced. . . .

While we think the enforced separation of the races, as applied to the internal commerce of the State, neither abridges the privileges or immunities of the colored man, deprives him of his property without due process of law, nor denies him the equal protection of the laws, within the meaning of the Fourteenth Amendment, we are not prepared to say that the conductor, in assigning passengers to the coaches according to their race, does not act at his peril, or that the provision of the second section of the act, that denies to the passenger compensation in damages for a re-fusal to receive him into the coach in which he properly belongs, is a valid exercise of the legislative power. Indeed, we understand it to be conceded by the State's attorney, that such part of the act as exempts from liability the railway company and its officers is unconstitutional. The power to assign to a particular coach obviously implies the power to determine to which race the passenger belongs, as well as the power to determine who, under the laws of the particular State, is to be deemed a white, and who a colored person. . . .

It is claimed by the plaintiff in error that, in any mixed community, the repu-tation of belonging to the dominant race, in this instance the white race, is *property*, in the same sense that a right of action, or of inheritance, is property. Conceding this to be so, for the purposes of this case, we are unable to see how this statute de-prives him of, or in any way affects his right to, such property. If he be a white man and assigned to a colored coach, he may have his action for damages against the company for being deprived of his so called property. Upon the other hand, if he be a colored man and be so assigned, he has been deprived of no property, since he is not lawfully entitled to the reputation of being a white man.

In this connection, it is also suggested by the learned counsel for the plaintiff in error that the same argument that will justify the state legislature in requiring railways to provide separate accommodations for the two races will also authorize them to require separate cars to be provided for the people whose hair is of a certain color, or who are aliens, or who belong to certain nationalities, or to enact laws requiring colored people to walk upon one side of the street, and white people upon the other, or requiring white men's houses to be painted white, and colored men's black, or their vehicles or business signs to be of different colors, upon the theory that one side of the street is as good as the other, or that a house or vehicle of one color is as good as one of another color. The reply to all this is that every exercise of the police power must be reasonable, and extend only to such laws as are enacted in good faith for the promotion for the public good, and not for the annoyance or oppression of a particular class. . . .

We consider the underlying fallacy of the plaintiff's argument to consist in the assumption that the enforced separation of the two races stamps the colored race with a badge of inferiority. If this be so, it is not by reason of anything found in the act, but solely because the colored race chooses to put that construction upon it. The argument necessarily assumes that if, as has been more than once the case, and is not unlikely to be so again, the colored race should become the dominant power in the state legislature, and should enact a law in precisely similar terms, it would thereby relegate the white race to an inferior position. We imagine that the white race, at least, would not acquiesce in this assumption. The argument also assumes that social prejudices may be overcome by legislation, and that equal rights cannot be secured to the negro except by an enforced commingling of the two races. We cannot accept this proposition. If the two races are to meet upon terms of social equality, it must be the result of natural affinities, a mutual appreciation of each other's merits and a voluntary consent of individuals.*

Plessy vs. Ferguson, 163 U.S. 537 *United States Reports: Cases Adjudged in the Supreme Court* (New York, Banks & Brothers, 1896).

18

United States Constitution: *Nineteenth Amendment (1920)*

Amendment XIX (ratified August 18, 1920). *Section 1.* The right of citizens of the United States to vote shall not be denied or abridged by the United States or by any State on account of sex.

Section 2. Congress shall have power to enforce this Article by appropriate legislation.

19

Korematsu v. United States, 1944

The present case involved perhaps the most alarming use of executive military authority in our nation's history. Following the bombing of Pearl Harbor in December, 1941, the anti-Japanese sentiment on the West Coast brought the residents of the area to a state of near hysteria; and in February, 1942, President Roosevelt issued an executive order authorizing the creation of military areas from which any or all persons might be excluded as the military authorities might decide. On March 2, the entire West Coast to a depth of about forty miles was designated by the commanding general as Military Area No. 1, and he thereupon proclaimed a curfew in that area for all persons of Japanese ancestry. Later he ordered the compulsory evacuation from the area of all persons of Japanese ancestry, and by the middle of the summer most of these people had been moved inland to "war relocation centers," the American equivalent of concentration camps. Congress subsequently made it a crime to violate these military orders. Of the 112,000 persons of Japanese ancestry involved, about 70,000 were native-born American citizens, none of whom had been specifically accused of disloyalty. Three cases were brought to the Supreme Court as challenging the right of the government to override in this manner the customary civil rights of these citizens. In Hirabayashi v. United States, 320 U.S. 81 (1943), the Court upheld the curfew regulations as a valid military measure to prevent espionage and sabotage. "Whatever views we may entertain regarding the loyalty to this country of the citizens of Japanese ancestry, we cannot reject as unfounded the judgment of the military authorities and of Congress that there were disloyal members of that population, whose number and strength could not be precisely and quickly ascertained. We cannot say that the war-making branches of the Government did not have ground for believing that in a critical hour such persons could not readily be isolated and separately dealt with, and constituted a menace to the national defense and safety. . . ." While emphasizing that distinctions based on ancestry were "by their very nature odious to a free people" the Court nonetheless felt "that in time of war residents having ethnic affiliations with an invading enemy may be a greater source of danger than those of a different ancestry."

While the Court, in the present case, held valid the discriminatory mass evacuation of all persons of Japanese descent, it also held in Ex parte Endo, 323 U.S. 283 (1944), that an American citizen of Japanese ancestry whose loyalty to this country had been established could not constitutionally be held in a War Relocation Center but must be unconditionally released. The government had allowed persons to leave the Relocation Centers under conditions and restrictions which aimed to guarantee that there should not be "a dangerously disorderly migration of unwanted people to unprepared communities." Permission to leave was granted only if the applicant had the assurance of a job and a place to live, and wanted to go to a place "approved" by the War Relocation Authority. The Court held that the sole purpose of the evacuation and detention program was to protect the war effort against sabotage and espionage. "A person who is concededly loyal presents no problem of espionage or sabotage. . . . He who is loyal is by definition not a spy or a saboteur." It therefore follows that the authority to detain a citizen of Japanese ancestry ends when his loyalty is established. To hold otherwise would be to justify his detention not on grounds of military necessity but purely on grounds of race.

Although no case reached the Court squarely challenging the right of the government to incarcerate citizens of Japanese ancestry pending a determination of their loyalty, the tenor of the opinions leaves little doubt that such action would have been sustained. The present case involved only the right of the military to evacuate such persons from the West Coast. Mr. Justice Murphy, one of the three dissenters, attacked the qualifications of the military to make sociological judgments about the effects of ancestry, and pointed out that the time consumed in evacuating these persons (eleven months) was ample for making an orderly inquiry into their individual loyalty.

Mr. Justice Black delivered the opinion of the Court, saying in part:

The petitioner, an American citizen of Japanese descent, was convicted in a federal district court for remaining in San Leandro, California, a "Military Area," contrary to Civilian Exclusion Order No. 34 of the Commanding General of the Western Command, U.S. Army, which directed that after May 9, 1942, all persons of Japanese ancestry should be excluded from that area. No question was raised as to petitioner's loyalty to the United States. The Circuit Court of Appeals affirmed, and the importance of the constitutional question involved caused us to grant certiorari.

It should be noted, to begin with, that all legal restrictions which curtail the civil rights of a single racial group are immediately suspect. That is not to say that all such restrictions are unconstitutional. It is to say that courts must subject them to the most rigid scrutiny. Pressing public necessity may sometimes justify the existence of such restrictions; racial antagonism never can.

In the instant case prosecution of the petitioner was begun by information charging violation of an Act of Congress, of March 21, 1942, 56 Stat. 173, which provides that ". . . whoever shall enter, remain in, leave, or commit any act in any military area or military zone prescribed, under the authority of an Executive order of the President, by the Secretary of War, or by any military commander designated by the Secretary of War, contrary to the restrictions applicable to any such area or zone or contrary to the order of the Secretary of War or any such military commander, shall, if it appears that he knew or should have known of the existence and extent of the restrictions or order and that his act was in violation thereof, be guilty of a misdemeanor and upon conviction shall be liable to a fine of not to exceed $5,000 or to imprisonment for not more than one year, or both, for each offense."

Exclusion Order No. 34, which the petitioner knowingly and admittedly violated was one of a number of military orders and proclamations, all of which were substantially based upon Executive Order No. 9066, 7 Fed. Reg. 1407. That order, issued after we were at war with Japan, declared that "the successful prosecution of the war requires every possible protection against espionage and against sabotage to national-defense material, national-defense premises, and national-defense utilities. . . ."

One of the series of orders and proclamations, a curfew order, which like the exclusion order here was promulgated pursuant to Executive Order 9066, subjected all persons of Japanese ancestry in prescribed West Coast military areas to remain in their residences from 8 p.m. to 6 a.m. As is the case with the exclusion order here, that prior curfew order was designed as a "protection against espionage and against sabotage." In Kiyoshi Hirabayashi v. United States, 320 U.S. 81, we sustained a conviction obtained for violation of the curfew order. The Hirabayashi conviction and this one thus rest on the same 1942 Congressional Act and the same basic executive and military orders, all of which orders were aimed at the twin dangers of espionage and sabotage.

The 1942 Act was attacked in the Hirabayashi case as an unconstitutional delegation of power; it was contended that the curfew order and other orders on which it rested were beyond the war powers of the Congress, the military authorities and of the President, as Commander in Chief of the Army; and finally that to apply the curfew order against none but citizens of Japanese ancestry amounted to a constitutionally prohibited discrimination solely on account of race. To these questions, we gave the serious consideration which their importance justified. We upheld the curfew order as an exercise of the power of the government to take steps necessary to prevent espionage and sabotage in an area threatened by Japanese attack.

In the light of the principles we announced in the Hirabayashi case, we are unable to conclude that it was beyond the war power of Congress and the Executive to exclude those of Japanese ancestry from the West Coast war area at the time they did. True, exclusion from the area in which one's home is located is a far greater deprivation than constant confinement to the home from 8 p.m. to 6 a.m. Nothing short of apprehension by the proper military authorities of the gravest imminent danger to the public safety can constitutionally justify either. But exclusion from a threatened area, no less than curfew, has a definite and close relationship to the prevention of espionage and sabotage. The military authorities, charged with the primary responsibility of defending our shores, concluded that curfew provided inadequate protection and ordered exclusion. They did so, as pointed out in our Hirabayashi opinion, in accordance with Congressional authority to the military to say who should, and who should not, remain in the threatened areas.

In this case the petitioner challenges the assumptions upon which we rested our conclusions in the Hirabayashi case. He also urges that by May 1942, when Order No. 34 was promulgated, all danger of Japanese invasion of the West Coast had disappeared. After careful consideration of these contentions we are compelled to reject them.

Here, as in the Hirabayashi case, ". . . we cannot reject as unfounded the judgment of the military authorities and of Congress that there were disloyal members of that population, whose number and strength could not be precisely and quickly ascertained. We cannot say that the warmaking branches of the Government did not have ground for believing that in a critical hour such persons could not readily be isolated and separately dealt with, and constituted a menace to the national defense and safety, which demanded that prompt and adequate measures be taken to guard against it."

Like curfew, exclusion of those of Japanese origin was deemed necessary because of the presence of an unascertained number of disloyal members of the group, most of whom we have no doubt were loyal to this country. It was because we could not reject the finding of the military authorities that it was impossible to bring about an immediate segregation of the disloyal from the loyal that we sustained the validity of the curfew order as applying to the whole group. In the instant case, temporary exclusion of the entire group was rested by the military on the same ground. The judgment that exclusion of the whole group was for the same reason a military imperative answers the contention that the exclusion was in the nature of group punishment based on antagonism to those of Japanese origin. That there were members of the group who retained loyalties to Japan has been confirmed by investigations made subsequent to the exclusion. Approximately five thousand American citizens of Japanese ancestry refused to swear unqualified allegiance to the United States and to renounce allegiance to the Japanese Emperor, and several thousand evacuees requested repatriation to Japan.

We uphold the exclusion order as of the time it was made and when the petitioner violated it. . . . In doing so, we are not unmindful of the hardships imposed by it upon a large group of American citizens. . . . But hardships are part of war, and war is an aggregation of hardships. All citizens alike, both in and out of uniform, feel the impact of war in greater or lesser measure. Citizenship has its responsibilities as well as its privileges, and in time of war the burden is always heavier. Compulsory exclusion of large groups of citizens from their homes, except under circumstances of direst emergency and peril, is inconsistent with our basic governmental institution. But when under conditions of modern warfare our shores are threatened by hostile forces, the power to protect must be commensurate with the threatened danger. . . .

[The Court dealt at some length with a technical complication which arose in the case. On May 30, the date on which Korematsu was charged with remaining unlawfully in the prohibited area, there were two conflicting military orders outstanding, one forbidding him to remain in the area, the other forbidding him to leave but ordering him to report to an assembly center. Thus, he alleged, he was punished for doing what it was made a crime to fail to do. The Court held the orders not to be contradictory, since the requirement to report to the assembly center was merely a step in an orderly program of compulsory evacuation from the area.]

It is said that we are dealing here with the case of imprisonment of a citizen in a concentration camp solely because of his ancestry, without evidence or inquiry concerning his loyalty and good disposition towards the United States. Our task would be simple, our duty clear, were this a case involving the imprisonment of a loyal citizen in a concentration camp because of racial prejudice. Regardless of the true nature of the assembly and relocation centers—and we deem it unjustifiable to call them concentration camps with all the ugly connotations that term implies—we are dealing specifically with nothing but an exclusion order. To cast this case into outlines of racial prejudice, without reference to the real military dangers which were presented, merely confuses the issue. Korematsu was not excluded from the Military Area because of hostility to him or his race. He was excluded because we are at war with the Japanese Empire, because the properly constituted military authorities feared an invasion of our West Coast and felt constrained to take proper security measures, because they decided that the military urgency of the situation demanded that all citizens of Japanese ancestry be segregated from the West Coast temporarily, and finally, because Congress reposing its confidence in this time of war in our military leaders—as inevitably it must—determined that they should have the power to do just this. There was evidence of disloyalty on the part of some, the military authorities considered that the need for action was great, and time was short. We cannot—by availing ourselves of the calm perspective of hindsight—now say that at that time these actions were unjustified.

Affirmed.

Mr. Justice Frankfurter wrote a concurring opinion. Justices Roberts, Murphy, and Jackson each wrote a dissenting opinion.

Brown v. Board of Education of Topeka, 1954

Mr. Chief Justice Warren delivered the opinion of the Court.

These cases come to us from the States of Kansas, South Carolina, Virginia, and Delaware. They are premised on different facts and different local conditions, but a common legal question justifies their consideration together in this consolidated opinion.[1]

In each of the cases, minors of the Negro race, through their legal representatives, seek the aid of the courts in obtaining admission to the public schools of their community on a nonsegregated basis. In each instance, they had been denied admission to schools attended by white children under laws requiring or permitting segregation according to race. This segregation was alleged to deprive the plaintiffs of the equal protection of the laws under the Fourteenth Amendment. In each of the cases other than the Delaware case, a three-judge federal district court denied relief to the plaintiffs on the so-called "separate but equal" doctrine announced by this Court in Plessy v. Ferguson, 163 U.S. 537. Under that doctrine, equality of treatment is accorded when the races are provided substantially equal facilities, even though these facilities be separate. In the Delaware case, the Supreme Court of Delaware adhered to that doctrine, but ordered that the plaintiffs be admitted to the white schools because of their superiority to the Negro schools.

The plaintiffs contend that segregated public schools are not "equal" and cannot be made "equal," and that hence they are deprived of the equal protection of the laws. Because of the obvious importance of the question presented, the Court took jurisdiction.[2] Argument was heard in the 1952 Term, and reargument was heard this Term on certain questions propounded by the Court. . . .[3]

In approaching this problem, we cannot turn the clock back to 1868 when the Amendment was adopted, or even to 1896 when Plessy v. Ferguson was written. We must consider public education in the light of its full development and its present place in American life throughout the Nation. Only in this way can it be determined if segregation in public schools deprives these plaintiffs of the equal protection of the laws.

Today, education is perhaps the most important function of state and local governments. Compulsory school attendance laws and the great expenditures for education both demonstrate our recognition of the importance of education to our democratic society. It is required in the performance of our most basic public responsibilities, even service in the armed forces. It is the very foundation of good citizenship. Today it is a principal instrument in awakening the child to cultural values, in preparing him for later professional training, and in helping him to adjust normally to his environment. In these days, it is doubtful that any child may reasonably be expected to succeed in life if he is denied the opportunity of an education. Such an opportunity, where the state has undertaken to provide it, is a right which must be made available to all on equal terms.

We come then to the question presented: Does segregation of children in public schools solely on the basis of race, even though the physical facilities and other "tangible" factors may be equal, deprive the children of the minority group of equal educational opportunities? We believe that it does.

In Sweatt v. Painter, in finding that a segregated law school for Negroes could not provide them equal educational opportunities, this Court relied in large part on "those qualities which are incapable of objective measurement but which make for greatness in a law school." In McLaurin v. Oklahoma State Regents, the Court, in requiring that a Negro admitted to a white graduate school be treated like all other students, again resorted to intangible considerations: ". . . his ability to study, to engage in discussions and exchange views with other students, and in general, to learn his profession." Such considerations apply with added force to children in grade and high schools. To separate them from others of similar age and qualifications solely because of their race generates a feeling of inferiority as to their status in the community that may affect their hearts and minds in a way unlikely ever to be undone. The effect of this separation on their educational opportunities was well stated by a finding in the Kansas case by a court which nevertheless felt compelled to rule against the Negro plaintiffs:

> Segregation of white and colored children in public schools has a detrimental effect upon the colored children. The impact is greater when it has the sanction of the law; for the policy of separating the races is usually interpreted as denoting the inferiority of the negro group. A sense of inferiority affects the motivation of a child to learn. Segregation with the sanction of law, therefore, has a tendency to [retard] the educational and mental development of negro children and to deprive them of some of the benefits they receive in a racial[ly] integrated school system.[4]

Whatever may have been the extent of psychological knowledge at the time of Plessy v. Ferguson, this finding is amply supported by modern authority.[5] Any language in Plessy v. Ferguson contrary to this finding is rejected.

We conclude that in the field of public education the doctrine of "separate but equal" has no place. Separate educational facilities are inherently unequal. Therefore, we hold that the plaintiffs and others similarly situated for whom the actions have been brought are, by reason of the segregation complained of, deprived of the equal protection of the laws guaranteed by the Fourteenth Amendment. This disposition makes unnecessary any discussion whether such segregation also violates the Due Process Clause of the Fourteenth Amendment.

Because these are class actions, because of the wide applicability of this decision, and because of the great variety of local conditions, the formulation of decrees in these cases presents problems of considerable complexity. On reargument, the consideration of appropriate relief was necessarily subordinated to the primary question—the constitutionality of segregation in public education. We have now announced that such segregation is a denial of the equal protection of the laws. In order that we may have the full assistance of the parties in formulating decrees, the cases will be restored to the docket, and the parties are requested to present further argument on Questions 4 and 5 previously propounded by the Court for the reargument this Term.[6] The Attorney General of the United States is again invited to participate. The Attorneys General of the states requiring or permitting segregation in public education will also be permitted to appear as amici curiae upon request to do so by September 15, 1954, and submission of the briefs by October 1, 1954.

It is so ordered.

NOTES

1. In the Kansas case, Brown v. Board of Education, the plaintiffs are Negro children of elementary school age residing in Topeka. They brought this action in the United States District Court for the District of Kansas to enjoin enforcement of a Kansas statute which permits, but does not require, cities of more than 15,000 population to maintain separate school facilities for Negro and white students. Kan. Gen. Stat. §72-1724 (1949). Pursuant to that authority, the Topeka Board of Education elected to establish segregated elementary schools. Other public schools in the community, however, are operated on a nonsegregated basis. The three-judge District Court, convened under 28 U.S.C. §§2281 and 2284, found that segregation in public education has a detrimental effect upon Negro children, but denied relief on the ground that the Negro and white schools were substantially equal with respect to buildings, transportation, curricula, and educational qualifications of teachers. 98 F. Supp. 797. The case is here on direct appeal under 28 U.S.C. §1253. [The Topeka, Kansas case would be analogous to a Northern school case inasmuch as the school segregation that existed in Topeka was not mandated by state law, and some of the system was integrated. It would be eighteen years before the Court would accept another such case for review. Keyes v. School District No. 1, Denver, 445 F.2d 990 (10th Cir. 1971), *cert. granted*, 404 U.S. 1036 (1972)].

In the South Carolina case, Briggs v. Elliot, the plaintiffs are Negro children of both elementary and high school age residing in Clarendon County. They brought this action in the United States District Court for the Eastern District of South Carolina to enjoin enforcement of provisions in the state constitution and statutory code which require the segregation of Negroes and whites in public schools. S.C. Const., Art. XI, §7; S.C. Code §5377 (1942). The three-judge District Court, convened under 28 U.S.C. §§2281 and 2284, denied the requested relief. The court found that the Negro schools were inferior to the white schools and ordered the defendants to begin immediately to equalize the facilities. But the court sustained the validity of the contested provisions and denied the plaintiffs admission to the white schools during the equalization program. 98 F. Supp. 529. This Court vacated the District Court's judgment and remanded the case for the purpose of obtaining the court's views on a report filed by the defendants concerning the progress made in the equalization program. 342 U.S. 350. On remand, the District Court found that substantial equality had been achieved except for buildings and that the defendants were proceeding to rectify this inequality as well. 103 F. Supp. 920. The case is again here on direct appeal under 28 U.S.C. §1253.

In the Virginia case, Davis v. County School Board, the plaintiffs are Negro children of high school age residing in Prince Edward County. They brought this action in the United States District Court for the Eastern District of Virginia to enjoin enforcement of provisions in the state constitution and statutory code which require the segregation of Negroes and whites in public schools. Va. Const., §140; Va. Code §22-221 (1950). The three-judge District Court, convened under 28 U.S.C. §§2281 and 2284, denied the requested relief. The court found the Negro school inferior in physical plant, curricula, and transportation, and ordered the defendants forthwith to provide substantially equal curricula and transportation and to "proceed with all reasonable diligence and dispatch to remove" the inequality in physical plant. But, as in the South Carolina case, the court sustained the validity of the contested provisions and denied the plaintiffs admission to the white schools during the equalization program. 103 F. Supp. 337. The case is here on direct appeal under 28 U.S.C. §1253.

In the Delaware case, Gebhart v. Belton, the plaintiffs are Negro children of both elementary and high school age residing in New Castle County. They brought this action in the Delaware Court of Chancery to enjoin enforcement of provisions in the state constitution and statutory code which require the segregation of Negroes and whites in public schools. Del. Const., Art. X, §2; Del. Rev. Code §2631 (1935). The chancellor gave judgment for the plaintiffs and ordered their immediate admission to schools previously attended only by white children, on the ground that the Negro schools were inferior with respect to teacher training, pupil-teacher ratio, extracurricular activities, physical plant, and time and distance involved in travel. 87 A.2d 862. The Chancellor also found that segregation itself results in an inferior education for Negro children (see note 4, infra), but did not rest his decision on that ground. Id., at 865. The Chancellor's decree was affirmed by the Supreme Court of Delaware, which intimated, however, that the defendants might be able to obtain a modification of the decree after equalization of the Negro and white schools had been accomplished. 91 A.2d 137, 152. The defendants, contending only that the Delaware courts had erred in ordering the immediate admission of the Negro plaintiffs to the white schools, applied to this Court for certiorari. The writ was granted, 344 U.S. 891. The plaintiffs, who were successful below, did not submit a cross-petition.

2. 344 U.S. 1, 141, 891.

3. 345 U.S. 972. The Attorney General of the United States participated both Terms as amicus curiae.

4. A similar finding was made in the Delaware case: "I conclude from the testimony that in our Delaware Society, State-imposed segregation in education itself results in the Negro children, as a class, receiving educational opportunities which are substantially inferior to those available to white children otherwise similarly situated." 87 A.2d 862, 865.

5. K. B. Clark, Effect of Prejudice and Discrimination on Personality Development (Midcentury White House Conference on Children and Youth, 1950); Witmer and Kotinsky, Personality in the Making (1952), c. VI; Deutscher and Chein, The Psychological Effects of Enforced Segregation: A Survey of Social Science Opinion, 26 J. Psychol. 259 (1948); Chein, What are the Psychological Effects of Segregation Under Conditions of

Equal Facilities?, 3 Int. J. Opinion and Attitude Res. 229 (1949); Brameld, Educational Costs, in Discrimination and National Welfare (MacIver, ed., 1949), 44–48; Frazier, The Negro in the United States (1949), 674–681. And see generally Myrdal, An American Dilemma (1944).

6. "4. Assuming it is decided that segregation in public schools violates the Fourteenth Amendment

"(a) would a decree necessarily follow providing that, within the limits set by normal geographic school districting, Negro children should forthwith be admitted to schools of their choice, or

"(b) may this Court, in the exercise of its equity powers, permit an effective gradual adjustment to be brought about from existing segregated systems to a system not based on color distinctions?

"5. On the assumption on which questions 4(a) and (b) are based, and assuming further that this Court will exercise its equity powers to the end described in question 4(b),

"(a) should this Court formulate detailed decrees in these cases;

"(b) if so, what specific issues should the decrees reach;

"(c) should this Court appoint a special master to hear evidence with a view to recommending specific terms for such decrees;

"(d) should this Court remand to the courts of first instance with directions to frame decrees in these cases, and if so what general directions should the decrees of this Court include and what procedures should the courts of first instance follow in arriving at the specific terms of more detailed decrees?"

21

Roe v. Wade, 1973

This historic decision legalized a woman's right to terminate her pregnancy by abortion. The ruling was based upon the right of privacy founded on both the Fourteenth and Ninth Amendments to the Constitution. The court ruled that this right of privacy protected the individual from interference by the state in the decision to terminate a pregnancy by abortion during the early portion of the pregnancy. At the same time, it recognized the interest of the state in regulating decisions concerning the pregnancy during the latter period as the fetus developed the capacity to survive outside the woman's body.

The Equal Rights Amendment (Defeated)

Equality of rights under the law shall not be denied or abridged by the United States or any State on account of sex.

Bowers v. Hardwick, 1986

Justice WHITE delivered the opinion of the Court.

In August 1982, respondent Hardwick (hereafter respondent) was charged with violating the Georgia statute criminalizing sodomy by committing that act with another adult male in the bedroom of respondent's home. After a preliminary hearing, the District Attorney decided not to present the matter to the grand jury unless further evidence developed.

Respondent then brought suit in the Federal District Court, challenging the constitutionality of the statute insofar as it criminalized consensual sodomy. He asserted that he was a practicing homosexual, that the Georgia sodomy statute, as administered by the defendants, placed him in imminent danger of arrest, and that the statute for several reasons violates the Federal Constitution. . . .

[2] This case does not require a judgment on whether laws against sodomy between consenting adults in general, or between homosexuals in particular, are

wise or desirable. It raises no question about the right or propriety of state legislative decisions to repeal their laws that criminalize homosexual sodomy, or of state-court decisions invalidating those laws on state constitutional grounds. The issue presented is whether the Federal Constitution confers a fundamental right upon homosexuals to engage in sodomy and hence invalidates the laws of the many States that still make such conduct illegal and have done so for a very long time. The case also calls for some judgment about the limits of the Court's role in carrying out its constitutional mandate.

We first register our disagreement with the Court of Appeals and with respondent that the Court's prior cases have construed the Constitution to confer a right of privacy that extends to homosexual sodomy and for all intents and purposes have decided this case. . . .

Accepting the decisions in these cases . . . we think it evident that none of the rights announced in those cases bears any resemblance to the claimed constitutional right of homosexuals to engage in acts of sodomy that is asserted in this case. No connection between family, marriage, or procreation on the one hand and homosexual activity on the other has been demonstrated, either by the Court of Appeals or by respondent. Moreover, any claim that these cases nevertheless stand for the proposition that any kind of private sexual conduct between consenting adults is constitutionally insulated from state proscription is unsupportable. Indeed, the Court's opinion in *Carey* twice asserted that the privacy right, which the *Griswold* line of cases found to be one of the protections provided by the Due Process Clause, did not reach so far. . . .

Precedent aside, however, respondent would have us announce, as the Court of Appeals did, a fundamental right to engage in homosexual sodomy. This we are quite unwilling to do. It is true that despite the language of the Due Process Clauses of the Fifth and Fourteenth Amendments, which appears to focus only on the processes by which life, liberty, or property is taken, the cases are legion in which those Clauses have been interpreted to have substantive content, subsuming rights that to a great extent are immune from federal or state regulation or proscription. Among such cases are those recognizing rights that have little or no textual support in the constitutional language. *Meyer, Prince,* and *Pierce* fall in this category, as do the privacy cases from *Griswold* to *Carey.*

Striving to assure itself and the public that announcing rights not readily identifiable in the Constitution's text involves much more than the imposition of the Justices' own choice of values on the States and the Federal Government, the Court has sought to identify the nature of the rights qualifying for heightened judicial protection. In *Palko v. Connecticut* . . . (1937), it was said that this category includes those fundamental liberties that are "implicit in the concept of ordered liberty," such that "neither liberty nor justice would exist if [they] were sacrificed." A different description of fundamental liberties appeared in *Moore v. East Cleveland* . . . (1977) (opinion of POWELL, J.), where they are characterized as those liberties that are "deeply rooted in this Nation's history and tradition.". . .

It is obvious to us that neither of these formulations would extend a fundamental right to homosexuals to engage in acts of consensual sodomy. Proscriptions against that conduct have ancient roots. . . . Sodomy was a criminal offense at common law and was forbidden by the laws of the original thirteen States when they ratified the Bill of Rights. In 1868, when the 24 States and the District of Columbia continue to provide criminal penalties for sodomy performed in private and between consenting adults. . . . Against this background, to claim that a right to engage in such conduct is "deeply rooted in this Nation's history and tradition" or "implicit in the concept of ordered liberty" is, at best, facetious.

[3] Nor are we inclined to take a more expansive view of our authority to discover new fundamental rights imbedded in the Due Process Clause. The Court is most vulnerable and comes nearest to illegitimacy when it deals with judge-made constitutional law having little or no cognizable roots in the language or design of the Constitution. . . .

Respondent, however, asserts that the result should be different where the homosexual conduct occurs in the privacy of the home. He relies on *Stanley v. Georgia*, . . . (1969), where the Court held that the First Amendment prevents conviction for possessing and reading obscene material in the privacy of one's home: "If the First Amendment means anything, it means that a State has no business telling a man, sitting alone in his house, what books he may read or what films he may watch." . . .

Stanley did protect conduct that would not have been protected outside the home, and it partially prevented the enforcement of state obscenity laws; but the decision was firmly grounded in the First Amendment. The right pressed upon us here has no similar support in the text of the Constitution, and it does not qualify for recognition under the prevailing principles for construing the Fourteenth Amendment. Its limits are also difficult to discern. Plainly enough, otherwise illegal conduct is not always immunized whenever it occurs in the home. Victimless crimes, such as the possession and use of illegal drugs, do not escape the law where they are committed at home. *Stanley* itself recognized that its holding offered no protection for the possession in the home of drugs, firearms, or stolen goods. . . . And if respondent's submission is limited to the voluntary sexual conduct between consenting adults, it would be difficult, except by fiat, to limit the claimed right to homosexual conduct while leaving exposed to prosecution adultery, incest, and other sexual crimes even though they are committed in the home. We are unwilling to start down that road.

[4] Even if the conduct at issue here is not a fundamental right, respondent asserts that there must be a rational basis for the law and that there is none in this case other than the presumed belief of a majority of the electorate in Georgia that homosexual sodomy is immoral and unacceptable. This is said to be an inadequate rationale to support the law. The law, however, is constantly based on notions of morality, and if all laws representing essentially moral choices are to be invalidated under the Due Process Clause, the courts will be very busy indeed. Even respondent makes no such claim, but insists that majority sentiments about the morality

of homosexuality should be declared inadequate. We do not agree, and are un-persuaded that the sodomy laws of some 25 States should be invalidated on this basis.

Accordingly, the judgment of the Court of Appeals is

Reversed.

The Law and the Lesbian and Gay Community

Paula L. Ettelbrick

The movement for equality for lesbians and gay men began in this country shortly after World War II. Gay men, on the one hand, and lesbians, on the other, estab-lished their first discussion groups and organizations where they could talk about who they are and begin to dismantle for themselves the internalized hatred they had learned so well from the society in which they lived. While these early groups form the base for the current lesbian and gay rights movement, the rebellion against the police raid of a Greenwich Village bar called the Stonewall Inn ignited a movement seeking not only equality but also liberation.

Police raids of gay bars, arrests of its patrons, and random violence had been common occurrences as it was illegal in many states to associate with known les-bians or gay men in an establishment serving alcohol. Fear of exposure in a hostile society kept many lesbians and gay men from challenging police action. Newspaper publication of an arrest for being in a known gay bar would undoubtedly result in loss of a job, public humiliation, and alienation from family and friends.

The Stonewall Rebellion, which occurred on June 28, 1969, is used as the his-torical marker between pre-Stonewall life, when most lesbians and gay men ac-cepted their lot in the darkness of the closet, and the post-Stonewall transition to challenging discriminatory laws and attitudes.

Prior to Stonewall, very little in the law reflected the existence of lesbians and gay men, much less their right to live freely in society. Their sexual conduct was prohibited by law; their children were routinely taken away from them; they did not dare "come out" at work because of the substantial likelihood that they would lose their jobs; and they could not form student groups on college campuses. Serving in the military was off-limits to them, and even the thought that their relationships would be treated with respect seemed unattainable until recently.

While many vestiges of this past clearly remain, the twenty-five years since the Stonewall Rebellion have marked nothing short of a revolutionary change in the attitudes that have kept lesbians and gay men less than worthy citizens. These changes were not made in a vacuum. As they are being realized, a great debt is owed to the African-American and other communities of color who struggled to make equality not only a legal right but a social value as well. Equal debt is owed to the feminist movement, which raised our national consciousness about the oppression caused by rigid gender roles and the treatment of women as the property of men and of the law. Often, it is the judicial opinions enforcing race and sex equality that provide both the legal and moral guidelines for lesbians and gay men in their struggle for liberation. Needless to say, the current state of the law is mixed at best.

Sodomy Laws

The status of lesbian and gay legal rights must always begin with a discussion of sodomy laws. These laws, which criminalize sexual relations between persons of the same sex, form the cornerstone for discrimination against lesbians and gay men. The potency of these laws lies mainly in their collateral effect. They are used as the basis for denying gay and lesbian parents the right to have custody of and visitation with their children. Sodomy laws have been used to deny them professional licenses, such as those required to practice law. They are used as "proof" of the moral character of lesbians and gay men, or at least to challenge their reputations. In contrast, while most sodomy laws also criminalize oral and anal sex between opposite sex partners, straight people are not routinely denied their children or fired from their job because they had oral sex. Nor are they stigmatized for the mere assumption that they engage in such prohibited behavior.

Before 1961, when Illinois became the first state to drop its sodomy law as part of general criminal law reform, every state in the country made it a crime to engage in oral or anal sex. The premier constitutional challenge to these laws resulted in a 1986 decision of the United States Supreme Court upholding the Georgia sodomy law on the grounds that there is no constitutional right to engage in same-sex sexual conduct. The case involved a gay man, Michael Hardwick, who missed his court date on a disorderly conduct citation. When an Atlanta police officer arrived at Hardwick's home to serve a warrant, a houseguest let him in and directed him to Hardwick's bedroom. The officer walked back to the bedroom, peered in the bedroom door and saw Hardwick engaged in sex with his male lover. The officer arrested Hardwick and charged him with violating Georgia's sodomy law. Though the charges were soon dropped, Hardwick filed a civil law suit challenging the law as an unconstitutional invasion of his right to be free of governmental intrusion into his personal life.

The Supreme Court rejected Hardwick's claim that he had a constitutional right to privacy that allowed him to engage in sex with another consenting adult free from government interference. The decision left the states free to retain their sodomy laws or to readopt laws that had already been dropped during the criminal law reforms of the 1960s.

While some religious right groups lauded the decision, most people—both gay and straight—expressed outrage over a decision that allows the government to enter one's home and arrest people for engaging in adult, consensual sexual conduct. Despite the legal devastation caused by a ruling that enforced a criminal view of lesbians and gay men, the case raised the consciousness of many in the general public about the way the law treats lesbians and gay men. Since the decision in Hardwick's case, the State of Nevada and the District of Columbia have repealed their sodomy laws, and courts in the states of Michigan, Texas, and Kentucky have struck down their laws as violative of state constitutional provisions securing the right to privacy and equal protection.

Federal Law

While some positive change has occurred, the federal government has an unsavory history of explicitly discriminating in both law and practice against lesbians and gay men. The FBI and the CIA, in particular, have long discriminated by denying security clearances to lesbians and gay men on the grounds that they present a security risk. Denying the security clearance is tantamount to denying the job. To justify their actions, the agencies claimed that lesbians and gay men are more capable of being blackmailed if threatened with exposure of their sexual orientation. Recently, such arguments have been widely disparaged. First, the government could not cite a single case of such blackmail. Second, it is unlikely and illogical that a lesbian or gay man who is open about their sexual orientation with family and friends can be blackmailed with the threat of exposure. As these justifications have fallen into disrepute, access to jobs in the federal government has expanded for lesbians and gay men.

Until 1990, federal law banned lesbians and gay men from entering the country. The immigration law prohibited entry to people with "psychopathic personalities," a category deemed to include lesbians and gay men. Anyone daring to enter the country—whether a tourist, a businessperson, or an immigrant—and found to be gay was detained by the Immigration and Naturalization Service (INS) and given the Hobson's choice of remaining in detention until a hearing could be held or going back home. Since it was not uncommon to wait a week for a hearing, most lesbians and gay men simply returned home.

The United States Supreme Court affirmed the ban in 1967. In 1979, the Public Health Service, responding to the American Psychiatric Association's and American Psychological Association's 1973 vote to remove homosexuality from the list of mental disorders, announced an end to the certification of lesbians and gay men as psychopathic personalities. However, the INS continued to harass and detain lesbians and gay men at the borders. Finally, in 1990, the Congress repealed the ban, and lesbians and gay men are now free to immigrate and travel to the United States.

In contrast, the struggles of lesbians and gay men who wish to serve in the military persist. For many years, military regulations explicitly banned lesbians and gay men from serving in any branch of the armed services. If discovered, they were discharged immediately and denied any veterans benefits to which they would otherwise have been entitled. Although gay and lesbian service members now receive honorable discharges, for decades they received dishonorable discharges because they were gay, resulting in service records that haunted them for the rest of their lives because they revealed their sexual orientation.

Despite years of lawsuits challenging the military ban, only recently have the courts begun to question the constitutionality of a regulation that bars lesbians and gay men from service without regard for their individual capabilities. A handful of federal judges have ruled that the ban is unconstitutional. However, some of these decisions are likely to be overturned as the judiciary struggles with its own history of deferring to military rationale and resisting arguments that lesbians and gay men deserve equal protection under the law.

Until recently, the military ban had been enforced through an administrative regulation. Shortly after his election, President Bill Clinton promised to issue an executive order to lift the ban by repealing the regulation, which would allow openly gay and lesbian service members to serve. The announcement caused an explosion among the all-male military brass. Bowing to pressure from the Pentagon (whose own studies have consistently concluded that one's sexual orientation has no bearing on one's ability to serve in the military), the president instead issued an order that left most of the regulation intact, except that the military may no longer ask its members whether they are gay. If their sexual orientation becomes known through other means, though, they may still be discharged.

In other areas, policies have changed. In 1990 Congress enacted the Hate Crimes Statistics Act, which requires states to monitor and report bias-motivated assaults that were based upon the victim's race, national origin, sexual orientation, and other categories. For the first time, sexual orientation appeared as an affirmative category in federal law. Sex, however, was not added as a category in this act, reflecting the persistent resistance to recognizing violence perpetrated against women. For many lesbians, it is often difficult to differentiate an assault based upon one's sexual orientation from one based upon one's sex. Thus, much of the crime perpetrated against lesbians will remain unacknowledged and, therefore, unremedied.

Finally, in late 1993, several federal agencies—including the White House, the Department of Justice, and the FBI—issued policies banning discrimination against employees based upon their sexual orientation, in addition to the typical characteristics of race, sex, religion, and others. Although not legally enforceable, these policies indicate growing support for the notion that characteristics irrelevant to one's ability to perform a job may not be used as the basis for discrimination.

Civil Rights

To date, no federal law bans discrimination in employment, housing, public accommodations, education, and other areas on the basis of sexual orientation, while laws do forbid discrimination on the basis of sex, race, national origin, religion, age, and disability. Not only would a federal law provide a legal remedy to the thousands of lesbians and gay men who endure discriminatory treatment each year, but it also would provide strong moral leadership on the ideal of equality for all people. In addition, it would provide a remedy for a persistent form of discrimination faced by lesbians and gay men: harassment. Despite the horror of cases in which employees have been subjected to public humiliation in the workplace, overtly demeaning behavior, and even assault by coworkers, courts have simply shrugged these cases off as lacking any legal remedy.

On the state and local level, sporadic protections exist. To date, eight states (Wisconsin, Connecticut, Massachusetts, Vermont, New Jersey, Hawaii, Minnesota, and California) and the District of Columbia ban sexual orientation-based discrimination. Several more states have come close to passing civil rights laws, and it is projected that by the end of the decade nearly half of the states will have enacted such laws. On the local level, nearly 100 cities, towns, and counties have likewise outlawed sexual orientation discrimination.

Family Rights

While family matters are not traditionally considered to be civil rights issues, lesbian and gay advocates have increasingly presented them as such because of the systematic way in which their relationships do not receive any of the fundamental social and economic benefits provided to straight couples who marry. Because the law defines family primarily through blood, marriage, and adoption, a good number of families, especially gay and lesbian couples who are barred by law from marriage, are routinely ignored. Regardless of the length of their relationship and the clear care and commitment they give to one another, their relationships have no legal relevance. As a result, if a lesbian becomes seriously ill and is admitted to an intensive care unit, her partner may be barred from seeing her, may be refused any medical update, or may not be given any voice in decisions regarding her care, including whether to discontinue life support. If she has no medical insurance, her partner cannot cover her on her employment plan as she could do for a surviving spouse. Nor would the partner be able to take time for family sick leave or bereavement leave in the event of death. If she dies without a will, her family can, by law, lay claim to all of her belongings. Additionally, the surviving partner would have no right to decide on funeral arrangements or to receive social security survivor's benefits, which are routinely available to surviving spouses to help them through old age. These are only a handful of the thousands of ways that unmarried couples face disadvantages that married couples do not encounter.

The law has slowly begun to respond to these injustices. When a group of lesbian and gay teachers sued the New York City Board of Education for the right to extend health benefits to their domestic partners, as married employees can do for their spouses, the court broke new ground in ruling that the teachers had stated a legal claim of discrimination and could pursue their case. (The case was recently settled and benefits are now available to the partners of all unmarried employees of the City of New York.) When a landlord tried to evict Miguel Braschi from the rent-controlled apartment he shared with his partner who died of AIDS because the law allowed only family members to remain in the apartment after the death of the named tenant, Mr. Braschi took his case to the highest court of New York. That court ruled that because Mr. Braschi and his partner had shared a committed, emotionally and financially interdependent relationship for eleven years, as a gay couple they were entitled to be considered as family. Mr. Braschi was allowed to remain in the apartment. When Karen Thompson fought for over eight years to remain in the life of her partner Sharon Kowalski, who had been disabled in a car accident and whose parents had forbidden visits from Karen after learning they were lesbians, a Minnesota court finally ruled that Karen would be the best legal guardian for Sharon given their close relationship. The court characterized their relationship as a "family of affinity."

Also, a number of cities and dozens of employers now provide domestic partner benefits for the partners and children of lesbian and gay employees. Health and dental benefits, paid sick leave to care for ill family members, and paid bereavement leave to mourn the loss of an immediate family member are provided to millions of employees through their workplace benefits plans. However, where these benefits are extended only to married spouses and biological/adoptive children, married employees are paid more by the company for their work than unmarried employees who do not receive such benefits for their partners or the children they may be raising with their partners. To remedy this pay inequity, some employers provide family benefits to unmarried employees who can establish that they are in a longtime, committed relationship and share the same residence with their partner. All of the cities that have adopted such policies extend the benefits to both gay/lesbian and straight couples. Most of the employers have opted to only extend them to lesbian/gay couples.

In addition to the cases that have broken barriers between the rights of married couples and those of unmarried couples, legal challenges to gain the right to marry for same-sex couples continue to be filed around the country. In the 1970s, courts unanimously rejected any claim that lesbian and gay couples should be entitled to marry. However, a significant breakthrough came in 1993 when the Hawaii Supreme Court ruled that the state marriage law may violate the constitutional right to equal protection. The court ordered the state to present its rationale for denying the privilege of marriage to same-sex partners. By law, the reasons must be compelling enough to justify the exclusion of an entire class of people from a right as fundamental as marriage. If the state is unable to offer a compelling justification, the court presumably will order that gay and lesbian couples be allowed to marry.

Relationships with children is another area where the law reflects society's bias against and false impressions of lesbians and gay men. Despite more than forty years of challenges to the belief that lesbians and gay men are unfit parents, it remains legal in many states to take children out of the home of a lesbian mother or a gay father. In fact, every study done in the last twenty years has concluded that the children of lesbian mothers are just as likely to be well adjusted as those of straight mothers.

There are, of course, many states where custody or visitation may not be denied without showing that the parent's sexual orientation would harm the child. Courts have steadily rejected the old prejudices that gay parents will molest their children (more than 90 percent of child sexual abuse is perpetrated by straight men); that the children will grow up gay (most lesbians and gay men were raised by straight parents whose sexual orientation clearly had little influence on their own); or that their behavior is illegal, thus immoral (the steady demise of sodomy laws has weakened this argument). Some courts still deny custody on the basis that the children will be stigmatized when it becomes known that the parent is lesbian or gay. These rulings play directly into the hands of bigots by taking children away merely because some others may make fun of these kids.

Yet, the openness of a growing number of lesbians and gay men who desire to raise children and who are doing so has led to remarkable changes in the law in other family areas. Although two states, Florida and New Hampshire, bar them from adopting, many states allow lesbians and gay men to adopt children, though for the most part only one member of the couple is allowed to be the adoptive parent. Most laws prohibit unmarried couples from adopting together. Lesbians are more likely to choose biological parenting by inseminating with the sperm of a donor. Because only the biological mother is recognized by law as the parent, the other mother has no legal relationship to the child despite the couple's desire to raise the children as equal parents. Lesbian families thus live in constant fear that the child could be taken away should the biological mother die or become otherwise unable to care for the child. In cases where the couple has separated, courts have been nearly unanimous in denying visitation rights to the nonbiological mother on the theory that only biological parents are real parents.

To provide greater family security to the children of lesbian mothers, some local courts have allowed the nonbiological parent to adopt her partner's children. These "second parent" adoptions allow both women to be legally recognized parents of the child. Thus, the child may inherit property from both parents, be assured of a continued relationship with both should one parent die or the couple separate, and both parents are obligated by law to provide financial support.

Despite attempts by the religious right-wing to characterize lesbians and gay families as being antifamily, the growing visibility of lesbian and gay couples in long-term committed relationships has begun to rebut such claims and their underlying prejudices. As one of the courts that granted a second parent adoption to a lesbian mother stated, in this world, children are lucky to have one parent who loves and cares for them, much less two mothers who do so.

Right Wing Antigay Initiatives

As they become successful, all social movements face a backlash from those who are threatened by change. Gains made to promote diversity in educational materials, to recognize that bias violence and speech cause real harm, by women to control their own bodies, and to protect the rights of those historically facing discrimination face challenges. Currently, the religious right wing has stirred up a backlash against the small gains made by lesbians and gay men to become equal citizens.

A striking example of this backlash occurred in 1993 when the citizens of Colorado voted to amend their state constitution so that lesbians and gay men would forever be denied the right to seek redress for discrimination based on their sexual orientation. Under this ballot initiative, promoted by a group calling itself Colorado for Family Values, lesbians and gay men would be denied access both to the state courts to bring their cases and to the political process to seek protection under the law, since Colorado's government would be barred from passing any law protecting the rights of lesbians and gay men. The courts in Colorado have struck down the amendment as unconstitutional and contrary to the democratic system, which allows each citizen the right to engage in the political process.

The religious right has fanned out across the country, promoting such initiatives in Oregon, Florida, Washington, Cincinnati, and dozens of other targeted cities and states. Because the promoters of these ballot initiatives are able to draw on people's fears and prejudices about a group of people they largely do not know or understand, most of these amendments have been passed by the voters. It is up to the courts, now, to uphold once again the premise upon which all of us rely: that each citizen is entitled to equality, regardless of race, sex, national origin, disability, religion—and sexual orientation.

Suggestions for Further Reading

Acuna, Rudolpho. *Occupied America: A History of Chicanos.* New York: Harper & Row, 1987.

Aptheker, B. *Woman's Legacy: Essays on Race, Sex, and Class in American History.* Amherst: University of Massachusetts Press, 1982.

Baxendall, R., L. Gordon, and S. Reverby. *America's Working Women: A Documentary History—1600 to the Present.* New York: Random House, 1976.

Berlin, Ira. *Free at Last?* Boston: Little, Brown, 1991.

Berry, M. F., and J. W. Blassingame. *Long Memory: The Black Experience in America.* New York: Oxford University Press, 1982.

Boyer, R. O., and H. Morais. *Labor's Untold Story.* New York: United Electrical, Radio and Machine Workers of America, 1972.

Cluster, D., ed. *They Should Have Served That Cup of Coffee.* Boston: South End Press, 1979.

Cott, Nancy F. *Root of Bitterness: Documents of the Social History of American Women.* Boston: Northeastern Press, 1986.

Deitz, James L. Economic *History of Puerto Rico: Institutional Change and Capitalist Development.* Princeton, N.J.: Princeton University Press, 1986.

Duberman, Martin Baum, Martha Vicinus, and George Chauncey, Jr. *Hidden from History: Reclaiming the Gay and Lesbian Past.* New York: New American Library, 1989.

DuBois, Ellen, and Vicki Ruis: *Unequal Sisters.* New York: Routledge and Kegan Paul, 1990.

Flexner, E. *Century of Struggle.* Cambridge, Mass.: Harvard University Press, 1976.

Gee, E., ed. *Counterpoint: Perspectives on Asian Americans.* Los Angeles: Asian American Studies Center, University of California, Los Angeles, 1976.

Giddings, P. *When and Where I Enter: The Impact of Black Women on Race and Sex in America.* New York: Bantam Books, 1976.

Jacobs, P., and S. Landau, eds. *To Serve the Devil.* Vol.1, *Natives and Slaves*; Vol.2, *Colonials and Sojourners: A Documentary Analysis of America's Racial History and Why It Has Been Kept Hidden.* New York: Vintage Books, 1971.

Katz, Jonathan. *Gay American History: Lesbians and Gay Men in the U.S.: A Documentary History.* New York: Avon Books, 1984.

Konig, Hans. *The Conquest of America: How the Indian Nations Lost Their Continent.* New York: Monthly Review Press, 1993.

Mintz, Sidney. *Caribbean Transformations.* Baltimore, Md.: Johns Hopkins Press, 1974.

Robson, Ruthann. *Lesbian (Out)Law: Survival under the Rule of Law.* Ithaca, N.Y.: Firebrand Books, 1992.

Stampp, K. M. *The Peculiar Institution: Slavery in the Ante-Bellum South.* New York: Vintage Books, 1956.

Takaki, Ronald. A *Different Mirror: Multicultural American History.* Boston: Little, Brown, 1993.

Takaki, Ronald. *From Different Shores: Perspectives on Race and Culture in America.* New York: Oxford University Press, 1987.

United States Commission on Human Rights. *Indian Tribes: A Continuing Quest for Survival.* Washington, D.C.: United States Commission on Human Rights, 1981.

Wagenheim, K., and O. J. Wagenheim, eds. *The Puerto Ricans: A Documentary History.* New York: Praeger, 1973.

Creating and Maintaining Hierarchy: Stereotypes, Language, Ideology, Violence, and Social Control

 T he most effective forms of social control are always invisible. Tanks in the streets and armed militia serve as constant reminders that people are not free and provide a focus for anger and an impetus for rebellion. More effective by far are the beliefs and attitudes a society fosters to rationalize and reinforce prevailing distributions of power and opportunity. It is here that stereotypes, ideology, and language have roles to play. They shape how we see ourselves and others; they affect how we define social issues; and they determine who we hold responsible for society's ills. Each plays a part in persuading people that differences in wealth, power, and opportunity are reflections of natural differences among people, not a result of the economic and political organization of society. If they are really effective, they go beyond rationalizing inequality to making it invisible. The social construction of gender, race, and class as hierarchy that we examined in Part I of this book is at the heart of the belief system that makes the prevailing distribution of wealth and opportunity appear natural and inevitable rather than arbitrary and alterable. In our society, stereotypes, ideology, and language have played a critical role in perpetuating racism, sexism, and class privilege even at those times when the law has been used as a vehicle to fight discrimination rather than maintain it.

The selections in Part VI examine some of the ways in which the unconscious beliefs we hold about ourselves and others reinforce existing social roles and class positions and blunt social criticism. Stereotypes and beliefs are perpetuated by the institutions in society. In addition to providing us with information and values, education, religion, and the family encourage us to adopt a particular picture of the world and our place in it. These institutions shape our perceptions of others and provide us with a sense of our own future. The curriculum from elementary school through college and beyond presents a world that is firmly anchored in white, male, European traditions and knowledge. Rather than identifying and contextualizing its perspective, the curriculum offers this narrow piece of the past and present as if it were coextensive with reality. In addition to severely limiting our understanding of the past and present, the curriculum defines what *counts* as knowledge and culture in ways that obliterate the contributions of all but a few. The mass media also provides us with information and values and teaches us who and what we should regard as important. Along with other institutions the mass media shapes our definition of community, painting a picture of a society divided between "us" and "them." By making inequities and suffering appear to be the result of personal or group deficiency rather than injustice, stereotypes, ideology, and language reconcile people to the way things are and prevent them from asking how things might be. Violence and the threat of violence reinforces ideology and threatens those who challenge the prevailing system or its stereotypes and prescriptions with pain or death.

In addition to creating and maintaining mistaken beliefs about the reason for unequal distribution of privilege, stereotypes can play an important role in reconciling individuals to discriminatory treatment. If stereotypes are really effective they can prevent individuals not only from recognizing discrimination but even from encountering it by ensuring that they do not seek opportunities that are unavailable to members of their groups.

In "Self-Fulfilling Stereotypes," Mark Snyder uses examples from current psychological research to show how important our expectations are in shaping our perceptions of others and in determining how we behave. These studies raise serious questions about the "objectivity" of our evaluations of job candidates or candidates for admission to educational programs and suggest that our perceptions often say more about unconscious stereotyping and expectations than about other people. As Snyder points out, some of the most interesting studies being done in the field of education show that teachers' expectations are at least as important as "innate ability" in determining how well young children do in school. These expectations are often shaped unconsciously by the racist and sexist stereotypes that pervade our language.

The many ways in which our language smuggles in negative images of women and people of color are explored in the selections by Robert B. Moore and Haig Bosmajian. Language can provide valuable clues to unconscious attitudes in a society, but some people have difficulty analyzing language because they dismiss it as trivial or because they have trouble believing that *what* we call something affects *how* we feel about it. These selections ask us to take language seriously. Taken together with Richard Mohr's discussion of gay stereotypes, Jean Kilbourne's account of images of women in advertising, and Gregory Mantsios's analysis of the media's portrayal of class, these selections suggest that language, stereotyping, and ideology often result in the creation of "the other," a way of seeing members of certain groups that strips them of their humanity and makes it possible for us to treat them in ways that would otherwise horrify us. Peggy Sanday's account of the role of gang rape in the social construction of masculinity provides another insight into this process, and Carole Sheffield's article on hate-violence, which follows, describes and analyzes some of the consequences of these depictions.

In Selection 8, William Chafe examines the impact of both race and gender stereotypes and ideology by drawing an analogy between sex and race. He argues persuasively that both racism and sexism function analogously as forms of social control. Although Chafe suggests he is comparing the experiences of white women with those of African-Americans, a careful reading of this essay suggests he is really comparing the experience of white women to those of Black men. The reader might be interested to see whether Chafe's claim about racism and sexism and social control holds up equally well when we construct similar accounts of the experiences of African-American women as well as members of other racial/ethnic groups discussed in this book. Chafe begins by analyzing how stereotypes, ideology, and language function to distort our expectations, perceptions, and experience and then proceeds to ask whose interests are served by this distortion.

Often, people become overwhelmed and discouraged when they realize how much our unconscious images and beliefs affect our ways of seeing each other and the world and, as a result, fail to go on to analyze the consequences of ideology. Believing that people are naturally prejudiced and can't change is one more bit of ideology that prevents us from taking control of our lives. And ideology is dangerous because it prevents us from questioning prevailing social and economic arrangements and asking whether they serve the best interest of all the people. By dividing us from each other and confusing us as to who really profits from these arrangements, ideology and stereotypes imprison us in a false world. In the final part of this book, a number of thinkers will offer their suggestions about how to move beyond race, class, and gender divisions.

Self-Fulfilling Stereotypes

Mark Snyder

Gordon Allport, the Harvard psychologist who wrote a classic work on the nature of prejudice, told a story about a child who had come to believe that people who lived in Minneapolis were called monopolists. From his father, moreover, he had learned that monopolists were evil folk. It wasn't until many years later, when he discovered his confusion, that his dislike of residents of Minneapolis vanished.

Allport knew, of course, that it was not so easy to wipe out prejudice and erroneous stereotypes. Real prejudice, psychologists like Allport argued, was buried deep in human character, and only a restructuring of education could begin to root it out. Yet many people whom I meet while lecturing seem to believe that stereotypes are simply beliefs or attitudes that change easily with experience. Why do some people express the view that Italians are passionate, blacks are lazy, Jews materialistic, and lesbians mannish in their demeanor? In the popular view, it is because they have not learned enough about the diversity among these groups and have not had enough contact with members of the groups for their stereotypes to be challenged by reality. With more experience, it is presumed, most people of good will are likely to revise their stereotypes.

My research over the past decade convinces me that there is little justification for such optimism—and not only for the reasons given by Allport. While it is true that deep prejudice is often based on the needs of pathological character structure, stereotypes are obviously quite common even among fairly normal individuals. When people first meet others, they cannot help noticing certain highly visible and distinctive characteristics: sex, race, physical appearance, and the like. Despite people's best intentions, their initial impressions of others are shaped by their assumptions about such characteristics.

What is critical, however, is that these assumptions are not merely beliefs or attitudes that exist in a vacuum; they are reinforced by the behavior of both prejudiced people and the targets of their prejudice. In recent years, psychologists have collected considerable laboratory evidence about the processes that strengthen stereotypes and put them beyond the reach of reason and good will.

My own studies initially focused on first encounters between strangers. It did not take long to discover, for example, that people have very different ways of treating those whom they regard as physically attractive and those whom they consider physically unattractive, and that these differences tend to bring out precisely those kinds of behavior that fit with stereotypes about attractiveness.

In an experiment that I conducted with my colleagues Elizabeth Decker Tanke and Ellen Berscheid, pairs of college-age men and women met and became acquainted in telephone conversations. Before the conversations began, each man received a Polaroid snapshot, presumably taken just moments before, of the woman he would soon meet. The photograph, which had actually been prepared before the experiment began, showed either a physically attractive woman or a physically unattractive one. By randomly choosing which picture to use for each conversation, we insured that there was no consistent relationship between the attractiveness of the woman in the picture and the attractiveness of the woman in the conversation.

By questioning the men, we learned that even before the conversations began, stereotypes about physical attractiveness came into play. Men who looked forward to talking with physically attractive women said that they expected to meet decidedly sociable, poised, humorous, and socially adept people, while men who thought that they were about to get acquainted with unattractive women fashioned images of rather unsociable, awkward, serious, and socially inept creatures. Moreover, the men proved to have very different styles of getting acquainted with women whom they thought to be attractive and those whom they believed to be unattractive. Shown a photograph of an attractive woman, they behaved with warmth, friendliness, humor, and animation. However, when the woman in the picture was unattractive, the men were cold, uninteresting, and reserved.

These differences in the men's behavior elicited behavior in the women that was consistent with the men's stereotyped assumptions. Women who were believed (unbeknown to them) to be physically attractive behaved in a friendly, likeable, and sociable manner. In sharp contrast, women who were perceived as physically unattractive adopted a cool, aloof, and distant manner. So striking were the differences in the women's behavior that they could be discerned simply by listening to tape recordings of the woman's side of the conversations. Clearly, by acting upon their stereotyped beliefs about the women whom they would be meeting, the men had initiated a chain of events that produced *behavioral confirmation* for their beliefs.

Similarly, Susan Anderson and Sandra Bem have shown in an experiment at Stanford University that when the tables are turned—when it is women who have pictures of men they are to meet on the telephone—many women treat the men according to their presumed physical attractiveness, and by so doing encourage the men to confirm their stereotypes. Little wonder, then, that so many people remain convinced that good looks and appealing personalities go hand in hand.

Sex and Race

It is experiments such as these that point to a frequently unnoticed power of stereotypes: the power to influence social relationships in ways that create the illusion of reality. In one study, Berna Skrypnek and I arranged for pairs of previously unacquainted students to interact in a situation that permitted us to control the information that each one received about the apparent sex of the other. The two people were seated in separate rooms so that they could neither see nor hear each other. Using a system of signal lights that they operated with switches, they negotiated a division of labor, deciding which member of the pair would perform each of several tasks that differed in sex-role connotations. The tasks varied along the dimensions of masculinity and femininity: sharpen a hunting knife (masculine), polish a pair of shoes (neutral), iron a shirt (feminine).

One member of the team was led to believe that the other was, in one condition of the experiment, male; in the other, female. As we had predicted, the first member's belief about the sex of the partner influenced the outcome of the pair's negotiations. Women whose partners believed them to be men generally chose stereotypically masculine tasks; in contrast, women whose partners believed that they were women usually chose stereotypically feminine tasks. The experiment thus suggests that much sex-role behavior may be the product of other people's stereotyped and often erroneous beliefs.

In a related study at the University of Waterloo, Carl von Baeyer, Debbie Sherk, and Mark Zanna have shown how stereotypes about sex roles operate in job interviews. The researchers arranged to have men conduct simulated job interviews with women supposedly seeking positions as research assistants. The investigators informed half of the women that the men who would interview them held traditional views about the ideal woman, believing her to be very emotional, deferential to her husband, home-oriented, and passive. The rest of the women were told that their interviewer saw the ideal woman as independent, competitive, ambitious, and dominant. When the women arrived for their interviews, the researchers noticed that most of them had dressed to meet the stereotyped expectations of their prospective interviewers. Women who expected to see a traditional interviewer had chosen very feminine-looking makeup, clothes, and accessories. During the interviews (videotaped through a one-way mirror) these women behaved in traditionally feminine ways and gave traditionally feminine answers to questions such as "Do you have plans to include children and marriage with your career plans?"

Once more, then, we see the self-fulfilling nature of stereotypes. Many sex differences, it appears, may result from the images that people create in their attempts to act out accepted sex roles. The implication is that if stereotyped expectations about sex roles shift, behavior may change, too. In fact, statements by people who have undergone sex-change operations have highlighted the power of such expectations in easing adjustment to a new life. As the writer Jan Morris said in recounting the story of her transition from James to Jan: "The more I was treated as a woman, the more woman I became."

The power of stereotypes to cause people to confirm stereotyped expectations can also be seen in interracial relationships. In the first of two investigations done at Princeton University by Carl Word, Mark Zanna, and Joel Cooper, white undergraduates interviewed both white and black job applicants. The applicants were actually confederates of the experimenters, trained to behave consistently from interview to interview, no matter how the interviewers acted toward them.

To find out whether or not the white interviewers would behave differently toward white and black job applicants, the researchers secretly videotaped each interview and then studied the tapes. From these, it was apparent that there were substantial differences in the treatment accorded blacks and whites. For one thing, the interviewers' speech deteriorated when they talked to blacks, displaying more errors in grammar and pronunciation. For another, the interviewers spent less time with blacks than with whites and showed less "immediacy," as the researchers called it, in their manner. That is, they were less friendly, less outgoing, and more reserved with blacks.

In the second investigation, white confederates were trained to approximate the immediate or the nonimmediate interview styles that had been observed in the first investigation as they interviewed white job applicants. A panel of judges who evaluated the tapes agreed that applicants subjected to the nonimmediate styles performed less adequately and were more nervous than job applicants treated in the immediate style. Apparently, then, the blacks in the first study did not have a chance to display their qualifications to the best advantage. Considered together, the two investigations suggest that in interracial encounters, racial stereotypes may constrain behavior in ways to cause both blacks and whites to behave in accordance with those stereotypes.

Rewriting Biography

Having adopted stereotyped ways of thinking about another person, people tend to notice and remember the ways in which that person seems to fit the stereotype, while resisting evidence that contradicts the stereotype. In one investigation that I conducted with Seymour Uranowitz, student subjects read a biography of a fictitious woman named Betty K. We constructed the story of her life so that it would fit the stereotyped images of both lesbians and heterosexuals. Betty, we wrote, never had a steady boyfriend in high school, but did go out on dates. And although we gave her a steady boyfriend in college, we specified that he was more of a close friend than anything else. A week after we had distributed this biography, we gave our subjects some new information about Betty. We told some students that she was now living with another woman in a lesbian relationship; we told others that she was living with her husband.

To see what impact stereotypes about sexuality would have on how people remembered the facts of Betty's life, we asked each student to answer a series of questions about her life history. When we examined their answers, we found that the students had reconstructed the events of Betty's past in ways that supported their own stereotyped beliefs about her sexual orientation. Those who believed that Betty was a lesbian remembered that Betty had never had a steady boyfriend in high school, but tended to neglect the fact that she had gone out on many dates in college. Those who believed that Betty was now a heterosexual tended to remember that she had formed a steady relationship with a man in college, but tended to ignore the fact that this relationship was more of a friendship than a romance.

The students showed not only selective memories but also a striking facility for interpreting what they remembered in ways that added fresh support for their stereotypes. One student who accurately remembered that a supposedly lesbian Betty never had a steady boyfriend in high school confidently pointed to the fact as an early sign of her lack of romantic or sexual interest in men. A student who correctly remembered that a purportedly lesbian Betty often went out on dates in college was sure that these dates were signs of Betty's early attempts to mask her lesbian interests.

Clearly, the students had allowed their preconceptions about lesbians and heterosexuals to dictate the way in which they interpreted and reinterpreted the facts of Betty's life. As long as stereotypes make it easy to bring to mind evidence that supports them and difficult to bring to mind evidence that undermines them, people will cling to erroneous beliefs.

Stereotypes in the Classroom and Work Place

The power of one person's beliefs to make other people conform to them has been well demonstrated in real life. Back in the 1960s, as most people well remember, Harvard psychologist Robert Rosenthal and his colleague Lenore Jacobson entered elementary-school classrooms and identified one out of every five pupils in each room as a child who could be expected to show dramatic improvement in intellectual achievement during the school year. What the teachers did not know was that the children had been chosen on a random basis. Nevertheless, something happened in the relationships between teachers and their supposedly gifted pupils that led the children to make clear gains in test performance.

It can also do so on the job. Albert King, now a professor of management at Northern Illinois University, told a welding instructor in a vocational training center that five men in his training program had unusually high aptitude. Although these five had been chosen at random and knew nothing of their designation as high-aptitude workers, they showed substantial changes in performance. They were absent less often than were other workers, learned the basics of the welder's trade in about half the usual time, and scored a full 10 points higher than other trainees on a welding test. Their gains were noticed not only by the researcher and by the welding instructor, but also by other trainees, who singled out the five as their preferred coworkers.

Might not other expectations influence the relationships between supervisors and workers? For example, supervisors who believe that men are better suited to some jobs and women to others may treat their workers (wittingly or unwittingly) in ways that encourage them to perform their jobs in accordance with stereotypes about differences between men and women. These same stereotypes may determine who gets which job in the first place. Perhaps some personnel managers allow stereotypes to influence, subtly or not so subtly, the way in which they interview job candidates, making it likely that candidates who fit the stereotypes show up better than job-seekers who do not fit them.

Unfortunately, problems of this kind are compounded by the fact that members of stigmatized groups often subscribe to stereotypes about themselves. That is what Amerigo Farina and his colleagues at the University of Connecticut found when they measured the impact upon mental patients of believing that others knew their psychiatric history. In Farina's study, each mental patient cooperated with another person in a game requiring teamwork. Half of the patients believed that their partners knew they were patients, the other half believed that their partners thought they were nonpatients. In reality, the nonpatients never knew a thing about any-one's psychiatric history. Nevertheless, simply believing that others were aware of their history led the patients to feel less appreciated, to find the task more difficult, and to perform poorly. In addition, objective observers saw them as more tense, more anxious, and more poorly adjusted than patients who believed that their status was not known. Seemingly, the belief that others perceived them as stigmatized caused them to play the role of stigmatized patients.

Consequences for Society

Apparently, good will and education are not sufficient to subvert the power of stereotypes. If people treat others in such a way as to bring out behavior that supports stereotypes, they may never have an opportunity to discover which of their stereotypes are wrong.

I suspect that even if people were to develop doubts about the accuracy of their stereotypes, chances are they would proceed to test them by gathering precisely the evidence that would appear to confirm them.

The experiments I have described help to explain the persistence of stereotypes. But, as is so often the case, solving one puzzle only creates another. If by acting as if false stereotypes were true, people lead others, too, to act as if they were true, why do the stereotypes not come to *be* true? Why, for example, have researchers found so little evidence that attractive people are generally friendly, sociable, and outgoing and that unattractive people are generally shy and aloof?

I think that the explanation goes something like this: Very few among us have the kind of looks that virtually everyone considers either very attractive or very unattractive. Our looks make us rather attractive to some people but somewhat less attractive to other people. When we spend time with those who find us attractive, they will tend to bring out our more sociable sides, but when we are with those who find us less attractive, they will bring out our less sociable sides. Although our actual physical appearance does not change, we present ourselves quite differently to our admirers and to our detractors. For our admirers we become attractive people, and for our detractors we become unattractive. This mixed pattern of behavior will prevent the development of any consistent relationship between physical attractiveness and personality.

Now that I understand some of the powerful forces that work to perpetuate social stereotypes, I can see a new mission for my research. I hope, on the one hand, to find out how to help people see the flaws in their stereotypes. On the other hand, I would like to help the victims of false stereotypes find ways of liberating themselves from the constraints imposed on them by other members of society.

2

Racism in the English Language

Robert B. Moore

Language and Culture

An integral part of any culture is its language. Language not only develops in conjunction with a society's historical, economic and political evolution; it also reflects that society's attitudes and thinking. Language not only *expresses* ideas and concepts but actually *shapes* thought.[1] If one accepts that our dominant white culture is racist, then one would expect our language—an indispensable transmitter of culture—to be racist as well. Whites, as the dominant group, are not subjected to the same abusive characterization by our language that people of color receive. Aspects of racism in the English language that will be discussed in this essay include terminology, symbolism, politics, ethnocentrism, and context.

Before beginning our analysis of racism in language we would like to quote part of a TV film review which shows the connection between language and culture.[2]

Depending on one's culture, one interacts with time in a very distinct fashion. One example which gives some cross-cultural insights into the concept of time is language. In Spanish, a watch is said to "walk." In English, the watch "runs." In German, the watch "functions." And in French, the watch "marches." In the Indian culture of the Southwest, people do not refer to time in this way. The value of the watch is displaced with the value of "what time it's getting to be." Viewing these five cultural perspectives of time, one can see some definite emphasis and values that each culture places on time. For example, a cultural perspective may provide a clue to why the negative stereotype of the slow and lazy Mexican who lives in the "Land of Manana" exists in the Anglo value system, where time "flies," the watch "runs" and "time is money."

A Short Play on "Black" and "White" Words

Some may blackly (angrily) accuse me of trying to blacken (defame) the English language, to give it a black eye (a mark of shame) by writing such black words (hostile). They may denigrate (to cast aspersions; to darken) me by accusing me of being blackhearted (malevolent), of having a black outlook (pessimistic, dismal) on life, of being a blackguard (scoundrel)—which would certainly be a black mark (detrimental fact) against me. Some may black-brow (scowl at) me and hope that a black cat crosses in front of me because of this black deed. I may become a black sheep (one who causes shame or embarrassment because of deviation from the accepted standards), who will be blackballed (ostracized) by being placed on a blacklist (list of undesirables) in an attempt to blackmail (to force or coerce into a particular action) me to retract my words. But attempts to blackjack (to compel by threat) me will have a Chinaman's chance of success, for I am not a yellow-bellied Indian-giver of words, who will whitewash (cover up or gloss over vices or crimes) a black lie (harmful, inexcusable). I challenge the purity and innocence (white) of the English language. I don't see things in black and white (entirely bad or entirely good) terms, for I am a white man (marked by upright firmness) if there ever was one. However, it would be a black day when I would not "call a spade a spade," even though some will suggest a white man calling the English language racist is like the pot calling the kettle black. While many may be niggardly (grudging, scanty) in their support, others will be honest and decent—and to them I say, that's very white of you (honest, decent).

The preceding is of course a white lie (not intended to cause harm), meant only to illustrate some examples of racist terminology in the English language.

Obvious Bigotry

Perhaps the most obvious aspect of racism in language would be terms like "nigger," "spook," "chink," "spic," etc. While these may be facing increasing social disdain, they certainly are not dead. Large numbers of white Americans continue to utilize these terms. "Chink," "gook," and "slant-eyes" were in common usage among U.S. troops in Vietnam. An NBC nightly news broadcast, in February 1972, reported that the basketball team in Pekin, Illinois, was called the "Pekin Chinks" and noted that even though this had been protested by Chinese Americans, the term continued to be used because it was easy, and meant no harm. Spiro Agnew's widely reported "fat Jap" remark and the "little Jap" comment of lawyer John Wilson during the Watergate hearings, are surface indicators of a deep-rooted Archie Bunkerism.

Many white people continue to refer to Black people as "colored," as for instance in a July 30, 1975 *Boston Globe* article on a racist attack by whites on a group of Black people using a public beach in Boston. One white person was quoted as follows:

> We've always welcomed good colored people in South Boston but we will not tolerate radical blacks or Communists. . . . Good colored people are welcome in South Boston, black militants are not.

Many white people may still be unaware of the disdain many African Americans have for the term "colored," but it often appears that whether used intentionally or unintentionally, "colored" people are "good" and "know their place," while "Black" people are perceived as "uppity" and "threatening" to many whites. Similarly, the term "boy" to refer to African American men is now acknowledged to be a demeaning term, though still in common use. Other terms such as "the pot calling the kettle black" and "calling a spade a spade" have negative racial connotations but are still frequently used, as for example when President Ford was quoted in February 1976 saying that even though Daniel Moynihan had left the U.N., the U.S. would continue "calling a spade a spade."

Color Symbolism

The symbolism of white as positive and black as negative is pervasive in our culture, with the black/white words used in the beginning of this essay only one of many aspects. "Good guys" wear white hats and ride white horses, "bad guys" wear black hats and ride black horses. Angels are white, and devils are black. The definition of *black* includes "without any moral light or goodness, evil, wicked, indicating disgrace, sinful," while that of *white* includes "morally pure, spotless, innocent, free from evil intent."

A children's TV cartoon program, *Captain Scarlet*, is about an organization called Spectrum, whose purpose is to save the world from an evil extraterrestrial force called the Mysterons. Everyone in Spectrum has a color name—Captain Scarlet, Captain Blue, etc. The one Spectrum agent who has been mysteriously taken over by the Mysterons and works to advance their evil aims is Captain Black. The person who heads Spectrum, the good organization out to defend the world, is Colonel White.

Three of the dictionary definitions of white are "fairness of complexion, purity, innocence." These definitions affect the standards of beauty in our culture, in which whiteness represents the norm. "Blondes have more fun" and "Wouldn't you really rather be a blonde" are sexist in their attitudes toward women generally, but are racist white standards when applied to third world women. A 1971 *Mademoiselle* advertisement pictured a curly-headed, ivory-skinned woman over the caption, "When you go blonde go all the way," and asked: "Isn't this how, in the back of your mind, you always wanted to look? All wide-eyed and silky blonde down to there, and innocent?" Whatever the advertising people meant by this particular woman's innocence, one must remember that "innocent" is one of the definitions of the word white. This standard of beauty when preached to all women is racist. The statement "Isn't this how, in the back of your mind, you always wanted to look?" either ignores third world women or assumes they long to be white.

Time magazine in its coverage of the Wimbledon tennis competition between the black Australian Evonne Goolagong and the white American Chris Evert described Ms. Goolagong as "the dusky daughter of an Australian sheepshearer," while Ms. Evert was "a fair young girl from the middle-class groves of Florida." *Dusky* is a synonym of "black" and is defined as "having dark skin; of a dark color; gloomy; dark; swarthy." Its antonyms are "fair" and "blonde." *Fair* is defined in part as "free from blemish, imperfection, or anything that impairs the appearance, quality, or character; pleasing in appearance, attractive; clean; pretty; comely." By defining Evonne Goolagong as "dusky," *Time* technically defined her as the opposite of "pleasing in appearance; attractive; clean; pretty; comely."

The studies of Kenneth B. Clark, Mary Ellen Goodman, Judith Porter and others indicate that this persuasive "rightness of whiteness" in U.S. culture affects children before the age of four, providing white youngsters with a false sense of superiority and encouraging self-hatred among third world youngsters.

Ethnocentrism or from a White Perspective

Some words and phrases that are commonly used represent particular perspectives and frames of reference, and those often distort the understanding of the reader or listener. David R. Burgest[3] has written about the effect of using the terms "slave" or "master." He argues that the psychological impact of the statement referring to "the master raped his slave" is different from the impact of the same statement substituting the words: "the white captor raped an African woman held in captivity."

> Implicit in the English usage of the "master-slave" concept is ownership of the "slave" by the "master," therefore, the "master" is merely abusing his property (slave). In reality, the captives (slave) were African individuals with human worth, right and dignity and the term "slave" denounces that human quality thereby making the mass rape of African women by white captors more acceptable in the minds of people and setting a mental frame of reference for legitimizing the atrocities perpetuated against African people.

The term slave connotes a less than human quality and turns the captive person into a thing. For example, two McGraw-Hill Far Eastern Publishers textbooks (1970) stated, "At first it was the slaves who worked the cane and they got only food for it. Now men work cane and get money." Next time you write about slavery or read about it, try transposing all "slaves" into "African people held in captivity," "Black people forced to work for no pay" or "African people stolen from their families and societies." While it is more cumbersome, such phrasing conveys a different meaning.

Passive Tense

Another means by which language shapes our perspective has been noted by Thomas Greenfield,[4] who writes that the achievements of Black people—and Black people themselves—have been hidden in

> the linguistic ghetto of the passive voice, the subordinate clause, and the "understood" subject. The seemingly innocuous distinction (between active/passive voice) holds enormous implications for writers and speakers. When it is effectively applied, the rhetorical impact of the passive voice—the art of making the creator or instigator of action totally disappear from a reader's perception—can be devastating.

For instance, some history texts will discuss how European immigrants came to the United States seeking a better life and expanded opportunities, but will note that "slaves *were brought* to America." Not only does this omit the destruction of African societies and families, but it ignores the role of northern merchants and southern slaveholders in the profitable trade in human beings. Other books will state that "the continental railroad *was built*," conveniently omitting information about the Chinese laborers who built much of it or the oppression they suffered.

Another example. While touring Monticello, Greenfield noted that the tour guide

> made all the black people at Monticello disappear through her use of the passive voice. While speaking of the architectural achievements of Jefferson in the active voice, she unfailingly shifted to passive when speaking of the work performed by Negro slaves and skilled servants.

Noting a type of door that after 166 years continued to operate without need for repair, Greenfield remarks that the design aspect of the door was much simpler than the actual skill and work involved in building and installing it. Yet his guide stated: "Mr. Jefferson designed these doors . . ." while "the doors **were installed** in 1809." The workers who installed these doors were African people whom Jefferson held in bondage. The guide's use of the passive tense enabled her to dismiss the reality of Jefferson's slaveholding. It also meant that she did not have to make any mention of the skills of those people held in bondage.

Politics and Terminology

"Culturally deprived," "economically disadvantaged" and "underdeveloped" are other terms which mislead and distort our awareness of reality. The application of the term "culturally deprived" and third world children in this society reflects a value judgment. It assumes that the dominant whites are cultured and all others without culture. In fact, third world children generally are bicultural, and many are bilingual, having grown up in their own culture as well as absorbing the dominant culture. In many ways, they are equipped with skills and experiences which white youth have been deprived of, since most white youth develop in a monocultural, monolingual environment. Burgest[5] suggests that the term "culturally deprived" be replaced by "culturally dispossessed," and that the term "economically disadvantaged" be replaced by "economically exploited." Both these terms present a perspective and implication that provide an entirely different frame of reference as to the reality of the third world experience in U.S. society.

Similarly, many nations of the third world are described as "underdeveloped." These less wealthy nations are generally those that suffered under colonialism and neo-colonialism. The "developed" nations are those that exploited their resources and wealth. Therefore, rather than referring to these countries as "underdeveloped," a more appropriate and meaningful designation might be "over exploited." Again, transpose this term next time you read about "underdeveloped nations" and note the different meaning that results.

Terms such as "culturally deprived," "economically disadvantaged" and "underdeveloped" place the responsibility for their own conditions on those being so described. This is known as "Blaming the Victim."[6] It places responsibility for poverty on the victims of poverty. It removes the blame from those in power who benefit from, and continue to permit, poverty.

Still another example involves the use of "non-white," "minority" or "third world." While people of color are a minority in the U.S., they are part of the vast majority of the world's population, in which white people are a distinct minority. Thus, by utilizing the term minority to describe people of color in the U.S., we can lose sight of the global majority/minority reality—a fact of some importance in the increasing and interconnected struggles of people of color inside and outside the U.S.

To describe people of color as "non-white" is to use whiteness as the standard and norm against which to measure all others. Use of the term "third world" to describe all people of color overcomes the inherent bias of "minority" and "non-white." Moreover, it connects the struggles of third world people in the U.S. with the freedom struggles around the globe.

The term third world gained increasing usage after the 1955 Bandung Conference of "non-aligned" nations, which represented a third force outside of the two world superpowers. The "first world" represents the United States, Western Europe and their sphere of influence. The "second world" represents the Soviet Union and its sphere. The "third world" represents, for the most part, nations that were, or are, controlled by the "first world" or West. For the most part, these are nations of Africa, Asia and Latin America.

"Loaded" Words and Native Americans

Many words lead to a demeaning characterization of groups of people. For instance, Columbus, it is said, "discovered" America. The word *discover* is defined as "to gain sight or knowledge of something previously unseen or unknown; to discover may be to find some existent thing that was previously unknown." Thus, a continent inhabited by millions of human beings cannot be "discovered." For history books to continue this usage represents a Eurocentric (white European) perspective on world history and ignores the existence of, and the perspective of, Native Americans. "Discovery," as used in the Euro-American context, implies the right to take what one finds, ignoring the rights of those who already inhabit or own the "discovered" thing.

Eurocentrism is also apparent in the usage of "victory" and "massacre" to describe the battles between Native Americans and whites. *Victory* is defined in the dictionary as "a success or triumph over an enemy in battle or war; the decisive defeat of an opponent." *Conquest* denotes the "taking over of control by the victor, and the obedience of the conquered." *Massacre* is defined as "the unnecessary, indiscriminate killing of a number of human beings, as in barbarous warfare or persecution, or for revenge or plunder." *Defend* is described as "to ward off attack from; guard against assault or injury; to strive to keep safe by resisting attack."

Eurocentrism turns these definitions around to serve the purpose of distorting history and justifying Euro-American conquest of the Native American homelands. Euro-Americans are not described in history books as invading Native American lands, but rather as defending *their* homes against "Indian" attacks. Since European communities were constantly encroaching on land already occupied, then a more honest interpretation would state that it was the Native Americans who were "warding off," "guarding" and "defending" their homelands.

Native American victories are invariably defined as "massacres," while the indiscriminate killing, extermination and plunder of Native American nations by Euro-Americans is defined as "victory." Distortion of history by the choice of "loaded" words used to describe historical events is a common racist practice. Rather than portraying Native Americans as human beings in highly defined and complex societies, cultures and civilizations, history books use such adjectives as "savages," "beasts," "primitive," and "backward." Native people are referred to as "squaw," "brave," or "papoose" instead of "woman," "man," or "baby."

Another term that has questionable connotations is *tribe*. The Oxford English Dictionary defines this noun as "a race of people; now applied especially to a primary aggregate of people in a primitive or barbarous condition, under a headman or chief." Morton Fried,[7] discussing "The Myth of Tribe," states that the word "did not become a general term of reference to American Indian society until the nineteenth century. Previously, the words commonly used for Indian populations were 'nation' and 'people.'" Since "tribe" has assumed a connotation of primitiveness or backwardness, it is suggested that the use of "nation" or "people" replace the term whenever possible in referring to Native American peoples.

The term *tribe* invokes even more negative implications when used in reference to American peoples. As Evelyn Jones Rich[8] has noted, the term is "almost always used to refer to third world people and it implies a stage of development which is, in short, a put-down."

"Loaded" Words and Africans

Conflicts among diverse peoples within African nations are often referred to as "tribal warfare," while conflicts among the diverse peoples within European countries are never described in such terms. If the rivalries between the Ibo and the Hausa and Yoruba in Nigeria are described as "tribal," why not the rivalries between Serbs and Slavs in Yugoslavia, or Scots and English in Great Britain, Protestants and Catholics in Ireland, or the Basques and the Southern Spaniards in Spain? Conflicts among African peoples in a particular nation have religious, cultural, economic and/or political roots. If we can analyze the roots of conflicts among European peoples in terms other than "tribal warfare," certainly we can do the same with African peoples, including correct reference to the ethnic groups or nations involved. For example, the terms "Kaffirs," "Hottentot" or "Bushmen" are names imposed by white Europeans. The correct names are always those by which a people refer to themselves. (In these instances Xhosa, Khoi-Khoin and San are correct.[9])

The generalized application of "tribal" in reference to Africans—as well as the failure to acknowledge the religious, cultural and social diversity of African peoples—is a decidedly racist dynamic. It is part of the process whereby Euro-Americans justify, or avoid confronting, their oppression of third world peoples. Africa has been particularly insulted by this dynamic, as witness the pervasive "darkest Africa" image. This image, widespread in Western culture, evokes an Africa covered by jungles and inhabited by "uncivilized," "cannibalistic," "pagan," "savage" peoples. This "darkest Africa" image avoids the geographical reality. Less than 20 per cent of the African continent is wooded savanna, for example. The image also ignores the history of African cultures and civilizations. Ample evidence suggests this distortion of reality was developed as a convenient rationale for the European and American slave trade. The Western powers, rather than exploiting, were civilizing and christianizing "uncivilized" and "pagan savages" (so the rationalization went). This dynamic also served to justify Western colonialism. From Tarzan movies to racist children's books like *Doctor Dolittle* and *Charlie and the Chocolate Factory*, the image of "savage" Africa and the myth of "the white man's burden" has been perpetuated in Western culture.

A 1972 *Time* magazine editorial lamenting the demise of *Life* magazine, stated that the "lavishness" of *Life's* enterprises included "organizing safaris into darkest Africa." The same year, the *New York Times'* C. L. Sulzberger wrote that "Africa has a history as dark as the skins of many of its people." Terms such as "darkest Africa," "primitive," "tribe" ("tribal") or "jungle," in reference to Africa, perpetuate myths and are especially inexcusable in such large circulation publications.

Ethnocentrism is similarly reflected in the term "pagan" to describe traditional religions. A February 1973 *Time* magazine article on Uganda stated, "Moslems account for only 500,000 of Uganda's 10 million people. Of the remainder, 5,000,000 are Christians and the rest pagan." *Pagan* is defined as "Heathen, a follower of a polytheistic religion; one that has little or no religion and that is marked by a frank delight in and uninhibited seeking after sensual pleasures and material goods." *Heathen* is defined as "Unenlightened; an unconverted member of a people or nation that does not acknowledge the God of the Bible. A person whose culture or enlightenment is of an inferior grade, especially an irreligious person." Now, the people of Uganda, like almost all Africans, have serious religious beliefs and practices. As used by Westerners, "pagan" connotes something wild, primitive and inferior—another term to watch out for.

The variety of traditional structures that African people live in are their "houses," not "huts." A *hut* is "an often small and temporary dwelling of simple construction." And to describe Africans as "natives" (noun) is derogatory terminology—as in, "the natives are restless." The dictionary definition of *native* includes: "one of a people inhabiting a territorial area at the time of its discovery or becoming familiar to a foreigner; one belonging to a people having a less complex civilization." Therefore, use of "native," like use of "pagan" often implies a value judgment of white superiority.

Qualifying Adjectives

Words that would normally have positive connotations can have entirely different meanings when used in a racial context. For example, C. L. Sulzberger, the columnist of the *New York Times*, wrote in January 1975, about conversations he had with two people in Namibia. One was the white South African administrator of the country and the other a member of SWAPO, the Namibian liberation movement. The first is described as "Dirk Mudge, who as senior elected member of the administration is a kind of acting Prime Minister. . . ." But the second person is introduced as "Daniel Tijongarero, an intelligent Herero tribesman who is a member of SWAPO. . . ." What need was there for Sulzberger to state that Daniel Tijongarero is "intelligent"? Why not also state that Dirk Mudge was "intelligent"—or do we assume he wasn't?

A similar example from a 1968 *New York Times* article reporting on an address by Lyndon Johnson stated, "The President spoke to the well-dressed Negro officials and their wives." In what similar circumstances can one imagine a reporter finding it necessary to note that an audience of white government officials was "well-dressed?"

Still another word often used in a racist context is "qualified." In the 1960's white Americans often questioned whether Black people were "qualified" to hold public office, a question that was never raised (until too late) about white officials like Wallace, Maddox, Nixon, Agnew, Mitchell, et al. The question of qualifications has been raised even more frequently in recent years as white people question whether Black people are "qualified" to be hired for positions in industry and educational institutions. "We're looking for a qualified Black" has been heard again and again as institutions are confronted with affirmative action goals. Why stipulate that

Blacks must be "qualified," when for others it is taken for granted that applicants must be "qualified."

Speaking English

Finally, the depiction in movies and children's books of third world people speaking English is often itself racist. Children's books about Puerto Ricans or Chicanos often connect poverty with a failure to speak English or to speak it well, thus blaming the victim and ignoring the racism which affects third world people regardless of their proficiency in English. Asian characters speak a stilted English ("Honorable so and so" or "Confucius say") or have a speech impediment ("roots or ruck," "very solly," "flied lice"). Native American characters speak another variation of stilted English ("Boy not hide. Indian take boy."), repeat certain Hollywood-Indian phrases ("Heap big" and "Many moons") or simply grunt out "Ugh'" or "How." The repeated use of these language characterizations functions to make third world people seem less intelligent and less capable than the English-speaking white characters.

Wrap-Up

A *Saturday Review* editorial[10] on "The Environment of Language" stated that language

> ... has as much to do with the philosophical and political conditioning of a society as geography or climate. ... people in Western cultures do not realize the extent to which their racial attitudes have been conditioned since early childhood by the power of words to ennoble or condemn, augment or detract, glorify or demean. Negative language infects the subconscious of most Western people from the time they first learn to speak. Prejudice is not merely imparted or superimposed. It is metabolized in the bloodstream of society. What is needed is not so much a change in language as an awareness of the power of words to condition attitudes. If we can at least recognize the underpinnings of prejudice, we may be in a position to deal with the effects.

To recognize the racism in language is an important first step. Consciousness of the influence of language on our perceptions can help to negate much of that influence. But it is not enough to simply become aware of the affects of racism in conditioning attitudes. While we may not be able to change the language, we can definitely change our usage of the language. We can avoid using words that degrade people. We can make a conscious effort to use terminology that reflects a progressive perspective, as opposed to a distorting perspective. It is important for educators to provide students with opportunities to explore racism in language and to increase their awareness of it, as well as learning terminology that is positive and does not perpetuate negative human values.

NOTES

1. Simon Podair, "How Bigotry Builds Through Language," *Negro Digest*, March '67

2. Jose Armas, "Antonio and the Mayor: A Cultural Review of the Film," *The Journal of Ethnic Studies*, Fall, '75

3. David R. Burgest, "The Racist Use of the English Language," *Black Scholar*, Sept. '73

4. Thomas Greenfield, "Race and Passive Voice at Monticello," *Crisis*, April '75

5. David R. Burgest, "Racism in Everyday Speech and Social Work Jargon," *Social Work*, July '73

6. William Ryan, *Blaming the Victim*, Pantheon Books, '71

7. Morton Fried, "The Myth of Tribe," *National History*, April '75

8. Evelyn Jones Rich, "Mind Your Language," *Africa Report*, Sept./Oct. '74

9. Steve Wolf, "Catalogers in Revolt Against LC's Racist, Sexist Headings," *Bulletin of Interracial Books for Children*, Vol. 6, Nos. 3&4, '75

10. "The Environment of Language," *Saturday Review*, April 8, '67

Also see:

Roger Bastide, "Color, Racism and Christianity," *Daedalus*, Spring '67

Kenneth J. Gergen, "The Significance of Skin Color in Human Relations," *Daedalus*, Spring '67

Lloyd Yabura, "Towards a Language of Humanism," *Rhythm*, Summer '71

UNESCO, "Recommendations Concerning Terminology in Education on Race Questions," June '68

3

The Language of Sexism

Haig Bosmajian

While the language of racial and ethnic oppression is often blatant and relatively easy to identify, the language of sexism is more subtle and pervasive. Our everyday speech reflects the "superiority" of the male and the "inferiority" of the female, resulting in a master-subject relationship. The language of sexism relegates the woman to the status of children, servants, and idiots, to being the "second sex" and to virtual invisibility. The progress implied in the advertising slogan "You've come a long way, baby" notwithstanding, the language of sexism remains with us and exerts an influence on the male's attitudes towards and control over women and the women's attitudes toward themselves. More accurate than the above slogan is the feminist's response: "If I've come such a long way, how come you still call me baby?"

The need to eradicate the language of sexism to bring about equality of the sexes has been recognized by a variety of writers. Deborah Rosenfelt and Florence Howe have pointed out that "a number of reputable linguists believe that linguistic systems are partially determined by underlying metaphysical assumptions about the structure of reality. Linguists argue about the precise nature of the interaction between language, thought, and culture, but it seems clear that language as a form of social behavior does both reflect and help to perpetuate deeply held cultural attitudes. Among these attitudes—and this is an area that traditional linguists have hardly touched upon—are those concerning the relationships between men and women."[1] "By calling attention to sexist usage," continue Rosenfelt and Howe, "feminists hope to change not only the language—the surface behavior—but the underlying attitudes that determine and, in a constant interaction, are determined by the behavior."[2] . . .

Our sexist language, according to Aileen Hernandez, past president of the National Organization for Women, makes it abundantly clear that "in all areas that really count, we discount women." Sexist language manifests itself in various ways:

"'Mankind' is the generic term for all people or all males, but there is no similar dual meaning for 'womankind.' The masculine pronoun is used to refer to both men and women in general discussions.

"The Constitution of the United States is replete with sexist language—Senators and Representatives are 'he'; the President is obviously 'he' and even the fugitive from justice is 'he' in our Constitution. . . .

"But just in case we as women manage to escape the brainwashing that assigns us to 'our place' in the order of things, the language continues to get the message across.

"There is a 'housewife' but no 'househusband'; there's a 'housemother' but no 'housefather'; there's a 'kitchenmaid' but no 'kitchenman'; unmarried women cross the threshold from 'bachelor girl' to 'spinster' to 'old maid,' but unmarried men are 'bachelors' forever."[3]

Writing in *Women: A Journal of Liberation*, Emily Toth has observed that "generally, women lack their own words for professional positions: a woman must be a 'female judge,' 'female representative,' 'madam chairman,' or—a ghastly pun—a 'female mailman'."[4] She notes that "one textbook defines Standard English as that language spoken by 'educated professional people and their wives.'"[5] She might have added the *Webster's New World Dictionary of the American Language* definition of "honorarium": "a payment to a professional man for services on which no fee is set or legally obtainable."

Alma Graham tells us in an article titled "The Making of a Nonsexist Dictionary" that "at every level of achievement and activity—from primitive man to the man of the hour—woman is not taken into account. Consider the congressman. He is a man of the people. To prove that he's the best man for the job, he takes his case to the man in the street. He is a champion of the workingman. He speaks for the little man. He has not forgotten the forgotten man. And he firmly believes: one man, one vote. Consider the policeman or fireman, the postman or milkman, the clergyman or businessman."[6] So ingrained is the language of sexism that it is with great effort and some resistance that people will refer to a "jurywoman," "chairwoman," "churchwoman," or "journeywoman." Instead, the females all end up "countrymen," "middlemen," "selectmen," "jurymen" when these groups are referred to generally.

Not only does the woman end up a "man," she also finds herself labeled "he" or "him" or "his" when the pronoun is used as a neuter to designate anyone, female or male.

Lynne T. White, former president of Mills College, has commented on this problem of women coming out male through the use of masculine pronouns: "The grammar of English dictates that when a referent is either of indeterminant sex or both sexes, it shall be considered masculine. The penetration of this habit of language into the minds of little girls as they grow up to be women is more profound than most people, including most women, have recognized: it implies that personality is really a male attribute, and that women are human subspecies. . . . It would be a miracle if a girl-baby, learning to use the symbols of our tongue, could escape some wound to her self-respect; whereas a boy-baby's ego is bolstered by the pattern of our language."[7]

In her study dealing with the response of individuals to the pronoun "he" Virginia Kidd found that "the use of the male pronoun as the generic is not generally interpreted as representative of a neutral antecedent; that in fact the antecedent is considered male; that this interpretation of the antecedent as male is stronger in cases where the societal stereotypes of the male role coincides with the pronoun is often strong enough to be indicated in cases where other traits of the antecedent are admittedly unknown."[8] Kidd concludes that the results of her study "seem eminently clear: use of the masculine pronoun as the generic simply does not accomplish the purpose for which it is intended. The masculine pronoun does not suffice as a verbal indicator in situations where persons of either sex could be the antecedent."[9]

Rosenfelt and Howe report that "at a summer workshop a Feminist Press staff member used a simple device to illustrate the feelings of invisibility that the 'universal' *he* can arouse in women. She substituted the feminine pronoun: 'the teacher . . . she.' Finally a principal (male) could take it no longer. 'Why are you doing that, Marj?' he asked plaintively; 'why do you keep saying *she?*' With all eyes on her, Marj responded pleasantly, without embarrassment, 'why, I'm using the word generically.' Then there was laughter, an explosive release of tension. But the point had been made, and as the workshop went on, the participants were careful to use either he/she or the plural. Perhaps *he* was not so generic after all?"[10] . . .

There are many occasions when "women and men" would be more appropriate than "men and women." In fact, one might argue that since women are a majority in this nation we should henceforth always speak of "the women and men of this nation" instead of "the men and women of this nation." The firstness of the male has always appeared evident when male and female names are put side by side: Jack and Jill, Hansel and Gretel, Romeo and Juliet, Antony and Cleopatra, Dick and Jane, John and Marsha. As for the firstness of the female, there isn't much more than Snow White and the Seven Dwarfs.

In the church we have the "clergyman," the "altar boy," the Father, Son, and the Holy Ghost. Males dominate in Christianity not only in language, but also in terms of the decision-making powers, a domination which can partly be attributed to the language of sexism. This male domination exists despite the fact that "every survey that measures sex differences in religiosity shows that females attend church more frequently than males, pray more often, hold firmer beliefs, cooperate more in church programs. This is true at all age levels from childhood to senior-citizen, and of both single and married women, of women gainfully employed and homemakers."[11] But what is a woman to do when in Scriptures she is told: "Wives, submit yourselves unto your own husbands, as unto the Lord"? This, in the same book, Ephesians, which tells children to obey their parents and tells servants to be obedient to their masters. Somehow, women, along with children and servants, end up subjects in the master-subject relationship.

The idea that women are to play a subservient role and not to be taken seriously has been perpetuated through the use of the word "lady." One might, at first glance, think that referring to a woman as a "lady" is something complimentary and desirable. Upon closer examination, however, "lady" turns out to be a verbal label connoting the non-seriousness of women.

Robin Lakoff has argued convincingly that "lady" is a euphemism. Of the euphemism generally she declares:

"When a word acquires a bad connotation by association with something people find unpleasant or embarrassing to think of, people will reach for substitutes for that word that do not have this uncomfortable effect—that is, euphemisms. What then happens is that, since feelings about the things or people referred to themselves are not altered by a change of name, the new name itself takes on the same old connotations, and a new euphemism must be found. It is no doubt possible to pick out those areas in which a society is feeling particular psychological strain or discomfort—areas where problems exist in a culture—by pinpointing those lexical items around which a great many euphemisms are clustered."[12] One has only to think of the numerous euphemisms we have for death, toilet, and certain dreaded diseases. Lakoff's point is that "unless we start feeling more respect for women, and at the same time less uncomfortable about them and their roles in society in relation to men, we cannot avoid *ladies* any more than we can avoid broads."[13]

In her discussion of the use of "lady" in job terminology, Lakoff writes: "For at least some speakers, the more demeaning the job, the more the person holding it (if female, of course) is likely to be described as a *lady*. Thus cleaning *lady* is at least as common as *cleaning woman*, *saleslady* or *saleswoman*. But one says, normally *woman doctor*. To say *lady doctor* is to be very condescending; it constitutes an insult. For men, there is no such dichotomy. *Garbage man* or *salesman* is the only possibility, never *garbage gentleman*."[14]

The non-seriousness of "lady" as contrasted to "woman" is exemplified further in the titles of organizations: "It seems that organizations of women who have a serious purpose (not merely that of spending time with one another) cannot use the world *lady* in their titles, but less serious ones may. Compare the *Ladies' Auxiliary* of a men's group, or the *Thursday Evening Ladies Browning and Garden Society* with *Ladies' Lib* or *Ladies Strike for Peace.*"[15]

One might try substituting "ladies" for "women" in the following: National Organization for Women; Harvard Medical and Dental School Committee on the Status of Women; Women's Studies Program; Radical Women; Black Women's Community Development Foundation. One seldom finds "lady" or "ladies" in titles of books which treat women seriously; substituting those terms for "woman" or "women" in the following titles clearly demonstrates that "lady" trivializes, denegrates: *The Natural Superiority of Women* by M. F. Ashley Montague; *Women and the Law* by Leo Kanowitz; *A Vindication of the Rights of Women* by Mary Wollstonecraft; *The Subjection of Women* by John S. Mill; *The Emancipation of Women* by V. I. Lenin; *The Ideas of the Woman Suffrage Movement* by Aileen Kraditor.

To those who say that the use of "lady" is simply a matter of being polite, Lakoff answers: "The concept of politeness thus invoked is the politeness used in dignifying or ennobling a concept that normally is not thought of as having dignity or nobility. It is this notion of politeness that explains why we have *cleaning lady*, but not normally *lady doctor*: a doctor does not need to be exalted by conventional expressions: she has dignity enough from her professional status. But a cleaning woman is in a very different situation, in which her occupational category requires ennobling. Then perhaps we can say that the very notion of womanhood, as opposed to manhood, requires ennobling since it lacks inherent dignity of its own; hence the word *woman* requires the existence of a euphemism like *lady*."[16] ...

Linguistically, we live in a world of professional men and only men; unless the professional is identified as a "lady" or "woman" we assume the person to be a male. As Casey Miller and Kate Swift have observed: "When a woman or girl makes news, her sex is identified at the beginning of a story, if possible in the headline or its equivalent. The assumption, apparently, is that whatever event or action is being reported, a woman's involvement is less common and therefore more newsworthy than a man's. If the story is about achievement, the media have developed a special and extensive vocabulary to avoid the constant repetition of 'woman.' The results, 'Grandmother Wins Nobel Prize,' 'Blonde Hijacks Airliner,' 'Housewife to Run for Congress,' convey the kind of information that would be ludicrous in comparable headlines if the subjects were men."[17]

The nonseriousness and the triviality of women and their accomplishments have been further conveyed in that special language used to describe females in news features which report on their personal and sexual characteristics, a language seldom ever used in news features about men.

More often than not, the woman is identified in terms of her husband, while the story about a man usually makes no reference to his wife. For example, "in the recent discussion of possible Supreme Court nominees, one woman was mentioned prominently. In discussing her general qualifications for the office, and her background, *The New York Times* saw fit to remark on her 'bathing-beauty figure.' Note that is not only a judgment on a physical attribute totally removed from her qualifications for the Supreme Court, but that it is couched in terms of how a man would react to her figure, rather than being merely descriptive. So it is conceivable that a male prospective nominee might (but was not) have been described by the *Times* as 'well-preserved,' or 'athletic,' the reference in this case not invoking a judgment on the part of the opposite sex, and not as 'sexy'; but a woman appointee is described as though an entrant in a beauty contest: even an aspirant to a Supreme Court seat is judged in terms of her physical attractiveness to men." [18]

Commenting on this double standard treatment, one time Presidential press secretary Bill Moyers has said: "The obsolete treatment of women in the press has, I think contributed greatly to the anger many women feel. Why does the press identify Golda Meir as a grandmother but not Georges Pompidou as a grandfather? Why does the press talk of a female politician's hair coloring and dress style, but not the hair dye or tailor used by a Presidential candidate or Senator?" [19] . . .

The language of sexism not only portrays women as nonserious, as trivial, and as the "second sex," but it also contributes to her invisibility. In a world of "chairmen," "spokesmen," "statesmen," "repairmen," et cetera, the woman loses visibility. We know of the Neanderthal Man, the Java Man, and the Cro-Magnon Man, but never have we had a comparable pre-historic woman. The invisible woman remains linguistically invisible as long as "the assumption is that unless otherwise identified, people in general—including doctors and beggars—are men. It is a semantic mechanism that operates to keep women invisible: *man* and *mankind* represent everyone; *he* in generalized use refers to either sex; the 'land where our fathers died' is also the land of our mothers—although they go unsung." [20] . . .

The woman's efforts to achieve self-identity has been further complicated by the "street language" which labels her a sexual child object. She is openly called "babe," "toots," "chick," "doll," et cetera. All of these labels are associated with children, helplessness, and immaturity.

Dictionary definitions tell us a "babe" is "1. a baby; infant; hence, 2. a naive, gullible, or helpless person. 3. [slang], a girl or young woman, especially a pretty one." A "chick" is "1. a young chicken. 2. a young bird. 3. a child: term of endearment." A "tootsy" is "1. a child's or woman's small foot. 2. "toots"; and a "toots" is "[slang], darling, dear: affectionate or playful term of address." If a woman is not a "babe," "toots," or "chick," she can be a "doll." Doll: "1. a children's toy made to resemble a baby, child or grown person. 2. a pretty but rather stupid or silly girl or woman. 3. a pretty child. 4. [slang], any girl or young woman." And if the woman is not labeled any of these, she still can be a "girl." No matter how high in professional status or how old she may be, the woman can always be the "girl."

Three of the definitions of "girl" given by *Webster's New World Dictionary of the American Langauge* are: "1. a female child. 2. a young, unmarried woman. 3. a female servant." Lakoff has said of the use of the term "girl": "One seldom hears a man past the age of adolescence referred to as a boy, save in expressions like 'going out with boys,' which are meant to suggest an air of adolescent frivolity and irresponsibility. But women of all ages are 'girls'. . . . It may be that this use of *girl* is euphemistic in the sense in which *lady* is an euphemism: in stressing the idea of immaturity, it removes the sexual connotations lurking in women."

All of these terms identifying women with babies and children result in a portrayal of mature females as weak, silly, irresponsible and dependent. The women are infantalized through language.

The language of sexism, like the language of racism, leads to circularity in our thinking and behavior. Our sexist language does affect our attitudes and behavior which in turn affect our language. . . .

NOTES

1. Deborah Rosenfelt and Florence Howe, "Language and Sexism A Note," *MLA Newsletter*, (December 1973), p. 5.

2. *Ibid.*, p. 6.

3. Aileen Hernandez, "The Preening of America," *Star-News* (Pasadena, Calif.), 1971 New Year's edition.

4. Emily Toth, "How Can A Woman MAN the Barricades? Or—Linguistic Sexism Up Against the Wall, *Women: A Journal of Liberation*, 2 (1970), p. 57.

5. *Ibid.*

6. Alma Graham, "The Making of a Nonsexist Dictionary," ETC., 31 (March 1974), p. 63.

7. Cited in Kate Miller and Casey Smith, "De-Sexing the English Language," *Ms.*, (Spring 1972), p. 7.

8. Virginia Kidd, "A Study of the Images Produced Through the Use of the Male Pronoun As the Generic," *Movements: Contemporary Rhetoric and Communication*, 1 (Fall 1971), p. 27.

9. *Ibid.*, p. 28.

10. Rosenfelt and Howe, p. 5.

11. Joseph Fichter, "Holy Father Church," *Commonweal*, 92 (1970), p. 216.

12. Robin Lakoff, "Language and Woman's Place," *Language in Society*, II, p. 57.

13. *Ibid.*, pp. 58–59.

14. *Ibid.*, pp. 59–60.

15. *Ibid.*, p. 60.

16. *Ibid.*, p. 61.

17. Casey Miller and Kate Smith, "One Small Step for Genkind," *New York Times Magazine*, (April 16, 1972), p. 100.

18. Lakoff, p. 65.

19. Cited in Midge Kovacs, "Women: Correcting the Myths," *New York Times*, August 26, 1972, p. 25.

20. Miller and Smith, "One Small Step for Genkind," p. 36.

Beauty and the Beast of Advertising

Jean Kilbourne

"You're a Halston woman from the very beginning," the advertisement proclaims. The model stares provocatively at the viewer, her long blonde hair waving around her face, her bare chest partially covered by two curved bottles that give the illusion of breasts and a cleavage.

The average American is accustomed to blue-eyed blondes seductively touting a variety of products. In this case, however, the blonde is about five years old.

Advertising is an over $145 billion a year industry and affects all of us throughout our lives. We are each exposed to over 1,500 ads a day, constituting perhaps the most powerful educational force in society. The average adult will spend one and one-half years of his/her life watching television commercials. But the ads sell a great deal more than products. They sell values, images and concepts of success and worth, love and sexuality, popularity and normalcy. They tell us who we are and who we should be. Sometimes they sell addictions.

Advertising's foundation and economic lifeblood is the mass media, and the primary purpose of the mass media is to deliver an audience to advertisers, just as the primary purpose of television programs is to deliver an audience for commercials.

Adolescents are particularly vulnerable, however, because they are new and inexperienced consumers and are the prime targets of many advertisements. They are in the process of learning their values and roles and developing their self-concepts. Most teenagers are sensitive to peer pressure and find it difficult to resist or even question the dominant cultural messages perpetuated and reinforced by the media. Mass communication has made possible a kind of nationally distributed peer pressure that erodes private and individual values and standards.

But what does society, and especially teenagers, learn from the advertising messages that proliferate in the mass media? On the most obvious level they learn the stereotypes. Advertising creates a mythical, WASP-oriented world in which no one is ever ugly, overweight, poor, struggling or disabled either physically or mentally (unless you count the housewives who talk to little men in the toilet bowls). And it is a world in which people talk only about products.

Housewives or Sex Objects

The aspect of advertising most in need of analysis and change is the portrayal of women. Scientific studies and the most casual viewing yield the same conclusion: Women are shown almost exclusively as housewives or sex objects.

The housewife, pathologically obsessed by cleanliness and lemon-fresh scents, debates cleaning products with herself and worries about her husband's "ring around the collar."

The sex object is a mannequin, a shell. Conventional beauty is her only attribute. She has no lines or wrinkles (which would indicate she had the bad taste and poor judgment to grow older), no scars or blemishes — indeed, she has no pores. She is thin, generally tall and long-legged, and, above all, she is young. All "beautiful" women in advertisements (including minority women), regardless of product or audience, conform to this norm. Women are constantly exhorted to emulate this ideal, to feel ashamed and guilty if they fail, and to feel that their desirability and lovability are contingent upon physical perfection.

Creating Artificiality

The image is artificial and can only be achieved artificially (even the "natural look" requires much preparation and expense). Beauty is something that comes from without; more than one million dollars is spent every hour on cosmetics. Desperate to conform to an ideal and impossible standard, many women go to great lengths to manipulate and change their faces and bodies. A woman is conditioned to view her face as a mask and her body as an object, as *things* separate from and more important than her real self, constantly in need of alteration, improvement, and disguise. She is made to feel dissatisfied with and ashamed of herself, whether she tries to achieve "the look" or not. Objectified constantly by others, she learns to objectify herself. (It is interesting to note that one in five college-age women have an eating disorder.)

"When *Glamour* magazine surveyed its readers in 1984, 75 percent felt too heavy and only 15 percent felt just right. Nearly half of those who were actually underweight reported feeling too fat and wanting to diet. Among a sample of college women, 40 percent felt overweight when only 12 percent actually were too heavy," according to Rita Freedman in her book *Beauty Bound*.

There is evidence that this preoccupation with weight begins at ever-earlier ages for women. According to a recent article in *New Age Journal*, "even grade-school girls are succumbing to stick-like-standards of beauty enforced by a relentless parade of wasp-waisted fashion models, movie stars and pop idols." A study by a University of California professor showed that nearly 80 percent of fourth-grade girls in the Bay Area are watching their weight.

A recent *Wall Street Journal* survey of students in four Chicago-area schools found that more than half the fourth-grade girls were dieting and three-quarters felt they were overweight. One student said, "We don't expect boys to be that handsome. We take them as they are." Another added, "But boys expect girls to be perfect and beautiful. And skinny."

Dr. Steven Levenkron, author of *The Best Little Girl in the World*, the story of an anorexic, says his blood pressure soars every time he opens a magazine and finds an ad for women's fashions. "If I had my way," he said, "every one of them would have to carry a line saying, 'Caution: This model may be hazardous to your health.'"

Women are also dismembered in commercials, their bodies separated into parts in need of change or improvement. If a woman has "acceptable" breasts, then she must also be sure that her legs are worth watching, her hips slim, her feet sexy, and that her buttocks look nude under her clothes ("like I'm not wearin' nothin'"). This image is difficult and costly to achieve and impossible to maintain (unless you buy the product)—no one is flawless and everyone ages. Growing older is the great taboo. Women are encouraged to remain little girls ("because innocence is sexier than you think"), to be passive and dependent, never to mature. The contradictory message—"sensual, but not too far from innocence"—places women in a double bind; somehow we are supposed to be both sexy and virginal, experienced and naive, seductive and chaste. The disparagement of maturity is, of course, insulting and frustrating to adult women, and the implication that little girls are seductive is dangerous to real children.

Influencing Sexual Attitudes

Young people also learn a great deal about sexual attitudes from the media and from advertising in particular. Advertising's approach to sex is pornographic; it reduces people to objects and de-emphasizes human contact and individuality. This reduction of sexuality to a dirty joke and of people to objects is the real obscenity of the culture. Although the sexual sell, overt and subliminal, is at a fevered pitch in most commercials, there is at the same time a notable absence of sex as an important and profound human activity.

There have been some changes in the images of women. Indeed, a "new woman" has emerged in commercials in recent years. She is generally presented as superwoman, who manages to do all the work at home and on the job (with the help of a product, of course, not of her husband or children or friends), or as the liberated woman, who owes her independence and self-esteem to the products she uses. These new images do not represent any real progress but rather create a myth of progress, an illusion that reduces complex sociopolitical problems to mundane personal ones.

Advertising images do not cause these problems, but they contribute to them by creating a climate in which the marketing of women's bodies—the sexual sell and dismemberment, distorted body image ideal and children as sex objects—is seen as acceptable.

This is the real tragedy, that many women internalize these stereotypes and learn their "limitations," thus establishing a self-fulfilling prophecy. If one accepts these mythical and degrading images, to some extent one actualizes them. By remaining unaware of the profound seriousness of the ubiquitous influence, the redundant message and the subliminal impact of advertisements, we ignore one of the most powerful "educational" forces in the culture—one that greatly affects our self-images, our ability to relate to each other, and effectively destroys any awareness and action that might help to change that climate.

5

Pulling Train

Peggy R. Sanday

This article discusses certain group rituals of male bonding on a college campus, in particular, a phenomenon called "pulling train." According to a report issued by the Association of American Colleges in 1985, "pulling train," or "gang banging" as it is also called, refers to a group of men lining up like train cars to take turns having sex with the same woman (Ehrhart and Sandler 1985, 2). This report labels "pulling train" as gang rape. Bernice Sandler, one of its authors, recently reported that she had found more than seventy-five documented cases of gang rape on college campuses in recent years (*Atlanta Constitution*, 7 June 1988). Sandler labeled these incidents gang rape because of the coercive nature of the sexual behavior. The incidents she and Julie K. Ehrhart described in their 1985 report display a common pattern. A vulnerable young woman, one who is seeking acceptance or who is high on drugs or alcohol, is taken to a room. She may or may not agree to have sex with one man. She then passes out, or is too weak or scared to protest, and a train of men have sex with her. Sometimes the young woman's drinks are spiked without her knowledge, and when she is approached by several men in a locked room, she reacts with confusion and panic. Whether too weak to protest, frightened, or unconscious, as has been the case in quite a number of instances, anywhere from two to eleven or more men have sex with her. In some party invitations the possibility of such an occurrence is mentioned with playful allusions to "gang bang" or "pulling train" (Ehrhart and Sandler 1985, 1–2).

The reported incidents occurred at all kinds of institutions: "public, private, religiously affiliated, Ivy League, large and small" (ibid.). Most of the incidents occurred at fraternity parties, but some occurred in residence halls or in connection with college athletics. Incidents have also been reported in high schools. . . .

Just a few examples taken from the Ehrhart and Sandler report (1985, 1—2) are sufficient to demonstrate the coercive nature of the sexual behavior.

> The 17-year-old freshman woman went to the fraternity "little sister" rush party with two of her roommates. The roommates left early without her. She was trying to get a ride home when a fraternity brother told her he would take her home after the party ended. While she waited, two other fraternity members took her into a bedroom to "discuss little sister matters." The door was closed and one of the brothers stood blocking the exit. They told her that in order to become a little sister (honorary member) she would have to have sex with a fraternity member. She was frightened, fearing they would physically harm her if she refused. She could see no escape. Each of the brothers had sex with her, as did a third who had been hiding in the room. During the next two hours a succession of men went into the room. There were never less than three men with her, sometimes more. After they let her go, a fraternity brother drove her home. He told her not to feel bad about the incident because another woman had also been "upstairs" earlier that night. (Large southern university)

> It was her first fraternity party. The beer flowed freely and she had much more to drink than she had planned. It was hot and crowded and the party spread out all over the house, so that when three men asked her to go upstairs, she went with them. They took her into a bedroom, locked the door and began to undress her. Groggy with alcohol, her feeble protests were ignored as the three men raped her. When they finished, they put her in the hallway, naked, locking her clothes in the bedroom. (Small eastern liberal arts college)

> A 19-year-old woman student was out on a date with her boyfriend and another couple. They were all drinking beer and after going back to the boyfriend's dorm room, they smoked two marijuana cigarettes. The other couple left and the woman and her boyfriend had sex. The woman fell asleep and the next thing she knew she awoke with a man she didn't know on top of her trying to force her into having sex. A witness said the man was in the hall with two other men when the woman's boyfriend came out of his room and invited them to have sex with his unconscious girlfriend. (Small midwestern college)

Although Ehrhart and Sandler boldly labeled the incidents they described as rape, few of the perpetrators were prosecuted. Generally speaking, the male participants are protected and the victim is blamed for having placed herself in a compromising social situation where male adolescent hormones are known, as the saying goes, "to get out of hand." For a number of reasons, people say, "She asked for it." As the above examples from the Ehrhart and Sandler report suggest, the victim may be a vulnerable young woman who is seeking acceptance or who is weakened by the ingestion of drugs or alcohol. She may or may not agree to having sex with one man. If she has agreed to some sexual activity, the men assume that she has agreed to all sexual activity regardless of whether she is conscious or not. In the minds of the boys involved the sexual behavior is not rape. On many campuses this opinion is shared by a significant portion of the campus community. . . .

The XYZ Express

I first learned about "pulling train" in 1983 from a student who was then enrolled in one of my classes. Laurel had been out of class for about two weeks. I noticed her absence and worried that she was getting behind on her work. When she came back to class she told me that she had been raped by five or six male students at a fraternity house after one of the fraternity's weekly Thursday night parties. Later, I learned from others that Laurel was drunk on beer and had taken four hits of LSD before going to the party. According to the story Laurel told to a campus administrator, after the party she fell asleep in a first-floor room and when she awoke was undressed. One of the brothers dressed her and carried her upstairs, where she was raped by "guys" she did not know but said she could identify if photographs were available. She asked a few times for the men to get off her, but to no avail. According to her account, she was barely conscious and lacked the strength to push them off her.

There is no dispute that Laurel had a serious drinking and drug problem at the time of the party. People at the party told me that during the course of the evening she acted like someone who was "high," and her behavior attracted quite a bit of attention. They described her as dancing provocatively to the beat of music only she could hear. She appeared disoriented and out of touch with what was happening. Various fraternity brothers occasionally danced with her, but she seemed oblivious to the person she was dancing with. Some of the brothers teased her by spinning her around in a room until she was so dizzy she couldn't find her way out. At one point during the evening she fell down a flight of stairs. Later she was pulled by the brothers out of a circle dance, a customary fraternity ritual in which only brothers usually took part.

After the other partyers had gone home, the accounts of what happened next vary according to who tells the story. The differences of opinion do not betray a Rashomon effect as much as they reflect different definitions of a common sexual event. No one disputes that Laurel had sex with at least five or six male students, maybe more. When Anna, a friend of the XYZ brothers, saw Laurel the next day and heard the story from the brothers, her immediate conclusion was that they had raped Laurel. Anna based her conclusion on seeing Laurel's behavior at the party and observing her the following day. It seemed to Anna that Laurel was incapable of consenting to sex, which is key for determining a charge of rape. Anna's opinion was later confirmed by the Assistant District Attorney for Sex Crimes, who investigated but did not prosecute the case.

The brothers claimed that Laurel had lured them into a "gang bang" or "train," which they preferred to call an "express." Their statements and actions during the days after the event seemed to indicate that they considered the event a routine part of their "little sisters program," something to be proud of. Reporting the party activities on a sheet posed on their bulletin board in the spot where the house minutes are usually posted, Anna found the following statement, which she later showed me:

Things are looking up for the [XYZ] sisters program. A prospective leader for the group spent some time interviewing several [brothers] this past thursday and friday. Possible names for the little sisters include [XYZ] "little wenches" and "The [XYZ] express."

. . . The ideology that promotes "pulling train" is seen in the discourse and practices associated with some parties on campus. Party invitations expressing this ideology depict a woman lying on a pool table, or in some other position suggestive of sexual submission. The hosts of the party promote behavior aimed at seduction. *Seduction* means plying women with alcohol or giving them drugs in order to "break down resistance." A drunken woman is not defined as being in need of protection and help, but as "asking for it." If the situation escalates into sexual activity, the brothers watch each other perform sexual acts and then brag about "getting laid." The event is referred to as "drunken stupidity, women chasing, and all around silliness." The drama enacted parodies the image of the gentleman. Its male participants brag about their masculinity and its female participants are degraded to the status of what the boys call "red meat" or "fish." The whole scenario joins men in a no-holds-barred orgy of togetherness. The woman whose body facilitates all of this is sloughed off at the end like a used condom. She may be called a "nympho" or the men may believe that they seduced her—a practice known as "working a yes out"—through promises of becoming a little sister, by getting her drunk, by promising her love, or by some other means. Those men who object to this kind of behavior run the risk of being labeled "wimps" or, even worse in their eyes, "gays" or "faggots."

The rationalization for this behavior illustrates a broader social ideology of male dominance. Both the brothers and many members of the broader community excuse the behavior by saying that "boys will be boys" and that if a woman gets into trouble it is because "she asked for it," "she wanted it," or "she deserved it." The ideology inscribed in this discourse represents male sexuality as more natural and more explosive than female sexuality. This active, "naturally" explosive nature of male sexuality is expected to find an outlet either in the company of male friends or in the arms of prostitutes. In these contexts men are supposed to use women to satisfy explosive urges. The women who satisfy these urges are included as passive actors in the enactment of a sexual discourse where the male, but not the female, sexual instinct is characterized as an insatiable biological instinct and psychological need.

Men entice one another into the act of "pulling train" by implying that those who do not participate are unmanly or homosexual. This behavior is full of contradictions because the homoeroticism of "pulling train" seems obvious. A group of men watch each other having sex with a woman who may be unconscious. One might well ask why the woman is even necessary for the sexual acts these men stage for one another. As fraternity practices described in this book suggest, the answer seems to lie in homophobia. One can suggest that in the act of "pulling train" the polymorphous sexuality of homophobic men is given a strictly heterosexual form.

Polymorphous sexuality, a term used by Freud to refer to diffuse sexual interests with multiple objects, means that men will experience desire for one another.

However, homophobia creates a tension between polymorphous sexual desire and compulsory heterosexuality. This tension is resolved by "pulling train": the brothers vent their interest in one another through the body of a woman. In the sociodrama that is enacted, the idea that heterosexual males are superior to women and to homosexuals is publicly expressed and probably subjectively absorbed. Thus, both homophobia and compulsory heterosexuality can be understood as strategies of knowledge and power centering on sex that support the social stratification of men according to sexual preference.

In group sex, homoerotic desire is simultaneously indulged, degraded, and extruded from the group. The fact that the woman involved is often unconscious highlights her status as a surrogate victim in a drama where the main agents are males interacting with one another. The victim embodies the sexual urges of the brothers; she is defined as "wanting it"—even though she may be unconscious during the event—so that the men can satisfy their urges for one another at her expense. By defining the victim as "wanting it," the men convince themselves of their heterosexual prowess and delude themselves as to the real object of their lust. If they were to admit to the real object, they would give up their position in the male status hierarchy as superior, heterosexual males. The expulsion and degradation of the victim both brings a momentary end to urges that would divide the men and presents a social statement of phallic heterosexual dominance.

By blaming the victim for provoking their own sexual aggression, men control and define acceptable and unacceptable female sexual behavior through the agency of fear. The fear is that a woman who does not guard her behavior runs the risk of becoming the target of uncontrollable male sexual aggression. Thus, although women are ostensibly the controlling agent, it is fear of the imagined explosive nature of male sexuality that ultimately reigns for both sexes. This fear instills in some men and women consciousness of their sexual and social identities.

In sum, the phenomenon of "pulling train" has many meanings. In addition to those meanings that have been mentioned, it is a bonding device that can permanently change a young man's understanding of masculinity. The bonding is accomplished by virtue of coparticipation in a "forbidden" act. As Ward Goodenough (1963) points out, sharing in the forbidden as part of initiation to a group is a powerful bonding device. For example, criminal gangs may require the initiate to perform a criminal act in order to be accepted as a member, an act that once performed is irrevocable. Participation in a "train" performs the same function of bonding the individual to the group and changing his subjectivity. Such bridge-burning acts of one kind or another are standard parts of ritualized identity-change procedures.

The Conditions Promoting "Pulling Train"

We cannot assume that all entering college students have well-established sexual and social identities or ethical positions regarding sexual harassment and abuse. Recent research by psychologists on human subjectivity argues that subjectivity is dynamic and changes as individuals move through the life cycle. The evidence presented here suggests that the masculine subjectivity of insecure males may be shaped, or at least reinforced, by experiences associated with male bonding at college.

[One] example is fraternity initiation rituals in which young men who admit to feelings of low self-esteem upon entering the college setting are forced to cleanse and purify themselves of the despised and dirty feminine, "nerdy," "faggot" self bonded to their mothers. The ritual process in these cases humiliates the pledges in order to break social and psychological bonds to parental authority and to establish new bonds to the brotherhood. The traumatic means employed to achieve these goals induces a state of consciousness that makes abuse of women a means to renew fraternal bonds and assert power as a brotherhood. . . .

. . . Cross-cultural research demonstrates that whenever men build and give allegiance to a mystical, enduring, all-male social group, the disparagement of women is, invariably, an important ingredient of the mystical bond, and sexual aggression the means by which the bond is renewed (Sanday 1981, 1986). As long as exclusive male clubs exist in a society that privileges men as a social category, we must recognize that collective sexual aggression provides a ready stage on which some men represent their social privilege and introduce adolescent boys to their future place in the status hierarchy.

Why has the sexual abuse of women and the humiliation of generations of pledges been tolerated for so long? The answer lies in a historical tendency to privilege male college students by failing to hold them accountable. Administrators protect young men by dissociating asocial behavior from the perpetrator and attributing it to something else. For example, one hears adult officials complaining about violence committed by fraternity brothers at the same time they condone the violence by saying that "things got out of hand" because of alcohol, adolescence, or some other version of "boys will be boys." Refusing to take serious action against young offenders promotes the male privilege that led to the behavior in the first place. At some level, perhaps, administrators believe that by taking effective action to end all forms of abuse they deny young men a forum for training for masculinity. Where this is the case women students cannot possibly experience the same social opportunities or sense of belonging at college as their male peers, even though they spend the same amount of money for the privilege of attending. As colleges and universities face an increasing number of legal suits deriving from rape, murder, and the other forms of abuse reported in fraternities, athletic settings, and dorms, change is clearly imminent. . . .

REFERENCES

Ehrhart, Julie K., and Bernice R. Sandler. 1985. "Campus Gang Rape: Party Games?" Washington, D.C.: Project on the Status of Women, Association of American Colleges.

Goodenough, Ward Hunt. 1963. *Cooperation in Change*. New York: Russell Sage Foundation.

Sanday, Peggy Reeves. 1981. "The Socio-Cultural Context of Rape." *Journal of Social Issues* 37: 5–27.

————. 1986. "Rape and the Silencing of the Feminine." In *Rape: A Collection of Essays,* edited by Roy Porter and Sylvana Tomaselli. London: Basil Blackwell.

Anti-Gay Stereotypes

Richard D. Mohr

A recent Gallup poll found that only one in five Americans reports having a gay acquaintance.[1] This finding is extraordinary given the number of practicing homosexuals in America. Alfred Kinsey's 1948 study of the sex lives of 5000 white males shocked the nation: 37 percent had at least one homosexual experience to orgasm in their adult lives; an additional 13 percent had homosexual fantasies to orgasm; 4 percent were exclusively homosexual in their practices; another 5 percent had virtually no heterosexual experience, and nearly 20 percent had at least as many homosexual as heterosexual experiences.[2] With only slight variations, these figures held across all social categories: region, religion, political belief, class, income, occupation, and education.

Two out of five men one passes on the street have had orgasmic sex with men. Every second family in the country has a member who is essentially homosexual, and many more people regularly have homosexual experiences. Who are homosexuals? They are your friends, your minister, your teacher, your bankteller, your doctor, your mailcarrier, your secretary, your congressional representative, your sibling, parent, and spouse. They are everywhere, virtually all ordinary, virtually all unknown.

What follows? First, the country is profoundly ignorant of the actual experience of gay people. Second, social attitudes and practices that are harmful to gays have a much greater overall negative impact on society than is usually realized. Third, most gay people live in hiding—in the closet—making the "coming out" experience the central fixture of gay consciousness and invisibility the chief social characteristic of gays.

Society's ignorance of gay people is, however, not limited to individuals' lack of personal acquaintance with gays. Stigma against gay people is so strong that even discussions of homosexuality are taboo. This taboo is particularly strong in academe, where it is reinforced by the added fear of the teacher as molester. So even within the hearth of reason irrational forces have held virtually unchallenged and largely unchallengeable sway. The usual sort of clarifying research that might be done on a stigmatized minority has with gays only just begun—haltingly—in history, literature, sociology, and the sciences.

Yet ignorance about gays has not stopped people from having strong opinions about them. The void which ignorance leaves has been filled with stereotypes. Society holds chiefly two groups of antigay stereotypes; the two are an oddly contradictory lot. One set of stereotypes revolves around alleged mistakes in an individual's gender identity: lesbians are women that want to be, or at least look and act like, men—bulldykes, diesel dykes; while gay men are those who want to be, or at least look and act like, women—queens, fairies, limp-wrists, nellies. Gays are "queer," which, remember, means at root not merely weird but chiefly counterfeit—"he's as queer as a three dollar bill." These stereotypes of mismatched or fraudulent genders provide the materials through which gays and lesbians become the butts of ethnic-like jokes. These stereotypes and jokes, though derisive, basically view gays and lesbians as ridiculous.

Another set of stereotypes revolves around gays as a pervasive, sinister, conspiratorial, and corruptive threat. The core stereotype here is the gay person as child molester and, more generally, as sex-crazed maniac. These stereotypes carry with them fears of the very destruction of family and civilization itself. Now, that which is essentially ridiculous can hardly have such a staggering effect. Something must be afoot in this incoherent amalgam.

Sense can be made of this incoherence if the nature of stereotypes is clarified. Stereotypes are not *simply* false generalizations from a skewed sample of cases examined. Admittedly, false generalizing plays a part in most stereotypes a society holds. If, for instance, one takes as one's sample homosexuals who are in psychiatric hospitals or prisons, as was done in nearly all early investigations, not surprisingly one will probably find homosexuals to be of a crazed and criminal cast. Such false generalizations, though, simply confirm beliefs already held on independent grounds, ones that likely led the investigator to the prison and psychiatric ward to begin with. Evelyn Hooker, who in the mid-fifties carried out the first rigorous studies to use nonclinical gays, found that psychiatrists, when presented with results of standard psychological diagnostic tests—but with indications of sexual orientation omitted—were able to do no better than if they had guessed randomly in their attempts to distinguish gay files from nongay ones, even though the psychiatrists believed gays to be crazy and supposed themselves to be experts in detecting craziness.[3] These studies proved a profound embarrassment to the psychiatric establishment, the financial well-being of which was substantially enhanced by 'curing' allegedly insane gays. Eventually the studies contributed to the American Psychiatric Association's dropping homosexuality from its registry of mental illnesses in 1973.[4] Nevertheless, the stereotype of gays as sick continues apace in the mind of America.

False generalizations *help maintain* stereotypes; they do not *form* them. As the history of Hooker's discoveries shows, stereotypes have a life beyond facts. Their origin lies in a culture's ideology—the general system of beliefs by which it lives—and they are sustained across generations by diverse cultural transmissions, hardly any of which, including slang and jokes, even purport to have a scientific basis. Stereotypes, then, are not the products of bad science, but are social constructions that perform central functions in maintaining society's conception of itself.

On this understanding, it is easy to see that the antigay stereotypes surrounding gender identification are chiefly means of reinforcing still powerful gender roles in society. If, as this stereotype presumes (and condemns), one is free to choose one's social roles independently of gender, many guiding social divisions, both domestic and commercial, might be threatened. The socially gender-linked distinctions would blur between breadwinner and homemaker, protector and protected, boss and sec-retary, doctor and nurse, priest and nun, hero and whore, saint and siren, lord and helpmate, and God and his world. The accusations "fag" and "dyke" (which recent philology has indeed shown to be rooted in slang referring to gender-bending, espe-cially cross-dressing)[5] exist in significant part to keep women in their place and to prevent men from breaking ranks and ceding away theirs.

The stereotypes of gays as child molesters, sex-crazed maniacs, and civilization destroyers function to displace (socially irresolvable) problems from their actual source to a foreign (and so, it is thought, manageable) one. Thus, the stereotype of child molester functions to give the family unit a false sheen of absolute innocence. It keeps the unit from being examined too closely for incest, child abuse, wife-battering, and the terrorism of constant threats. The stereotype teaches that the problems of the family are not internal to it, but external.

Because this stereotype has this central social function, it could not be dislodged even by empirical studies, paralleling Hooker's efforts, that showed heterosexuals to be child molesters to a far greater extent than the actual occurrence of heterosex-uals in the general population.[6] But one need not even be aware of such debunking empirical studies in order to see the same cultural forces at work in the social belief that gays are molesters as in its belief that they are crazy. For one can see them now in society's and the media's treatment of current reports of violence, especially domestic violence. When a mother kills her child or a father rapes his daughter—regular Section B fare even in major urbane papers—this is never taken by re-porters, columnists, or pundits as evidence that there is something wrong with het-erosexuality or with traditional families. These issues are not even raised.

But when a homosexual child molestation is reported it is taken as confirming evidence of the way homosexuals are. One never hears of heterosexual murders, but one regularly reads of "homosexual" ones. Compare the social treatment of Richard Speck's sexually motivated mass murder in 1966 of Chicago nurses with that of John Wayne Gacy's serial murders of Chicago youths. Gacy was in the culture's mind taken as symbolic of gay men in general. To prevent the possibility that The Family was viewed as anything but an innocent victim in this affair, the mainstream press knowingly failed to mention that most of Gacy's adolescent victims were homeless hustlers, even though this was made obvious at his trial.[7] That knowledge would be too much for the six o'clock news and for cherished beliefs.

The stereotype of gays as sex-crazed maniacs functions socially to keep individuals' sexuality contained. For this stereotype makes it look as though the problem of how to address one's considerable sexual drives can and should be answered with repression, for it gives the impression that the cyclone of dangerous psychic forces is *out there* where the fags are, not within one's own breast. With the decline of the stereotype of the black man as raping pillaging marauder (found in such works as *Birth of a Nation*, *Gone with the Wind*, and *Soul on Ice*), the stereotype of gay men as sex-crazed maniacs has become more aggravated. The stereotype of the sex-crazed threat seems one that society desperately needs to have somewhere in its sexual cosmology.

For the repressed homosexual, this stereotype has an especially powerful allure — by hating it consciously, he subconsciously appears to save himself from himself, at least as long as the ruse does not exhaust the considerable psychic energies required to maintain it, or until, like ultraconservative Congressmen Robert E. Bauman (R-Md.) and Jon C. Hinson (R-Miss.), he is caught importuning hustlers or gentlemen in washrooms.[8] If, as Freud and some of his followers thought, everyone feels an urge for sex partners of both genders, then the fear of gays works to show us that we have not "met the enemy and he is us."[9]

By directly invoking sex acts, this second set of stereotypes is the more severe and serious of the two — one never hears child-molester jokes. These stereotypes are aimed chiefly against men, as in turn stereotypically the more sexed of the genders. They are particularly divisive for they create a very strong division between those conceived as "us" and those conceived as "them." This divide is not so strong in the case of the stereotype of gay men as effeminate. For women (and so the woman-like) after all do have their place. Nonstrident, nonuppity useful ones can even be part of "us," indeed, belong, like "our children," to "us." Thus, in many cultures with overweening gender-identified social roles (like prisons, truckstops, the armed forces, Latin America, and the Islamic world) only passive partners in male couplings are derided as homosexual.[10]

Because "the facts" largely do not matter when it comes to the generation and maintenance of stereotypes, the effects of scientific and academic research and of enlightenment generally will be, at best, slight and gradual in the changing fortunes of gays. If this account of stereotypes holds, society has been profoundly immoral. For its treatment of gays is a grand scale rationalization and moral sleight-of-hand. The problem is not that society's usual standards of evidence and procedure in coming to judgments of social policy have been misapplied to gays, rather when it comes to gays, the standards themselves have simply been ruled out of court and disregarded in favor of mechanisms that encourage unexamined fear and hatred.

Partly because lots of people suppose they do not know a gay person and partly though their willful ignorance of society's workings, people are largely unaware of the many ways in which gays are subject to discrimination in consequence of widespread fear and hatred. Contributing to this social ignorance of discrimination is the difficulty for gay people, as an invisible minority, even to complain of discrimination. For if one is gay, to register a complaint would suddenly target one as a stigmatized person, and so, in the absence of any protections against discrimination, would in turn invite additional discrimination.

Further, many people, especially those who are persistently downtrodden and so lack a firm sense of self to begin with, tend either to blame themselves for their troubles or to view their troubles as a matter of bad luck or as the result of an innocent mistake by others—as anything but an injustice indicating something wrong with society. Alfred Dreyfus went to his grave believing his imprisonment for treason and his degradation from the French military, in which he was the highest ranking Jewish officer, had all just been a sort of clerical error, merely requiring recomputation, rather than what it was—lightning striking a promontory from out of a storm of national bigotry.[11] The recognition of injustice requires doing something to rectify wrong; the recognition of systematic injustices requires doing something about the system, and most people, especially the already beleaguered, simply are not up to the former, let alone the latter.

For a number of reasons, then, discrimination against gays, like rape, goes seriously underreported. What do they experience? First, gays are subject to violence and harassment based simply on their perceived status rather than because of any actions they have performed. A recent extensive study by the National Gay and Lesbian Task Force found that over 90 percent of gays and lesbians had been victimized in some form on the basis of their sexual orientation.[12] Greater than one in five gay men and nearly one in ten lesbians had been punched, hit, or kicked; a quarter of all gays had had objects thrown at them; a third had been chased; a third had been sexually harassed and 14 percent had been spit on—all just for being perceived to be gay.

The most extreme form of antigay violence is queerbashing—where groups of young men target another man who they suppose is gay and beat and kick him unconscious and sometimes to death amid a torrent of taunts and slurs. Such seemingly random but in reality socially encouraged violence has the same social origin and function as lynchings of blacks—to keep a whole stigmatized group in line. As with lynchings of the recent past, the police and courts have routinely averted their eyes, giving their implicit approval to the practice.

Few such cases with gay victims reach the courts. Those that do are marked by inequitable procedures and results. Frequently judges will describe queerbashers as "just All-American Boys." In 1984, a District of Columbia judge handed suspended sentences to queerbashers whose victim had been stalked, beaten, stripped at knife point, slashed, kicked, threatened with castration, and pissed on, because the judge thought the bashers were good boys at heart—after all they went to a religious prep school.[13]

In the summer of 1984, three teenagers hurled a gay man to his death from a bridge in Bangor, Maine. Though the youths could have been tried as adults and normally would have been, given the extreme violence of their crime, they were tried rather as children and will be back on the streets again automatically when they turn twenty-one.[14]

Further, police and juries simply discount testimony from gays.[15] They typically construe assaults on and murders of gays as "justified" self-defense—the killer need only claim his act was a panicked response to a sexual overture.[16] Alternatively, when guilt seems patent, juries will accept highly implausible insanity or other "diminished capacity" defenses. In 1981 a former New York City Transit Authority policeman, later claiming he was just doing the work of God, machine-gunned down nine people, killing two, in two Greenwich Village gay bars. His jury found him innocent due to mental illness.[17] The best known example of a successful "diminished capacity" defense is Dan White's voluntary manslaughter conviction for the 1978 assassination of openly gay San Francisco city councilman Harvey Milk—Hostess Twinkies, his lawyer successfully argued, made him do it.[18]

These inequitable procedures and results collectively show that the life and liberty of gays, like those of blacks, simply count for less than the life and liberty of members of the dominant culture. . . .

NOTES

1. "Public Fears—And Sympathies," *Newsweek*, August 12, 1985, p. 23.

2. Alfred C. Kinsey, et al., *Sexual Behavior in the Human Male* (Philadelphia: Saunders, 1948), pp. 650–51. On the somewhat lower incidences of lesbianism, see Alfred C. Kinsey, et al., *Sexual Behavior in the Human Female* (Philadelphia: Saunders, 1953), pp. 472–75.

3. Evelyn Hooker, "The Adjustment of the Male Overt Homosexual," *Journal of Projective Techniques* (1957) 21:18–31, reprinted in Hendrik M. Ruitenbeck, ed., *The Problem of Homosexuality*, pp. 141–61, epigram quote from p. 149 (New York: Dutton, 1963).

4. See Ronald Bayer, *Homosexuality and American Psychiatry* (New York: Basic Books, 1981).

5. See Wayne Dynes, *Homolexis: A Historical and Cultural Lexicon of Homosexuality* (New York: Gay Academic Union, Gai Saber Monograph No. 4, 1985), s.v. dyke, faggot.

6. For studies showing that gay men are no more likely—indeed, are less likely—than heterosexuals to be child molesters and that the most widespread and persistent sexual abusers of children are the children's fathers, stepfathers or mother's boyfriends, see Vincent De Francis, *Protecting the Child Victim of Sex Crimes Committed by Adults* (Denver: The American Humane Association, 1969), pp. vii, 38, 69–70; A. Nicholas Groth, "Adult Sexual Orientation and Attraction to Underage Persons," *Archives of Sexual Behavior* (1978) 7:175–81; Mary J. Spencer, "Sexual Abuse of Boys," *Pediatrics* (July 1986) 78(1):133–38.

7. See Lawrence Mass, "Sanity in Chicago: The Trial of John Wayne Gacy and American Psychiatry," *Christopher Street* [New York] (June 1980) 4(7):26. See also Terry Sullivan, *Killer Clown* (New York: Grosset & Dunlap, 1983), pp. 219–25, 315–16; Tim Cahill, *Buried Dreams* (Toronto: Bantam Books, 1986), pp. 318, 352–53, 368–69.

8. For Robert Bauman's account of his undoing, see his autobiography, *The Gentleman from Maryland* (New York: Arbor House, 1986).

9. On Freud, see Timothy F. Murphy, "Freud Reconsidered: Bisexuality, Homosexuality, and Moral Judgment," *Journal of Homosexuality* (1984) 9(2–3):65–77.

10. On prisons, see Wayne Wooden and Jay Parker, *Men Behind Bars: Sexual Exploitation in Prison* (New York: Plenum, 1982). On the armed forces, see George Chauncey Jr., "Christian Brotherhood or Sexual Perversion? Homosexual Identities and the Construction of Sexual Boundaries in the World War One Era," *Journal of Social History* (1985) 19: 189–211.

11. See Jean-Denis Bredin, *The Affair: The Case of Alfred Dreyfus*, trans. Jeffrey Mehlman (1983; New York: George Braziller, 1986), pp. 486–96.

12. National Gay and Lesbian Task Force, *Anti-Gay/Lesbian Victimization* (New York: National Gay and Lesbian Task Force, 1984). See also, "Anti-Gay Violence," Subcommittee on Criminal Justice, Committee on the Judiciary, House of Representatives, 99th Congress, 2nd Session, October 9, 1986, serial no. 132.

13. "Two St. John's Students Given Probation in Assault on Gay," *The Washington Post*, May 15, 1984, p. I.

The 1980 Mariel boatlift, which included thousands of gays escaping Cuban internment camps, inspired U.S. Federal District Judge A. Andrew Hauk in open court to comment of a Mexican illegal alien caught while visiting his resident alien daughter: "And he isn't even a fag like all these faggots we're letting in." *The Advocate* [Los Angeles], November 27, 1980, no. 306, p. 15. Cf. "Gay Refugees Tell of Torture, Oppression in Cuba," *The Advocate*, August 21, 1980, no. 299, pp. 15–16.

14. See *The New York Times*, September 17, 1984, p. D17 and October 6, 1984, p. 6.

15. John D'Emilio writes of the trial of seven police officers caught in a gay bar shakedown racket: "The defense lawyer cast aspersions on the credibility of the prosecution witnesses . . . and deplored a legal system in which 'the most notorious homosexual may testify against a policeman.' Persuaded by this line of argument, the jury acquitted all of the defendants." *Sexual Politics, Sexual Communities: The Making of a Homosexual Minority in the United States, 1940–1970* (Chicago: University of Chicago Press, 1983), p. 183.

16. See for discussion and examples, Pat Califia, "'Justifiable' Homicide?" *The Advocate*, May 12, 1983, no. 367, p. 12 and Robert G. Bagnall, et al., "Burdens on Gay Litigants and Bias in the Court System: Homosexual Panic, Child Custody, and Anonymous Parties," *Harvard Civil Rights-Civil Liberties Law Review* (1984) 19:498–515.

17. *The New York Times*, July 25, 1981, p. 27, and July 26, 1981, p. 25.

18. See Randy Shilts, *The Mayor of Castro Street: The Life and Times of Harvey Milk* (New York: St. Martin's, 1982), pp. 308–25.

Media Magic:
Making Class Invisible

Gregory Mantsios

Of the various social and cultural forces in our society, the mass media is arguably the most influential in molding public consciousness. Americans spend an average twenty-eight hours per week watching television. They also spend an undetermined number of hours reading periodicals, listening to the radio, and going to the movies. Unlike other cultural and socializing institutions, ownership and control of the mass media is highly concentrated. Twenty-three corporations own more than one-half of all the daily newspapers, magazines, movie studios, and radio and television outlets in the U.S.[1] The number of media companies is shrinking and their control of the industry is expanding. And a relatively small number of media outlets is producing and packaging the majority of news and entertainment programs. For the most part, our media is national in nature and single-minded (profit-oriented) in purpose. This media plays a key role in defining our cultural tastes, helping us locate ourselves in history, establishing our national identity, and ascertaining the range of national and social possibilities. In this essay, we will examine the way the mass media shapes how people think about each other and about the nature of our society.

The United States is the most highly stratified society in the industrialized world. Class distinctions operate in virtually every aspect of our lives, determining the nature of our work, the quality of our schooling, and the health and safety of our loved ones. Yet remarkably, we, as a nation, retain illusions about living in an egalitarian society. We maintain these illusions, in large part, because the media hides gross inequities from public view. In those instances when inequities are revealed, we are provided with messages that obscure the nature of class realities and blame the victims of class-dominated society for their own plight. Let's briefly examine what the news media, in particular, tells us about class.

About the Poor

The news media provides meager coverage of poor people and poverty. The coverage it does provide is often distorted and misleading.

The Poor Do Not Exist

For the most part, the news media ignore the poor. Unnoticed are forty million poor people in the nation—a number that equals the entire population of Maine, Vermont, New Hampshire, Connecticut, Rhode Island, New Jersey, and New York combined. Perhaps even more alarming is that the rate of poverty is increasing twice as fast as the population growth in the United States. Ordinarily, even a calamity of much smaller proportion (e.g., flooding in the Midwest) would garner a great deal of coverage and hype from a media usually eager to declare a crisis, yet less than one in five hundred articles in the *New York Times* and one in one thousand articles listed in the *Readers Guide to Periodic Literature* are on poverty. With remarkably little attention to them, the poor and their problems are hidden from most Americans.

When the media does turn its attention to the poor, it offers a series of contradictory messages and portrayals.

The Poor Are Faceless

Each year the Census Bureau releases a new report on poverty in our society and its results are duly reported in the media. At best, however, this coverage emphasizes annual fluctuations (showing how the numbers differ from previous years) and ongoing debates over the validity of the numbers (some argue the number should be lower, most that the number should be higher). Coverage like this desensitizes us to the poor by reducing poverty to a number. It ignores the human tragedy of poverty—the suffering, indignities, and misery endured by millions of children and adults. Instead, the poor become statistics rather than people.

The Poor Are Undeserving

When the media does put a face on the poor, it is not likely to be a pretty one. The media will provide us with sensational stories about welfare cheats, drug addicts, and greedy panhandlers (almost always urban and Black). Compare these images and the emotions evoked by them with the media's treatment of middle class (usually white) "tax evaders," celebrities who have a "chemical dependency," or wealthy businesspeople who use unscrupulous means to "make a profit." While the behavior of the more affluent offenders is considered an "impropriety" and a deviation from the norm, the behavior of the poor is considered repugnant, indicative of the poor in general, and worthy of our indignation and resentment.

The Poor Are an Eyesore

When the media does cover the poor, they are often presented through the eyes of the middle class. For example, sometimes the media includes a story about community resistance to a homeless shelter or storekeeper annoyance with panhandlers. Rather than focusing on the plight of the poor, these stories are about middle-class opposition to the poor. Such stories tell us that the poor are an inconvenience and an irritation.

The Poor Have Only Themselves to Blame

In another example of media coverage, we are told that the poor live in a personal and cultural cycle of poverty that hopelessly imprisons them. They routinely center on the Black urban population and focus on perceived personality or cultural traits that doom the poor. While the women in these stories typically exhibit an "attitude" that leads to trouble or a promiscuity that leads to single motherhood, the men possess a need for immediate gratification that leads to drug abuse or an unquenchable greed that leads to the pursuit of fast money. The images that are seared into our mind are sexist, racist, and classist. Census figures reveal that most of the poor are white not Black or hispanic, that they live in rural or suburban areas not urban centers, and hold jobs at least part of the year.[2] Yet, in a fashion that is often framed in an understanding and sympathetic tone, we are told that the poor have inflicted poverty on themselves.

The Poor Are Down on Their Luck

During the Christmas season, the news media sometimes provide us with accounts of poor individuals or families (usually white) who are down on their luck. These stories are often linked to stories about soup kitchens or other charitable activities and sometimes call for charitable contributions. These "Yule time" stories are as much about the affluent as they are about the poor: they tell us that the affluent in our society are a kind, understanding, giving people—which we are not.* The series of unfortunate circumstances that have led to impoverishment are presumed to be a temporary condition that will improve with time and a change in luck.

Despite appearances, the messages provided by the media are not entirely disparate. With each variation, the media informs us what poverty is not (i.e., systemic and indicative of American society) by informing us what it is. The media tells us that poverty is either an aberration of the American way of life (it doesn't exist, it's

---

*American households with incomes of less than $10,000 give an average of 5.5 percent of their earning to charity or to a religious organization, while those making more than $100,000 a year give only 2.9 percent. After changes in the 1986 tax code reduced the benefits of charitable giving, taxpayers earning $500,000 or more slashed their average donation by nearly one-third. Furthermore, many of these acts of benevolence do not help the needy. Rather than provide funding to social service agencies that aid the poor, the voluntary contributions of the wealthy go to places and institutions that entertain, inspire, cure, or educate wealthy Americans—art museums, opera houses, theaters, orchestras, ballet companies, private hospitals, and elite universities. (Robert Reich, "Secession of the Successful," *New York Times Magazine*, February 17, 1991 p. 43.)

just another number, it's unfortunate but temporary) or an end product of the poor themselves (they are a nuisance, do not deserve better, and have brought their predicament upon themselves).

By suggesting that the poor have brought poverty upon themselves, the media is engaging in what William Ryan has called "blaming the victim."[3] The media identify in what ways the poor are different as a consequence of deprivation, then define those differences as the cause of poverty itself. Whether blatantly hostile or cloaked in sympathy, the message is that there is something fundamentally wrong with the victims—their hormones, psychological makeup, family environment, community, race, or some combination of these—that accounts for their plight and their failure to lift themselves out of poverty.

But poverty in the United States is systemic. It is a direct result of economic and political policies that deprive people of jobs, adequate wages, or legitimate support. It is neither natural nor inevitable: there is enough wealth in our nation to eliminate poverty if we chose to redistribute existing wealth or income. The plight of the poor is reason enough to make the elimination of poverty the nation's first priority. But poverty also impacts dramatically on the nonpoor. It has a dampening effect on wages in general (by maintaining a reserve army of unemployed and underemployed anxious for any job at any wage) and breeds crime and violence (by maintaining conditions that invite private gain by illegal means and rebellion-like behavior, not entirely unlike the urban riots of the 1960s). Given the extent of poverty in the nation and the impact it has on us all, the media must spin considerable magic to keep the poor and the issue of poverty and its root causes out of the public consciousness.

About Everyone Else

Both the broadcast and the print news media strive to develop a strong sense of "we-ness" in their audience. They seek to speak to and for an audience that is both affluent and like-minded. The media's solidarity with affluence, that is, with the middle and upper class, varies little from one medium to another. Benjamin DeMott points out, for example, that the *New York Times* understands affluence to be intelligence, taste, public spirit, responsibility, and a readiness to rule and "conceives itself as spokesperson for a readership awash in these qualities."[4] Of course, the flip side to creating a sense of "we" or "us," is establishing a perception of the "other." The other relates back to the faceless, amoral, undeserving, and inferior "underclass." Thus, the world according to the news media is divided between the "underclass" and everyone else. Again the messages are often contradictory.

The Wealthy Are Us

Much of the information provided to us by the news media focuses attention on the concerns of a very wealthy and privileged class of people. Although the concerns of a small fraction of the populace, they are presented as though they were the concerns of everyone. For example, while relatively few people actually own stock, the news media devotes an inordinate amount of broadcast time and print space to business news and stock market quotations. Not only do business reports cater to a particular narrow clientele, so do the fashion pages (with $2,000 dresses), wedding announcements, and the obituaries. Even weather and sports news often have a class bias. An all news radio station in New York City, for example, provides regular national ski reports. International news, trade agreements, and domestic policies issues are also reported in terms of their impact on business climate and the business community. Besides being of practical value to the wealthy, such coverage has considerable ideological value. Its message: the concerns of the wealthy are the concerns of us all.

The Wealthy (as a Class) Do Not Exist

While preoccupied with the concerns of the wealthy, the media fails to notice the way in which the rich as a class of people create and shape domestic and foreign policy. Presented as an aggregate of individuals, the wealthy appear without special interests, interconnections, or unity in purpose. Out of public view are the class interests of the wealthy, the interlocking business links, the concerted actions to preserve their class privileges and business interests (by running for public office, supporting political candidates, lobbying, etc.). Corporate lobbying is ignored, taken for granted, or assumed to be in the public interest. (Compare this with the media's portrayal of the "strong arm of labor" in attempting to defeat trade legislation that is harmful to the interests of working people.) It is estimated that two-thirds of the U.S. Senate is composed of millionaires.[5] Having such a preponderance of millionaires in the Senate, however, is perceived to be neither unusual nor anti-democratic; these millionaire senators are assumed to be serving "our" collective interests in governing.

The Wealthy Are Fascinating and Benevolent

The broadcast and print media regularly provide hype for individuals who have achieved "super" success. These stories are usually about celebrities and superstars from the sports and entertainment world. Society pages and gossip columns serve to keep the social elite informed of each others doings, allow the rest of us to gawk at their excesses, and help to keep the American dream alive. The print media is also fond of feature stories on corporate empire builders. These stories provide an occasional "insiders" view of the private and corporate life of industrialists by suggesting a rags to riches account of corporate success. These stories tell us that corporate success is a series of smart moves, shrewd acquisitions, timely mergers, and well thought out executive suite shuffles. By painting the upper class in a positive light, innocent of any wrongdoing (labor leaders and union organizations usually get the opposite treatment), the media assure us that wealth and power are benevolent. One person's capital accumulation is presumed to be good for all. The elite, then, are portrayed as investment wizards, people of special talent and skill, who even their victims (workers and consumers) can admire.

The Wealthy Include a Few Bad Apples

On rare occasions, the media will mock selected individuals for their personality flaws. Real estate investor Donald Trump and New York Yankees owner George Steinbrenner, for example, are admonished by the media for deliberately seeking publicity (a very un-upper class thing to do); hotel owner Leona Hemsley was caricatured for her personal cruelties; and junk bond broker Michael Milkin was condemned because he had the audacity to rob the rich. Michael Parenti points out that by treating business wrongdoings as isolated deviations from the socially beneficial system of "responsible capitalism," the media overlook the features of the system that produce such abuses and the regularity with which they occur. Rather than portraying them as predictable and frequent outcomes of corporate power and the business system, the media treats abuses as if they were isolated and atypical. Presented as an occasional aberration, these incidents serve not to challenge, but to legitimate the system.[6]

The Middle Class Is Us

By ignoring the poor and blurring the lines between the working people and the upper class, the news media create a universal middle class. From this perspective, the size of one's income becomes largely irrelevant: what matters is that most of "us" share an intellectual and moral superiority over the disadvantaged. As *Time* magazine once concluded, "Middle America is a state of mind."[7] "We are all middle class," we are told, "and we all share the same concerns:" job security, inflation, tax burdens, world peace, the cost of food and housing, health care, clean air and water, and the safety of our streets. While the concerns of the wealthy are quite distinct from those of the middle class (e.g., the wealthy worry about investments, not jobs), the media convinces us that "we [the affluent] are all in this together."

The Middle Class Is a Victim

For the media, "we" the affluent not only stand apart from the "other"—the poor, the working class, the minorities, and their problems—"we" are also victimized by the poor (who drive up the costs of maintaining the welfare roles), minorities (who commit crimes against us), and by workers (who are greedy and drive companies out and prices up). Ignored are the subsidies to the rich, the crimes of corporate America, and the policies that wreak havoc on the economic well-being of middle America. Media magic convinces us to fear, more than anything else, being victimized by those less affluent than ourselves.

The Middle Class Is Not a Working Class

The news media clearly distinguish the middle class (employees) from the working class (i.e., blue collar workers) who are portrayed, at best, as irrelevant, outmoded, and a dying breed. Furthermore, the media will tell us that the hardships faced by blue collar workers are inevitable (due to progress), a result of bad luck (chance circumstances in a particular industry), or a product of their own doing (they priced themselves out of a job). Given the media's presentation of reality, it is hard to believe that manual, supervised, unskilled, and semiskilled workers actually represent more than 50 percent of the adult working population.[8] The working class, instead, is relegated by the media to "the other."

In short, the news media either lionizes the wealthy or treats their interests and those of the middle class as one in the same. But the upper class and the middle class do not share the same interests or worries. Members of the upper class worry about stock dividends (not employment), they profit from inflation and global militarism, their children attend exclusive private schools, they eat and live in a royal fashion, they call on (or are called upon by) personal physicians, they have few consumer problems, they can escape whenever they want from environmental pollution, and they live on streets and travel to other areas under the protection of private police forces.*[9]

The wealthy are not only a class with distinct life-styles and interests, they are a ruling class. They receive a disproportionate share of the country's yearly income, own a disproportionate amount of the country's wealth, and contribute a disproportionate number of their members to governmental bodies and decision-making groups—all traits that William Domhoff, in his classic work *Who Rules America*, defined as characteristic of a governing class.[10]

This governing class maintains and manages our political and economic structures in such a way that these structures continue to yield an amazing proportion of our wealth to a minuscule upper class. While the media is not above referring to ruling classes in other countries (we hear, for example, references to Japan's ruling elite),[11] their treatment of the news proceeds as though there were no such ruling class in the United States.

Furthermore, the news media inverts reality so that those who are working class and middle class learn to fear, resent, and blame those below, rather than those

---

*The number of private security guards in the United States now exceeds the number of public police officers. (Robert Reich, "Secession of the Successful", *New York Times Magazine*, February 17, 1991, p. 42.)

above them in the class structure. We learn to resent welfare, which accounts for only two cents out of every dollar in the federal budget (approximately $10 billion) and provides financial relief for the needy,* but learn little about the $11 billion the federal government spends on individuals with incomes in excess of $100,000 (not needy),[12] or the $17 billion in farm subsidies, or the $214 billion (twenty times the cost of welfare) in interest payments to financial institutions.

Middle-class whites learn to fear African Americans and Latinos, but most violent crime occurs within poor and minority communities and is neither interracial** nor interclass. As horrid as such crime is, it should not mask the destruction and violence perpetrated by corporate America. In spite of the fact that 14,000 innocent people are killed on the job each year, 100,000 die prematurely, 400,000 become seriously ill, and 6 million are injured from work-related accidents and diseases, most Americans fear government regulation more than they do unsafe working conditions.

Through the media, middle class—and even working class—Americans learn to blame blue collar workers and their unions for declining purchasing power and economic security. But while workers who managed to keep their jobs and their unions struggled to keep up with inflation, the top 1 percent of American families saw their average incomes soar 80 percent in the last decade.[13] Much of the wealth at the top was accumulated as stockholders and corporate executives moved their companies abroad to employ cheaper labor (56 cents per hour in El Salvador) and avoid paying taxes in the United States. Corporate America is a world made up of ruthless bosses, massive layoffs, favoritism and nepotism, health and safety violations, pension plan losses, union busting, tax evasions, unfair competition, and price gouging, as well as fast buck deals, financial speculation, and corporate wheeling and dealing that serve the interests of the corporate elite, but are generally wasteful and destructive to workers and the economy in general.

It is no wonder Americans cannot think straight about class. The mass media is neither objective, balanced, independent, nor neutral. Those who own and direct the mass media are themselves part of the upper class, and neither they nor the ruling class in general have to conspire to manipulate public opinion. Their interest is in preserving the status quo, and their view of society as fair and equitable comes naturally to them. But their ideology dominates our society and justifies what is in reality a perverse social order—one that perpetuates unprecedented elite privilege and power on the one hand and widespread deprivation on the other. A mass media that did not have its own class interests in preserving the status quo would acknowledge that inordinate wealth and power undermines democracy and that a "free market" economy can ravage a people and their communities.

---

*A total of $20 billion is spent on welfare when you include all state funding. But the average state funding also comes to only two cents per state dollar.

**In 92 percent of the murders nationwide the assailant and the victim are the same race (46 percent are white/white, 46 percent are black/black), 5.6 percent are black on white, and 2.4 percent are white on black. (FBI and Bureau of Justice Statistics, 1985–1986, quoted in Franklin p. 108)

NOTES

1. Martin Lee and Norman Solomon, *Unreliable Sources*, Lyle Stuart (New York, 1990), p. 71. See also, Ben Bagdikian, *The Media Monopoly*, Beacon Press (Boston, 1990).

2. Department of Commerce, Bureau of the Census, "Poverty in the United States: 1992," *Current Population Reports, Consumer Income*, Series P60–185, pp. xi, xv, 1.

3. William Ryan, *Blaming the Victim*, Vintage (New York, 1971).

4. Benjamin Demott, *The Imperial Middle*, William Morrow (New York, 1990), p. 123.

5. Fred Barnes, "The Zillionaires Club," *The New Republic*, January 29, 1990, p. 24.

6. Michael Parenti, *Inventing Reality*, St. Martin's Press (New York, 1986), p. 109.

7. *Time*, January 5, 1979, p. 10.

8. Vincent Navarro, "The Middle Class—A Useful Myth," *The Nation*, March 23, 1992, p. 1.

9. Charles Anderson, *The Political Economy of Social Class*, Prentice Hall (Englewood Cliffs, N.J., 1974), p. 137.

10. William Domhoff, *Who Rules America*, Prentice Hall (Englewood Cliffs, N.J., 1967), p. 5.

11. Lee and Solomon, *Unreliable Sources*, Lyle Stuart (New York, 1990), p. 179.

12. *Newsweek*, August 10, 1992, p. 57.

13. *Business Week*, June 8, 1992, p. 86.

⑧

Sex and Race:
The Analogy of Social Control

William Chafe

. . . Analogies should not be limited to issues of substance alone, nor is their purpose to prove that two categories or objects are exactly identical. According to the dictionary, an analogy is "a relation of likeness . . . consisting in the resemblance not of the things themselves but of two or more attributes, circumstances or effects." Within this context, the purpose of an analogy is to illuminate a process or relationship which might be less discernible if only one or the other side of the comparison were viewed in isolation. What, then, if we look at sex and race as examples of how social control is exercised in America, with the primary emphasis on what the analogy tells us about the modes of control emanating from the dominant culture? Throughout the preceding discussion, the strongest parallels dealt with the use of stereotypes and ascribed attributes to define the respective position of women and blacks in the society. Thus what if the nature of the analogy is not in the *substance* of the material existence which women and blacks have experienced but in the *forms* by which others have kept them in "their place" and prevented them from challenging the status quo?

The virtues of such an approach are many. First, it provides greater flexibility in exploring how the experience of one group can inform the study of another. Second, it has the potential of developing insights into the larger processes by which the status quo is perpetuated from generation to generation. In this sense, it can teach us about the operation of society as a whole and the way in which variables like sex and race have been made central to the division of responsibilities and power within the society. If the forms of social control used with blacks and women resemble each other in "two or more attributes, circumstances, or effects," then it may be possible to learn something both about the two groups and how the status quo has been maintained over time. The best way to pursue this, in turn, is through looking closely at the process of social control as it has operated on one group, and then comparing it with the process and experience of the second group.

In his brilliant autobiographical novel *Black Boy*, Richard Wright describes what it was like to grow up black in the Jim Crow South. Using his family, the church, his classmates, his jobs, and his fantasies as stage-pieces for his story, Wright plays out the themes of hunger, fear, and determination which permeated his young life. Above all, he provides a searing account of how white Southerners successfully controlled the lives and aspirations of blacks. A series of concentric circles of social control operated in devastating fashion to limit young blacks to two life options—conformity to the white system, or exile.*

The outermost circle of control, of course, consisted of physical intimidation. When Richard asked his mother why black men did not fight white men, she responded, "The white men have guns and the black men don't." Physical force, and ultimately the threat of death, served as a constant reminder that whites held complete power over black lives. Richard saw that power manifested repeatedly. When his Uncle Hoskins dared to start his own saloon and act independently of the white power structure, he was lynched. The brother of one of Richard's schoolmates suffered a similar fate, allegedly for fooling with a white prostitute. When Richard worked for a clothing store, he frequently saw the white manager browbeat or physically attack black customers who had not paid their bills on time. When one woman came out of the store in a torn dress and bleeding, the manager said, "That's what we do to niggers when they don't pay their bills."[1]

---

*Despite the problems created by using a novel for purposes of historical analysis, the interior perspective that is offered outweighs the limitations of "subjectiveness." Wright has been criticized for being overly harsh and elitist in his judgment of his black peers. His depiction of the conditions blacks had to cope with, on the other hand, corresponds well with the historical record. In the cases of both women and blacks, novels provide a vividness of detail and personal experience necessary to understand the larger processes at work in the society, but for the most part unavailable in conventional historical sources.

The result was pervasive fear, anchored in the knowledge that whites could unleash vicious and irrational attacks without warning. Race consciousness could be traced, at least in part, to the tension which existed between anger at whites for attacking blacks without reason, and fear that wanton violence could strike again at any time, unannounced and unrestrained. "The things that influenced my conduct as a Negro," Richard wrote, "did not have to happen to me directly; I needed but to hear of them to feel their full effects in the deepest layers of my consciousness. Indeed the white brutality that I had not seen was a more effective control of my behavior than that which I knew . . . as long as it remained something terrible and yet remote, something whose horror and blood might descend upon me at any moment, I was compelled to give my entire imagination over to it, an act which blocked the springs of thought and feelings in me."[2]

The second circle of control rested in white domination of the economic status of black people. If a young black did not act the part of "happy nigger" convincingly, the employer would fire him. Repeatedly, Richard was threatened with the loss of work because he did not keep his anger and independence from being communicated to his white superiors. "Why don't you laugh and talk like the other niggers?" one employer asked. "Well, sir, there is nothing much to say or smile about," Richard said. "I don't like your looks nigger. Now git!" the boss ordered. Only a limited number of economic roles were open to blacks, and if they were not played according to the rules, the job would be lost. A scarce supply of work, together with the demand that it be carried out in a deferential manner, provided a powerful guarantee that blacks would not get out of line.[3]

Significantly, the highest status jobs in the black community—teachers, ministers, civil servants—all depended ultimately upon acting in ways that pleased the white power structure.* One did not get the position at the post office or in the school system without being "safe"—the kind of person who would not make trouble. The fundamental precondition for success in the black community, therefore, was acting in ways that would not upset the status quo. When Richard tried to improve his own occupational chances and learn the optical trade, the white men who were supposed to teach him asked: "What are you trying to do, get smart, nigger?"[4]

The third circle of control consisted of the psychological power of whites to define and limit the reach of black aspirations. The sense people have of who they are and what they might become is tied intimately to the expectations communicated to them by others. The verbal cues, the discouragement or encouragement of authority figures, the picture of reality transmitted by friends or teachers—all of

---

*There is an important distinction, of course, between jobs which were tied to white support and those with an indigenous base in the black community. Black doctors, morticians, and barbers, for example, looked to the black community itself for their financial survival; hence they could be relatively free of white domination. On the other hand, the number of such independent positions was small. Although many people would include ministers in such a category, the visibility of the ministerial role created pressure from blacks concerned with the stability and safety of their churches for ministers to avoid a radical protest position. That started to change during the civil rights movement.

these help to shape how people think of themselves and their life chances. Stated in another way, human beings can envision careers as doctors and lawyers or a life of equality with others only to the extent that someone holds forth these ideals as viable possibilities.

Within this realm of social psychology, white Southerners exerted a pervasive and insidious control upon blacks. When Richard took his first job in a white household, he was given a bowl of molasses with mold on it for breakfast, even as his employers ate bacon and eggs. The woman he worked for asked what grade he was in, and when he replied the seventh, she asked, "Then why are you going to school?" When he further answered, "Well, I want to be a writer," she responded: "You'll never be a writer . . . who on earth put such ideas into your nigger head?" By her response, the woman attempted to undercut whatever sense of possibility Richard or other young blacks might have entertained for such a career. In effect, the woman had defined from a white perspective the outer boundaries of a black person's reality. As Richard noted, "She had assumed that she knew my place in life, what I felt, what I ought to be, and I resented it with all my heart . . . perhaps I would never be a writer; but I did not want her to say so." In his own time Richard Wright was able to defy the limits set upon his life by white people. But for the overwhelming majority of his fellow blacks, the ability of whites to intimidate them psychologically diminished the chance that they would be able to aspire realistically to a life other than that assigned them within a white racist social structure.[5]

The most devastating control of all, however, was that exercised by the black community itself out of self-defense. In the face of a world managed at every level by white power, it became an urgent necessity that black people train each other to adapt in order to survive. Thus the most profound and effective socialization toward accepting the racial status quo came from Richard's own family and peer group. It was Richard's mother who slapped him into silence "out of her own fear" when he asked why they had not fought back after Uncle Hoskins's lynching. To even ask the question posed a threat to safety. Similarly, it was Richard's Uncle Tom who insisted that Richard learn, almost by instinct, how to be accommodating. If Richard did not learn, the uncle said, he would never amount to anything and would end up on the gallows. Indeed, Richard would survive only if somebody broke his spirit and set the "proper" example.[6]

The instances of social control from within the black community abound in Wright's *Black Boy*. It was not only the white employer, but almost every black he knew, who opposed Richard's writing aspirations. "From no quarter," he recalled, "with the exception of the Negro newspaper editor, had there come a single encouraging word . . . I felt that I had committed a crime. Had I been aware of the full extent to which I was pushing against the current of my environment, I would have been frightened altogether out of my attempts at writing." The principal of his school urged vehemently that Richard give a graduation speech written by the principal rather than by Richard himself so that the proper tone of accommodation could be struck; the reward for going along was a possible teaching job. Griggs,

Richard's best friend, was perhaps the most articulate in demanding that Richard control his instincts. "You're black and you don't act a damn bit like it." When Richard replied, "Oh Christ, I can't be a slave," Griggs responded with the ultimate lesson of reality: "But you've got to eat . . . when you are in front of white people, think before you act, think before you speak . . . you may think I'm an Uncle Tom, but I'm not. I hate these white people, hate them with all my heart. But I can't show it; if I did, they'd kill me." No matter where he went or whom he talked to in his own community, Richard found, not support for his protest, but the warning that he must behave externally in the manner white people expected. Whatever the hope of ultimate freedom, survival was the immediate necessity. One could not fight another day if one was not alive.[7]

Paradoxically, even the outlets for resistance within the system provided a means of reinforcing it. There were many ways of expressing unhappiness with one's lot, and all were essential to let off steam. The gang on the corner constantly verbalized resentment and anger against the white oppressor. Yet the very fact that the anger had to be limited to words and out of the earshot of whites meant that in practical terms it was ineffectual. Humor was another form of resistance. Richard and his friends joked that, if they ate enough black-eyed peas and buttermilk, they would defeat their white enemies in a race riot with "poison gas." But the end of the joke was an acknowledgment that the only way in reality to cope with the "mean" white folks was to leave.[8]

Indeed, the most practical form of resistance—petty theft—almost seemed a ploy by white people to perpetuate the system. Just as modern-day department store owners tolerate a certain degree of employee theft as a means of making the workers think they are getting away with something so they will not demand higher wages, so white employers of black people appear to have intentionally closed their eyes to a great deal of minor stealing. By giving blacks a small sense of triumph, white employers were able to tie them even more closely into the system, and prevent them from contemplating outright defiance. As Wright observed:[9]

> No Negroes in my environment had ever thought of organizing . . . and petitioning their white employers for higher wages . . . They knew that the whites would have retaliated with swift brutality. So, pretending to conform to the laws of the whites, grinning, bowing, they let their fingers stick to what they could touch. And the whites seemed to like it.
>
> But I, who stole nothing, who wanted to look them straight in the face, who wanted to talk and act like a man, inspired fear in them. The southern whites would rather have had Negroes who stole work for them than Negroes who knew, however dimly, the worth of their own humanity. Hence, whites placed a premium upon black deceit; they encouraged irresponsibility, and their rewards were bestowed upon us blacks in the degree that we could make them feel safe and superior.

From a white point of view, a minor exercise of indirect and devious power by blacks was a small price to pay for maintaining control over the entire system. Thus, whites held the power to define black people's options, even to the point of controlling their modes of resistance.*

The result of all this was a system that functioned smoothly, with barely a trace of overt protest or dissension. Everyone seemed outwardly content with their place. At a very early age, Wright observed, "the white boys and the black boys began to play our traditional racial roles as though we had been born to them, as though it was in our blood, as though we were guided by instinct." For most people, the impact of a pervasive system of social control was total: resignation, a lowering of aspirations, a recognition of the bleakness of the future and the hopelessness of trying to achieve major change. In Wright's images life was like a train on a track; once headed in a given direction, there was little possibility of changing one's course.[10]

Wright himself, of course, was the exception. "Somewhere in the dead of the southern night," he observed, "my life had switched onto the wrong track, and without my knowing it, the locomotive of my heart was rushing down a dangerously steep slope, heading for a collision, heedless of the warning red lights that blinked all about me, the sirens and the bells and the screams that filled the air." Wright had chosen the road of exile, of acute self-consciousness and alienation. For most blacks of his era, though, the warning red lights, the sirens, the bells, and the screams produced at least outward conformity to the status quo. In the face of forms of social control which effectively circumscribed one's entire life, there seemed no other choice.[11]

Obviously, women have not experienced overtly and directly the same kind of consistent physical intimidation that served so effectively to deter the black people of Richard Wright's childhood from resisting their condition. On the other hand, it seems clear that the physical strength and alleged dominance of men have been an important instrument of controlling women's freedom of action. The traditional image of the male as "protector" owes a great deal to the notion that women cannot defend themselves and that men must therefore take charge of their lives physically. The same notion of male strength has historically been responsible for restricting jobs involving heavy labor to men. Nor is the fear with which women view the potential of being struck or raped by a male lover, husband, or attacker an insignificant reality in determining the extent to which women historically have accepted the dominance of the men in their lives. Richard Wright observed that "the things that influenced my conduct . . . did not have to happen to me directly; I needed but to hear of them to feel their full effects. . . ." Similarly, women who have grown up with the image of powerful and potentially violent men need not have experienced a direct attack to share a sense of fear and intimidation. "Strength," the psychologist

*It is important to remember that there existed a life in the black community less susceptible to white interference on a daily basis. Black churches, lodges, and family networks provided room for individual self-expression and supplied emotional reinforcement and sustenance. In this connection it is no accident that black institutions are strongest in the South where, until recently, the vast majority of blacks resided. On the other hand, the freedom which did exist came to a quick end wherever blacks attempted to enter activities, occupations, or areas of aspiration involving whites; or defined as white-controlled. Thus even the realm where freedom existed was partially a reflection of white control.

Jerome Kagan has observed, "is a metaphor for power." Thus, despite the substantive difference in the way women and blacks have been treated, the form of social control represented by physical strength has operated similarly for both groups.[12]

An even stronger case can be made for the way in which economic controls have succeeded in keeping blacks and women in their place. In 1898 Charlotte Perkins Gilman argued in *Women and Economics* that the root of women's subjection was their economic dependency on men. As long as women were denied the opportunity to earn their own living, she argued, there could never be equality between the sexes. The fact that women had to please their mates, both sexually and through other services, to ensure their survival made honest communication and mutual respect impossible. The prospect of a "present" from a generous husband, or a new car or clothes, frequently served to smooth over conflict, while the implicit threat of withholding such favors could be used to discourage carrying conflict too far.[13]

In fact, the issue of women not controlling their own money has long been one of the most painful and humiliating indexes of inequality between the sexes, especially in the middle class. Since money symbolizes power, having to ask others for it signifies subservience and an inferior status. Carol Kennicott, the heroine of Sinclair Lewis's *Main Street*, recognized the problem. After begging prettily for her household expenses early in her marriage, she started to demand her own separate funds. "What was a magnificent spectacle of generosity to you," she told her husband, "was a humiliation to me. You *gave* me money—gave it to your mistress if she was complaisant." Beth Phail, a character in Marge Piercy's novel *Small Changes*, experienced the same conflict with her husband, who was immediately threatened by the idea of her economic autonomy. Indeed, few examples of psychological control seem more pointed than those represented in husbands' treating their wives as not mature enough to handle their own money.[14]

Even the women who held jobs reflected the pattern by which economic power was used to control women's freedom of action. Almost all women workers were concentrated in a few occupations delineated as "woman's" work. As secretaries, waitresses, cooks, and domestic workers, women on the job conformed to the "service" image of their sex. Significantly, the highest status jobs available—nurses and teachers—tended to reinforce a traditional image of women and the status quo between the sexes, just as the highest jobs available within the black community—teachers and civil servants—reinforced a pattern of accommodation with the existing white power structure. Any woman who chose a "man's job" automatically risked a loss of approval, if not total hostility. For most, the option simply did not exist.

Even those in the most prestigious positions illustrated how money could be used as an instrument of social control. If they were to succeed in raising funds, college administrators in black and women's schools frequently found that they had to shape their programs in conformity to social values that buttressed the status quo. Booker T. Washington represented the most outstanding example of this phenomenon. Repeatedly he was forced to appease white racist presumptions in order to get another donation for Tuskegee. As the funnel through which all white philanthropic aid to blacks was channeled, Washington had to ensure that no money would be spent in a way which might challenge the political values of his contributors, even though privately he fought those political values. But Washington was not alone. During the 1830's Mary Lyons, head of Mt. Holyoke Seminary, agreed not to attend trustee meetings lest she offend male sensibilities, and Mary Alice Baldwin, the very effective leader of the Women's College of Duke University, felt it necessary to pay homage to the conservative tradition of "the Southern lady" as the price for sustaining support of women's education at Duke.[15]

In all of these instances, economic controls functioned in parallel ways to limit the freedom of women and blacks. If a group is assigned a "place," there are few more effective ways of keeping it there than economic dependency. Not only must the group in question conform to the expectations of the dominant class in order to get money to live; those who would do otherwise are discouraged by the fact that no economic incentives exist to reward those who challenge the status quo. The absence of financial support for those who dare to deviate from prescribed norms has served well to perpetuate the status quo in the condition of both women and blacks. "I don't want to be a slave," Richard Wright observed. "But you have to eat," Griggs replied.

The strongest parallel, however, consists of the way in which blacks and women have been given the psychological message that they should be happy with their "place." In both instances, this form of control has effectively limited aspiration to non-conventional roles. Although Beth Phail of *Small Changes* wanted to go to college and law school, her family insisted that her highest aspiration should be marriage and homemaking. A woman should not expect a career. Similarly, when Carol Kennicott told her college boy friend, "I want to do something with my life," he responded eagerly: "What's better than making a comfy home and bringing up some cute kids . . . ?" The small town atmosphere of Gopher Prairie simply reinforced the pressure to conform. Carol was expected to be a charming hostess, a dutiful wife, and a good homemaker, but not a career woman. Thus, as Sinclair Lewis observed, she was a "woman with a working brain and no work." The messages Carol received from her surroundings were not designed to give her high self-esteem. Her husband called her "an extravagant little rabbit," and his poker partners, she noted simply expected her "to wait on them like a servant."[16]

Although Carol's personality was atypical, her social experience was not. When high school girls entertained the possibility of a career, they were encouraged to be nurses, not doctors. The qualities that received the most praise were those traditionally associated with being a "lady," not an assertive individual ready to face the world. Significantly, both women and blacks were the victims of two devices designed to discourage non-conformity. Those who sought to protest their status, for example, were subjected to ridicule and caricature. The black protestor was almost certain to be identified with subversive activity, just as the women's rights advocate was viewed as unsexed and a saboteur of the family. (Ordinary blacks and females were subject to a gentler form of humor, no less insidious, as in the characters of Amos 'n Andy's "King Fish" or Lucille Ball's "Lucy.") In addition, it was not uncommon for blacks to be set against blacks and women against women in a competition which served primarily the interests of the dominant group. According to Judith Bardwick and Elizabeth Douvan, girls are socialized to use oblique forms of aggression largely directed at other females, while men's aggression is overt. The stereotype of women doing devious battle over an attractive man is an ingrained part of our folk tradition. Nor is the "divide and conquer" strategy a stranger to the history of black people, as when white workers sowed seeds of suspicion between Richard Wright and another black worker in order to make them fight each other for the entertainment of whites.[17]

In both cases the psychological form of social control has operated in a similar fashion. The aspirations, horizons, and self-images of blacks and women have been defined by others in a limiting and constrictive way. More often than not, the result historically has been an acceptance of society's perception of one's role. The prospect of becoming an architect, an engineer, or a carpenter is not easy to sustain in an environment where the very idea is dismissed as foolish or unnatural. Instead of encouragement to aspire to new horizons of achievement, the message transmitted to blacks and women has been the importance of finding satisfaction with the status quo.

But in the case of women, as with blacks, the most effective instrument of continued control has been internal pressure from the group itself. From generation to generation, mothers teach daughters to please men, providing the instruction that prepares the new generation to assume the roles of mothers and housewives. Just as blacks teach each other how to cope with "whitey" and survive within the system, women school each other in how to win a man, how to appear charming, where to "play a role" in order to avoid alienating a potential husband. When Beth in *Small Changes* rebelled against her husband and fought the idea of tying herself down with a child, it was the other women in her family who urged her to submit and at least give the *appearance* of accepting the role expected of her.[18]

In fact, dissembling in order to conform to social preconceptions has been a frequent theme of women's socialization. As Mirra Komarovsky has demonstrated, college women in the 1940's were taught to hide their real ability in order to make their male friends feel superior. "My mother thinks that it is very nice to be smart in college," one of Komarovsky's students noted, "but only if it doesn't take too much effort. She always tells me not to be too intellectual on dates, to be clever in a light sort of way." It is not difficult to imagine one woman saying to another as Griggs said to Richard Wright, "When you are around white people [men] you have to act the part that they expect you to act." Even if deception was the goal, however, the underlying fact was that members of the "oppressed" group acted as accomplices in perpetuating the status quo.[19]

The most effective device for maintaining internal group discipline was to ostracize those who did not conform. Richard Wright found himself singled out for negative treatment because he refused to accept authority and to smile and shuffle before either his teachers or white people. Beth Phail was roundly condemned by her sisters and mother for not pleasing her husband, and above all for not agreeing to have a child. And Carol Kennicott received hostile glances when she violated her "place" by talking politics with men or seeking to assume a position of independent leadership in the community of Gopher Prairie. The disapproval of her female peers was the most effective weapon used to keep her in line, and, when it appeared that she finally was going to have a child, her women friends applauded the fact that in becoming a mother she would finally get over all her strange ideas and settle down. As Sinclair Lewis observed, "She felt that willy-nilly she was being initiated into the assembly of housekeepers; with the baby for hostage, she would never escape."[20]

The pressure of one's own group represented a double burden. In an environment where success was defined as marriage, and fulfillment as being a happy homemaker, it was hard enough to fight the tide in the first place. If one did, however, there was the additional problem of being seen as a threat to all the other members of the group who had conformed. The resistance of blacks toward Richard Wright and of women toward Carol Kennicott becomes more understandable in light of the fact that in both cases the individual protestors, through their refusal to play the game according to the rules, were also passing judgment on those who accepted the status quo. Thus, historically, women and blacks have kept each other in line not only as a means of group self-defense—protecting the new generation from harm and humiliation—but also as a means of maintaining self-respect by defending the course they themselves have chosen.

Indeed, for women as well as for blacks, even the vehicles for expressing resentment became reinforcements of the status quo. For both groups, the church provided a central emotional outlet—a place where solidarity with one's own kind could be found, and where some protest was possible. Women's church groups provided not only a means of seeking reform in the larger society but also for talking in confidence to other women about the frustrations of being a woman in a male-dominated society. What social humorists have called "hen-sessions" were in fact group therapy encounters where women had a chance to voice their gripes. Humor was frequently a vehicle for expressing a bittersweet response to one's situation, bemoaning, even as one laughed, the pain of being powerless. But as in the case with blacks, venting one's emotions about a life situation—although necessary for survival—was most often an instrument for coping with the situation, rather than for changing it.

Perhaps the most subversive and destructive consequence of a pervasive system of social control is how it permeates every action, so that even those who are seeking to take advantage of the "enemy" end up supporting the system. When Shorty, the elevator man in *Black Boy* known for his wit and hostility to whites, needed some money for lunch one day, he told a white man he would not move the elevator until he got a quarter. "I'm hungry, Mr. White Man. I'm dying for a quarter," Shorty said. The white man responded by asking what Shorty would do for a quarter. "You can kick me for a quarter," Shorty said, bending over. At the end of the elevator ride, Shorty had his quarter. "This monkey's got the peanuts," he said. Shorty was right. He had successfully used racial stereotypes and his own role as a buffoon to get

himself some lunch money. But in the process, the entire system of racial imbalance had been strengthened.[21]

Similar patterns run through the history of women's relationships to men. The
coquette role is only the most extreme example of a type of manipulative behavior
by women that seems to confirm invidious stereotypes. In the classic case of a wife
trying to persuade her husband to go along with a desired course of action, the
woman may play up to a man's vanity and reinforce his stereotyped notions about
being a tower of strength and in control. Similarly, a female employee wishing
advancement may adopt a flirtatious attitude toward a male superior. By playing a
semi-seductive role and implying a form of sexual payoff for services rendered, she
may achieve her immediate goal. But in each of these cases, the price is to become
more entrapped in a set of distorted and unequal sex role stereotypes. The fact that
overt power is not available and that the ability to express oneself honestly and
openly has been denied leads to the use of covert and manipulative power. Thus,
a woman may play dumb or a black may act deferential—conforming in each case
to a stereotype—as a means of getting his or her way. But the result is pathological
power that simply perpetuates the disease. The irony is that, even in trying to outwit
the system of social control, the system prevails.

Basic to the entire system, of course, has been the extent to which a clearly
defined role was "woven into the texture of things." For blacks the crucial moment
might come as soon as they developed an awareness of whites. In the case of women,
it more likely took place at puberty when the need to begin pleasing potential husbands was emphasized. In either case, what Richard Wright said about the process
of socialization could be said of both groups. "I marveled," he wrote[22]:

> at how smoothly the black boys [women] acted out the role . . . mapped out for
> them. Most of them were not conscious of living a special, separate, stunted way of
> life. Yet I knew that in some period of their growing up—a period that they had no
> doubt forgotten—there had been developed in them a delicate, sensitive controlling
> mechanism that shut off their minds and emotions from all that the white race
> [society] had said was taboo. Although they lived in America where in theory there
> existed equality of opportunity, they knew unerringly what to aspire to and what not
> to aspire to.

The corollary for both women and blacks, at least metaphorically, has been that
those unable or unwilling to accept the role prescribed for them have been forced
into a form of physical or spiritual exile. Richard Wright understood that continued
accommodation with the white Southern system of racial oppression would mean
the destruction of his integrity and individuality. "Ought one to surrender to authority even if one believed that the authority was wrong?" Wright asked. "If the
answer was yes, then I knew that I would always be wrong, because I could never
do it. . . . How could one live in a world in which one's mind and perceptions
meant nothing and authority and tradition meant everything?" The only alternative
to psychological death was exile, and Wright pursued that course, initially in Chicago, later in Paris. In her own way Carol Kennicott attempted the same journey.

"I've got to find out what my work is," she told her husband. "I've been ruled too long by fear of being called things. I'm going away to be quiet and think. I'm—I'm going. I have a right to my own life." And Beth Phail finally fled her home and family because it was the only way to grow up, to find out what "she wanted," to learn how to be a person in her own right in the world.[23]

Although in reality only a few blacks and women took the exact course adopted by Richard Wright, Carol Kennicott, and Beth Phail, all those who chose to resist the status quo shared to some extent in the metaphor of exile. Whether the person was a feminist like Charlotte Perkins Gilman, a pioneer career woman such as Elizabeth Blackwell, a runaway slave like Frederick Douglass, or a bold race leader like W. E. B. Du Bois, the act of challenging prevailing norms meant living on the edge of alienation and apart from the security of those who accepted the status quo. Until and unless protest generated its own community of support which could provide a substitute form of security and reinforcement, the act of deviance promised to be painful and solitary.

This condition, in turn, reflected an experience of marginality which many blacks and women shared. In sociological terms, the "marginal" personality is someone who moves in and out of different groups and is faced with the difficulty of adjusting behavior to the norms of the different groups. By definition, most blacks and most women have participated in that experience, especially as they have been required to accommodate the expectations of the dominant group of white males. The very fact of having to adopt different modes of behavior for different audiences introduces an element of complexity and potential conflict to the lives of those who are most caught up in a marginal existence. House slaves, for example, faced the inordinately difficult dilemma of being part of an oppressed group of slaves even as they lived in intimacy with and under the constant surveillance of the white master-class, thereby experiencing in its most extreme form the conflict of living in two worlds.[24]

Ordinarily, the tension implicit in such a situation is deflected, or as Richard Wright observed, "contained and controlled by reflex." Most house slaves seemed to learn how to live with the conflict by repressing their anger and uneasiness. Coping with the situation became a matter of instinct. But it is not surprising that many slave revolts were led by those house slaves who could not resolve the conflict by reflex, and instead were driven to alienation and protest. For the minority of people who misinterpreted the cues given them or learned too late how to cope, consciousness of the conflict made instinctive conformity impossible. As Richard Wright observed, "I could not make subservience an automatic part of my behavior. . . . while standing before a white man . . . I had to figure out how to say each word . . . I could not grin . . . I could not react as the world in which I lived expected me to." The pain of self-consciousness made the burden almost unbearable. As Maya Angelou has written, awareness of displacement "is the rust on the razor that threatens the throat." In an endless string of injuries, it was the final insult.[25]

Dissenting blacks and women have shared this experience of being "the outsider." Unable to accept the stereotyped behavior prescribed for their group, they have, in Vivian Gornick's words, "stood beyond the embrace of their fellows." With acute vision, Gornick writes, the outsider is able to "see deeply into the circle, penetrating to its very center, his vision a needle piercing the heart of life. Invariably, what he sees is intolerable." On the basis of such a vision, exile is the only alternative available. Yet, ironically, it too serves to reinforce the status quo by removing from the situation those most likely to fight it. Until the members willing to resist become great enough, the system of social control remains unaltered.[26]

It seems fair to conclude, therefore, that a significant resemblance has existed in the forms of social control used to keep women and blacks in their "place." Despite profound substantive differences between women and blacks, and white women and black women, all have been victims of a process, the end product of which has been to take away the power to define one's own aspirations, destiny, and sense of self. In each case a relationship of subservience to the dominant group has been perpetuated by physical, economic, psychological, and internal controls that have functioned in a remarkably similar way to discourage deviancy and place a premium on conformity. "It was brutal to be Negro and have no control over my life," Maya Angelou observes in her autobiography. "It was brutal to be young and already trained to sit quietly." From a feminist perspective, the same words describe the process of control experienced by most women.[27]

The core of this process has been the use of a visible, physical characteristic as the basis for assigning to each group a network of duties, responsibilities, and attributes. It is the physical foundation for discriminatory treatment which makes the process of social control on sex and race distinctive from that which has applied to other oppressed groups. Class, for example, comes closest to sex and race as a source of massive social inequity and injustice. Yet in an American context, class has been difficult to isolate as an organizing principle. Because class is not associated with a visible physical characteristic and many working class people persist in identifying with a middle-class life-style, class is not a category easy to identify in terms of physical or psychological control. (The very tendency to abjure class consciousness in favor of a social mobility ethic, of course, is its own form of psychological control.) Ethnicity too has frequently served as a basis for oppression, but the ease with which members of most ethnic minorities have been able to "pass" into the dominant culture has made the structure of social control in those cases both porous and complicated. Thus although in almost every instance invidious treatment has involved the use of some form of physical, economic, psychological, or internal controls, the combinations have been different and the exceptions frequent.

The analogy of sex and race is distinctive, therefore, precisely to the extent that it highlights in pure form the process of social control which has operated to maintain the existing structure of American society. While many have been victimized by the same types of control, only in the case of sex and race—where physical attributes are ineradicable—have these controls functioned systematically and clearly to define from birth the possibilities to which members of a group might aspire. Perhaps for that reason sex and race have been cornerstones of the social system, and the source of values and attitudes which have both reinforced the power of the dominant class and provided a weapon for dividing potential opposition.

Finally, the analogy provides a potential insight into the strategies and possibilities of social change. If women and blacks have been kept in their "place" by similar forms of social control, the prerequisites for liberation may consist of overcoming those forms of social control through a similar process. In the case of both women and blacks, the fundamental problem has been that others have controlled the power to define one's existence. Thus, to whatever extent women and blacks act or think in a given way solely because of the expectation of the dominant group rather than from their own choice, they remain captive to the prevailing system of social control. The prototypical American woman, writes Vivian Gornick, is perceived as "never taking, always being taken, never absorbed by her own desire, preoccupied only with whether or not she is desired." Within such a context, the "other" is always more important than the "self" in determining one's sense of individual identity. It is for this reason that efforts by blacks and women toward group solidarity, control over one's own institutions, and development of an autonomous and positive self-image may be crucial in breaking the bonds of external dominance.[28]

Yet such a change itself depends on development of a collective consciousness of oppression and a collective commitment to protest. As long as social and political conditions, or the reluctance of group members to participate, preclude the emergence of group action, the individual rebel has little chance of effecting change. Thus the issue of social control leads inevitably to the question of how the existing cycle is broken. What are the preconditions for the evolution of group protest? How do external influences stimulate, or forestall, the will to resist? And through what modes of organization and action does the struggle for autonomy proceed? For these questions too, the analogy of sex and race may provide a useful frame of reference.

Whatever the case, it seems more productive to focus on forms of control or processes of change than to dwell on the substantive question of whether blacks and women have suffered comparable physical and material injury. Clearly, they have not. On the other hand when two groups exist in a situation of inequality, it may be self-defeating to become embroiled in a quarrel over which is more unequal or the victim of greater oppression. The more salient question is how a condition of inequality for both is maintained and perpetuated—through what modes is it reinforced? By that criterion, continued exploration of the analogy of sex and race promises to bring added insight to the study of how American society operates.

NOTES

1. Richard Wright, *Black Boy* (New York, 1937), pp. 48, 52, 150, 157. Quotations used by permission of the publishers Harper and Row, New York.

2. Wright, pp. 65, 150–51.

3. Wright, p. 159.

4. Wright, p. 164.

5. Wright, pp. 127–29.

6. Wright, pp. 139–40.

7. Wright, pp. 147, 153–55, 160–61.

8. Wright, pp. 68–71, 200.

9. Wright, p. 175.

10. Wright, p. 72.

11. Wright, p. 148.

12. Wright, pp. 150–51; Brownmiller, *Against Our Will*; Jerome Kagan and H. A. Moss, *Birth to Maturity* (New York, 1962).

13. Degler, "Introduction," *Women and Economics*.

14. Lewis, *Main Street*, pp. 74, 167; Marge Piercy, *Small Changes* (Greenwich, Conn., 1972), p. 33.

15. Louis P. Harlan, *Booker T. Washington 1856–1901* (New York, 1972); Ralph Ellison, *Invisible Man* (New York, 1952); Flexner, *Century of Struggle*, p. 33; and Dara DeHaven, "On Educating Women—The Co-ordinate Ideal at Trinity and Duke University," Masters thesis, Duke University, 1974.

16. Piercy, *Small Changes*, pp. 19–20, 29, 40–41; Lewis, *Main Street*, pp. 14–15, 86, 283.

17. Bardwick and Douvan, "Ambivalence: The Socialization of Women"; Wright, *Black Boy*, pp. 207–13.

18. Piercy, *Small Changes*, pp. 31, 34, 316–17.

19. Piercy, pp. 30–31, 34, 39; Mirra Komarovsky, "Cultural Contradictions and Sex Roles," *American Journal of Sociology* 52 (November 1946).

20. Lewis, *Main Street*, p. 234.

21. Wright, *Black Boy*, p. 199.

22. Wright, p. 172.

23. Wright, p. 144; Lewis, *Main Street*, pp. 404–5; Piercy, *Small Changes*, p. 41.

24. See Everett Hughes, "Social Change and Status Protest: An Essay on the Marginal Man," *Phylon* 10 (December 1949); and Robert K. Merton, *Social Theory and Social Structure* (New York, 1965), pp. 225–50.

25. Wright, *Black Boy*, p. 130; Maya Angelou, *I Know Why the Caged Bird Sings*, p. 3.

26. Vivian Gornick, "Woman as Outsider," in Moran and Gornick, pp. 126–44.

27. Angelou, p. 153.

28. Gornick, p. 140.

9

Hate-Violence

Carole Sheffield

Hate-violence is not a new phenomenon in the United States. Our history reveals a pattern of violence, brutality, and bigotry against those defined as "other." The campaign of genocide against native peoples is the prototype of American hate-violence. In the first three hundred years of American history, hate-violence was often institutionally organized and sanctioned. The government and its agents were the perpetrators. State violence was committed against Native Americans, captured and enslaved Africans, African-Americans, workers, and citizens who protested against domestic and foreign policies. Hate-violence, however, has also always been spontaneous and unorganized. Violence against women and gay and lesbian people has been documented since the earliest settlements and illuminates the central role of violence in American life. Women's diaries, newspaper accounts, and case records of social work agencies (which date as far back as 1870) chronicle the high incidence of rape, sexual abuse of children, and wife beating. Men were executed for sodomy as early as 1624. Lesbian women and gay men have, for three centuries, been subjected to many forms of institutional violence including forced psychiatric treatment, castration and clitoridectomy (the removal of the clitoris), felony imprisonment and fines, and dishonorable discharge from the military (Herek 1989, p. 949).

Organized hate groups have played key roles in maintaining an environment of fear for minority Americans. The most well-known organized hate group, the Ku Klux Klan, was organized in 1865 out of the resentment and hatred many white Southerners felt after the Civil War, and emancipated Africans were its principal targets. The KKK has been responsible for some of the most brutal violence in our history. It has used whips, dynamite, hanging, acid-burning, tar-and-feathering, torture, shooting, stabbing, clubbing, fire-branding, castration, and other forms of mutilation (Bullard 1988, p. 24). Between 1889 and 1941, 3,811 black people were lynched in the United States. In 1981, Klansmen in Mobile, Alabama, stopped nineteen-year old Michael Donald as he was walking home from visiting relatives, cut his throat and hanged him from a tree limb in a residential neighborhood, because, as one of them put it, "they wanted to kill a black person" (Bullard 1988, p. 25). While the menace of the KKK has fluctuated over the years, it has never vanished. During the Civil Rights Movement, a particularly "active" time for the Klan, and up to the present, the Klan has developed ties with a number of hate groups, including the White Citizens Councils (organized to defy U.S. Supreme

Court-ordered desegregation), the Skinheads, and the Aryan Nation and its various subsidiaries. The Christian Identity Movement, which includes the Order, the Covenant, the Sword, the Arm of the Lord, seeks to unite religious people with the white supremacy movement (Ostling 1986, p. 74).

The Center for Democratic Renewal reports that gay people are now included with Jews and African-Americans as the "favorite target for hate groups" (Herek 1989, p. 952). For example, a hate group called "Crusade Against Corruption" published a pamphlet entitled "Praise God for AIDS," which claimed that "AIDS is a racial disease of jews and negroids that also exterminates sodomites." They called for the segregation of high risk AIDS groups "so as to protect innocent white people from AIDS" (Herek 1989, p. 952). Similarly, the National States Rights Party's newspaper *Thunderbolt*, in a front page headline "Bisexuals Infect white Women with AIDS," claimed that "most bisexuals are Negroes who often seek affairs with White females" (Herek 1989, p. 952). Here the linkage between race-hate, gay-hate, and misogyny is evident. It is important to note that racism, anti-Semitism, and hatred of gay and lesbian people are not caused by Klan and neo-Nazi organizations; these groups merely attract individuals whose prejudice and bigotry have already developed.

The Incidence of Hate-Violence

The latter part of the twentieth century has seen an alarming rise of individual acts of hate-violence. While organized hate groups do advocate and promulgate violence, much, if not most, hate-violence is not the work of people associated with organized hate groups. Singling out individuals for apparently random attack because of their sex, skin color, ethnicity, religion, presumed or known affectional identification is a pattern of both historical and contemporary significance. Recent examples include cross burnings on the front lawns of African-American families; an attack on African-Americans who moved into a predominately white neighborhood in Philadelphia; continued attacks by neighborhood youths on families of Cambodian refugees who had to flee Brooklyn; the shootings of African-American joggers; the beating to death of a Chinese-American because he was presumed to be Japanese; the harassment of Laotian fishermen in Texas; the brutal attack on two men in Manhattan by a group of knife-and bat-wielding teenage boys shouting "Homos!" and "Fags!"; the assault on three women in Portland, Maine, after their assailant yelled anti-lesbian epithets at them; the stalking of two lesbian women while camping in Pennsylvania, and the brutal murder of one of them; the gang rape with bottles, lighted matches, and other implements of a gay man who was repeatedly told, "this is what faggots deserve"; the stabbing to death of a heterosexual man in San Francisco because he was presumed to be gay; and the gang rapes of a female jogger in Central Park and a mentally handicapped teenager in Glen Ridge, N.J. Unfortunately, the list goes on and on.

While no national data on the incidence of racial, ethnic, anti-gay and lesbian, and sexual violence exists, there is a remarkable and generally unchallenged consensus that hate-violence is not only extensive but that it may well be increasing, both in incidence and in brutality (Hernandez 1990, p. 845–6; Finn and McNeil 1988, p. 2; Lutz 1987, p. 11; Wexler and Marx 1986, p. 205). The data which support this view come from a variety of sources, including twelve states who monitor hate crime statistics (in advance of the recent federal mandate to do so); hearings; reports from various municipalities; the FBI Uniform Crime Reports and the National Crime Surveys data on rape; statistics collected by a number of concerned interest groups; and the media. For example, the Anti-Defamation League of B'nai B'rith reports that anti-Semitic incidents, ranging from desecration to murder, reached their highest level in 1989 since the organization began collecting statistics eleven years ago (Toner 1990, p. A16). The National Gay and Lesbian Task Force (NGLTF) reports that the incidence of anti-gay violence and victimization reported to its Violence Project has risen steadily—an increase of 142 percent from 1985 to 1986 and an increase of 42 percent in 1987. In 1988, there were seventy "gay-motivated" or "gay-related" murders (Herek 1989, p. 950).

The Center for Democratic Renewal conducted a nation-wide study on racist violence and documented nearly 3,000 incidents of race hate-violence between 1980 and 1986 (Lutz 1987, p. 91). The study also revealed a notably high level of violence aimed at interracial couples (p. 13). The Puerto Rican Legal Defense and Education Fund reports a significant increase in hate crimes against Latinos (Hernandez 1990, p. 846). In 1988, thirty state attorneys general reported that violence against individuals based on race is increasing (Hernandez 1990, p. 846, note 2). Despite the high incidence revealed by these varied sources, most also agree that there is considerable underreporting of hate-violence. As with sexual violence, insensitivity and prejudice of officials, blaming the victim (especially true of women, gay men, and lesbian women, who are often accused of "flaunting" their sexuality), shame, fear of exposure, and fear that little or nothing will be done contribute to underreporting.

Finally, recent studies and reports suggest that the incidence of hate-violence on college campuses is quite high. During the 1986–1987 academic year, the National Institute Against Prejudice and Violence documented racist incidents on 130 college campuses (Farrell and Jones 1988, p. 214). However, most colleges and universities do not have adequate reporting procedures and this data is also seriously underrepresentative of the actual incidence of campus hate-violence.

The Roots of Hate-Violence

Hate-violence is neither accidental nor coincidental. It is the result of acquired beliefs, stereotypes, expectations, and images that we have of ourselves and others. These beliefs, etc. are called "ideologies." An ideology is a system of beliefs about how things are and how things should be. As such, an ideology is both descriptive and prescriptive. It helps us to process and evaluate information and events, to determine what is right or wrong, good or bad. It helps us locate and understand our place in a complex world.

Ideologies, commonly known as "isms," address questions of social, economic, political, religious, and even scientific relations. The "isms" that are of primary concern in understanding the roots of hate-violence are racism, sexism, classism, and heterosexism. Each of these "isms" is based on conceptualizations of superiority and inferiority. In racism, white people are defined as naturally superior to people of color; in sexism, men are defined as superior to women; in classism, richer people are considered superior to poorer people; and in heterosexism, heterosexual people are considered superior to homosexual or bisexual people. Within each "ism" is an elaborate network of beliefs and stereotypes that attempts to justify and maintain the dominance and privilege of the superior group. Dominance is maintained by an allocation of scarce resources (employment, education, housing, health care, status, acceptance, etc.), which favors the "superior" group. Indeed, members of those groups defined as superior are taught to expect greater advantages and rewards than those who are defined as inferior and therefore less deserving.

Dominance is translated by the ideology(ies) into specific interests and privileges, which while collectively defined (by race, sex, ethnicity, religion, sexual orientation) are manifested in individual expectations of resources and privileges. Harassing people of color who move into white middle-class neighborhoods and gay and lesbian people who demonstrate affection are examples of hate-violence based on what the perpetrators of such violence often feel is a betrayal of what they were taught to expect about how the world is and should be. Because ideologies establish a framework for determining who is most and least deserving of opportunities for success and fulfillment, economic conditions play a key role in organizing hate and bigotry. Economic hardship is blamed on "reverse discrimination," inflated welfare rolls, and unfair advantages "given" to racial minorities and women by "lowering standards" in the competition for fewer jobs and shrinking resources. This is known as "scapegoating"; a process of placing blame for society's problems on people who are defined as inferior. Another striking example of scapegoating is the dramatic rise in anti-gay and lesbian violence since the beginning of the AIDS epidemic. AIDS, however, is not the cause of such violence but rather the rationale used by bigots to justify their acts of hatred.

Dominance is also maintained through the threat of force and the use of actual violence against those defined as inferior. All systems of oppression employ violence and the threat of violence as an institutionalized mechanism for maintaining the interests and privileges of the "superior" group. Indeed, while there are differences in the manifestations of racism, sexism, heterosexism, and classism, the commonality that underlies these ideologies is force and its threat. No aspect of well-being is more fundamental than freedom from ideologically motivated and justified violence; that is, personal harm that is motivated by hatred and fear of one's ascribed characteristics (Sheffield 1987, p. 171). Richard Wright (1945), in his autobiography *Black Boy*, makes explicit the fear and control of racial terrorism:

> The things that influenced my conduct as a Negro did not have to happen to me directly. I needed but to hear of them to feel their full effects in the deepest layers

of my consciousness. Indeed, the white brutality that I had not seen was a more effective control of my behavior than that which I knew . . . as long as it remained something terrible and yet remote, something whose horror and blood might descend upon me at any moment, I was compelled to give up my entire imagination over to it, an act which blocked the springs of thought and feelings in me (p. 190).

Sexual Terrorism

Violence against women constitutes a system of sexual terrorism—a system by which males frighten and, by frightening, dominate and control females (Sheffield 1987, pp. 171–189; Sheffield 1989, pp. 3–19). Sexual terrorism is manifested through actual and implied violence; and all females, irrespective of race, class, physical or mental abilities, and sexual orientation, are potential victims—at any age, at any time, or in any place. Sexual terrorism employs a variety of means: rape, battery, incestuous abuse, sexual abuse of children, sexual harassment, pornography, prostitution and sexual slavery, and murder.

Pervasive sexual danger is a basic reality for American women. The level of violence against women is at an all-time high and many believe that it is increasing. Also, many acts of sexual violence are more severe and brutal than ever before. There is an apparent increase in gang rapes, serial rapes, sexual torture, and sexualized murder. Approximately 1,500 women are killed every year by husbands and lovers (Uniform Crime Reports 1987, p. 11). Nine out of every ten females who are murdered are murdered by men (Uniform Crime Reports 1989, p. 11). "In 1990, more women were raped than in any year in United States history," according to research conducted for the U.S. Senate Judiciary Committee (Majority Staff Report 1991, p. i). The FBI reports that in 1990 12 rapes were committed every hour, one every five minutes, close to 300 per day (Majority Staff Report 1991, p. 2). FBI data, however, does not reflect the actual incidence of rape due to the significant underreporting of this crime. Furthermore, the rape rate has increased four times faster than the overall crime rate during the last decade (Majority Staff Report 1991, p. 4). Every 18 seconds a woman is beaten. An estimated 3 million to 4 million women a year are battered, largely by their husbands or men they know (Rasky 1990, p. A19). Domestic violence is the single largest cause of injury to women in the U.S.; 22–35 percent of emergency room visits by women are for injuries caused by battering (Warshaw 1989, pp. 506–507). The March of Dimes (Brygger 1990, p. 1) reports that domestic violence is a major cause of birth defects in the U.S. Research indicates that there are nearly 38 million adults who have been sexually abused as children; 8 million who have been the victims of childhood incest (Crewdson 1988, p. 81).

Violence and its corollary, fear, function to terrorize females and to maintain the patriarchal definition of woman's subordinate place (Sheffield 1987, p. 171). How much do women worry about rape? According to Margaret T. Gordon and Stephanie Riger's (1989) study of female fear, about a third of women said they worry once a month about being raped—or more often; many said more than once a day. When they think about rape, they feel terrified and somewhat paralyzed. Another third of women indicated that the fear of rape is "part of the background," "one of those things that's always there." Another third said they never worried about rape but admitted taking precautions, "sometimes elaborate ones," to try to avoid being raped (pp. 21–22).

Women's attempts to avoid rape and other forms of sexual assault and intrusion take many forms. Women change/restrict their behavior, lifestyles, bodies, and appearances; they will pay higher costs for housing, purchase and maintain cars in order to avoid public transportation, refuse employment in certain areas or at certain times—all in attempts to avoid sexual assault. In a system of sexual terrorism where unpredictable, indiscriminate, and arbitrary violence is an essential component of social control, these self-protective acts serve as ways for women to feel some measure of control over their lives. Adaptive behaviors are used by all victims of oppression and are functional, although not without cost, for one's psychological, if not physical, survival.

Not only are women's lives controlled by the threat or reality of men's sexual violence, but the research shows that for many women it is the men they know— those with whom they live, work, spend leisure time—who are the most likely to victimize them. A study of acquaintance rape on 32 college campuses revealed that 1 in 4 women were victims of rape or attempted rape; that 84 percent of those raped knew their attacker; and that 57 percent of the rapes occurred while on dates (Warshaw 1988, p. 11). This reality, in large measure, sets sexual violence apart from other forms of hate-violence. Victims of race-hate or religious or ethnic intolerance have the most to fear from strangers. While gay and lesbian youth are often subject to abuse in the home, the perpetrators of anti-lesbian and gay violence are also mostly strangers.

Violence against women by acquaintances or by strangers is an assertion of the individual power of males as well as the power of men as a class. In this way, the beliefs and attitudes which support male interests and privileges are reinforced and perpetuated in women's and men's daily lives. Furthermore, we live in a culture that celebrates aggressive masculinity and denigrates female sexuality. Female sexuality is defined as insatiable, lustful, even desirous of male aggression. The pervasive patriarchal myth that "all women secretly want to be raped" provides the lens through which women and girls are blamed for their victimization. This belief that women/girls are responsible for assaults committed against them is a primary reason for the low conviction rate of rapists (Stanko 1985; LaFree 1989).

Moreover, the image of the male as warrior and the female as enemy is concretized in films, television, advertising, music, literature, and pornography. Every day and everywhere, in the most routine and mundane ways, women and female children are reminded visually and verbally that they are sexually objectified and are potential targets of violence. This commodification of women as sex is a multibillion dollar industry and further distinguishes sex hate from other forms of hate-violence.

Sexuality does, however, play a role in other forms of hate-violence. Sexual arrangements are socially constructed and are political in nature. They are often organized, imposed, propagandized, and enforced by a dominant group in order to further its aims. For example, the racist construction of the sexuality of Africans during slavery defined African men as sexual savages and particularly as rapists. This view provided the justification for lynchings, castration, and other brutal punishments designed to terrorize and control African men and the slave community as a whole. Similarly, African women were defined as sexual savages, as depraved, immoral, loose; available and eager for sexual relations with any man. These constructions of the sexuality of enslaved Africans were translated into stereotypes that persist today and influence the way society processes sexual assaults committed by African-American men or against African-American women. That African-American women are treated poorly by the criminal justice system when they are victims of sexual assault is well documented (hooks 1981; LaFree 1989).

Constructions of sexuality play a key role in hate-violence directed against lesbian women and gay men. Homosexuality has been constructed as deviant, sinful, sick, and dangerous. Homosexuality is seen as a perversion of heterosexuality: that is, a deviation from the "norm" of the aggressive, masculine man having sex with the passive, feminine woman. Thus, gay men are often denigrated with language infused with misogyny—"you faggot bitch." Lesbian women are often raped by men claiming that "sex" with them could turn them into heterosexuals. As with sexual violence, victim-blaming is pervasive in how society evaluates violence against lesbian and gay people. Recently, two college students were beaten in Philadelphia by several assailants who called them "faggots" and "pretty boys." The police refused to take a report on the assault because, they said, the victims provoked the incident by "sitting like that" (Roskey 1988, p. 18).

Hate-Violence and Social Control

The assessment of the impact and harm of hate-violence is a complex one, and a critical one as it points to the uniqueness and insidiousness of such violence. Hate-violence is motivated by social and political factors and is bolstered by belief systems which (attempt to) legitimate such violence. The intent of hate-violence is to harm both the individual victim and the group to which the victim belongs. It reveals that the personal is political; that such violence is *not* a series of isolated incidents but rather the consequence of a political culture which allocates rights, privilege and prestige according to biological or social characteristics. This is what distinguishes all forms of hate-violence from the random acts of violence that occur daily in this society. Ann Pellegrini (1990) argues that "hate crimes are not random acts. They target a person because of who she or he is; because of what she or he is taken to represent. The only thing random about a hate crime is which woman, which Korean-American, which African-American, which family with AIDS, is raped, assaulted, beaten with bats, left for dead, burned out of their home" (p. E13).

Furthermore, the harm from swastikas and other graffiti, racial epithets, cross-burnings, broken windows and other property destruction extends far beyond the material damage. Names and words that assail a person's basic identity and dignity are profoundly injurious. Many studies of raped and/or battered women reveal that the name-calling that accompanied the violence was described by the victims as being as hurtful as the actual violence. The manifestation of sexual violence, race-hate, religious intolerance, and hatred of gay and lesbian people in the form of assault or murder goes beyond the injured person or taken life. Hate-violence is a demonstration of power over the victim and the class to which the victim belongs; therefore, hate-violence victimizes an entire class of people. It functions to intimidate every member of the target group. Its purpose is to limit the rights and privileges of individuals/groups and to maintain the superiority of one group—its beliefs, values, and privileges—through terrorism.

Conclusion

On April 23, 1990 President George Bush signed the "Federal Hate Crimes Statistics Act." The Act requires the Justice Department to conduct a five-year statistical study on crimes that "manifest evidence of prejudice based on race, religion, sexual orientation, or ethnicity, including crimes of murder; non-negligent manslaughter; forcible rape; aggravated assault; simple assault; intimidation; arson; and destruction, damage or vandalism of property" (Rosenthal 1990, p. A14).

This law, noteworthy in that it represents a far-ranging consensus about the need to address hate-violence in America, and historic in that it recognizes that violence against gay and lesbian people is a crime of hatred and bigotry, is seriously flawed by its omission of sexual violence.* Counting hate crimes against women would reveal that 52 percent of the population is in serious jeopardy (Pellegrini 1990, p. E13). The exclusion of sex-hate as a form of hate-violence is not only a profound denial of the most pervasive form of violence in the United States but an attempt to deny the reality of patriarchal/sexist oppression and its interaction with other structures of power and privilege such as race, class, and sexuality. It is an attempt to have it both ways: that is, to rage against such hate-violence when the victims are males (and occasionally females) and yet protect male superiority over women. The denial of sexual violence as a hate crime is purposeful for the status quo, for it would be detrimental to the social order to define men's violence against women as a serious, hateful crime. The basic reality of sexual violence is that ordinary women are victimized every day by ordinary men. In denying this, the law sets the stage for viewing other forms of hate-violence as something committed by

---

*The Act was supported by a coalition, "The Coalition on Hate Crimes," of sixty civil rights, religious, peace, gay and lesbian, and ethnic rights groups. It received the support of both liberal Democrats and conservative Republicans. Women's rights groups such as the National Organization for Women and the National Coalition Against Domestic Violence were deliberately excluded from "The Coalition on Hate Crimes" (de santis 1990, p. 1).

the "extremists," "irrational," "socially maladjusted"—and not as a function of our shared political and cultural myths. Therefore, the basic social order will remain essentially unchallenged.

NOTES

Brygger, Mary Pat. 1990. "Beginning of National Domestic Violence Awareness Month." Washington, D.C.: National Woman Abuse Prevention Project.

Bullard, Sara (ed.). 1988. *The Ku Klux Klan: A history of racism and violence* (3rd. ed.). Montgomery, Alabama: The Southern Poverty Law Center.

Crewdson, John. 1988. *By Silence Betrayed: Sexual Abuse of Children in America.* New York: Harper and Row, Publishers.

Conyers, J. 1986. *Hearings on anti-gay/lesbian violence.* Washington, D.C.: U.S. House of Representatives Committee on the Judiciary, Subcommitte on Criminal Violence.

de santis, marie. 1990. "Hate Crimes Bill Excludes Women." *off our backs* xx: p. 1.

Farrell, Walter C. Jr., and Cloyzelle K. Jones. 1988. "Recent Racial Incidents in Higher Education: A Preliminary Perspective." *The Urban Review* 20:211–226.

Finn, Peter and Taylor McNeil. 1988. "Bias Crime and the Criminal Justice Response: A Summary Report Prepared for the National Criminal Justice Association." Washington, D.C.: U.S. Department of Justice.

Gordon, Linda. 1988. *Heroes of Their Own Lives: The Politics and History of Family Violence.* New York: Penguin Books.

Gordon, Margaret T. and Stephanie Riger. 1989. *The Female Fear.* New York: The Free Press.

Herek, Gregory M. 1989. "Hate Crimes Against Lesbians and Gay Men: Issues for Research and Policy." *American Psychologist* 44: 948–955.

Hernandez, Tanya Kateri. 1990. "Bias Crimes: Unconscious Racism in the Prosecution of 'Racially Motivated Violence'." *The Yale Law Journal* 99:845–864.

hooks, bell. 1981. *Ain't I A Woman: black women and feminism.* Boston: South End Press.

LaFree, Gary D. 1989. *Rape and Criminal Justice: The Social Construction of Sexual Assault.* Belmont, California: Wadsworth, Inc.

Lutz, Chris (compiler). 1987. *They Don't All Wear Sheets: A Chronology of Racist and Far Right Violence—1980–1986.* Atlanta: Center for Democratic Renewal.

Majority Staff Report. 1991. "Violence Against Women: The Increase of Rape in America 1990." Washington, D.C.: U.S. Senate, Committee on the Judiciary.

National Gay and Lesbian Task Force. 1990. "Anti-Gay Violence, Victimization and Defamation in 1989." Washington, D.C.

Ostling, Richard N. 1986. "A Sinister Search for 'Identity'." *Time* (October 20): 74.

Rasky, Susan F. 1990. "Bill on Sex Crime Assessed in Senate." *New York Times* (June 21): Sec. A, 19.

Rosenthal, Andrew. 1990. "President Signs Law for Study of Hate Crimes." *New York Times* (April 24): Sec. A, 14.

Roskey, Michael L. 1988. *Ideology in Instances of Anti-Gay Violence.* University of California at Irvine, unpublished dissertation.

Sheffield, Carole J. 1987. "Sexual Terrorism and the Social Control of Women." Pp. 177–189 in *Analyzing Gender*, edited by B. Hess and M. Marx Ferree. Newbury Park, California: Sage.

_____ 1989. "Sexual Terrorism." Pp. 3–19 in *Women: A Feminist Perspective*, edited by Jo Freeman. Palo Alto, California: Sage.

Stanko, Elizabeth A. 1985. *Intimate Intrusions: Women's Experience of Male Violence.* Boston: Routledge and Kegan Paul.

Toner, Robin. 1990. "Senate, 92 to 4, Wants U.S. Data on Crimes that Spring From Hate." *New York Times* (February 9): Sec. A, 16.

Uniform Crime Reports. 1987. Washington, D.C.: U.S. Department of Justice.

_____ 1989. Washington, D.C.: U.S. Department of Justice.

Walker, Lenore E. 1984. *The Battered woman Syndrome.* New York: Springer.

Warshaw, Carole. 1989. "Limitations of the Medical Model in the Care of Battered Women." *Gender & Society* 3: 506–517.

Warshaw, Robin. 1988. *I Never Called It Rape.* New York: Harper and Row, Publishers.

Wexler, Chuck and Gary T. Marx. 1986, "When Law and Order Works: Boston's Innovative Approach to the Problem of Racial Violence." *Crime and Delinquency* 32: 205–223.

Wright, Richard. 1945. *Black Boy.* New York: Harper and Row, Publishers.

Suggestions for Further Reading

Bastow, Susan. *Gender Stereotypes: Traditions and Alternatives*, 2d ed. Pacific Grove, Calif.: Brooks/Cole Publishing Company, 1986.

Fass, Paula S. *Outside In.* New York: Oxford University Press, 1989.

Harding, S., and M. B. Hintikka. *Discovering Reality: Feminist Perspectives on Epistemology, Metaphysics, Methodology, and Philosophy of Science.* Boston: D. Reidel Publishing Co., 1983.

Hartman, Paul, and Charles Husband. *Racism and the Mass Media.* Totowa, N.J.: Rowman and Littlefield, 1974.

Kramarae, C., M. Schultz, and W. M. O'Barr, eds. *Language and Power.* Beverly Hills, Calif.: Sage Press, 1984.

Lee, Martin A., and Norman Solomon. *Unreliable Sources.* New York: Lyle Stuart, 1990.

Marcuse, H. *One-Dimensional Man.* Boston: Beacon Press, 1964.

Michaels, Leonard, et. al., eds. *The State of the Language.* Berkeley: University of California Press, 1979.

Parenti, Michael. *Inventing Reality.* New York: St. Martin's Press, 1986.

Sadker, Myra, and David Sadker. *Failing at Fairness: How America's Schools Cheat Girls.* New York: Scribner's, 1994.

Spender, D. *Man Made Language*, 2d ed. Boston: Routledge and Kegan Paul, 1985.

Vetterling-Braggin, M. *Sexist Language.* Totowa, N.J.: Littlefield, Adams, 1981.

Wolf, Naomi. *The Beauty Myth.* New York: Doubleday Anchor, 1992.

PART VII

Revisioning the Future

Developing an adequate understanding of the nature and causes of race, class, and gender oppression is a critical first step toward moving beyond them. Solutions to problems are generated, at least in part, by the way we pose them. That is why so much of this book is devoted to defining and analyzing the nature of the problem. Only when we appreciate the complex, subtle factors that operate together to create a society in which wealth, privilege, and opportunity are unequally divided will we be able to formulate viable proposals for changing those conditions.

What, then, have the selections in this book told us about racism, sexism, heterosexism, and class divisions? First, that there is no single cause. Eliminating these forms of oppression will involve changes at the personal, social, political, and economic levels. It will require that we learn to think differently about ourselves and others and see the world through new categories. We will have to learn to pay close attention to our language, our attitudes, and our behavior and ask what values and forms of relationships are being created and maintained both consciously and unconsciously by them. It will mandate that we reevaluate virtually every institution in society and critically appraise the ways in which it intentionally or unintentionally perpetuates the forms of discrimination we have been studying, and that we act to change them. In short, we will have to scrutinize every aspect of our economic, political, and social life with a view to asking whose interests are served and whose are denied by organizing our world in this way.

In the first two selections in this part Audre Lorde and Gloria Anzaldúa suggest that we will need to begin by redefining and rethinking the idea of difference. While acknowledging that real differences of race, age, and sex exist, Lorde argues that it is not these differences that separate us as much as it is our refusal to acknowledge them and the role they play in shaping our relationships and our society. Denying or distorting those differences keeps us apart; embracing those differences can provide a new starting point for us from which to work together to reconstruct our world. Gloria Anzaldúa is concerned with the way women of color deal with differences among themselves, and argues that many women of color have learned to see each other through the categories of inferiority/superiority that white people have constructed. She urges women of color to reject these categories and stand "on the ground of our own ethnic being." The poem that follows by Cherríe Moraga illustrates what it might mean to rethink difference. Moraga writes of discovering differences that were previously hidden from her and, in this way, of finding a new basis for human community.

Ruth Sidel turns our attention to social policy. She suggests that young women today have unrealistic expectations about the kind of life they are likely to lead as adults. Caught up in a version of the American Dream that promises you can have it all, young women today are unprepared for the difficult choices they will have to make in a world where class, race, and gender inequities shape people's lives. After offering a brief survey of these unrealistic expectations, Sidel goes on to suggest the kinds of social policies that are necessary if we are to create a more humane society. Among them are fundamental changes in the workplace, education, and health care, and the availability of sex education and abortion. Arguing that the American Dream cannot and never could work for the vast majority of people in this society, Sidel suggests that a humane society will be one organized around the public good, not private profit.

A new vision of society will require new choices and possibilities for men as well as women. Cooper Thompson is profoundly critical of the way this society socializes boys to believe that violence is an acceptable, even desirable, way to establish their manhood and to negotiate difference. He believes that this socialization leads to both misogyny and homophobia and makes it difficult for men to form warm and loving friendships with members of both sexes. Because the social costs of prevailing conceptions of masculinity are so high, he urges us to develop a new vision of manhood, one that allows boys to claim many of the qualities previously defined as "feminine." Thompson concludes his essay with the warning that "the survival of our society may rest on the degree to which we are able to teach men to cherish life."

Like Thompson, Suzanne Pharr is concerned with the role that misogyny and homophobia play in perpetuating oppression; like Ruth Sidel, she is concerned with the relationship between economic policy and social justice. She argues that in a society organized to create and maintain an extremely unequal distribution of wealth, economics is "the underlying, driving force that keeps all oppression in place." Beginning with an analysis of our economic system, Pharr goes on to examine the ways in which homophobia and heterosexism operate as weapons of sexism that threaten all women with violence and keep race, class, and gender sub-ordination and domination in place. She concludes her discussion by asking us to imagine what the world might be like, for both women and men, without homo-phobia in it.

Like Pharr, bell hooks is concerned with understanding the way in which sex, race, and class function as interlocking, mutually supportive, systems of domina-tion. Like Lorde and Anzaldúa she urges us to rethink difference. While acknowl-edging past failures of much feminist theory to adequately deal with issues of race, racism, and class, hooks maintains that a revisioned feminism can provide the most comprehensive perspective from which to challenge all forms of oppression and domination. This is true because sexism is the form of oppression we confront throughout our daily lives; "sexism directly shapes and determines relations of power in our private lives, in familiar social spaces, in that most intimate context—home—and in that most intimate sphere of relations—family." hooks envisions a process of education and consciousness raising where women from diverse back-grounds come together in small groups to talk about feminism and to learn from each other, but she calls upon men as well as commit themselves to overthrowing patriarchal domination.

This Part, and this book, concludes with poems by Maya Angelou and Marge Piercy that celebrate survival, transformation, and the human spirit. They remind us of the strength oppressed people have called upon to help them survive under inhumane conditions, and they encourage us with their vision of an indomitable human spirit that will not merely survive but, as William Faulkner once wrote, will prevail.

Age, Race, Class, and Sex:
*Women Redefining Difference**

Audre Lorde

Much of Western European history conditions us to see human differences in simplistic opposition to each other: dominant/subordinate, good/bad, up/down, superior/inferior. In a society where the good is defined in terms of profit rather than in terms of human need, there must always be some group of people who, through systematized oppression, can be made to feel surplus, to occupy the place of the dehumanized inferior. Within this society, that group is made up of Black and Third World people, working-class people, older people, and women.

As a forty-nine-year-old Black lesbian feminist socialist mother of two, including one boy, and a member of an interracial couple, I usually find myself a part of some group defined as other, deviant, inferior, or just plain wrong. Traditionally, in american society, it is the members of oppressed, objectified groups who are expected to stretch out and bridge the gap between the actualities of our lives and the consciousness of our oppressor. For in order to survive, those of us for whom oppression is as american as apple pie have always had to be watchers, to become familiar with the language and manners of the oppressor, even sometimes adopting them for some illusion of protection. Whenever the need for some pretense of communication arises, those who profit from our oppression call upon us to share our knowledge with them. In other words, it is the responsibility of the oppressed to teach the oppressors their mistakes. I am responsible for educating teachers who dismiss my children's culture in school. Black and Third World people are expected to educate white people as to our humanity. Women are expected to educate men. Lesbians and gay men are expected to educate the heterosexual world. The oppressors maintain their position and evade responsibility for their own actions. There is a constant drain of energy which might be better used in redefining ourselves and devising realistic scenarios for altering the present and constructing the future.

Institutionalized rejection of difference is an absolute necessity in a profit economy which needs outsiders as surplus people. As members of such an economy, we have *all* been programmed to respond to the human differences between us with fear and loathing and to handle that difference in one of three ways: ignore it, and

*Paper delivered at the Copeland Colloquium, Amherst College, April 1980.

if that is not possible, copy it if we think it is dominant, or destroy it if we think it is subordinate. But we have no patterns for relating across our human differences as equals. As a result, those differences have been misnamed and misused in the service of separation and confusion.

Certainly there are very real differences between us of race, age, and sex. But it is not those differences between us that are separating us. It is rather our refusal to recognize those differences, and to examine the distortions which result from our misnaming them and their effects upon human behavior and expectation.

Racism, the belief in the inherent superiority of one race over all others and thereby the right to dominance. Sexism, the belief in the inherent superiority of one sex over the other and thereby the right to dominance. Ageism. Heterosexism. Elitism. Classism.

It is a lifetime pursuit for each one of us to extract these distortions from our living at the same time as we recognize, reclaim, and define those differences upon which they are imposed. For we have all been raised in a society where those distortions were endemic within our living. Too often, we pour the energy needed for recognizing and exploring difference into pretending those differences are insurmountable barriers, or that they do not exist at all. This results in a voluntary isolation, or false and treacherous connections. Either way, we do not develop tools for using human difference as a springboard for creative change within our lives. We speak not of human difference, but of human deviance.

Somewhere, on the edge of consciousness, there is what I call a *mythical norm*, which each one of us within our hearts knows "that is not me." In america, this norm is usually defined as white, thin, male, young, heterosexual, christian, and financially secure. It is with this mythical norm that the trappings of power reside within society. Those of us who stand outside that power often identify one way in which we are different, and we assume that to be the primary cause of all oppression, forgetting other distortions around difference, some of which we ourselves may be practicing. By and large within the women's movement today, white women focus upon their oppression as women and ignore differences of race, sexual preference, class, and age. There is a pretense to a homogeneity of experience covered by the word *sisterhood* that does not in fact exist.

Unacknowledged class differences rob women of each others' energy and creative insight. Recently a women's magazine collective made the decision for one issue to print only prose, saying poetry was a less "rigorous" or "serious" art form. Yet even the form our creativity takes is often a class issue. Of all the art forms, poetry is the most economical. It is the one which is the most secret, which requires the least physical labor, the least material, and the one which can be done between shifts, in the hospital pantry, on the subway, and on scraps of surplus paper. Over the last few years, writing a novel on tight finances, I came to appreciate the enormous differences in the material demands between poetry and prose. As we reclaim our literature, poetry has been the major voice of poor, working class, and Colored women. A room of one's own may be a necessity for writing prose, but so are reams of paper, a typewriter, and plenty of time. The actual requirements to produce the visual arts also help determine, along class lines, whose art is whose. In this day of inflated prices for material, who are our sculptors, our painters, our photographers? When we speak of broadly based women's culture, we need to be aware of the effect of class and economic differences on the supplies available for producing art.

As we move toward creating a society within which we can each flourish, ageism is another distortion of relationship which interferes with our vision. By ignoring the past, we are encouraged to repeat its mistakes. The "generation gap" is an important social tool for any repressive society. If the younger members of a community view the older members as contemptible or suspect or excess, they will never be able to join hands and examine the living memories of the community, nor ask the all important question, "Why?" This gives rise to a historical amnesia that keeps us working to invent the wheel every time we have to go to the store for bread.

We find ourselves having to repeat and relearn the same old lessons over and over that our mothers did because we do not pass on what we have learned, or because we are unable to listen. For instance, how many times has this all been said before? For another, who would have believed that once again our daughters are allowing their bodies to be hampered and purgatoried by girdles and high heels and hobble skirts?

Ignoring the differences of race between women and the implications of those differences presents the most serious threat to the mobilization of women's joint power.

As white women ignore their built-in privilege of whiteness and define *woman* in terms of their own experience alone, then women of Color become "other," the outsider whose experience and tradition is too "alien" to comprehend. An example of this is the signal absence of the experience of women of Color as a resource for women's studies courses. The literature of women of Color is seldom included in women's literature courses and almost never in other literature courses, nor in women's studies as a whole. All too often, the excuse given is that the literatures of women of Color can only be taught by Colored women, or that they are too difficult to understand, or that classes cannot "get into" them because they come out of experiences that are "too different." I have heard this argument presented by white women of otherwise quite clear intelligence, women who seem to have no trouble at all teaching and reviewing work that comes out of the vastly different experiences of Shakespeare, Molière, Dostoyefsky, and Aristophanes. Surely there must be some other explanation.

This is a very complex question, but I believe one of the reasons white women have such difficulty reading Black women's work is because of their reluctance to see Black women as women and different from themselves. To examine Black women's literature effectively requires that we be seen as whole people in our actual complexities—as individuals, as women, as human—rather than as one of those problematic but familiar stereotypes provided in this society in place of genuine images of Black women. And I believe this holds true for the literatures of other women of Color who are not Black.

The literatures of all women of Color recreate the textures of our lives, and many white women are heavily invested in ignoring the real differences. For as long as any difference between us means one of us must be inferior, then the recognition of any difference must be fraught with guilt. To allow women of Color to step out of stereotypes is too guilt provoking, for it threatens the complacency of those women who view oppression only in terms of sex.

Refusing to recognize difference makes it impossible to see the different problems and pitfalls facing us as women.

Thus, in a patriarchal power system where whiteskin privilege is a major prop, the entrapments used to neutralize Black women and white women are not the same. For example, it is easy for Black women to be used by the power structure against Black men, not because they are men, but because they are Black. There-fore, for Black women, it is necessary at all times to separate the needs of the oppres-sor from our own legitimate conflicts within our communities. This same problem does not exist for white women. Black women and men have shared racist oppres-sion and still share it, although in different ways. Out of that shared oppression we have developed joint defenses and joint vulnerabilities to each other that are not duplicated in the white community, with the exception of the relationship between Jewish women and Jewish men.

On the other hand, white women face the pitfall of being seduced into joining the oppressor under the pretense of sharing power. This possibility does not exist in the same way for women of Color. The tokenism that is sometimes extended to us is not an invitation to join power; our racial "otherness" is a visible reality that makes that quite clear. For white women there is a wider range of pretended choices and rewards for identifying with patriarchal power and its tools.

Today, with the defeat of ERA, the tightening economy, and increased conser-vatism, it is easier once again for white women to believe the dangerous fantasy that if you are good enough, pretty enough, sweet enough, quiet enough, teach the children to behave, hate the right people, and marry the right men, then you will be allowed to co-exist with patriarchy in relative peace, at least until a man needs your job or the neighborhood rapist happens along. And true, unless one lives and loves in the trenches it is difficult to remember that the war against dehumanization is ceaseless.

But Black women and our children know the fabric of our lives is stitched with violence and with hatred, that there is no rest. We do not deal with it only on the picket lines, or in dark midnight alleys, or in the places where we dare to verbalize our resistance. For us, increasingly, violence weaves through the daily tissues of our living—in the supermarket, in the classroom, in the elevator, in the clinic and the schoolyard, from the plumber, the baker, the saleswoman, the bus driver, the bank teller, the waitress who does not serve us.

Some problems we share as women, some we do not. You fear your children will grow up to join the patriarchy and testify against you, we fear our children will be dragged from a car and shot down in the street, and you will turn your backs upon the reasons they are dying.

The threat of difference has been no less blinding to people of Color. Those of us who are Black must see that the reality of our lives and our struggle does not make us immune to the errors of ignoring and misnaming difference. Within Black communities where racism is a living reality, differences among us often seem dangerous and suspect. The need for unity is often misnamed as a need for homogeneity, and a Black feminist vision mistaken for betrayal of our common interests as a people. Because of the continuous battle against racial erasure that Black women and Black men share, some Black women still refuse to recognize that we are also oppressed as women, and that sexual hostility against Black women is practiced not only by the white racist society, but implemented within our Black communities as well. It is a disease striking the heart of Black nationhood, and silence will not make it disappear. Exacerbated by racism and the pressures of powerlessness, violence against Black women and children often becomes a standard within our communities, one by which manliness can be measured. But these woman-hating acts are rarely discussed as crimes against Black women.

As a group, women of Color are the lowest paid wage earners in america. We are the primary targets of abortion and sterilization abuse, here and abroad. In certain parts of Africa, small girls are still being sewed shut between their legs to keep them docile and for men's pleasure. This is known as female circumcision, and it is not a cultural affair as the late Jomo Kenyatta insisted, it is a crime against Black women.

Black women's literature is full of the pain of frequent assault, not only by a racist patriarchy, but also by Black men. Yet the necessity for and history of shared battle have made us, Black women, particularly vulnerable to the false accusation that anti-sexist is anti-Black. Meanwhile, womanhating as a recourse of the powerless is sapping strength from Black communities, and our very lives. Rape is on the increase, reported and unreported, and rape is not aggressive sexuality, it is sexualized aggression. As Kalamu ya Salaam, a Black male writer points out, "As long as male domination exists, rape will exist. Only women revolting and men made conscious of their responsibility to fight sexism can collectively stop rape."[1]

Differences between ourselves as Black women are also being misnamed and used to separate us from one another. As a Black lesbian feminist comfortable with the many different ingredients of my identity, and a woman committed to racial and sexual freedom from oppression, I find I am constantly being encouraged to pluck out some one aspect of myself and present this as the meaningful whole, eclipsing or denying the other parts of self. But this is a destructive and fragmenting way to live. My fullest concentration of energy is available to me only when I integrate all the parts of who I am, openly, allowing power from particular sources of my living to flow back and forth freely through all my different selves, without the restrictions of externally imposed definition. Only then can I bring myself and my energies as a whole to the service of those struggles which I embrace as part of my living.

A fear of lesbians, or of being accused of being a lesbian, has led many Black women into testifying against themselves. It has led some of us into destructive alliances, and others into despair and isolation. In the white women's communities, heterosexism is sometimes a result of identifying with the white patriarchy, a rejection of that interdependence between women-identified women which allows the self to be, rather than to be used in the service of men. Sometimes it reflects a diehard belief in the protective coloration of heterosexual relationships, sometimes a self-hate which all women have to fight against, taught us from birth.

Although elements of these attitudes exist for all women, there are particular resonances of heterosexism and homophobia among Black women. Despite the fact that woman-bonding has a long and honorable history in the African and African-american communities, and despite the knowledge and accomplishments of many strong and creative women-identified Black women in the political, social and cultural fields, heterosexual Black women often tend to ignore or discount the existence and work of Black lesbians. Part of this attitude has come from an understandable terror of Black male attack within the close confines of Black society, where the punishment for any female self-assertion is still to be accused of being a lesbian and therefore unworthy of the attention or support of the scarce Black male. But part of this need to misname and ignore Black lesbians comes from a very real fear that openly women-identified Black women who are no longer dependent upon men for their self-definition may well reorder our whole concept of social relationships.

Black women who once insisted that lesbianism was a white woman's problem now insist that Black lesbians are a threat to Black nationhood, are consorting with the enemy, are basically un-Black. These accusations, coming from the very women to whom we look for deep and real understanding, have served to keep many Black lesbians in hiding, caught between the racism of white women and the homophobia of their sisters. Often, their work has been ignored, trivialized, or misnamed, as with the work of Angelina Grimke, Alice Dunbar-Nelson, Lorraine Hansberry. Yet women-bonded women have always been some part of the power of Black communities, from our unmarried aunts to the amazons of Dahomey.

And it is certainly not Black lesbians who are assaulting women and raping children and grandmothers on the streets of our communities.

Across this country, as in Boston during the spring of 1979 following the unsolved murders of twelve Black women, Black lesbians are spearheading movements against violence against Black women.

What are the particular details within each of our lives that can be scrutinized and altered to help bring about change? How do we redefine difference for all women? It is not our differences which separate women, but our reluctance to recognize those differences and to deal effectively with the distortions which have resulted from the ignoring and misnaming of those differences.

As a tool of social control, women have been encouraged to recognize only one area of human difference as legitimate, those differences which exist between women and men. And we have learned to deal across those differences with the urgency of all oppressed subordinates. All of us have had to learn to live or work or coexist with men, from our fathers on. We have recognized and negotiated these differences, even when this recognition only continued the old dominant/subordinate mode of human relationship, where the oppressed must recognize the masters' difference in order to survive.

But our future survival is predicated upon our ability to relate within equality. As women, we must root our internalized patterns of oppression within ourselves if we are to move beyond the most superficial aspects of social change. Now we must recognize differences among women who are our equals, neither inferior nor superior, and devise ways to use each others' difference to enrich our visions and our joint struggles.

The future of our earth may depend upon the ability of all women to identify and develop new definitions of power and new patterns of relating across difference. The old definitions have not served us, nor the earth that supports us. The old patterns, no matter how cleverly rearranged to imitate progress, still condemn us to cosmetically altered repetitions of the same old exchanges, the same old guilt, hatred, recrimination, lamentation, and suspicion.

For we have, built into all of us, old blueprints of expectation and response, old structures of oppression, and these must be altered at the same time as we alter the living conditions which are a result of those structures. For the master's tools will never dismantle the master's house.

As Paulo Freire shows so well in *The Pedagogy of the Oppressed*,[2] the true focus of revolutionary change is never merely the oppressive situations which we seek to escape, but that piece of the oppressor which is planted deep within each of us, and which knows only the oppressors' tactics, the oppressors' relationships. .

Change means growth, and growth can be painful. But we sharpen self-definition by exposing the self in work and struggle together with those whom we define as different from ourselves, although sharing the same goals. For Black and white, old and young, lesbian and heterosexual women alike, this can mean new paths to our survival.

> We have chosen each other
> and the edge of each others battles
> the war is the same
> if we lose
> someday women's blood will congeal
> upon a dead planet
> if we win
> there is no telling
> we seek beyond history
> for a new and more possible meaning.[3]

NOTES

1. From "Rape: A Radical Analysis, An African-American Perspective" by Kalamu ya Salaam in *Black Books Bulletin*, vol. 6, no. 4 (1980).

2. Seabury Press, New York, 1970.

3. From "Outlines," unpublished poem.

En rapport, In Opposition:
Cobrando cuentas a las nuestras

Gloria Anzaldúa

Watch for Falling Rocks

The first time I drove from El Paso to San Diego, I saw a sign that read *Watch for Falling Rocks*. And though I watched and waited for rocks to roll down the steep cliff walls and attack my car and me, I never saw any falling rocks. Today, one of the things I'm most afraid of are the rocks we throw at each other. And the resultant guilt we carry like a corpse strapped to our backs for having thrown rocks. We colored women have memories like elephants. The slightest hurt is recorded deep within. We do not forget the injury done to us and we do not forget the injury we have done another. For unfortunately we do not have hides like elephants. Our vulnerability is measured by our capacity for openness, intimacy. And we all know that our own kind is driven through shame or self-hatred to poke at all our open wounds. And we know they know exactly where the hidden wounds are.

> I keep track of all distinctions. Between past and present. Pain and pleasure. Living and surviving. Resistance and capitulation. Will and circumstances. Between life and death. Yes. I am scrupulously accurate. I have become a keeper of accounts.
> —Irena Klepfisz[1]

One of the changes that I've seen since *This Bridge Called My Back* was published[2] is that we no longer allow white women to efface us or suppress us. Now we do it to each other. We have taken over the missionary's "let's civilize the savage role," fixating on the "wrongness" and moral or political inferiority of some of our sisters, insisting on a profound difference between oneself and the *Other*. We have been indoctrinated into adopting the old imperialist ways of conquering and dominating, adopting a way of confrontation based on differences while standing on the ground of ethnic superiority.

452

In the "dominant" phase of colonialism, European colonizers exercise direct control of the colonized, destroy the native legal and cultural systems, and negate non-European civilizations in order to ruthlessly exploit the resources of the sub-jugated with the excuse of attempting to "civilize" them. Before the end of this phase, the natives internalize Western culture. By the time we reach the "neocolonialist" phase, we've accepted the white colonizers' system of values, attitudes, morality, and modes of production.[3] It is not by chance that in the more rural towns of Texas Chicano neighborhoods are called *colonias* rather than *barrios*.

There have always been those of us who have "cooperated" with the colonizers. It's not that we have been "won" over by the dominant culture, but that it has exploited pre-existing power relations of subordination and subjugation within our native societies.[4] The great White ripoff and they are still cashing in. Like our ex-ploiters who fixate on the inferiority of the natives, we fixate on the fucked-upness of our sisters. Like them we try to impose our version of "the ways things should be"; we try to impose one's self on the *Other* by making her the recipient of one's negative elements, usually the same elements that the Anglo projected on us. Like them, we project our self-hatred on her; we stereotype her, we make her generic.

Just How Ethnic Are You?

One of the reasons for this hostility among us is the forced cultural penetration, the rape of the colored by the white, with the colonizers depositing their perspective, their language, their values in our bodies. External oppression is paralleled with our internalization of that oppression. And our acting out from that oppression. They have us doing to those within our own ranks what they have done and continue to do to us—*Othering* people. That is, isolating them, pushing them out of the herd, ostracizing them. The internalization of negative images of ourselves, our self-hatred, poor self-esteem, makes our own people the *Other*. We shun the white-looking Indian, the "high yellow" Black woman, the Asian with the white lover, the Native woman who brings her white girl friend to the Pow Wow, the Chicana who doesn't speak Spanish, the academic, the uneducated. Her difference makes her a person we can't trust. *Para que sea "legal,"* she must pass the ethnic legitimacy test we have devised. And it is exactly our internalized whiteness that desperately wants boundary lines (this part of me is Mexican, this Indian) marked out and woe to any sister or any part of us that steps out of our assigned places, woe to anyone who doesn't measure up to our standards of ethnicity. *Si no cualifica,* if she fails to pass the test, *le aventamos mierda en la cara, le aventamos piedras, la aventamos.* We throw shit in her face, we throw rocks, we kick her out. *Como gallos de pelea nos atacamos unas a las otras—mexicanas de nacimiento contra* the born-again *mexicanas.* Like fighting cocks, razor blades strapped to our fingers, we slash out at each other. We have turned our anger against ourselves. And our anger is immense. *Es un acido que corroe.*

Internal Affairs *o las que niegan a su gente*

Tu traición yo la llevo aquá muy dentro,
la llevo dentro de mi alma
dentro de mi corazón.
Tu traición.
  —Cornelio Reyna[5]

I get so tired of constantly struggling with my sisters. The more we have in common, including love, the greater the heartache between us, the more we hurt each
other. It's excruciatingly painful, this constant snarling at our own shadows. Anything can set the conflict in motion: the lover getting more recognition by the community, the friend getting a job with higher status, a break-up. As one of my friends
said, "We can't fucking get along."

So we find ourselves *entreguerras*,[6] a kind of civil war among intimates, an in-
class, in-race, in-house fighting, a war with strategies, tactics that are our coping
mechanisms, that once were our survival skills and which we now use upon one another,[7] producing intimate terrorism—a modern form of *las guerras floridas*, the war
of flowers that the Aztecs practiced in order to gain captives for the sacrifices. Only
now we are each other's victims, we offer the *Other* to our politically correct altar.

El deniego. The hate we once cast at our oppressors we now fling at women
of our own race. Reactionary—we have gone to the other extreme—denial of our
own. We struggle for power, compete, vie for control. Like kin, we are there for each
other, but like kin we come to blows. And the differences between us and this new
Other are not racial but ideological, not metaphysical but psychological. *Nos nega-*
mos a si mismas y el deniego nos causa daño.

Breaking Out of the Frame

I'm standing at the sea end of the truncated Berkeley pier. A boat had plowed into
the black posts gouging out a few hundred feet of structure, cutting the pier in two. I
stare at the sea, surging silver-plated, between me and the loped-off corrugated arm,
the wind whipping my hair. I look down, my head and shoulders, a shadow on the sea.
Yemaya pours strings of light over my dull jade, flickering body, bubbles pop out of my
ears. I feel the tension easing and, for the first time in months, the litany of work yet
to do, of deadlines, that sings incessantly in my head, blows away with the wind.

  Oh, Yemaya, I shall speak the words
    you lap against the pier.
But as I turn away I see in the distance a ship's fin fast approaching. I see fish heads
lying listless in the sun, smell the stench of pollution in the waters.

From where I stand, *queridas carnalas*—in a feminist position—I see, through a
critical lens with variable focus, that we must not drain our energy breaking down
the male/white frame (the whole of Western culture) but turn to our own kind and

change our terms of reference. As long as we see the world and our experiences through white eyes—in a dominant/subordinate way—we're trapped in the tar and pitch of the old manipulative and strive-for-power ways.

Even those of us who don't want to buy in get sucked into the vortext of the dominant culture's fixed oppositions, the duality of superiority and inferiority, of subject and object. Some of us, to get out of the internalized neocolonial phase, make for the fringes, the Borderlands. And though we have not broken out of the white frame, we at least see it for what it is. Questioning the values of the dominant culture which imposes fundamental difference on those of the "wrong" side of the good/bad dichotomy is the first step. Responding to the *Other* not as irrevocably different is the second step. By highlighting similarities, downplaying divergences, that is, by *rapprochement* between self and *Other* it is possible to build a syncretic relationship. At the basis of such a relationship lies an understanding of the effects of colonization and its resultant pathologies.

We have our work cut out for us. Nothing is more difficult than identifying emotionally with a cultural alterity, with the *Other*. *Alter:* to make different; to castrate. *Altercate:* to dispute angrily. *Alter ego:* another self or another aspect of oneself. *Alter idem:* another of the same kind. Nothing is harder than identifying with an interracial identity, with a mestizo identity. One has to leave the permanent boundaries of a fixed self, literally "leave" oneself and see oneself through the eyes of the *Other.* Cultural identity is "nothing more nor less than the mean between selfhood and otherness. . . ."[8] Nothing scares the Chicana more than a quasi Chicana; nothing disturbs a Mexican more than an acculturated Chicana; nothing agitates a Chicana more than a Latina who lumps her with the *norteamericanas.* It is easier to retreat to the safety of difference behind racial, cultural and class borders. Because our awareness of the *Other* as object often swamps our awareness of ourselves as subject, it is hard to maintain a fine balance between cultural ethnicity and the continuing survival of that culture, between traditional culture and an evolving hybrid culture. How much must remain the same, how much must change.

For most of us our ethnicity is still the issue. Ours continues to be a struggle of identity—not against a white background so much as against a colored background. *Ya no estamos afuera o atras del marco de la pintura*—we no longer stand outside nor behind the frame of the painting. We are both the foreground, the background and the figures predominating. Whites are not the central figure, they are not even in the frame, though the frame of reference is still white, male and heterosexual. But the white is still there, invisible, under our skin—we have subsumed the white.

*El desengaño/*Disillusionment

And yes I have some criticism, some self-criticism. And no I will not make everything nice. There is shit among us we need to sift through. Who knows, there may be some fertilizer in it. I've seen collaborative efforts between us end in verbal abuse, cruelty and trauma. I've seen collectives fall apart, dumping their ideals by the wayside and treating each other worse than they'd treat a rabid dog. My momma said, "Never tell other people our business, never divulge family secrets." Chicano dirt you do not air out in front of white folks, nor lesbian dirty laundry in front of heterosexuals. The cultural things stay with la Raza. Colored feminists must present a united front in front of whites and other groups. But the fact is we are not united. (I've come to suspect that unity is another Anglo invention like their one sole god and the myth of the monopole.[9]) We are not going to cut through *la mierda* by sweeping the dirt under the rug.

We have a responsibility to each other, certain commitments. The leap into self-affirmation goes hand in hand with being critical of self. Many of us walk around with reactionary, self-righteous attitudes. We preach certain political behaviors and theories and we do fine with writing about them. Though we want others to live their lives by them, we do not live them. When we are called on it, we go into a self-defensive mode and denial just like whites did when we started asking them to be accountable for their race and class biases.

*Las opuestas/*Those in Opposition

In us, intra- and cross-cultural hostilities surface in not so subtle put-downs. *Las no comprometidas, las que negan a sus gente. Fruncemos las caras y negamos toda responsabilidad.* Where some of us racially mixed people are stuck in now is denial and its damaging effects. Denial of the white aspects that we've been forced to acquire, denial of our sisters who for one reason or another cannot "pass" as 100% ethnic—as if such a thing exists. Racial purity, like language purity, is a fallacy. Denying the reality of who we are destroys the basis needed from which to talk honestly and deeply about the issues between us. We cannot make any real connections because we are not touching each other. So we sit facing each other and before the words escape our mouths the real issues are blanked in our consciousness, erased before they register because it hurts too much to talk about them, because it makes us vulnerable to the hurt the *carnala* may dish out, because we've been wounded too deeply and too often in the past. So we sit, a paper face before another paper face—two people who suddenly cease to be real. *La no compasiva con la complaciente, lo incomunicado atorado en sus gargántas.*

We, the new Inquisitors, swept along with the "swing to the right" of the growing religious and political intolerance, crusade against racial heretics, mow down with the sickle of righteous anger our dissenting sisters. The issue (in all aspects of life) has always been when to resist changes and when to be open to them. Right now, this rigidity will break us.

*Recobrando/*Recovering

Una luz fria y cenicienta bañada en la plata palida del amanecer entra a mi escritorio and I think about the critical stages we feminists of color are going through, chiefly that of learning to live with each other as *carnalas, parientes, amantes,* as kin, as friends, as lovers. Looking back on the road that we've walked on during the last decade, I see many emotional, psychological, spiritual, political gains — primarily developing an understanding and acceptance of the spirituality of our root ethnic cultures. This has given us the ground from which to see that our spiritual lives are not split from our daily acts. *En recobrando* our affinity with nature and her forces (deities), we have "recovered" our ancient identity, digging it out like dark clay, pressing it to our current identity, molding past and present, inner and outer. Our clay-streaked faces acquiring again images of our ethnic self and self-respect taken from us by the *colonizadores.* And if we've suffered losses, if often in the process we have momentarily "misplaced" our *carnala*hood, our sisterhood, there beside us always are the women, *las mujeres.* And that is enough to keep us going.

By grounding in the earth of our native spiritual identity, we can build up our personal and tribal identity. We can reach out for the clarity we need. Burning sage and sweetgrass by itself won't cut it, but it can be a basis from which we act.

And yes, we are elephants with long memories, but scrutinizing the past with binocular vision and training it on the juncture of past with present, and identifying the options on hand and mapping out future roads will ensure us survival.

So if we won't forget past grievances, let us forgive. Carrying the ghosts of past grievances *no vale la pena.* It is not worth the grief. It keeps us from ourselves and each other; it keeps us from new relationships. We need to cultivate other ways of coping. I'd like to think that the in-fighting that we presently find ourselves doing is only a stage in the continuum of our growth, an offshoot of the conflict that the process of biculturation spawns, a phase of the internal colonization process, one that will soon cease to hold sway over our lives. I'd like to see it as a skin we will shed as we are born into the 21st century.

And now in these times of the turning of the century, of harmonic conversion, of the end of *El Quinto Sol* (as the ancient Aztecs named our present age), it is time we began to get out of the state of opposition and into *rapprochment,* time to get our heads, words, ways out of white territory. It is time that we broke out of the invisible white frame and stood on the ground of our own ethnic being.

NOTES

1. Irena Klepfisz, *Keeper of Accounts* (Montpelier, VT: Sinister Wisdom, 1982), 85.

2. According to Chela Sandoval, the publication of *Bridge* marked the end of the second wave of the women's movement in its previous form. *U.S. Third World Feminist Criticism: The Theory and Method of Oppositional Consciousness,* a dissertation in process.

3. Abdul R. JanMohamed, "The Economy of Manichean Allegory: The Function of Racial Difference in Colonialist Literature," *"Race," Writing, and Difference,* ed. Henry Louis Gates, Jr. (Chicago: University of Chicago Press, 1985), 80–81.

4. JanMohamed, 81.

5. A Chicano from Texas who sings and plays *bajo-sexto* in his *música norteña/conjunto. "Tu Traición"* is from the album *15 Exitasos,* Reyna Records, 1981.

6. *Entreguerras, entremundos/Inner Wars Among the Worlds* is the title of a forthcoming book of narratives/novel.

7. Sarah Hoaglund, "Lesbian Ethics: Intimacy & Self-Understanding," *Bay Area Women's News*, May/June 1987, vol. 1, no. 2, 7.

8. Nadine Gordimer is quoted in JanMohamed's essay, 88.

9. Physicists are searching for a single law of physics under which all other laws will fall.

Up Against the Wall

Cherríe Moraga

The cold in my chest comes
from having to decide

while the ice builds up on *this* side
of my new-york-apt.-bldg.-window
whose death
has been marked
upon the collective forehead
of this continent, this
shattering globe
the most indelibly.

Indelible. A catholic word
I learned
when I learned
that there were catholics and there
were not.
        But somehow
we did not count the Jews
among the have-nots, only protestants
with their cold & bloodless god
with no candles/no incense/no bloody
sacrifice or spirits
lurking.
Protestantism. The white people's
religion.

. . .

First time I remember
seeing pictures of the Holocaust
was in the ninth grade and the moving pictures
were already there in my mind
somehow *before* they showed me
what I already understood
that these people were killed
for the spirit-blood
that runs through them.

They were like us in this.
Ethnic people with long last names
with vowels at the end or the wrong
type of consonants
combined   a colored kind of white people.

But let me tell you
first time I saw an actual
picture glossy photo of a lynching
I was already grown & active
& living & loving Jewish.
Black. White. Puerto
Rican.
     And the image blasted
my consciousness   split it
wide   I
had never thought   seen
heard   of such a thing
never imagined the look
of the man   the weight
dead
hanging
swinging
heavy
the fact   of the white people
cold
bloodless
looking on   It
had never occurred to me
I tell you   I
the nuns
failed to mention

this could happen, too
how *could* such a thing happen?

because somehow dark real dark
was not quite real
people killed
but some
thing not
taken to heart
in the same way it feels
to see white shaved/starved
burned/buried
the boned bodies stacked & bulldozed
into huge craters made by men
and machines
and at fifteen
before that movie screen
I kept running through my mind
and I'm only one
count one
it could be me
it could be me
I'm nothing
to this cruelty.

. . .

Somehow tonight,
is it the particular coldness
where I sleep with a cap
to keep it out
that causes me to toss
and turn the events of the last weeks
the last years of my life
around in my sleep?

Is it the same white coldness
that forces my back up
against the wall—*choose.*
Choose.

I cannot
choose nor forget
how simple

to fall back
upon rehearsed racial memory.

I work to remember
what I never dreamed possible
what my consciousness could never
contrive.

Whoever I am

I must believe
I am not
and will never be
the only
one
who suffers.

Toward a More Caring Society

Ruth Sidel

We have listened as young women have talked about their dreams: their dreams of work, of success, of affluence; their dreams of love, of child rearing, of intimacy; their dreams of affiliation and of independence. We have also heard their concerns: concerns about balancing work and family, about needing to be able to go it alone, about finding that close personal relationship so many seek. And we have heard their despair: the despair of those who cannot envision a future beyond tomorrow, of those whose lives have been shaped at a young age by personal circumstances and social and economic forces often beyond their control, of eighteen- and nineteen-year-olds who seem old before their time.

In listening to these young women it is clear that twenty-five years after the publication of *The Feminine Mystique*, much has changed and much has remained the same. Women are attending college and graduate school in greater numbers than ever before. In the area of work, women have made great strides: the vast increase in the number of women in the labor force; the once unimaginable increase in the number of women in high-status, high-income professions; the growing acceptance, both on the part of women and on the part of many men, that women are competent, committed workers who can get the job done and achieve a considerable amount of their identity through their work roles. In keeping with their greatly increased presence in the world of work, women are often pictured by the media, by the fashion industry, even by politicians as serious, significant members of the labor force.

In recent years women have also gained greater control over their bodies. Largely because of the feminist movement, women have far greater understanding of how their bodies work, more control over their own fertility, and far greater participation in the process of childbirth. As this is being written, some of that control is under siege, particularly the right to abortion; but there have been significant strides nonetheless.

And, perhaps most important, many women recognize that they must make their own way in the world, that they must develop their own identity rather than acquire that identity through a relationship with a man. Woman after woman detailed her plan for becoming a full-fledged person, able to survive on her own; and woman after woman recognized that she must be able to support herself and, if she has them, her children as well.

But in other areas over this quarter-century there has been very little change, and some aspects of women's lives have deteriorated dramatically. Women are still all too often depicted in advertising, in films, on television, and by the fashion industry as sex objects. Women are still encouraged to focus on their looks—their bodies, their clothes, their makeup, their image. How women are supposed to look may have changed; but the tyranny of physical attractiveness, compounded by the need to appear "fit" and youthful, is omnipresent. Even in an event such as the women's final of the 1988 U.S. Open tennis tournament, in which Steffi Graf was trying to win her fourth major tournament of the year, thereby winning the "Grand Slam"—a feat accomplished by only four other players in the history of tennis—the good looks of her opponent, Gabriela Sabatini, were mentioned numerous times by the male television announcers, who were otherwise scrupulously nonsexist. It is noteworthy that in the record-breaking four-hour-and-fifty-four-minute men's final, which pitted Mats Wilander against Ivan Lendl, there was no mention of Wilander's rugged good looks. It is not, after all, simply how well women play the game but how they look while playing that counts as well.

The area of sex is still extraordinarily problematic for young women today. Of all the mine fields women must navigate, sex is one of the most complex and treacherous. The pressures to have sex are enormous and the pressures not to plan for sex nearly as great. Many young women are caught in this incredible bind: some are caught by ignorance, others by the desire to be part of the group; some by fear, others by the need to be held or "loved." And many are caught by the notion that having sex is cool, sophisticated, a rite of passage somehow required in today's culture. But it is still widely seen as something you do inadvertently, almost as an afterthought, for if a fifteen-, sixteen-, or seventeen-year-old plans for sex, goes to the local family-planning clinic for contraception, acknowledges her intention, takes responsibility for her actions, truly takes control, she is often seen by her peers, her family, even her community as deviant, as a "bad girl." To acquiesce is permissible; to choose clearly and consciously to embark on a sexual relationship is somehow reprehensible. One is reminded of many magazine advertisements that picture women being "carried away" by feeling or literally carried away by men, vignettes that are clearly metaphors for sex. Are we really saying that being carried away is appropriately feminine while being in control of one's actions is not?

But it is not only the objectification of women that remains a fact of life but the marginalization of women as well, particularly in the workplace and in positions of power. Contrary to the expectations of the young women I interviewed, female workers still occupy the lowest rungs of most occupations, including the prestigious professions they have recently entered in such large numbers. Women may have entered the labor market in record numbers in recent years, but they are still working predominantly in the lowest-paying jobs within the lowest-paying occupations.

In addition, it has become clear over the past decade that proverty dominates and determines the lives of millions of women in the United States. Today two out of three poor adults are women. Teen mothers, female heads of families, divorced women, many working women, elderly women, the "new poor" as well as those who have grown up in poverty are all at substantial risk of spending a significant part of their lives at or below the poverty line. And, of course, if women are poor, their children are poor. One out of five children under the age of eighteen and one out of four under the age of six live in poverty today. One out of every two young black children is officially poor. Perhaps most disturbing, moreover, are the sharp increases over the past decade in the number of children in families with incomes below the poverty line, a group that has been termed "the poorest of the poor." The vast majority of these families are headed by women.

Within this context, within the reality of women's true economic situation, what is surprising in talking with young women from various parts of the country—black women, white women, and Hispanic women; affluent, middle-class, and poor women; women who are headed for Ivy League colleges as well as high school dropouts—is the narrowness of their image of success, the uniformity of their dreams. The affluent life as symbolized by the fancy car, the "house on a hill," the "Bloomingdale's wardrobe," "giving everything to my children," was described yearningly time and time again. As if programmed, the same words, the same dreams tumbled out of the mouths of young women from very different backgrounds and life experiences. Success was seen, overwhelmingly, in terms of what they would be able to purchase, what kind of "life-style" they would have. The ability to consume in an upper-middle-class manner was often the ultimate goal. . . .

Few spoke of becoming a reporter or a journalist, of teaching or entering the ministry. Rarely did anyone speak of caring for the sick or helping the poor; only occasionally did someone hope to make difference in the lives of others. Even those planning to become social workers or nurses (and there were very few) spoke mainly of their concern that these professions would pay enough to enable them to live the life-style they hoped for. Are these young women programmed or "brainwashed," or are they too reflecting the tone—and the economic reality—or their time?

Are young women focusing on material possessions in part because they are at least something to hold on to, symbols of identity and security in an era of fragmented family life, insecure, often transient work relationships, and a vanishing sense of community? In any case, young women are surely reflecting the omnipresent message of television. As Todd Gitlin has stated:

> With few exceptions, prime time gives us people preoccupied with personal ambition . . . Personal ambition and consumerism are the driving forces in their lives. The sumptuous and brightly lit settings of most series amount to advertisements for a consumption-centered version of the good life, and this doesn't even take into consideration the incessant commercials, which convey the idea that human aspirations for liberty, pleasure, accomplishment, and status can be fulfilled in the realm of consumption.

Given the reality of the job market for women, what will become of their dreams of affluence? Given the reality of the structure of work and the availability of child care, what will become of their image of mothering? Have these young women, in fact, been sold a false dream? Have young women become encouraged to raise their expectations, only to see those expectations unfulfilled because there has not been comparable change within society? Have the major institutions that influence public opinion—the media, advertising, the fashion industry, as well as the industries that produce consumer goods and parts of the educational establishment—fostered these rising expectations because it suits their purposes and, in some cases, their profits? Has the dream of equal opportunity for women and men, of at least partial redistribution of power both within the family and in the society at large, been coopted and commodified, turned into a spirit for consumer goods rather than a long march toward a more humane life for all of us?

Have we indeed over the last quarter-century persuaded women that they, too, are entitled to their fair share of the American Dream, in their own right, not merely as appendages to the primary players, without changing the rules of the game in ways that would permit them truly to compete and succeed? Have women, in short, been hoodwinked into believing that they can "have it all, do it all, be it all" while society itself changes minimally? And have we somehow communicated to them that they must make it on their own, recreating the myth of the rugged individualist seeking the American Dream—alone? . . .

Much has been written about the difficult choices women currently have: how to balance marriage and career; how to balance motherhood and career; the timing of conception; the problems of a demanding job versus the demands and joys of motherhood. But these books, articles, television programs, and occasionally films put forth a largely false message: that the majority of women in late-twentieth-century America indeed have these choices to make. The illusion is abroad in the land that a young woman can simply "choose" to postpone pregnancy and marriage, acquire the education of her choice (which should, of course, be in a field in which jobs are available and well paying), and then step into the job of her choice. At that point, if she wishes, the man of her dreams will miraculously appear (and will be single and interested in "commitment"!), and, despite years of contraception and possibly even an abortion or two, she will promptly conceive, have a healthy baby or two, and live happily ever after. But of course we know life is not like that—at least not for the vast majority of women.

Most women do not have these magnificent choices. The education of many women is circumscribed by economics, by inferior schooling, and by the expectations of their social group. The jobs they will take are dictated far more by the economy, by what jobs are "open" to women, and by their own economic need than by individual choice. And, as we know all too well, controlling and timing fertility can be an extremely difficult and delicate task. Not only do many women become pregnant when they are unprepared for motherhood, but many cannot seem to have a child when they have been planning and longing for one for years. Moreover, many women grow up hungry, homeless, and hopeless, part of the underside of a society that is increasingly coming to resemble a third-world nation with its very rich and privileged and its very poor and despairing.

This illusion of choice is a major impediment to the establishment of conditions that would enable women—and indeed all people—to have real choices. Young women recognize that they are likely to participate actively in both work and home, in "doing" and "caring," but they fail to recognize what they must have in order to do so: meaningful options and supports in their work lives; in childbearing, child rearing, and the structure of their families; in housing, health care, and child care; and, above all, in the values by which they live their lives. Does emphasis on fashion, consumerism, and the lives of the rich and famous create the illusion of choice while diverting attention from serious discussion of policies that would give women genuine options? It is significant that during the 1988 presidential campaign legislation to raise the minimum wage, to provide parental leave, and to improve and expand the child care system—measures that would have significantly increased the life options of women and of all family members—were defeated, the latter two by a Republican filibuster. Despite the much-touted gender gap, little real attention was paid to policies that relate primarily to the well-being of women and children during the national campaign, a time when these issues could have been thoroughly discussed and debated. Do politicians really believe that women are not watching and listening? Are women perhaps *not* watching and listening? Or have they given up on a society that does not seem interested in addressing their needs?

For women to have real choices, we must develop a society in which women and children and indeed families of all shapes and sizes are respected and valued. Despite the mythology of American individualism, it is clear that most women cannot truly go it alone. The young women I interviewed know that they must be prepared to be part of the labor force and still be available to care for others—for children, for older family members, for friends, for lovers—but these often mutually exclusive tasks will be possible only when we develop a society that supports doing and caring. Men must take on caring functions; the society must take some of the responsibility for caring and above all must be restructured to permit, even to encourage, doing and caring. Women simply cannot do it all and cannot do it alone.

To suggest that aspects of American society must be significantly altered may seem to some to be utopian or at best visionary. In a time of corporate takeovers, insider trading, and lavish levels of private consumption, calling for fundamental restructuring of social and economic priorities may seem fatuous or at best naive. I do not mean to suggest that such restructuring will be accomplished easily or in the near future, but while many of these changes may take years or even decades to accomplish, if we are to bring about significant change in the twenty-first century, discussion and debate must be ongoing and must involve all sectors of society. It must be stressed, moreover, that most of these proposals have been outlined before and will be explored again and again. It is my hope that this discussion will add to the debate and will thereby further the process of developing a more humane environment in which we can all live, work, and care for one another.

First, I believe that fundamental change must be made in the workplace. Traditionally male-dominated professions cannot continue to expect their workers to function as if there were a full-time wife and mother at home. Most male workers no longer live in that never-never land; female workers surely do not. Alternative paths to partnerships, professorships, and promotion must be developed that will neither leave women once again at the bottom of the career ladder without real power and equal rewards nor force them to choose between a demanding work life and a demanding personal life.

Nor should women have to choose a middle ground between work and mothering. One compromise has been described as "sequencing"—establishing a career, leaving it to bring up the children, and then resuming work in a way that does not conflict with domestic responsibilities. Isn't that what many of us did in the fifties? Most women, clearly, cannot afford to sequence. Try telling a stitcher in a garment factory to sequence—or a waitress or a clerical worker. In addition to the loss of income, status, and seniority, the problem with these upper-middle-class "solutions," which are often unsatisfactory even for those who can afford them, is that once again they give the illusion of choice. For the vast majority of American women, sequencing is not possible, or even desirable. What we must develop are options for the millions of women who must work and for the millions of women who *want* to work, not the illusion of options applicable only to that minority of women who are part of affluent two-parent families and are willing to sacrifice their careers, their earning power, and often the real pleasure they obtain from work because the larger society is unwilling to meet women and families even halfway.

Another compromise suggested recently is institutionalizing within corporations one track for "'career primary'" women, who can "be worked long hours, promoted, relocated and generally treated like a man," and another for "career and 'family'" women, who will accept "lower pay and little advancement in return for a flexible schedule that allows . . . [them] to accommodate to family needs." This proposal clearly would legitimize the second-class status of any parent, mother, or father who wished to spend a significant amount of time on family responsibilities. Once again, we would be insisting that individuals and families bend to norms that are defined by employers and that primarily serve the needs of employers.

We must reevaluate our system of economic rewards. Do we really want our entertainers, our stockbrokers, our corporate executives, and our divorce lawyers making millions while our nurses and day-care workers barely scrape by? Do we really want the rich to get richer while the poor get poorer and the middle class loses ground? Do we really want to tell our young women that they must play traditional male roles in order to earn a decent living and that caregiving no longer counts, is no longer worth doing? . . .

Market forces cannot be permitted to rule in all spheres of American life. If our society is to be a caring, humane place to live, to rear our children, and to grow old, we must recognize that some aspects of life—the education of our young people, health care, child care, the texture of community life, the quality of the environment—are more important than profit. We as a nation must determine our priorities and act accordingly. If teaching, the care of young children, providing nursing care, and other human services are essential to the quality of life in the United States, then we must recruit our young people into these fields and pay them what the job is really worth. Only then will we be giving them, particularly our young women, real choices. If we want nurses to care for our sick, we must indicate by decent wages and working conditions that the job is valued by society. We must give nurses and other health workers real authority, a meaningful voice in the health-care system, and then, and only then, will some of our best and brightest and most caring women and men choose to enter nursing. Whatever happened to careers in community organizing, urban planning, Legal Aid, and public-health nursing? Young women and men will be able to consider these options only if they are decently paid, have a future and some degree of security and respect.

In this fin de siècle period of U.S. history characterized (in the words of John Kenneth Galbraith) by "private affluence" and "public squalor," it may be difficult to see our way clear to putting significantly larger amounts of money into health care, community organizing, education, or even a meaningful effort to deter young people from drug abuse, but we must recognize that these issues are central to the well-being of families and thus central to the very fabric and structure of American society. While the 1980s have surely been characterized by absorption with personal advancement and well-being (particularly economic and physical well-being), there are many indications that Americans are also concerned about the well-being of the society as a whole. Poll after poll has demonstrated that people *are* concerned about issues such as education and homelessness and *are* willing to make sacrifices to enable the society to deal more effectively with those problems.

Furthermore, it is often said that there is no money to truly make this into a "kinder, gentler nation" but we must remember that the United States spends $300 billion annually on arms, the U.S. Congress has approved the Bush administration's savings and loan bailout proposal that will cost nearly $160 billion over the next ten years, and the United States has one of the lowest tax rates, particularly for the wealthy, in the industrialized world. I suggest that the money *is* there. The issue is how we choose to allocate it.

What should our priorities be? Among them, parents must have some time at home with their children. Why can't parents of young children work a shorter day or week and not risk losing their jobs? Why aren't parents at the time of the birth or adoption of a baby guaranteed some paid time together with that infant when virtually every other industrialized country has some statutory maternity or parental leave? The parental leave bill that was killed during the 100th Congress called for unpaid leave for the parents of a newborn or newly adopted child. It would have affected only 5 percent of all businesses and 40 percent of all workers (the firms affected would have been those with fifty or more employees). It was estimated by Senator John H. Chafee, Republican of Rhode Island, that the cost would have been $160 million per year, which averages out to one cent per day for each covered employee. The bill also would have provided unpaid leave for parents with seriously ill children. As Senator Christopher J. Dodd, Democrat of Connecticut, a sponsor of the legislation, stated:

> Today fewer than one in ten American families have the luxury of having the mother at home with the children while the father is at work.
>
> In this nation today there are 8.7 million women as the sole providers of their families. They are taking care of 16 million kids who have no father at home. And when that child becomes sick or that employee becomes sick, we ought not to say to that family struggling to make ends meet: "Choose. Choose your child or choose your job."

No, women cannot make it alone. They cannot work and parent and care for their elderly relatives as well without a caring society. They cannot work and care for others without sufficient income, parental leave, real flex time, and a work environment that recognizes and understands that a rewarding private life takes time and energy.

Furthermore, that work environment must make it possible for both fathers and mothers to care for others. It must become acceptable in the United States for fathers to take leave to care for a new baby, to stay home with sick children, to leave work in time to pick up a child from day care or after-school care; for sons to attend to the needs of aging parents. It must even become acceptable for fathers to attend a school play or a Halloween party during the work day. Changing male roles may take years of resocialization and structural change within the society, but we must attempt it nonetheless. Mothers can no longer play the solitary domestic role—not while participating in the work force as well. If women are to do and to care, men must also do and care.

Perhaps a vignette from the life of one family and one work site illustrates the need to humanize the workplace. On November 21, 1985, the U.S. Senate agreed not to cast any votes between seven and nine p.m. The following letter was the reason for this unusual action:

Dear Senator Dole:

I am having my second-grade play tonight. Please make sure there aren't any votes between 7 and 9 so my daddy can watch me. Please come with him if you can.

Love,
Corinne Quayle

What is particularly remarkable about this incident is that when the final version of the Parental and Medical Leave Act was being written by the Senate Labor and Human Resources Committee, Vice-President J. Danforth Quayle, then a senator, vehemently opposed it and, according to one observer, "offered an amendment in committee that would assure that an employer enjoys the right to fire an employee who takes as much as one day off to be with a seriously ill child." As Judy Mann, the *Washington Post* columnist who brought this incident to light, wrote: "Quayle lives by a set of special rules for the privileged and well-connected and doesn't hesitate to impose another set of rules and obligations, harsher and devoid of compassion, on those who were not to the manner born. Either he doesn't know anything about the reality of most workers' lives, or he doesn't care."

The United States must also finally decide where it stands on the care of preschool children. By 1995 two-thirds of all preschool children (approximately 15 million) and more than three-quarters of all school-age children (approximately 34.4 million) will have mothers in the work force. In addition, 3.7 million mothers receiving welfare with 3.1 million children under six and 2.9 million school-age children will with the passage of recent welfare legislation be required to enter the work force or to participate in education and job-training courses. Day care must be provided for those single-parent families for at least one year. Today only 23 percent of all children of working parents attend full or part-time centers, which vary enormously in quality; an additional 23 percent are cared for in family day care, most of which is unlicensed and unsupervised. As Edward Zigler, director of the Bush Center in Child Development and Social Policy at Yale and one of the founders of the Head Start program, has recently stated, "All over America today we have hundreds of thousands of children in child-care settings that are so bad that their development is being compromised. . . . We are cannibalizing our children. I know that sounds awful, but when you see 13 babies in cribs and one adult caretaker . . . you see children who are being destroyed right after birth."

How will 50 to 60 million children whose mothers will be in the work force be cared for during the 1990s? The New York-based Child Care Action Campaign, whose blue-ribbon board includes experts in child care from all over the country, has urged every level of society to become involved in solving this child-care crisis. It has urged the federal government to establish a national child-care office and a "new and separate funding stream" for child care, to expand Head Start, and to set federal regulations on minimum standards. It has urged state and local governments to establish school-age-child-care programs, expand resource and referral programs, and raise the professional status and working conditions of child-care workers. It has urged employers to adopt flexible work schedules, to support community efforts to expand day-care centers and family day care, to invest in on-site centers, to help parents to pay for regular day care and emergency day care, and to allow employees to use their sick leave to care for ill children. . . .

One of the central components of all of these recommendations is adequate training, recompense, employment security, and status for caregivers at every level. By demeaning the role of caregiver, society demeans all women and indeed, to one extent or another, exploits all caregivers. It also sets up the exploitation of one group of women by another. The ripples are endless: from the middle-or upper-middle-class career mother who is "stressed out" by trying to do it all to the single mother who really *is* doing it all to the day-care worker who is working in inadequate conditions earning inadequate pay to the child-care worker/domestic who is often shamefully exploited in the home, society's fundamental disregard for caregivers and for raising children diminishes us all. Ultimately, of course, it is the children who suffer, but women at all levels suffer as well. And the poor, the nonwhite, those with least choice suffer the most.

Any society that really wants to enable women to be in control of their lives must provide a comprehensive program of sex education and contraception. Perhaps one of the most startling aspects of my interviews with young women and with relevant professionals was the sense that many young women are buffeted about by conflicting attitudes toward sexuality and indeed find it exceedingly difficult to determine what they themselves think and want. By the time they figure it out, it is often too late. They are pregnant and faced with a real Hobson's choice: to abort, or to have a baby at a time in their life when they are ill-prepared—economically, physically, socially, or psychologically—to care for a child. We know what it can do to both the mother and the child when the pregnancy is unplanned and the mother is unable to care for the infant properly. We must do everything possible to make every child a planned child, to make every child a wanted child.

We must learn from the experience of other industrialized countries, whose rate of unintended and teenage pregnancy is so much lower than our own. We must institute sex education in our schools at all levels. The ignorance on the part of young women is astonishing and serves no useful purpose. Moreover, in this era of AIDS and other sexually transmitted diseases, such ignorance can literally be life-threatening. We must increase the accessibility of contraceptives, whether through school-based clinics or community-based health centers. We should consider staffing these centers with midwives or other health professionals whose primary task would be to relate to young people, understand their needs, and help them to understand their choices. The empowerment of young women and men in the area of sexuality should be the central goal—empowerment through knowledge, empowerment through emotional maturity, empowerment through access to the health-care system. And teenagers must be assured of confidentiality whenever they are dealing with contraception or abortion.

As Lisbeth Schorr so forcefully points out in her recent book *Within Our Reach: Breaking the Cycle of Disadvantage,* "The knowledge necessary to reduce the growing toll of damaged lives is now available." We know what to do; we know what works. A school-based program in Baltimore, Maryland, illustrates what can be done. Starting in January 1982, professionals at Johns Hopkins University and the Baltimore Health Department and School Board collaborated in bringing sex education, reproduction-related medical services, and counseling to students in the junior high school and senior high school closest to Johns Hopkins Hospital. Both schools had all-black student bodies. Many of the young people lived in nearby high-rise public housing, and in the junior high school 85 percent were poor enough to qualify for the free-lunch program.

A nurse midwife and a social worker were placed in one school; a nurse practitioner and a social worker were placed in the other. The same professionals were available every afternoon, with physician backup if necessary, to provide relevant medical services at a clinic across the street. The teams gave classroom presentations, counseled individuals and small groups, and made appointments for further consultation, education, and treatment at the clinic. Medical services, including physical exams and contraceptives, were provided during a single visit and at no cost. Every effort was made to ensure that the students would see the same professionals each time they came, "in the belief that consistency of relationships builds trust, helps youngsters to synthesize what they have learned, and makes it possible for them to share very private concerns."

The demonstration program continued until June 1984. During the two-and-a-half years of its existence, the proportion of sexually active high-school students who had babies went down 25 percent; the proportion of girls who became sexually active by age fourteen dropped 40 percent, and the median age at which girls became sexually active rose by seven months, from age fifteen and a half before the program was started to a little over age sixteen at the program's end. This experience is yet another piece of evidence that knowledge about reproduction and access to contraception and to caring people who can discuss a young person's options rationally, with concern and yet with objectivity, can and does lessen the critical problem of teenage pregnancy.

Michael Carrera and Patricia Dempsey, director and former program coordinator of the Teen Primary Pregnancy Prevention Program of the Children's Aid Society in New York City, claim that what is needed is a "holistic approach." "It is our belief," they state, "that the teen pregnancy problem is largely a symptomatic response to greater social ills and because of this, it must concurrently be attacked on several levels. For example, unintended pregnancies among poor, urban teens can be more effectively curtailed if we reduce the impact of the institutional racism that is systemic in our society; if we provide quality education for everyone; and if we create more employment opportunities for young people and adults. If we could accomplish this, we would probably impact, in a more meaningful way, on the lives of teens than can any school or agency sexuality program."

Continued access to abortion must be guaranteed. Efforts to overturn or limit women's right to abortion must be vigorously resisted. For many young women, abortion is the only barrier between them and a life of poverty and despair. Until we stop giving our young women mixed messages—that it is desirable and sometimes even de rigueur to have sex but not legitimate to protect against pregnancy—abortion remains the only resource. Saying that one is for adoption, not abortion, may sound reasonable and "pro life"; but once young women are pregnant and decide to have the baby, giving it up for adoption is a wrenching decision, particularly for those young women who see little opportunity to make another life for themselves. Indeed, among the women I interviewed those who were most despairing about their lives were often those who had babies at a young age and could see no way out of the trap in which they found themselves. I am not suggesting that any of these issues—particularly ones as personal and as controversial as sex education and abortion—are easy to resolve in our complex heterogeneous society, but we must somehow develop a public policy that will help our young people become mature before they are thrust into parenting roles. Other societies have developed such policies; we must learn from them and develop our own.

In addition to giving women greater choice over sex and childbearing, we must stop exploiting women as sex objects. As long as the message of jean manufacturers, cereal companies, automobile conglomerates, and perfume distributors is that women are for sale along with the product, that women are, in a very real sense, just another commodity to be bought, used, and traded in when the model wears out, both men and women will perceive women in this way. And until we enable young women to responsibly say either yes or no to sex, to understand their options and the risks involved, we are not permitting them to be in charge of their own destiny. But we cannot expect young women to take control of their own destiny unless they can see alternatives, pathways that will lead to a rewarding life.

It is ironic that young women, a group outside the cultural mainstream in at least two fundamental ways, age and gender, have internalized that most mainstream of ideologies, the American Dream. After examining the realities of women's lives today, it is clear that the American Dream, at least as conventionally conceived, cannot be the blueprint for the majority of women. The fundamental components of the American Dream—an almost devout reliance on individualism; the notion that American society, particularly at the end of the twentieth century and the beginning of the twenty-first, is fluid enough to permit substantial upward mobility; the belief that hard work will lead to economic rewards, even for women, a group that has always been at the margins of the labor force; and the determined optimism in the face of massive social and economic problems—will not serve women well.

We must recognize that even for most men the American Dream, with its belief in the power of the individual to shape his or her own destiny, was a myth. Men usually did not "make it" alone; they did not, as the image goes, tame the West, develop industrial America, and climb the economic ladder alone—and they certainly did not do it while being the primary caregiver for a couple of preschoolers. Most of those men who "made it" in America, whom we think of when we reaffirm our belief in the American Dream, had women beside them every step of the way—women to iron their shirts, press their pants, mend their socks, cook their meals, bring up their children, and soothe them at the end of a hard day. They did not do it alone. They *still* don't do it alone. How can women do it alone? Who is there to mend and press their clothes, cook their meals, bring up their children, and soothe them at the end of a hard day? How can women possibly make it alone when they earn 65 percent of what men earn, when housing is virtually unaffordable for millions of families, when child care is scarce and all too often second-rate or worse? And where did they get the notion that they *should* be able to make it alone? It may be progress that many young women now realize that they cannot depend on marriage and a man for their identity, their protection, their daily bread; but is it progress or is it illusion for them to believe that they can do the caring and the doing and do it all on their own in a society that has done very little to make women truly independent?

The American Dream cannot really work for any of the groups of women I interviewed. Yes, some women will accomplish their dreams and live productive, rewarding lives; but most of them will have to make substantial compromises, scale down their ambitions, not be quite the kind of parent they hoped they would be. How will the New American Dreamers make it in law, medicine, or oceanography when the rules were made for men with an elaborate support system? How will they get to the top of their fields when our image of authority is still someone who is six feet tall in a blue suit, striped shirt, and not-too-bold red tie? How will they afford the co-op, the BMW, and the trips to Europe when they must often choose between sequencing, the "Mommy" track, part-time work, or leaving their field entirely in order to parent? And how will they resolve their guilt about what they are likely to perceive as less-than-adequate parenting when they must work to remain competitive in their field, to contribute to the maintenance of the family, or to function as its sole support?

Nor does the ideology of the American Dream serve the Neo-traditionalists well. Many of them place their faith in a loving, lasting marriage and hope to spend much of their lives caring for others. But what happens if disaster strikes or the marriage fails? Will they be prepared to go it alone? Will they really be prepared and able to take care of themselves and their children—and possibly their aging parents—with relatively few societal supports? And what if they cannot be home at three o'clock for cookies and milk? How will they feel about themselves as mothers?

And finally, of course, the ideology of the American Dream fails the Outsiders most abysmally and most tragically. Those who are truly outside the system—the homeless and the hungry, the poor and the near-poor, who know that America as it enters the 1990s has largely forgotten them, the millions of nonwhites who feel permanently outside the culture, the young people who leave high school functionally illiterate, those who feel like a "circle within a square," those who try to forget their sadness and anger through alcohol or drugs or, tragically, through suicide—what can the American Dream mean to them? To many it means that their inability to find the path to success is their own fault; for imbedded in the ideology of the American Dream, inherent in that "I think I can" mentality, is the presumption that if we do not succeed in this land of milk and honey, in this world of infinite opportunity, it must be our fault. If everyone is so rich on "Dallas,"

"Dynasty," and "L.A. Law," if even blacks have made it on "The Cosby Show" and its spin-offs, if single women like Kate and Allie and married couples like Hope and Michael and rural/suburban people like Bob Newhart and his support group and urban people like Sam Malone and his gang at "Cheers" all live comfortable and relatively happy, contented lives, what must be wrong with those who feel like Outsiders, either temporarily or permanently? If the biggest problems are solvable in twenty-two minutes, what hope can there be for those of us so beyond the pale that we cannot think of solutions at all?

We must have the courage and the wisdom as a society to recognize that we need a new vision of America for the twenty-first century, perhaps even a new American Dream. We need a vision that recognizes that we cannot survive without one another, that families must have supports in order to thrive, that women cannot make it alone any more than men ever have.

We must provide many more paths toward a gratifying, economically secure life. Traditional male occupations cannot be the only routes to the good life; traditional female work must be restructured so that it too can lead to power, prestige, and a life of plenty. And the traditional male work style must give way, for both women and men, to the recognition that work is merely one aspect of life and that private concerns, family life, leisure activities, and participation in community life help to define who we are and must be seen as important both to the individual and to the society.

We must find ways of opening up American society to those who feel outside the system, to those who feel hopeless and despairing. We must educate all of our young people, not simply the most privileged. We must provide them with adequate housing, health care, nutrition, safe communities in which to grow, and, above all, a meaningful role in society. So many of them feel extraneous because so many of them are treated as extraneous, except, possibly, in their roles as consumers. Moreover, providing decent lives for the millions of young people who are Outsiders will provide decent jobs for millions of other Americans and, even more, the sense that one is participating in a worthwhile way in the life of the nation. But, of course, we will not make the society accessible to those who now consider themselves Outsiders unless power and wealth are distributed far more equitably. It has been said before, it will be said again, but it cannot be said too often: there is a greater gap today between the rich and the poor than at any point since the Bureau of the Census began collecting these data in 1947. In 1987 the wealthiest 40 percent of American families received 67.8 percent of the national family income, the highest percentage ever recorded, while the poorest 40 percent received 15.4 percent, the lowest percentage (along with that of 1986) ever recorded. Until we address these fundamental inequities we cannot hope to enable our young people to become fully participating members of society.

These changes will not come about all at once or even, perhaps, in the near future. Changing our priorities is exceedingly difficult without strong national leadership pointing the way, but until we have representatives in Washington who will promote the public good rather than private gain we must develop leadership at the local level and work toward a more humane society step by step. We can raise these issues in our own communities and places of work. We can select one concern, such as child care or parental leave or flexible work hours, and together with others place that issue on the agenda of our employer, our union, or our local legislator. We can work with major national organizations to place family policy concerns on the national agenda. We must recognize that these concerns transcend the traditional barriers of class, race, gender, and age and form common cause with those who share our priorities.

Above all, we must develop a vision that recognizes that caring is as important as doing, that caring indeed *is* doing, and that caregivers, both paid and unpaid, are the foundation of a humane society and must be treasured and honored. We need a vision of America that recognizes that we must reorganize our social institutions — our family life, our schools, our places of work, and our communities—to enable all people to care for one another, to enable all people to work and to participate in the public life of the nation. Our courageous, insightful, persevering, and often wise young women deserve no less. Our young men deserve no less. Future generations deserve no less.

A New Vision of Masculinity

Cooper Thompson

I was once asked by a teacher in a suburban high school to give a guest presentation on male roles. She hoped that I might help her deal with four boys who exercised extraordinary control over the other boys in the class. Using ridicule and their status as physically imposing athletes, these four wrestlers had succeeded in stifling the participation of the other boys, who were reluctant to make comments in class discussions.

As a class we talked about the ways in which boys got status in that school and how they got put down by others. I was told that the most humiliating put-down was being called a "fag." The list of behaviors which could elicit ridicule filled two large chalkboards, and it was detailed and comprehensive; I got the sense that a boy in this school had to conform to rigid, narrow standards of masculinity to avoid being called a fag. I, too, felt this pressure and became very conscious of my mannerisms in front of the group. Partly from exasperation, I decided to test the seriousness of these assertions. Since one of the four boys had some streaks of pink in his shirt, and since he had told me that wearing pink was grounds for being called a fag, I told him that I thought he was a fag. Instead of laughing, he said, "I'm going to kill you."

Such is the stereotypic definition of strength that is associated with masculinity. But it is a very limited definition of strength, one based on dominance and control and acquired through the humiliation and degradation of others.

Contrast this with a view of strength offered by Pam McAllister in her introduction to *Reweaving the Web of Life*:

> The 'Strength' card in my Tarot deck depicts, not a warrior going off to battle with his armor and his mighty sword, but a woman stroking a lion. The woman has not slain the lion nor maced it, not netted it, nor has she put on it a muzzle or a leash. And though the lion clearly has teeth and long sharp claws, the woman is not hiding, nor has she sought a protector, nor has she grown muscles. She doesn't appear to be talking to the lion nor flattering it, nor tossing it fresh meat to distract its hungry jaws.
>
> The woman on the 'Strength' card wears a flowing white dress and a garland of flowers. With one hand she cups the lion's jaws, with the other she caresses its nose. The lion on the card has big yellow eyes and a long red tongue curling out of its mouth. One paw is lifted and the mane falls in thick red curls across its broad torso. The woman. The lion. Together they depict strength.

This image of strength stands in direct contrast to the strength embodied in the actions of the four wrestlers. The collective strength of the woman and the lion is a strength unknown in a system of traditional male values. Other human qualities are equally foreign to a traditional conception of masculinity. In workshops I've offered on the male role stereotype, teachers and other school personnel easily generate lists of attitudes and behaviors which boys typically seem to not learn. Included in this list are being supportive and nurturant, accepting one's vulnerability and being able to ask for help, valuing women and "women's work," understanding and expressing emotions (except for anger), the ability to empathize with and empower other people, and learning to resolve conflict in nonaggressive, noncompetitive ways.

Learning Violence

All of this should come as no surprise. Traditional definitions of masculinity include attributes such as independence, pride, resiliency, self-control, and physical strength. This is precisely the image of the Marlboro man, and to some extent, these are desirable attributes for boys and girls. But masculinity goes beyond these qualities to stress competitiveness, toughness, aggressiveness, and power. In this context, threats to one's status, however small, cannot be avoided or taken lightly. If a boy is called a fag, it means that he is perceived as weak or timid—and therefore not masculine enough for his peers. There is enormous pressure for him to fight back. Not being tough at these moments only proves the allegation.

Violence is learned not just as a way for boys to defend allegations that they are feminized, but as an effective, appropriate way for them to normally behave. In "The Civic Advocacy of Violence" [*M.*, Spring 1982] Wayne Ewing clearly states:

> I used to think that we simply tolerated and permitted male abusiveness in our society. I have now come to understand rather, that we advocate physical violence. Violence is presented as effective. Violence is taught as the normal, appropriate and necessary behavior of power and control. Analyses which interweave advocacy of male violence with 'SuperBowl Culture' have never been refuted. Civic expectations—translated into professionalism, financial commitments, city planning for recreational space, the raising of male children for competitive sport, the corporate ethics of business owner-ship of athletic teams, profiteering on entertainment—all result in the monument of the National Football League, symbol and reality at once of the advocacy of violence.

Ultimately, violence is the tool which maintains what I believe are the two most critical socializing forces in a boy's life: *homophobia*, the hatred of gay men (who are stereotyped as feminine) or those men believed to be gay, as well as the fear of being perceived as gay; and *misogyny*, the hatred of women. The two forces are targeted at different classes of victims, but they are really just the flip sides of the same coin. Homo-phobia is the hatred of feminine qualities in men while misogyny is the hatred of feminine qualities in women. The boy who is called a fag is the target of other boys' homophobia as well as the victim of his own homophobia. While the overt message is the absolute need to avoid being feminized, the implication is that females—and all that they traditionally represent—are contemptible. The United States Marines have a philosophy which conveniently combines homophobia and misogyny in the belief that "When you want to create a group of male killers, you kill 'the woman' in them."

The pressures of homophobia and misogyny in boys' lives have been poignantly demonstrated to me each time that I have repeated a simple yet provocative activity with students. I ask them to answer the question, "If you woke up tomorrow and discovered that you were the opposite sex from the one you are now, how would you and your life be different?" Girls consistently indicate that there are clear advan-tages to being a boy—from increased independence and career opportunities to decreased risks of physical and sexual assault—and eagerly answer the question. But boys often express disgust at this possibility and even refuse sometimes to answer the question. In her reports of a broad-based survey using this question, Alice Baum-gartner reports the following responses as typical of boys: "If I were a girl, I'd be stupid and weak as a string;" "I would have to wear makeup, cook, be a mother, and yuckky stuff like that;" "I would have to hate snakes. Everything would be miserable;" "If I were a girl, I'd kill myself."

The Costs of Masculinity

The costs associated with a traditional view of masculinity are enormous, and the damage occurs at both personal and societal levels. The belief that a boy should be tough (aggressive, competitive, and daring) can create emotional pain for him.

While a few boys experience short-term success for their toughness, there is little security in the long run. Instead, it leads to a series of challenges which few, if any, boys ultimately win. There is no security in being at the top when so many other boys are competing for the same status. Toughness also leads to increased chances of stress, physical injury, and even early death. It is considered manly to take extreme physical risks and voluntarily engage in combative, hostile activities.

The flip side of toughness—nurturance—is not a quality perceived as masculine and thus not valued. Because of this boys and men experience a greater emotional distance from other people and few opportunities to participate in meaningful interpersonal relationships. Studies consistently show that fathers spend very small amounts of time interacting with their children. In addition, men report that they seldom have intimate relationships with other men, reflecting their homophobia. They are afraid of getting too close and don't know how to take down the walls that they have built between themselves.

As boys grow older and accept adult roles, the larger social costs of masculinity clearly emerge. Most women experience male resistance to an expansion of women's roles; one of the assumptions of traditional masculinity is the belief that women should be subordinate to men. The consequence is that men are often not willing to accept females as equal, competent partners in personal and professional settings. Whether the setting is a sexual relationship, the family, the streets, or the battlefield, men are continuously engaged in efforts to dominate. Statistics on child abuse consistently indicate that the vast majority of abusers are men, and that there is no "typical" abuser. Rape may be the fastest growing crime in the United States. And it is men, regardless of nationality, who provoke and sustain war. In short, traditional masculinity is life threatening.

New Socialization for Boys

Masculinity, like many other human traits, is determined by both biological and environmental factors. While some believe that biological factors are significant in shaping some masculine behavior, there is undeniable evidence that cultural and environmental factors are strong enough to override biological impulses. What is it, then, that we should be teaching boys about being a man in a modern world?

- Boys must learn to accept their vulnerability, learn to express a range of emotions such as fear and sadness, and learn to ask for help and support in appropriate situations.
- Boys must learn to be gentle, nurturant, cooperative and communicative, and in particular, learn nonviolent means of resolving conflicts.
- Boys must learn to accept those attitudes and behaviors which have traditionally been labeled feminine as necessary for full human development—thereby reducing homophobia and misogyny. This is tantamount to teaching boys to love other boys and girls.

Certain qualities like courage, physical strength, and independence, which are traditionally associated with masculinity, are indeed positive qualities for males, provided that they are not manifested in obsessive ways nor used to exploit or dominate others. It is not necessary to completely disregard or unlearn what is traditionally called masculine. I believe, however, that the three areas above are crucial for developing a broader view of masculinity, one which is healthier for all life.

These three areas are equally crucial for reducing aggressive, violent behavior among boys and men. Males must learn to cherish life for the sake of their *own* wholeness as human beings, not just *for* their children, friends, and lovers. If males were more nurturant, they would be less likely to hurt those they love.

Leonard Eron, writing in the *American Psychologist*, puts the issue of unlearning aggression and learning nurturance in clear-cut terms:

> Socialization is crucial in determining levels of aggression. No matter how aggression is measured or observed, as a group males always score higher than females. But this is not true for all girls. There are some girls who seem to have been socialized like boys who are just as aggressive as boys. Just as some females can learn to be aggressive, so males can learn *not* to be aggressive. If we want to reduce the level of aggression in society, we should also discourage boys from aggression very early on in life and reward them too for others' behaviors; in other words, we should socialize boys more like girls, and they should be encouraged to develop socially positive qualities such as tenderness, cooperation, and aesthetic appreciation. The level of individual aggression in society will be reduced only when male adolescents and young adults, as a result of socialization, subscribe to the same standards of behavior as have been traditionally encouraged for women.

Where will this change in socialization occur? In his first few years, most of a boy's learning about masculinity comes from the influences of parents, siblings and images of masculinity such as those found on television. Massive efforts will be needed to make changes here. But at older ages, school curriculum and the school environment provide powerful reinforcing images of traditional masculinity. This reinforcement occurs through a variety of channels, including curriculum content, role modeling, and extracurricular activities, especially competitive sports.

School athletics are a microcosm of the socialization of male values. While participation in competitive activities can be enjoyable and healthy, it too easily becomes a lesson in the need for toughness, invulnerability, and dominance. Athletes learn to ignore their own injuries and pain and instead try to injure and inflict pain on others in their attempts to win, regardless of the cost to themselves or their opponents. Yet the lessons learned in athletics are believed to be vital for full and complete masculine development, and as a model for problem-solving in other areas of life.

In addition to encouraging traditional male values, schools provide too few experiences in nurturance, cooperation, negotiation, nonviolent conflict resolution, and strategies for empathizing with and empowering others. Schools should become places where boys have the opportunity to learn these skills; clearly, they won't learn them on the street, from peers, or on television.

Setting New Examples

Despite the pressures on men to display their masculinity in traditional ways, there are examples of men and boys who are changing. "Fathering" is one example of a positive change. In recent years, there has been a popular emphasis on child-care activities, with men becoming more involved in providing care to children, both professionally and as fathers. This is a clear shift from the more traditional view that child rearing should be delegated to women and is not an appropriate activity for men.

For all of the male resistance it has generated, the Women's Liberation Movement has at least provided a stimulus for some men to accept women as equal partners in most areas of life. These are the men who have chosen to learn and grow from women's experiences and together with women are creating new norms for relationships. Popular literature and research on male sex roles is expanding, reflecting a wider interest in masculinity. Weekly news magazines such as *Time* and *Newsweek* have run major stories on the "new masculinity," suggesting that positive changes are taking place in the home and in the workplace. Small groups of men scattered around the country have organized against pornography, battering, and sexual assault. Finally there is the National Organization for Changing Men which has a pro-feminist, pro-gay, pro-"new man" agenda, and its ranks are slowly growing.

In schools where I have worked with teachers, they report that years of efforts to enhance educational opportunities for girls have also had some positive effects on boys. The boys seem more tolerant of girls' participation in coed sports activities and in traditionally male shops and courses. They seem to have a greater respect for the accomplishments of women through women's contributions to literature and history. Among elementary school aged males, the expression of vulnerable feelings is gaining acceptance. In general, however, there has been far too little attention paid to redirecting male role development.

Boys Will Be Boys

I think back to the four wrestlers and the stifling culture of masculinity in which they live. If schools were to radically alter this culture and substitute for it a new vision of masculinity, what would that look like? In this environment, boys would express a full range of behaviors and emotions without fear of being chastized. They would be permitted and encouraged to cry, to be afraid, to show joy, and to express love in a gentle fashion. Extreme concern for career goals would be replaced by a consideration of one's need for recreation, health, and meaningful work. Older boys would be encouraged to tutor and play with younger students. Moreover, boys would receive as much recognition for artistic talents as they do for athletics, and, in general, they would value leisure-time, recreational activities as highly as competitive sports.

In a system where maleness and femaleness were equally valued, boys might no longer feel that they have to "prove" themselves to other boys; they would simply accept the worth of each person and value those differences. Boys would realize that it is permissable to admit failure. In addition, they would seek out opportunities to learn from girls and women. Emotional support would be commonplace, and it would no longer be seen as just the role of the female to provide the support. Relationships between boys and girls would no longer be based on limited roles, but instead would become expressions of two individuals learning from and supporting one another. Relationships between boys would reflect their care for one another rather then their mutual fear and distrust.

Aggressive styles of resolving conflicts would be the exception rather than the norm. Girls would feel welcome in activities dominated by boys, knowing that they were safe from the threat of being sexually harassed. Boys would no longer boast of beating up another boy or of how much they "got off" of a girl the night before. In fact, the boys would be as outraged as the girls at rape or other violent crimes in the community. Finally, boys would become active in efforts to stop nuclear proliferation and all other forms of military violence, following the examples set by activist women.

The development of a new conception of masculinity based on this vision is an ambitious task, but one which is essential for the health and safety of both men and women. The survival of our society may rest on the degree to which we are able to teach men to cherish life.

Homophobia as a Weapon of Sexism

Suzanne Pharr

Patriarchy—an enforced belief in male dominance and control—is the ideology and sexism the system that holds it in place. The catechism goes like this: Who do gender roles serve? Men and the women who seek power from them. Who suffers from gender roles? Women most completely and men in part. How are gender roles maintained? By the weapons of sexism: economics, violence, homophobia.

Why then don't we ardently pursue ways to eliminate gender roles and therefore sexism? It is my profound belief that all people have a spark in them that yearns for freedom, and the history of the world's atrocities—from the Nazi concentration camps to white dominance in South Africa to the battering of women—is the story of attempts to snuff out that spark. When that spark doesn't move forward to full flame, it is because the weapons designed to control and destroy have wrought such intense damage over time that the spark has been all but extinguished.

Sexism, that system by which women are kept subordinate to men, is kept in place by three powerful weapons designed to cause or threaten women with pain and loss. . . .

We have to look at economics not only as the root cause of sexism but also as the underlying, driving force that keeps all the oppressions in place. In the United States, our economic system is shaped like a pyramid, with a few people at the top, primarily white males, being supported by large numbers of unpaid or low-paid workers at the bottom. When we look at this pyramid, we begin to understand the major connection between sexism and racism because those groups at the bottom of the pyramid are women and people of color. We then begin to understand why there is such a fervent effort to keep those oppressive systems (racism and sexism and all the ways they are manifested) in place to maintain the unpaid and low-paid labor.

Susan DeMarco and Jim Hightower, writing for *Mother Jones*, report that *Forbes* magazine indicated that "the 400 richest families in America last year had an average net worth of $550 million each. These and less than a million other families— roughly one percent of our population—are at the prosperous tip of our society. . . . In 1976, the wealthiest 1 percent of America's families owned 19.2 percent of the nation's total wealth. (This sum of wealth counts all of America's cash, real estate, stocks, bonds, factories, art, personal property, and anything else of financial value.) By 1983, those at this 1 percent tip of our economy owned 34.3 percent of our wealth. . . . *Today, the top 1 percent of Americans possesses more net wealth than the bottom 90 percent.*" (My italics.) (*May, 1988, pp. 32–33*)

In order for this top-heavy system of economic inequity to maintain itself, the 90 percent on the bottom must keep supplying cheap labor. A very complex, intricate system of institutionalized oppressions is necessary to maintain the status quo so that the vast majority will not demand its fair share of wealth and resources and bring the system down. Every institution—schools, banks, churches, government, courts, media, etc—as well as individuals must be enlisted in the campaign to maintain such a system of gross inequity.

What would happen if women gained the earning opportunities and power that men have? What would happen if these opportunities were distributed equitably, no matter what sex one was, no matter what race one was born into, and no matter where one lived? What if educational and training opportunities were equal? Would women spend most of our youth preparing for marriage? Would marriage be based on economic survival for women? What would happen to issues of power and control? Would women stay with our batterers? If a woman had economic independence in a society where women had equal opportunities, would she still be thought of as owned by her father or husband?

Economics is the great controller in both sexism and racism. If a person can't acquire food, shelter, and clothing and provide them for children, then that person can be forced to do many things in order to survive. The major tactic, worldwide, is to provide unrecompensed or inadequately recompensed labor for the benefit of those who control wealth. Hence, we see women performing unpaid labor in the home or filling low-paid jobs, and we see people of color in the lowest-paid jobs available.

The method is complex: limit educational and training opportunities for women and for people of color and then withhold adequate paying jobs with the excuse that people of color and women are incapable of filling them. Blame the economic victim and keep the victim's self-esteem low through invisibility and distortion within the media and education. Allow a few people of color and women to succeed among the profitmakers so that blaming those who don't "make it" can be intensified. Encourage those few who succeed in gaining power now to turn against those who remain behind rather than to use their resources to make change for all. Maintain the myth of scarcity—that there are not enough jobs, resources, etc., to go around—among the middleclass so that they will not unite with laborers, immigrants, and the unemployed. The method keeps in place a system of control and profit by a few and a constant source of cheap labor to maintain it.

If anyone steps out of line, take her/his job away. Let homelessness and hunger do their work. The economic weapon works. And we end up saying, "I would do this or that—be openly who I am, speak out against injustice, work for civil rights, join a labor union, go to a political march, etc.—if I didn't have this job. I can't afford to lose it." We stay in an abusive situation because we see no other way to survive. . . .

Violence against women is directly related to the condition of women in a society that refuses us equal pay, equal access to resources, and equal status with males. From this condition comes men's confirmation of their sense of ownership of women, power over women, and assumed right to control women for their own means. Men physically and emotionally abuse women because they *can*, because they live in a world that gives them permission. Male violence is fed by their sense of their *right* to dominate and control, and their sense of superiority over a group of people who, because of gender, they consider inferior to them.

It is not just the violence but the threat of violence that controls our lives. Because the burden of responsibility has been placed so often on the potential victim, as women we have curtailed our freedom in order to protect ourselves from violence. Because of the threat of rapists, we stay on alert, being careful not to walk in isolated places, being careful where we park our cars, adding incredible security measures to our homes—massive locks, lights, alarms, if we can afford them—and we avoid places where we will appear vulnerable or unprotected while the abuser walks with freedom. Fear, often now so commonplace that it is unacknowledged, shapes our lives, reducing our freedom. . . .

Part of the way sexism stays in place is the societal promise of survival, false and unfulfilled as it is, that women will not suffer violence if we attach ourselves to a man to protect us. A woman without a man is told she is vulnerable to external violence and, worse, that there is something wrong with her. When the male abuser calls a woman a lesbian, he is not so much labeling her a woman who loves women as he is warning her that by resisting him, she is choosing to be outside society's protection from male institutions and therefore from wide-ranging, unspecified, ever-present violence. When she seeks assistance from woman friends or a battered women's shelter, he recognizes the power in woman bonding and fears loss of her servitude and loyalty: the potential loss of his control. The concern is not affectional/ sexual identity: the concern is disloyalty and the threat is violence.

The threat of violence against women who step out of line or who are disloyal is made all the more powerful by the fact that women do not have to do anything— they may be paragons of virtue and subservience—to receive violence against our lives: the violence still comes. It comes because of the woman-hating that exists throughout society. Chance plays a larger part than virtue in keeping women safe. Hence, with violence always a threat to us, women can never feel completely secure and confident. Our sense of safety is always fragile and tenuous.

Many women say that verbal violence causes more harm than physical violence because it damages self-esteem so deeply. Women have not wanted to hear battered women say that the verbal abuse was as hurtful as the physical abuse: to acknowledge that truth would be tantamount to acknowledging that *virtually every woman is a battered woman*. It is difficult to keep strong against accusations of being a bitch, stupid, inferior, etc., etc. It is especially difficult when these individual assaults are backed up by a society that shows women in textbooks, advertising, TV programs, movies, etc., as debased, silly, inferior, and sexually objectified, and a society that gives tacit approval to pornography. When we internalize these messages, we call the result "low self-esteem," a therapeutic individualized term. It seems to me we should use the more political expression: when we internalize these messages, we experience *internalized sexism*, and we experience it in common with all women living in a sexist world. The violence against us is supported by a society in which woman-hating is deeply imbedded.

In "Eyes on the Prize," a 1987 Public Television documentary about the Civil Rights Movement, an older white woman says about her youth in the South that it was difficult to be anything different from what was around her when there was no vision for another way to be. Our society presents images of women that say it is appropriate to commit violence against us. Violence is committed against women because we are seen as inferior in status and in worth. It has been the work of the women's movement to present a vision of another way to be.

Every time a woman gains the strength to resist and leave her abuser, we are given a model of the importance of stepping out of line, of moving toward freedom. And we all gain strength when she says to violence, "Never again!" Thousands of women in the last fifteen years have resisted their abusers to come to this country's 1100 battered women's shelters. There they have sat down with other women to share their stories, to discover that their stories again and again are the same, to develop an analysis that shows that violence is a statement about power and control, and to understand how sexism creates the climate for male violence. Those brave women are now a part of a movement that gives hope for another way to live in equality and peace.

Homophobia works effectively as a weapon of sexism because it is joined with a powerful arm, heterosexism. Heterosexism creates the climate for homophobia with its assumption that the world is and must be heterosexual and its display of power and privilege as the norm. Heterosexism is the systemic display of homophobia in the institutions of society. Heterosexism and homophobia work together to enforce compulsory heterosexuality and that bastion of patriarchal power, the nuclear family. The central focus of the rightwing attack against women's liberation is that women's equality, women's self-determination, women's control of our own bodies and lives will damage what they see as the crucial societal institution, the nuclear family. The attack has been led by fundamentalist ministers across the country. The two areas they have focused on most consistently are abortion and homosexuality, and their passion has led them to bomb women's clinics and to recommend deprogramming for homosexuals and establishing camps to quarantine people with AIDS. To resist marriage and/or heterosexuality is to risk severe punishment and loss.

It is not by chance that when children approach puberty and increased sexual awareness they begin to taunt each other by calling these names: "queer," "faggot," "pervert." It is at puberty that the full force of society's pressure to conform to heterosexuality and prepare for marriage is brought to bear. Children know what we have taught them, and we have given clear messages that those who deviate from standard expectations are to be made to get back in line. The best controlling tactic at puberty is to be treated as an outsider, to be ostracized at a time when it feels most vital to be accepted. Those who are different must be made to suffer loss. It is also at puberty that misogyny begins to be more apparent, and girls are pressured to conform to societal norms that do not permit them to realize their full potential. It is at this time that their academic achievements begin to decrease as they are coerced into compulsory heterosexuality and trained for dependency upon a man, that is, for economic survival.

There was a time when the two most condemning accusations against a woman meant to ostracize and disempower her were "whore" and "lesbian." The sexual revolution and changing attitudes about heterosexual behavior may have led to some lessening of the power of the word *whore*, though it still has strength as a threat to sexual property and prostitutes are stigmatized and abused. However, the word *lesbian* is still fully charged and carries with it the full threat of loss of power and privilege, the threat of being cut asunder, abandoned, and left outside society's protection.

To be a lesbian is to be *perceived* as someone who has stepped out of line, who has moved out of sexual/economic dependence on a male, who is woman-identified. A lesbian is perceived as someone who can live without a man, and who is therefore (however illogically) against men. A lesbian is perceived as being outside the acceptable, routinized order of things. She is seen as someone who has no societal institutions to protect her and who is not privileged to the protection of individual males. Many heterosexual women see her as someone who stands in contradiction to the sacrifices they have made to conform to compulsory heterosexuality. A lesbian is perceived as a threat to the nuclear family, to male dominance and control, to the very heart of sexism.

Gay men are perceived also as a threat to male dominance and control, and the homophobia expressed against them has the same roots in sexism as does homophobia against lesbians. Visible gay men are the objects of extreme hatred and fear by heterosexual men because their breaking ranks with male heterosexual solidarity is seen as a damaging rent in the very fabric of sexism. They are seen as betrayers, as traitors who must be punished and eliminated. In the beating and killing of gay men we see clear evidence of this hatred. When we see the fierce homophobia expressed toward gay men, we can begin to understand the ways sexism also affects males through imposing rigid, dehumanizing gender roles on them. The two circumstances in which it is legitimate for men to be openly physically affectionate with one another are in competitive sports and in the crisis of war. For many men, these two experiences are the highlights of their lives, and they think of them again and again with nostalgia. War and sports offer a cover of all-male safety and dominance to keep away the notion of affectionate openness being identified with homosexuality. When gay men break ranks with male roles through bonding and affection outside the arenas of war and sports, they are perceived as not being "real men," that is, as being identified with women, the weaker sex that must be dominated and that over the centuries has been the object of male hatred and abuse. Misogyny gets transferred to gay men with a vengeance and is increased by the fear that their sexual identity and behavior will bring down the entire system of male dominance and compulsory heterosexuality.

If lesbians are established as threats to the status quo, as outcasts who must be punished, homophobia can wield its power over all women through lesbian baiting. Lesbian baiting is an attempt to control women by labeling us as lesbians because our behavior is not acceptable, that is, when we are being independent, going our own way, living whole lives, fighting for our rights, demanding equal pay, saying no to violence, being self-assertive, bonding with and loving the company of women, assuming the right to our bodies, insisting upon our own authority, making changes that include us in society's decision-making; lesbian baiting occurs when women are called lesbians because we resist male dominance and control. And it has little or nothing to do with one's sexual identity.

To be named as lesbian threatens all women, not just lesbians, with great loss. And any woman who steps out of role risks being called a lesbian. To understand how this is a threat to all women, one must understand that any woman can be called a lesbian and there is no real way she can defend herself: there is no way to credential one's sexuality. ("The Children's Hour," a Lillian Hellman play, makes this point when a student asserts two teachers are lesbians and they have no way to disprove it.) She may be married or divorced, have children, dress in the most feminine manner, have sex with men, be celibate—but there are lesbians who do all those things. *Lesbians look like all women and all women look like lesbians.* There is no guaranteed method of identification, and as we all know, sexual identity can be kept hidden. (The same is true for men. There is no way to prove their sexual identity, though many go to extremes to prove heterosexuality.) Also, women are not necessarily born lesbian. Some seem to be, but others become lesbians later in life after having lived heterosexual lives. Lesbian baiting of heterosexual women would not work if there were a definitive way to identify lesbians (or heterosexuals).

We have yet to understand clearly how sexual identity develops. And this is disturbing to some people, especially those who are determined to discover how lesbian and gay identity is formed so that they will know where to start in eliminating it. (Isn't it odd that there is so little concern about discovering the causes of heterosexuality?) There are many theories: genetic makeup, hormones, socialization, environment, etc. But there is no conclusive evidence that indicates that heterosexuality comes from one process and homosexuality from another.

We do know, however, that sexual identity can be in flux, and we know that sexual identity means more than just the gender of people one is attracted to and has sex with. To be a lesbian has as many ramifications as for a woman to be heterosexual. It is more than sex, more than just the bedroom issue many would like to make it: it is a woman-centered life with all the social interconnections that entails. Some lesbians are in long-term relationships, some in short-term ones, some date, some are celibate, some are married to men, some remain as separate as possible from men, some have children by men, some by alternative insemination, some seem "feminine" by societal standards, some "masculine," some are doctors, lawyers and ministers, some laborers, housewives and writers: what all share in common is a sexual/affectional identity that focuses on women in its attractions and social relationships.

If lesbians are simply women with a particular sexual identity who look and act like all women, then the major difference in living out a lesbian sexual identity as opposed to a heterosexual identity is that as lesbians we live in a homophobic world that threatens and imposes damaging loss on us for being *who we are*, for choosing to live whole lives. Homophobic people often assert that homosexuals have the choice of not being homosexual; that is, we don't have to act out our sexual identity. In that case, I want to hear heterosexuals talk about their willingness not to act out their sexual identity, including not just sexual activity but heterosexual social interconnections and heterosexual privilege. It is a question of wholeness. It is very difficult for one to be denied the life of a sexual being, whether expressed in sex or in physical affection, and to feel complete, whole. For our loving relationships with humans feed the life of the spirit and enable us to overcome our basic isolation and to be interconnected with humankind.

If, then, any woman can be named a lesbian and be threatened with terrible losses, what is it she fears? Are these fears real? Being vulnerable to a homophobic world can lead to these losses:

- *Employment.* The loss of job leads us right back to the economic connection to sexism. This fear of job loss exists for almost every lesbian except perhaps those who are self-employed or in a business that does not require societal approval. Consider how many businesses or organizations you know that will hire and protect people who are openly gay or lesbian.

- *Family.* Their approval, acceptance, love.
- *Children.* Many lesbians and gay men have children, but very, very few gain custody in court challenges, even if the other parent is a known abuser. Other children may be kept away from us as though gays and lesbians are abusers. There are written and unwritten laws prohibiting lesbians and gays from being foster parents or from adopting children. There is an irrational fear that children in contact with lesbians and gays will become homosexual through influence or that they will be sexually abused. Despite our knowing that 95 percent of those who sexually abuse children are heterosexual men, there are no policies keeping heterosexual men from teaching or working with children, yet in almost every school system in America, visible gay men and lesbians are not hired through either written or unwritten law.
- *Heterosexual privilege and protection.* No institutions, other than those created by lesbians and gays—such as the Metropolitan Community Church, some counseling centers, political organizations such as the National Gay and Lesbian Task Force, the National Coalition of Black Lesbians and Gays, the Lambda Legal Defense and Education Fund, etc.,—affirm homosexuality and offer protection. Affirmation and protection cannot be gained from the criminal justice system, mainline churches, educational institutions, the government.
- *Safety.* There is nowhere to turn for safety from physical and verbal attacks because the norm presently in this country is that it is acceptable to be overtly homophobic. Gay men are beaten on the streets; lesbians are kidnapped and "deprogrammed." The National Gay and Lesbian Task Force, in an extended study, has documented violence against lesbians and gay men and noted the inadequate response of the criminal justice system. One of the major differences between homophobia/heterosexism and racism and sexism is that because of the Civil Rights Movement and the women's movement racism and sexism are expressed more covertly (though with great harm); because there has not been a major, visible lesbian and gay movement, it is permissible to be overtly homophobic in any institution or public forum. Churches spew forth homophobia in the same way they did racism prior to the Civil Rights Movement. Few laws are in place to protect lesbians and gay men, and the criminal justice system is wracked with homophobia.
- *Mental health.* An overtly homophobic world in which there is full permission to treat lesbians and gay men with cruelty makes it difficult for lesbians and gay men to maintain a strong sense of well-being and self-esteem. Many lesbians and gay men are beaten, raped, killed, subjected to aversion therapy, or put in mental institutions. The impact of such hatred and negativity can lead one to depression and, in some cases, to suicide. The toll on the gay and lesbian community is devastating.
- *Community.* There is rejection by those who live in homophobic fear, those who are afraid of association with lesbians and gay men. For many in the gay and lesbian community, there is a loss of public acceptance, a loss of allies, a loss of place and belonging.

- *Credibility.* This fear is large for many people: the fear that they will no longer be respected, listened to, honored, believed. They fear they will be social outcasts.

The list goes on and on. But any one of these essential components of a full life is large enough to make one deeply fear its loss. A black woman once said to me in a workshop, "When I fought for Civil Rights, I always had my family and community to fall back on even when they didn't fully understand or accept what I was doing. I don't know if I could have borne losing them. And you people don't have either with you. It takes my breath away."

What does a woman have to do to get called a lesbian? Almost anything, sometimes nothing at all, but certainly anything that threatens the status quo, anything that steps out of role, anything that asserts the rights of women, anything that doesn't indicate submission and subordination. Assertiveness, standing up for oneself, asking for more pay, better working conditions, training for and accepting a non-traditional (you mean a man's?) job, enjoying the company of women, being financially independent, being in control of one's life, depending first and foremost upon oneself, thinking that one can do whatever needs to be done, but above all, working for the rights and equality of women.

In the backlash to the gains of the women's liberation movement, there has been an increased effort to keep definitions man-centered. Therefore, to work on behalf of women must mean to work against men. To love women must mean that one hates men. A very effective attack has been made against the word *feminist* to make it a derogatory word. In current backlash usage, *feminist* equals *man-hater* which equals *lesbian*. This formula is created in the hope that women will be frightened away from their work on behalf of women. Consequently, we now have women who believe in the rights of women and work for those rights while from fear deny that they are feminists, or refuse to use the word because it is so "abrasive."

So what does one do in an effort to keep from being called a lesbian? She steps back into line, into the role that is demanded of her, tries to behave in such a way that doesn't threaten the status of men, and if she works for women's rights, she begins modifying that work. When women's organizations begin doing significant social change work, they inevitably are lesbian-baited; that is, funders or institutions or community members tell us that they can't work with us because of our "man-hating attitudes" or the presence of lesbians. We are called too strident, told we are making enemies, not doing good. . . .

In my view, homophobia has been one of the major causes of the failure of the women's liberation movement to make deep and lasting change. (The other major block has been racism.) We were fierce when we set out but when threatened with the loss of heterosexual privilege, we began putting on brakes. Our best-known nationally distributed women's magazine was reluctant to print articles about lesbians, began putting a man on the cover several times a year, and writing articles about women who succeeded in a man's world. We worried about our image, our being all right, our being "real women" despite our work. Instead of talking about the elimination of sexual gender roles, we stepped back and talked about "sex role stereotyping" as the issue. Change around the edges for middleclass white women began to be talked about as successes. We accepted tokenism and integration, forgetting that equality for all women, for all people—and not just equality of white middleclass women with white men—was the goal that we could never put behind us.

But despite backlash and retreats, change is growing from within. The women's liberation movement is beginning to gain strength again because there are women who are talking about liberation for all women. We are examining sexism, racism, homophobia, classism, anti-Semitism, ageism, ableism, and imperialism, and we see everything as connected. This change in point of view represents the third wave of the women's liberation movement, a new direction that does not get mass media coverage and recognition. It has been initiated by women of color and lesbians who were marginalized or rendered invisible by the white heterosexual leaders of earlier efforts. The first wave was the 19th and early 20th century campaign for the vote; the second, beginning in the 1960s, focused on the Equal Rights Amendment and abortion rights. Consisting of predominantly white middleclass women, both failed in recognizing issues of equality and empowerment for all women. The third wave of the movement, multi-racial and multi-issued, seeks the transformation of the world for us all. We know that we won't get there until everyone gets there; that we must move forward in a great strong line, hand in hand, not just a few at a time.

We know that the arguments about homophobia originating from mental health and Biblical/religious attitudes can be settled when we look at the sexism that permeates religious and psychiatric history. The women of the third wave of the women's liberation movement know that *without the existence of sexism, there would be no homophobia.*

Finally, we know that as long as the word lesbian can strike fear in any woman's heart, then work on behalf of women can be stopped; the only successful work against sexism must include work against homophobia.

7

Feminism:
A Transformational Politic

bell hooks

We live in a world in crisis—a world governed by politics of domination, one in which the belief in a notion of superior and inferior, and its concomitant ideology—that the superior should rule over the inferior—effects the lives of all people everywhere, whether poor or privileged, literate or illiterate. Systematic dehumanization, worldwide famine, ecological devastation, industrial contamination, and the possibility of nuclear destruction are realities which remind us daily that we are in crisis. Contemporary feminist thinkers often cite sexual politics as the origin of this crisis. They point to the insistence on difference as that factor which becomes the occasion for separation and domination and suggest that differentiation of status between females and males globally is an indication that patriarchal domination of the planet is the root of the problem. Such an assumption has fostered the notion that elimination of sexist oppression would necessarily lead to the eradication of all forms of domination. It is an argument that has led influential Western white women to feel that feminist movement should be *the* central political agenda for females globally. Ideologically, thinking in this direction enables Western women, especially privileged white women, to suggest that racism and class exploitation are merely the offspring of the parent system: patriarchy. Within feminist movement in the West, this has led to the assumption that resisting patriarchal domination is a more legitimate feminist action than resisting racism and other forms of domination. Such thinking prevails despite radical critiques made by black women and other women of color who question this proposition. To speculate that an oppositional division between men and women existed in early human communities is to impose on the past, on these non-white groups, a world view that fits all too neatly within contemporary feminist paradigms that name man as the enemy and woman as the victim.

   Clearly, differentiation between strong and weak, powerful and powerless, has been a central defining aspect of gender globally, carrying with it the assumption that men should have greater authority than women, and should rule over them. As significant and important as this fact is, it should not obscure the reality that women can and do participate in politics of domination, as perpetrators as well as victims—that we dominate, that we are dominated. If focus on patriarchal domination masks this reality or becomes the means by which women deflect attention from the real conditions and circumstances of our lives, then women cooperate in suppressing and promoting false consciousness, inhibiting our capacity to assume responsibility for transforming ourselves and society.

Thinking speculatively about early human social arrangement, about women and men struggling to survive in small communities, it is likely that the parent-child relationship with its very real imposed survival structure of dependency, of strong and weak, of powerful and powerless, was a site for the construction of a paradigm of domination. While this circumstance of dependency is not necessarily one that leads to domination, it lends itself to the enactment of a social drama wherein domination could easily occur as a means of exercising and maintaining control. This speculation does not place women outside the practice of domination, in the exclusive role of victim. It centrally names women as agents of domination, as potential theoreticians, and creators of a paradigm for social relationships wherein those groups of individuals designated as "strong" exercise power both benevolently and coercively over those designated as "weak."

Emphasizing paradigms of domination that call attention to woman's capacity to dominate is one way to deconstruct and challenge the simplistic notion that man is the enemy, woman the victim; the notion that men have always been the oppressors. Such thinking enables us to examine our role as women in the perpetuation and maintenance of systems of domination. To understand domination, we must understand that our capacity as women and men to be either dominated or dominating is a point of connection, of commonality. Even though I speak from the particular experience of living as a black woman in the United States, a white-supremacist, capitalist, patriarchal society, where small numbers of white men (and honorary "white men") constitute ruling groups, I understand that in many places in the world oppressed and oppressor share the same color. I understand that right here in this room, oppressed and oppressor share the same gender. Right now as I speak, a man who is himself victimized, wounded, hurt by racism and class exploitation is actively dominating a woman in his life — that even as I speak, women who are ourselves exploited, victimized, are dominating children. It is necessary for us to remember, as we think critically about domination, that we all have the capacity to act in ways that oppress, dominate, wound (whether or not that power is institutionalized). It is necessary to remember that it is first the potential oppressor within that we must resist — the potential victim within that we must rescue — otherwise we cannot hope for an end to domination, for liberation.

This knowledge seems especially important at this historical moment when black women and other women of color have worked to create awareness of the ways in which racism empowers white women to act as exploiters and oppressors. Increasingly this fact is considered a reason we should not support feminist struggle even though sexism and sexist oppression is a real issue in our lives as black women (see, for example, Vivian Gordon's *Black Women, Feminism, Black Liberation: Which Way?*). It becomes necessary for us to speak continually about the convictions that inform our continued advocacy of feminist struggle. By calling attention to interlocking systems of domination—sex, race, and class—black women and many other groups of women acknowledge the diversity and complexity of female experience, of our relationship to power and domination. The intent is not to dissuade people of color from becoming engaged in feminist movement. Feminist struggle to end patriarchal domination should be of primary importance to women and men globally not because it is the foundation of all other oppressive structures but because it is that form of domination we are most likely to encounter in an ongoing way in everyday life.

Unlike other forms of domination, sexism directly shapes and determines relations of power in our private lives, in familiar social spaces, in that most intimate context—home—and in that most intimate sphere of relations—family. Usually, it is within the family that we witness coercive domination and learn to accept it, whether it be domination of parent over child, or male over female. Even though family relations may be, and most often are, informed by acceptance of a politic of domination, they are simultaneously relations of care and connection. It is this convergence of two contradictory impulses—the urge to promote growth and the urge to inhibit growth—that provides a practical setting for feminist critique, resistance, and transformation.

Growing up in a black, working-class, father-dominated household, I experienced coercive adult male authority as more immediately threatening, as more likely to cause immediate pain than racist oppression or class exploitation. It was equally clear that experiencing exploitation and oppression in the home made one feel all the more powerless when encountering dominating forces outside the home. This is true for many people. If we are unable to resist and end domination in relations where there is care, it seems totally unimaginable that we can resist and end it in other institutionalized relations of power. If we cannot convince the mothers and/or fathers who care not to humiliate and degrade us, how can we imagine convincing or resisting an employer, a lover, a stranger who systematically humiliates and degrades?

Feminist effort to end patriarchal domination should be of primary concern precisely because it insists on the eradication of exploitation and oppression in the family context and in all other intimate relationships. It is that political movement which most radically addresses the person—the personal—citing the need for transformation of self, of relationships, so that we might be better able to act in a revolutionary manner, challenging and resisting domination, transforming the world outside the self. Strategically, feminist movement should be a central component of all other liberation struggles because it challenges each of us to alter our person, our personal engagement (either as victims or perpetrators or both) in a system of domination.

Feminism, as liberation struggle, must exist apart from and as a part of the larger struggle to eradicate domination in all its forms. We must understand that patriarchal domination shares an ideological foundation with racism and other forms of group oppression, that there is no hope that it can be eradicated while these systems remain intact. This knowledge should consistently inform the direction of feminist theory and practice. Unfortunately, racism and class elitism among women has frequently led to the suppression and distortion of this connection so that it is now necessary for feminist thinkers to critique and revise much feminist theory and the direction of feminist movement. This effort at revision is perhaps most evident in the current widespread acknowledgement that sexism, racism, and class exploitation constitute interlocking systems of domination—that sex, race, and class, and not sex alone, determine the nature of any female's identity, status, and circumstance, the degree to which she will or will not be dominated, the extent to which she will have the power to dominate.

While acknowledgement of the complex nature of woman's status (which has been most impressed upon everyone's consciousness by radical women of color) is a significant corrective, it is only a starting point. It provides a frame of reference which must serve as the basis for thoroughly altering and revising feminist theory and practice. It challenges and calls us to re-think popular assumptions about the nature of feminism that have had the deepest impact on a large majority of women, on mass consciousness. It radically calls into question the notion of a fundamentally common female experience which has been seen as the prerequisite for our coming together, for political unity. Recognition of the inter-connectedness of sex, race, and class highlights the diversity of experience, compelling redefinition of the terms for unity. If women do not share "common oppression," what then can serve as a basis for our coming together?

Unlike many feminist comrades, I believe women and men must share a common understanding—a basic knowledge of what feminism is—if it is ever to be a powerful mass-based political movement. In *Feminist Theory: from margin to center*, I suggest that defining feminism broadly as "a movement to end sexism and sexist oppression" would enable us to have a common political goal. We would then have a basis on which to build solidarity. Multiple and contradictory definitions of feminism create confusion and undermine the effort to construct feminist movement so that it addresses everyone. Sharing a common goal does not imply that women and men will not have radically divergent perspectives on how that goal might be reached. Because each individual starts the process of engagement in feminist struggle at a unique level of awareness, very real differences in experience, perspective, and knowledge make developing varied strategies for participation and transformation a necessary agenda.

Feminist thinkers engaged in radically revisioning central tenets of feminist thought must continually emphasize the importance of sex, race and class as factors which *together* determine the social construction of femaleness, as it has been so deeply ingrained in the consciousness of many women active in feminist movement that gender is the sole factor determining destiny. However, the work of education for critical consciousness (usually called consciousness-raising) cannot end there. Much feminist consciousness-raising has in the past focussed on identifying the particular ways men oppress and exploit women. Using the paradigm of sex, race, and class means that the focus does not begin with men and what they do to women, but rather with women working to identify both individually and collectively the specific character of our social identity.

Imagine a group of women from diverse backgrounds coming together to talk about feminism. First they concentrate on working out their status in terms of sex, race, and class using this as the standpoint from which they begin discussing patriarchy or their particular relations with individual men. Within the old frame of reference, a discussion might consist solely of talk about their experiences as victims in relationship to male oppressors. Two women—one poor, the other quite wealthy— might describe the process by which they have suffered physical abuse by male partners and find certain commonalities which might serve as a basis for bonding. Yet if these same two women engaged in a discussion of class, not only would the social construction and expression of femaleness differ, so too would their ideas about how to confront and change their circumstances. Broadening the discussion to include an analysis of race and class would expose many additional differences even as commonalities emerged.

Clearly the process of bonding would be more complex, yet this broader discussion might enable the sharing of perspectives and strategies for change that would enrich rather than diminish our understanding of gender. While feminists have increasingly given "lip service" to the idea of diversity, we have not developed strategies of communication and inclusion that allow for the successful enactment of this feminist vision.

Small groups are no longer the central place for feminist consciousness-raising. Much feminist education for critical consciousness takes place in Women's Studies classes or at conferences which focus on gender. Books are a primary source of education which means that already masses of people who do not read have no access. The separation of grassroots ways of sharing feminist thinking across kitchen tables from the spheres where much of that thinking is generated, the academy, undermines feminist movement. It would further feminist movement if new feminist thinking could be once again shared in small group contexts, integrating critical analysis with discussion of personal experience. It would be useful to promote anew the small group setting as an arena for education for critical consciousness, so that women and men might come together in neighborhoods and communities to discuss feminist concerns.

Small groups remain an important place for education for critical consciousness for several reasons. An especially important aspect of the small group setting is the emphasis on communicating feminist thinking, feminist theory, in a manner that can be easily understood. In small groups, individuals do not need to be equally literate or literate at all because the information is primarily shared through conversation, in dialogue which is necessarily a liberatory expression. (Literacy should be a goal for feminists even as we ensure that it not become a requirement for participation in feminist education.) Reforming small groups would subvert the appropriation of feminist thinking by a select group of academic women and men, usually white, usually from privileged class backgrounds.

Small groups of people coming together to engage in feminist discussion, in dialectical struggle make a space where the "personal is political" as a starting point for education for critical consciousness can be extended to include politicization of the self that focusses on creating understanding of the ways sex, race, and class to-gether determine our individual lot and our collective experience. It would further feminist movement if many well known feminist thinkers would participate in small groups, critically re-examining ways their works might be changed by incorporating broader perspectives. All efforts at self-transformation challenge us to engage in on-going, critical self-examination and reflection about feminist practice, about how we live in the world. This individual commitment, when coupled with engagement in collective discussion, provides a space for critical feedback which strengthens our efforts to change and make ourselves new. It is in this commitment to feminist prin-ciples in our words and deeds that the hope of feminist revolution lies.

Working collectively to confront difference, to expand our awareness of sex, race, and class as interlocking systems of domination, of the ways we reinforce and perpetuate these structures, is the context in which we learn the true meaning of solidarity. It is this work that must be the foundation of feminist movement. With-out it, we cannot effectively resist patriarchal domination; without it, we remain estranged and alienated from one another. Fear of painful confrontation often leads women and men active in feminist movement to avoid rigorous critical encounter, yet if we cannot engage dialectically in a committed, rigorous, humanizing manner, we cannot hope to change the world. True politicization—coming to critical con-sciousness—is a difficult, "trying" process, one that demands that we give up set ways of thinking and being, that we shift our paradigms, that we open ourselves to the unknown, the unfamiliar. Undergoing this process, we learn what it means to struggle and in this effort we experience the dignity and integrity of being that comes with revolutionary change. If we do not change our consciousness, we can-not change our actions or demand change from others.

Our renewed commitment to a rigorous process of education for critical con-sciousness will determine the shape and direction of future feminist movement. Until new perspectives are created, we cannot be living symbols of the power of feminist thinking. Given the privileged lot of many leading feminist thinkers, both in terms of status, class, and race, it is harder these days to convince women of the primary of this process of politicization. More and more, we seem to form select interest groups composed of individuals who share similar perspectives. This limits our capacity to engage in critical discussion. It is difficult to involve women in new processes of feminist politicization because so many of us think that identifying men as the enemy, resisting male domination, gaining equal access to power and privilege is the end of feminist movement. Not only is it not the end, it is not even the place we want revitalized feminist movement to begin. We want to begin as women seriously addressing ourselves, not solely in relation to men, but in relation to an entire structure of domination of which patriarchy is one part. While the struggle to eradicate sexism and sexist oppression is and should be the primary thrust of feminist movement, to prepare ourselves politically for this effort we must first learn how to be in solidarity, how to struggle with one another.

Only when we confront the realities of sex, race, and class, the ways they divide us, make us different, stand us in opposition, and work to reconcile and resolve these issues will we be able to participate in the making of feminist revolution, in the transformation of the world. Feminism, as Charlotte Bunch emphasizes again and again in *Passionate Politics*, is a transformational politics, a struggle against domination wherein the effort is to change ourselves as well as structures. Speaking about the struggle to confront difference, Bunch asserts:

> A crucial point of the process is understanding that reality does not look the same from different people's perspective. It is not surprising that one way feminists have come to understand about differences has been through the love of a person from another culture or race. It takes persistence and motivation—which love often engenders—to get beyond one's ethnocentric assumptions and really learn about other perspectives. In this process and while seeking to eliminate oppression, we also discover new possibilities and insights that come from the experience and survival of other peoples.

Embedded in the commitment to feminist revolution is the challenge to love. Love can be and is an important source of empowerment when we struggle to confront issues of sex, race, and class. Working together to identify and face our differences— to face the ways we dominate and are dominated—to change our actions, we need a mediating force that can sustain us so that we are not broken in this process, so that we do not despair.

Not enough feminist work has focussed on documenting and sharing ways individuals confront differences constructively and successfully. Women and men need to know what is on the other side of the pain experienced in politicization. We need detailed accounts of the ways our lives are fuller and richer as we change and grow politically, as we learn to live each moment as committed feminists, as comrades working to end domination. In reconceptualizing and reformulating strategies for future feminist movement, we need to concentrate on the politicization of love, not just in the context of talking about victimization in intimate relationships, but in a critical discussion where love can be understood as a powerful force that challenges and resists domination. As we work to be loving, to create a culture that celebrates life, that makes love possible, we move against dehumanization, against domination. In *Pedagogy of the Oppressed*, Paulo Freire evokes this power of love, declaring:

> I am more and more convinced that true revolutionaries must perceive the revolution, because of its creative and liberating nature, as an act of love. For me, the revolution, which is not possible without a theory of revolution—and therefore science—is not irreconcilable with love ... The distortion imposed on the word "love" by the capitalist world cannot prevent the revolution from being essentially loving in character, nor can it prevent the revolutionaries from affirming their love of life.

That aspect of feminist revolution that calls women to love womanness, that calls men to resist dehumanizing concepts of masculinity, is an essential part of our struggle. It is the process by which we move from seeing ourselves as objects to acting as subjects. When women and men understand that working to eradicate patriarchal domination is a struggle rooted in the longing to make a world where everyone can live fully and freely, then we know our work to be a gesture of love. Let us draw upon that love to heighten our awareness, deepen our compassion, intensify our courage, and strengthen our commitment.

Still I Rise

Maya Angelou

You may write me down in history
With your bitter, twisted lies,
You may trod me in the very dirt
But still, like dust, I'll rise.

Does my sassiness upset you?
Why are you beset with gloom?
'Cause I walk like I've got oil wells
Pumping in my living room.

Just like moons and like suns,
With the certainty of tides,
Just like hopes springing high,
Still I'll rise.

Did you want to see me broken?
Bowed head and lowered eyes?
Shoulders falling down like teardrops,
Weakened by my soulful cries.

Does my haughtiness offend you?
Don't you take it awful hard
'Cause I laugh like I've got gold mines
Diggin' in my own back yard.

You may shoot me with your words,
You may cut me with your eyes,
You may kill me with your hatefulness,
But still, like air, I'll rise.

Does my sexiness upset you?
Does it come as a surprise
That I dance like I've got diamonds
At the meeting of my thighs?

Out of the huts of history's shame
I rise
Up from a past that's rooted in pain
I rise
I'm a black ocean, leaping and wide,
Welling and swelling I bear in the tide.

Leaving behind nights of terror and fear
I rise
Into a daybreak that's wondrously clear
I rise
Bringing the gifts that my ancestors gave,
I am the dream and the hope of the slave.
I rise
I rise
I rise.

The woman in the ordinary*

Marge Piercy

The woman in the ordinary pudgy downcast girl
is crouching with eyes and muscles clenched.
Round and pebble smooth she effaces herself
under ripples of conversation and debate.
The woman in the block of ivory soap
has massive thighs that neigh,

*From *Circles on the Water* by Marge Piercy.

great breasts that blare and strong arms that trumpet.
The woman of the golden fleece
laughs uproariously from the belly
inside the girl who imitates
a Christmas card virgin with glued hands,
who fishes for herself in other's eyes,
who stoops and creeps to make herself smaller.
In her bottled up is a woman peppery as curry,
a yam of a woman of butter and brass,
compounded of acid and sweet like a pineapple,
like a handgrenade set to explode,
like goldenrod ready to bloom.

Suggestions for Further Reading

Bowser, B. P., and R. G. Hunt. *Impacts of Racism on White Americans.* Beverly Hills, Calif.:
Sage Publications, 1981.

deLone, Richard H. *Small Futures.* New York: Harcourt Brace Jovanovich, 1979.

Economists Policy Group on Women's Issues. *Women's Policy Agenda.* Washington, D.C.:
Institute for Women's Policy Research, 1992.

Eisenstein, Z. R. *Feminism and Sexual Equality.* New York: Monthly Review Press, 1984.

Harvey, Philip. *Securing the Right to Employment: Social Welfare Policy and the Unemployed
in the United States.* Princeton, N.J.: Princeton University Press, 1989.

Kaufman, Michael, ed. *Beyond Patriarchy.* Toronto: Oxford University Press, 1987.

Lynch, James. *Prejudice Reduction in the Schools.* New York: Nichols Publishing Company,
1987.

Marable, M. *Black American Politics from the Washington Marches to Jesse Jackson.* New
York: Schocken, 1985.

National Displaced Homemakers Network. *The Women's Job Training Agenda.* Washington,
D.C.: National Displaced Homemakers Network, 1993.

Pogrebin, L. C. *Growing Up Free.* New York: Bantam Books, 1981.

Shalom, S. *Socialist Visions.* Boston: South End Press, 1980.

Stoltenberg, Jon. *The End of Manhood: A Book for Men of Conscience.* New York: Dutton,
1993.

Vogel, Lise. *Mothers on the Job: Maternity Policy in the U.S. Workplace.* New Brunswick,
N.J.: Rutgers University Press, 1993.

West, Cornel. *Race Matters.* Boston: Beacon Press, 1993.

"Deconstructing the Underclass," by Herbert Gans. Reprinted by permission of the *Journal of the American Planning Association* 271, Summer 1990.

"Domination and Subordination," from *Toward a New Psychology of Women*, by Jean Baker Miller. Copyright © 1976 by Jean Baker Miller. Reprinted by permission of Beacon Press.

"The Problem: Discrimination," from *Affirmative Action in the 1980s*, U.S. Commission on Civil Rights, 65, January 1981, pp. 9–15.

"Oppression," from *The Politics of Reality*. Copyright © 1983 by Marilyn Frye, published by The Crossing Press, Freedom, CA. Reprinted by permission of the publisher.

"Racism: Something about the Subject Makes It Hard to Name," by Gloria Yamato, from Cochran, et al, *Changing Our Power*. Copyright © 1991 by Kendall/Hunt Publishing Company. Used with permission.

"Smells like Racism," by Rita Chaudhry Sethi, from *The State of Asian America*, ed. Karin Aguilar-San Juan. Copyright © 1994 by South End Press. Reprinted by permission of the publisher.

"Death of a Teenager Widens a Racial Rift between Two Towns," by Alex Kotlowitz, from *The Wall Street Journal*, February 26, 1993. Copyright © 1993 by The Wall Street Journal. Reprinted by permission.

"Little Sympathy or Surprise," by David Gonzalez with Garry Pierre-Pierre, from *The New York Times*, November 21, 1993. Copyright © 1993 by The New York Times Company. Reprinted by permission.

"No Cure for Sexism in the Medical Profession," by Kathy K. Astor, was originally published in *New Directions for Women*, Sept.–Oct. 1993. Copyright held by Kathy K. Astor. Reprinted by permission of the author.

"Imagine a Country," by Holly Sklar. An earlier version appeared in Z Magazine, November 1992. Permission is granted by the author.

"Class in America: Myths and Realities," by Gregory Mantsios, is used by permission of the author.

"The Wage Gap: Myths and Facts," by the National Committee on Pay Equity.

"Women Face Glass Walls as well as Ceilings," by Julie Amparano Lopez, from *The Wall Street Journal*, March 3, 1992. Copyright © 1992 by The Wall Street Journal. Reprinted by permission.

"Three Realities: Minority Life in America." Permission granted by The Business—Higher Education Forum, c/o American Council on Education, One Dupont Circle, Suite 800, Washington, DC 20036.

"Middle Class Blacks Try to Grip a Ladder While Lending a Hand," by Isabel Wilkerson, from *The New York Times*, November 26, 1990. Copyright © 1990 by The New York Times Company. Reprinted by permission.

"The Poverty Industry," by Theresa Funiciello, is reprinted by permission of *Ms.* Magazine, © 1990.

"Racial and Ethnic Minorities: An Overview," adapted by Beth B. Hess with the permission of Macmillan College Publishing Company from *Sociology*, 4th ed., by Beth B. Hess, Elizabeth W. Markson, and Peter J. Stein. Copyright 1991 by Macmillan College Publishing Company, Inc.

"Sun Chief: Autobiography of a Hopi Indian," ed. Leo W. Simmons. Copyright © 1942 by Yale University Press. Used with permission.

"Then Came the War," by Yuri Kochiyama, © 1991, 1992 by Joann Faung Jean Lee. Reprinted by permission of The New Press.

"The Media's Image of Arabs," by Jack G. Shaheen, from *New Worlds of Literature*, Norton, 1989. Used by permission of the author.

"The Circuit," by Francisco Jiménez, from *The Arizona Quarterly* (Autumn, 1973). Used by permission of the author.

"The Myth of the Latin Woman: I Just Met a Girl Named Maria," by Judith Ortiz Cofer, from *The Latin Deli*, Copyright © 1993 by The University of Georgia Press. Used by permission.

"Suicide Note," excerpted from *Shedding Silence* by Janice Mirikitani. Used by permission of Celestial Arts, P.O. Box 7327, Berkeley, CA 94707.

"The Gap between Striving and Achieving: The Case of Asian American Women," by Deborah Woo, from *Making Waves* by Asian Women United. Copyright © 1989 by Asian Women United. Reprinted by permission of Beacon Press.

"Black Hispanics: The Ties That Bind," by Vivian Brady, from *Centro*.

"Blacks and Hispanics: A Fragile Alliance," by Jacqueline Conciatore and Roberto Rodriguez, from *Black Issues in Higher Education*, Oct. 11, 1990. Used by permission.

"Black Intellectuals, Jewish Tensions: How to End the Impasse," by Cornel West, from *The New York Times*, April 14, 1993. Copyright © 1993 by The New York Times Company. Reprinted by permission.

"Pigskin, Patriarchy, and Pain," by Don Sabo, from *Changing Men*, Summer 1986. Reprinted by permission of the author.

"He Defies You Still: The Memoirs of a Sissy," by Tommi Avicolli, in *Radical Teacher*, #24, pp. 4–5. Copyright © 1985 by Tommi Avicolli. Reprinted by permission of the author.

"With No Immediate Cause," copyright © 1972, 1974, 1975, 1976, 1977, 1978 by Ntozake Shange. From the book *Nappy Edges*. Reprinted with permission from St. Martin's Press, Inc., New York, NY.

"The Tyranny of Slenderness," from *The Obsession: Reflections on the Tyranny of Slenderness*, by Kim Chernin. Copyright © 1981 by Kim Chernin. Reprinted by permission of HarperCollins Publishers, Inc.

"The Triangular Tube of Pink Lipstick," by Gail Watnick, from *Twenty-first Century Challenge: Lesbians and Gays in Education—Bridging the Gap*, ed. Sue McConnell-Celi, published by Lavender Crystal Press, Red Bank, NJ. Copyright © 1993 by Sue McConnell-Celi. Reprinted by permission of the author and publisher.

"'We Are Who You Are': Feminism and Disability," by Bonnie Sherr Klein, from *Ms. Maqazine*, © 1990.

"The Case of Sharon Kowalski and Karen Thompson: Ableism, Heterosexism, and Sexism," by Joan L. Griscom. Reprinted by permission of the author.

"Silent Scream," by Carole R. Simmons. Reprinted by permission of the author.

"Poem for the Young White Man Who Asked Me How I, an Intelligent, Well-read Person Could Believe in the War between Races," is reprinted from *Emplumada*, by Lorna Dee Cervantes, by permission of the University of Pittsburgh Press. Copyright © 1981 by Lorna Dee Cervantes.

"Requiem for the Champ," from *Technical Difficulties* by June Jordan. Copyright © 1992 by June Jordan. Reprinted by permission of Pantheon Books, a division of Random House, Inc.

"C. P. Ellis," from *American Dreams* by Studs Terkel. Copyright © 1980 by Studs Terkel. Reprinted by permission of Pantheon Books, a division of Random House, Inc.

"Indian Tribes: A Continuing Quest for Survival." Reprinted by permission of U.S. Commission on Civil Rights.

"Race and the American Legal Process," by A. Leon Higginbotham, Jr., from *In The Matter of Color: Race and the American Legal Process: The Colonial Period* by A. Leon Higginbotham, Jr. Copyright © 1978 by Oxford University Press, Inc. Reprinted by permission.

"Declarations of Sentiments and Resolutions, Seneca Falls Convention, 1848," excerpts from *Up from the Pedestal*, by Aileen S. Kraditor, published by Times Books, a division of Random House, Inc.

"The Antisuffragists: Selected Papers, 1852–1887," excerpts from *Up from the Pedestal*, by Aileen S. Kraditor, published by Times Books, a division of Random House, Inc.

"*People v. Hall*," from Rogers Daniels and Harry H. L. Kitano, *American Racism: Exploration of the Nature of Prejudice*, Prentice Hall, Englewood Cliffs, NJ, 1970. Used by permission of R. Daniels and H. H. L. Kitano.

"The Black Codes," from *Black Reconstruction* by W. E. B. Du Bois (Harcourt Brace Jovanovich, Inc., 1935). Reprinted by permission of David G. Du Bois.

"*Bradwell v. Illinois*, 1873," reprinted from *Cases and Materials on Sex-Based Discrimination*, 2nd edition, edited by Herma Hill Kay, with permission of the West Publishing Company.

"*Bowers v. Hardwick*, 1986," reprinted from 106 S. Court 2841 by permission of the West Publishing Company.

"The Law and the Lesbian and Gay Community," by Paula L. Ettelbrick. Reprinted by permission of the author.

"Self-Fulfilling Stereotypes," by Mark Snyder. Reprinted with permission of *Psychology Today* Magazine. Copyright © 1982 (Sussex Publishers, Inc.).

"Racist Stereotyping in the English Language," by Robert B. Moore. Reprinted by permission from *Racism in the English Language*. New York: The Council on Interracial Books for Children, P.O. Box 1263, New York, NY 10023.

"The Language of Sexism," by Haig Bosmajian, from *The Language of Oppression*, Public Affairs Press, 1974.

"Beauty and the Beast of Advertising," by Jean Kilbourne. From *Media&Values Magazine: Redesigning Women*, Winter 1990. Reprinted by permission of the Center for Media Literacy.

"Pulling Train," by Peggy R. Sanday, from *Fraternity Gang Rape*, Copyright © 1990 by New York University Press. Used by permission.

"Anti-Gay Stereotypes," from *Gays/Justice: A Study of Ethics, Society, and Law* by Richard D. Mohr. Copyright © by Columbia University Press, New York. Reprinted with permission of the publisher.

"Media Magic: Making Class Invisible," by Gregory Mantsios, is used by permission of the author.

"Sex and Race: The Analogy of Social Control," by William Chafe. From *Women and Equality: Changing Patterns in American Culture* by William H. Chafe. Copyright © 1977 by Oxford University Press, Inc. Reprinted by permission.

"Hate-Violence," by Carole Sheffield, is reprinted by permission of the author.

"Age, Race, Class, and Sex: Women Redefining Difference," from *Sister Outsider*, copyright © 1984 by Audre Lorde, published by The Crossing Press, Freedom, Calif.

"En Rapport, In Opposition: Cobrando cuentas a las nuestras," by Gloria Anzaldúa, from *Making Face, Making Soul/Haciendo Caras: Creative and Critical Perspectives by Feminists of Color*. Copyright © 1990 by Gloria Andzaldúa. Reprinted with permission from Aunt Lute Books (415) 558–8116.

"Up Against the Wall," by Cherríe Moraga, from *Loving in the War Years*. Copyright © 1983 by South End Press. Reprinted by permission of the publisher.

Index